Hypnosis and Behavior Modification: Imagery Conditioning

WILLIAM S. KROGER, M.D.

Clinical Professor, Department of Anesthesiology, University of California Los Angeles School of Medicine; Consultant to the Pain Clinic, University of California Los Angeles; Consulting Psychiatrist (Department of Neurology), City of Hope Medical Center, Century City and Los Angeles New Hospitals; Teaching Consultant, Department of Psychiatry, Cedars-Lebanon Medical Center, Los Angeles, California; Co-founder, Society for Clinical and Experimental Hypnosis; Co-founder, American Society of Clinical Hypnosis; Member, American Psychiatric Association; Executive Director, Institute for Comprehensive Medicine, Beverly Hills, California

and

WILLIAM D. FEZLER, Ph.D.

Associate Director, Institute for Comprehensive Medicine, Beverly Hills, California

J. B. Lippincott Company
Philadelphia · Toronto

ISBN 0-397-50362-8

Library of Congress Catalog Card Number 76-20586

Printed in the United States of America
6 5 4 3 2

Library of Congress Cataloging in Publication Data

Kroger, William S
  Hypnosis and behavior modification.

  Bibliography: p.
  Includes index.
  1. Fantasy—Therapeutic use. 2. Hypnotism—
Therapeutic use. 3. Behavior therapy. I. Fezler,
William D., joint author. II. Title.
RC489.F35K76   616.8'914   76-20586
ISBN 0-397-50362-8

To my wife, Jimmy Louise, whose unstinting love, devotion and assistance enabled me to complete this book.

WILLIAM S. KROGER, M.D.

To my parents for their years of patience and understanding.

WILLIAM D. FEZLER, Ph.D.

Foreword

It is an honor and a pleasure to introduce Drs. Kroger and Fezler's new volume on hypnosis and behavior modification. It is a book of remarkable scope, written by pioneers with broad interests. In many ways it is a timely volume—a number of leading behavior therapists have advocated the use of hypnotic technics to facilitate the therapeutic process, while several therapists identified with hypnotherapy have borrowed some of the technology of behavior modification.

Behavior therapy, tracing its origins to the animal laboratory and experimental psychology, has scrupulously tried to externalize all constructs and avoid concepts that might be construed as mentalistic, such as the ego or the self. As behavior therapy has become more widely used and its technics have multiplied, behavior therapists have continued to share a common vocabulary and a commitment to phrase all activities in objective terms despite increasing difficulties as they seek to modify more molar units of behavior and deal with covert events.

This volume has a profoundly pragmatic orientation toward treatment and focuses on the technology developed by behavior therapy without necessarily concerning itself with phrasing what is done in the careful language that usually characterizes this literature. This feature may trouble some behavior therapists, but is likely to be appreciated by many clinical readers unfamiliar with the field. The volume deals analogously with the use of hypnosis in treatment. Here again conceptual problems, such as the relationship of trance depth to the therapeutic process, are not emphasized. There is a brief chapter presenting various theories of hypnosis. However, the authors see hypnosis as an exceedingly broad concept intended to include all special states of consciousness, suggestion, the placebo effect, and all forms of persuasive communication, while ignoring individual differences in patient responsivity. Though many investigators and some clinicians will find themselves discomfitted by the authors' decision to disregard many potentially important distinctions, some of the strength of the volume may lie in the simplified framework within which technics are outlined. The bridge between hypnosis and behavior therapy is the use of guided imagination, perhaps most central to this volume. This technic is widely used in behavior therapy and basic to all hypnotic approaches.

The authors are first and foremost pragmatic clinicians and do not seek to critically synthesize the various views. The many sections of this volume which cover the gamut of psychoneuroses, psychosis, psychosomatic disorders, and disorders of self-indulgence are characterized by brevity and an attempt to offer the readers simple therapeutic prescriptions. Further, it provides a focused review of relevant work, using either hypnosis or behavior therapeutic approaches for each of its many sections. Little effort is made to distinguish between the relatively reliable reports or systematic studies as opposed to controversial or anecdotal reports based on single cases. For the most part, the authors have chosen to withhold comment except when they report on their own work.

It is important that the reader understand the aim of this volume. It is to provide him with a considerable number of potentially useful clinical technics for the treatment of a broad range of symptoms. The material is presented lucidly and with conviction. The topical bibliographies will allow the serious clinician to review what little solid data is available in each of these areas, and thus the book is intended as a useful beginning to allow the clinician to learn about these matters. From the point of view of the practitioner, the emphasis on the technology of treatment rather than its theory makes this a volume likely to be useful for years to come.

MARTIN T. ORNE, M.D., PH.D.
The Institute of Pennsylvania Hospital
and University of Pennsylvania

Foreword

There has been very little interaction between behaviour therapy and hypnosis, a failure of mutual understanding which I think is very much to be deplored. The book here offered is the first to try and reconcile these two strangers, and bring them together in cooperative endeavour; for this we are all in the debt of the authors. I believe that hypnotic techniques are powerful enough to add both to our theoretical understanding and to our practical application of psychological methods in the treatment of psychiatric problems; only the future will be able to decide on the true value of hypnotic techniques, although the case for them made out here is certainly strong. I think it would be wrong of us to refuse even to experiment with these techniques, on the basis of too little scientific understanding; that excuse would have stifled effectively all medical advance since the time of Hippocrates!

One obvious difficulty in the way of using hypnosis in the practice of behaviour therapy is of course the simple fact that few psychologists are trained in these procedures, and that few courses give any instruction on hypnosis. It is very much to be hoped that such instruction will in future be given to all students of psychology; they ought to be familiar with one of the most striking phenomena in the whole of their science, and they ought certainly to be familiar with the current theories advanced to explain these phenomena. We really cannot go on and treat hypnosis as an outcast; to do so is unscientific in the extreme. Even though it may be more a problem than many other phenomena, let us remember that most of our explanations of psychological phenomena are far from adequate, and that fundamentally most of our problems are still unsolved—even as is the problem of hypnosis. This does not impede us from using intelligence tests (do we know what intelligence is?), from applying principles of conditioning (do we really know what conditioning is?), or from using concepts of personality (who would claim to know the basic nature of personality?). The existence of a textbook, such as this, is a good augury for future advance along these lines; I hope that the marriage between hypnosis and behaviour therapy here proposed will be consummated in the near future!

H. J. Eysenck
Institute of Psychiatry
University of London

Preface

There is a growing need in all fields of psychotherapy today for more effective methods of treatment. Successful therapy should facilitate the patient's gaining increased mastery over himself so that he can learn to cope with and to overcome his problems. The majority of psychotherapeutic methods are either too limited in their applications, too lengthy, or too costly. Powerful voices are now asking the psychotherapist to give evidence of the efficacy of his particular school of therapy. This means that the recovery rate as judged by empirical observations can be meaningful only if it exceeds the 65 per cent cure rate—the placebo effect.

At present, behavior modification therapy, a form of treatment derived from experimental psychology, is the cynosure of the psychotherapeutic world. There is an explosive increase in literature on behavior therapy. Its indications and contraindications are constantly being explored. However, many emotionally disturbed patients—even those presenting themselves with an existential crisis—seem to respond to behavior therapy.

The American Psychiatric Task Force to study behavior therapy recommends that it be used together with dynamic psychiatry. Currently, many psychotherapists would like to see a greater interchange between the psychodynamic approach and behavior therapy. They believe there is much value in incorporating the best of both traditions. This endeavor is a step in the right direction. Additionally, there is a need for the integration of hypnotherapeutic technics not only to supplement the other approaches but to act synergistically with them.

Some leaders in the behavior movement are conversant with the current advances in modern scientific hypnosis. They are aware that some of their technics have been pioneered and employed by hypnotherapists for years. The latter have used these intuitively in conjunction with learning theory in a manner unmistakably recognized as behavior therapy.

Hypnotherapists admit that suggestion utilized at different levels of awareness is one of the vectors responsible for the effectiveness of their methods. We appreciate that the acceptance of hypnotherapeutic technics is generally retarded by philosophical differences in orientation. This accounts for one school's rejecting rival theories. We hope that our book will demonstrate that behavior therapists need not consider hypnosis antithetical to their theory and practice. We, as well as others, have effectively used behavior technics with suggestion and/or hypnosis and know that behavior therapists can use suggestion and/or hypnosis technics within the context of behavior therapy.

At present, the didactic principles of learning theory and behavior therapy are rapidly being incorporated into medical education at the premedical, medical school, and residency levels. Behavior therapists are playing a significant role within a wide variety of mental health settings such as community centers, family medical practice, state hopitals, and school systems. There are also more colleges and medical schools offering training in hypnosis at the postgraduate and undergraduate levels. "Cross-fertilization" between hypnosis and behavior therapy, therefore, is inevitable.

In keening through the psychiatric literature, one finds a fair number of studies that utilize sophisticated hypnotic technics within a behavioral model. We offer numerous examples that this combined approach—the hypnobehavioral model—provides an innovative method that enables the psychotherapist to come to grips with refractory problems encountered either in his clinical practice or a hospital in-patient setting. The hypnobehavioral model is effective, in part, because suggestions given at hypnotic levels are more incisively received and acted upon. Individuals under hypnosis generally respond with a pinpoint precision or literalness to what is being said to them because the greater relaxation, concentration, and exquisite receptivity leads to greater objectivity. This ability to view the self is ordinarily difficult to attain with conventional therapies.

The hypnagogic images we describe also play an important role in our therapeutic approach. This internalization in the patient's own psyche makes imagery an effective agent for behavioral change. Seemingly forgotten is the fact that modern psychiatry has its roots deeply embedded in the various suggestive procedures and imagery originally practiced by saints, priests, and exorcists. Also, the Western world is now avidly embracing Eastern philosophic-religious healing methods, especially Zen and Yoga. These rely heavily on suggestion, relaxation, imagery, and fantasy evocation—all the *bêtes noires* of anxiety. Since this is the cornerstone of a great deal of behavior therapy and hypnosis, it is obvious that the circle has been completed. No single all-embracing theory underlies the hypnobehavioral model.

Therefore, the purpose of this book will be to take the knowledge gained from the basic sciences and clinical research in psychology, cross-cultural psychiatry, psychodynamics, hypnosis, and behavior therapy and integrate it into a new and useful frame of reference. We are not implying that our model is the answer to solving all problem behaviors. We are well aware that faith in a specific cure leads to the success of that cure! We stress this so as not to invite the same criticisms leveled at the Skinnerian school, namely, that they are mechanistic and disavow the humanistic approach.

As mentioned, our thesis is that hypnosis and behavior therapy are compatible and need not be warring factions. The best features of each can be fused as a multimodal form of therapy and can be carried out effectively in a medical-psychological setting. This multidisciplinary therapeutic approach to patient management can thus be directed to substituting positive, constructive, healthy, and adaptive responses for negative, destructive, harmful, and maladaptive responses. The neural pathways by which individuals develop emotional disorders are the same pathways by which these inappropriate responses can be eradicated, particularly if the patient learns the necessary mechanisms to reverse the processes that have conditioned him adversely. In other words, the target behavior to be treated has been learned, and therefore can be unlearned by introducing a new pattern of behavior. Although the method takes into consideration personality factors, it is primarily directed to a *here* and *now* approach.

The technics developed by the behavior modifiers as observational learning or "modeling" to develop greater ability to cope with maladaptive behavior and the step-by-step progression called a "hierarchy" are ingenious. The latter approach is individually constructed from the history and designed to bring about gradual desensitization. However, we shall describe how these methods can be reinforced by the strategies used by hypnotherapists.

The behavior modifiers do not use technics such as age regression or progression, time distortion (consisting of time expansion or time condensation), "glove anesthesia," dissociation, revivification, and negative or positive hallucinations. There are numerous other subtle hypnotic methods such as syptom-manipulation and communication utilizing double-blind strategies. These might be equated as basic determinants of behavior analogous to reflex conditioning and learning as they help the patient substitute more adaptive forms of behavior for incapacitating behaviors. These technics have been described but not conceptually integrated into behavior therapy per se. We shall illustrate how the integration of the aforementioned technics expedites therapy for specific disorders and also how hypnosis intensifies the perceptual and cognitive factors involved in "visual voyages" or hypnagogic experiences, evocation of fantasies, feeling states, and "altered states of consciousness" to bring about behavioral changes.

This is the first book to describe the kinds of standard images for reversal of specific conditioned responses ("symptoms")—by sensory imagery conditioning. These images can be readily incorporated into the hypnobehavioral therapist's armamentarium. This is also one of the first books to combine the most practical approaches offered by behavior modifiers and the most useful technics developed by contemporary hypnotherapists. It is also the first to discuss the similarities and dissimilarities between the two disciplines. We also have presented the various verbalizations for hypnotic induction and sensory-imagery conditioning used for managing patients with a wide variety of clinical problems. There are illustrative case histories to better acquaint the reader with our technics. We hope that the reader will make full use of these as well as the references and source material at the end of each chapter. By these means the reader can enhance his knowledge on any subject of particular interest to him. Some repetition throughout the text is necessary for greater clarity, particularly for those readers interested only in specific chapters.

A practical therapeutic approach based on our clinical experience with hypnosis and behavior modification has been presented. Even though there is an extensive literature, we have included the studies and therapeutic technics we considered of practical clinical import. Finally, we are confident that amalgamating the fundamental principles of hypnosis and the practical features of psychodynamics with behavior therapy will have a salutary effect on the practice of psychology and psychiatry. It should also be a boon for providing a fertile field for further research.

Acknowledgments

We wish to acknowledge the work of those intrepid pioneers, most of whom are mentioned in this volume, who contributed to the advancement of hypnosis, behavior therapy, and imagery psychotherapy. It is impossible to give credit to everyone who enlightened the scientific community to these disciplines.

We wish to thank our publishers, the J. B. Lippincott Co., for their confidence in the merits of our efforts. We are particularly grateful to J. Stuart Freeman, Jr. for his guidance and infinite patience with the production of the manuscript. He particularly stressed that the material be immediate and clinically practical. Also, we are indebted to Fred Zeller, who had the foresight and courage to catalyze our seminal ideas into fruition of this book. We cannot adequately express our gratitude to Carole Baker, Copy Editor, and her staff for the superb editorial assistance.

We also are grateful to the many students whom we have taught at the undergraduate and postgraduate levels as well as our patients; both gave us many penetrating insights into those areas required to make our endeavors a basic textbook of interest to the student, researcher, and clinician. We are most appreciative to Professors Martin T. Orne and H. J. Eysenck, who are, respectively, editors of the prestigious International Journal of Clinical and Experimental Hypnosis and the Journal of Behavior Research and Therapy. Both have honored us with their forewords.

Finally, we acknowledge the efforts of Jimmy Louise Kroger, who spent many months on the research, typing, and preparation of the manuscript. Even though the two collaborators practice together, she often had to modify our behavior in her own special way when we disagreed on how, why, and what material was to be presented. Thus we were able to achieve a harmonious and balanced approach.

We trust the reader will realize there are numerous gaps in our present knowledge of the art and science of hypnosis and behavior therapy, but hope that future researchers will build on our hypnobehavioral model.

W. S. KROGER, M.D.
Beverly Hills, California

W. D. FEZLER, PH.D.
Beverly Hills, California

Contents

Part Five NEUROSES AND PSYCHOSES

Nothing should be omitted in an art which interests the whole world, one which may be beneficial to suffering humanity and which does not risk human life or comfort.

HIPPOCRATES

PART ONE

History, Foundations, Technics

1

Historo-Diagnosis

In this chapter we shall discuss history-taking in the emotionally disturbed patient. We shall describe briefly the differences in the methods employed by psychodynamically oriented therapists and behavior modifiers, irrespective of whether they employ hypnosis. Though the technics of the two groups are similar in many respects, there are important differences. In the former, more emphasis is placed on past events and how they relate to current behaviors. In behavior modification, more attention is directed to the current needs for the various maladaptive behaviors that have been learned. There is also more emphasis on the "here and now" (see p. 67 for a more complete description). We have combined the best features of both approaches so that historo-diagnosis can be a more flexible tool for applying our hypnobehavioral model.

HANDLING THE INITIAL INTERVIEW

Before discussing our hypnobehavioral model, we shall describe how our patients are handled from the initial visit. They usually are tense and apprehensive. We have noted that the anxiety-laden patient is more at ease if we casually sit in front of our desk alongside the patient using two chairs of similar construction and height. The first few minutes are crucial, so everything possible is done to make him feel that we are interested in hearing his story. The average patient is ashamed, often a bit distrustful at first, and fearful. Putting him at ease also allays fear. Presence of fear increases the defenses and this causes the patient to withdraw, thus concealing his anxiety and need for help. A stereotyped history from a form is not used nor should one talk above the patient's intellectual level. Also, seldom is the patient's narration interrupted. It is difficult for the

3

anxious patient to talk when full attention is not paid to his overt or implied communications. Since his problem cannot be seen but only heard, he wonders if the therapist will understand his dilemma. So let him talk.

The old adage, "If the patient opens his mouth enough times, he will put his foot into it," has merit. Listen carefully with "the third ear" for important or "hot" material; pay at least as much attention to what he does not say as to his verbalizations. Do not ask routine questions, because routine questions deserve only routine answers. Patients can ignore an important one by answering an unimportant one. Avoid patronizing questions such as What can I do for you? What's wrong with you? Avoid rapid-fire questions, as this only invites glib answers. If one asks factual questions without obvious embarrassment, the patient will continue talking.

When seeking answers to why the patient is disturbed, try to control your intonation and choice of words so that you do not bias his replies. Try to convey that you are seriously interested in him, eager to help, prepared to listen without interrupting, and capable of understanding and responding to his needs. Look for slips of the tongue or accidental remarks, frequent sighing, inordinate laughing or crying. Note particularly if flushing or blanching of the face occurs, flickering or lowering of the eyes, tensing of the jaws or fists, and most important, assess the quality of the patient's speech, particularly stammering. These are usually cues that highly charged material has been touched.

If a patient blocks while relating embarassing material or if he is silent for any length of time, say, "Just take your time. Don't talk until you can do so without effort." The apprehensive patient is grateful for being helped, and usually the brief period of silence is followed by spontaneous expressions involving his difficulties. As soon as he realizes that he has the freedom to choose when and what to say, he feels more secure in your presence and will then usually reveal meaningful material. At this time, pointed questions about what has been omitted can be asked. Too much explaining should be avoided, as this may only confuse the apprehensive patient. The therapist unfamiliar with history-taking is unlikely to obtain the information essential for making an accurate diagnosis.

THE EMOTIONAL NEEDS FOR SYMPTOMS

Patients who consult a therapist seldom recognize their inordinate need for their symptoms. Some of the commonest of these are the need to inadvertently exaggerate the severity of their complaints as a means of getting more attention, to avoid the responsibilities of marriage or parenthood, to dominate their home environment in a neurotic manner in order to compensate for their complete inability to deal with their problems in a realistic and mature manner, and, finally, to use symptoms as a means of self-punishment for guilty fears.

Many such patients, even if aware of their deep-seated needs, are unable to face their emotional problems. They resist psychological probing with puzzled silence or offer only vague replies when questioned. For such difficult cases the skillful therapist may wish to devote several multi-evaluation sessions for more in-depth history-taking. These diagnostic sessions will be more productive if he does not pontificate or make judgmental statements. The patient has not come in for lessons in ethics. If the therapist is a generalist, he can get important information during the physical examination. It is here, during an unguarded moment, that much valuable knowledge can be gathered. After this, he can discuss the present complaints, the pertinent facts that led up to it, and, more important, the patient's attitudes toward these facts. If the therapist knows what he is looking for, particularly if there is too much digression, he can gently guide the patient to tell his story. How to obtain sexual and other intimate information is discussed in Chapter 11.

DIFFERENTIAL DIAGNOSIS

Differentiation of the types of emotional disorders can be accomplished as follows: Are they connected to or aggravated by emotional upsets? Is there any evidence of a previous personality disturbance? What was the patient's reaction to other environmental difficulties? How have acute or chronic illnesses interfered with emotional adjustments? Are the complaints compatible with the physical findings? Negative examinations should not contribute to the common error of diagnosing a neurosis by exclusion, but rather a valid diagnosis of neurosis should be made by positive signs that an emotional conflict exists, which the therapist must recognize or learn to recognize. The emotionally disturbed patient with a ''denial of illness'' syndrome often presents the real problem.

One should not accept statements at their face value. Patients are often confused about the nature of their problems, both past and present, and tend to exaggerate or unnecessarily minimize their importance. Careful inquiry will usually reveal the reasons behind such attitudes. Prominent personality features have their opposites in sharp contrast, such as amiability and hostility, dependence and independence, submissiveness and aggressiveness. The therapist must help the patient to understand the needs for these contradictory traits, and how they relate to his problem.

After obtaining his information, the therapist, if unskilled, may want to discuss the history material with a trained psychotherapist in order to better understand the significance of data and to recommend whatever therapy is indicated. Even the psychologically trained physician at times seeks this consultation, and certainly the doctor who has not had psychiatric training will save himself much time and trouble if he recognizes the need for and accepts this type of help.

2

Historical Development of Hypnosis

We shall briefly describe the historical development of hypnosis. A cursory review of all psychological healing methods indicates that hypnosis has been practiced in one form or another in the civilized and uncivilized world under many different labels since the dawn of history (Bromberg 1954, Kroger 1963, Tinterow 1970, and Kiev 1974). Persian Magi and the Greek oracles used rituals similar to hypnotic procedures, calling them "temple sleep." There are many allusions to it in the Bible. Kroger (1963) and Mac Hovec (1973) have reviewed the history of hypnosis, and the reader is referred to their presentations on the subject.

ANCIENT METHODS

Exorcist-hypnotic methods were used by Assyro-Babylonian physician-priests to destroy the demons responsible for illnesses (Gordon 1949, Bettman 1956). Almost simultaneously, Egyptian soothsayers and priests, about 5000 B.C., used similar technics to placate the wrath of the gods responsible for healing (Sigerist 1951). Often, imagery oriented around "visions" of improvement was employed to cope with the invisible "wounds" of the supplicant.

Such Greek-Roman healers as Hippocrates (c. 460–370 B.C.) and Plato (c. 427–347 B.C.) replaced magic-mystical-religious approaches by concepts that "natural phenomena had natural explanations" and posited various types of "humors" responsible for mental disorders, (Alexander and Selesnick 1966). These were implicated even by Galen 700 years later.

The ancient Hebrews, though they used magical rites and incantations, invoked a monotheistic God with prayers of mercy. They deliberately omitted

6

references to demons and magic (Castiglione 1947) and allusions to exorcism (Felman 1966). They also used meditation accompanied by chanting, breathing exercises, and fixation on the letters in the Jewish alphabet that spelled God or that developed other names for God (Bokser 1954). Bowers and Glasner (1958), the latter a rabbi, have noted that these ritualistic practices were similar to autohypnosis and that they are crystallized in the "ecstasy" state of *kavanah*. In the Talmud, *kavanah* implies relaxation, concentration, correct intention (motivation), and all enhanced the ritualistic procedures. Scholem (1967), after studying Abulafia, a rabbi in the 13th century, gives the impression that his own works are a Judaized treatise on Yoga. Methodical meditation, breathing exercises, and ecstasy states are similar to the practices of Yoga, Zen Buddhism, Hinduism, Shintoism (Fujisawa 1959), Sufism (Trimingham 1971), and Christian meditation, including the repetitive prayers developed in the Byzantine Church (Norwich and Sitwell 1966).

The philosophy of the early Chinese dealt with balance and inner harmony achieved by Yin (darkness and death) and Yang (light of life). In conjunction with these principles, Taoism (the Right Way) found further expression in the teachings of Lao-Tzu (c. 604 B.C.). Folk tales were embraced as healing methods of the lower classes. Vivid images and fantasies were built upon a "nether world of witches and wizardry, of animal disease and ancestral spirits, all of which can bring madness as well as cure" (Vieth 1963). To cope with the demons responsible for disease, priest-magicians claimed to represent Yang (positive forces), which empowered them to overcome Yin (negative forces).

These historical developments have recently been described by Benson et al. (1974). He also cites other traditional religious practices capable of achieving "altered states of consciousness" and the "relaxation response." Though he mentions hypnosis, autogenic training, progressive relaxation, and transcendental meditation, he does not emphasize that all of these as well as the philosophical-religious states described above are all forms of hypnosis. It is obvious, however, that the cadence and intonations of prayer in a relaxing environment, posture, eye fixation on an altar or religious symbol, and rhythmic chanting are hypnagogic. Finally, the self-contemplation, self-absorption characterizing prayer and meditation are practically identical with modern-day autohypnosis.

The best source of historical data on the ancient use of hypnosis is the Aesculapian cult that thrived in ancient Greece about 500 B.C. There were literally hundreds of temples throughout Greece and the Roman Empire. A special room was allocated for "dream healing," which at that time was considered the best form of therapy. The Aesculapian priests, after interpreting the supplicants' dreams, then formulated what they considered to be the best treatment for the specific disease of that particular patient. They also used special prayers to cast out evil spirits. According to Mac Hovec (1975), the repetitive nature of these suggestions acted as reinforcements similar to the technics of modern-day behavior modification. He also points out that the Zen, Buddhist, Tibetan, and Yogic literature is replete with guided fantasies that were given to a patient while he was deeply relaxed and in a reflective, contemplative state of mind. It is interesting that these technics were similar to what is now called guided affective imagery (G.A.I.) (Leuner 1969). By using every sensory modality, altered states of consciousness were produced. For instance, mantras were chanted in darkened rooms and there was the scent of incense, sound of wind chimes, soft music, dripping of water, or perfect silence. Thus, by repetitively using all the senses, they increased awareness and established a receptive condition that closely resembles the modern-day hypnotic state. (We mention this since such modern-day hypnotists as Rochkind and Conn [1974] have revived the use of fantasy evocation.) We shall stress the utilization of specific images for stimulating all five sensory modalities (described in Chap. 10). These are somewhat similar to those used in ancient times.

MODERN METHODS

Aesculapian priests sometimes used a brush to literally "brush away" symptoms or disease. They also used a cloth or touch of the hand. Mesmer did much the same with his iron magnets and with his hands. In 1771, Mesmer also borrowed exorcist-like technics from Father Gassner and ideas from Father Hell, a pioneer in the application of steel plates to the body. He also incorporated Maxwell's "universal fluid" as magnetic energy that acted as a curative agent. Mesmer coined the term "animal magnetism" and unwittingly laid the cornerstone for modern-day psychiatry. A commission was set up in 1784 by the Academie des Sciences to investigate Mesmer's animal magnetism cures; it concluded that "magnetism without the imagination produces nothing." Deslon, a member of the committee stated, "If the imagination is so effective, why do we not use it?" His question has been ignored for 200 years, as it is only recently that imagery technics are being employed in psychiatry. This is surprising, as all religions control behavior by imagery conditioning.

Braid (1889), an English physician, became the father of modern hypnotism when he coined the term *hypnotism* from the Greek word *hypnos,* meaning sleep. Unfortunately the term has created great confusion and has long prevented the acceptance of its curative effects by orthodox medicine. Many pioneers who espoused hypnotism have been called charlatans by their colleagues. Among these were Elliotson, one of the most able physicians in England, who introduced the stethoscope, Esdaile, who performed numerous painless surgical operations, and Bramwell; all braved the titter of the herd to hear their thoughts called absurd. Two French physicians, Liébeault and Bernheim (1947), who taught Freud, treated over 12,000 cases. They refuted Charcot's observations that hypnosis was a form of hysteria.

Through Breuer, Freud became interested in hypnosis, but unfortunately he thought of it as a doctor-directed modality. He did not understand that the patient in reality hypnotized himself. Nor did he utilize self-hypnosis or patient-centered technics. As a result, he erroneously thought it stripped the patient of his defenses. He also admitted he was baffled by the riddle of suggestion. He never really abandoned it (Kline 1958), but unfortunately did not realize that his system of therapy was based largely upon the very faith he disavowed.

Sidis, Prince, McDougall, and Janet took issue with Freud's postulates regarding hypnosis. Those who still espouse the outmoded belief that hypnosis is a temporary cure are not aware that hypnosis is a meaningful interpersonal relationship that does not merely involve symptom removal but that can effectively form and shape adaptive behavior. This contemporary approach is vastly different from the outmoded concept of directive hypnosis utilized by Freud.

Pavlov, Platonov, Hull, Williams, Young, Estabrooks, and many other psychologists became interested in hypnosis and ushered in the current scientific era. Formation of the Society for Clinical and Experimental Hypnosis and the American Society for Clinical Hypnosis rapidly brought hypnosis into respectable circles. Kline, Conn, Raginsky, Erickson, Barber, Hilgard, Weitzenhoffer, Schneck, Spiegel, Watkins, Wolberg, Meares, Edmonston, and others too numerous to mention played important roles in the teaching and acceptance of scientific hypnosis.

In 1955, the British Medical Association reported its approval of hypnosis for treatment of psychoneuroses and hypnoanesthesia. The report also advised that all physicians and medical students receive fundamental training in hypnosis. In 1958, the American Medical Association recommended that, in view of our increasing knowledge, medical schools should include hypnosis in their curricula. It further emphasized that in the hands of properly trained persons, it had definite uses in medicine and dentistry. The report also said that even though certain areas remained controversial, more research should be encouraged.

Since these reports and the publication of over a dozen journals worldwide, there has been a tremendous explosion in the literature. This contains numerous studies conducted in academic circles that explain the rationale and indications for hypnosis. During this tortuous history, behavior modifiers, like Wolpe (1958) and some of his disciples, became interested in combining desensitization procedures and other behavioral technics with hypnotic relaxation. Often the latter was referred to as progressive relaxation or autogenic training; both are modifications of hypnotic technics.

At last the therapeutic and research potentialities of hypnosis are being recognized by serious-minded scientists. The links forged by Mesmer, Bernheim, and Liébeault, which led to Freud's misunderstanding the nature of hypnosis, are now used to make this ancient modality a better understood and more fully accepted therapeutic tool.

The historical development of hypnosis eventuated in methods for rapid and effective therapy. Study of transcultural psychological therapies from antiquity reveals that the *liet motif* of all healing methods is the "relaxation response" (Benson 1974, 1975). This is patently induced by suggestion, hypnosis, or both. Since no one knows where the latter begins and the former ends, it is obvious that all interpersonal psychotherapies, particularly those that use ritual, involve some degree of suggestion, hypnosis, or both.

We have taken hypnosis a step further by using sensory-imagery conditioning and other specialized technics described in the next chapter to systematically change behavioral responses. Thus, from Mesmer's unwitting use of the imagination evolved a more sophisticated directive application of the use of imagery under hypnosis. This fascinating aspect, with the addition of behavior modification therapy, adds a new chapter in the historical development of hypnosis.

REFERENCES

Alexander, F. G. and Selesnick, S. T.: The History of Psychiatry. New York, Harper and Row, 1966.

Benson, H.: The Relaxation Response. New York, Morrow, 1975.

Benson, H., Beary, J. F. and Carol, M. P.: The relaxation response. Psychiatry, *37:*37–46, 1974.

Bernheim, H.: Suggestive Therapeutics. New York, London Book Co., 1947.

Bettman, C. L.: A Pictorial History of Medicine. Springfield, Ill., Charles C Thomas, 1956.

Bokser, Rabbi Ben Zion: From the World of the Cabbalah. New York, Philosophical Library, 1954.

Bowers, M. and Glasner, S.: Auto-hypnotic aspects of the Jewish cabbalistic concept of kavanah. J.C.E.H., *6:*50, 1958.

Braid, J.: Neurypnology. London, Redway, 1899.

Bromberg, W.: Man Above Humanity. Philadelphia, J. B. Lippincott, 1954.

Castiglione, A. A.: A History of Medicine, ed. 2. New York, Alfred A. Knopf, 1947.

Felman, Y. M.: Cutis, *2:*984, 1966.

Fusawa, C.: Zen and Shinto. New York, Philosophical Library, 1959.

Gordon, B. L.: Medicine Throughout Antiquity. Philadelphia, F. A. Davis, 1949.

Kiev, A.: Magic Faith In Healing. New York, Free Press, 1974.

Kroger, W. S.: Clinical and Experimental Hypnosis. Philadelphia, J. B. Lippincott, 1963.

Leuner, H.: Guided Affective Imagery (G.A.I.): A method of intensive psychotherapy. Am. J. Psychother., *23:*4, 1969.

Mac Hovec, F. J.: Hypnosis before Mesmer. Am. J. Clin. Hypn., *17:*215, 1973.

Norwich, J. J. and Sitwell, R.: Mount Athos. New York, Harper and Row, 1966.

Rochkind, M. and Conn, J. H.: Guided fantasy encounter. Am. J. Psychother., *27:*516, 1974.

Scholem, G. G.: Jewish Mysticism. New York, Schocken Books, 1967.

Sigerist, H. E.: A History of Medicine. vol. 1. New York, Oxford University Press, 1951.

Tinterow, M. M.: Foundations of Hypnosis, From Mesmer to Freud. Springfield, Ill., Charles C Thomas, 1970.

Trimingham, J. S.: Sufi Orders in Islam. Oxford, Clarendon Press, 1971.
Veith, I.: Bull. Hist. Med., *37:*139, 1963.
Wolpe, J.: Psychotherapy by Reciprocal Inhibition. Stanford, Stanford University Press, 1958.

SUGGESTED READINGS

Boudreau, L.: Transcendental meditation and yoga as reciprocal inhibitors. J. Behavior Therapy, *3:*97–98, 1972.
Daniels, L. K.: The treatment of psychophysiological disorders & severe anxiety by behavior therapy, hypnosis & transcendental meditation. Am. J. Clin. Hypn., *17:*267–270, 1975.
Kline, M. V.: Freud and Hypnosis. New York, Julian Press, 1958.
Schultz, J. H. and Luthe, W.: Autogenic Training. New York, Grune & Stratton, 1950.

3

Foundations of Hypnosis

Since many clinicians are not acquainted with the technics and terms used by hypnotherapists, we shall briefly describe some of these as they relate to suggestion and hypnosis. It is the hallmark of a scientist that he defines his terms, for only then can semantic confusion be eliminated. We shall first define the term *suggestion,* a word commonly used in medicine and psychology but admittedly subject to different interpretations.

PHENOMENA OF SUGGESTION

Suggestion

There are four types of suggestion. *Verbal,* which includes preverbal or subverbal, refers to communication by any type of sound. *Nonverbal* applies to gestures and facial expressions, which meaningfully enhance suggestibility. *Intraverbal* applies to the intonation of words; vocal inflections greatly influence suggestibility. The last is *extraverbal,* the implications of words and gestures; these facilitate acceptance of ideas. The latter is the most powerful type of suggestion. For instance, if one says, "Why don't you stand up?" in a peremptory tone of voice, such a suggestion usually mobilizes a critical attitude and resistance. But if one asks softly: "Are you not a little tired of sitting down?" the suggestion carries no tone of criticism. As a result it has a better chance of influencing an individual without the latter's realizing that he is being influenced!

Extraverbal suggestions are reinforced when words are accompanied by appropriate gestures symbolic of the desired act. Thus, the choice of words, man-

12

nerisms, inflections of the voice, as well as the implied meaning of the phrases used, play an important role in mediating perception, cognition, and behavioral response. These are potent factors in influencing suggestibility.

Suggestibility refers to a suggested act that is uncritically carried out without the individual's logical processes participating in the response. Suggestibility is potentiated whenever an individual repetitively hears any one of the four types of suggestions, either singularly or in combination, that is, by progressive contiguity.

Suggestibility, naturally, is also influenced to a great degree by motivation as well as by other factors that we shall describe below. The extent to which motivation is increased depends upon a favorable attitude and an "inhibitory mental set." The latter invariably is produced by misdirection of attention, that is, by some type of ritual. The inhibitory mental set increases responsiveness by blocking inappropriate stimuli opposed to the suggested and desired responses. These stimuli are either *sensory* (those derived via any of the neural pathways for transmitting sensations) or *cognitive* (permanent recordings of past experiences). For instance, the thought or idea of food (cognitive stimulus) can be initiated by the smell of food (sensory stimulus) or the thought of a restaurant where one experienced a pleasant meal (cognitive stimulus; Barrios 1969). We shall describe how we use these various types of stimuli emanating from the *signal input environment*—the external or internal milieu—for enhancing suggestibility via sensory imagery conditioning or recall.

The degree of suggestibility depends not only upon the technics used to produce it, but also on the prestige, expectation, and other variables such as the "emotional contagion" associated with group susceptibility. Another important variable is the quality of the relationship established between therapist and subject—the rapport—an important ingredient for potentiating suggestibility. This aspect will be discussed more fully below.

Whenever a suggestion is repeated again and again, the sensory spiral of belief is compounded from the outset into conviction. This automatically produces a conditioned response. Such conditioning, in part, helps explain the role that suggestibility plays in the production of hypnotic behavior. However, increased suggestibility alone does not explain the complex processes associated with hypnotic behavior. Rather, one might state that increased suggestibility (hypersuggestibility) is a constant feature of hypnosis. Before discussing hypersuggestibility, it must be emphasized that the term and the manner in which we use it must be differentiated from gullibility; the latter implies use of deception.

Hypersuggestibility. As mentioned, when specific stimuli are responded to more readily as a result of inhibition of competing ones, this leads to hypersuggestibility. Thus, whenever *selective attention* (cortical excitation) to relevant stimuli occurs with *concomitant selective inattention* (partial cortical inhibition) to irrelevant ones, the resultant hypersuggestibility accounts in part for what we refer to (for want of a better term) as hypnosis.

We are continually being bombarded by suggestions. There is no fine line of demarcation between suggestibility and hypnotizability. Thus, where suggestibility ends and hypnotizability begins is not known. However, susceptibility to suggestion is apparently increased during hypnosis. This is one of the prime reasons for using it. For a more complete discussion of suggestibility and hypersuggestibility and how they relate to hypnosis, the reader is referred to Wolberg (1945), Barber (1965), Weitzenhoffer (1953), Meares (1960), Kroger (1963a), Hilgard (1965), Erickson (1967), and Barrios (1970).

THEORIES OF HYPNOSIS

There are as many definitions of hypnosis as there are definers. To provide a better understanding we shall discuss separately the induction procedures, phenomena, and posthypnotic responses even though they are interrelated. There is a vast and mutually contradictory literature on the theoretical formulations of hypnosis. We do not wish to get involved in the current dispute as to whether or not hypnosis is a habit (Hull 1933), a goal-directed behavior (White 1941), selective hypersuggestibility (Weitzenhoffer 1953, 1957), an atavism (Meares 1960), role playing (Sarbin and Coe 1972), a trance (Erickson 1967), a state (Orne 1959; Hilgard 1965), a non-state (Barber 1969) or an adaptative regression (Gill and Brenman 1959; Gill 1972). All of these formulations concerning a theory of hypnosis certainly have broadened our understanding of the subject. However, because of the polymorphous nature of hypnosis, considerable confusion still exists.

Barber (1969), the chief protagonist of the non-state view, in numerous publications contends that "hypnosis cannot be related in a linear fashion to the phenomena." He does not intimate that "hypnosis does not exist" (Barber 1967). Rather he contends that denotable antecedent, intervening, and dependent variables account for the elusive altered state of awareness called hypnosis. He has raised some pertinent questions that challenge our prevailing notions about what constitutes hypnosis.

We believe that there is some modicum of truth to the above-mentioned theoretical formulations. For instance, there are some individuals who "role play" but soon find themselves going along with the therapist's suggestions to become hypersuggestible. The problem of role playing is negated by hypnoanesthesia, with which one of us has had extensive experience (Kroger 1960, 1963).

The problem of role playing, or shamming, was advanced to explain Mesmeric anesthesia at the turn of the last century. Esdaile (1850) reported hundreds of painless surgical procedures, and the question of shamming arose. He stated: "I see only two ways of accounting for it; my patients on returning home either say to their friends similarly afflicted 'What a soft man the Doctor is: he cut me to pieces for 20 minutes and I made him believe that I did not feel it. Isn't it a capital joke? Do go and play him the same trick,' or they may say to their brother sufferers, 'Look at me; I have got rid of my burden'—20, 30, 40, 50, 60 or 80 lbs., as it may be (scrotal tumors)—'I am restored to the use of my body and can work for my bread. This I assure you, the doctor did when I was asleep, and I knew nothing about it.' '' (Marcuse 1959).

There is no doubt that patients capable of entering the deepest or plenary state of hypnosis, somnambulism, are in a so-called trance. No professional actor or actress could respond so realistically to the suggestions of the hypnotist. There also is a great deal of merit to the theory propounded by Orne (1959)—that hypnotic subjects develop "trance logic" or a "tolerance for incongruity," that is, people buy things that do not add up. This makes more sense than equating hypnosis with trance, magic, and occultism.

FACTORS INFLUENCING HYPNOTIC INDUCTION

Most factors discussed in this section apply not only to the hypnotic induction procedure with its associated changes in awareness, but also to the relaxation process used by behavior therapists. We are not implying that hypnosis and behavior therapy are identical. Rather we wish to illustrate that each method contains a number of commonalities important for understanding the behavioral changes noted in both procedures (see Chap. 8).

Concentration

The greater a patient's ability to concentrate the more he will relax, and the greater the probability of success of the hypnotic induction.

Prestige

A therapist who is in a "one up" position commands respect from the supplicant who is in a "one down" position. If the latter regards the therapist with awe and respect, particularly if he is an authority, the prestige increases success of the hypnotic induction. We do not equate a hypnotic induction technic with the psychodynamic concept of transference. For instance, if the child-parent type transference is present, it does not necessarily facilitate hypnotic induction.

Expectation

Expectations can influence the induction procedure and relaxation response negatively or positively. Fears and strong desires relevant to being hypnotized are examples of negative and positive effects. Fears can consist of mistrust, fear of revealing secrets or of being dominated by the hypnotist; all interfere with the hypnotic induction. However, the authors obviate these misconceptions by a preinduction talk designed to produce an acceptance and a positive attitude.

If the patient either has a preconceived notion of what hypnosis is like or has already experienced the procedure, the expectation influences the hypnotic induction. Expectation certainly plays a major role in the goal-directed (White 1941), role-playing (Sarbin and Coe 1972) theories of hypnosis. In essence, responses to hypnotic suggestions are goal striving in an expectant subject. The individual, therefore, behaves like a hypnotized person, as this role is continuously being defined by the hypnotist and understood by the subject (Barber 1961).

Motivation

Lack of motivation decreases effectiveness of both the suggestions for producing hypnotic induction and the associated relaxation. The patient who always wants to be in control is difficult to hypnotize or relax. This can be obviated if he is told, *"You* control the entire induction procedure," which indeed is true. Too-strong motivation for hypnotization often can evoke negative responses and interfere with the induction procedure. Skepticism also interferes with the positive responses necessary for hypnotic induction.

Imagination

The imagination plays an important role not only in hypnotic induction, but for evoking the imagery so essential for deep relaxation and facilitation of conditioning. The readier response to imagery definitely increases the susceptibility to hypnotic induction.

Age

Susceptibility varies with age. Language ability plays an important role. Since the hypnotic induction responses are evoked by words, it is understandable why children below 5 or 6 make poor subjects. With increasing age, the patient's inability to concentrate also lessens the degree of responsivity.

Other Factors

Imbeciles, morons, senile persons, and completely detached individuals are difficult, if not impossible, to hypnotize. The ability to concentrate on one idea at a time facilitates induction. Braid tried to change the name of hypnosis to *monoideism*—the ability to think of one thing at a time so as to exclude irrelevant ideas—but did not succeed. Cultural factors often determine susceptibility to suggestion. People think and act according to the way they have been "programmed." The stage entertainer-hypnotist capitalizes on this factor. The feelings and temperament of the hypnotherapist at the time of induction often can be an important determinant of the outcome. This is seldom considered as an important antecedent variable. His confident manner also influences the induction procedure. Conviction of hypnosis leads to hypnosis!

From the foregoing, we can conclude that hypnotic induction is influenced by the "misdirection of attention," or ritual that inhibits stimuli (sensory or cognitive) that are incompatible with those task-motivated suggestions given by the hypnotherapist. This facilitates the readiness to accept desired suggestions, resulting in increased responsiveness.

NATURE OF THE HYPNOTIC INDUCTION

The hypnotic induction to be described on pages 30, 31, and 32 consists of a sequential series of double-bind suggestions given in such a manner that a positive response to a prior suggestion conditions the subject to react with hyper-suggestibility to the next suggestion so that relaxation results.

Wolpe (1958) states:

> Patients who cannot relax will not make progress with this method. Those who cannot or will not be hypnotized but who can relax will make progress, although apparently more slowly than when hypnosis is used.

The hypnotic induction is *not* produced by passes, gestures, or the "evil eye" characterizing the Svengali-Trilby-Rasputin concept of hypnosis. It can be produced by literally dozens of modalities involving stimulation of any one or all of the senses. Often, too, there is no need for a formalized induction technic. Rather, it can be induced by exhortations such as those seen at evangelical, shrine or faith healing meetings. Contrary to popular opinion, the hypnotherapist need not have a powerful personality; hypnotic susceptibility is a function of the subject's capacity to respond!

We do not conceptualize hypnosis as a state of unconsciousness or a sleep-state. It is as natural to the organism as sleep and wakefulness, which are merely other arbitrary delineations of awareness. One can be "asleep while awake and awake while asleep"! One important difference is that in hypnosis there is a narrowing of the perceptual fields, which results in a heightened attention span. The resultant hyperacuity increases susceptibility to suggestion and enhances voluntary and involuntary performance. Thus, the individual "can tap forgotten assets and hidden potentials" that he always possessed, but did not realize how to utilize. When this occurs, belief is compounded into conviction! The induction of hypnosis is the induction of conviction! Hence we can summarize that in the presence of *appropriate motivation, a favorable mental set, misdirection of attention, belief, confidence, and expectation—catalyzed by the imagination or experiential background (the sum total of an individual's life experiences)—all lead to conviction or "programmed faith."* This is what differentiates hypnosis from forceful suggestion and persuasion. The latter two mobilize resistance, whereas hypnosis allows faith-laden suggestions to be accepted uncritically.

Because of the popular misconceptions about hypnosis that prevail, even among the scientific community, we wish to re-emphasize that, as mentioned in the preceding chapter, hypnosis is a *patient-centered mechanism rather than a doctor-directed modality.* This theme has been elaborated on in "It's Indeed a Wise Hypnotist Who Knows Who Is Hypnotizing Whom" (Kroger 1962), and in *Illusion and Reality* (Kubie 1972).

Barrios (1969) posits that if a series of suggestions are given to the subject, the probability of inducing hypnosis will be greater if the suggestions are given in gradually increasing order of difficulty rather than in random order. Each positive response increases the probability of success of the following suggestion. It is interesting to look at some of Barber's results in this light (1961, 1965). Barrios (1973) astutely points out that Barber obtained a good many hypnotic phenomena by means of waking suggestions, that is, without the need of a hypnotic induction. Barber considers a hypnotic induction in terms of the giving of sleep or relaxation suggestions. Since Barber usually gives his suggestions in increasing order of difficulty, he actually uses hypnosis without a formal induction technic to obtain the responses.

Many misconceptions have arisen from Barber's (1969) work. One is likely to get the mistaken impression that hypnosis is not uniquely effective, and those unfamiliar with hypnosis might conclude that since hypnosis is relatively ineffective it is not worth investigating. This is not Barber's intention. He is attempting to clarify the nature of hypnosis and place it on a more scientific basis. He is *not* explaining it *away,* rather he is attempting to explain it (Barrios 1973).

PHENOMENA OF HYPNOSIS

Hypnotic phenomena occur in the course of our everyday existence. For example, "waking hypnosis" in the form of repetitive radio and television commercials, advertising, propaganda, and the performance of a good orator or actor—all heighten the attention span in a meaningful manner to enhance suggestibility. Since the brain can develop negative and positive hallucinations during dreams, it can be used to develop such phenomena during hypnosis. We shall show how all the phenomena subsumed under the rubric of hypnosis can readily be explained in terms of everyday experiences. Other examples of waking hypnosis may be noted in someone engrossed in a daydream or watching a film; varying degrees of emotions are registered as we get caught up in the action sequences. The phenomena of hypnosis occur whenever reality is made out of unreality!

Autohypnosis

Autohypnosis or self-hypnosis results from heterosuggestions. However, the autosuggestions appear to originate spontaneously within the individual rather than to be instituted by another person. Whenever an individual believes that these are *his* suggestions, they are apt to be followed more readily because criticalness and resistances are greatly reduced. Irrespective of whether autohypnosis originates from within or from without the person, it allows the individual to tap a tremendous reservoir of potential strength. A prime example of autohypnosis is prayer and meditation. Here varying degrees of autosuggestion in no small measure account for the success of religious healing.

Rapport

Rapport refers to the harmonious relationship between therapist and patient. Hypnosis produces a close interpersonal relationship where "the space between" is filled by the closeness of the concentration existing between therapist and patient. As a result of this special relationship, suggestions from the therapist (heterosuggestions) are more readily followed. In addition, greater attention is paid to a therapist when this rapport exists. The rapport is enhanced by the prestige of the therapist. When a subject is in good rapport with a therapist under hypnosis, he usually responds with a pinpoint literalness or precision to suggestions, particularly if these are in accord with his wishes and other emotional needs.

Persons in good rapport with a therapist will even respond to a written order. Others will respond on hearing the therapist's voice on a telephone, provided they have been cued for this suggestion beforehand. The rapport can even be transferred to an associate who need have no knowledge of the patient's relationship with his previous therapist. Also, a prearranged signal can induce hypnosis readily in a willing subject whenever strong rapport is present.

One must not confuse rapport with undue emotional dependency on the therapist. Undue dependency is usually fostered either by the needs of the patient or the therapist, not by the rapport. The shared qualities of rapport, an important psychological phenomena of hypnosis, require more research. Who can deny that the important vector in any type of psychotherapeutic relationship is the establishment of good rapport?

As an important variable, rapport during hypnosis is more intense and provides therapist and patient with an emotional satisfaction seldom achieved by other forms of psychotherapy. Rapport is a specific requisite for hypnotic induction, utilization of the hypnotic process, and for production of subsequent behavioral changes.

Catalepsy

Catalepsy is a state characterized by involuntary contractions of any part or all of the body musculature. The counterpart of catalepsy is seen in humans during fright when they became rigid as a result of an alarm reaction. Animals also go into a catalepsy-like state known as "tonic immobility" where they "freeze" in order to blend into the landscape and escape detection. This is for protective purposes. The ability of an individual to develop catalepsy thus may be an atavism (Kroger and Freed 1951, Meares 1960).

When a limb is cataleptic, it will remain in any position in which it is placed. The plasticity of the fingers and extremities is referred to as flexibilitas cerea. When the eyeballs are cataleptic, they remain fixed when the head moves. This is at variance with eyeball movement at nonhypnotic levels; here quick darting of the eyes and lid blinking usually occurs. A cataleptic limb involuntarily resists counterpressure, and this usually indicates that medium or deep hypnosis has been reached. The whole body can be made cataleptic. When the muscles are balanced against each other, certain groups become rigid *without the subject's knowledge.*

Ideosensory Activities

Ideosensory activity refers to the capacity of the individual to develop sensory images that may be kinesthetic, olfactory, visual, auditory, tactile, or gustatory. This group of phenomena are of particular import for the images to be described in Chapter 10 on fantasy evocation and imagery conditioning. Recall of any past experience using any or all of the five senses constitutes an ideosensory activity. For example, the memory of the smell of a pine tree is a *positive ideosensory activity.* A *negative ideosensory activity* involves the denial of a given sensory experience; for instance, not seeing one's keys on the desk or not hearing one's name called are typical examples of negative ideosensory activity.

In order for an individual to make effective use of the images that we describe in Chapter 10, the patient must be involved in as many ideosensory experiences as possible. This facilitates conditioning, particularly if he utilizes his own memories, ideas, and sensations. The section on our imagery technics will illustrate how ideosensory activities are employed to affect physiologic responses. Understanding the nature of ideosensory activities is the sine qua non for understanding the operation of not only hypnosis but also for some of the "imagogic" technics used in behavior therapy.

Ideomotor Activities

Ideomotor activity also facilitates suggestibility. It refers to the involuntary capacity of muscles to respond to external stimuli. The thud of the boxer's glove on the jaw automatically causes an observer to wince, thus indicating his suggestibility. The induction technic, in part, depends on the patient's being unaware that he has made such physical responses to suggestion. Little does he realize they are a function of his own thoughts in response to external stimulation. However *he* thinks he is making the responses. This further heightens his belief and expectations of the success of future suggestions.

Hence, the hypersuggestibility leading to production of a great many hypnotic phenomena is brought about by the resultant of two forces, ideosensory and ideomotor activities. When ideosensory and ideomotor activities are paired, they bypass criticalness and are interpreted as reality. The resultant synergistic effect in part, leads to hypnosis.

Amnesia

Amnesia or forgetting is a common mechanism that everyone experiences at one time or another. A typical example of amnesia at a nonhypnotic level is when one introduces his best friend at a cocktail party and his name drops right out of one's mind. Amnesia during hypnosis can occur spontaneously or it can be suggested. Good subjects usually are unaware of most of the events that occurred during the hypnotic sessions. However, subsequent recall of the amnestic material can usually be obtained by appropriate posthypnotic suggestions. Either spontaneous or suggested amnesia is a very important dynamism in hypnotherapy. Painful segments of an individual's life, for instance, can be forgotten. However the durability of such amnesia is not predictable.

Dissociation

Though somewhat similar to amnesia, dissociation refers to the ability of the hypnotized patient to detach himself from his immediate environment. Dissociation occurs at nonhypnotic levels during reverie states, daydreaming, or when one fantasizes himself performing many activities. We use specific images to produce dissociation. This ability to ''step out'' of one's self has far-reaching implications for treatment of many types of problems including pain, insomnia, and sexual dysfunction. Its explicit use will be discussed in this and other chapters. The term *depersonalization* often is used to refer to a type of dissociation in which the patient is told to forget who he is and assume the identity of the person he would like to be.

Hypermnesia or Memory Recall

This term refers to the ability of the subject to recall events in greater detail than they can be recalled at nonhypnotic levels. Good hypnotic subjects can retrieve a tremendous amount of information. One must always consider the possibility of inaccuracy in the recall. This is due to *screen memories,* wherein an individual *misremembers* the actuality of events he *believes* he recalls. A typical example is the adult who thinks he has recalled an actual scene that occurred when he was two or three years old, but had forgotten that the event was described to him by his mother when he was four or five. Hypermnesia is used in criminology to recall pertinent information in the reconstruction of crimes. This phenomenon must not be confused with *revivification* described below.

Glove Anesthesia

The entire hand can be made insensitive to stimuli in a circumscribed area from the fingertips to the wrist. The depth of "anesthesia," achieved in good subjects is such that the area feels as numb and "wooden" as if an anesthetic agent has been injected. We shall describe how we use glove anesthesia for mitigating pain, and in treating other conditions.

Revivification and Age Regression

Revivification refers to actual reliving of earlier events. Usually, in true revivification, all memories that occurred after experiencing the prior events are not subject to recall. In age regression or pseudorevivification, the hypnotized person relives the past events but in the framework of present time. One must always be on guard for screen memories. During revivification, there is a marked change in demeanor, and the actions are truly compatible with the age of the subject at the period he is reliving. Recall of important memories is greatly facilitated by hypnosis. Various degrees of revivification and age regression can occur simultaneously, depending on the depth of the hypnosis. When spontaneous age regression is associated with some degree of revivification, it is referred to as retrogression. This often occurs when the conversation is carried on in the past tense. This helps to establish more firmly the clarity of the images to be recalled.

Revivification and age regression can be used by the therapist to exhume earlier portions of an individual's life experiences. This, as described in a chapter on hypnoanalysis, is of great import to the psychodynamically trained therapist. We use revivification and age regression to recover desired mnemonic data that we wish to use for changing future adaptive responses.

Age Progression

Age progression is artificially induced disorientation of a hypnotized subject who hallucinates living in the future, but at his present chronologic age. We use a great deal of age progression in the form of pseudo-orientation in time to understand how a hypnotized patient might react in the future to stressful conditions that are suggested to him now. Many of our images in Chapter 10 make full use of these phenomena, particularly in treating refractory sexual problems.

Hypnotic Analgesia and Anesthesia

Analgesia produced by hypnosis is much more effective than "biting the bullet" or volitional control of pain. We have had an extensive experience with childbirth (Kroger 1961) and surgical analgesia and anesthesia (see Chap. 35).

As mentioned above, we do not believe that analgesia and anesthesia can be explained solely by role playing (Barber, Spanos and Chavez 1974). Those who adhere to this theory are not clinicians, and their observations usually have been made on subjects who were asked to imagine a heavy weight on a finger or the hand immersed in ice water. In the latter instance, there is little or no motivation for pain relief, an important variable for attaining hypnoanalgesia. Placebos are more effective in persons whose stress and anxiety are real and thus greatly intensified (Beecher 1955).

Hypnoanesthesia refers to a state where the pain is there but there is no awareness of it. (The other side of the coin familiar to clinicians is "hysterical anesthesia" which follows no known segmental nerve distribution.) Our empirical observations lead us to believe that the degree of anesthesia is usually correlated with the depth of hypnosis and the strength of motivation.

We also see the "port-of-last-call patient" with chronic pain syndromes (Kroger 1963). Our results with hypnoanesthesia are not due to such relevant variables as placebo effects and desire to please the hypnotherapist. However, those with organic pain problems do better because they are more highly motivated to obtain pain relief. For fuller explanation of hypnoanesthesia see Chapters 34 and 35.

Negative and Positive Hallucinations

A negative hallucination is not sensing a stimulus that exists, while a positive hallucination is experiencing a stimulus that does not exist in external reality. Such negative and positive hallucinations involving any of the senses can be produced in good subjects. These are similar to such everyday experiences and distortions of reality that occur during fantasies, reverie states, and dreams. By appropriate suggestions, alterations in all the sensory modalities can be produced. "Blindness" and "deafness" can be induced in some patients by hypnosis. This is undoubtedly similar to hysterical blindness and deafness. Even "color-blindness" has reportedly been induced (Erickson 1939), although this has been refuted by Barber (1964).

However, even though some of the hallucinations may be due to simulation or role playing, they act as potent stimuli to influence behavioral responses. Hypnotherapists make full use of these suggested hallucinatory experiences in imagery conditioning, especially in scene visualization and fantasy evocation. We also use hallucinatory experiences produced by our images for altering perceptual processes and effecting the desired behavioral responses.

Somnambulism

This refers to one of the deepest stages of hypnosis. It is similar to the Nirvana state of Yoga and the Satori state of Zen and other trancelike states. This is an important phenomenon of hypnosis. It occurs also, at nonhypnotic levels—as in sleepwalking and sleep-talking. Often a conversation can be carried on while the person is asleep and without his knowledge.

Most individuals who are somnambulists exhibit spontaneously many other phenomena of hypnosis: dissociation, analgesia, anesthesia, revivification, and amnesia. Oddly enough, a formal induction technic usually is not needed to attain somnambulism. It just occurs. Such persons constitute about 10 per cent of the general population. Often they are erroneously classified as having "multiple personalities."

Somnambulism is not sleep, even though the person appears to be in a dreamlike state. Often, however, it can be transformed to true sleep. It also is generally associated with catalepsy. The eyes may be opened or closed. As a rule, the somnambulist cannot recall events during hypnosis unless told to do so, even though his memory is enhanced. Suggestions are accepted by the subject as convictions. The lack of criticalness together with amnesia and an inability to appraise reality explains somnambulism. One need not postulate "regression of the ego" (Gill and Brenman 1959) or the subject being in the "power of the hypnotist". It is a natural adaptive response mechanism, "built into" the human organism. Nearly all the important hypnotic responses can readily be demonstrated on somnambules. When present, we captitalize on it for readily obtaining maximal results.

Automatic Writing

This refers to the material produced by a good hypnotic subject able to write while he is engaged in conversation irrelevant to the material being written. The person often has no awareness at the time of *what* he is writing, but later under hypnosis often can make meaningful associations to the writings. It is utilized by hypnoanalysts (see p. 53).

Time Distortion

Time distortion is one of the most interesting and clinically valuable phenomena of hypnosis. It refers to the remarkable capacity of the brain to "expand" or "condense" time. This dynamism is also noted during everyday experiences. For instance, time can drag during a boring lecture during which 2 minutes seems like 20 minutes. Or, when one is pleasantly engaged in conversation over the phone, time passes quickly (condensation or time contraction). Briefly, 1 minute of brain, subjective, or experiential time can be equated with 10 minutes of world, clock, or chronologic time (time expansion). How time distortion is utilized to facilitate hypnotherapy has been described in a pioneering work by Cooper and Erickson (1954).

We shall refer to time distortion—time condensation and expansion—especially in the chapter on imagery conditioning. We have found it most advantageous in mitigating the duration of pain; evaluating the emotional sequelae associated with sterilization in the male and female (Kroger 1963 b); lengthening the duration of erection in men with premature ejaculation and in helping women who require prolonged sexual stimulation.

Posthypnotic Responses

Actions carried out after the termination of hypnosis are called posthypnotic responses. Periodic reinforcement tends to increase the effectiveness of a posthypnotic response; repeated elicitation does not weaken it. Strength of the response depends on the patient's motivation to accept the suggestion. Therefore, posthypnotic suggestions should be in keeping with the subject's needs and goals. Likewise posthypnotic responses, too, are part of our everyday existence. Our lives are full of such relationships—"waking hypnosis." Whenever reality thinking is neutralized, responses to suggestion occur more readily. Here we see how posthypnotic responses occur as a result of the subjects being rendered suggestible to ordinary experiences.

Posthypnotic suggestions may be remembered or forgotten when the suggested act is carried out. Hence response to posthypnotic suggestions can be compared to the manner in which we respond to waking hypnosis (propaganda and advertising slogans)—all reduce resistance and enhance suggestibility. However, ridiculous posthypnotic suggestions will not be carried out. The patient responds also to the nuances of the hypnotherapist's words. As mentioned, an extraverbal approach is more effective than a direct command to perform a given act. Purposeless commands are readily forgotten, like similar instructions given at nonhypnotic levels.

Posthypnotic suggestions are more effective if simpler suggestions are given initially and then built up to a higher order of complexity. Posthypnotic responses also are more likely to be carried out when ideosensory and ideomotor activities are used synergistically as reinforcement. Since the initial sensations were felt, the more complex task-motivated instructions will be accepted more readily. The fulfillment of a posthypnotic suggestion is the result of a series of conditioned sensory impressions and muscular activities. Good patients accept the reality of a posthypnotic suggestion as readily as any belief associated with cognitive and perceptual stimuli.

PRINCIPLES OF SUGGESTION AND HYPNOSIS

Law of Concentrated Attention

There are several important principles or "laws" that should be kept in mind by the practitioner using hypnosis. The first is the law of concentrated attention, defined as follows: Whenever attention is concentrated on an idea over and over again, it spontaneously tends to realize itself. This is more effective than simple or direct persuasion, as the critical faculties or resistances to acceptance of an idea are bypassed. A typical example is the influence that advertising—a type of waking hypnosis—can have on buying patterns. The prospective buyer's decision making is altered without his realizing that he is being influenced. This is a simple example of how behavior can be shaped by manipulation of external stimuli.

Law of Reversed Effect

The second principle is: The harder one tries to do something by using his will, the less chance he has of succeeding. For instance, the harder one wills himself to remember a name or to fall asleep, the less chance he has of success. It is also axiomatic that whenever the imagination and the will come into conflict the imagination invariably wins. Therefore, the sophisticated hypnotherapist employs the principles embodied in stressing "imagination power" rather than "will power." For instance, when one is trying to develop glove anesthesia for pain relief, it is incorrect and counterproductive to suggest, "I want your hand to get numb." Rather, one must use a descriptive, imagistic verbalization such as:

Imagine that you are putting your hand into a pitcher of very cold ice water. As soon as you can visualize this, you will feel your hand developing a numb, heavy, wooden feeling, the same as if you had been sitting on it, or the same as if you had anesthetic injected into it.

Stimulating the imagination in this manner is more likely to produce the desired response. This principle is similar to that of reciprocal inhibition developed by the behavior therapists.

Law of Dominant Effect

This principle is based on the axiom that a strong emotion tends to replace a weaker one. Attaching a strong emotion to a suggestion helps to make the suggestion more effective. Thus when a person is having a pleasurable emotional experience and sudden danger arises, the latter displaces the former, particularly if the danger is pronounced. These laws or principles are the basis for the success of the various technics used by hypnotherapists. They should be followed carefully.

This survey should give the reader a good background in the foundations for the various types of suggestion and hypnosis. We have explained the latter by arbitrarily dividing it into three categories: the factors influencing hypnotic induction, phenomena, and posthypnotic responses. We purposefully have eschewed becoming involved in any extensive discussion pertaining to the numerous theories advanced to explain hypnosis. We wish to emphasize that hypnosis facilitates any type of conditioning and is of far-reaching relevance for potentiating the conditioning involved in behavior therapy. This will be amplified in subsequent chapters dealing with hypnobehavioral therapy.

REFERENCES

Barber, T. X.: Experimental evidence for a theory of hypnotic behavior: II. Experimental controls in hypnotic age-regression. Int. J. Clin. Exp. Hypn., *9:*181, 1961.

————: Hypnotic "colorblindness," "blindness," and "deafness." Dis. Nerv. Syst., *25:*529, 1964.

————: Physiological effects of "hypnotic suggestions": A critical review of recent research (1960–1964). Psychological Bull. *63:*201, 1965.

————: An empirically-based formulation of hypnotism. Amer. J. Clin. Hypn., *12:*100, 1969.

Barber, T. X., Spanos, N. P., and Chaves, J. F.: Hypnotism: Imagination, and Human Potentialities. New York, Pergamon Press, 1974.

Barrios, A. A.: Toward Understanding the Effectiveness of Hypnotherapy: A Combined Clinical, Theoretical and Experimental Approach. (Unpublished Doctoral Dissertation, University of California) Los Angeles, 1969.

————: Hypnotherapy: a reappraisal. Psychother. Theor. Res. Pract., *7:*2, 1970.

————: Posthypnotic suggestion as higher-order conditioning: A methodological and experimental analysis. Int. J. Clin. Exp. Hypn., *21:*32, 1973.

Beecher, H. K.: The powerful placebo. J.A.M.A., *159:*1602, 1955.

Cooper, L. F., and Erickson, M. H.: Time Distortion in Hypnosis. Baltimore, Williams & Wilkins, 1954.

Erickson, M. H.: The induction of color blindness by a technique of hypnotic suggestion. J. Gen. Psychol., *20:*61, 1939.

————: Advanced techniques of hypnosis and therapy. *In* Haley, J.: Selected Papers of Milton H. Erikson. New York, Grune and Stratton, 1967.

Esdaile, J.: Mesmerism in India. Hartford, England, S. Andrus & Son, 1850.

Gill, M. M.: Hypnosis as an altered and regressed state. Int. J. Clin. Exper. Hypn., *20:*224, 1972.

Gill, M. M., and Brenman, M.: Hypnosis and Related States. New York, 1959. International Universities Press.

Hilgard, E. R.: Hypnotic Susceptibility. New York, Harcourt, Brace & Jovanovich, 1965.

Hull, C. L.: Hypnosis and Suggestibility. New York, Appleton-Century-Crofts, 1933.

Kroger, W. S.: Hypnoanesthesia in surgery. West. J. Surg. Obst. Gynecol. *68:*25, 1960.

————: Childbirth With Hypnosis. New York, Doubleday, 1961.

————: It is a wise hypnotist who knows who is hypnotizing whom! Brit. J. Med. Hypn., *13:*4, 1961.

————: Clinical and Experimental Hypnosis. Philadelphia, J. B. Lippincott, 1963.

————: Hypnotic pseudo-orientation in time as a means of determining the psychological effects of surgical sterilization in the male and female. J. Fertil. Steril., *14:*535, 1963.

Kroger, W. S., and Freed, S. C.: Psychosomatic Gynecology: Including Problems of Obstetrical Care. Philadelphia, W. B. Saunders, 1951.

Kubie, L. S.: Illusion and reality in the study of sleep, hypnosis, psychosis and arousal. Int. J. Clin. Hypn., *20:*205, 1972.

Marcuse, E. L.: Hypnosis: Fact or Fiction. Baltimore, Penguin Books, 1959.

Meares, A.: A System of Medical Hypnosis. Philadelphia, W. B. Saunders, 1960.

Orne, M. T.: The nature of hypnosis: artifact and essence. J. Abnormal Soc. Psycho. *46:*213, 1959.

Sarbin, T. R., and Coe, W. C.: Hypnosis: A Social Psychological Analysis of Influence and Communication. New York, Holt, Rinehart & Winston, 1972.

Weitzenhoffer, A. M.: Hypnotism: An Objective Study in Suggestibility. New York, John Wiley & Sons, 1953.

————: General Techniques of Hypnotism. New York, Grune & Stratton, 1957.

White, R. W.: A preface to a theory of hypnotism. J. Abnormal Soc. Psychol. *36:*477, 1941.

Wolberg, L.: Medical Hypnosis. New York, Grune & Stratton, 1945.

Wolpe, J.: Psychotherapy by Reciprocal Inhibition. Stanford, Stanford University Press, 1958.

SUGGESTED READINGS

Barber, T. X.: Measuring "hypnotic-like" suggestibility with and without "hypnotic induction"; psychometric properties, norms, and variables influencing response to the Barber Suggestibility Scale (BSS). Psych. Reports, *16:*809, 1965.

————: Reply to Conn and Conn's "Discussion of Barber's 'hypnosis' as a causal variable . . ." Int. J. Clin. Exp. Hypn., *15:*111, 1967.

Brenman, M. and Gill, M. M.: Hypnotherapy: A Survey of the Literature. New York, International Universities Press, 1972.

Check, D. B., and Le Cron, L. M.: Clinical Hypnotherapy. New York, Grune & Stratton, 1968.

Chertor, L.: Hypnosis. New York, Pergamon Press, 1965.

Crasilneck, H. B. and Hall, J. H.: Clinical Hypnosis: Principles and Applications. New York, Grune & Stratton, 1975.

Dengrove, E.: Hypnosis and Behavior Therapy. Springfield, Ill., Charles C Thomas, 1975.

Erickson, M. H., Rossi, E. L., and Rossi, S. I.: Hypnotic Realities: The Induction of Clinical Hypnosis and the Indirect Forms of Suggestion. New York, Irving Publishers, Halsted-Wiley Press, 1976.

Fromm, E. and Shor, R.: Hypnosis: Research Developments & Perspectives. Chicago, Aldine-Atherton, 1972.

Haley, J.: Uncommon Therapy: The Psychiatric Techniques of Milton H. Erickson, M.D. New York, W. W. Norton, 1973.

Hartland, J.: Medical and Dental Hypnosis. Baltimore, Williams & Wilkins, 1971.

Hilgard, J. R.: Personality and Hypnosis: A Study of Imaginative Involvement. Chicago, Univ. Chicago Press, 1970.

————: Imaginative involvement: Some characteristics of the highly hypnotizable and the non-hypnotizable. Int. J. Clin. Exper. Hypn., *22:*138, 1974.

Kubie, L. S.: Illusion and reality in the study of sleep, hypnosis, psychosis and arousal. Int. J. Clin. Hypn., *20:*205, 1972.

Moss, C. S.: Hypnosis in Perspective. New York, Macmillan, 1965.

Shor, R. E.: Expectancies of being influenced and hypnotic performance. Int. J. Clin. Exper. Hypn., *19:*154, 1971.

Van Nuys, D.: Meditation, attention, and hypnotic susceptibility: A correlational study. Int. J. Clin. Exper. Hypn., *21:*59, 1973.

4

Hypnotic Technics

SPECIALIZED INDUCTION TECHNICS

After the diagnostic assessment is made the patient is usually taught hypnosis and autohypnosis during his first session, as this often is his expectation. The nature of hypnosis must always be explained to the subject before the induction is begun. He may be informed as follows:

Hypnosis is a process whereby, because you relax better, you hear better. And whenever you hear better, whatever I say to you or whatever you say to yourself will "sink in" better. If it sinks in better, you will respond better. This allows greater awareness. Since you are more aware, you naturally cannot be asleep. You go into a superalert state whenever you desire and you come out of it whenever you wish. You are always in control. You will remember everything you said during the induction procedure. There is never a time when you cannot get up off the couch, walk around the room or do whatever you wish. You can do anything during hypnosis that you can do out of it, but you can do it more effectively under hypnosis because your concentration is greater and there is less distraction. This means you can talk, dance, or take an examination while in hypnosis!

Authors' Double-Bind Hypnotic Induction Technic

While a great array of procedures has been used to induce hypnosis, the authors have found the following verbalization to be most effective for most patients. This is an interesting technic because therapy is initiated from the onset of the induction. The structured nuances of the induction technic also build in a "control" system. The patient has no alternative but to go into some level of

29

hypnosis because of the "double-bind" nature of the approach. We have used this technic on thousands of patients. Suggestibility tests are not necessary, provided the verbalizations are given as described below. It is suggested to the patient that if he wishes to learn to control the symptoms he presents, he first must learn to control very simple feeling states such as heaviness, tightness, coldness, warmth, limpness, stiffness, and relaxation. After he has mastered these he can then learn to control more complex feeling states involved in the behavior requiring change. Words, thoughts, and ideas act as conditioned stimuli for eliciting these states, even though the original stimulus has been forgotten. As Pavlov stated, "Suggestion is the simplest form of a conditioned reflex."

First you will look at a spot directly above your forehead. Pick a spot on the ceiling just above your hairline. Keep staring at it. As you keep staring at it the first sensation that you will learn how to control is that of *heaviness.* Your lids are getting *very, very heavy.* Getting *heavier* and *heavier.* Your eyes are beginning to blink. [If the patient's eyes blink or the individual swallows one can say "see you just blinked" or swallowed, as the case may be. These act as reinforcers to suggest that the patient is doing fine.] Your eyes are blinking and you just swallowed, that's a good sign that you are going deeper and deeper relaxed. And now at the count of 3 if you *really* wish to gain mastery and control over your symptom [one can mention whatever the symptom may be] you will gently control the closing of your lids. At this point you will notice that you want to close your lids because they are getting very, very tired. Promptly, precisely and exactly at the count of 3 you will close your lids, not because you have to but because you really want to. Don't close your lids too rapidly, but close them gently at the count of 3. Your eyes are closing, lids are closing *tighter* and *tighter* together. And I really want you to feel that *tightness,* good, this is still another sensation that you are gaining control over.

Now let your eyeballs roll up into the back of your head. [At this point the operator can place his thumb and forefinger gently over the forehead just above the eyes.] Now let the eyeballs roll back down into their normal position. And as they return to their normal position you will notice that your lids are *stuck* even *tighter* and *tighter* together. [Here the operator can lightly place his thumb and forefinger over each eyelid to reinforce the suggestion.]

Now I'd like to have you imagine that your entire body from your head to your toes is becoming very, very relaxed. However, your body will not relax just because you tell it to do so. Rather, it will only relax if you pair this suggestion with the memory which once produced the desired response. Perhaps it would be nice if you would imagine yourself taking a soothing warm bath. You are relaxing *deeper* and *deeper.* And the more vividly that you can see *all* the familiar sights of your own bathroom, the deeper relaxed you will go. And the more vividly that you can see yourself in your own bathtub, the deeper relaxed you will go. And the more vividly that you feel the

imaginary warm water up to your armpits, the deeper relaxed you will go. *reassure*
You are doing fine, just fine. Your breathing is getting slower, deeper, more
regular, slower, deeper and more regular. [It is at this point the patient
needs reinforcement because he is wondering how he is doing.]

Now if you *really* wish to go deeper, and gain more mastery over yourself
so that *you* can control the removal of your symptoms you will first learn
how to raise your arm in a controlled fashion. Listen very carefully for the
following instructions. Carry these out to the best of your ability. The better
you control the raising of your arm the better you will be able to control
your symptom. [This heightens motivation.] You may raise either your right   *doubly*
arm or your left arm, whichever arm you choose. But raise it in the following   *bind*
fashion [the patient thinks he has been given a choice, but actually this
double-bind remark gives him no choice but to raise one arm or the other].
Here are the instructions for the raising of your arm. Listen carefully for the
instructions. Raise either your right arm or your left arm about 2 or 3 inches
at a time and then pause 30 or 40 seconds. During this pause perhaps you
might be willing to suggest that as your arm lifts higher and higher, with
each cogwheel-like movement it will get lighter and lighter—another sensation that you are controlling. And the lighter your arm gets as it rises, the   *phenomena*
deeper relaxed you will go. You will raise your arm at the count of 3, not   *reinforcing*
because you have to but because you really want to! Now do not raise it too   *phenomena*
rapidly [another double bind] 1,2,3, slowly the arm is lifting, lifting, lifting,
lifting, and as it lifts higher and higher with each movement notice how your
arm is getting lighter and lighter. And as the arm gets lighter and lighter notice how your state of relaxation is getting deeper and deeper. You are
doing fine.

Your breathing is getting slower, deeper, more regular. [At this point the
arm is allowed to slowly rise to a 75-degree angle. The patient does not realize the operator is one up and the subject in reality is one down. Since the
former is setting the rules of the game, the patient does not know what to
expect. However, since he has begun to notice certain feeling states occurring, he attributes these to the suggestions of the operator. Little does he
realize that *he* is producing them.]

As your arm is now approaching a straight, vertical, perpendicular position you will notice that you can develop still another sensation, that of *stiffness*. Your arm is now lifting higher and higher to where your fingers, hand,
forearm, and arm are all stretched straight toward the ceiling. Paradoxically,
you will notice that the *stiffer* your arm gets from the fingers to the hand, to
the wrist, to the elbow to the shoulder, the *deeper relaxed* you will go. Your
arm is now stiff, very rigid, like a bar of steel from the fingertips down to the
elbow to the shoulder. [At this point no challenges are issued such as "you
can't bend your arm," rather it is suggested that the stiffer the arm gets the
deeper relaxed the patient will be and the better he will be able to control
the symptom.

Here the operator can gently stroke the outstretched arm from the
fingers to the shoulder. Utilizing the ideosensory response with an ideomotor response produces a synergistic effect. The stroking must be performed

very lightly, because it is precisely at this point that the arm develops cata-lepsy.] Notice the stiffness of your outstretched arm. You are doing fine.

Now, if you wish to control other sensations and gain still more mastery over your symptom, listen very carefully to the following suggestions. At the count of 3 you will slowly, ever so slowly, about an inch or two at a time allow your arm to fall to your side and with each 2 inches or so that it falls, your arm will become as limp as a wet noodle. It will become limper and limper as it slowly drops to your side. Is it not surprising how many sensa-tions that you are gaining control over? Also, is it not remarkable how many sensations are built into your body? Now don't let the arm drop too rapidly [another double-bind remark]. Allow it to drop very, very *slowly*. And with each motion that your arm moves downward, perhaps, you might be willing to suggest to yourself that when your arm returns to your side or touches any part of your body, that will be a cue or signal for every *muscle* and every *fiber* in your body to develop complete relaxation. [Notice how we are work-ing within the framework of the patient's own personality in a permissive manner even though the technic is authoritative in nature]. Now as your arm is about to reach your side or touch the chair (or couch) perhaps you could allow that to be a cue for every muscle in your body to relax completely. [The arm now falls limply to the side.

At this point it is wise to use a positive reinforcing maneuver such as lift-ing the arm gently between the forefinger and thumb at the patient's wrist and letting the arm slip from between the operator's fingers. If the patient is male, one can insert the middle finger under the sleeve and lift the arm up about 6 or 8 inches and allow it to slip away so that it drops with a thud.]

Now you are in a very deep state of relaxation and I am going to give you several suggestions for terminating it. One route you will be able to control. The other route will be one that I can use, provided and if it is with your per-mission. Any time that I touch you on your right shoulder with your permis-sion you will promptly close your eyes, let your eyeballs roll up into the back of your head [the operator can lightly touch the lids and the forehead above the eyes with his thumb and forefinger]. You will let your eyeballs roll up into the back of your head to prevent yourself from falling asleep. As you know, for many individuals lid closure can trigger the onset of sleep. We want to trigger the onset of super-alertness! Next you will let the eyeballs roll back down into their normal position and you will quickly drop into a deep state of relaxation.

A touch on the left shoulder will be the signal for you to open your eyes, feeling wonderful, refreshed, relaxed. Notice that at no time did I use the words sleep, trance, or unconsciousness. [This is emphasized again and again as many patients will state, "Doctor, I know I wasn't hypnotized, I heard everything you said." This makes it clear to the patient that hypnosis is not a sleep state.] Now you can put yourself into this deep, meditative, self-reflective, contemplative state by yourself. [A touch on the left shoulder is the one which enables the patient to open his eyes. A touch on the right is the cue to enter into hypnosis.] In many thousands of inductions using the above technics we have never had a patient fail to open his eyes.

biofeedback in nature?

The next one or two sessions can be used to deepen the hypnosis by scene visualization such as the images described in Chapter 10. Where possible, all five senses are utilized in the visualization of these images. We want to emphasize that scene visualization should be practiced as often as possible.

Vogt's Fractionation Technic

Another deepening technic that can be utilized is Vogt's (1894, 1896) fractionation technic. Before dehypnotization, the subject is asked to relate the thoughts, feelings, and sensations he experienced at the moment of maximal relaxation. The individual is then dehypnotized by the shoulder cue. Then these sensations are fed back when he is rehypnotized. He is told that he will go deeper with *each* rehypnotization. For instance, if he states, "I felt that I was floating on fleecy white clouds," this is incorporated into the next induction procedure by stating, "You will go deeper and deeper as you feel yourself floating on fleecy white clouds." If he remarks, "I saw all kinds of colored flashes of light," tell him, "Now as soon as you see these colored flashes, you will relax deeper and deeper."

Vogt's fractionation technic simply depends on the subject's being dehypnotized, questioned, and then rehypnotized by feeding in those relaxing sensations that he has just described. This procedure is repeated again and again until deep relaxation is achieved. This technic is effective because it obviates the possibility of suggesting sensations that may antagonize the subject. Another advantage is that the information used is conducive to deep hypnotization. The fractionation method can be used in conjunction with a hand-levitation method for subsequent inductions.

Some readily hypnotized patients may prefer to simply go into hypnosis themselves and then let the therapist give them the appropriate posthypnotic suggestions. In the majority of our cases, however, we always give the patient some form of formal induction. In all cases the hypnosis is terminated by the verbalization "I am now going to count to 3. At the count of 3 you will open your eyes. You will be totally refreshed, completely relaxed. 1 . . . 2 . . . 3." There are many other technics for inducing hypnosis through a wide variety of sensory modalities; the reader is referred to Wolberg (1948), Weitzenhoffer (1957), Meares (1960), Kroger (1963), and Erickson (1967).

Deepening

Deepening can be more effective if words such as "deeper and deeper" and "heavier and heavier" are given to coincide with the patient's actual breathing. The patient is told to follow the procedure as outlined below for practicing autohypnosis, three times a day, 5 to 10 minutes each time, at home. Practice is very important for the patient to obtain proper self-control.

DEHYPNOTIZATION

To bring yourself out of autohypnosis simply say to yourself, "I am now going to count to 3. At the count of 3 I will come out of hypnosis feeling totally refreshed, completely relaxed, 1 . . . 2 . . . 3."

EXPLANATION OF HYPNOTIC PROCEDURES

After the first hypnotic session the patient is asked how he feels and whether he has any questions. He often will state that he did not think he was hypnotized and that he merely tried to please the therapist. He must be assured without argumentation that he was indeed in a relaxed or light state of hypnosis as evidenced by his rapid lid fluttering or, if his arm became cataleptic, by the increased muscle tone.

The same classical conditioning procedure as described in Chapter 5 in reference to Pavlov's dog experiment occurs in the beginning of the induction of the hypnotic "state." In this case, the verbal suggestion, "Your lids are getting very, very *heavy*," is the conditioned stimulus (CS) and the lid heaviness is the unconditioned stimulus (UCS). Fixing one's eyes on a focal point *inevitably* leads to physiological tiring of the lid muscles and ensuing heaviness just as presentation of food naturally produces salivation. After repeated associations of the verbal suggestion for heaviness with actual heaviness (due to eyestrain) the verbal suggestion will elicit lid heaviness just as the bell elicits salivation.

It is interesting that most subjects believe it to be the other way around. They think from the beginning that the suggestion is producing the lid closure when in fact the lid closure or *tightness* is reinforcing the suggestion. It is only later after conditioning has occurred that the suggestion actually is influential in bringing about a desired effect. Once the suggestion for lid heaviness is capable of producing this effect it lends credibility to further auto-suggestions. Thus, a belief system is built in and expectation leads to actualization.

This belief system is continually reinforced by other procedures in the induction. For instance, during arm levitation the raising of the arm 2 or 3 inches at a time is associated with *lightness*. By pairing the lightness with total bodily *relaxation*, the latter is reinforced. Just as the arm reaches a vertical position, *stiffness* is suggested. The subject is told, "If you really want to overcome your problem, your arm will become rigid." Likewise, this suggestion is paired with *limpness* as the arm slowly falls to the side. This pairing of ideosensory and ideomotor activities is a subtle conditioning of an inhibitory mental set.

The same holds true for the suggestion, "Your lids are locked so tight you can't open them." Of course the subject can open his eyes if he wants to. The point is he *wants* to feel as if he cannot perform these acts. By giving himself these suggestions he increases the heaviness of the eyelids and the tightness of the lid closure and thus becomes more motivated to accept other suggestions.

Authors' Feedback Technic for Autohypnosis

After the individual is aware that he can readily enter into hypnosis, usually all that is required is the prearranged cue or shoulder signal. The individual is then instructed in autohypnosis. During autohypnosis, full use of the imagination is used to relive past experiences similar to changes suggested. The following technic is most effective:

It has been stated that one picture is worth a thousand words. For instance, if you say, "I will be confident," the words must be implemented by a picture of yourself as the confident person you want to be. If you keep fortifying this image with appropriate suggestions, eventually these mental impressions will give rise to the confident feelings that you seek.

I know that this technic seems simple, but if you keep implanting positive images into your mind, they will become a part of your personality. Do not expect immediate results when you begin to use autohypnosis and don't ask, "what's wrong?" All you have to do to attain autohypnosis is to use what we call sensory or visual-imagery conditioning. This is an old technic that has been the basis for many different types of prayer.

Anyone can learn and practice autohypnosis, but to achieve the best results you must carefully consider what you wish to accomplish. Through self-exploration you can establish reasonable goals for improvement. Don't think that you have to be "out of this world" to be in autohypnosis. This idea has been produced by novels, comic strips and motion pictures. Actually, you will only be in a very deep state of relaxation and concentration. You may develop a feeling of detachment or you may experience a very pleasant sinking feeling, or you may get a feeling of peace and serenity. At times you may not even feel a definite change; it may just seem as if you had your eyes closed and heard everything at all times. However, if you aim for a deeply relaxed state, you will reach it.

After you are satisfied that you have achieved autohypnosis you may give yourself further suggestions to deepen it if you wish. Also, remember that it is not too important to reach a deep state on your initial attempts. Just realize that you are trying to establish a conditioned response which will cause you to react instantly to any cue that you wish to use. Through frequent repetition, the cue will bring on the autohypnosis.

During every attempt to achieve autohypnosis, visualize yourself going *deeper* and *deeper*. At first you may experience some difficulty, but as you stick to it you will be able to picture yourself deeply *relaxed*. Always use the visual imagery technics whether or not you think you are under hypnosis. The images will become clear as you constantly repeat the appropriate suggestions. As you continue to work with yourself, you will develop confidence in giving yourself suggestions. To be effective, they cannot be given in a hesitant manner but with enthusiasm and anticipation. If you follow these instructions, you will see results of your suggestions and efforts.

When you practice this on your own at home, begin by selecting a quiet place and arrange to spend an uninterrupted 10 minutes three times a day practicing there. Seat yourself in a comfortable chair with your hands resting in your lap and your feet on the floor, or recline in the position in which you are now, fix your eyes on a spot on the ceiling above eye level.

Then begin counting to yourself slowly from 1 to 10. Direct your attention to your eyelids and, between numbers, tell yourself repeatedly that your eyelids are getting *very, very heavy,* and that your eyes are getting *very, very tired.* Again and again say: "My lids are getting *heavier* and *heavier.* I feel my lids getting so *heavy,* and the *heavier* they get, the *deeper relaxed* I will become, and the better able I will be to follow all suggestions I give myself. My lids are getting *very heavy.* It will feel so good to close my eyes."

By the time you count to 2, think of enough suggestions like the ones just mentioned so that you actually feel the heaviness of your eyelids. When you are sure that your lids are indeed heavy, count to 3 and let your eyes roll up into the back of your head for a few seconds. Then say, "My lids are now locked so tight that I doubt very much that I can open them. My lids shut tighter and tigher and tighter, and as my lids lock tight, I begin to feel a nice, calm, soothing, relaxed feeling beginning in my toes, moving into my legs and into my thighs as I keep counting. It's the same feeling that I have in my jaws when my dentist injects Novocaine into them; the same feeling that I have when I fall asleep on my arm; the same feeling that I have when I sit too long in one position; the identical feeling that I would have in my legs if I sat cross-legged on them for very long. A numb, wooden feeling starting in my toes is beginning to move up, up, up from my toes into my legs."

Next, count to 4 and say, "By the time I have counted to 5, my legs from my toes to my thighs will be just as heavy as lead. I can feel my legs relaxing from my toes to my thighs. I can feel them getting *heavier* and *heavier* and *heavier* . . . 5. They are so *heavy* now that I don't think I can move them." Then double back for repetition. "My eyelids are locked *tight,* so *tight* that I don't believe I can open them. My legs from my toes to my thighs are completely *relaxed.*" Each time you retrace these autosuggestions, you stamp in the learned response pattern.

You continue in this way, "By the time I have counted to 6 and 7, my fingers, hands and arms will be very, very *heavy.* I am beginning to feel that same numbness moving up from my fingers to my shoulders. A *heavy,* detached feeling is moving up from my fingers to my hand, to my wrist, past my elbows, up to my arm, to my shoulder. Both my arms, from my hands to my shoulders, are getting very numb—a heavy woodlike numbness. When I have counted to 7, my arms will be just as *heavy* and relaxed as my eyelids, as numb as my legs are now, as if I have been sleeping on them."

Don't worry if you forget the exact words. The exact words are far less important than the effect that you are trying to achieve: a feeling of numbness all the way from the fingertips to the wrist, to the elbow, to the shoulder, to the neck. In practice, this may be a bit more difficult to accomplish in the first few sessions at home, but the feeling will come faster in subsequent attempts. It is most important that you never become discouraged and that you not tire yourself by spending more than 30 minutes a day in practice.

When you finally reach the point where, by the count of 7, your limbs are sufficiently relaxed, you repeat again all the suggestions you have given yourself, adding: "My legs are so *heavy* that I don't believe I can move them. My eyes are locked so tight that I doubt that I can open them. My arms are so *heavy* that I cannot lift them, and, by the time I have counted from 7 to 8, my trunk will be *relaxed.*"

Now go back to the lids, legs, and arms. Then say, "By the time I count from 8 to 9, my chest will have relaxed, too. With every breath I take, I can just feel myself going *deeper* and *deeper* into a *relaxed* state. My back and abdomen are getting very, very *numb.* I can feel the muscles in my chest *relaxing* . . . 8. My entire body, from my neck down, is *relaxed* . . . 9. I am completely *relaxed.* I can't open my eyes. I can't move my legs. I can't move my arms. I feel my whole body *relaxed,* thoroughly and deeply. It is so refreshing to remain in this deep, quiet state."

"I will now relax my neck and head, so that, at the count of 10, I will be completely relaxed from my head to my toes. I can feel that with every breath I take I am becoming calmer and *deeper relaxed* . . . *deeper* and *deeper relaxed* . . . into a calm, soothing, *refreshing* state. Everything is just getting more and more *relaxed.* I feel as if I am floating away . . . falling *deeper* and *deeper* . . . not asleep, but just thoroughly relaxed . . . 10. I am completely relaxed. My eyes and limbs are as heavy as lead. My entire body feels numb, heavy, woodenlike, as I go *deeper* and *deeper.*"

By picturing yourself deeply *relaxed* in your mind's eye, you will go *deeper.* If you can imagine yourself in your own bed comfortably *relaxed,* this can be a stimulus for *deepening* the relaxation. If you think of this again and again, you set in motion a response that ultimately will allow you to achieve a *profound* state of relaxation. As you become more proficient with autohypnosis, your practice sessions become shorter until finally the mere blinking and closing of the eyes will trigger hypnosis. Rapidity with which autohypnosis can be induced increases with practice.

It is well to remember that you deepen the autohypnosis by your own efforts and that the depth depends largely on how well you follow the principles that you are learning. It also is most important to have the proper frame of mind if you wish to achieve effective autohypnosis. If you approach it with a "prove-it-to-me" attitude, nothing will happen. To attain ultimate success, self-confidence and persistence are necessary!

INDICATIONS FOR AUTOHYPNOSIS

We inform patients they should learn autohypnosis for the following reasons: (1) They will have a feeling of pride and self-esteem that they removed the symptom; (2) They will not be dependent upon us or any other physicians after they are rid of the symptom; (3) If the original symptom returns they can use the same autosuggestions that once removed it; (4) Should a substitute symptom replace the removed one (and this is highly equivocal), they can readily remove it as they did the original symptom. Symptom-substitution does not occur if the patient eliminates the original symptom. Hypnotherapists consider it ridiculous that they should be criticized for only curing symptoms when other, nonhypnotic methods are employed solely for symptom removal.

IMAGERY OR SCENE VISUALIZATION
IN CONDITIONING

After sufficient practice with autohypnosis, the patient is given a specific image to produce relaxation. The image is always given immediately after the standard induction described earlier and serves to reinforce and thus deepen the hypnosis. If direct hypnotic suggestions are given, they are delivered immediately after the image since at this point hypnotic depth is greatest. The patient is instructed to practice this image a minimum of three times and a maximum of five times daily (5 to 10-minute sessions) while in hypnosis.

In any form of counterconditioning the degree of relaxation produced is crucial. The deeper the relaxation produced the stronger will be the counterconditioning and the greater the rapidity with which it can be induced. The depth of relaxation produced is largely a function of the subject's concentration and sensory recall. The more vivid the patient's relaxing image (to be described later) the greater will be the relaxation and the more vivid his anxiety-inhibiting image, the more real will be the counterconditioning (that is, the greater will be the generalization from imagined object to real object).

Vivid images are accomplished by focusing on the development of a subject's sensory recall. Every image should be experienced in all five senses if possible, and just as if it were really happening. A sensation once experienced is never forgotten. It is recorded forever. We have the ability to recall a sensation in its entirety but we seldom utilize this potential. A sensation is created by imaginarily going back in time to a point where that particular sensation was received and re-experiencing it. For example, if the relaxing image is seeing yourself on the *beach,* you smell the salt not by saying over and over, "I smell salt," but by recalling a particular point in time when you experienced that smell and reliving it.

In excellent hypnotic subjects it may be necessary only for the therapist to give instructions to focus on a spot, notice a blurring around its periphery (Troxler phenomenon), close the eyes tightly when the lids feel heavy, roll back the eyeballs 30 seconds, and feel a rhythmic wave of relaxation starting in the toes, moving through the legs, fingers, hands, arms, stomach, chest, neck, and head. Imagery or scene visualization is utilized at this point. Scene visualization should be practiced as often as possible. Continual reinforcement eventually leads to increased control over volitional and even resistant autonomic responses. During subsequent sessions, the patient is taught to make full use of imaginative capacities.

After sufficient practice, autohypnosis is attained by a triggering cue such as closure of the eyelids. This bypasses the need for continually repeating the autohypnotic technic. In this relaxed state, specific autosuggestions given for counterconditioning are repeated long enough, strongly enough, and often enough to build in and reinforce positive conditioned responses. The negative ones associated with the problems are thus inhibited. This approach is permissive and patient-centered.

TECHNIC OF DEHYPNOTIZATION

The patient is now taught the standard dehypnotization affirmations. Briefly they are: (1) I'll go deeper the next time to the best of my ability; (2) I'll follow all the suggestions that I give to myself to the best of my capacity; (3) I'll open my eyes and feel complete confidence that this approach will help me.

RATIONALE FOR AUTONOMIC CONTROL AND CONDITIONED REFLEX THERAPY

If the four premises mentioned on p. 37 are understood, we then suggest appropriate autosuggestions required for dissolution of the symptom. We prefer to have these repeated by interoceptive conditioning, as we all have "bells in our brain that we can ring." "Inner speech" based on the scene visualization of past experiences (sensory-imagery conditioning), or "visual voyages," and "self-feeling talk" enhance autonomic nervous system control. This, as mentioned, is relatively easy if control of the nonlearned, nonconditioned, or *involuntary* reflexes such as heaviness and lightness is taught first. These ideosensory activities are functions of the primary signaling system described by Pavlov. Because they are either present (on) or absent (off), they have been compared to "digital" notions in sensory information processing and control of higher central nervous system functioning and behavior (Miller, Galanter, and Pribram, 1959).

Patients are also trained in stimulus transfer. They can be taught by posthypnotic suggestion to transfer "heat" by imagining their hand being placed in a tub of hot water, and "cold" or numbness by imagining their hand being put in a tub of ice water (glove anesthesia). After these ideosensory experiences are perceived as real, then the more complex feeling states related to specific desired responses are developed by recalling the representations of pleasurable thoughts. Such thoughts or symbolic activities are *learned, conditioned,* and *voluntary.* They are part of the secondary signaling system of higher nervous elaboration. Since they act slowly by comparison or analogy, they have been referred to as *analogic notions* in higher central nervous system functioning and processing of information (Kroger 1963). This method is not new but differs from the classical type of Pavlovian and instrumental conditioning initially produced by external stimuli, exteroceptive conditioning. (For further discussion, see Chap. 5.)

This approach is similar to the extraordinary "mind-body" conditioning of responses used by Yoga, Zen and other Eastern therapies. All rely on similar principles for facilitation of the positive sensory images derived from internalized signals. In other words, internalized biofeedback cues can trigger and reinforce responses by association with recall of pleasant states in a manner similar to the alpha "beeps" of biofeedback training (BFT). As proof, well-trained Yogins and Zennists do not need an external device to alter pulse, blood pressure, and other autonomic conditioned reflexes.

Recent data also indicate that the conditioned reflexes established under autohypnosis are more durable and less likely to be extinguished. We have taken this type of conditioning one step further by employing sophisticated hypnotic technics with reinforcement learning to establish corrective behavioral changes. The punishment and reward alternatives implicit in operant conditioning can be incorporated. Auto- and posthypnotic suggestions (PHS) are oriented around the patient's emotional needs, to shape and modify desired adaptive behavioral responses. It is recommended that the autosuggestions be used at least four to five times a day during autohypnosis. As reinforcement learning increases, desired responses become a reward, and the failure to derive therapeutic results acts as punishment.

HOLISTIC APPROACH

To expedite therapy, most of the patients are given an interview-in-depth and a complete psychometric evaluation. This saves time and brings many hidden facets of the personality into focus. Patients also can be reconditioned or "immunized" in a stepwise manner to specific and nonspecific stressors. The associated relaxation allows anxiety-provoking material to be presented in "threshold doses" in fantasy, and then later when they are able to, patients can deal with these in reality. This is similar to the hierarchy and de-sensitization approaches used by behavior modifiers. As Conn (1959) has described, there are needs inherent in all anxiety-ridden persons, that is, the need to talk, the need to be told what to do, the need to be accepted, the need to be one's real self, and the need to emancipate oneself from any undue dependency on the therapist.

The therapeutic design is structured around the following: (1) How much of the behavior do you really have to keep? Could some actions be channeled into other, less significant outlets? (2) What are you trying to achieve by maintaining your abnormal behavior? (3) How rapidly can your personality get rid of the emotional needs to keep the behavior? (4) How could you convert your inappropriate feelings to more appropriate ones? (5) How would you feel without the problem?

There are only three therapeutic avenues open to anxiety-ridden patients: (1) they can "develop a thicker skin" and learn to live with their problems; (2) they can retreat from their difficult life situations to fight another day when stronger; or (3) they can come to grips with their difficulties, provided, and if, the therapist—on the basis of his experience, wisdom and judgment—gives them the necessary coping mechanisms.

Patients sense the hypnotherapist's interest, empathy, and warmth. During hypnosis the therapist tries to motivate the patient to achieve self-mastery over his behavior. This can be achieved by the best co-pilot any healer can have— Faith. Successful hypnotic conditioning is therefore a collaborative and reciprocal effort between therapist and patient; each learns from the other.

SPECIALIZED HYPNOTHERAPEUTIC TECHNICS

We shall describe some of the specialized technics that can be used in conjunction with behavior therapy. They are especially effective for patients who do not completely respond to hypnosis or who are resistant to hypnosis. The therapist who is psychodynamically trained or oriented also can incorporate some of these technics into his approach.

Haley (1961) describes Erickson's approach for controlling behavior from the initial meeting. Erickson was one of the first hypnotherapists to employ what today would be termed a behavioral approach. He emphasizes directly or indirectly that the patient can either talk or be silent; such permissiveness establishes rapport and facilitates ventilation of the target behaviors that require changing. Whatever the patient does, he is encouraged to continue doing, but always *under the direction of the therapist.*

In this approach few resistances develop. For instance, if a person refuses to speak, he is complimented on being able to communicate at least, by nodding or shaking the head. The patient is then asked if he can write, and if he nods his head in the affirmative, a pencil is placed in the non-dominant hand. He is then asked, "How do you feel about communicating with me that way?" In such a structured situation, the patient has to talk since he cannot write.

Other ingenious ploys Erickson uses are to always emphasize the positive aspects of the patient's behavior. If a person feels he is a failure, he is complimented on whatever determination he shows. If he is a passive personality, he is complimented on his ability to endure. If aggressive, on his ambition. Thus, since the patient cannot object to such compliments, the positive aspects of the behavior are accepted and utilized so that the foundation for change (or behavioral modification) can be produced. Symptomatic behavior is encouraged, but always as defined by the therapist. For instance, a highly resistant, obese patient was instructed to *overeat* enough to maintain a weight of 260 pounds instead of her current 270 pounds. Thus, her needs to overeat, to lose weight, and to rebel were satisfied at the same time.

Another resistant obese woman was deliberately instructed to *gain* from 15 to 25 pounds. While gaining she was asked to speculate on how she would go about losing the weight. Despite her reluctance to gain more weight, the therapist insisted that she gain 20 pounds. Then she was "permitted" to stop gaining weight, which subsequently led to a permanent loss. The acceptance of the need to gain weight is encouraged, and, as a result, the patient looks to the therapist for further direction. In general, the method involves the self-respect, the needs, and the desire of the patient to give up the symptom by committing him, as Haley states, to "some activity which he does not like (but preferably feels he should accomplish) and persuading him to go through with the activity as directed."

Often resistance can be circumvented by hypnotically directing attention to other activities rather than to the symptom itself. Erickson instructed an enuretic to walk when he wet the bed. This served a two-fold purpose: the enuresis indirectly came under the control of the therapist; the walking was self-punishment. An insomniac was told to deliberately stay awake, but to polish the floor all night for self-punishment reasons. A migraine sufferer was told to remember what her headache felt like in order to alter it within a month. The hidden meaning implied is, "You might consider the possibility of skipping your headache for 3 weeks or a month." Patients who are controlled without knowing it are usually unable to resist the directives (extraverbal suggestions): for instance, a casual comment arouses a patient's interest in a topic, and the later mentioning of another apparently unrelated topic "unconsciously" connects the two in his mind.

BRIEF HYPNOTHERAPY BY SYMPTOM-MANIPULATION

Symptom-Substitution

Erickson (1954, 1959) intentionally manipulates target behaviors to be corrected in those patients inaccessible to a total approach (symptom-manipulation). In these, direct symptom-removal by hypnosis invariably fails and usually results in resistance to further therapy. The neurotic manifestations are continuously maintained until a satisfactory change is achieved.

Illustrative is a patient who desperately needed to keep his neurotic disability. Since the underlying maladjustments were impossible to correct, Erickson substituted another neurotic disability that was similar to the existing one, but nonincapacitating in character. Shifting attention from anxiety-provoking symptoms to less urgent problems makes the patient less preoccupied with his present difficulties. The substitutive symptom also satisfies the personality needs and, as a result, a healthy adjustment to reality occurs. Erickson concludes, "Regardless of how farcical, the above technic met his symptomatic needs."

Symptom-substitution should be used to trade down to a less handicapping symptom; the new substitute symptom is more readily removed. The poorly motivated individual, the "psychiatric veteran," or the geriatric patient responds well to symptom-substitution; fortunately, deep hypnosis is seldom required. Autohypnosis and sensory-imagery conditioning can be combined with symptom-substitution. A more effective response to suggestions occurs during autohypnosis, and this in turn depends upon the effort that the patient puts forth and how often and how well he practices. However, the therapist must never get himself out on a limb by raising the patient's hopes too high. This approach works well in the patient who has an inordinate need for attention-getting symptoms.

One of the authors (W.S.K.) was called in consultation to see a 57-year-old male who developed a paralysis of both arms following a "whiplash injury" incurred in a minor auto collision. He had a bilateral hysterical paralysis of the legs sustained 28 years earlier, which had been diagnosed as *astasia abasia*, and which necessitated the use of crutches and braces on both legs. In the presence of the referring neuropsychiatrist, a pseudo-erudite discussion of a placebo diagnosis was conducted (while the patient was under hypnosis) as follows: "This is a typical case of a partial compression of the cervical vertebrae; several nerves are pinched, and this accounts for the paralysis of both arms. They usually *run a typical course* and clear up in 6 weeks. However, for some unknown reason, the little finger on each hand does not recover full motion. But, it, too, eventually clears up." It was suggested that the patient work on one arm first, and that he imagine under autohypnosis that he was able to move it up slowly—about an inch or two each day. He practiced faithfully, and at the end of almost 6 weeks he regained full function of both arms. He complained bitterly of the involvement of the little finger on each hand for some time. When it was suggested that he might be able eventually to walk without his crutches and braces, he stated, "I want to rest for a while before undergoing more therapy." Since the personality needs were met sufficiently to achieve a satisfying, constructive, personal success, it was decided to abide by his decision. As yet he has not returned for further therapy.

This patient had been in the limelight for many years as a well-known actor. When he no longer was noticed, he developed the "paralysis." It would have been useless to confront him with this fact or to use logical persuasion. My discussion with his physicians made use of concealed suggestions that were really directed toward him. Inasmuch as he was not aware that he was being influenced, his criticalness was decreased, and he was thus made much more receptive to the suggestions. The placebo diagnosis fitted in with his needs and the emphasis on "run a typical course" placed the recovery *within him*. Most important, the rug was not pulled from under his feet; he was left with a temporary paralysis of the little finger. However, during therapy he was "allowed" to remove this symptom—but, of course, not too rapidly. Orienting the therapy around the patient's accomplishing the results and taking full credit for these is the key to a successful outcome.

Symptom-Removal by Symptom-Transformation

It is generally the authors' policy to teach the patient how to control specific ideomotor and ideosensory activities such as thermal changes, alterations in size and shape of the limbs, arm-levitation, and breathing. When assured that he can produce these changes readily, the patient realizes that he can either remove or develop other somatization reactions through autohypnosis. Our standardized images are also of great value in changing the body image.

A middle-aged woman because of an intense hostility toward her mother-in-law, developed a hysterical tic. She was treated by symptom-transformation. She was instructed, under hypnosis, to transfer the twitching of the face to the little finger of her left hand; all her symptomatology could be "condensed" into the finger. She could, if she wished, choose the time of day that this would occur. After this occurred, permission was given to allow the twitching of the little finger to increase or decrease. In the meantime, the facial tic disappeared. She was then given a powerful but concealed posthypnotic suggestion: "You will gradually lose the twitching of your little finger. Perhaps it will be next week, next month, or within the year. I am sure that when I see you, at any time during the next 5 or 10 months, you will be free from all involuntary movements."

In other words, there was no question that she would be relieved within a year, or sooner. When such individuals realize that they can transfer their difficulties to other areas, they realize that self-mastery over their symptom is now possible. A specific time limit is not set. Symptom-transformation should never be attempted until the patient can follow posthypnotic suggestions readily and develop a posthypnotic amnesia. Attainment of these are proof positive that he will comply with suggested alterations in either sensory or motor areas. Although this approach seems similar to symptom-substitution, the neurotic behavior is utilized by transformation of the symptom to a less noxious one *without changing the character of the symptom itself.*

Symptom-Amelioration

This approach is indicated when the patient is inaccessible to most types of intensive psychotherapy.

A 15-year-old boy, who had been in therapy with several excellent psychiatrists, was referred with a hysterical reaction which involved the continual plucking of his eyelashes. Although he recognized that it was a masturbatory-equivalent symptom, it had gotten worse. Under hypnosis, it was suggested that he alternately increase and decrease the plucking. His symptom was ameliorated on the basis that whatever can be increased can be decreased.

However, not all cases respond as dramatically. Good rapport, motivation, and a warm sympathetic approach are indispensable, particularly in this approach.

Symptom-Utilization

Symptom-utilization consists in encouraging, accepting, and redefining behavior in order to control it. Typical was the uncooperative patient who continually paced the floor during the therapeutic sessions described below. By having his acting-out behavior shifted into more cooperative activity, the patient eventually followed other directions. These technics utilize the subject's own attitudes, thoughts, feelings, and behavior in a manner similar to that in which an induction procedure makes full use of the patient's own ideomotor and ideosensory responses. This differs from the more commonly used hypnotic technics for symptom removal. These are particularly applicable for stressful situations or for those not amenable to direct hypnotic symptom removal. The reader is referred to Erickson's excellent and extensive writings for a more detailed description of his technics (Haley 1973).

Recently, an agitated, suicidally depressed patient, was seen in psychiatric consultation. As he walked up and down in the office, gesticulating wildly, he stated, "No doctor can take care of me. My condition is hopeless." I asked him why he felt this way. He stated, "I must keep walking all the time, can't sit still, and I make every therapist nervous. They all gave me up as a bad job." I softly remarked, "You know, your walking is most refreshing to me. After all, *every* other patient either sits or lies down, and at least you are different." Taken aback, he said, "Do you really mean that?" I stated, "Of course I do. But there is one thing I must ask of you. Notice my pictures on the wall. They are all in line and not askew. Now you can walk as much as you wish, but please walk in a perfect square." Needless to say, he was readily hypnotized and eventually recovered.

Also, an experience that happened to the therapist or to another person can be related and a definitive idea to change can be included, which the patient recognizes as applicable to himself and defends himself against. However, while he is defending himself against the idea, other suggestions can encourage change by misdirection. There is seldom a need to work with resistances, as control of a symptom can be achieved by requesting that it be manifested at a different time than usual, or in a different context or purpose. When a relapse is inevitable, the conditions for its occurrence can be suggested so that it becomes part of a cooperative endeavor rather than a result of resistance by the patient. Symptoms are encouraged to remain until there is no need for their utilization. If a resistant patient states that he is getting worse, Erickson accepts this idea and negates it by remarking, "Since you are worse, might it not be time for a change?"

Insight, transference interpretations, or connections between past and present are not employed. Erickson's fundamental purpose is to "bring about a change in the patient, not to focus on his mental or emotional structure." His clever structuring of the therapeutic situation is most rewarding.

Symptom-Intensification

A symptom or target behavior requiring change can be intensified. If it can voluntarily be made worse, then often it can volitionally be made better. With sufficient practice, the patient can decondition himself to the symptom.

CORRECTIVE EMOTIONAL RESPONSES OBTAINED BY IDEOMOTOR SIGNALING

Time and effort are saved, and unrecognized needs for acting-out behavior can be understood when repressed material is brought into awareness by hypnotic self-exploration. Deeply hypnotized patients are instructed to review material long since forgotten, and, after the material is verbalized, its significance is revealed to the patient. It has been observed that the ease with which understanding occurs is most impressive; often an apparently hopeless situation turns into an understandable, logical, and ready accomplishment.

In this technic (Cheek 1959), it is carefully impressed upon the subject that his "unconscious mind" will reveal information pertinent to his problem that was heretofore inaccessible. However, the information revealed is seldom in an immediately recognized form. To understand it, ideomotor signaling (finger responses that are involuntarily given to indicate "yes" or "no") is resorted to so that the "unconscious" can meaningfully answer questions that it cannot answer at the so-called conscious level. The authors do not believe one can talk to the unconscious. Rather the ideomotor finger signaling acts like a projective technic, and as such can elicit valuable information.

RATIONALE OF BRIEF HYPNOTHERAPEUTIC METHODS

Direct suggestions to elicit physiologic responses are generally ineffective. Scene or picture visualization should be used in a dissociated state. For instance, in treating the insomniac, posthypnotic suggestions should be that he "see" himself in a deep state of repose, that he "see" his chest moving up and down rhythmically, and, finally, that he "picture" himself deep asleep. This is more effective than the direct posthypnotic command, "You will get drowsy and fall asleep as soon as you lie down on your pillow." Where there is no apparent progress, the therapist should make full use of extraverbal suggestions irrespective of the degree of improvement. For example, a patient can be asked to report when he slept one minute longer. When the patient concedes this, the groundwork is laid for further recovery by pointing out that, at least, he has taken a "turn for the better."

During symptom-removal by brief hypnotherapy, continual reinforcement at monthly intervals is necessary for most cases. These sessions can also be used to follow the patient's progress and provide the necessary adjustments to changing conditions.

When therapist-centered hypnosis is used, the patient gives up the symptom to please him; it will disappear only as long as the patient has faith in the all-powerful therapist. Relapse occurs because the enforced dependency fosters ambivalence (the co-existence of love and hate) toward the therapist. As soon as the resentment gains the upper hand, the symptom returns. Therefore, all patients are informed as soon as they are taught autohypnosis, "You are now on your own, and each day you will have less dependency on me."

Janet, Freud, and many of the older hypnotists contended that even though a temporary cessation could be achieved dramatically by hypnosis, symptom-removal was not lasting. This was true because of *the way in which they used hypnosis*. They seldom made full use of auto-hypnosis, sensory-imagery conditioning, and other sophisticated refinements. Had they been oriented in the technics of brief hypnotherapy described in this chapter, symptom-removal would have been more permanent. Irrespective of the therapeutic goals, symptom-removal by brief hypnotherapy provides many despondent patients with faith and hope.

MISCELLANEOUS SPECIALIZED TECHNICS OF HYPNOTHERAPY

Throughout this volume the authors espouse the dictum that anything and everything that helps the patient should be employed. Therefore, we do not hesitate to use hypnosis and behavior therapy with psychopharmacologic agents. Wolberg (1945) has described how healthy relationships based on guidance, reassurance, persuasion, reeducation, and reconditioning (desensitization) under hypnosis can raise the threshold to anxiety-provoking stimuli. Kroger and Freed (1951) used these hypnobehavioral technics with psychodynamic therapy for psychosomatic disorders.

Yoga or Y-State of Hypnosis

Meares (1960) uses the Yoga or Y-state of hypnosis for those who readily enter Transcendental Meditation, prayer or reverie states. The Y-state is more suitable for autohypnotherapeutic technics.

Religious Hypnotherapy

Rodriguez (1960) makes full use of a religious approach in conjunction with hypnotherapy. Today, many clergymen, especially those who are also psychologists, are employing hypnotherapy with astonishing success. Since they are already a sort of father-confessor to many of their parishioners, they are in an enviable position to help them because of well-established faith. Pastoral counseling has made rapid strides recently, and it is only a matter of time until there will be more clergymen making use of hypnotherapy.

Suggestive "Sleep"

Platonov (1959) in a psychophysiologic treatise on psychotherapy and hypnosis, describes how he has used suggestive "sleep" for achieving positive therapeutic effects in thousands of patients. He concurs with Pavlov, namely, that hypnosis affords curative protective inhibition (regenerative self-healing) of neurons disturbed by excitatory processes.

Platonov's hypnotherapy utilizes direct symptom-eliminating suggestions as follows:

What you have suffered belongs already to the past and does not trouble you any more. You have forgotten all your suffering, and when you remember it, it does not distress you.

This indicates that hypnosis represents an inhibitory conditioned reflex directed toward the suppression of the excitatory "trigger zone" in the cortex. The deranged regulatory activity of the cortex rather than the symptom is treated, and this is accomplished by the use of appropriate word stimuli. Platonov (1959) and his associates, who have hypnotized many thousands of persons in the Soviet Union for over half a century, remarks:

> We have never observed any harmful influence on the patient which could be ascribed to the method of hypnosuggestive therapy, presumably leading to the development of an "unstable personality", "Slavish subordination", "weakening of the will", or an "increase or pathological urge for hypnosis."

Active-Complex Psychotherapy

Another hypnotherapeutic approach similar to the Pavlovian model is Volgyési's (1951) Active Complex Psychotherapy. He utilized conditioned reflexology under hypnosis and a psychosomatic approach. In his book (1960) he described how he treated over 56,500 patients by a combination of group psychotherapy, hypnosis, and supportive technics.

Hypnosynthesis

Conn (1949) utilizes hypnotherapy without extensive probing—hypnosynthesis. The patient uses it as he sees fit without being given any symptom-eliminating suggestion, preconceived interpretations, or directions. With this method, in which no importance is attached to the depth of the hypnosis or recall of unpleasant memories, Conn has obtained very satisfactory results in a wide variety of emotional disorders. His experience substantiates our contentions, namely, that the hypnotherapist only "sets the stage" for an emotionally corrective experience. It is the patient who induces the "trance" by doing what is expected of him (Conn 1959).

Solovey and Milechnin (1960) base their approach on Conn's principles but, in addition, they incorporate extraverbal suggestions intended to increase the well-being of the patient. They, too, find that light hypnosis usually is adequate for giving the stimuli to induce "emotional stabilization."

AUTOGENIC TRAINING   ? for use with biofeedback

Chief Principles

Autogenic training is being employed with increasing frequency by the behavior modifiers, biofeedback therapists, acupuncturists, and a wide variety of lay and medical healers. Because of its growing popularity and its effectiveness, the authors would like to briefly describe its chief principles. It was developed by Schultz (1954) over 60 years ago and was considered a form of autohypnosis. During the induction, subjects are taught to develop various types of sensations through appropriate images to induce self-relaxation. Autogenic training, according to Schultz and Luthe (1959), is a basic therapeutic method of a series of psychophysiologically-oriented approaches that are different from other medical or psychological forms of relaxation. It involves the simultaneous regulation of mental and somatic functions by passive concentration upon phrases of preselected words. Specific somatic responses obtained during the preliminary training bring under voluntary control such feeling states as heaviness in the limbs, warmth in the extremities, control of heart rate, sense of warmth in the abdomen, and cooling of the forehead.

Schultz then uses ideosensory and ideomotór activities to induce a sleeplike stage by sensory-imagery conditioning. We use similar technics but constantly reinforce the idea that *control* over nonvoluntary or autonomic sensations will ultimately lead to increasing control over whatever symptom the patient manifests. This is an important difference as it involves building in a degree of control, that is, from simpler feeling states to the more complex ones associated with the symptom. Throughout this book, we shall refer to autogenic training not only in its relationship to therapy of a wide variety of psychosomatic disorders, but also in its use in hypnoanesthesia and acupunctural analgesia.

Other Autogenic Technics

Volgyési's (1955) "Active-Complex Concentration," Jacobson's (1938) "Progressive Relaxation," and "Transcendental Meditation" are rather similar in method and purpose. However, when these technics were first introduced, they were invariably paired with anxiety reduction, but were not employed in conjunction with systematic desensitization. It is also interesting that some good subjects can develop a great many responses that are not suggested—by generalization. For instance, some subjects develop some degree of anesthesia without its being specifically suggested. Also, many subjects develop deep self-relaxation states without the instructor's presence. Autogenic training teaches self-reliance and makes the subject feel he is doing something helpful. It also builds in the feeling that he himself can actualize his potentials. This enhances his self-esteem and creates a better self-image. We have also used Schultz's (1954) autogenic training for relieving pain of surgery *without the use of any type of analgesia and anesthesia*. All patients are prepared by autohypnosis, "glove anesthesia," and the rehearsal technic described in Chapter 34 on pain.

Many therapists familiar with autogenic training are now aware that the therapeutic benefits of biofeedback training and the current crop of esoteric therapies often are largely due to the relaxation produced by the autogenic training exercises, the conviction of success, and an expectant attitude. It is becoming more self-evident that the more one responds to his own healthy mental pictures the more likely his healthy fantasies will become healthy realities.

Rationale for Autogenic Training

The results with autogenic training depend on repetitive sessions involving the images derived from stimulation of all the sensory modalities. It also requires the individual's developing the capability for "passive concentration." The exercises for the beginner are called standard exercises and are directed specifically toward attaining physiological response. The verbal formula that is consistently mentioned is "My right arm is heavy," and after some hours of applying this formula to various parts of the body, the patient utilizes exercises to induce warmth. After the mastery of bodily relaxation exercises, the patient progresses to meditation exercises that concentrate on visual imagery. From the imagery of simple elements such as color, he will continue with imagination of objects and finally with abstract concepts. Still later, one's own feelings are explored until the deepest level of meditation is achieved. The reader will recognize the similarity between autogenic training, Yoga, Zen, Judaism, Sufi, Karma, and other Eastern meditative philosophies. All of these have been compared with modern hypnosis and other conditioning technics (Kroger 1966 a & b).

Standard Exercises for Autogenic Training

Autogenic training is based on six psychophysiologic exercises. These are practiced several times a day until the subject is able to voluntarily shift to a wakeful *low-arousal* state. The "Standard Exercises" are practiced in a quiet environment, in a horizontal position, and with closed eyes (Luthe 1969). Exercise 1 focuses on the feeling of heaviness in the limbs, and Exercise 2 on the cultivation of the sensation of warmth in the limbs. Exercise 3 deals with cardiac regulation, while Exercise 4 consists of passive concentration on breathing. In Exercise 5, the subject cultivates the sensation of warmth in his upper abdomen, and exercise 6 is the cultivation of feelings of coolness in the forehead. Exercises 1 through 4 most effectively elicit the relaxation and trophotropic response, while Exercises 5 and 6 are reported to have different effects (Luthe 1969). The subject's attitude toward the exercise must not be intense and compulsive, but rather of a quiet, "let it happen," nature. This is referred to as *passive concentration* and is deemed absolutely essential (Luthe 1972).

HYPNOANALYSIS

Hypnosis and psychoanalysis can be used together (Wolberg 1945). This combined method is referred to as hypnoanalysis. Every therapist knows that alterations in awareness are constantly taking place during every session. Neurophysiologists agree that the brain's attention span varies from second to second. Therefore, patients and therapists themselves are never in a static state but rather they fluctuate along the broad continuum of the sleep-wakefulness cycle. Thus, they can be alert (wakefulness), super-alert (hypnosis), or less alert (sleep). Psychoanalysts have observed that at times the patient may appear to be in a trancelike state that has been compared with the feeling states experienced during free association. Freud, who learned the technic from Liébeault, a French hypnotist, reported that he sometimes reassuringly placed his hand on the patient's forehead suggesting that this would increase relaxation, facilitating free association and dream recall.

When hypnosis is used with psychodynamic procedures, deeply repressed material is readily abreacted, and with the appropriate technics the meaningfulness of this material can be integrated into sensory awareness. This also more readily allows the patient insight into the hidden reasons for his behavior. Psychoanalysis derives from hypnosis incisive tools that speed up what ordinarily is a slow method.

Applicability

Nearly all individuals can be hypnotized to a degree. Those who attain deeper stages make the best subjects for the sophisticated hypnoanalytic technics described below. It is estimated that about 20 per cent of the population fall into this classification. However, another 20 per cent can be trained to develop many of the phenomenological responses associated with deep hypnosis, such as somnambulism.

Contraindications

Hypnoanalysis should be used only by psychotherapists trained in psychodynamic theory and practice. They must be capable of dealing with highly charged emotions when these appear. Cases for hypnoanalysis also must be carefully selected. The fearful individual with weak and inadequate characterological defenses also requires careful handling. Those likely to be overwhelmed by the intensity of their verbalizations likewise require careful consideration. Presence of a severe psychosis is a prime contraindication to hypnoanalysis.

Indications for Hypnoanalysis

Hypnoanalysis is indicated for those who do not respond to short-term therapy. It is very valuable for the poorly motivated patient. Posthypnotic suggestions can bind such patients to therapy. This allows time for rapport to be established. Even though dependency is fostered deliberately in such instances, it can be worked through and resolved during later sessions. This approach can shore up a weak ego and hold a symptom on leash until the need for it in the patient's emotional economy is worked through.

Hypnoanalysis has been particularly effective in the treatment of phobias and compulsions. An indication for hypnoanalysis is extreme depression and suicidal tendencies in a patient. On more than one occasion we have used age regression to revert the patient to a point in his life in which he was not depressed. A protective posthypnotic amnesia for the traumatic material is engrafted and removed only after the patient improves.

Methodology

Others, particularly those suffering from severe psychoneuroses, with diligent training can be taught to follow posthypnotic suggestions to develop amnesia, age regression, and revivification of past experiences. At each step the subject can be questioned as to his emotional reactions experienced while entering hypnosis, being in it, or coming out of it.

As in a classical analysis, the transference neurosis, resistances, and defenses can be analyzed. The process makes full use of the technics of free association, dream analysis, and interpretations by the therapist. An advantage of hypnoanalysis is in the handling of marked resistances. These are not removed through direct hypnotic suggestion per se, but rather are handled through discussion, interpretation, and evocation of the reasons for maintaining these and other defensive mechanisms. The reasons for the desire to maintain the chronicity of the symptom, for example, for secondary gain, and the ability to abreact traumatic events often can be facilitated by hypnoanalysis.

In good hypnotic patients, recovery of repressed or forgotten memories can be obtained by the "interim phenomenon" (Lindner 1953). In this interesting technic, a posthypnotic amnesia is engrafted for the repressed material obtained during hypnosis. The patient is then slowly prepared to assimilate the information at nonhypnotic levels. The usual cause for repression of traumatic material is anxiety. However, in a relaxed, anxiety-free state, harmful thoughts filter to consciousness and can more readily be worked through. In other words, the patient is now prepared to accept what he formerly defended himself against. Generally, repressed material for which the amnesia was imposed may slowly filter into awareness either after the termination of the hypnotic session or during the subsequent visits. Importantly, the patient participates with full awareness. A distinct advantage when working with highly charged material is that patients can be instructed that if the material is too traumatic to discuss during a specific session, it can be the basis for a dream between now and the next visit. Thus, if a symbolic correlation results between the highly charged material and the dream content, the validity of the exhumed material can be cross-validated by this approach.

Posthypnotic suggestion can be used to help the patient resolve difficult situations. Such suggestions can be used for helping in the dissolution of the transference relationship. As mentioned, since the rapport during hypnosis is closer and more intense than with conventional therapy, suggestions are more readily carried out. It is this feature that accounts for the rapidity with which exploration of deeply repressed material can take place in hypnoanalysis. Freud (1955) denied the use of suggestions in his therapeutic approach. Despite this denial or lack of awareness, he stated:

> Thus, it becomes possible for us to derive entirely new benefits from the *power of suggestion;* we are able to control it; the patient no longer manages his suggestibility to his own liking, but insofar as he is amenable to its influence at all, we *guide his suggestibility*.

Horizontal Exploration

Horizontal exploration of the nature of a symptom-complex can be obtained by sensory recall under hypnosis. In this approach the therapist identifies himself as a friend of the parents. The patient can be asked, How did things go with you today? or, What seems to be bothering you today? If the therapist can engraft an amnesia for his own identity and assume the role of a sibling, friend, teacher, employer, or parent, the patient's verbalizations and behavior will often reveal the way he felt toward such significant persons in his life at different age levels.

Vertical Exploration

Vertical exploration can be used to trace the development of specific attitudes. By interweaving the chronological past with the present, one can rapidly assess earlier attitudes. In this technic, age regression is used. In good hypnotic patients, an individual can be asked "You are eight years old *now* are you not? Tell me what you are doing this afternoon." The richness and detail of the recalled material often is dramatic.

Age "progression" may be used to advance an age-regressed individual through earlier years of development. Love, hate, fear, and other attitudes toward significant figures in the individual's life can be elicited. Considerable light can be shed in the genesis of these emotional attitudes, and how these affected the personality structure to produce symptoms.

Automatic Handwriting

Though we seldom use this technic, it can be of distinct value for those patients who are affect-blocked, and also for ascertaining the reasons for a specific conflict. Posthypnotic suggestions are given that the hand will be "dissociated'' and will write answers to specific questions while the patient is being engaged in conversation far removed from the desired answers. Here, too, automatic writing, in reality a form of "doodling," can be combined with age regression. Posthypnotic suggestions can be used to help interpret what looks like unintelligible writing. All patients should be "restored" to their present chronological age and the dissociated hand "returned" to normal. A protective amnesia can be employed if the automatic writing contains material too traumatic to be faced at the present time.

Projective Hypnoanalysis

In this technic, psychometric materials such as Rorschach ink blots are presented within what seems to be nonsense material. Since the patients are not on guard, highly significant verbalizations can be elicited. The Thematic Apperception Test, in which subjects are asked to imagine and tell a story from various picture cards, can also be used for this purpose. However, Watkins (1949) points out that the less structured the eliciting stimulus, the more significant the data gathered from it.

Hypnodrama

These methods are similar to those used in psychodrama. The conflict situation can be dramatized while the person is under hypnosis. The therapist or professional actor can play one of the roles. Posthypnotic suggestions can be given to the patient to play a specific character having relevance to conflicts in his life. Both the patient and the therapist can help dramatize the situations in which the inner conflicts of the imaginary character with whom the patient has identified are portrayed.

The personality structure can be dissociated for separate study. The patient can act out both roles. The dissociation should be along the lines of the inferred conflict. In this way the patient actually reenacts his own inner conflicts. Age regression, automatic handwriting, and any one of the projective technics can be used with hypnodrama. For a fuller explanation of this approach, the reader is referred to Greenberg's (1974) excellent book on the subject.

Abreactions

Reenacting past traumatic experiences with resultant release of affects can readily be obtained in good hypnotic subjects. This approach is helpful for reduction of hysterical or severe anxiety reactions of recent origin. The nature of the repressed impulses can be studied to determine their purpose. Following release of inhibited aggression, guilt, and fear impulses, emotional integration can be readily accomplished.

Affect-Bridge

Watkins (1971) describes this as a technic whereby a patient is moved experientially from the present to a past incident over an affect common to the two events rather than through an overlapping "idea" as is usual in psychoanalytic practice. The current affect is vivified and all other aspects of the present experience hypnotically ablated. The patient is then asked to return to some earlier experience during which the affect was felt and to relive the associated event. Significant conflict material so secured can be "brought forward" to the present to achieve "insight" and "work-through" conflictual material to produce an emotional abreaction. The technic also resembles sensory recall. This approach should be used only by experienced hypnotherapists.

Narcohypnoanalysis or Narcosynthesis

Skillful hypnotherapists seldom use drugs. However, occasionally a refractory patient may be given a small amount of sodium pentothal; this often allows the patient to talk more freely. The patient who benefits most by this approach is the one who states, "I doubt if I can by hypnotized." Other individuals, who associate hypnotizability with gullibility, respond well to various drugs such as scopolamine. Such patients are merely looking for some excuse not to directly respond to the suggestions of the therapist; they do not feel stigmatized by drug-induced "hypnosis."

Artificial Induction of Dreams

Meares (1960b) describes special procedures to facilitate hypnoanalysis. He makes use of dream analysis through directive or nondirective posthypnotic suggestions. He has found that this technic is valuable where age regression or abreaction cannot be induced.

Induced Hallucinations

Conflicts inaccessible to hypnoanalysis often can be revealed by suggesting positive hallucinations wherein the individual visualizes himself on a theatre or television screen. Analysis of the hallucinatory experiences may often provide considerable insight into the nature of the repressed conflicts.

Unstructured Hallucinations

Unstructured hallucinations are induced without structuring the therapeutic situation. Merely by asking the subject, while he is in a deep hypnosis, to relate what is happening may reveal significant material, and spontaneous regression and abreaction often occur.

Production of Experimental Conflicts

Through posthypnotic suggestions an artificial situation that resembles the patient's conflict situation may often provide him with insight as to how and why he is reacting to his own conflict. He reacts to the elicited emotions with his own specific behavioral response. Posthypnotic suggestions are directed toward recall of those experiences and feelings that the patient had while hypnotized. Thus, while observing the reaction to an imaginary conflict, the therapist gains insight into the nature of the conflict.

Hypnography

Meares (1957) describes hypnography as a "technique in hypnoanalysis in which the hypnotized patient projects psychic material in black and white painting." He believes that graphic expressions of conflicts has a greater therapeutic effect than verbal expressions of the same conflicts. Suppressed and repressed material is disclosed more readily, and there is greater emotional participation of the patient in the treatment. Symptomatic improvement manifests itself by a change of the paintings. For a more complete account of hypnography, the reader is referred to Meares' (1957) excellent monograph on this subject.

Hypnoplasty

In this technic, the hypnotized patient uses clay to model whatever he wishes to make. His conflicts find expression in plastic rather than graphic form. Specific meanings and the nature of the conflict that has motivated the making of a particular model are brought to light when the patient is asked to associate to the model. Meares (1960) presents a more complete account of hypnoplasty. This specialized technic has been described in more detail by Raginsky (1962).

REFERENCES

Specialized Induction Technics

Conn, J. H.: Psychobiologic therapy. Maryland State Med. J., *8:*192, 1959.

Erickson, M. H.: Advanced Techniques of Hypnosis and Therapy. *In* Haley, J. (ed.): Selected Papers of Milton H. Erickson. New York, Grune & Stratton, 1967.

Kroger, W. S.: Clinical and Experimental Hypnosis. Philadelphia, J. B. Lippincott, 1963.

Meares, A.: A System of Medical Hypnosis. Philadelphia, W. B. Saunders, 1960.

Miller, G. A., Galanter, E., and Pribram, K.: Plans and the Structure of Behavior. New York, Holt, Rinehart & Winston, 1960.

Weitzenhoffer, A. M.: General Techniques of Hypnotism. New York, Grune & Stratton, 1957.
Wolberg, L.: Medical Hypnosis. vol. 1. New York, Grune & Stratton, 1948.

Specialized Hypnotherapeutic Technics

Cheek, D. B.: Unconscious perception of meaningful sounds during surgical anesthesia as revealed under hypnosis. Am. J. Clin. Hypn., *1:*101, 1959.
Conn, J. H.: Hypnosynthesis; hypnosis as a unifying interpersonal experience. J. Nerv. Ment. Dis. *109:*9, 1949.
————: Cultural and clinical aspects of hypnosis, placebos, and suggestibility. Inter. J. Clin. Exper. Hypn., *7:*179, 1959.
Erickson, M. H.: Special techniques of brief hypnotherapy. J. Clin. Exper. Hypn., *2:*109, 1954.
————: Further clinical technics of hypnosis: utilization techniques. Am. J. Clin. Hypn., *2:*3, 1959.
Haley, J.: Control in brief psychotherapy. A.M.A. Arch. Gen. Psychiat., *4:*139, 1961.
Kroger, W. S., and Freed, S. C.: Psychosomatic Gynecology: Including Problems of Obstetrical Care. Philadelphia, W. B. Saunders, 1951.
Meares, A.: The Y-State: an hypnotic variant. J. Clin. Exper. Hypn., *8:*237, 1960.
Platonov, K.: The Word as a Physiological and Therapeutic Factor. Moscow, Foreign Languages Publishing House, 1959.
Raginsky, B. B.: Sensory hypnoplasty with case illustrations. Int. J. Clin. Exp. Hypn. *10:*205–219, 1962.
Rodriquez, R. quoted in: Solovey, G., and Milechnin, A.: Hypnosis as the substratum of many different psychotherapies. Am. J. Clin. Hypn., *3:*9, 1960.
Volgyési, F. A.: On the psycho-therapeutic importance of hypnotic sleep and sleep protective inhibition. Brit. J. Med. Hypnotism, *3:*2, 1951.
————: Ueber Aktiv-Komplexe Psychotherapie und die Blivegung "Schule der Kranken". Berlin, Verlag Volk & Gesundheit, 1960.
Wolberg, L.: Medical Hypnosis. New York, Grune & Stratton, 1945.

Autogenic Training

Geissman, P.: La relaxation recherches ilectroenciphalographiqes. (Relaxation, E.E.G. research). Rev. Med. Psychosom. *4:*75–84, 1962.
Jacobson, E.: Progressive Relaxation. Chicago, Univ. Chicago Press, 1938.
Kroger, W. S.: Clinical and Experimental Hypnosis. Philadelphia, J. B. Lippincott, 1963.
————: Comparative evaluation of Zen, Yoga, Judaism with Conditioning Technics and Psychotherapy. pp. 175–180. Amsterdam, Excerpta Medica Foundation, 1966a.
————: Newer trends in psychosomatic medicine and hypnosis as related to Yoga. *In* Shri Yogendra, (ed.): Yoga in Modern Life, pp. 135–144. Yoga Institute of Bombay, 1966b.
Luthe, W. (ed): Autogenic Therapy, vols. 1–5. New York, Grune & Stratton, 1969.
Luthe, W.: Autogenic therapy: excerpts on applications to cardiovascular disorders and hypercholesterolemia, *In* Biofeedback and Self-Control 1971. New York, Aldine-Atherton, 1972.

Schultz, J. H.: Some remarks about technics of hypnosis as anesthesia. Brit. J. Med. Hypnotism, *5:*23, 1954.
Schultz, J. H., and Luthe, W.: Autogenic Training. New York, Grune & Stratton, 1959.
Volgyési, F. A.: Franz Andreas Volgyési: Pioneer of Hypnotherapy. Brit. J. Med. Hypn., *6:*18, 1955.

Hypnoanalysis

Freud, S.: Complete Psychological Works. (J. Strachey, trans.) vols. 5 & 11. London, Hogarth Press, 1955.
Greenberg, I.: Psychodrama. New York, Behavioral Publications, 1974.
Kroger, W. S.: Clinical and Experimental Hypnosis. Philadelphia, J. B. Lippincott, 1963.
Lindner, R. M.: Hypnoanalysis as a psychotherapeutic technique. *In* Bychowski, G., and Despent, J. L. (eds.): Specialized Techniques in Psychotherapy. New York, Basic Books, 1953.
Meares, A.: Hypnography. Springfield, Ill., Charles C Thomas, 1957.
————: Shapes of Sanity. Springfield, Ill., Charles C Thomas, 1960a.
————: A System of Medical Hypnosis. Philadelphia, W. B. Saunders, 1960b.
Watkins, J.: The Affect Bridge: A hypnoanalytic technique. Int. J. Clin. Exper. Hypn., *19:*21, 1971.
Watkins, J.: Hypnotherapy of War Neuroses. New York, Ronald Press, 1949.
Wolberg, L. R.: Hypnoanalysis. New York, Grune & Stration, 1945.

SUGGESTED READINGS

Specialized Induction Techniques

Eliseo, T. S.: The hypnotic induction profile and hypnotic susceptibility. Int. J. Clin. Exp. Hypn. *22:*320, 1974.
Sacerdote, P.: Some individualized hypnotherapeutic techniques. Int. J. Clin. Exp. Hypn., *20:*1, 1972.
Todd, F. J., and Kelley, R. J.: The use of hypnosis to facilitate conditioned relaxation responses. Behav. Ther. Exp. Psychiat:, *1:*295, 1970.

Hypnoanalysis

Gill, M. M., and Brenman, M.: Hypnosis and Related States: Psychoanalytic Studies in Regression. New York, International Univ. Press, 1959.
Klempeser, E.: Techniques of hypnosis and hypnoanalysis. Int. J. Clin. Exper. Hypn., *17:*137, 1969.
Kline, M. V.: (ed.): Hypnodynamic Psychology: An Integrative Approach To The Behavior Sciences. New York, Julian Press, 1955.
Schneck, J. M.: Hypnoanalysis. Personality, *1:*307, 1951.
————: Hypnoanalysis. Int. J. Clin. Exper. Hypn., *10:*1, 1962.

5

Historical Development of Behavior Modification

OLDER CONCEPTS

The context of the development of current concepts of behavior modification may be understood by reviewing John Locke's (1632–1704) doctrine of the child's mind as a *tabula rasa*. Locke's views were opposed to the prevailing Cartesian doctrine that man's ideas (and therefore the sources of his behavior) are innate. Ideas, according to Locke, are not inborn but come from interaction with the external environment, that is, from experience. Aristotle had also believed that experience determines behavior, but it was Locke who made this concept central to philosophy and psychology.

The concept of associationism originated by David Hartley (1705–1757) was another major philosophical and psychological step toward current viewpoints. Although the idea of association of thoughts through "temporal continuity" can be found in Aristotle and others, including Locke, Berkley, Hume, and Hobbes, it was Hartley who observed a fundamental law of behavior. He labeled his observation as association and elaborated it into a psychological system, thus creating a formal doctrine and a new "school."

NEWER CONCEPTS

The Russian physiologist Ivan Sechenov (1829–1905) was particularly influenced by Locke's views. Sechenov argued in his monograph *Reflexes of the Brain* (1863) that all animal and human behavior was "reflexive" in origin and nature, that is, wholly determined by measurable units and combinations of units of neuromotor (or sensorineuromotor) action. Reflexes are learned, the mechanism of learning is association, which in itself is reflexive. Association, and not the innate nature of reflexes, determines "psychic content." Sechenov tried to account for all psychic phenomena within the framework of the reflex arc.

At the same time, also in Russia, another movement was growing that placed emphasis on the connection between man's behavior and "environmental" stimuli. This developed from the work of Pavlov and Bechterev, which came to be accepted as representative of a scientifically based behavioristic movement. Pavlov's (1840–1936) work on conditioned reflexes began in 1899 and continued until his death. In his basic and now classic experimental procedure, he sounded a tuning fork while applying a given quantity of powdered meat (the primary reinforcer) on a dog's tongue and repeated this procedure at intervals until the tuning fork alone, without the meat, produced a reasonably constant flow of saliva. This was the "conditioned reflex" method; the reflex was conditional upon the fact that a given stimulus had been presented together with one that was originally adequate to elicit it.

He stated, "Owing to the entire preceding life of the human adult, a word is connected with all the external and internal stimuli coming to the cerebral hemispheres, signals all of them, replaces all of them and can, therefore, evoke all the actions and reactions of the organism which these stimuli produce" (Pavlov, 1951). Also the notion of speech as a secondary signal system was introduced by Pavlov. Speech, which is unique to man, follows the same rules of conditioning as the primary signaling system of behavior. In the human being, words, thoughts, and ideas activate primary signaling processes by associated reflexes. The verbal signal or word becomes in time the conditioned stimulus to elicit primary signaling system activities. This is unique to humans, and it is for this reason that we can use images in the form of verbal instructions to control the primary signaling system processes.

A contemporary of Pavlov's, Bechterev, also investigated human learning and thought processes with objective technics. It was his argument that reflexes are elicited not only by the few stimuli which are in themselves sufficient to arouse them (for example, electric shock for retraction of the finger) but by many other associated stimuli (Bechterev 1932). For example, the sights and sounds present at the time of the reflex may come to elicit the reflex without the presence of the original (adequate) stimulus.

Watson (1878–1958) argued that abnormal behavior was the result of a "training" process. He contended that if the history of human maladjustments were fully known they all could be explained in terms of conditioning (Watson 1919). Watson pioneered studies in infant conditioning: in collaboration with Rayner (Watson and Rayner 1920) he demonstrated how a fear reaction could be developed in a young child. This experiment had a major effect on American psychology, in that it supported Watson's contention that not only simple motor habits but even emotional tendencies may be "built into" the child by conditioning. One of Watson's major concepts was that the phenomena of "inner" life could be explained in terms of the functioning of mechanisms that are objective, although not as observable, as gross muscular contractions. For example, imagination and thought may be expressed in terms of "implicit" muscle behavior, especially the behavior of the speech organs. His classification of verbal report as an explicit response represented a major link between introspection and behaviorism. Once verbal report is treated as an explicit response, all introspection becomes observable behavior.

Four other investigators considered to be direct progenitors of current concepts in behavior modification are Thorndike, Guthrie, Hull, and Skinner. The origin of present-day operant conditioning procedures may be traced, in part, to the 1898 doctoral dissertation at Columbia University of E. L. Thorndike. From his early studies of animal escape behavior, Thorndike formulated, in 1911, his Law of Effect, based on his observation that when a behavior is followed by satisfying (rewarding) consequences, it is likely to be learned, and when it is followed by punishment, failure, or an annoying state of affairs, it is less likely to recur. He defined his terms as follows:

> By a satisfying state of affairs is meant one which the animal does nothing to avoid, often doing things which maintain or renew it. By an annoying state of affairs is meant one which the animal does nothing to preserve, often doing things which put an end to it (1913).

A useful form of behaviorism was next espoused by Guthrie (1935, 1938, 1942), who returned to the principles of associative learning rather than starting with the Pavlovian conditioned reflex as his basic paradigm of learning, as Watson had done. Guthrie's one law of learning was as follows: "A combination of stimuli which has accompanied a movement will on its recurrence tend to be followed by that movement" (1935). A second statement completes his postulates about learning: "A stimulus pattern gains its full associative strength on the occasion of its first pairing with a response" (1942).

The similarity of Guthrie's language and concepts to the formulation of maladaptive behavior as conceived by present-day behavior modifiers is illustrated by the following. He states that

> to break a habit it is first necessary to know the stimuli responsible for its release . . . also, redirect the person to do something else. A habit may be circumvented by interrupting it at its onset and initiating some other action. . . . The patient may, by having the action deprived of success in the sense that it removes the motivating stimulus, bring about by trial and error behavior his own substitution for the unwanted act. In all these cases we are merely insuring that a cue which was once followed by the undesirable action is *once* followed by something else. If practice of the substitution is required, this is because the undesired act had more than one cue and it is necessary to recondition all its cues (Guthrie 1938).

Hull (1884–1952) was another major contributor to hypnosis and behaviorism. Hull (1943, 1951) attempted to develop quantitative laws for the prediction of human behavior. Skinner's publication in 1938 of *The Behavior of*

Organisms was a major landmark in the behavioral approach to the study of abnormal behavior. Despite Pavlov's influence, Skinner claimed that the physiological activity Pavlov thought he was studying was inferential. Skinner's contention was that it was not necessary to become involved with physiological or cognitive data in order to understand and work directly with human and animal behavior (Skinner 1938, 1953). The experimental basis, scientific spirit, and objective approach to behavior seen in much of the current work in behavior modification is an extension of Skinner's early efforts.

More recently, Wolpe (1958), Lazarus (1971), Bandura (1969) and other pioneers in the field of behavior modification have extended these principles to the field of applied psychology dealing with human behavior. We shall describe these contributions in other chapters and add our own observations, particularly those incorporating hypnosis into the behavioral model.

REFERENCES

Bandura, A.: Principles of Behavior Modification. New York, Holt, Rinehart & Winston, 1969.

Bechterev, V. M.: General Principles of Human Reflexology. New York, International Universities Press, 1932.

Guthrie, E. R.: The Psychology of Learning. New York, Harper & Brothers, 1935.

————: The Psychology of Human Conflict. New York, Harper & Brothers, 1938.

————: Conditioning: a theory of learning in terms of stimulus, response, and association. pp. 17–60. *In* The Psychology of Learning (Chap. 1). Washington, D.C., National Social Studies Education, 1942, 41st yearbook (Part 2).

Hull, C. L.: Principles of Behavior. New York, Appleton-Century Co., 1943.

————: Essentials of Behavior. New Haven, Yale Univ. Press, 1951.

Lazarus, A. A.: Behavior Therapy and Beyond. New York, McGraw-Hill, 1971.

Pavlov, I. P.: Twenty Years of Objective Study of the Higher Nervous Activity Behavior of Animals. Moscow, Medzig Publishing House, 1951.

Sechenov, I. M.: Reflexes of the Brain (1863). Reprinted in Selected Works. Moscow, Bookmiga, 1935.

Skinner, B. F.: The Behavior of Organisms. New York, Appleton-Century Co., 1938.

————: Science and Human Behavior. New York, Macmillan, 1953.

Thorndike, E. L.: The Psychology of Learning. New York, Teachers College, 1913.

Vogt, O.: Zur Kenntnis des Wesens und der psychologischen Bedeutung des Hypnotismus. Z. Hypnotismus, 1894–95: pp. 3, 277; 1896: pp. 4, 32, 122, 229.

Watson, J. B.: Psychology from the Standpoint of a Behaviorist. Philadelphia, J. B. Lippincott, 1919.

Watson, J. B., and Rayner, R.: Conditioned emotional reactions. J. Exp. Psychol., *3*:1, 1920.

Wolpe, J.: Psychotherapy by Reciprocal Inhibition. Stanford, Stanford Univ. Press, 1958.

6

Foundations of Behavior Modification

CLASSICAL OR RESPONDENT CONDITIONING

The core of learning theory has been derived from animal experiments. However, the principles evolving from the research in these areas can now be successfully applied to modifying human responses. The technics can be subsumed under the rubric of behavioral modification therapy. The basic classical conditioning paradigm is to closely associate in time a conditioned stimulus (CS) and an unconditioned stimulus (UCS). As a function of this pairing or association, the conditioned stimulus will take on properties of the unconditioned stimulus. The response made to the unconditioned stimulus is the unconditioned response (UCR). The response made to the conditioned stimulus is the conditioned response (CR). For example, when Pavlov presented food powder (UCS) to a dog, the animal salivated (UCR). This was the animal's normal reaction to contacting food. If however, a bell (CS) immediately preceded or coincided with the presentation of food (UCS), the animal would, after several pairings of bell and food, salivate (CR) merely to the sound of the bell even if food did not follow. The close association in time of the bell and food led to the bell's taking on properties of the food—namely the ability of the food to elicit salivation.

The conditioned stimulus is also called a secondary reinforcer (Sr) because it has taken on qualities of a primary reinforcer (Pr)—food. Keller and Schoenfeld (1950) clarify the concept of secondary reinforcement when they state, "a stimulus which is not originally reinforcing can become so through repeated association with one that is. That is, reinforcing power may be acquired by a stimulus through being present when an original reinforcement is given" (p. 232).

Primary reinforcers are intrinsically rewarding (e.g., food and water) while the value or desirability of a secondary reinforcer has been learned. The concept of primary reinforcement is inadequate to account for a great deal of learning which takes place over relatively protracted sequences. The concept of primary reinforcement must, therefore, be supplemented by the concept of secondary reinforcement if learning is to be explained. It has been found that reinforcement power, which has been transmitted to a hitherto neutral stimulus through repeated associations, can be transferred from this to another neutral stimulus. This can eventuate in a chain or series whose length is limited only by the conditions that bring about the repeated associations. Skinner (1953) states,

> Only a small part of behavior is immediately reinforced with food, water, sexual contact, or other events of obvious biological importance. Although it is characteristic of human behavior that primary reinforcers may be effective after a long delay, this is presumably only because intervening events become conditioned reinforcers.

Money is the prime example of a secondary reinforcer. There is nothing intrinsically rewarding about the paper it is printed on, but it has taken on great reinforcing properties through association with so many other forms of reinforcement. It is not money itself but what it can buy that is important.

A conditioned stimulus loses its reinforcing properties when the associations stop. *Extinction* of the salivation response is produced by sounding the bell and not pairing it with the food. The number of times the bell will elicit salivation after the food pairings have stopped is a function of several parameters. These include the number of primary reinforcements, magnitude of primary reinforcement, time interval between presentation of secondary and primary reinforcers, drive intensity (degree of hunger) during training and during testing, and the schedule of reinforcement in training. The schedule of reinforcement refers to the frequency with which the bell is paired with food during the time the association is being formed (training period). If the food is always paired with the bell, the schedule is one of continuous reinforcement; if it is not always paired with the bell, the schedule is one of intermittent reinforcement.

The terms *reinforcement* and *schedules* are generally used more with instrumental conditioning, which will be discussed next. However, since there is much debate as to whether there actually are two different forms of conditioning (classical and instrumental), there is no need, in our opinion, to restrict the terminology. A great deal of research, especially on animals, has identified the parameters involved in the establishment of a secondary reinforcer. The reader is referred to Wike (1966) for an exhaustive treatise on the parameters necessary for establishment of a secondary reinforcer. These principles can be applied in psychotherapeutic conditioning in humans.

INSTRUMENTAL OR OPERANT CONDITIONING

A fundamental question regarding learning has been: can conditioning by association alone (classical conditioning), without reinforcement (instrumental conditioning), exist? Even if association *and* reinforcement are operating in both forms of conditioning, there is a practical methodological difference between instrumental and classical conditioning: the conditioning paradigms are different. The standard dichotomy between classical (respondent) and instrumental conditioning (operant) is that in the former, the response to be conditioned is "elicited," whereas in instrumental conditioning, the response to be conditioned is "emitted." To classically condition salivation to the sound of a bell, the salivary response is elicited in the presence of or immediately after the bell sound by presenting food.

To instrumentally condition salivation, the salivary response would first have to be emitted by the subject and then reinforced. For example, every time there was an increase in salivation following the sounding of a bell (incidence would be random at first) the animal would be given some sort of reinforcement. While it was previously thought that classical conditioning was limited to the autonomic nervous system and instrumental to the skeletal system, this dichotomy no longer stands. Miller (1969) has demonstrated that autonomic responses such as alpha wave, heartbeat, and blood pressure can be instrumentally conditioned. A person's blood pressure can be elevated or lowered by reinforcing him whenever he emits the appropriate response: an increase or decrease in blood pressure.

Shaping, or the Method of Successive Approximations

It can be very tedious waiting around for an organism to emit a desired response so that it can be reinforced. In fact, some responses that we want may not occur in the subject's behavioral repertoire at all. This is where the concept of "shaping" is invaluable. Shaping involves Skinner's method of *successive approximations* whereby the subject is reinforced for pieces of behavior in increasing degrees of similarity to the final, desired response. For example, if we want to increase the frequency of the behavior of walking on the hind legs in the rat, the rat would first be reinforced for lifting one leg one inch, then one leg two inches, two legs one inch, and so forth, until the response of walking on the hind legs had been properly shaped. The method of successive approximations is used very effectively in psychotherapy with the concept of the hierarchy which we will describe later.

Reinforcement and Punishment

Reinforcers are of two types, positive and negative. In reference to these two types, Skinner (1953, p. 73) says, "Some reinforcements consist of *presenting* stimuli, of adding something—for example, food, water, or sexual contact—to the situation. These, as mentioned, we call *positive* reinforcers. Others consist of *removing* something—for example, a loud noise, a very bright light, extreme cold or heat, or electric shock—from the situation. These we call *negative* reinforcers.'' Both positive and negative reinforcers increase the probability of responding. Ferster and Skinner (1957, pp. 730, 723) now employ the term "aversive stimulus" in place of "negative reinforcer." By pairing stimuli with these two classes of primary reinforcers, two types of conditioned reinforcers are developed: positive and negative conditioned reinforcers. Using the more recent terminology of Ferster and Skinner (1957, pp. 723), the second type will be called "conditioned aversive stimuli."

Punishment, on the other hand, reduces the probability of responding. Azrin and Holz (1966) define punishment as "'a reduction of the future probability of a specific response as a result of the immediate delivery of a stimulus for the response.'' A punishing stimulus is thus "a consequence of behavior that reduces the future probability of the behavior (p. 381)." The definitions of punishment and reinforcement are the same except that punishment results in a *decrease* and reinforcement results in an *increase* in the future probability of a behavior following the contingent delivery of a stimulus for that behavior. Certain variables have been found crucial for maximizing the effectiveness of punishment procedures (Azrin and Holz 1966). The reader is referred to the work of these authors.

When a learned operant response is no longer followed by a reinforcer (positive or negative) or punishment, it will eventually return to the original strength; it extinguishes. A procedure in which desirable behavior is reinforced and less desirable behavior extinguished or punished is called "differential reinforcement." An environmental event correlated with reinforcement is called a "discriminative stimulus." This stimulus comes to excercise a controlling function over the behavior, so that the behavior tends to occur primarily in the presence of the environmental event. For example, if only a particular staff person gives out the tokens when patients in a "token economy" socialize (see p. 73) the patients tend to socialize only when that person is around. The staff member is a discriminative stimulus for the desirable behavior. This process, resulting in behavior occurring in only some situations or stimulus settings, is called "discrimination."

Classically conditioned responses will be elicited by conditioned stimuli that have been paired with unconditioned stimuli, and not by stimuli that are different from the conditioned stimuli. Operant behavior will occur in environments in which it has been reinforced, but not in environments very different from those associated with reinforcement. For example, if a response is reinforced in a hospital setting but not in the patient's home, it will be strong in the hospital but less likely to occur elsewhere. The process resulting in behavior occurring in an environment in which it has *not* previously been reinforced is termed *generalization*. The degree to which a behavior will generalize to another situation is a function of the similarity between the situation in which it was reinforced and the new situation. This is why it is important that the imagery used in covert conditioning procedures (to be described later) must be vivid. The more real the activities of the imagery seem, the more they will generalize to reality.

CLINICAL ASPECTS OF BEHAVIOR MODIFICATION

Behavior therapy begins with an objective description and survey to define the antecedent variables accounting for the problem behavior. This is a multifaceted study of the personality. The behavior therapist focuses on that which is observable and measurable. He is particularly on the *qui vive* for the specific situations where the faulty or maladaptive behavior occurs or does not occur. The therapist using this approach emphasizes the modification of the presenting behavior that requires changing, rather than emphasizing the etiogenesis or presumed unconscious conflicts responsible for the symptoms.

The treatment program pays special attention to systematic manipulation of the environmental determinants and behavioral variables that are thought to be functionally related to the disturbing behavior or performance. Finally the therapist, whenever possible, attempts to identify the initial problem and formulate the treatment program. Behavior therapists, furthermore, can present evidence of change by offering graphs or charts of the patient's progress.

The person making the observations may be either the therapist, a friend of the patient, or the patient himself. It is important to find out how he thinks or feels about his everyday activities. He should report anxieties, feelings of guilt, distressing fantasies, and also how he faces his work, school, or family, or how he reacts toward others. Is he withdrawn, abusive, or loving to members of his family? For instance, overeating, stuttering, or aggressive outbursts can be tallied. One can also determine how highly motivated the patients are in relinquishing untoward behavioral manifestations. In addition to what the patient does and does not do, the behavior therapist attempts to find out how the maladaptive behavior relates to physiological and environmental variables. The astute therapist will be on the lookout for the antecedent problematic behaviors as well as the consequences. He will try to determine under what circumstances the behavioral abnormalities occur. In this kind of behavioral assay, the individuality of each patient is explicitly recognized and the therapy is tailored to the individual case.

In brief, the therapist is in a good position to formulate the reasons for the origin and maintenance of maladaptive behaviors. He makes full use of the general principles of conditioning and learning theory. He also combines this with the observations he has made on previous patients and their social environments in the hospital, clinic and natural environment.

In contrast to psychodynamic therapy, behavior therapy permits the testing of such clinical hypotheses by the systematic manipulation of behavioral and environmental variables thought to be functionally related to the patient's difficulties. The principal goal of behavior therapy is to change and modify the behavior. We shall define and describe the important methods that are currently being utilized as we individually cover each specific problem behavior. New methods are continually being developed and evaluated by clinical researchers. The most common of these are systematic desensitization and token economies with operant principles.

Operant principles in conditioning are being adapted from animal conditioning to human conditioning. A fundamental principle is that the organism first must be deprived in one or more areas. Then when appropriate reinforcers are given in contiguity or close in time to the desired response, that response will tend to increase in frequency. Contrarily, responses not rewarded or reinforced close in time tend to go into extinction. Thus, when successive approximations are employed, the ultimately desired behavior is shaped through differential reinforcement.

Tugender and Ferinden (1972) state, "The astonishing discovery is that shaping behaviors is possible as a psychic experience solely." We agree completely. All the images to be presented in later chapters serve as psychic reinforcers. They further stress that use of hypnosis with mental operants should not be confused with Wolpe's reciprocal inhibition and desensitization technics wherein hypnosis was used merely to relax the patient *a priori.*

REFERENCES

Azrin, N. H. and Holz, W. C.: Punishment. In W. K. Honig (ed.): Operant Behavior: Areas of Research and Application. pp. 380–447. New York, Appleton-Century-Crofts, 1966.

Ferinden, W. E. and Tugender, H. S.: Handbook of Hypno-Operant Behavior Techniques. Orange, N.J., Power Publ., 1973.

Ferster, C. B. and Skinner, B. F.: Schedules of Reinforcement. New York, Appleton-Century-Crofts, 1957.

Keller, F. S. and Schoenfeld, W. N.: Principles of Psychology. New York, Appleton-Century-Crofts, 1950.

Miller, N. E.: Learning of visceral and glandular responses. Science, *163:*434, 1969.

Skinner, B. F.: Science and Human Behavior. New York, Macmillan, 1953.

Tugender, H. J. and Ferinden, W. E.: An Introduction to Hypno-Operant Therapy. Orange, N.J., Power Publ., 1972.

Wike, E. L.: Secondary Reinforcement. New York, Harper & Row, 1966.

SUGGESTED READINGS

American Psychiatric Association Task Force Report: Behavior Therapy in Psychiatry. July, 1973.

Fethke, G. C.: Token economies: a further comment. Behav. Res. Ther., *11:*225, 1973.

Hallam, R. and Rachman, S.: Theoretical problems of aversion therapy. Behav. Res. Ther., *10:*341, 1972.

Harlow, H. F., Gluck, J. P. and Suomi, S. J.: Generalization of behavioral data between nonhuman and human animals. Amer. Psychol., *27:*709, 1972.

Jernstedt, G. C.: Pattern of reinforcement and intertrial interval effects on acquisition and extinction performance in humans. Psychol. Rep., *34:*107, 1974.

Johnston, J. M.: Punishment of human behavior. Amer. Psychol., *27:*1033, 1972.

Kanfer, F. H. and Matarazzo, J. D.: Secondary and generalized reinforcement in human learning. J. Exp. Psychol., *58:*400, 1959.

Rettig, E. B. and Clement, P. W.: Peak versus mean amount of reinforcement in operant conditioning with children. Psychol. Rep., *34:*139, 1974.

Reynolds, W. F., Pavlik, W. B., and Goldstein, E.: Secondary reinforcement effects as a function of reward magnitude training methods. Psychol. Rep., *15:*7, 1964.

Wirth, P. W. and Maples, E. G.: Contiguous approach conditioning: a model for positive reinforcement. Psych. Rep., *34:*129, 1974.

Young, G. C. and Morgan, R. T.: Analysis of factors associated with the extinction of a conditioned response. Behav. Res. Ther., *11:*219, 1973.

7

Behavioral Technics

There are no standard behavioral technics that can (or should) be incorporated into this model in a routine fashion. Essentially each case represents a new problem to be tackled in its own right. Thus far, a bewildering variety of technics has been used by behavior therapists. Counterconditioning in the form of sensitization (aversion therapy) or desensitization is the basic tool of the behavior therapist. This, combined with specific scheduled rewards and punishment for desired behaviors, constitutes the core of behavior modification. Since many specific technics have only been used in relation to a single case study, it would be superfluous to describe them in detail in this chapter.

While there are many technics as mentioned, there are few concepts or general principles involved in behavior therapy. In terms of technics, Bandura (1961) organized his survey of behavior therapy around extinction, discrimination learning, methods of reward, punishment, and social imitation. Grossberg (1964) reviewed aversion, negative practice, positive conditioning, reinforcement withdrawal, and desensitization. Kalish (1965) stressed classical conditioning and argued that the various technics could be reduced to extinction and conditioning. Ullman and Krasner (1969) remark that although all technics are important, none of them, as such, define behavior therapy. These authors state, "Rather, behavior therapy can be summarized as involving many procedures that utilize systematic environmental contingencies to alter directly the subject's response to stimuli" (p. 253). The following are some of the basic technics used in the field of behavior modification.

SYSTEMATIC DESENSITIZATION

Systematic desensitization is the progressive exposure to feared situations to reduce maladaptive anxiety and avoidance behavior. The procedure is pre-planned and performed piecemeal or in graduated steps. A typical example is the phobic child who during a period of hunger is given food to eat while the feared object is slowly brought nearer to him. Care must be taken to keep the phobic stimulus sufficiently far away so as not to interfere with his eating. As the phobic object is brought closer, the child's tolerance increases and eventually he is able to touch it without alarm, whether or not food is available. Wolpe (1958) has developed other procedures for neutralizing anxiety. He believes that if a response antagonistic to anxiety can be made to occur in the presence of anxiety-evoking stimuli, the bond between these stimuli and the anxiety will be weakened. Mere exposure to the anxiety-eliciting stimuli is un-likely to extinguish the fear unless an incompatible response such as relaxation is paired with the fear-provoking stimulus.

The treatment of specific anxiety responses is performed by setting up the patient's fears into a hierarchy. The therapist must be careful to see that there are relatively small gradations between successive fear-provoking items. Concomitantly, patients are taught relaxation technics, which may consist of either progressive relaxation or hypnosis. Under relaxation, successively higher doses of anxiety-provoking material in the hierarchy can be presented. The patient is asked to signal by lifting his finger if the specific scenes prove disturbing. When this occurs, they are immediately withdrawn and the relaxation is deepened. The distressful scene is then presented repeatedly in small doses until the patient can picture the distressing scene without reporting subjective anxiety.

There are numerous clinical reports describing the use of systematic desensitization for a wide variety of problems. Some of the questions asked are: To what degree is systematic desensitization a method of counterconditioning? Does it act by producing extinction? What is the role of the various types of relaxation? How much of a role does an attitude expectant of improvement play? How important is the setting up of hierarchies?

The APA task force that investigated behavior therapy feels that the critical issues to its employment are the indications and contraindications. For example, they point out that schizophrenic syndromes respond better to chemotherapy than to behavior therapy. We are not wholly in agreement with this contention. Both modes should be used. We also feel that in borderline schizophrenics, the relaxation, whether at hypnotic or non-hypnotic levels, is a crucial variable in accounting for cure. How else can one account for success rates reported for psychotics with hypnosis? (See Chap. 28 for fuller explanation.) One salient factor emerges, namely that the practicing therapist will find that although the technic of setting up the hierarchy is rather tedious, it is a relatively direct technic for dealing with anxiety, especially the type precipitated by identifiable stimuli.

SENSITIZATION OR AVERSION THERAPY

While desensitization concerns itself with getting an individual to like or at least not fear a given object or situation, sensitization or aversion therapy attempts to condition a dislike or at least eliminate a like for an object or situation. Sensitization has commonly been used for cigarette smoking, alcoholism, obesity, and sexual deviations. Stimuli associated with undesirable behavior are paired with a painful or unpleasant stimulus, resulting in suppression of the undesired behavior. For example, the taste and smell of certain fattening foods would be paired with drug-induced nausea so that the obese patient would feel conditioned nausea when attempting to eat nondietetic foods.

PUNISHMENT

Punishment involves the addition of an aversive stimulus or removal of a positive stimulus *after* the inappropriate behavior. In the first case a child's hand may be slapped for talking out of turn in class while in the second case, the child would lose a privilege or forfeit a token for having talked. In either of these "aversive control" technics, if the patient does not perform the undesirable behavior, he is able to avoid being punished.

FLOODING AND IMPLOSION THERAPY

In this type of behavior therapy, the situation most deeply dreaded by the patient is presented in *intense* forms, either in imagination ("in vitro") or in real life ("in vivo") without benefit of associated relaxation. Implosion therapy, unlike flooding, is based on several psychodynamic assumptions out of the scope of this volume. Theoretically, the anxiety elicited by these technics finally extinguishes by the absence of the patient's usual reinforcement: escape avoidance. Experience of anxiety in the absence of any real aversive consequences leads to extinction.

MASSED OR NEGATIVE PRACTICE

This method seeks to extinguish a habit by exhausting repetition. For example, a typist who repeatedly makes the same spelling errors may be asked to type the word *incorrectly* a thousand times. The technic has been used most frequently in the treatment of tics, and its rationale and methodology are more fully described in that chapter.

THOUGHT STOPPING

In thought stopping whenever a negative or undesirable thought comes to mind the patient is to subvocally or out loud yell "STOP." This maneuver will interrupt a chain of thought leading to a negative feeling state or undesired behavior. Since negative thoughts trigger many undesirable responses, this technic has wide applicability.

ASSERTIVE TRAINING

In this type of behavior therapy, patients are taught to give appropriate and direct expression of ongoing feelings, both positive and negative. Maladaptive fear or rage reactions may inhibit dominant (not aggressive or domineering) responses and need to be desensitized or counterconditioned. People who habitually fail to stand up for their rights as well as those who typically overreact with rage to real or imagined slights from others are appropriate candidates for assertive training.

ROLE PLAYING OR BEHAVIORAL REHEARSAL

Using this technic in the context of behavior therapy, the therapist assumes the role of significant persons in the patient's life. A series of increasingly exacting scenes is enacted within the protective confines of the therapist's office. The patient's verbal content, mode of expression, tone of voice, inflection, and resonance are monitored by the therapist during rehearsal. Feedback, with or without tape recorded sequences, is used by the therapist in a behavior-shaping, role-playing paradigm that eventually enables the patient to remove apologetic hesitations or querulous overtones. Also modified is non-verbal behavior such as posture, gait, eye contact, and facial expression.

TOKEN ECONOMIES AND OPERANT PRINCIPLES

A wide variety of operant conditioning technics have been described for ward or group management problems. Positive reinforcement is used to develop and maintain appropriate behavior. Removal of positive reinforcement can be used to decrease the frequency of inappropriate behaviors. The token economy system, which we have described in the chapter on schizophrenia, is essentially a work-payment incentive system. In order for the token economy program to be successful, the staff who manages it may delineate the desired behaviors to develop a currency system that includes some kind of token to be dispensed by the staff and exchanged by patients. The program must also provide enough positive or reinforcing consequences obtainable through token exchange.

MODELING, IMITATION, OR OBSERVATIONAL LEARNING

Virtually all learning phenomena resulting from direct experiences can occur on a vicarious basis through observation of other persons' behavior and its consequences for them. Using these technics, emotional responses can be conditioned observationally by having the patient witness the affective reactions of others undergoing painful or pleasurable experiences. Fearful and avoidant behavior is extinguished vicariously through observation of modeled approach behavior toward feared objects without any adverse consequences accruing to the performer. Inhibitions or suppression of behavior can be induced by witnessing the behavior of others punished. Also the expression of well-learned responses can be enhanced and socially regulated through the actions of influential models. Modeling procedures therefore have a wide application, including elimination of behavioral deficits, reduction of excessive fears and inhibitions, transmission of self-regulating systems and social facilitation of behavioral patterns on a group scale. For a more detailed description of the use of modeling and vicarious processes in behavior modification the reader is referred to the excellent work of Bandura (1969).

Aversive control with aversion therapy and punishment technics, flooding, massed practice, assertive training, modeling, role playing, thought stopping, contingency management, and metronome-conditioned relaxation will be described in more detail later in the appropriate chapters.

Thus far, we have not only discussed the research in experimental psychology, but also its clinical application in the form of behavior therapy. Inasmuch as the authors have a rich background in behavior therapy and hypnosis, we readily recognize that a cross-fertilization exists between both fields. We believe on the basis of our clinical experience that when behavior therapy and hypnosis are used together, a synergistic effect results. For this reason, we have introduced the hypnobehavioral model that will be discussed in the following chapters. This approach is indicated for those patients refractory to either method alone, and it should have a salutary effect on the practice of psychology and psychiatry.

REFERENCES

Bandura, A.: Psychotherapy as a learning process. Psychol. Bull., *58:*143, 1961.
————: Principles of Behavior Modification. New York, Holt, Rinehart & Winston, 1969.
Grossberg, J. M.: Behavior therapy: a review. Psychol. Bull., *62:*73, 1964.
Kalish, H. I.: Behavior therapy. *In* Wolman, B. B. (ed.): Handbook of Clinical Psychology. New York, McGraw-Hill, 1965.
Ullmann, L. P. and Krasner, L.: A Psychological Approach to Abnormal Behavior. Englewood Cliffs, Prentice-Hall, 1969.

Wolpe, J.: Psychotherapy by Reciprocal Inhibition. Stanford, Stanford Univ. Press, 1958.

SUGGESTED READINGS

Bernstein, D. A. and Borkovec, T. D.: Progressive Relaxation Training. A Manual for the Helping Professions. Champaign, Ill., Research Press, 1973.

Calhoun, K. S., Adams, H. E. and Mitchell, K. M.: Innovative Treatment Methods in Psychopathology. New York, John Wiley and Sons, 1974.

Franks, C. M. and Wilson, G. T. (eds.): Annual Review of Behavior Therapy: Theory and Practice. New York, Brunner/Mazel, 1974.

Rimm, D. C. and Masters, C.: Behavior Therapy: Techniques and Empirical Findings. New York, Academic Press, 1974.

8

Similarities and Dissimilarities Between Hypnosis and Behavior Therapy

Several authors have reported that hypnosis can play an important part in the practice of behavior therapy (Barrios 1973, Astor 1973, Dengrove 1973, Cautela 1975, Kroger 1975). Astor states:

> Treatment time is telescoped through the use of hypnosis because of the emotional intensity of the experience, the lowered resistance, the increased motivation, the by-passing of defenses, and the therapist's ability to make in-depth use of dream induction imagery, and relaxation techniques.

In addition, one can use the specialized hypnotic technics described in Chapter 4. The therapeutic experience is deepened under hypnosis, and the imagery produced by the patient is more vivid and realistic. In addition to the need to stimulate behavior therapists to inquire about the possibility of making their treatment approach more effective by employing hypnotic induction procedures, there is also a definite need to alert hypnotherapists to the possibility of systematically employing covert conditioning procedures (Cautela 1975). Weitzenhoffer (1972) makes the point that a survey of behavior therapy literature does not justify the limited view of the utility of hypnosis that behavior therapists seem to hold. The use of hypnosis in connection with the application of learning principles has been essentially limited to systematic desensitization. On the other hand, review of the hypnotherapeutic literature indicates that hypnotic technics are being successfully used in conjunction with learning principles in many ways that qualify as recognized behavior-therapeutic technics. However, hypnotherapists who use learning principles often do so on an intuitive basis and usually not too systematically. A greater awareness of the potentialities inherent in both approaches could generate a more effective use of psychotherapy.

Therapists of both persuasions make use of expectancies, demand characteristics, and reinforcement principles. Both reinforce their patient's efforts with praise. Also, both maximize the probability of patient success by not demanding too much too soon. For example, the hypnotherapist may suggest to his patient that a desired feeling such as anesthesia is just beginning to develop and is growing. It may happen this session or at home in practice; no demand is made for immediate production of a given response. The same tactic of shaping, or successive approximations, is used by the behaviorist. He may desensitize a patient to stage fright, for example, by first having him see himself in front of one person in a living room, then a small group of friends in a meeting room, and finally in front of an audience in an auditorium.

Realizing the complexity of human behavior, both therapies personalize their approach. The patient is not forced into a procedural mold; if one method fails, others are available. In both approaches current situations are of major concern. Both therapies also stress ''homework'' between treatment sessions. In hypnotherapy this involves practice in self-hypnosis and giving of autosuggestions. In behavior therapy, homework assignments may consist of overt behavior practice, such as saying ''no'' to certain demands at work or ignoring a spouse's complaining. Similarities also exist in specific technics. These are described below.

AVERSION THERAPY AND HYPNOTHERAPY

Weitzenhoffer (1972) was puzzled by the omission in the behavior literature of the use of hypnosis with aversive technics. Its use dates back to the late nineteenth century or earlier, during which nicotinism, morphinism, and alcoholism were thus treated in Europe. Commonly, hypnotic suggestions ranging from moderate disgust to nausea and vomiting were associated with the patient's contact with the addictive substance (Bernheim 1903, Tuckey 1907, Moll 1909, Forel 1927, Grasset 1904). Use of this type of hypnotic aversion therapy continues to the present (Kroger 1942, 1970; Hershman 1955, 1956; Erickson 1954; Wolberg 1948; Abrams 1964; Femster and Brown 1963; Von Dedenroth 1964a, 1964b).

COUNTERCONDITIONING AND HYPNOTHERAPY

Counterconditioning is a so-called behavior modification technic which is also found in the hypnosis literature but under different labels. Wolberg (1948) gives two of the earliest accounts of hypnosis applied in the context of counterconditioning (he called it *reconditioning*). One patient experienced an intense dislike for orange juice while another experienced profound unease and discomfort in the presence of people. Treatment for both patients consisted of hypnotically inducing fantasies in which the problem stimulus (oranges, people) was experienced in association with hypnotically induced feelings of pleasure, happiness, relaxation, and peace. Erickson (1955) used hypnosis to countercondition two patients with cosmetic problems caused by dental defect by associating positive feelings with these defects. Kroger and Freed (1951) used hypnosis to countercondition the itching associated with pruritus vulvae.

POSITIVE REINFORCEMENT AND HYPNOTHERAPY

Hypnotherapists have also made use of the behaviorist's principles of positive reinforcement in their treatment. Hershman (1955, 1956) and Kroger (1970) used hypnosis to make their patients associate pleasant, positive feelings with the desired behavior (abstinence from smoking, consuming less food, and eating only the right foods). Peterson and London (1964) included in their treatment of a child with dyscopresis, the hypnotic suggestion that the act of defecation be rewarded by a good feeling (self-reinforcement). Von Dedenroth (1964a, 1964b) describes a treatment for tobaccomania where, through hypnotic suggestions, various good feelings are associated with a particular sequence of activities in which smoking is prohibited. Kroger (1967) describes in detail how good feelings are associated with not smoking.

MISCELLANEOUS TECHNICS

Other so-called behavior therapy technics have hypnotherapeutic analogues. "Thought stopping," a behavioristic technic described elsewhere in this book, closely resembles a hypnotic procedure used by Ludwig et al. (1964) for treating drug addicts. In this case, complex posthypnotic suggestions were employed to evoke hallucinations which acted as automatic thought-stoppers. The hallucinations were triggered by thoughts of using drugs. Another instance of thought-stopping in hypnotherapy is described by Spiegel (1970) in the treatment of smokers. Here the patient is instructed under hypnosis to perform a meditative exercise oriented around maintaining good health in self-hypnosis whenever he feels the urge to smoke.

Self-reinforcement as an active agent is an important factor in many hypnotherapeutic procedures. Meyer and Tilker (1969) gave two of their patients with character disorders posthypnotic suggestions to reward their own appropriate actions by strong, immediate self-approval. A modeling technic was used by Ludwig et al. (1964) in an attempt to cure drug addiction. Hypnotized drug addicts were repeatedly instructed to "watch" a fantasized television show in which the hero overcame his desire for drugs.

DIFFERENCES BETWEEN BEHAVIOR THERAPY AND TRADITIONAL HYPNOTHERAPY

While it can be seen from the above discussion that there are many similarities between behavior therapy and hypnotherapy, there are some basic differences. The primary focus of behavior modification is to change and sustain behavior with reinforcement; attitude change will naturally follow. Traditionally, hypnotherapists attempt attitude change first and assume that behavioral change will follow. The behaviorists claim "you are what you do" and if you can change the behavior, you will in time come to feel the role you are playing.

The school of traditional psychotherapy to which most hypnotherapists have belonged argue that one must first develop insight before any change can take place. For example, they felt it wrong to merely help a patient stop smoking without first determining why he was smoking. They feared that the presenting problem, smoking in this case, was merely a symptom of an underlying conflict which must first be resolved. If smoking was stopped without understanding its origin, they believed, another symptom would manifest itself in its place. There is no evidence, however, that such symptom substitution does exist.

The hypnobehavioral model accepts the tenets of both schools of thought. Attitude change leads to behavioral change and behavioral change leads to attitude change. However, we attempt to change both attitude and behavior *in conjunction*. It is not necessary to work on only one, hoping the other will follow; both are dealt with directly and simultaneously. If, for example, an individual is driven to smoke through anxiety caused by a nagging spouse, we counsel the couple in an attempt to produce attitude changes toward each other, but also in the meantime begin hypno-aversion therapy directed toward elimination of the smoking behavior.

A second basic difference is found in the therapeutic relationship. Historically the behavior therapist has been less permissive. While the hypnotherapist is receptive and interested in everything said by the patient in an attempt to maximize free expression, the behaviorist pays little attention to the patient's discussion of historical information. Verbalized feelings of hopelessness or despair ("sick talk") or emissions of maladaptive behaviors are ignored. Moss and Bremer (1973), in reference to behavior therapy, state,

> Primary focus is on the development of assets, so talk of liabilities is minimized. . . . Approval is made deliberately contingent rather than unconditional. . . . [In reference to hypnotherapy these authors state that] the hypnotherapist sets the stage for hypnosis, guides the patient into the production of hypnotic dreams and fantasy material, and stimulates discussion and integration of the meaningfulness of symbols for the patient's current life. He does not structure the hypnotic dream.

While the hypnobehavioral model encourages free expression by the patient, it is directive to the point of encouraging recall of positive feeling states so that the patient can "turn them on" as he needs them. Hypnotic recall of past trauma may provide insight or understanding and serve to desensitize the patient to his fears. However, the patient is also encouraged to recall positive feeling states, and often the hypnotic dream or image is structured. The images described in Chapter 10 are structured to enable the patient to gain control over creation of positive feeling states. In our years of clinical practice we have not found it sufficient to merely suggest to the patient that he recall a past pleasant experience. While this suggestion is helpful, it is in many cases more effective to construct the positive image for the patient (as is done in Chapter 10). While the behaviorist and hypnobehaviorist is relatively directive, he is not authoritarian. Like the traditional hypnotherapist, he constantly searches for clarification and patients' feedback.

According to Sloan et al. (1975a, 1975b), behavior therapy, as opposed to psychotherapy, makes little use of interpretation of the transference, the resistances, dreams, and lengthy exhumation of early childhood memories. On the other hand, directive suggestions, relaxation training, desensitization, and assertive training are used by behavior therapists. However, both are similar in that they take a history, may identify the original cause or causes of the disorder, attempt to reduce anxiety, correct misconceptions, and outline objectives. They also both may extend therapy to the family and other significant figures in the patient's life.

Treatment is always a mutual endeavor in which belief and faith that the method will work are involved. The universality of suggestion in any type of psychotherapy needs no reiteration. Thigpen and Cleckley (1964), in a discussion of psychoanalysis, hypnosis, and faith healing and the role of the latter in the conditioning therapies suggest:

> If we learn that we are working chiefly through the imperfectly understood but powerful effects of faith, let us admit it to be so, use it with more insight, and seek better and more straightforward means of application.

REFERENCES

Abrams, S.: An evaluation of hypnosis in the treatment of alcoholics. Amer. J. Psychiat., *120:*1160, 1964.

Astor, M. H.: Hypnosis and behavior modification combined with psychoanalytic psychotherapy. Int. J. Clin. Exp. Hypn., *21:*18, 1973.

Barrios, A. A.: Posthypnotic suggestion as higher-order conditioning: A methodological and experimental analysis. Int. J. Clin. Exp. Hypn., *21:*32, 1973.

Bernheim, H.: Hypnotisme, Suggestion, Psychotherapie. Paris, Octave Doin, 1903.

Cautela, J. R.: The use of covert conditioning in hypnotherapy. Int. J. Clin. Exp. Hypn., *23:*15, 1975.

Dengrove, E.: The uses of hypnosis in behavior therapy. Int. J. Clin. Exp. Hypn., *21:*13, 1973.

Erickson, M. H.: Indirect hypnotic therapy of an enuretic couple. Int. J. Clin. Exp. Hypn., *2:*171, 1954.

————: Hypnotherapy of two psychosomatic dental problems. J. Am. Soc. Psychosom. Dentistry, *1:*6, 1955.

Femster, J. H., and Brown, J. E.: Hypnotic aversion to alcohol: Three-year follow-up on one patient. Am. J. Clin. Hypn., *6:*164, 1963.

Forel, A.: Hypnotism or Suggestion and Psychotherapy. New York, Allied Publishing Company, 1927.

Grasset, P.: L'Hypnotisme et la Suggestion. Paris, Octave Doin, 1904.

Hershman, S.: Hypnosis in the treatment of obesity. Int. J. Clin. Exp. Hypn., *3:*136, 1955.

————: Hypnosis and excessive smoking. Int. J. Clin. Exp. Hypn., *4:*27, 1956.

Kroger, W. S.: The conditioned reflex treatment of alcoholism. J.A.M.A., *120:*714, 1942.

————: Thanks Doctor, I've Stopped Smoking. Springfield, Ill., Charles C Thomas, 1967.

————: Comprehensive management of obesity. Am. J. Clin. Hypn., *12:*165, 1970.

————: Behavior modification and hypnotic conditioning. *In* Dengrove, E. (ed.): Hypnosis and Behavior Therapy. pp. 379–388. Springfield, Ill., Charles C Thomas, 1975.

Kroger, W. S., and Freed, S. C.: Psychosomatic Gynecology: Including Problems of Obstetrical Care. Philadelphia, W. B. Saunders, 1951.

Ludwig, A. M., Williams, H. L., Jr., and Miller, J. S.: Group hypnotherapy techniques with drug addicts. Int. J. Clin. Exp. Hypn., *12:*53, 1964.

Meyer, R. G. and Tilker, H. A.: The clinical use of direct hypnotic suggestion: A traditional technique in the light of current approaches. Int. J. Clin. Hypn., *17:*81, 1969.

Moll, A.: Hypnotism. London, Walter Scott, 1909.

Moss, C. S., and Bremer, B.: Exposure of a "medical modeler" to behavior modification. Int. J. Clin. Exp. Hypn., *21:*1, 1973.

Peterson, D. R., and London, P.: Neobehavioristic psychotherapy: Quasi-hypnotic suggestion and multiple reinforcement in the treatment of a case of post-infantile dyscopresis. Psychol. Rec., *14:*469, 1964.

Sloan, B., *et al.:* Psychotherapy versus Behavior Therapy. Cambridge, Harvard University Press, 1975a.

Sloan, B., *et al.:* Short-term analytically oriented therapy. Am. J. Psychiat., *132:*373, 1975b.

Spiegel, H.: A single-treatment method to stop smoking using ancillary self-hypnosis. Int. J. Clin. Exp. Hypn., *18:*235, 1970.

Thigpen, C. H., and Cleckley, H. M.: Some Reflections on Psychoanalysis, Hypnosis and Faith Healing in the Conditioning Therapies. Wolpe, Salter and Reyna. New York, Holt, Rinehart & Winston, 1964.

Tuckey, C. L.: Treatment by Hypnotism and Suggestion. London, Baillière, Tindall and Cox, 1907.

Von Dedenroth, T. E.: The use of hypnosis with "tobaccomaniacs." Am. J. Clin. Hypn., *6:*326, 1964a.

————: Further help for the "tobaccomaniacs." Am. J. Clin. Hypn., *6:*332, 1964b.

Weitzenhoffer, A. M.: Behavior therapeutic techniques and hypnotherapeutic methods. Am. J. Clin. Hypn., *15:*71, 1972.

Wolberg, L. R.: The Principles of Hypnotherapy. Vol. 1: Medical Hypnosis. New York, Grune & Stratton, 1948.

SUGGESTED READINGS

Kroger, W. S.: Clinical and Experimental Hypnosis. Philadelphia, J. B. Lippincott, 1963.

————: Behavior modification and hypnotic conditioning. The Osteopathic Physician, *40:*109, 1973.

PART TWO

Integration of Hypnotherapy and Behavior Therapy

9

Preview of the Hypnobehavioral Model

The purpose of this chapter is to present a brief description of the authors' hypnobehavioral therapeutic model to provide a better understanding of the rest of the book. The similarities and dissimilarities of behavioral, psychodynamic, and hypnotic therapies were discussed in the preceding chapter. Also mentioned is the need for their integration into a new model of therapy. To fully benefit from this model, a solid foundation in the basic tenets of learning theory and hypnotic phenomena discussed below are required. Additional chapters describe the integration of these tenets into a holistic form of therapy. Hypnobehavioral therapy at first appears to be a simplistic approach; however, it soon becomes evident that it is a multifaceted approach to problem solving, worthy of much further study and evaluation, particularly a working knowledge of the complexities of learning theory.

ROLE OF LEARNING THEORY

Learning theory postulates that a neurotic symptom is a learned or maladaptive response. The unlearning of it has been called behavior modification. The method has been gaining momentum among psychologists and psychiatrists who formerly espoused the classical psychodynamic approach. Of the various methods of behavioral modification derived from learning theory, those based on the principle of counterconditioning are playing a prominent role. Two methods of behavior modification employing counterconditioning are covert sensitization and covert desensitization. These are discussed more fully in the next chapter. The purpose of covert desensitization is to desensitize a person to any harmful stimulus that is making him anxious, such as snakes, heights, water, public speaking, or his mother-in-law. If unpleasant or negatively equated events are repeatedly associated with pleasant or positive experiences, the harmful stimuli gradually lose their aversive quality.

This beneficial result is achieved by eliciting activities incompatible with anxiety, such as relaxation or the pleasures associated with eating. Contrarily, in covert sensitization, if the sensations afforded by pleasant habit patterns such as eating, alcohol consumption, or cigarette smoking are repeatedly associated with unpleasant experiences such as nausea or shock, the stimuli associated with the noxious habit lose their positive qualities. The procedures to accomplish these aims are termed covert because the stimuli, pleasant or unpleasant, to be reconditioned are to be imagined rather than actually experienced. For example, to treat an alcoholic via covert sensitization, the procedure is to have him associate a foul, nauseating taste or smell with the thought of imbibing alcohol. After repeated pairings with an aversive smell, the pleasant effect of alcohol eventually becomes disgusting and even loathsome.

HYPNOSIS

The behavioral technics of counterconditioning (desensitization and sensitization) are the same procedures that have been used by hypnotherapists for decades. Treating a phobic with hypnotic suggestion is actually using covert desensitization. To illustrate, a snake phobic while in hypnosis is told, "You are not afraid of snakes." The mention of the word *snake* by a posthypnotic suggestion triggers the subject's visualization of the fearful object. However, since the subject is hypnotized and thus deeply relaxed, the fear-provoking image causes no anxiety because he is psychologically immunized against the fear-provoking stimulus. Repetition of the snake image associated with hypnotic relaxation eliminates the snake as a feared object. The hypnotherapist can utilize other posthypnotic suggestions that lead to further scene visualizations such as, "See yourself handling several snakes. . . . There are snakes all around but still you have no fear."

Likewise, treating an alcoholic by hypnosis utilizes the principles of covert sensitization. The hypnotherapist can say to the subject, "You will not want to drink. The very thought of it will make you sick to your stomach." Since sensory recall is so acute under hypnosis, it is relatively easy for the subject to remember the sensation of nausea and pair it with the image of himself taking a drink (Kroger 1942). Tilker and Meyer (1972) used a hypnotic induction procedure in the treatment of an overweight person. Their results were excellent, but they ask, "Why did the hypnotic procedures apparently facilitate use of a nonhypnotic technic?" The answer to this question is simple. Hypnosis is a state of profound relaxation and concentration characterized by increased receptivity and objectivity; these attributes enhance an image more vividly than one induced by nonhypnotic means. Its use, therefore, strengthens the standard covert desensitization models used by the behavior modifiers. Conditioning of reflexes under hypnosis is more durable, rapid, and less likely to extinguish (Platonov 1959).

The reason that hypnosis, in one form or another, has been so effective throughout history as the basis for hundreds of different therapies in numerous geographical locations is that it effectively neutralizes the affective reactions produced by most emotional disturbances. Therefore, hypnotic relaxation is the antithesis of anxiety and tension. Even the effectiveness of a placebo to reduce anxiety is enhanced in the presence of relaxation (Evans 1973). Anxiety, then, is unquestionably, at the root of a preponderance of emotional turmoil. If the muscular tension constituting anxiety can be removed by relaxation, irrespective of what the technic is called, functioning will be improved. Tension manifests itself in many ways: overeating, chain smoking, impotency, premature ejaculation, inability to achieve orgasm, phobias, compulsions, depression, and a myriad of psychosomatic complaints such as ulcers, asthma, hypertension, and, to a large degree, certain types of cardiac disorders. The severity of these ailments is directly proportional to the amount of anxiety present: in a day filled with more aggravation than normal, the cigarette smoker will smoke more, the phobic will be more fearful, and the ulcer patient will experience more pain. The following patient's history is illustrative:

> A 52-year-old woman had extreme fear of losing control under a wide variety of circumstances. She would not climb stairs for fear of throwing herself off the stairway; she would not cross streets for fear of hurling herself into oncoming traffic; she would not even handle sharp kitchen utensils for fear of stabbing herself or her children. This fear became more and more overwhelming until the patient could not leave the house alone. When she and her husband attended a movie, the thought of sitting in the balcony section terrified her. She was led up the stairs and she described clinging to her husband's arm during the beginning of the picture. As the film commenced, however, she grew more and more relaxed and by the end she was sitting calmly and experienced no fear in descending the stairs. She had become so involved in the imagery on the screen that she relaxed and her fears were dissipated.

SENSORY RECALL

As mentioned, fear and relaxation are incompatible responses. It is impossible to be relaxed and anxious at the same time. Just as the imagery projected on the screen can produce relaxation, so the imagery projected in the mind's eye, or the mind's ear, can produce relaxation. It is easy by means of sensory recall under hypnosis to reconstruct an image as clear as reality. Hypnotherapists refer to this mechanism as pseudo-revivification. This type of recall under hypnosis is even more vivid than that produced by a film because it can utilize the senses of smell, taste, and touch as well as those of hearing and sight. Any sensation that has ever been experienced can be recalled just as it was originally felt. The brain stores all memories; nothing is ever forgotten! Therefore, the brain can construct an image even more potent in the production of relaxation than can the movie screen.

Disciples of Eastern healing methods have developed remarkable control over many of their autonomic bodily functions. One cannot remember a particular sensation without actually experiencing or feeling it to a degree. When one imagines placing his hand into a bucket of ice, he actually feels the cold and his teeth chatter. Later, the mere thought of this act under appropriate circumstances produces some degree of coldness. Through repetition of appropriate sensory images, the feelings of numbness and coldness and other sensations can be increased in intensity. Concentration on the desired responses increases with each trial or dry run and, therefore, greater proficiency in controlling autonomic responses ensues.

This capacity to recall and control basic sensations such as warmth, stiffness and various gradations of pressure are very important in the modification of sexual problems such as impotency, premature ejaculation, and orgasmic dysfunction. By recalling the experiential sensations associated with a past pleasurable orgasmic response, it is possible to climax even without physical stimulation of the sex organs. Sensory recall involves going back to when the subject actually experienced a given sensation and reliving it. Hypnosis facilitates this age regression or revivification. Even if the subject never experienced a climax per se, it is possible to recall and combine its component sensations of warmth, pressure, and pulsation and amalgamate them into producing an orgasmic response. We shall present several cases of sexual dysfunction to illustrate how the hypnobehavioral model works in Chapters 11 and 12.

ANXIETY REDUCTION BY IMAGERY CONDITIONING

The primary question, however, pertaining to most severe emotional problems, is, How do we eliminate anxiety? How can one use sensory recall and relaxation to improve his own life? Anxiety is produced by specific or nonspecific stressors, that is, certain conditions that elicit strong emotions. These conditions are varied, ranging from a nagging spouse to fear of the dark. There are three alternatives open to a person when he is faced with an anxiety-arousing situation: (1) he can avoid the situation; (2) he can change the situation; or (3) he can change his reaction to the situation. For example, in the case of the nagging spouse, one can (1) leave him; (2) get him to stop nagging; or (3) recondition oneself so that the nagging no longer upsets the partner. It is expedient to always consider 1 and 2 first, but often these alternatives are not satisfactory.

The best way to change one's feelings about a given situation is to respond with a different sensory reaction to the particular stimulus that previously produced the anxiety. The nagging behavior of the spouse has become a *cue,* signaling anxiety. A chained, conditioned response or pair bonding effect has been established whereby nagging from the spouse always precedes anxiety in the mate. If, however, whenever the spouse nagged, the mate responded with relaxation instead of anxiety, the nagging would in time become a cue for relaxation rather than for anxiety. Now, of course, the question is raised, "How can one relax when one is being nagged?" Again, the answer is simple. By using imagery that will produce relaxation. Any pleasant scene that can be constructed in the mind's eye will produce relaxation. You don't produce relaxation by gritting your teeth and saying, "I will relax," but rather by imagining yourself in a situation that is relaxing. The more vivid the image, the deeper the relaxation, and the sooner the counterconditioning can be accomplished. Pairing a stimulus (nagging) that elicits anxiety with a stimulus (pleasant image) that elicits an incompatible response such as relaxation is a good example of counterconditioning.

How is it possible to construct an image powerful enough for such counterconditioning to occur? The most vivid image utilizes all the sensory modalities and requires deep concentration. The best means to obtain control over sensory recall is the induction procedure used in hypnosis. The subject is told to fixate on an object and give himself suggestions that his eyes are becoming *very, very, very* heavy—this leads to a sensory recall of *heaviness*. When the eyes close, the subject is told to lock them *tightly* and let his eyes roll up into the back of his head with the suggestion that it will be very, very, difficult for him to open his eyes—sensory recall of *tightness* and *pressure*. Heaviness in the legs, arms, trunk, and chest is then suggested along with images appropriate for *relaxing* each portion of the body. What is achieved in hypnosis is a profound state of relaxation and concentration by means of sensory recall.

Once a suitably relaxing scene and the basic technics of relaxation and hypnosis are mastered, the scene can be turned on and off at will. In the beginning, whenever the spouse nags (the anxiety-eliciting stimulus) the mate voluntarily "turns on" a specific scene that leads him to relax. Scenes are tailored to the individual's specific needs. A common one, which we describe in detail on p. 102, employing all five senses, is picturing oneself walking along a deserted beach, *feeling* the warmth of the sand on his feet and the heat of the sun on his face, *smelling* and *tasting* the salty air, *hearing* the breezes rustle through the trees, *seeing* the blue of the sky and water, and whiteness of the sand. It is important to *really* recall these primary sensations.

After many pairings of nagging with relaxation, the nagging will automatically produce the pleasant, relaxing scene. Thus any stimulus can induce relaxation by being paired with relaxation. This classical conditioning paradigm is the basis for learning theory and behavior modification. However, most of the behavior modification literature does not make use of hypnosis per se to potentiate conditioning. This seems strange since, as mentioned, a conditioned reflex is more readily established and less likely to be extinguished when hypnosis is employed. However behavior modifiers often use autogenic training (Schultz and Luthe 1959).

As stated earlier, hypnosis utilizes a profound muscular relaxation. When the hypnotherapist says, "You will not be afraid," the subject cannot be afraid because the associated relaxation neutralizes fears. Thus, pairing the fearful thought with hypnotic relaxation is a counterconditioning procedure that results in loss of the fear reaction.

A primary difference, then, between hypnosis and covert desensitization and sensitization is the method of producing relaxation. Relaxation for covert desensitization is usually initially produced by directly manipulating various muscle groups (Jacobson 1938). This method is often inferior, however, because it does not utilize sensory recall to induce relaxation. Being able to induce relaxation through sensory imagery gives the patient far more control than resorting to direct muscular manipulation as employed by Jacobson's progressive relaxation technics. Also, a much deeper state of relaxation can be achieved through sensory recall than through direct muscle manipulation. Both hypnosis and standard behavior modification make use of sensory imagery conditioning, but the former results in more control even over much autonomic functioning. The autonomic nervous system is not as autonomic as commonly assumed. With practice, a large portion of this system can come under volitional control. The hypnotic process with its associated relaxation, therefore, is advocated for all forms of behavior therapy.

THE HIERARCHY

On the other hand, there is one very important technic used by the behavior modifiers that has been relatively neglected by the hypnotherapists. That is the use of the hierarchy, or Skinner's method of successive approximations. In all forms of desensitization under hypnosis, the therapist should utilize the hierarchy. The common procedure in hypnosis has been to have the subject imagine he is doing whatever he desires while he is deeply relaxed. The water phobic, for example, sees himself swimming, totally relaxed and confident. The thought of swimming is paired with hypnotic relaxation and is thus counterconditioned. It is best, however, not to start with the final goal as the first hypnotic image. Rather it is advisable to first construct a hierarchy of activities according to the degree of anxiety each one elicits. The first item should be relatively anxiety free and the last item the ultimate goal. An example of such a hierarchy for the water phobic could be: (1) putting on the bathing suit indoors; (2) sitting in the pool; (3) wading; (4) immersion to the neck; (5) holding breath under water. The subject is instructed to think of an image of himself putting on a bathing suit with the instructions that if at any point in the image he experiences any anxiety, he will signal by lifting his right index finger, whereupon the therapist will immediately switch this scene off and begin describing a pleasurable, relaxing image. It is imperative that the patient not experience prolonged anxiety at any time during the imagery, as this will only condition more anxiety to the feared object. The particular construction of a hierarchy requires much creativity, intuition, and knowledge on the part of the therapist. The successive approximations or steps may require many subdivisions in order to make a smooth transition from step to step. If, for example, the patient can imagine getting into his bathing suit without feeling anxious but experiences anxiety when picturing himself by the pool, an intermediate step will need to be devised, such as looking at the pool from the kitchen window.

The patient is instructed to practice self-hypnosis three times a day, for 10 minutes each session. During each session, he induces self-hypnosis, then visualizes himself through the various steps of the hierarchy. The moment he feels any anxiety, he switches off the anxiety-eliciting scene and turns to a relaxing one. He does not go back to this step of the hierarchy during that particular session. This procedure leads to the onset of any inordinate degree of anxiety becoming the triggering cue for the production of relaxation. Every time the subject feels anxiety, he switches on a specific relaxing scene, which produces relaxation. The scene must be a familiar one, involving as many sensory inputs as possible. After several pairings, the subjective feelings of anxiety automatically trigger relaxation. The punishing stimulus, anxiety, has now become a discriminative stimulus for reinforcement (relaxation). The usual punishing effect of the punishing stimulus (anxiety) can be negated if it automatically signals the opportunity for reinforcement (relaxation). This was thoroughly demonstrated in a laboratory study using psychotic female patients (Ayllon and Azrin 1966). In this study, when a stimulus (noise) previously shown to be punishing was paired with positive reinforcement, the subjects responded to produce the noise. The noise no longer was punishing inasmuch as it led to an increased probability of future responding. The noise produced no anxiety as it lost its aversive quality. In fact, the noise became a pleasant stimulus, which the subjects worked to produce.

SUMMARY

A more detailed discussion of hierarchy construction, hypnotic suggestions for relaxation, sensory recall, and image making will be described in detail in future chapters on specific problems. The basic premise in the hypnobehavioral model is that maladaptive responses are anxiety-mediated. It is, therefore, important to understand how much anxiety a patient can tolerate and under what circumstances he can best deal with it.

It is axiomatic that any time one works *directly* with a faulty conditioned behavior, one is using a behavioral approach. This is in contrast to "talk therapy," where the primary objective is to develop insight as to *why* a neurosis manifests itself as a symptom. Also therapy is directed more to reconditioning the faulty behavior now rather than fishing in the past. Hypnobehavioral therapy is more present- and future-directed.

REFERENCES

Ayllon, T. and Azrin, N. H.: Punishment as a discriminative stimulus and conditioned reinforcer with humans. J. Exp. Anal. Behav., *9:*411, 1966.

Barber, T. X. and DeMoor, W.: A theory of hypnotic induction. Am. J. Clin. Hypn. *15:*112, 1972.

Evans, F. J.: Placebo response in pain reduction. *In* Bonica, J. J.: Pain. New York, Raven Press, 1973.

Jacobson, E.: Progressive Relaxation. Chicago, Univ. Chicago Press, 1938.

Kroger, W. S.: The conditioned reflex treatment of alcoholism. J.A.M.A., *120:*714, 1942.

Platonov, K.:The Word as a Physiological and Therapeutic Factor. Moscow, Foreign Languages Publishing House, 1959.

Schultz, J. H. & Luthe, W.: Autogenic Training. New York, Grune and Stratton, 1959.

Tilker, H. A. and Meyer, R. G.: The use of covert sensitization and hypnotic procedures in the treatment of an overweight person: a case report. Amer. J. Clin. Hypn., *15:*15, 1972.

10

The Hypnobehavioral Model

RATIONALE FOR THE HYPNOBEHAVIORAL MODEL

The Relaxation Response; Altered States of Consciousness

There is fervent interest throughout the world in nonpharmacological, self-induced, altered states of consciousness as a means of dealing with tension and stress. During any one of these states, individuals describe feelings of increased creativity, of infinity, of immortality—all associated with the vanishing of mental and physical suffering. Data exist (Benson et al. 1974) supporting the hypothesis that an integrated central nervous system reaction, the relaxation response, underlies this altered state of consciousness. The response results in generalized decreased sympathetic nervous system activity, and perhaps also increased parasympathetic activity. Its activation leads to hypo- or adynamic skeletal musculature, decreased blood pressure, decreased respiratory rate, and pupillary constriction. Daily elicitation of this response is of value in situations where excessive sympathetic activity or anxiety is present. Termed the "trophotropic response" as first described by Hess (1957), it was conceptualized as

a protective mechanism against overstress belonging to the trophotropic-endophylactic system and promoting restorative processes . . . these adynamic effects are opposed to ergotropic reactions which are oriented toward increased oxidative metabolism and utilization of energy (1957 p. 40).

Hess's "ergotropic" reactions are analogous to the "emergency reaction" first described by Cannon and popularly referred to as the "fight or flight response."

93

SENSORY IMAGERY CONDITIONING

The authors in their psychotherapeutic approach stress the use of sensory imagery conditioning rather than direct suggestions to obtain such trophotropic or autonomic responses. We shall illustrate where and how *imaginative involvement* can be used to elicit the relaxation response as well as to facilitate alterations in sensory experiences, fantasy evocation, and altered states of consciousness.

 We shall also describe how hypnosis affords a wider spectrum of therapeutic strategies and shortens therapy. It also facilitates deeper relaxation than Jacobson's technics, particularly if practiced as self-hypnosis. Furthermore, use of self-assertive autosuggestions associated with imagery technics obviates dependency on the therapist. This shifts the responsibility for recovery to the patient. Posthypnotic suggestions can also be used to encourage those insufficiently motivated. Such suggestions also raise the patient's threshold for anxiety so he can deal with his life problems with greater equanimity. We advise that the therapist wishing to utilize the hypnobehavioral model seek training in these disciplines to augment his resourcefulness and competence.

Pioneers in the successful amalgamation of the two disciplines are Cautela (1975) and Tugender and Ferinden (1972). The latter investigators have advanced the novel concept of psychic reinforcers administered while patients are hypnotized. They have observed that it is a more effective means of shaping behaviors. They create deprivation states by use of age regression, time distortion, or hypermnesia. They then administer the psychic reinforcers to shape behavior similar to the way in which ordinary operants (approval or disapproval) are used at nonhypnotic levels. We are in accord with their views that a psychic reinforcer is largely formed from imagery. As emphasized throughout the following chapters, the recall of scene visualization is sharper in hypnosis.

We have also observed that the more bizarre the imagery, the stronger the effect and subsequent responses. For instance, suggestions of physical space travel and mental travel such as the mind leaving the body in dissociation are more readily accepted, particularly during deep hypnosis. Hilgard (1974) has shown that subjects who are deeply hypnotized were capable of far greater imaginative involvement than subjects scoring low on hypnotizability scales.

ROLE OF FANTASY EVOCATION IN CONDITIONING

It is difficult to explain how fantasy evocation affects cognitive performances. Nevertheless, these fantasies, which have many definitions, (Klinger 1971) consist of positive and gratifying suggestions that modify and shape behavior. There is a wide latitude for fantasies under hypnosis that allow the patient to expand his horizons to better deal with realities. For example, a person who is immersed in the beauty and relaxation of our beach scene (described below) can use this fantasy to achieve the relaxation response. Who can deny that fantasies are the grist that feeds the mills of realities? Also, do not fantasies of a harmful nature often lead to harmful behavioral responses? If one can make himself sick from what one thinks, so can one make himself well by his thoughts. There are unquestionably large individual differences in people's fantasizing capabilities. These will vary from person to person and even change during the life span of the same individual. However, one incontrovertible fact stands out, namely that these differences are related to the ability of an individual to enter into hypnosis and that they also are correlated with its depth.

Use of these images seems to deepen hypnosis. This in turn heightens feeling states and imaginative capacities. The capacity for seeing a beautiful sunset, smelling the salt of a sea breeze, feeling the coolness of waves washing over the feet, tasting a picnic lunch, and hearing the crashing of water against rocks involves all five senses. If all the sensory inputs are stimulated, there is a greater likelihood that autosuggestions and posthypnotic suggestions will more readily be followed. It is unfortunate that this has not been recognized except by hypnotherapists and by a few clinical psychologists working in the areas of hypnosis and altered states of consciousness.

Abel and Blanchard (1974) describe how sexual fantasy plays a critical role in the treatment of sexual deviations. These investigators as well as other behaviorally oriented therapists have reported successful treatment of a wide variety of disorders by using sexual fantasy to alter responses. Although there are as yet no controlled studies to prove that fantasy evocation is the relevant variable leading to the alteration of sexual behavioral patterns, sexual problems can be alleviated through this process. Hypnosis can alter characterological or ideological beliefs and potentiate subsequent responses. The combination of behavior therapy and hypnosis provides the clinician with a wide variety of sophisticated and more powerful technics for treating problems refractory to conventional psychotherapies.

Gottschalk (1974) notes the paucity of studies on possible relationships involving *self-induced* visual imagery or emotional states and the evoking of autonomic accompaniments by unverbalized introspection. He believes these correlates would shed light not only on relationships between internalized mental processes and visceral responses but also on the limitations of behavior and conditioning theory with respect to mind-body relationships. He notes that the Method school of acting teaches an actor to evoke a realistic emotional state by thinking of an actual experience that he wants to portray. No one has asked an actor to evoke emotional states, or recorded the A.N.S. reactions influenced by such affective arousals, and asked the actor to specify what elicited such responses.

Zikmund (1972) reviewed the literature on physiological correlates of visual imagery. He described a variety of physiological changes that occur during visual imagery. He could find no relationship between A.N.S. reactions and the visual imagery. However, he ignored the subject matter of the visual imagery. Also, since these studies did not incorporate the profound effects of hypnosis on self-induced imagery, such images naturally could not be as vivid or have the impact of the images described in this section. Our standardized images deal not only with affects such as love, hate, and anger, but also with pure feelings embodied in all sensory modalities.

Rochkind and Conn (1973) advocate guided fantasy encounter as an effective and usually short-term therapy for a wide variety of difficult crisis situations. Their approach consists of a combination of gestalt, implosive therapy, encounter, Zen meditation, and hypnosynthesis, the latter described in Chapter 4. Their methods are closely related to the depth psychologic approach of Progoff (1963), which stresses opening up new avenues of meaning. A ''Zen slap'' maneuver is used during which personal, highly charged material is thrust into the patient's awareness. The hypnotic relaxation and supportive relationship makes this maneuver possible. Material that is potentially overwhelming and, therefore, normally avoided is thus dealt with. These authors state, ''when these significant meanings are faced, they illuminate, motivate, and give purpose to a new way of life.''

Their monograph, based on over 100 cases, includes many illuminating case reports. Most patients were seen only one to six times. Brief psychotherapy often consisted of a single interview in crisis intervention, especially if the goals were clearly defined. Their approach closely resembles Leuner's (1969) symbol-drama, McKellar's succession of lantern slides, Kretschmer's (1959) picture strip thinking and Kosbab's (1974) guided affective imagery conditioning (G.A.I.). The difference between their approach and ours is that the strong mutual involvement induced by hypnotic rapport is not as pronounced. The spiritual bond between patient and therapist brought about by hypnosis is so real that it feels as if the experiences could almost be touched. Development of this bond is a demanding process for the therapist.

Singer (1974) in an elegant review has shown that imagery and daydreaming capacities can be examined within the context of psychodynamic psychotherapy and behavior modification. He surveys uses of imagery and fantasy processes in these fields and also brings together the work of McKellar (1957), Richardson (1969), Horowitz (1970), Klinger (1970), Segal (1971), Sheehan (1972), Shorr (1972), Paivio (1971), Kosbab (1972, 1974), Singer (1966, 1971 a,b), and various European researchers beginning with Jung's ''active imagination'' approach (1968), Bachélard (1971), Schultz (Schultz and Luthe 1959), who is the originator of autonomic biofeedback, Happich (1932), Desoille (1966), Frétigny and Virel (1968), Leuner (1969), Rigo (1962), and Assagioli (1965).

The interested reader is urged to read Singer's broad review of the psychotherapeutic uses of fantasy and imagery. His discussion ranges from Esalen-type imagery games, the Humanistic approach, Gestalt (Perls, et al. 1951), T-group imagery games, Transcendental and Zen Meditation therapies, Moreno's (1967) Psychodrama, Berne's (1964) Transactional Analysis, Ellis' (1973) Rational-emotive therapy to hypnosis, Kubie's (1943) classical psychoanalysis, Reyher's (1963) ''emergent uncovering'' (in which the patient produces images in sequence similar to free association and describes them to gain insight), and the usage of imagery in the behavior therapies such as systematic desensitization (Wolpe 1969), covert conditioning (Cautela 1967), and symbolic modeling (Bandura 1971).

ROLE OF DIFFERENT TYPES OF IMAGERY IN COVERT CONDITIONING

Our standardized images also differ from guided fantasy and imagery in that we use images for gaining mastery of simple feedback systems and then for control of the more complex systems. Unlike guided fantasy encounter, it is not always necessary to give the patient affect-laden material from his past. We are more concerned with sensory material rather than with specific past traumatic events. Since everyone has experienced feelings of touch, taste, smell, sound, and sight, it is possible to give the same images to several patients. The images can thus be standardized. After all, depression or anxiety is as much a feeling or sensation as is elation or the smell of a summer breeze.

Other technics that utilize images to a degree are Schultz's (1950) autogenic training, Jacobson's (1938) progressive relaxation and Kretchmer's (1959) fractional-active hypnosis. They all greatly facilitate the appearance of hypnagogic images and can be produced by appropriate scene visualization. O'Hare et al. (1975) have described the effects of guided fantasy in facilitating hypnotherapy. We would also like to remind the reader that all forms of covert conditioning involve imagery.

It is interesting that the wheel has made a complete turn. As mentioned, all healing originally was performed by magic, religious rites, and ritual. Even the ancient priests resorted to such hypnosis-like procedures as exorcism. For thousands of years the "soul" and the "mind" were treated by a wide variety of suggestive procedures consisting of theological concepts, imagery of a hell and heaven, and a pot pourri of incantations. Concomitantly with the advent of modern psychiatry are witnessed Coueism, spiritualistic and metaphysical healing methods, and finally in the last 40 years, hypnotherapy. At present, intense interest is centered on such Eastern metaphysical concepts as Yoga, Zen, and Shintoism. These fit into a hypnotic conditioning paradigm (Kroger 1966a, 1966b).

REASONS FOR SUCCESS OF THE HYPNOBEHAVIORAL MODEL

During the last decade, hypnosis and behavior therapy have come into their own, and many psychiatrists are abandoning traditional psychodynamic therapies. Yet even the most sophisticated of these investigators are now delving into Transcendental Meditation and other mystical approaches for expanding consciousness and mind control (Benson et al., 1974). Thus, we are back again to ritualistic healing not too unlike the oracle at Delphi. The reader may have reservations about the verbalizations used in our images, yet the use of prayer, communion, and the concept one holds of God, heaven, and hell are, in reality, highly reinforcing images that are conducive to a feeling of well-being.

We have been amazed that it has taken so long for modern-day psycho-therapists to utilize imagery of one type or another for potentiating their approach. In even difficult problems, we have found that an approach based upon common sense, ability to construct vivid images, and particularly the presentation of these at the appropriate time all provide therapeutic gains. If relaxation and the various hypnotic technics are added to the above model, these highly therapeutic tools per se increase possibilities for recovery. The neutralizing effects of the images when added to the hypnosis provide the positive reinforcements for change. For these reasons we are advancing our hypnobehavioral model.

The success of the hypnobehavioral model can be attributed to the following. First, the therapist, because of his authoritative position, can utilize prestige suggestions. Second, the therapist forces the patient to look at himself with a detached objectivity ordinarily difficult to attain with nonhypnotic psycho-therapy. Third, the patient, because of his expectant attitude or appropriate mental set, processes belief, faith, and confidence into conviction that a behavioral change will occur. The foregoing all fall into the realm of conviction phenomena!

IMAGERY OR COVERT CONDITIONING

Imagery has been used by hypnotherapists to aid hypnotic induction and to treat maladaptive behaviors. The use of imagery to change behavior has been termed "covert conditioning" by the behavior modifiers. Cautela (1975) defines covert conditioning as

> Conditioning procedures in which the stimuli and responses are presented in imagination *via* instructions. . . . The main assumption underlying the covert conditioning procedures is that stimuli presented in imagination *via* instructions affect covert and overt behavior in a manner similar to stimuli presented externally, i.e., if an individual is asked to imagine a noxious stimulus just after he has imagined a response, the probability of the response will decrease. Also, if a pleasant or reinforcing stimulus is presented to a S just after he has imagined a particular response, then we can expect the probability of that response to increase in a manner similar to external reinforcement.

Covert conditioning is easier to apply since no external apparatus is needed. Therefore, it enables the patient to bring his own behavior under his own control any time it is needed; the therapist's presence or the clinical setting is not necessary once the patient learns the proper procedure. There are four primary covert conditioning technics, which will be described below.

Covert Sensitization (Punishment)   *punish maladaptive response*

This technic was first described in detail by Cautela (1966, 1967). The patient is to imagine a scene in which he is committing the act he wishes to eliminate. The imaginal performance of this act is paired with imagined negative consequences, which serves to punish the undesired behavior. For example, a person who wishes to stop smoking is instructed to imagine himself in a typical situation, such as talking on the telephone, when he normally smokes. The scene is to be experienced with all five senses and to be as real as possible. He is not just to *see* himself there, but actually *be* there. Next he imagines a nauseous feeling coming over him from the smoke, an urge to gag, and finally, to vomit. The scene may be intensified by having the patient imagine himself dipping the cigarette in the vomit and sucking it through the tobacco, thus continuing the pairing of taste and smell of tobacco with the noxiousness of the vomit. The vomiting also causes considerable embarassment by the horrified reaction of the person listening on the other end of the telephone line. As soon as the patient imagines himself out of the sight, taste, and smell of the cigarette he is to feel better.

The scene is constructed beforehand by asking under what particular circumstances the patient emits the maladaptive behavior. A good behavior analysis will lead to a scene typical to the patient's response repertoire. After imagining the scene, the patient is questioned as to the clarity of his imagery—the stronger the imagery the more potent the conditioning. He is then instructed to practice covert sensitization several times a day.

Evidence from the behavioral literature indicates covert sensitization to be effective in reducing maladaptive approach behaviors such as smoking (Wagner and Bragg 1970), alcoholism (Ashem and Donner 1968) and sexual deviations (Barlow, Leitenberg and Agras 1969; Cautela and Wisocki 1971; Davison 1968). Hypnotherapists have also commonly used covert-sensitization-like procedures in treating maladaptive approach behaviors including alcoholism (Kroger, 1942; Feamster and Brown 1963, Wolberg 1948), face picking (Hollander 1958) and nail biting (Secter 1961).

Covert Positive Reinforcement   *reward adaptive response*

Learning theory explains response increase or decrease by the consequence following that response; a response will increase if it is rewarded and decrease if it is punished. Therapy involves punishing inappropriate responses and reinforcing appropriate ones.

The patient is asked to imagine himself performing a response completely opposed to his usual maladaptive one and then rewarding himself for this appropriate response by imagining a pleasant scene. For example, the smoker could imagine himself at home watching television and craving a cigarette next to him. Rather than thinking or saying "I sure would like a smoke," he is to imagine saying such words to the contrary as, "Boy, that cigarette smells bad, I can't imagine why people smoke." He then immediately rewards himself for the act of resisting the cigarette by changing the scene to a very pleasant and beautiful surrounding such as described in the images in this chapter. While he could ordinarily still feel tempted or anxious at being deprived of the cigarette, the reinforcing image introduces a relaxed and pleasant feeling after making an adaptive response. Once again, the imagery should be clear and should be experienced in all five senses. The more real the pleasant image is to the patient, the more reinforcing it will be. The patient may now use covert reinforcement (COR) whenever he is tempted to engage in a maladaptive behavior. COR, like other covert conditioning procedures, is self-controlled.

Experimental validation for COR was found in reducing phobic responses (Flannery 1972), reducing test anxiety (Wisocki 1971), changing attitudes toward the mentally retarded (Cautela, Walsh, and Wish 1971) and modifying self-concepts in children (Krop, Calhoon, and Verrier 1971). Successful use was also substantiated in changing perception of circle-sizes in college students (Cautela, Steffen and Wish, in press) and in schizophrenic subjects (Steffen 1971). The hypnotherapeutic literature provides examples of COR used to elicit eating of disliked foods (Shibata 1967), to improve reading in children (Krippner 1966), and to alleviate phobias (Wolberg 1948).

Covert Negative Reinforcement   *remove punishment for adaptive response* –

This technic developed by Cautela (1970) rewards the patient for an appropriate response by allowing him to escape or terminate a very unpleasant situation. The technic is especially useful for patients who claim there is nothing reinforcing in their lives and are thus not amenable to covert reinforcement. For example, patients with a fear of flying may be instructed to imagine they are caught in a burning building. They are trapped by walls of shooting flames. Just as the building is ready to collapse a helicopter appears at the window and takes them away into the clear blue sky. Flying thus becomes an activity associated with terminating a very unpleasant situation where before it was itself a frightening event.

It is important that the scene change be complete so that properties of the aversive scene are not associated with the imagined desirable behavior. Covert negative reinforcement (CNR) does not punish a maladaptive response (as does covert sensitization), it reinforces an adaptive one. Experimental data to indicate that CNR can increase response probability has been presented by Ascher and Cautela (1972). The hypnotherapeutic use of CNR was demonstrated by Abraham (1968) in the treatment of a hysterical paralysis of the legs. The hypnotized patient was told to imagine sitting on a beach in uncomfortably cold water and that he could only escape the cold water (negative situation) by lifting his legs out of it.

Covert Extinction   *ignoring maladaptive response*

This technic was developed by Cautela (1971). Many patients' undesirable behavior is being maintained by high reinforcement from individuals or situations which are not under the therapist's control. Somatic complaints of headache, fatigue, backache, asthmatic wheezing, and even paralysis in cases of conversion hysteria are often maintained by secondary gain in the form of attention by loved ones. To eliminate the expectancy of this gain of attention, the patient is asked to imagine performing the undesirable behavior. At the same time the therapist makes it clear that there is absolutely no reaction to his behavior from other people. For example, a young woman may begin wheezing whenever her husband wishes to leave the house without her. If no amount of pleading by the therapist convinces the husband to ignore these symptoms (he may consider it a lack of consideration not to comfort and attend to his wife's ailments), the patient may be instructed to imagine the following scene.

You are playing with the dog when suddenly your husband announces he is going jogging on the beach with a friend. Immediately you feel a shortness of breath and begin wheezing. You implore him to remain a little longer. He smiles and says, "You'll be all right without me . . . Goodbye."

We have used the technic of covert extinction in combination with hypnosis successfully for several problems. In one case a woman had an extreme fear she would expose herself, although this had never happened. In hypnosis, she was instructed to imagine running down the street holding her skirt over her head exposing herself to all, from the waist down. All onlookers were to show no reaction, completely ignoring this exhibition. In another case, a young man would have anxiety attacks in social situations accompanied by profuse sweating. While hypnotized he was told to imagine himself in a restaurant with a group of people. Sweat was pouring down his face; but the attack was completely ignored by everyone. In both cases, the patients' maladaptive behavior extinguished when it was no longer attended to imaginally.

Cautela (1975) makes the point, "In all of the covert conditioning procedures, as many possible different reinforcing and aversive stimuli are used to avoid satiation or adaptation." There is a need for many pleasant or aversive images. These will be described in the following sections.

STANDARD STRUCTURED IMAGES

The following section is devoted to a description of some of the relaxing images used in hypnobehavioral therapy. These images are flexible and may be deleted or tailored to the individual needs of a patient. They do, however, provide a useful reference and core for the discussion of the hypnobehavioral model. The relaxing image is usually given after the initial standard induction and before any posthypnotic or autohypnotic suggestions are utilized. They are also given before any situations relating specifically to the presenting problems.

A primary purpose of the following standardized images is to produce relaxation and deepen the hypnosis so that conditioning will be stronger and more rapid. Since nearly all presenting problems are anxiety-mediated, anxiety reduction plays an important part in therapy for any condition. Anxiety manifests itself in different ways in different people: one individual may react to tension by smoking too much while another may develop an ulcer. In any event, the bulk of the problem behaviors to be discussed in this volume are the product of a person's faulty coping with anxiety in his life.

The images are presented in order of increasing complexity. Each image serves to further deepen the hypnosis and associated relaxation. The reader should not be misled to believe that it is necessary to use all the images described herein to treat a patient. It is explained to the patient that the process of hypnotherapy is an infinite system. The hypnotic depth will be developed until sufficient anxiety reduction is achieved to alleviate the presenting problem. We have had patients who were successfully treated after only one image. On the other hand, we have had a few patients on whom we used as many as 80 different images in the course of their treatment. However with 95 per cent of our patients we have used less than 25 images. Also, a few would not accept this method. In those who refused, the reason was that the therapy was contrary to the patient's expectations. If, after explanation of the rationale for the use of imagery, the patient was still unwilling to accept it as a treatment modality, we did not use imagery in the therapy. In these cases we relied solely on a standard hypnotic induction, posthypnotic suggestions related directly to the problem, and behavioral technics (to be described).

While the images are usually given in sequence (one each session or possibly two, depending on how good a hypnotic subject the patient is), some of the standardized images are especially suited for specific problems and are delineated in the appropriate clinical chapters. These may be given after Image I, before going on in the sequence. The patient should have some experience practicing pleasant hypnotic imagery of a more general nature to develop a facility for sensory recall before working on images (whether among the 25 listed in this chapter or constructed by the individual therapist) tailored for his specific problem. All imagery to be used in covert behavioral procedures will be stronger and more effective if the subject first practices Image I, or one of that nature. This develops his ability to vividly experience an image in all five sense modalities. The stronger the patient's hypnotic imagery, the greater will be the generalization to reality.

These images are to be used in conjunction with the behavioral and hypnotic technics described in this book. We are not presenting imagery as a panacea but merely as an adjunctive method for decreasing anxiety, and developing self-control and hypnotic concentration.

suggest ideomotor indicator of stress [handwritten]

Image I

The first image is usually given in the second session after the subject has had one week to practice self-hypnosis. Its focus is on the recall of five basic senses emphasizing tactile feelings of warmth and cold, visual colors, the basic taste and smell of salt, and rhythmic sound. The therapist paints the picture as follows: *need the experience of barefooted* [handwritten]

Beach Scene. You are walking along the beach; it is mid-July. It is very, very warm. It is five o'clock in the afternoon. The sun has not yet begun to set but it is getting low on the horizon. The sun is a golden blazing yellow, the sky a brilliant blue, the sand a dazzling glistening white in the sunlight. Feel the cold, wet, firm, hard-packed sand beneath your feet. . . . Taste and smell the salt in the air. There is a residue of salt deposited on your lips from the ocean spray. You can taste it if you lick your lips. Hear the beating of the waves, the rhythmic lapping to and fro, back and forth of the water against the shore. Hear the far-off cry of a distant gull as you continue to walk. . . .

Suddenly you come to a sand dune, a mound of pure white sand. . . . Covering the mound are bright yellow buttercups, deep pink moss roses. You sit down on its crest and look out to sea. The sea is like a mirror of silver reflecting the sun's rays, a mass of pure white light, and you are gazing intently into this light. As you continue to stare into the sun's reflection off the water, you begin to see flecks of violet, darting spots of purple intermingled with the silver. Everywhere there is silver and violet. There is a violet line along the horizon . . . a violet halo around the flowers. Now the sun is beginning to set. With each movement, with each motion of the sun into the sea you become deeper and deeper relaxed. (It is important to pair physical sensations such as breathing with elements in the image so that the imaginal elements will cue relaxation.) The sky is turning crimson, scarlet, pink, amber, gold, orange as the sun sets . . . you are engulfed in a deep purple twilight, a velvety blue haze . . . you look up to the night sky. It is a brilliant starry night. The beating of the waves, the smell and taste of the salt, the sea, the sky, . . . and you feel yourself carried upward and outward into space, one with the universe . . . I am now going to count to 3. At the count of 3, you will open your eyes, you will feel completely refreshed, totally relaxed. 1, 2, 3. (The subject is always brought out of hypnosis by reciting the above three lines.)

The last two lines in this image should produce a feeling of detachment and often dissociation.

Image II

Once again emphasis is on tactile feelings of warmth and cold. Patients usually experience the most difficulty with recall of taste and smell. Visual and auditory recall are easiest, and tactile recall intermediary.

Mountain Cabin Scene. You are in a cabin in the mountains. It is midnight. It is the dead of winter. Outside the wind is howling. Inside you are sitting in front of a fireplace, gazing fixedly into the embers, staring intently into the coals. Feel the warmth of the flames against your body, feel the heat from the fire against your skin. There is a prickling almost itching sensation in your thighs) the heat on the front of your body is so intense. Hear the crackling of the logs as the sap hits the fire. Smell the smoke from the burning pine logs. See the flickering shadows on the wall. The only source of light comes from the fire. The rest of the cabin is in darkness.

Now you get up. You walk over to the window. There is a lace-like pattern of frost on the window pane. You put your warm fingertips to the cold, hard glass of the windowpane. Feel the heat from your fingers melt the frost. You look outside. The moon is full and silver, the snow a dazzling, sparkling white in the moonlight. There are tall, dark green fir trees casting deep purple shadows across the snowy whiteness. You are going to open the window. Feel it give way against the pressure of your hand. It opens. You take a big deep breath of cool, clean, crisp, fresh, pure mountain air. (The subject should actually take a deep breath at this point and the therapist takes a big breath while recounting it.) Your entire rib cage collapses in total, utter relaxation. It feels so good to breathe. Smell the pine!

Now you close the window. You walk to the fire. Feel its warmth. You lie down beside the fire on a bearskin rug. A drowsy feeling is coming over you. The howling of the wind, the warmth from the fire, the smell of the smoke, the crackling of the logs . . . all those sights and sounds and smells getting very, very far away . . . as you drift . . . and float and dream in that cabin that winter night (The word *very* is often said in rhythm with the subject's inhalations and exhalations).

Image III

The main emphasis in this scene is recall of taste and smell. Patients are told that if they are having any difficulty recalling taste and smell they may use lemons, oranges, and roses as props. When in the scene they bite into the orange or lemon or smell the rose, they should do likewise in reality. Pairing the actual taste and smell of lemons and oranges or the smell of the rose with the imagery potentiates the entire scene.

Garden Scene. You are in the middle of a vast garden. It is midnight. It is mid-summer. The air is warm and balmy. The garden stretches for miles and miles. You are walking down a path on either side of which are orange trees. The moon is full and yellow. The orange trees are deep green with brilliant orange oranges, phosphorescent in the moonlight. There are oranges on the ground. They are very ripe. The smell of orange is heavy in the air. You reach up. You pick an orange from the branch. Bite into the orange . . . the sweet orange juice squirts into your mouth, running down your throat and into your stomach. Taste the orange. Now you continue walking till you come to a place where two paths cross . . . you turn right, walking down a path on either side of which are lemon trees, bright yellow in the moonlight. You pick a lemon. Feel the rough outer texture of the lemon peel. You peel the lemon. Smell the lemony fragrance of the lemon rind. You sink your teeth into the lemon. The sour lemon juice squirts into your mouth. Taste the lemon. The saliva flows. Your mouth puckers as you swallow the sour lemon juice. You continue walking, the taste and smell of lemon lingering with you.

Suddenly before you is a long, descending, white marble staircase. Dazzling white in the moonlight. You begin to descend the stairs. With every step downward you become deeper and deeper relaxed. When you reach the base of the stairs you will be in a profound state of relaxation . . . you are now standing at the base of the stairs. In front of you is a huge marble swimming pool. All around the *fountain* pool are red and white and yellow roses, velvety soft in the moonlight, covered with dew. The smell of roses is heavy in the air. You take off your clothes. You glide into the pool. The pool is filled with billions of rose petals. You float on your back in the rose water looking up at the stars, buoyant in the water. Now you get out of the water. You stand up. The cool night air touches your wet body. It sends chills down your spine. You are shivering. Goose flesh appears. Suddenly you smell smoke. You look to the direction from which the smell is coming. There is a wooded area on the other side of the pool. You walk over toward the forest, the smell of smoke growing ever stronger in intensity as you approach the wooded area. You walk into the forest. There before you is a blazing bonfire of burning leaves. It smells like fall, it smells like autumn. You lie down beside the fire in a bed of dry leaves. The smell of wet earth beneath you, the smell of burning leaves beside you, the starry sky above you; you drift, you float, you dream . . . that mid-summer's night.

[handwritten: It is coming from a cigarette between your fingers. Your eyes tear from the prickling irritation of the smoke. The garden fades from view. The fragrance of ... are obscured.]

Image IV

In this image, the patient is taken back to the cabin scene with some deletions and embellishments in order to develop glove anesthesia, a sensory hallucination resulting in numbness of the hand from the fingers to the wrist. From the beginning of hypnotherapy the subject has been learning autonomic control of vasoconstriction. A concentration of blood in a given area produces congestion and warmth, and its absence produces numbness and chill. Suggestions for the production of numbness were given in the first hypnotic session, and by now the subject should be fairly adept at creating a feeling of numbness at least in the extremities. Therefore it is good that the subject has already had some experience with this image as the procedure for glove anesthesia requires his undivided attention.

[handwritten margin: You feel your hand bring the foul thing to your lips where ...]

The ability to produce glove anesthesia has far-ranging therapeutic benefits and the patient should be given encouragement during the training states. It

[handwritten: the nauseating stale tobacco takes over from the exciting lemon and wondrous sweet orange. Your lungs inhale hot smoke burning your mouth, your throat. You choke, you cough. You run from the cigarette]

should be emphasized that he is not expected to master it in one week even though he will be given a new image next time. The production of glove anesthesia in Image IV is to be worked on periodically throughout treatment. The other images are used only for the week they are given. An image can fade out, losing its vividness after repeated usage. Patients need a continual supply of new fantasy material. Glove anesthesia has been mentioned in the chapter on hypnotic technics. It has no analogue in behavior modification technics but lends itself admirably to behavior therapy. It is literally possible to transcend the pain threshold by using glove anesthesia. Any technic that permits this is certainly worthy of study.

Our world comprises two sets of stimuli, exteroceptive—those impinging on us from without in the external world—and interoceptive—those coming to us from inside our bodies. Glove anesthesia produces control over both exteroceptive and interoceptive tactile stimulation. We can receive inputs or we can choose not to receive them. Pain is a danger signal and should be responded to by seeing a physician. Once the reason for the discomfort is known and dealt with, however, the subject can decide whether or not he wants to continue to receive the signal. It is theoretically possible to control all sensory inputs, not only tactile ones.

Much research in perceptual defense shows that an individual will see what he wants to see. For example, when a list of words containing a taboo or "dirty" word is tachistoscopically presented for a fraction of a second many subjects do not recall this particular word. They just did not see it. Audio defense is also evident; many of us hear only what we want to. It is well known that when attention is directed to one thing, we become oblivious to sounds around us. For example, someone can speak to us while we are reading and we will not even hear them. We have shut out extraneous stimuli; since we are not attending to them, we are not receiving them. Such selective deafness is an everyday phenomenological response seen at both nonhypnotic and hypnotic levels of awareness.

Although we know of no research of olfactory defense or taste defense, such phenomena exist. We are reminded of a female patient who came with the presenting problem that her husband demanded she frequently perform fellatio on him. The taste made her ill. She was afraid that if she did not become more receptive and proficient in the act, he would leave her. Through sensory recall and appropriate pairing and conditioning, she was able to imagine the taste of a sloe gin fizz during fellatio. Hypnotic conditioning trials consisted of recalling the smell and taste of a sloe gin fizz in conjunction with the image of sexual intercourse with her husband. Not only was she able to shut out smells and tastes associated with fellatio, she was also able to revive any pleasant smell or taste she desired when engaging in this act. She had gone one step further from shutting out stimuli to actually creating her own gestalt. She combined her current inputs on the visual, auditory, and tactile modalities (exteroceptive stimuli) with a recall of the desired olfactory and gustatory modalities (interoceptive stimuli). Once a sensation has been experienced, it is on tap forever. Human organisms can take these experiences and recall them in any combination and at any rate (time distortion) they wish; they can shut out or control the rate and degree of reception of all external stimuli. They can in fact make their own world.

Mountain Cabin Scene with Glove Anesthesia. You are in a cabin in the mountains. It is midnight. Outside the wind is howling. Inside you are sitting in front of a fireplace, staring into the embers, gazing fixedly into the coals. Feel the heat from the fire. Feel the warmth from the flames against your skin. There is a prickling, almost itching sensation in your thighs; the heat on the front of your body is so intense. See the flickering shadows on the wall. Hear the crackling of the pine logs as the sap hits the fire. Smell the smoke from the burning pine logs. The only source of light comes from the fire; the rest of the cabin is in darkness.

Now you get up. You are going to go outside. You bundle up. You put on a coat, gloves, cap, boots. You go to the door. Feel the door gives way against the pressure of your hand. You are outside in the cold winter air! Take a big deep breath of cool, fresh, pure, mountain air. Smell the pine. It feels so good to breathe! Your entire rib cage collapses in total, utter relaxation. The door closes behind you. The moon is full and silvery. It is 20 degrees below zero, bitter cold. You can see your breath in white puffs. You begin walking down a path on either side of which are tall deep green pine trees laden with snow. The snow is knee deep. Everything has a bluish tinge to it; even the snow looks blue. Ten minutes pass, twenty minutes, thirty minutes. You stop, take the glove off your right hand and thrust your warm hand into the snow making a fist compressing the snow into an ice ball in the palm of your hand. . . . You feel a numb, wooden, leathery-like sensation beginning in your right palm, spreading throughout your hand. When you feel this sensation I want you to place your right hand upon your right cheek. [The subject does as directed.] Good, now let all that numbness drain from your hand into your cheek. Your cheek is becoming numb, leathery, wooden, just as if Novocaine had been injected into it. Your hand is becoming warm, alive; the blood is rushing back into it. When all the numbness has drained from your hand into your cheek, place your hand once again at your side. [The subject does as directed.] Now once again place your hand on your cheek and let all the numbness in your cheek drain back into your hand. Your hand is becoming numb, leathery, woodenlike, just like a block of wood with nails in it. Your cheek is becoming hot, flushed, the blood is rushing to the surface of the skin in your cheek. When all that numbness has drained from your cheek back into your hand once again place your hand at your side. [The subject does so.]

Good! Now place the glove back on your right hand. You turn around and begin tracing your footsteps back to the cabin. Ten minutes pass, twenty minutes, thirty minutes. You are back to the cabin. You go inside. You take off your outer wraps and walk over to the fire. Hold your hands over the fire. Feel the warmth spreading throughout your body. (This suggestion elimi- nates the numbness and returns the hand to its normal condition.) You lie down beside the fire on a bearskin rug. The warmth of the fire, the smell of the pine smoke, the crackling of the logs, the howling outside of the wind, all these sights, and smells and sounds seem very, very far away as you drift further and further away.

Image V

This scene is the subject's first exposure to recall of external pressure. It should be noted that there are many sensations in each scene that enhance the potential for sensory recall. The authors remark only on things of special inter- est in each scene.

Desert Scene. Everything is very, very dark. It is pitch black. It is warm. You are barefoot. Beneath your feet you can feel coarse, cracked clay. The ground is perfectly flat. Now it is beginning to get light. Every breath you take, the sky gets bluer and bluer. Every breath you take, it gets warmer and warmer. You now see that there is nothing but sunbaked clay as far as the eye can see. Everything is perfectly flat. There are no mountains, no hills, no vegetation . . . nothing but clay to the horizon line, to the vanishing point. It is like a surrealistic landscape. It is getting warmer and warmer, hotter and hotter, 80 degrees, 90 degrees, 100 degrees, 110 degrees. Beads of perspi- ration are running down your back, down your armpits. Your hair is matted to your forehead. Clothes are clinging and sticking to your body. Eyes are stinging from the salt in your perspiration. You are wringing wet with sweat. Throat is getting parched . . . lips are dry . . . tongue is thickening. You are having difficulty swallowing.

Suddenly before you is a large, freshwater sea . . . a vast expanse of cool, fresh, pure water. You take off your clothes. You glide into the water. It is crystal clear. You drink, quenching your thirst. You float on your back in the water gazing up at the blue desert sky. Night falls. You get out of the water. The cool night air touches your wet body. It sends chills down your spine. You are shivering. Goose flesh appears. You wade to shore. Your feet touch the sand, which is still warm from the day, still retaining the heat from the sun. You lie down. A gentle breeze begins to cover you with a warm blanket of sand, inch by inch, layer by layer . . . feel the ever increasing pressure as the shifting sand covers you layer by layer. You are protected in a warm cocoon, safe, secure, at peace with the world, tranquil under the desert stars.

Image VI

Here is an example of how we produce time distortion. The specific posthyp- notic suggestion for time expansion is always given before the image. This scene also often produces a feeling of detachment and altered perspective. Kinesthetic sense is also greatly altered. The rationale for this particular image is that in 5 minutes of actual time (the approximate time it takes to describe this scene) an eternity of imaginal time elapses. If the scene is at all real to the subject, it will seem as if more than 5 minutes had lapsed. It is not uncommon to report a threefold expansion of time on the first session although the suggestion is usually that time will expand tenfold.

Space Scene. One minute of actual time will seem like 10 minutes to you. Time will go by very, very slowly. It will seem like an eternity. In less than 10 minutes you can watch an entire motion picture again and actually see it better than when you first saw it.

You are lying on your back on a large round bed in a gigantic circular, black marble room. It is midnight. You are looking up at the ceiling, which is a glass dome, a clear, transparent bubble. The night is clear. The sky is filled with stars. You are gazing at the heavens.

Suddenly you notice that the room is beginning to turn. Ever so slightly at first, gradually picking up momentum. It is revolving like a turntable on a record player. Going round, and round and round, and round, and round [The therapist continues saying this faster and faster] and the room is spinning. You are hurled upward and outward off the bed. The dome opens and you shoot out into space, traveling at an incredible rate of speed, going faster than the speed of light, a dizzy sensation in the pit of your stomach. Flashes of light streak into view as you pass other planets, other solar systems, other galaxies, hurling wildly through space.

Now you are beginning to fall. You are falling back to the point from which you came. Falling through space. You are now back to your source, but there is no bed, there is no room, there is no Earth. The Earth has long ceased to exist. You have been gone billions of Earth years. You are suspended in space, in a vacuum. No sound, no touch, no smell . . . suspended animation.

Image VII

In the second scene for time expansion, the amount of imaginal time passing is a morning. This is certainly less than an eternity and will probably be easier for the subject to identify with. Once again, if the scene is real for the subject, it will seem as if more than the actual 5 minutes taken to describe the scene had lapsed.

Farm Scene. You are in a very warm, snug, comfortable bed. It is very early morning. The covers feel so good. You are in a farmhouse in Kansas. It is late August. You hear a rooster crow. It is 5:30 in the morning. You drift off back to sleep. Suddenly you are awakened by the shrill sound of an alarm clock. It is 6:00 in the morning. You get out of bed and go to the window. The sun is just beginning to rise. The sky is turning scarlet, crimson, gold, orange, amber. Every breath you take the sky gets bluer and bluer.

You go into the kitchen. There on a blue platter is a sizzling stack of smoked bacon, hot from the frying pan. Next to it on a white platter are piping hot squares of corn bread covered with rich melted butter. You sink your teeth into the bacon; feel it crunch between your teeth. Taste the smoky flavor. Now you eat the corn bread, feel the coarse texture of the bread and creamy taste of the butter. It is 6:30 in the morning.

You go out onto the porch. You sit down in a rocking chair and rock back and forth, to and fro, listening to the creaking of the porch boards beneath the weight of the rocker. You look out over the farm yard. You see the mud yard with ruts from the tractor, a white henhouse, a red barn, a garden with cucumbers, tomatoes, lettuce, squash, pumpkins, radishes, peas, and carrots, a ditch, a gravel road, bright green corn field, brilliant blue sky. Suddenly off to your left you hear the voices of children. You turn your head and see three boys, age 8, hurrying off to school. It is five minutes to nine and they are late. They rush down the gravel road, up the hill to your right, and disappear into a white schoolhouse. You continue rocking. You are getting hungry again. It is now 10:00. You go back into the kitchen. There on the table is a blue platter with a piping hot stack of blueberry muffins fresh from the oven. You sink your teeth into a muffin. The ripe blueberries burst in your mouth. Taste the sweet blueberry juice. Taste the nutty flavor of the muffin.

You go back out onto the porch and continue to rock. Now you walk down the porch steps, across the farm yard, down the ditch, over the gravel road and into the corn field. Feel the dry corn rustle against your body. Now you come out into a field of sunflowers. Huge yellow flowers against the bright blue sky with large round brown centers. Next you find yourself in a field of clover. It smells like honey. Butterflies are darting back and forth among the clover blossoms. You lie down in the clover, the smell of wet earth beneath you, the smell of honey around you. You look at a wisp of a cloud in the blue sky. The sun is straight above you. It is high noon. A lazy, hazy August day. You drift, you float, you doze, in the summer sun, not a care in the world.

Image VIII

This scene is the subject's first real taste of dissociation. Many persons report that they can actually feel themselves shrinking during this image. There is a euphoric sense of timelessness akin to free floating. Time expansion has also been reported by patients from this scene. One patient exclaimed that the shrinking period seemed to last for an hour (actually 30 seconds); she felt herelf getting large again during the therapist's counting to three to end the scene, and this time period seemed like another hour.

Jungle Scene. It is very warm, very humid, very close. It is dark. You are in a sleeping bag. You can hear insects humming. Now it is beginning to get light. You sit up. All around you is dense tropical foliage. There are giant ferns and lilies. You are in the middle of a rain forest, a jungle. You hear monkeys chattering, birds cawing. There is steam rising off the jungle floor. It is very early morning. Sunlight is filtering through the canopy of leaves above you, casting a lacelike pattern of light on the jungle floor. You get up. You begin making your way through the dense undergrowth cutting your way through with a machete. The ground is spongelike. It feels like steam heat, like a sauna bath. Perspiration is running down your armpits, the small of your back. Your clothing is clinging to your skin, soaked in sweat. Hair is matted to your forehead, blurring your vision. You continue cutting, making your way forward.

Suddenly you come to a clearing, to a grotto, a mineral hot spring. The grotto is composed of a white chalklike substance resembling coral, which crunches under the weight of your feet. The strong smell of sulfur is in the air. Interspersed in this white chalky substance are pools of brilliant aqua-blue mineral water. You walk over to one of these pools. You take off your clothes. You glide into the warm mineral water. It is like a whirlpool. Your muscles become soft and pliant. Now you notice a curious thing. The pool is getting larger. First the size of a pond, then a baseball field, then a small lake. You look up and see that the trees are miles high into the sky. You realize that the pool has not been getting larger, you have been getting smaller. You are shrinking. Getting smaller and smaller. A large orange Monarch butterfly lights beside you. You crawl onto his back. He soars high up into the blue sky, dipping and soaring like a roller coaster. Feel that sinking feeling in the pit of your stomach. And you continue to shrink, until finally there is nothing left at all.

This is a good technic for achieving hypnotic dissociation. The reader should not be perturbed by such verbalizations, as we have never seen the slightest danger from using this image.

Image IX

The purpose of this image is threefold. First of all, it is designed to enhance the intensification of recall of temperature. Second, it is the beginning of a series of images constructed to start the subject in recalling feeling components that concentrate on combinations of sensation. All experiences are comprised of combinations of given sensations. When all the sensations comprising a past experience can be recalled, the experience is totally revivified. For example, the sensation of the erection constitutes several feeling components. The two primary ones are warmth and congestion or pressure. By recalling the sensations of warmth and pressure in the genital area, an erection can be produced. Fortunately, most males suffering from impotence have experienced warmth and pressure in the genital area or an erection, and they work at merely recalling a given experience when they had an erection. Image IX concentrates on the combinations of the feeling components of cold-wet, hot-dry, hot-wet, and cold-dry, in that order.

Sometimes, however, the sensation we wish to produce has never occurred in the area we now wish to experience it in. We then have to recall the sensation in an area where we have felt it before and transfer it to the desired area. The transfer of numbness or glove anesthesia has already been described in relation to Image IV. We have all experienced anesthesia in some parts of our body. Legs and feet often "go to sleep" or become numb when we cut off the circulation, and numbness in the cheeks from the dentist's Novocaine is a common experience. Numbness in an area like the stomach, for example, is not so common and many people may never have experienced this sensation, or lack of sensation, in the stomach area. Anesthesia in the stomach has several uses including calming stomach contractions and quelling hunger pangs for weight control. If the subject has never experienced a numb stomach, he must first recall numbness in an area where he has experienced it, such as the hand, and then transfer it to the stomach area. It is important that the subject work on transferring all the sensations he is learning to recall so that he will be adept in this procedure when the time comes to utilize it.

This brings us then to the third function of Image IX, focus on the transfer of heat. The same procedure is used as was utilized in the transfer of numbness. Heat is first felt in the hand, then transferred to the cheek and transferred back to the hand. Whenever a sensation is induced, it is always necessary to give a suggestion later that the affected area will return to its normal state. Sometimes this can be incorporated directly into the image, as in the mountain cabin scene when the subject is told at the end of the scene to hold his hands over the fire and feel the warmth running through them. The recall of warmth in the hands necessitates the alleviation of the numbness in that area without giving a direct suggestion such as, "The numbness will now leave your hands and they will return to their normal state."

The ability to transfer heat has special import in cases of sexual inadequacy. While most impotent males have experienced an erection and can recall one, many females have never experienced a climax. Primary components of the orgasm are heat, congestion and sudden release of tension. The non-orgasmic female must recall these feeling components in areas of her body where she has experienced them and combine them by transferring them to the genital area. The male can produce an erection by transferring heat and pressure to the genital area. Sexually arousing imagery should be used in conjunction with this physical transfer. The sensory recall of given feeling components, their transfer and combination is the use of Skinner's method of successive approximations. It is truly shaping behavior. The orgasm and the erection thus can be shaped by the method of successive approximations. Any feeling or experience can be shaped by the right recall and combination of components.

Pool Scene. You are sitting on a white ice-cream chair beside a table out of the center of which is a yellow and blue striped umbrella. It is mid-August. It is very, very hot—95 degrees. Next to you is a large swimming pool and sunken garden. All around the pool are brilliantly colored red hibiscus and coconut palms with monkeys chattering in them. You can also see multicolored parrots in the palms with orange, chartreuse, and purple plumage. On the far side of the pool are Arabian night-like cabanas of vari-colored stripes. In front of you on the table is a cold glass of lemonade. Moisture has condensed in beads running down the cold slippery surface of the glass. You pick up the *wet, cold* glass in your warm right hand. You are wearing nothing but a white bathing suit. You stand up and walk toward the pool. Your bare feet touch the *dry, hot* cement of the pool area. You run to the edge of the pool where water has been splashed. The wet cement is still hot but not as hot as where it is dry. You stand there on the *hot, wet* cement in the blazing sun holding the lemonade. You put the glass to your lips. Hear the ice cubes clatter against the glass. Feel the ice cold liquid touch your lips, go down your throat and into your stomach. Feel the cold radiate out from the center of your body. Feel the contrast of the hot sun on the outside of your stomach against the cold on the inside of your stomach.

Now you go over and lie down on a chaise longue. You are getting hotter and hotter, thirstier and thirstier. You see a Coke machine on the other side of the pool. You get up and walk over to the machine. You press your warm, moist body against the *cold, dry* metal of the Coke machine. You press your cheeks, your stomach, your thighs against the machine. It takes your breath away. Now you put the money into the machine. The Coke is dispensed. Feel the carbonation, the bubbles against your nose as you drink the Coke. Taste it. You walk back over to the edge of the pool. You squat down. You place your right hand flat on the hot, wet cement. When you feel the heat in your hand, I want you to place your right hand against your right cheek. [The subject does as directed.] Good. Now let all that heat drain from your hand into your cheek. Your cheek is becoming warm, flushed, your hand is becoming cool. When all the heat has drained from your hand into your cheek, place your hand once again at your side. [The subject does so.] Now, once again place your right hand upon your right cheek. Let all the heat in your cheek drain back into your hand. Your hand is becoming warm, hot, your cheek is becoming cool, as if a gentle evening breeze were blowing over it. When all the heat has drained from your cheek back into your hand, once again place your hand at your side. [The subject does as directed.] Now, you stand up. You walk over to a grove of palms. You sit down in the shade. A cool breeze blows through the grove. Hear the wind rustling through the palm leaves. It lulls you into a dreamy, drowsy state. You feel limp all over as you drift away.

Image X

Extreme changes in temperature are experienced during this scene. This is the first scene in which combinations of feelings are transferred. The combinations of components to be transferred are hot-dry and hot-wet. No particular scenes for transfer of cold have been devised, as the sensation of cold is usually recalled in conjunction with the transfer of numbness in Image IV due to the nature of the scene (that is, thrusting one's hand in snow to produce numbness.)

Arctic Scene. It is very, very cold. It is 30 degrees below zero. All you can see is bright blue and stark white. There are masses of white snow and mountains of glistening ice. You are at the polar ice cap, you are at the North Pole. The sky is vivid blue, the sun a cold, pale yellow. You are making your way through the snow. You see the mouth of a cavern. All around the mouth are long, slender icicles sparkling in the sunlight. You walk up to the cavern, you take the glove off your right hand, you grasp an icicle. The heat from your hand begins to melt the ice. You run your hand up and down the *cold, wet* surface of the icicle. Put your glove back on. Now you walk into the cave. In the center of the cave is a large pool of ice cold water, dark and deep. You take a tin cup from a knapsack on your back. You scoop up the water, holding the cup between your hands, you bring the *cold, dry* metal to your lips. The cold liquid pours down your throat and into your stomach. Feel the cold radiating from the center of your body.

Now you walk to the mouth of the cave. Your footsteps resound among the cavern walls. You stand looking at the white snow. Suddenly above, you hear a shrill mechanical sound. You look up and see a helicopter. A wind is created from the motion of the rotors. It lands. You walk over to the helicopter. You take off the glove from your right hand. You place your hand on the *hot, dry* metal of the copter where the engine is. When you feel that dry heat in your hand I want you to place your right hand upon your right cheek. [The subject does as instructed.] Now let the dry heat in your right hand drain into your cheek. Your cheek is becoming hot and flushed, the blood is running to the surface of the skin. It feels as if hot air is blowing against it. Your hand is becoming cold. When all the heat has drained from your hand into your cheek, once again place your hand at your side. [The subject does so.] Good. Now once again place your right hand upon your right cheek. Let the dry warmth in your cheek drain back into your hand. When all that warmth has drained back into your hand, once again place your hand at your side. Your hand is becoming hot and dry, your cheek is becoming cool. [The subject places his hand at his side.] Good.

You get into the helicopter. You fasten your seat belt. Feel the pressure around your midsection. The copter begins to ascend. You are surrounded by a silver mist as you continue to go higher and higher. You look at the altitude gauge. You are now 5,000 feet above sea level. When you go back down to 2,000 feet above sea level, you will land. In front of you on a tray is a sizzling T-bone steak and a bowl of crisp green salad. You begin eating the steak. It tastes delicious. Now you eat the salad. You keep eating and eating and your stomach begins to distend. Notice the contrast between the pressure on the inside of your stomach from the food and the pressure on the outside of your stomach from the seat belt.

Now the copter is beginning to descend. Feel that sinking feeling in the pit of your stomach . . . 5,000 feet, 4,000 feet, 3,000 feet, 2,000 feet, 1,000 feet. This is strange. You were to land at 2,000 feet above sea level, but the copter continues to descend. As the plane goes lower and lower it gets hotter and hotter inside the compartment . . . 1,000 feet, 80 degrees above zero, sea level, 90 degrees above zero, −1,000 feet, 100 degrees above zero, −2,000 feet, 110 degrees above zero. At 3,000 feet below sea level the copter lands. Beads of perspiration are running down your forehead and your armpits. Clothes are clinging to your body. The inside of the compartment is steamed up. Hair is matted to your forehead. It is very stuffy. You open the door. You get out. There before you is the world as it existed millions of years ago, a primeval forest. There are giant redwoods, colossal ferns—thick jungle with gigantic, gnarled trees. You walk over to a river of boiling water. You hold your hand above it. Feel the *hot, wet* steam collecting on the palm of your right hand. When you feel this wet heat on your right hand, place your right hand upon your right cheek and let that wet heat drain into your cheek. [The subject does as directed.] The cheek is getting wet and hot and sweaty, the hand is cool as if being held in front of a fan. When all the wet heat has drained from your hand into your cheek, once again place your hand at your side. [The subject does so.] Now once again place your right hand upon your right cheek and let the wet heat in your cheek drain back into your hand. When all the wet heat in your cheek has drained back into your hand, once again place your hand at your side. Your cheek is becoming cool and dry, your hand is moist and hot as if being held over a pressure cooker. [The subject places his hand again at his side.] Good. Now you lie down beside the river. The smell of wet earth beneath you, you drift in a world as it existed millions of years ago . . . drifting and floating . . . and dreaming. . . .

DISCUSSION OF TIME EXPANSION IMAGES

At this point, it is often beneficial to go back to the two time expansion scenes, Images VI and VII. This time the therapist pauses 2 minutes after giving the posthypnotic suggestion for time expansion. He then asks the subject to estimate, "How long has it been since last I spoke?" The common and desired response is that he will estimate more than 2 minutes. Regardless of what response the subject makes, the therapist then goes on to describe the particular time distortion image. The therapist makes no response of any kind to the subject's estimated time lapse. If the subject says he does not know how much time has passed, he is requested to guess.

After the image has been described, the therapist pauses 5 minutes. He then once again asks for the subject's estimation of time lapse. Once the subject has responded, the therapist terminates the hypnosis in the usual manner. The pauses of 2 and 5 minutes are arbitrary and may be varied. These particular time lapses have generally been found to work well, since shorter periods do not lead to expansion and longer periods may result in the subject's mind straying or even in his falling asleep. As the subject becomes more adept at hypnosis and the induction of time expansion, he will be able to maintain the distortion for hours at a time. The subject is asked to estimate time lapse so that the therapist can evaluate his progress within this dimension. The patient is told how much time actually elapsed during these two periods and whether he was successful in expanding the time. It is very reinforcing for the subject to learn he has been successful in the expansion of time, and this gives him greater motivation to go on to greater levels of relaxation and sensory control.

It has been our experience that in almost all cases, subjects are very good at time expansion. Ideally the sense of time expansion should be greater or at least equal to the sense of expansion experienced immediately after the posthypnotic suggestion for it. The mere suggestion for it may be enough for its production in very suggestible subjects, but more often an image is needed in conjunction with the suggestion in order to produce the feeling that time is going by very slowly. Once the subject has experienced the feeling of time expansion on several occasions by means of the image, he will be able to immediately recall it without the image. This ability for immediate recall of time expansion is most useful whenever the subject feels himself under a time pressure. Whether he is on a tight schedule, works as a court reporter, or is merely uptight for no apparent reason, the recall of time expansion will give the subject a chance to wind down and get a second breath.

Time distortion is basically a hypnotic technic. It is utilized mainly in research and therapy by hypnotherapists. It has never been included as such by behavior modifiers, and it is difficult to think of a behavioral analogue. Of all the hypnotic technics described, this one has produced some of the most amazing results. Its induction is much simpler and more subjects respond than we would ever have expected. It can be used with all subjects to relieve the sense of time pressure generally associated with the coronary-prone patient. It also has some very specific applications in such areas as test anxiety and sexual inadequacy, which will be dealt with later.

It should be noted that the phenomenon of hypnotic relaxation itself often produces time expansion. Subjects often say it seemed as if hours had passed during their 30- or 40-minute session. For some, however, time concentration ensues as a function of the hypnosis, and those subjects report that it seems as if they had just begun. This general orientation of the subject should be taken into account when assessing his progress.

Image XI

At this point, another type of time should be developed, that of time condensation or concentration. The phenomena of time expansion and time condensation are fairly common in everyday activities. Time expansion is usually experienced in an unpleasant situation such as waiting for a taxi on a cold, rainy day—it seems as if the minutes were hours. Time condensation occurs during pleasant times such as during a good movie; compare the old adage, ''Time flies when you're having fun.'' The ideal state, however, is to prolong the good times or peak experiences and shorten the negative or bad experiences. For example, time expansion is very valuable in prolonging a period of sexual arousal for the impotent male so that he can maintain an erection longer. Conversely, periods of depression or trauma could be much better handled if their duration could be condensed.

The following is a practical application using time condensation to shorten a negative experience.

> A young woman of 26 came to us complaining that she had a fear of riding in airplanes, especially trans-Atlantic flights, which lasted several hours. In addition to counterconditioning her to the image of her flying, which involved an elaborate hierarchy leading up to the closing of the plane doors, she was taught to condense time so that a 10-hour flight seemed like 1 hour and very little anxiety was generated in that time.

In the following scene, a clock tower chimes the hour of midnight while various events are unfolding. The rationale in terms of time condensation is that while it takes approximately 30 seconds for a clock to chime the hour of midnight, the description of the events ensuing in that imaginal 30 seconds takes 5 minutes. If the scene seems real, the subject will feel that 30 seconds have lapsed (the amount of time lapsing in the scene), while in reality, 5 minutes have passed.

The feeling of weightlessness described in this scene is also important in that it serves to enhance the subject's ability to recall pressure, weightlessness being an absence of external pressure. Likewise, developing the potential for condensing time increases the capacity for expanding time. Whether time is expanded or condensed, the object is to control the time sense; whether the suggestion is to feel heavy or light, the purpose is to control pressure; and whether one attempts to regulate hot or cold, the goal is to control temperature.

Clock Scene. Ten minutes of actual time will seem like 1 minute to you. Time will go by very rapidly. It will seem like an instant. In less than 1 hour you can accomplish an entire day's work and accomplish it more effectively than you would ordinarily.

You are in a room on the second floor of a house. It is almost midnight. You are looking at a large bay window with starched white curtains. Moonlight is flooding in, illuminating the room, bathing it in silver. There is a toy chest, wooden toy soldiers, a raggedy Ann doll, a large bed with a canopy. It is a child's bedroom. Outside is a city with a tall clock tower, a winding river like a ribbon of silver in the moonlight, a bridge, and rolling countryside. Now the clock tower is beginning to toll the hour of midnight.

It strikes for the first time. You see clouds drift over the moon, transparent in the moonlight. The clock strikes a second time. A breeze blows in the window, ruffling the curtains; it smells like spring. On the third strike of the clock you notice the sweet, heavy scent of lilacs in the air. The clock strikes for the fourth time. You hear a dog bark beneath the window. On the fifth strike of the clock you notice the taste of honey from tea and honey you had earlier that evening. On the sixth chime of the clock you look outside and see what appears to be stardustlike sparklers. The clock strikes for the seventh time. The stardust comes into the room, filling it with a golden glow. On the eighth strike of the clock you feel a sensation of weightlessness. When the clock strikes for the ninth time, you feel your body carried upward and out the window. The tenth strike of the clock sounds very distant. On the eleventh chime you hear a faraway dog bark. When the clock strikes the hour of midnight all sorts of happy childhood memories come to mind . . . sleigh bells, cotton candy, Christmas trees, carnivals, ferris wheels, circuses, rainbows, pots of gold, Easter eggs. You float over the city, over the river, over the countryside, and then straight up toward the stars.

Image XII

This is the second image for the production of time condensation. It consists of a bluebird flying from a branch to the outstretched arms of the subject. The imaginal time elapsing during the 5-minute description is approximately 5 seconds, a much shorter amount of imaginal time than in the previous clock scene. Again, if the scene seems real, it will appear that less than 5 minutes has passed during the imagery. Time condensation is usually much more difficult to elicit than time expansion.

Bluebird Scene. Ten minutes of actual time will seem like one minute to you. Time will go by very, very rapidly. It will seem like an instant. In less than 1 hour you can accomplish an entire day's work and accomplish it more effectively than you would ordinarily.

You are sitting on the bank of a river looking up at the branch of a tree on which is perched a bluebird. It is spring. Smell the freshness in the air. Now the bird has left his perch and is starting to fly toward you. Hear the babbling of the river as the water rushes over the rocks. The bird is drawing closer. Look up the river. At its head you see a pink castle with flags waving from the turrets. The bird is getting still closer. A breeze blows from out of the woods bringing to your nostrils the salty smell of ham from a picnic lunch which is spread before you on a checkered cloth. There is ham, French bread, cheese, and wine. Notice the pattern of the red and white checks in the spread. You feel a feather brush against your hand, tickling your skin. Now you feel the weight and heat of the bird as it lights in your hand. You look into the eyes of the bird. You see in his eyes the reflection of you sitting under a tree by a river. You are surrounded by patches of white and yellow daisies. The tree becomes transparent, turns to glass. Hanging from its branches are long strands of a glittering mosslike substance. The bird closes his eyes. The scene is gone.

Image XIII

Once again we return to the recall of feeling or sensory components. This scene deals with combinations of the components of temperature and pressure: light-hot, heavy-hot, light-cold, and heavy-cold, in that order. The sequence of combinations is arbitrary.

Lake Scene. You are walking barefoot down a gravel road. It is mid-June. It is very warm. You are walking down to the lake. On your right is a thatched-roof cottage with a white picket fence around it. There is a small garden with cucumbers, tomatoes, carrots, rutabagas, radishes, and lettuce growing in it. Beside the garden is an incinerator burning paper. Particles of *light, hot* paper ash are blowing in the wind. They brush against your skin. They are warm and light and tickling against your flesh.

Now you come to a long flight of stone steps leading down a steep bank to the shoreline. You begin descending the steps. They are cool and moist beneath your feet. There is a cool metal railing of pipe. The bank is forested. There are wildflowers growing—lupine, columbine, tiger lilies. You reach the base of the steps and there before you is a wooden dock and a boat house. A dock boy comes out of the boat house. He is loading a white wooden boat, which is tied to the dock. He brings out cushions and oars. You get into the boat. Feel it rock beneath the pressure of your body. The dock boy brings a large red gas can, which he places on the dock. It gets very warm in the sun. He hands you the gas can, which is *hot* and *heavy* in your lap. He loads the motor and takes the can from you, placing it in the bottom of the boat. Feel the release of pressure in your lap when the can is removed. The boat is untied and pushed away with an oar. The dock boy starts the motor. Hear the roar of the engine. The boat speeds out into the lake. The water is like glass. Your hair is blowing from the wind created by the motion of the boat. Feel the *cold, light* spray against your face. It is exhilarating!

You reach the other side of the lake where there are tall rushes growing over 8 feet high. The motor is shut off and you begin to row through the channels of water in the rushes. Feel the pulling in your muscles as you dip and pull the oars. Hear the reeds pressing against the boat. You come to a small clearing in the rushes. The boat is anchored. You lie in the bttom of the boat gently rocking back and forth, to and fro by the motion of the ripples on the water. The summer sun makes you feel so lazy. You drift there for hours. Now it is time to go back. The dock boy pulls up the anchor and places it in your lap; it is *cold* and *heavy*. He starts the motor and takes the anchor from you, which he places in the bottom of the boat. Feel the release of pressure in your midsection. The boat speeds out of the rushes and heads straight for the opposite shore and the dock. The boat approaches shore, the motor is turned off, and it is docked. You get out of the boat, walk down the dock, up the cool stone steps, and back down the gravel road, going home.

Image XIV

Component combinations for this scene are light-dry, light-wet, heavy-wet, and heavy-dry. This scene ends the series of four images focusing on the combinations of the external components of hot-cold, wet-dry, and light-heavy.

Thundershower Scene. You are sitting on a patio surrounded by a white fence and flowers. It is mid-June. It is one o'clock in the afternoon. It is 80 degrees above zero. You are looking at the flowers. There are bells of Ireland, sweet peas, zinnias, Canterbury bells, sweet William, roses, and iris. Past the fence are two box elder trees with a clothesline running between them. There is a long lawn of green grass, a large garden surrounded by poplar trees with silver leaves rustling in the wind, and past that a railroad track and a lake. White sheets are billowing on the clothesline. You get up. You gather the sheets in your arms. They are *light* and fluffy and *dry*. They smell sweet and fresh and clean. You carry them over to a table on the patio. Running the length of the lawn is a hose with small holes in it, out of which a fine mist of water is being forced. There is a rainbow in the mist. You strip to your underwear and run the length of the hose feeling the *light, wet* mist against your skin. You sit back down in a chair on the patio in the sun to dry.

Off to the west it is beginning to get dark. Large thick clouds are building up. It is getting cooler. Storm clouds are rolling in. It is three o'clock in the afternoon but it is dark. It is very still. Now a wind begins. It picks up, and soon branches are being torn from the trees as the wind increases in velocity, and it gets still colder: you go into the house and put on a heavy wool sweater. You come back outside and sit. A bolt of lightning streaks across the sky. You hear deafening clashes of thunder. The sky is black and gray with yellow streaks of lightning electricity. It begins to pour rain. Your sweater is soaked. You are cold and shivering. . . . Everything is deep, deep green. The sweater is *heavy* and *wet* against your skin.

You go back into the house. You walk down a long corridor and up a winding flight of stairs to the master bedroom. The room is large with a massive oak, wide-beamed ceiling. There is a blazing fire in the fireplace. You crawl into an old Victorian bed with a high needlepoint headboard. Feel the pressure of the *dry, heavy* quilts over your body. You remove your clothes under the blankets. Smell the smoke from the burning logs, hear the patter of the rain against the window pane . . . the sweet sound of the rain, the warmth of the fire. You are completely calm, totally secure.

DISCUSSION OF TIME CONDENSATION IMAGES

Just as we returned to time expansion, we also return to time condensation at this point in order to further develop it and evaluate the subject's progress in achieving it. Procedure for evaluation is the same as was used in evaluation of time expansion. The subject is asked to estimate the time lapse immediately after the posthypnotic suggestion for time condensation and then again after the scene has been described.

Image XV

The primary goal here is to gain greater control over the basic human systems: digestive, circulatory, skeletal, and excretory. Since relaxation directly controls the respiratory system from the beginning of hypnotic instruction (breathing becomes deeper and more regular as relaxation increases) it need not be dealt with separately as are the other four systems mentioned above. The same combinations of the components of hot-cold, wet-dry, and light-heavy as were recalled externally in the last series are now to be recalled or created internally in these four major systems. We will now be dealing with the gaining of control over interoceptive rather than exteroceptive stimuli.

This image begins a new and important series. Since many of the sensations that will need to be produced internally have never been experienced in this manner to any appreciable degree, if at all, it will often be necessary for the subject to transfer the recall of an external sensation to an internal area. He will internalize the recall of external sensations via sensory stimulus transference. Thus, the acquisition of the ability to internalize previously primarily external sensations will give the subject greater control over autonomic and skeletal functioning. He can already control blood pressure or vasoconstriction as well as subjective body temperature by producing warmth or numbness. It will be remembered that warmth and numbness were originally produced by going back in time to a period when the subject was actually experiencing these sensations and by recalling these incidents. Because some of these sensations are seldom, if ever, experienced internally, the images in this sequence may seem quite bizarre. Such an image does, however, provide some sort of identification for the subject and aid in the production of the given sensation. The images in this series also serve to further develop the subject's hypnotic depth and powers of concentration, since the patient is now called upon to "create" certain sensations rather than merely "recall" them. In the following image the sensory components, hot-dry, cold-wet, hot-wet, and cold-dry are recalled internally in relation to the digestive system.

Mansion Scene. You are walking down a very busy street. Hear the traffic, the horns blowing, the brakes screeching. The air is smoggy and polluted. It is mid-July. It is very hot and scorching. Now you turn left and take a side street that winds its way up into the hills. Every step you take the air gets fresher and fresher. Every step you take it gets quieter and quieter. . . . You walk for half an hour. You come to a large iron gate. You look beyond the gate and see a gigantic gray stone mansion built during the 20s in the golden era of Hollywood. You walk through the gate. Hear the creak and grate of its hinges. You are in a field of dandelions gone to seed, brightly lit by sunlight, a field of golden light. You walk over to one of the dry dandelions; it looks like a puff of fluff or cotton. You put the seed in your mouth and begin eating large quantities of them. They are dry like feathers in your mouth. They taste like sunflower seeds. They absorb all the moisture in your mouth making it dry and cottony. You swallow the seeds. They are *hot* and *dry* in your stomach.

Next you do down a flight of stone stairs to another part of the garden. You see a white gazebo yellowing with age covered with ivy. You go over to it and sit down. In front of you is a large glass of limeade. Moisture has condensed on the glass. Beads of water are running down the cool container. You put the glass to your mouth, listening to the ice cubes rattle against the glass. You begin drinking, you swallow one of the ice cubes. It is *cold* and *wet* in the pit of your stomach. Feel the cold radiating out from the center of your body.

You get up and go into the house. You find yourself in a large banquet hall. There is a large oak table that seats 30 people. On the walls is painted a hunting mural with men in redcoats riding horses after a fox. You sit down at the table. There before you is a hot bowl of vegetable soup. You eat the soup. It is tangy and delicious. Feel the *hot, wet* liquid in your mouth going down your throat and into your stomach. A radiating wave of warmth spreads from your stomach throughout your body. Now you leave the table and go outside behind the house. There is a large rock garden, a waterfall, and a grove of weeping willow trees. You sit on a cool bench under the willows listening to the falling of the water. There materializes in your right hand a cherry snow cone. The cone is not composed of ordinary ice but of dry ice. You eat the cone. Taste the sweet cherry flavor. The ice is *dry* and *cold* in your stomach. It absorbs the moisture from your body. Now you lie down under the willows listening to the steady fall of the water, drifting and floating . . . drifting and floating . . . at peace . . . lulled to sleep.

Image XVI

Here we have the internalized combinations of the following components: hot-dry, cold-dry, cold-wet, and hot-wet in relation to the circulatory and skeletal systems. This has proven to be a particularly powerful scene and patients have been observed to shiver with goose flesh and flush with heat at the appropriate places in the imagery.

Scuba Diving Scene. You are on a fishing boat in the Florida Keys. It is very warm. The sky is vivid blue, the sun a blazing yellow. The shore is lined with glistening white sand and palm trees. Brilliantly colored flowers are everywhere along the coast. You are wearing gear for skin diving with an oxygen tank on your back. You are perched on the edge of the boat ready to dive. Feel your body turning over, somersaulting into the water, going round and round, head over heels into the warm, tropical water. As you go deeper and deeper the water gets cooler and cooler. As you go deeper and deeper, it gets darker and darker. There are bright salmon-colored coral, fan-shaped plants, multicolored fish. Glinting goldfish and lime green and orange angelfish catch the sunlight as they flash by. Now you see an ice-blue network object. You approach and touch it. It sends a jolt of electricity through you. It feels as if you had touched an electric wire or light socket. The feeling is pleasant, very stimulating, like electricity running through your bones making them *hot* and *dry*.

As you continue to go deeper, you get colder and colder. You become encased in ice, encapsulated in a block of ice. Your skin and body are numb, woodenlike. The block of ice surfaces and floats to shore, drifting up onto the hot sand. There it melts in the heat of the sun. Your muscles feel like jelly as they thaw. Your bones are still frozen solid, *cold* and *dry*. Blood is cold like ice-water, *wet* and *cold* in your body, forcing its way through your arteries and veins. You begin to shiver with chills in the blazing tropic sun. Suddenly your eye is caught by the sight of a bottle washed up on shore. You go over to it. It is a bottle of rum. You begin drinking. You become intoxicated, euphoric. Your blood is *hot, wet,* on fire. You lie down on the sand. All the vivid colors around you begin to mesh and swirl becoming molten. . . . spinning round and round. You feel yourself whirling and spinning in a state of complete euphoria, seeing liquid purples, greens, reds and golds. Then all is calm, all is gray, and you sleep.

Image XVII

The picnic scene internalizes the following combination of components: cold-wet, cold-dry, hot-wet, and hot-dry in relation to the excretory and skeletal systems. This is the subject's first exposure to recall of the excretory function.

Picnic Scene. You are walking down a gravel road in the country. It is late July. It is a warm summer day. You walk off the road and into a ditch of grass. Crawling under a barbed-wire fence, you find yourself in a forested area of tall elms and thick, shortly cropped grass. There is a river winding its way through the woods, which you follow to a spring of crystal clear water shooting up out of the earth. In the water are ice-cold cans of beer, which you begin drinking. You drink can after can, gradually becoming intoxicated. You feel an urge to urinate. You go behind a bush and expel the beer, which comes out as *wet* and *cold* as it was when you drank it.

Now you remove your clothes and wade into the river. The water is ice-cold and flowing rapidly. You let the river carry you downstream, your body becoming numb from the cold. You feel frozen right down to the marrow, your bones are *cold* and *dry*. The river takes you into a pond of warm water. There is a wooden mill with a paddlewheel turning water and a dock. You float in the warm water, looking up at the sky. Suddenly you spot a bottle on the dock. You swim over to it. It is tequila. You begin drinking the liquor. Your body seems on fire as you become intoxicated with the tequila. Once again you urinate. The urine feels *wet* and *hot* as it is expelled. Now you get out of the water and climb onto the dock. You walk away from the pond into a forest coming out into a pasture. The grass is cropped very short like a golf green. You lie down on the grass carpet in the sun. Your skin reflects the sun's heat and your bones feel *dry* and *hot* in the sunlight.

Image XVIII

This image begins a series of three that deal with internalized pressure in the alimentary, circulatory, excretory, and skeletal systems. The following scene emphasizes the internalization and control of dryness-wetness and pressure in the alimentary and skeletal systems. The object of all images is greater control over physical functioning. The following combinations of sensory components are internalized: light-dry, heavy-wet, light-wet, and heavy-dry.

Shangri-La Scene. You are in a vast meadow with a huge expanse of blue sky above you. It is early spring. Smell the freshness in the air. In the distance you can see snow-covered mountains like the Alps or Himalayas. The meadow is green and covered with white daisies and other wildflowers. You wish to scale the mountaintops. You take an air pump and place the rubber hose in your mouth. You begin pumping your body with air, filling up like a balloon. The *light, dry* air inside your body gives you a sensation of weightlessness. You begin to float up into the blue sky. You are approaching the mountain peaks. It is getting colder as the altitude increases. The cold causes the air inside you to contract. You begin to descend, landing on the ridge of the mountain. It is freezing cold. The wind is blowing bitterly. With your back to the sheer side of the mountain, you inch your way along the ledge, snow blowing in your face.

You come to a pass. On the other side of the pass is another world. You cross the threshold and find yourself in an orchard of peaches. It is warm, like summer. There are fountains and marble statues. Passing through the orchard, you come to a long flight of stone stairs leading to a rock palace. You walk up the steps and into the temple, finding yourself in a large stone chamber. There before you is a teak table on which is a stack of piping-hot pancakes covered with butter and syrup. Next to them is a pitcher of milk. You begin eating the pancakes, washing them down with the milk. You are starved! They taste delicious and you eat and eat, shovelling the food down. The pancake batter or dough is getting heavier and heavier in the pit of your stomach, weighing you down with a *wet, heavy* mass. You cannot even stand up. Suddenly a gong rings. It echoes throughout the chamber. A sliding stone panel opens and an ancient man with a long white beard enters, bearing a frothing glass of pink liquid. It is an ancient yeast drink, a health-food drink. He gives it to you and you drink. The yeast inside your stomach makes you feel lighter and lighter. The *light, wet* bubbles inside you make you feel airy as a feather. You float along the stone floor as if there were no gravity.

You glide along the floor, out the temple arch, down the steps, and to a river. You float like an innertube in the river to the very point where you entered the orchard. You are once again at the pass. Immediately you feel a heaviness in your bones . . . *dry, heavy* bones. They weigh down your arms and legs as if they were made of lead. You recline to the sound of the wind on the mountain ridge.

Image XIX

The emphasis here is on internalization and control of pressure and dryness/wetness in the circulatory and alimentary systems. Components are dry-heavy, wet-heavy, wet-light, and dry-light, in that order.

Chalk Cliff Scene. You are standing on the edge of a cliff overlooking the sea. Wind is blowing through your hair and the smell of salt from the ocean is strong. There is a great stretch of light blue sky as you stand almost a mile above the sea. Behind you is a cottage with a stone fence around it. The grass is undulating in the wind. Patches of heather are scattered along the cliff side. You begin walking down the cliff. The path is white, composed of chalk. You bend down and pick up some lumps of chalk. You put them in your mouth. They are dry and absorb the moisture in your mouth. You swallow them. They are *dry* and *heavy* in the pit of your stomach, soaking up the internal moisture. The chalk mixes with the chemical composition of your blood . . . blood feels *wet,* and *heavy.* You can feel the thick blood forcing itself through your veins and arteries. The weight from the chalk causes you to fall. You somersault head over heels down the cliff path. The motion of your body causes air to mix with the blood forming bubbles, making it lighter.

You bounce the remainder of the way down the path to the sand. Your blood is *wet* and *light.* You are now in a cove. The beach stretches for over a mile before the water begins. There are strange natural-rock formations like bridges and pinnacles formed from the water's washing away of the rock over the centuries. It looks like a surrealistic landscape. You begin walking to the sea, watching the white sea gulls circling above you in the sky. You come upon an old abandoned ship washed up on a reef from long ago. Climbing onto the deck of the ship you look out to sea. From your pocket you take a package of soda crackers. You begin eating them. They are dry and flaky in your mouth, absorbing the moisture, making your mouth feel dry and cottonlike. You swallow the *light, dry* cracker crumbs; they feel dry in your stomach. You lie down on the ship deck looking up at the clouds. Feel the sea breeze. You dream, and doze, and sleep.

Image XX

The emphasis in this scene is on internalization and control of feelings of pressure and wetness-dryness in the excretory system. This is the first image where there is recall of solid excrement as well as gas in this system.

Sensory components recalled are heavy-wet, light-dry, heavy-dry, and light-wet. This is also the first scene in which colors intensify and matter changes form. This is equivalent to giving a suggestion for various medicated states. Many patients come to treatment wishing to phase themselves off medication or narcotics. It often is possible in a hypnotic state to recall the drug state so that no medication is ever needed. Hypnosis is first used in conjunction with medication and then it is gradually phased out.

Intensification of color and distortion of form are not uncommon in deep states of hypnosis. Eastern philosophies posit different levels of consciousness that one must pass through to attain the Universal One. After color and form distortion, there come more pronounced states of dissociation wherein the subject feels he is outside his body, looking at himself—a state known as ''mind leaving the body.'' The next level enables the dissociated self to travel and finally to attain a state known as ''astral projection'' or ''mind-expanded consciousness.'' In the ultimate level, the subject reaches a point of no return wherein he has become one with the cosmic forces. At this point, however, we will be satisfied with a subject's perception of a bluer blue or a slight alteration in physical perspective, such as undulating walls or infinitely regressing vanishing points.

Volcano Scene. You are standing at the mouth of a large, inactive volcano. It is very cold. The landscape is barren and desolate. Dead, twisted trees are silhouetted against the bleak silver-gray sky. Hear the whistling of the wind. All is dank and sterile. You are looking into the mouth of the volcano. It appears interminably deep and dark. As you continue to gaze into the depths, you feel yourself falling. You are falling down the mouth of the volcano. Tumbling down an infinitely large funnel. Falling and falling. Suddenly you bounce as if on a trampoline. You have landed in a bed of giant mushrooms, bouncing up and down. Your body now remains still and you look around you. The walls are sheer, radiating a purple light like ultraviolet. You begin eating the mushroom. The mushroom changes the chemical composition of the fluid in your body. You urinate. The urine is *wet* and *heavy,* liquid, but heavy. Your body fluids have become deuterium or ''heavy water.'' Feel the wet pressure on urination. Now the walls are turning phosphorescent purple, orange, and charteuse. They are beginning to waver and ripple and flow.

You leave the mushroom bed, coming out into an underground field of alfalfa. The sky above is molten red and orange lava, swirling in a spiral. You begin eating the alfalfa sprouts. They form a silage in your stomach, creating much heat and gas. You leave the field, coming to a large lake. Removing your clothes, you glide into the water and float on your back. You begin expelling the *light, dry* gas from your stomach via your anus. The gas propels you through the water. Feel the bubbles and churning of the water. This brings you to the other side where you walk up on shore. You expel the alfalfa in *dry, heavy* pellets. You walk through a fringe of ferns into a crystal garden. There are mountains of diamonds, rubies, sapphires, and emeralds, all reflecting multicolored light in streaks like spotlights. Before you is a high amethyst cliff with a waterfall. The liquid comprising the waterfall is very volatile, like alcohol. You drink it. You urinate a fine, purple mist, *light* and *wet.* You are engulfed in purple.

Image XXI

Images XV, XVI, and XVII were concerned with the internalization of temperature and dryness/wetness in relation to the alimentary, circulatory, excretory, and skeletal systems. Images XVIII, XIX, and XX treated the internalization of pressure and dryness/wetness in relation to these four systems. The present scene begins a series of four that emphasizes the internalized recall of combinations of components of temperature and pressure in relation to these four systems. The alimentary system is in focus in the cantina scene. Sensory components to be recalled are hot-heavy, cold-heavy, cold-light, and hot-light.

This is also the first scene used to produce sexual arousal. If the presenting problem of the patient is sexual in nature, however, he will have been given sexually arousing imagery long before this. It is also interesting to note that several of the preceding images have on occasion aroused patients sexually. Each scene is responded to somewhat differently by each patient, so it is always wise to ask the patient what his feelings were during hypnosis when the session is over. Much valuable information can be evoked through the administration of these images. Consider the following examples.

A young woman presented the problem that she had no sex drive, which was frustrating her husband into overeating. The husband had been told by his therapist that his weight gain was due to his sexual frustration and he had therefore requested his wife to seek assistance. When doing Image III, the garden scene, she became very aroused sexually while imagining herself standing nude in front of the marble pool. This led to recall of past experiences when she had been aroused by reflections of herself in the mirror. These incidents had been repressed, but they were uncovered in this hypnotic image. She was then able to go on to discuss her ambivalent sexual feelings and the guilt they had produced in relation to her husband.

A middle aged woman complained she could not concentrate and would soon lose her job as a secretary if her memory did not improve. When doing Image V, the desert scene, she regressed in age to her childhood in Arizona. She wept long while recalling the happy family life she had had and expressed under hypnosis how much she missed her parents, who had died a year earlier. References to her parents' death up to this time in therapy had been very brief and were not affect-laden. During hypnotic relaxation, the feelings that she had previously denied were expressed and she was able to work them through. Memory and powers of concentration greatly improved once she could deal with her separation anxiety. All her energy before had been directed toward denying her feelings of loss; there was none left for her job.

Examples such as these in which the images trigger previously repressed memories and emotions are quite common generalizations, and the mechanism certainly is invaluable in therapy.

As already stated, there are three basic primary drives: hunger, thirst, and sex. While we certainly cannot satisfy these drives purely by psychological means, we can induce them psychologically. Hunger, thirst, and sexual arousal can be induced by recalling times when one was hungry, thirsty, or sexually aroused. Suggestions for hunger are given in Images III (garden), VII (farm), X (arctic), XV (mansion), XVIII (Shangri-La), XIX (chalk cliffs), and XX (volcano). Suggestions for thirst were given in Images V (desert), IX (pool), X (arctic), XV (Mansion), XVI (scuba-diving), XVII (picnic), XVIII (Shangri-La), and XX (chalk cliffs). The present scene deals with hunger, thirst, and sexual arousal.

The hypnobehavioral model can be used either to induce or increase these drives or to reduce them. One would, for example, wish to increase the respective drives in cases of underweight and impotence or sexual apathy. Drive reduction would be desired in cases of obesity, alcoholism, premature ejaculation, and nymphomania. More specific means of application are discussed later in this book.

Cantina Scene. You are riding a burro through the desert. It is beginning to get dark. It is dusk. The sand is golden yellow, the hills deep purple. There is a cool breeze blowing. In the distance you can see lights from a small village. You can hear guitars. See the orange light coming from the town. You ride into town, dismount in front of a cantina, tie up your burro. The sky is aflame with pink and crimson from the sunset. Large saguaro cacti are silhouetted against the red. You hear laughter emanating from the cantina. You are very hungry, having ridden all day. You walk inside. Everyone is shouting and laughing. Women are dancing in the center of the room. Drunken men are coaxing them on. You sit down at a table and are served hot tamales with red peppers. You take a large bite of the red pepper. It sets your system on fire. Sweat appears on your forehead. You take gulp after gulp of the hot tamales loaded with Tabasco sauce. They are *hot* and *heavy* in your stomach. You are sweating profusely. You take a large glass of cold water and swallow the ice cubes. They are *cold* and *heavy* in your stomach. Feel the cold radiating out from the center of your body. Next you drink a large glass of Coke. The carbonation is very strong and produces a *cold, light* gas in your stomach. You are next presented with a bubbling vessel of hot Alka-Seltzer, which you down in one gulp. Feel the *hot, light* bubbles in your stomach.

There are now two dancers in the middle of the floor, a young man and woman. They are moving lustily and seductively. The man/woman comes over to you and puts his/her hand on your thighs, massaging them. He/she puts his/her hand in your pants and begins manipulating your genitals. The music grows louder. The heat increases. You feel congestion, a build and surge. You climax! You get up and run out of the cantina into the cool night air. You cross the dirt road to a stable. You lie down in the hay looking at the desert sky, a heavy, throbbing sensation in your loins. A groggy feeling comes over you and you sleep.

Image XXII

This scene's subject matter is the internalized recall of combinations of the components of temperature and pressure relative to the circulatory system. The combinations are hot-light, cold-light, cold-heavy, hot-heavy.

Hayloft Scene. It is late afternoon. It is late summer. You are lying in a hayloft on the second floor of a barn. You are looking out at rolling hills where sheep are grazing. Some of them are winding their way homeward. The landscape is like a Rembrandt, dark siennas and browns and golds; deep, rich colors. Long, dark shadows are being thrown by the trees. The loft is golden from the dust of wheat and hay. The last rays of sunlight filter in, illuminating the grain. The smell of smoke from burning leaves is in the air. You are drinking hot brandy; a pleasant, soothing, wave of relaxation and intoxication is spreading over your body. The alcohol is mixing with your blood; it is becoming lighter and lighter: *hot* and *light* in your circulatory system. You leave the loft, sweat pouring down your forehead, your body drenched with perspiration. You climb down a wooden ladder to the ground floor.

You open a large metal door which leads into a walk-in freezer. Hunks of frozen meat are hanging from the ceiling. Your blood becomes *cool* and *light*. You sit down in the freezer. Your blood begins to thicken from the cold; it is *cold* and *heavy* in your system, forcing its way through your body. You get up and walk out of the freezer. The massive door slams behind you. You walk out of the barn to the back. Beef is being barbequed. Smell the beef. In a pit are piles of red-hot coals. You walk among these piles, finally reaching the center of the pit. You stand there in the heat and smoke, sweating profusely. More and more water evaporates from your system. Your blood becomes *heavy* and *hot,* pushing its way to the surface of your skin. You are hot and flushed. All the moisture is now gone from your body. You ignite. You become fire! [Thinking of yourself as fire will raise your subjective body temperature, just as thinking of yourself as ice will lower it.]

Image XXIII

The emphasis in this scene is the internalized recall of combinations of the components of temperature and pressure relative to the excretory system. Combinations employed are as follows: cold-light, hot-heavy, cold-heavy, hot-light.

Sand Pit Scene. "You are walking through a birch forest. It is winter. It is two o'clock in the afternoon. It is 40 degrees above zero and the snow is melting. Smell the wet earth. The sky is vivid blue and clear. There is not a sign of a cloud. The snow is stark white, the birch trees are stark white. You come to a sand pit. There are patches of exposed sand where the snow has melted. It is now getting cooler. The sky is turning silver grey. It begins to sleet. You open your mouth. The sleet goes into your mouth and out every opening in your body; it is *cold* and *light*. You walk through the sand pit into a forest of maple trees. Driven into the trees are tent stakes shaped like troughs down which is running maple sap into wooden buckets. You go over to one of the buckets and drink the thin, white, sweet liquid coming from the maple trees.

Now you continue walking through the woods till you come to a blazing fire of burning logs. There is a large black cauldron over the fire, filled with thick maple syrup. The air is heavy with the sweet smell of maple syrup. You drink the hot, heavy syrup. You feel the urge to urinate. The syrup comes out *hot* and *heavy*. Feel the heat and the pressure created by the syrup forcing its way through your urinary tract. It is now getting darker and darker. The sky is lead grey. You are sitting in front of the blazing crimson fire. It begins to hail large balls of ice. You open your mouth and swallow the hail. You expel balls of ice through every other opening in your body. They are *cold* and *heavy* coming through and out your excretory tracts. You move closer to the fire. Feel the intense heat on the front of your body. The heat melts the hail in your stomach turning it to steam. You urinate *hot, light* steam. Feel the release of pressure and heat. You feel like a pressure cooker.

Leaving the fire, you walk down a wooded path and come to a frozen pond. The ice is like glass. You walk over the slippery ice and sit down in the snow. You feel warm all over, the snow serving as insulation. A pleasant glowing feeling is stealing over your entire body.

Image XXIV

This scene focuses on the internalized recall of combinations of components of temperature and pressure relative to the skeletal system. Combinations are: hot-heavy, hot-light, cold-light, cold-heavy.

Mine Scene. "You are standing at the mouth of a mine shaft. There is a long tunnel running steeply downhill with a rail for boxcars. You get into a boxcar. It begins ever so slowly to move down the rail. Hear the rusty, grating sound of the wheels as they begin to turn after years of disuse. The car is gradually picking up momentum. There are flecks of sparkling gold dust in the black walls. The car is now racing downward like a roller coaster. Feel that sinking feeling in the pit of your stomach as the boxcar speeds downward at an ever-accelerating pace. It stops abruptly and you are hurled out into the air, landing in a vat of a liquid-gold-like substance. It is hot but does not burn. Your body absorbs the liquid. The surface of your bones takes in the metallic substance. Your dry bones feel *hot* and *heavy* weighing you down. The marrow of your bones dissolves. Now a blast of hot air comes down upon you from an air furnace above you. The hot air blows through your bones which are now hollow like tubes of aluminum, they are *hot* and *light*. The air is becoming cooler and cooler, turning frigid. Bones are now *cold* and *light*.

Suddenly from above there descends a glass elevator. You climb into the elevator. It starts its ascent, rapidly picking up speed. Millions of multicolored neon lights pass you by as you shoot upward—flashes and streaks of orange, magenta, chartreuse, amber, platinum, ice blue. The elevator stops. You are in a world of rainbow-colored snow. There are peaks and valleys of glistening snow in every color of the spectrum. Orange shading into red into purple into blue into aqua into green into chartreuse—swirls of brilliant sparkling ice and snow. You feel very light, a sense of weightlessness as you begin walking through the snow. You come to a round tundra or barren area the color of caramel. You stand in the center of this area. It begins to slowly revolve like a turntable on a record player, going round and round and round and round—picking up momentum, round and round and round and round, and it is spinning! The spinning motion creates heat, and the caramel turns to spun caramel cotton candy. You are enveloped in a sugary floss of cotton candy. Your body sinks into the candy and the centers of your bones fill with caramel becoming very heavy. The spinning stops, a chill sets in from the surrounding snow and your bones feel very *cold* and *heavy*. The spinning motion begins once again, a wave of warmth coming over you. You are hurled off the turntable, upward into space, drifting and floating, a beautiful, detached feeling coming over you as you coast through space in a state of complete tranquillity.

Image XXV

Although age regression may occur in any of the previous images, this is the first scene designed expressly for that purpose. During deeper states of age regression, the subject will exhibit the same speech patterns he did when he was the age he has regressed to in the image. The scene incorporates activities the subject would probably have engaged in as a child. The recall of these experiences will trigger other childhood associations and thoughts. The subject will then be thinking the same thoughts he did as a child. Affects associated with these thoughts will also be recalled and he will feel like a child again.

Age regression has been most commonly used to uncover traumatic or repressed data in the subject's past. Psychodynamically oriented therapists contend that this knowledge is necessary to understand the present. There are, however, other benefits to be derived from this phenomenon. Feeling younger gives the subject the perspective on life he had at that particular age. He sees the world through the eyes of a child again. Many of the good aspects of life that have since been tainted by negative experiences are once again apparent; the world looks fresh again. Many patients have remarked after age regression,

"I'd forgotten how beautiful the world used to be." The session involving age regression is a poignant illustration of the degree to which the world's beauty and ugliness is a function of our own perception. It is an impetus for changing and evaluating present values and our own outlook on life. Another example of the use of age regression in a more practical vein comes from a description of the following case:

> A young actor in his mid-20s came to one of us stating that he was doing the part of a man with the intelligence and mannerisms of a 12-year-old. He had tried observing 12-year-olds and emulating their mannerisms, but his attempts at being a child looked forced and contrived. Using age regression he was able to recall his own feelings and mannerisms at 12. He received rave reviews and the critics called his mannerisms and voice modifications remarkable.

The age regression image also places an emphasis on the recall of kinesthetic sensations like running, jumping, diving, and springing.

Autumn Scene. It is a beautiful autumn day. The smell of burning leaves is in the air. You are 12 years old. Remember what was on your mind in the fall of your 12th year. Who were your friends? What activities were you in? Who was your teacher? What classes were you taking? What did you look like? What did you want to be? What did you think about when you were 12? What did the world look like when you were 12? Think. Feel. Remember. You are standing on the edge of a forest. Leaves of orange, gold, and red are falling all around you. Hear them crunch beneath your feet. Squirrels are scurrying among the dry leaves.

On the edge of the forest is a pumpkin field. A light frost has turned the pumpkins brilliant orange and the vines a deep brown. Past the pumpkins are shocks of dry golden corn shaped like tepees. You walk through the pumpkins and corn shocks, coming to a tall haystack. Climb to the top of the hay stack. The sky is a glorious blue; big fluffy, white clouds roll in the sky. You can see over the fields to a farm house and a big, red barn. You jump up into the air . . . landing in the soft spongy hay. A golden dust goes up around you as you smell the sweet scent of hay. You climb again and jump again, sailing through the air into the hay.

You leave the haystack, coming to a chain of granite quarries. Jagged, high rocks surround pools of clear water, reflecting the orange and gold of the trees. You are standing high above the water on a rock. You take off your clothes. The sun is hot against your skin. You take a deep breath and dive. Feel the air rushing past your skin as you fall through the air and into the cold, clear water. It takes your breath away when you make contact with the water—cold and invigorating! Your whole body feels tingling and alive. You swim over to the rocks, feeling the water move against your body and lift yourself up on the warm granite. You bask nude in the sun on the hot rocks.

Now, you rise and walk along a stretch of granite, coming to another pool. In the center of the pool is a diving raft, a pontoon. You jump feet first into the water and swim to the raft. Climbing up on the raft you feel the warm sun against your wet body. You step onto the diving board. Feel the coarse burlap which covers the diving board under your feet. You walk to the end of the board and begin springing up and down. Feel the resiliency of the board beneath the weight of your body. You spring higher and higher, finally tucking your knees into your chest and somersaulting head over heels through the air and into the water. Your body shoots downward deeper and deeper and then scoops upward. You surface, taking a deep gulp of clean, fresh air. You swim to shore and lie on the warm granite, browning in the sun. You feel young, alive, vibrant, full of health and vigor.

The images described above can have a potent effect in altering responses at any level. The hypnobehavioral therapist will find that he can soon become proficient in the use of these images. He also will rapidly ascertain when and how and for what conditions the effects produced by these images are most useful. Initially the therapist can read the verbalizations aloud to the hypnotized patient. After this has been done a number of times, the therapist will find that he remembers even the minutest details of each image. Naturally, these must be presented with confidence and certainty so that the patient is not able to discern that the material is being read. To enable the patient to remember them, the images may be taped on a cassette during actual therapy for replay in private sessions.

Although in clinical sections in this book we indicate where these images can be used for specific problems, we rely on the ingenuity of the individual therapist for further applications. As mentioned, there is nothing new about fantasy evocation and imagery conditioning. What is new is that we have presented a standardized set of images to be used for eliciting some of the phenomena of hypnosis and also for alleviating specific problems. This offers a fertile field for research and we hope that other investigators will be stimulated to use these methods. Imagery technics have been used in psychiatry for over a century (Kosbab 1974). However, these technics have been employed primarily for diagnostic and exploratory purposes. They have not been explicitly structured to any degree, rather they have relied upon giving a simple, basic theme to a patient and allowing him to elaborate upon it. Rather than using imagery technics to find out about a patient, we are using them to produce definite effects that the patient can use himself for his own benefit. Also, previous imagery technics have focused heavily on the visual modality to the exclusion of the other four senses (Richardson 1969). Since the world comes to us through five senses not one, all senses must be developed, directed, and controlled. Our goal is to enable the patient to gain control over his sensory world, not merely to watch him free associate to a projective stimulus.

Imagery technics open up a resource which enables the therapist to better understand what goes on in the private or inner world of the patient. Also it allows for increased self-control and greater expression of his expectations. The wide range of imagery technics characterizing the above mentioned therapies point out the need for integration of the basic principles of fantasy and imagery into a new and practical form of psychotherapy. We fulfill this aim by presenting structured imagery conditioning and its relationship to affective states within the framework of the hypnobehavioral model.

REFERENCES

Rationale for the Hypnobehavioral Model

Abel, G. G. and Blanchard, E. B.: The role of fantasy in the treatment of sexual deviation. Arch. Gen. Psych., *30:*467, 1974.

Benson, H., Beary, J. F. and Carol, M. P.: The relaxation response. Psychiatry, *37:*37, 1974.

Cautela, J. R.: Covert conditioning in hypnotherapy. Internat. J. Clin. Exp. Hypn., *23:*15, 1975.

Conn, J. H.: Hypnosynthesis. Am. J. Clin. Hypn., *13:*208, 1971.

Hess, W. R.: Functional Organization of the Diencephalon. New York, Grune & Stratton, 1957.

Hilgard, J. R.: Imaginative involvement: Some characteristics of the highly hypnotizable and the non-hypnotizable. Internat. J. Clin. Exp. Hypn., *22:*138, 1974.

Jacobson, E.: Progressive Relaxation. Chicago, University of Chicago Press, 1938.

Klinger, E.: Structures and Functions of Fantasies. New York, John Wiley & Sons, 1971.

Kosbab, F. P.: Imagery techniques in psychiatry. Arch. Gen. Psych., *31:*283, 1974.

Kretschmer, E.: Gestufte aktiv hypnose. Zweigleisige standard-methode. *In* Handbuch der Neurosenlehre und Psychotherapie. Munich and Berlin, Urband Schwarzenberg, 1959.

Kroger, W. S.: Newer trends in psychosomatic medicine and hypnosis as related to Yoga. *In* Yogendra, S. (ed.): Yoga in Modern Life. Bombay, Yoga Institute, 1966a.

————: Comparative evaluation of Zen, Yoga, Judaism with Conditioning techniques and psychotherapy. Excerpta Medica Foundation Prac. Amsterdam, Sept. 1966b.

Leuner, H.: Guided affective imagery (GAI): A method of intensive psychotherapy. Am. J. Psychother., *23:*4, 1969.

O'Hare, C., *et al.:* An experiment in ''step wise'' mutual hypnosis and shared guided fantasy. Am. J. Clin. Hypn., *17:*239, 1975.

Progoff, I.: The Symbolic and the Real. New York, Julian Press, 1963.

Richardson, A.: Mental Imagery. New York, Springer, 1969.

Rochkind, M., and Conn, J. H.: Guided fantasy encounter. Am. J. Psychother., *27:*516, 1973.

Schultz, J. H., and Luthe, W.: Autogenic Training: A Physiologic Approach in Psychotherapy. New York, Grune & Stratton, 1950.

Tugender, H. S., and Ferinden, W. E.: An Introduction to Hypno-Operant Therapy. Orange, N.J., Power Publishers, Inc., 1972.

Fantasy Evocation in Conditioning

Assagioli, R.: Psychosynthesis: A manual of principles and techniques. New York, Hobbs, Dorman, 1965.

Bachélard, G.: On Poetic Imagination and Reverie. Indianapolis, Bobbs-Merrill, 1971.

Bandura, A.: Psychological Modeling. New York, Adline-Atherton, 1971.

Berne, E.: Games People Play. New York, Grove Press, 1964.

Cautela, J. R.: Covert sensitization. Psychological Reports. *20:*459, 1967.

Desoille, R.: Groupe d'études de rêve éveille dirigé en psychotherapie. Séance du 26 mai 1966. Bulletin de la Societe de recherches psychotherapiques de langue franciase, *4:*52, 1966.

Ellis, A.: The no cop-out theory. Psychology Today, *7:*56, 1973.

Frétigny, R., and Virel, A.: L'imagerie mentale. Geneva, Mont-Blanc, 1968.

Gottschalk, Louis A. Self-induced visual imagery, affect arousal, and autonomic correlates. Psychosomatics, *4:*166, 1974.

Happich, C.: Das Bildewusstein als anstelle psychischer Behandlung. Zentralblatt Psychotherapie, *5:*21–26, 1932.

Horowitz, M. J.: Image Formation and Cognition. New York, Appleton-Century-Crofts, 1970.

Jung, C. C.: Man and His Symbols. New York, Dell, 1968.

Klinger, E.: Structure and Function of Fantasy. New York, John Wiley & Sons, 1970.

Kosbab, F. P.: Symbolism, Self-experience and the deductic use of affective imagery in psychiatric training. Zeitschrift fur Psychotherapie und Medizinische Psychologie, *22:*210, 1972.

Kubie, L.: The use of induced hypnotic reveries in the recovery of repressed amnesic data. Bulletin of the Menninger Clinic, *7:*172, 1943.

Leuner, H.: Guided affective imagery (GAI): A method of intensive psychotherapy. Am. J. of Psychother., *23:*4, 1969.

McKellar, P.: Imagination and Thinking. New York, Basic Books, 1957.

Moreno, J. L.: Reflections on my method of group psychotherapy and psychodrama. *In* H. Greenwald (ed.): Active Psychotherapy. New York, Atherton, 1967.

Paivio, A.: Imagery and Verbal Processes. New York, Holt, Rinehart & Winston, 1971.

Perls, F., Goodman, P., and Hefferline, R.: Gestalt Therapy. New York, Dell, 1951.

Reyher, J.: Free imagery: An uncovering procedure. J. Clin. Psych., *19:*454, 1963.

Rigo, L. L.: La psicoterapia con il réve éveillé dirigé. Archivio de Psicologia, Neurologia e Psiquiatria, *25:*45, 1962.

Schultz, J. H., and Luthe, W.: Autogenie Training: A Physiologic Approach in Psychotherapy. New York, Grune & Stratton, 1959.

Segal, S. J. (ed.): Imagery: Current Cognitive Approaches. New York, Academic Press, 1971.

Sheehan, P.: The Function and Nature of Imagery. New York, Academic Press, 1972.

Shorr, J. E.: Psycho-imagination Therapy. New York, Intercontinental Medical Book Corporation, 1972.

Singer, J. L. Daydreaming. New York, Random House, 1966.

————: Imagery and daydream techniques employed in psychotherapy: Some practical and theoretical implications. *In* Spielberger, C. (ed.): The Control of Aggression and Violence. New York, Academic Press, 1971.

————: Imagery and Daydream Methods in Psychotherapy and Behavior Modification. New York, Academic Press, 1974.

Wolpe, J.: The Practice of Behavior Therapy. New York, Pergamon, 1969.

Zikmund, V.: Physiological correlates of visual imagery. *In* Sheehan, P. W. (ed.): The Function and Nature of Imagery. New York, Academic Press, 1972.

Imagery or Covert Conditioning

Abraham, H. A.: Hypnosis used in the treatment of somatic manifestations of a psychiatric disorder. Amer. J. Clin. Hypn., *10:*304, 1968.

Ascher, L. M., and Cautela, J. R.: Covert negative reinforcement: an experimental test. J. Behav. Ther. Exp. Psychiat., *3:*1, 1972.

Ashem, B., and Donner, L.: Covert sensitization with alcoholics: A controlled replication. Behav. Res. Ther., *6:*7, 1968.

Barlow, D. H., Leitenberg, H., and Agras, W. S.: Experimental control of sexual deviation through manipulation of the noxious scene in covert sensitization. J. Abnorm. Psychol., *74:*596, 1969.

Cautela, J. R.: Treatment of compulsive behavior by covert sensitization. Psychol. Rec., *16:*33, 1966.

————: Covert sensitization. Psychol. Rep., *20:*459, 1967.

————: Covert negative reinforcement. J. Behav. Ther. Exp. Psychiat., *1:*273, 1970.

————: Covert extinction. Behav. Ther., *2:*192, 1971.

Cautela, J. R., Steffen, J., and Wish, P.: Covert reinforcement: an experimental test. J. Clin. Consult. Psychol., [in press].

Cautela, J. R., Walsh, K., and Wish, P.: The use of covert reinforcement in the modification of attitudes toward the mentally retarded. J. Psychol., *77:*257, 1971.

Cautela, J. R., and Wisocki, P. A.: Covert sensitization for the treatment of sexual deviation. Psychol. Rec., *21:*37, 1971.

Davison, G. C.: Elimination of a sadistic fantasy by a client-controlled countyerconditioning technique: a case study. J. Abnorm. Psychol., *73:*84, 1968.

Feamster, J. F., and Brown, J. E.: Hypnotic aversion to alcohol: Three-year follow-up of one patient. Am. J. Clin. Hypn., *6:*164, 1963.

Flannery, R. B., Jr.: A laboratory analogue of two covert reinforcement procedures. J. Behav. Ther. Exp. Psychiat., *3:*171, 1972.

Hollander, M. B.: Excoriated acne controlled by post-hypnotic suggestion. Am. J. Clin. Hypn., *1:*122, 1958.

Krippner, S.: The use of hypnosis with elementary and secondary school children in a summer reading clinic. Amer. J. Clin. Hypn., *3:*261, 1966.

Kroger, W. S.: The conditioned reflex treatment of alcoholism. *J.A.M.A., 120:*8, 1942.

Krop, H., Calhoon, B., and Verrier, R.: Modification of the "self-concept" of emotionally disturbed children by covert reinforcement. Behav. Ther., *2:*201, 1971.

O'Hare, C., While, G., Macphillamy, D. and Lund, B.: Interaction of attitudes toward hypnosis and involvement in everyday imaginative activities on hypnotic susceptibility. Am. J. Clin. Hypn., *17:*247–252, 1975

Secter, I. I.: Tongue thrust and nail biting simultaneously treated during hypnosis: a case report. Am. J. Clin. Hypn., *4:*51, 1961.

Shibata, J.: Hypnotherapy of patients taking unbalanced diets. Am. J. Clin. Hypn., *10:*81, 1967.

Steffen, J.: Covert reinforcement with hospitalized patients. Paper presented at the meeting of the Ass. Adv. Behav. Ther., Washington, D.C., 1971.

Wagner, M. K., and Bragg, R. A.: Comparing behavior modification approaches to habit decrement—smoking. J. Consult. Clin. Psychol., *34:*258, 1970.

Wisocki, P. A.: An application of covert reinforcement to the treatment of test anxiety. (Unpublished doctoral dissertation, Boston College), 1971.

Wolberg, L. R.: Medical Hypnosis. 2 vols. New York, Grune & Stratton, 1948.

PART THREE

Sexual Problems

11

Impotence and Premature Ejaculation

Impotence and premature ejaculation are very common problems. Anxiety associated with this type of sexual inadequacy often contributes to obesity, smoking, alcoholism, and depressive reactions. It is strange, in view of its prevalence, that there is so little in the literature utilizing behavior modification for its treatment.

Most research in sexual areas has been directed to problems of deviance. Patients with deviant behavior seldom come in for treatment inasmuch as they seldom wish to change. Most patients with impotency and premature ejaculation, however, definitely want these inadequacies modified or alleviated. Since sexual inadequacy is not thoroughly covered in the literature or taught in many schools, colleges and universities, a detailed discussion of impotence and frigidity will be undertaken in separate chapters.

ETIOLOGIC FACTORS

Organic impotency, the causes of which are too numerous to discuss in this chapter, can be established or ruled out by the patient's history. Heredity, physical factors, and age are predisposing factors to impotency. In impotency, premature ejaculation, or both, it is important to determine whether dysfunction occurs during both intercourse and masturbation. If nocturnal emissions or morning erections occur, this is a good sign.

The psychological causes may be due to anxieties produced by faulty attitudes toward sex, fear of failure brought on by intense mental activity, preoccupation, fatigue, or repeated episodes of failure, hostility, and lack of affection. Abstinence also leads to impotence. One who thinks that sex is wicked, sinful, and dirty may equate his mate with his mother and become impotent.

However, some may be potent with other women and not with their mates (facultative impotency). Another common factor is a deep-seated need to reject the mate for various reasons. Other factors such as a too aggressive or experienced sex partner may intimidate the passive male. The female who shows revulsion for the sex act or has the desire to get it over in a hurry can render the male impotent. The psychophysiology of impotence, erection, and ejaculation have been described in detail by Masters and Johnson (1966, 1970).

TREATMENT

Drugs such as testosterone to increase the libido, anesthetic ointments to abolish sensitivity of the glans penis, and prostatic massage seem to help only by a placebo effect. Long-standing premature ejaculation often is refractory to all types of psychotherapy. Misconceptions and faulty attitudes toward sexual matters must be corrected by reeducation. The male who has occasional episodes of impotency requires only superficial psychotherapy.

BEHAVIOR MODIFICATION THERAPY

Behavior treatment in these areas has largely involved systematic desensitization technics aimed at reducing the anxiety associated with the approach to sexual intercourse (Cooper 1963, Kushner 1965, Wolpe 1958). Indirect treatment has also been attempted. The method used in indirect treatment has usually been to train the patient to be more assertive in social relationships, particularly with women (Lazarus 1965, Wolpe 1958). Kraft and Al-Issa (1968) reported on behavior therapy for premature ejaculation. They constructed a stimulus hierarchy of seven items related to increasing degrees of sexual intimacy. Systematic desensitization was carried out with the use of Brevital to produce relaxation during training. The patients were also given sexual instruction to overcome their inexperience. All of the patients were helped. On the other hand, Kockott et al. (1975) in a controlled study found that systematic desensitization when used alone for erectile impotency was only of limited therapeutic effect. They did not use hypnosis. However, the Masters and Johnson technic helped three-fourths of the unimproved patients.

Before discussing treatment of impotence and premature ejaculation using the hypnobehavioral model, comment will be made on the use of medication to aid relaxation or induction of hypnosis. In our experience, medication such as tranquilizers seldom deepens hypnotic relaxation as it dulls receptivity.

HYPNOTHERAPY

Strong reassurance under hypnosis often establishes confidence for the prematurist. Many forms of impotence have been treated by suggestion and directive hypnotherapy. The first step is to demonstrate that the patient is capable of an erection. Recovery is initiated once self-confidence is strengthened and reinforced. The constant preoccupation with the symptom can be reduced if an indifferent attitude over failure is suggested. Forcing the sex act is harmful, as it creates demand performance (Masters and Johnson 1970).

More recently, technics have been developed utilizing revivification of previous satisfactory sex contacts under autohypnosis. This effectively conditions the prematurist to perform adequately. In others, especially in those who have never had a satisfactory sex act, the premature ejaculation can be treated by reversing the fear of too-rapid ejaculation. The following posthypnotic suggestion is illustrative.

You might consider the possibility of being very concerned over *not* being able to ejaculate, regardless of how hard you try. The more you try, the more difficult it will be to lose your erection.

Time distortion can be employed to prevent premature ejaculation in a good subject by making him think that he has maintained an erection for a relatively long time. During deep hypnosis, it is suggested that 30 seconds of subjective or experiential time *will seem* like two minutes of world, clock, or chronologic time. Thus, if the prematurist maintains an erection for only 30 seconds, he will think that he had it for 2 minutes. This positive hallucination by which time is expanded can be reinforced through further posthypnotic suggestions. Time expansion rapidly helps to restore confidence in the patient's staying ability (Kroger 1958). The wife should be apprised of the situation and told to praise her husband's ability. Naturally, the husband is not made aware of this.

Such hypnotic technics can be incorporated into supportive psychotherapy. If the patient feels accepted by the therapist, he will wittingly or unwittingly reveal the basis for the fears and anxieties associated with his sexual inadequacy. Guidance directed toward breaking up the harmful patterns enables the individual to react to his problem in a healthier manner. Extensive probing and attempting to exhume the past is fruitless, especially for the impotent male who has never been erectively and ejaculatively potent. What should be emphasized is that the spiritual relationship between the partners influences the performance of the sex act (Kroger 1972).

We have found the *symptom-utilization* technics described by Erickson (1973) very helpful in treating impotence. Here the patient's own patterns of response and behavior, including the actual illness can more readily be controlled. *Symptom-substitution* is also a valuable technic. Through posthypnotic suggestion (PHS) one can "trade up" to other sexual behaviors depending on the effects desired. For example, substituting vaginal sensations during penile friction for those derived from masturbatory ones is trading up. In *symptom-transformation,* inadequate feelings associated with impotence can be transferred by appropriate PHS to other behaviors such as physical exercise involving aggressiveness in sports. Dissolution of sexual inhibitions often can occur by transformation of the symptom into healthier outlets without directly attacking the character of the symptom itself. In *symptom-amelioration* the premature ejaculation is reduced. Also it can be deliberately *worsened* by PHS on the supposition that if this is done volitionally by the patient, it eventually can be *improved* by his own efforts. These technics differ from mere symptom removal by direct suggestion.

Other adjuvant technics that help the prematurist involve the PHS that he can concentrate on contracting the anal spincter during intercourse. This is an old Yoga method for preventing premature ejaculation. Still another valuable technic lost to modern medicine is having the patient thrust his tongue back to slow down rapid breathing which increases his excitation level. Pavlovians have long recognized that when two conditioned reflexes reach cortical awareness, one must be dominant and the other recessive or inhibitory. This is dependent on the mental set at the time of the stimulus. This is *the principle of dominant effect:* attaching a strong emotion to a suggestion makes it more effective.

Any one or all of these technics can be used in various combinations in conjunction with imposing a double bind. In a typical double-bind maneuver, a patient's insistence that he cannot help himself to stop his faulty behavior is *accepted* rather than opposed. He is directed in such a way that he must stop behaving in the way he does or stop denying that he is behaving in that way!

THE STANDARD HYPNOBEHAVIORAL MODEL

Before training in hypnosis and desensitization is begun, it is necessary to talk at length with the parties involved. Feelings of hostility and guilt must be explored. A male cannot expect to be potent with a female he would rather clobber than have sexual relations with, and vice versa. Also, many sexual problems stem from ignorance, so the therapist must serve as an instructor in sexual technics.

IMAGERY CONDITIONING

Use of our standard images as described in Chapter 10 deepen hypnosis, aid sensory recall, and produce greater revivification. Mastery of these relaxing images potentiates sexual imagery or recall of past gratifying sexual experiences. Since the standard images described in Chapter 10 are used to deepen the hypnosis they, therefore, always precede the specifically tailored images and suggestions given the patient. This procedure is also used in the practice sessions at home and generally for all other disorders to be described in the following pages. The subject induces autohypnosis, recalls a given standard relaxing image, then utilizes the suggestions and imagery related to his particular problem. It should be noted, however, that even the standard images are often changed and embellished to meet the needs of individual subjects. Certain preferred smells, tastes, and sounds are often substituted in these scenes to make them more pleasurable and thus more relaxing for the subject.

Since impotency and premature ejaculation are often seen together, the patient must learn to turn on the response of sexual arousal by recalling or creating a sexually arousing image. This requires the combination of feeling sensual components in the genital area associated with an erection. To prevent premature ejaculation, he must turn off or decrease his level of sexual arousal at a given moment to prevent too rapid a climax.

There are also many cases when impotency and premature ejaculation occur in isolation. To modify premature ejaculation, the subject is taught to lower his level of sexual excitement by focusing his attention on a subject of a nonsexual nature. Often he flashes on a particular relaxing image to lower arousal level. The substitute subject matter should be pleasant, but neutral in regard to its potential for eliciting sexual arousal. In order to achieve orgasm, the individual involved must be thinking thoughts of a sexual nature. No amount of genital manual manipulation will lead to a climax if it is not coupled with the appropriate thoughts. During intercourse, the patient may switch from neutral to sexual images several times to maintain an appropriate balance of arousal great enough to maintain an erection but reduced enough to delay orgasm. Since the prematurist is usually easily excited he seldom needs to recall or create sexual imagery per se. When he wishes to start building arousal levels again after diverting his attention from the sex act, he simply focuses his attention back on what he is doing and the present situation is sexually arousing enough to produce orgasm without any additional imagery. The following case illustrates a standard treatment of a case of premature ejaculation.

D.L., age 45, came to therapy primarily at the request of his wife who was not being satisfied sexually. He was a rather shy, undemonstrative professional man always on a time schedule. Mrs. L. said she felt that even sex was on schedule and she was always aware of a time pressure. She also was concerned about whether her husband felt uncomfortable around women as he never flirted, was seldom aroused spontaneously sexually, and was tight mouthed when kissing.

Mr. and Mrs. L. were seen conjointly for the first two sessions. Various sexual positions and technics were discussed to determine which were mutually compatible. Most importantly, avenues of communication were opened so that this topic was no longer taboo and could be discussed freely.

Mr. L. was trained in hypnosis and taught to recall appropriate sexually neutral images when he felt himself coming to a premature climax. This method was very successful, and he was finally able to maintain an erection for 10 to 15 minutes, lasting longer than his wife. Another technic used with him which worked well was to have him hypnotically produce an image of himself maintaining an erection for a long period of time. It is always good to have the subject imagine himself in a vivid hypnotic image performing whatever act it is he wishes to achieve.

It was also suggested that he attempt to climax more than once during each sexual encounter. This is often suggested in cases of premature ejaculation. A sort of deal or understanding is developed between the sex partners of ''one for you and one for me.'' The male has his climax, withdraws, repenetrates, and thrusts until his partner is satisfied. The premature ejaculator is usually able to delay a climax longer the second time around. This type of arrangement prevents the female from developing hostility and anger when the male climaxes prematurely. If she knows she will still be satisfied later, his first climax is met with enthusiasm rather than hostility. Often women become cold or angry in response to the male's premature climax and thus turn off and intimidate a sex partner who would otherwise have gone on to a second, longer lasting erection.

D.L. also had cluster headaches. Mrs. L. reported that her husband would say, "Wait till tonight," in regard to sex and then he would develop a cluster headache. Through the development of glove anesthesia and the resolution of his sexual problems, the headaches disappeared.

Mrs. L. was also trained in hypnotic relaxation and sensory recall. She was preoccupied with the question, "Will he make it?" during intercourse. This overconcern with whether her husband would last long enough for her to achieve satisfaction was causing her much anxiety during intercourse. She was taught to focus attention on sexual imagery of an arousing nature during intercourse and thus divert her mind from rumination over fear of poor performance by her partner. This change in her also reduced anxiety in Mr. L. caused by pressure to perform.

Mrs. L. stated that there was not enough foreplay. This is a common criticism among women; they need more time to stimulate their sexual desires. She said that she would like at least 20 minutes of foreplay and D.L.'s behavior was changed in this respect. One of the greatest gains from the therapy, Mrs. L. felt, was that it had opened up communication. She now felt much closer to her husband. In her own words she said, "If you can communicate, you can copulate."

While many of these technics may seem quite mechanical at first, they soon become natural and reflexive. Once subjects become desensitized to discussing sexual matters, progress is rapid. In cases of impotence, the male is not able to control his level of sexual arousal sufficiently to obtain or maintain an erection. Most often, the patient either has difficulty achieving an erection but is fine once he has, or he is potent during foreplay but loses it during penetration. Hypnobehavioral technics designed for increasing potency involve sexual imagery and recall of combinations of feeling components constituting the sensation of an erection.

SCENE VISUALIZATION IN IMPOTENCE

Sexual imagery is of two primary types: 1. Recall of a specific sexually arousing experience. 2. Creation of an erotic image. Both types have their advantages and, therefore, both types of images are used consecutively in therapy. Recall of a specific situation has the advantage of drawing on an actual memory. The fact that such an experience really occurred means that it is possible to reexperience it in its entirety without the vagueness or ambiguity one might encounter in a scene one has created. Also, in recalling a specific situation, one also recalls the sexual affect one experienced during that time. In creating a new image, one is sexually aroused in the present by the image but does not recall sexual arousal as he does when an actual experience is revivified. The advantage in creating an image is that one can combine the best parts of various sexual experiences or fantasies to create a scene, which if experienced in reality would in all probability be the best sexual experience the subject would ever have. The disadvantage is that the subject who has had no prior sexual experience cannot recall the sensation of an erection in association with this scene.

A modification that can be used with either recalled or created sexual images is to have the subject imagine the scene as if it had been filmed and is now being projected on a screen. This is particularly effective when working with a hierarchy, and when the subject is having difficulty bridging one of the steps. He is told that he is to imagine that he had a very pleasurable and successful sexual experience. It has been filmed, he has seen the film before, and he is now merely viewing it again. There is no way he can fail in this image because it is a *fait accompli*. Imaginal review of this scene reinforces the patient's self-concept as a virile and potent man. He literally sees himself as potent and begins to think of himself as such. One failure can make a person feel inadequate and trigger a chain of failures. Likewise, making a person feel adequate through reconditioning of his self-image can trigger a chain of successes. The subject changes his self-image by seeing himself in hypnosis as the person he wants to be. He is using a classical conditioning paradigm, pairing the image of himself with the desired potency. In time when he thinks of himself, he will think of potency behavior.

While it is necessary to focus on sexually arousing imagery to achieve orgasm, it is possible to physically produce an erection through control over vasoconstriction. As the erection is produced by the engorgement of the organ with blood, the transference of blood to that area can be accomplished by recalling the component sensations associated with an erection. The two primary components are heat and pressure. It will be recalled that when vasocongestion occurs, it produces warmth and that detumescence results in inability to respond to sensory input. The transfer or recall of warmth and pressure in the genital area produces congestion and thus an erection. Congestion also produces pressure. Thus the recall or transference of pressure to the genital area also produces an erection. As emphasized, recall and transference of warmth and pressure to the genital area should be combined with imagery of a sexually arousing nature in the production of an erection.

This same procedure is used to produce sexual arousal in the female. The male as well as the female orgasm is a combination of the basic sensational components heat, pressure, and wetness. In Image II (mountain cabin) subjects are given the suggestion of a prickling, almost itching-like sensation in the thighs due to the intense heat produced from the fireplace. They are, in effect, recalling the basic component of heat in the genital area, which actually serves to produce sexual arousal. In Image IX (pool) the patient learns to transfer heat so that he may recall it in the area where it is most often experienced (the easiest place) and then transfer it to the genital area. The office procedure involves transferring heat from the hand to the cheek with instructions to practice at home transferring heat from the hand to the genital area.

Recall of heat and pressure in the genital area is introduced in Image V (desert). Here the patient is instructed to feel the ever-increasing pressure as he is covered layer by layer with a warm blanket of sand. The components of heat and wetness are combined in a transfer to the genital area in Image X (Arctic). Most patients are able to achieve good enough recall and transfer of heat, pressure, and wetness by the tenth session to produce strong sexual arousal. If erection and orgasm are still not achieved by this time, Images XIII to XXIV are employed to further develop and intensify the patient's facility for production of these three basic sensations in the genital area. The images are given as written in Chapter 10 with the addition of an instruction to transfer the appropriate sensory components to the genital area.

Images I (beach), VIII (jungle), and XXII (hayloft) are excellent for producing dissociation. The feeling of detachment derived from dissociation, when combined with erotic imagery, produces a feeling of uninhibited sexual abandon. There is no thought of past failures or fear of future ones. The patient dissociates himself from his apprehension and inhibition and lives only for the present sexual experience. Patients are instructed to use dissociation during actual intercourse once it has been developed hypnotically through practice. As mentioned earlier, any of the 25 images listed in this book may be eroticized by adding a sexual partner and situation pleasing to the patient.

Images VI (space) and VII (farm) are used for time expansion in patients with sexual inadequacy to prolong and heighten the periods of actual sexual arousal. These time distortion images are also used to develop time expansion in the prematurist so that he believes his arousal is lasting longer than it actually is, which will build his self confidence. In time, this illusion of long maintenance will become a reality.

Image XXV (autumn) employs age regression and may be effectively used to regress a patient back to a time when his sex drive was strongest, such as shortly after puberty. Control over the recall of these past strong sexual urges keeps them on tap for present use.

Image III (garden) is very useful in the treatment of the sexually inadequate patient as it develops their sensitivity to taste, touch, and smell. These three senses evolutionarily have been the primary elicitors of sexual arousal. Faulty conditioning has caused many people to inhibit these senses and feel that tastes and smells associated with the sex act are ''dirty.'' All five senses are capable of eliciting arousal and therefore all five senses should be used and developed to attain a strong and balanced sexual response.

While all images progressively serve to develop concentration, deepen relaxation, and gain greater control over basic physiological processes, some are outstanding for treatment of certain problems and will be highlighted in the appropriate chapters that follow. The following case illustrates further the standard methods used in the treatment of impotency:

T. M., age 28, had not had intercourse until he was 25. His parents had been overprotective, and he now felt much hostility toward them. First sexual encounters had been relatively successful, but the last three experiences had ended in his losing his erection on penetration. He thus had not attempted intercourse in over a year. If able to penetrate, he could maintain an erection without any problems. He also voiced considerable dissatisfaction with personal relationships, stating he did not know what love was as he had never experienced it. Dating had been restricted to very prudish girls, and he started feeling more comfortable with girls who resisted his sexual advances. He was very threatened by sexually aggressive females.

[In order to achieve a sexually arousing image, it is necessary to discuss with the patient what situations arouse him sexually. Sometimes the therapist may create a sexually arousing image for the patient based on this discussion. One should also discuss masturbatory fantasies, as these are important sources of information for clues to components to be used in the construction of sexual images.] This patient reported that photos of nude females and literary descriptions of intercourse were arousing to him. He was then instructed to attempt the elicitation of sexual arousal in hypnosis by recalling these photos and passages. He practiced this for a week.

Next, he was asked to age-regress under hypnosis to specific successful sexual experiences and recall them with as much physical and affective detail as possible. With practice, the recall of these experiences became so vivid that very fine details such as the room temperature and dialogue were readily remembered. He was then asked to modify his scene visualization by manually manipulating himself during the imagined intercourse. Imagery became even more vivid, he reported, if he undulated up and down during the imagery. Finally he manipulated himself to climax in conjunction with muscular undulations during imaginal intercourse in scene recall. [Pairing of actual orgasms and manual stimulation with the imagery made the imagery on future recall more potent. When the subject uses imagery recall during actual sex play, it must be as potent as possible in order for an erection to be maintained.]

From the beginning of therapy, T.M. had been dating a very proper and sexually reserved girl. At this point in treatment he reported they had their first kiss. Next, the sexual imagery was preceded by the posthypnotic suggestion for time expansion. The standard time expansion images had been given earlier. [The purpose of interjecting time expansion is to prolong periods of sexual arousal, so that the erection can be stronger and last longer.] Sexual imagery at this point was very vivid, and the patient was able to get strong erections. He reported, ''The orgasm in hypnosis was most intense . . . so much pressure it was almost frightening.''

The next step in treatment was instructing the patient to recall the sensation of heat in the genital area. A prop was used for this. T.M. was told to put a hot wet towel between his legs, remove it, and then immediately recall the sensation. [This type of practice of immediate recall can be done at either a normal or a hypnotic level. A prop is also often used in the recall of numbness in glove anesthesia. In this case the subject holds an ice cube in his hand, producing numbness, removes the cube, and then immediately recalls that sensation.] The next strategy was to pair the heat from the wet towel with the recall of the sexual experiences. Pairing the heat with the sexual imagery made future imagery stronger.

The patient's next scene in his hierarchy of sexual images was to see himself penetrating a girl from one of his past experiences several times in the same session. He reported experiencing no anxiety from imaginal initial penetration, but that he did experience some anxiety on repenetration. A subhierarchy was then constructed around this step. This hierarchy was engineered on the premise that the reason for repenetration would have bearing on the amount of anxiety experienced. The following reasons for repenetration would elicit an increasing amount of anxiety on a scale from 1 to 5; the first reason would cause little if any anxiety on repenetration, the last reason would make repenetration quite traumatic: (1) The subject has a stiff erection, but withdraws because he is close to climaxing. (2) The subject has a stiff erection, but he withdraws in order to change positions. (3) The subject has a stiff erection, but he slips out due to making too long a thrust. (4) There is a semi-erection, and he withdraws to change position. (5) There is a semi-erection, and he slips out because it is not hard enough. The patient was told to desensitize himself to each of these situations in rank order by pairing hypnotic relaxation with the image of the particular situation.

The relationship with his girl was progressing well at this point. They had undressed to the waist and embraced. He had also discussed the fact with her that he had some sexual problems although he was not specific as to their nature. This discussion made him more comfortable and eased his performance anxiety in that she would no longer expect him to be vigorous sexually at this point in their relationship. In their next sexual encounter, they undressed each other down to their underpants.

The subject's next sexual image was a change from recall of sex with previous sexual partners to the creation of a sexual scene with his present girl. These images were projections into the imagined future—pseudo-orientation in time. These consisted of activities one step ahead of what was actually transpiring in his present affair. In this image he was to see himself and his girl fondling each other's genitals while still wearing their underpants. The following image was to see themselves nude and embracing.

At this point in their affair they both stripped and embraced. He reported that she was more affectionate and intimate emotionally and physically. He manually manipulated her to orgasm but she did not do the same to him. He lost his erection while pressing his penis against her labia. A woman had never manually manipulated him to climax, and he was disgusted by the idea of cunnilingus.

In his next image he was to see himself holding his penis next to her genital area. Following this image he was able to maintain an erection over a two-hour period and engage in several minor penetrations of the labia. She performed fellatio on him but not to orgasm, although he reported a very strong erection and he felt he could penetrate.

(It is important to note here that he has a contract with the therapist not to attempt penetration at this time regardless of how potent he feels. He is to take stepwise progressions both imaginally and in practice. As mentioned above, small, controlled, successive approximations—shaping the desired behavior—to the desired goal is the key to all problems of this nature.)

The next image involved his making successively deeper penetrations. Then the image constituted his penetrating once, making a rapid thrust, and withdrawing. At this point their sexual encounters were lasting entire weekends. He said, "I think I love her." He reported being aroused all the time they were near and she had asked him, "Are you always like this?" referring to his erection.

The patient was still reporting some anxiety on penetration in his image, so he was told to see the image as if it were on a screen. The mental set was that he had had sex with his girl, it was great, and he was potent throughout. Now he was to view it on film. This method deconditioned anxiety to this image. The patient reported that he had performed cunnilingus and enjoyed it. Also, he had had a climax on genital-to-genital friction. This was his first climax with a girl in over a year.

Intensified practice in the recall and transfer of heat was the next focus of instruction. In addition to the washcloth prop for immediate recall, the patient was instructed to use red peppers and later niacin for the production of heat so that practice could be undertaken in immediate recall of these recent sensations. On the next visit, the patient reported a successful penetration and climax. He said he hoped the therapist was not angry about his breaking the contract and penetrating—the therapist wasn't.

The dictum for treating impotence is that confidence begets confidence and nothing succeeds like success. Positive reinforcement and hypnobehavioral technics can salvage many cases of intractable impotence. Whenever possible, it is advisable to treat the husband and wife as a unit. The character of the marital relationship greatly influences potency. The effort is not easy; it may be tedious; but it is rewarding.

REFERENCES

Cooper, A. J.: A case of fetishism and impotence treated by behavior therapy. Brit. J. Psychiat., *109:*649, 1963.

Erickson, M. H.: Psychotherapy achieved by a reversal of the neurotic processes in a case of ejaculatio precox. Amer. J. Clin. Hypn., *15:*217, 1973.

Kockott, G., Dittmar, F. and Nusselt, L.: Systematic desensitization of erectile impotence: A controlled study. Arch. Sexual Behavior., *4:*493, 1975.

Kraft, T. and Al-Issa, I.: The use of methohexitone sodium in the systematic desensitization of premature ejaculation. Brit. J. Psychiat., *114:*351, 1968.

Kroger, W. S.: Psychosomatic aspects of frigidity & impotence. Int. Rec. of Med. *171:*469, 1958.

Kushner, M.: The reduction of a long-standing fetish by means of aversive conditioning. *In* Ullmann, L. P. and Krasner, L. (ed.): Case Studies in Behavior Modification, pp. 243–245. New York, Holt, Rinehart, & Winston, 1965.

Lazarus, A. A.: The treatment of a sexually inadequate man. *In* Ullmann, L. P., and Krasner, L. (eds.): Case Studies in Behavior Modification. New York, Holt, Rinehart, & Winston, 1965.

Masters, W. H. and Johnson, V. E.: Human Sexual Response. Boston, Little, Brown, 1966.

————: Human Sexual Inadequacy. Boston, Little, Brown, 1970.

Wolpe, J.: Psychotherapy by Reciprocal Inhibition. Stanford, Stanford Univer. Press, 1958.

SUGGESTED READINGS

Kaplan, H. S. et al.: Group treatment of premature ejaculation. Arch. Sex. Behav., *3:*443, 1974.

Kroger, W. S.: Comprehensive approach to ecclesiogenic neuroses. J. Sex Research, *5:*2, 1969.

————: Help the impotent male to help himself. Consultant. *10:*37–39, 1972.

12

Frigidity, Dyspareunia, and Vaginismus

This section will be directed to some of the newer concepts for treating nonorgasmic females (primary orgasmic dysfunction) some of whom have dyspareunia and vaginismus. Before discussing various therapeutic modalities, it should be emphasized that the majority of sexual dysfunctions are due to psychological factors. One of the most important of these is the failure to understand the meaningfulness of the sexual relationship, especially as it relates to each of the partner's unrealistic expectations (Caplan and Black 1974). Others include the kind of early psychosexual development, prior sexual experiences, parental and religious attitudes, and many other complex factors. Still another cause is the sexual revolution with its new ideas, such as "sex for sex's sake." The latter has resulted in the "mechanization of sex" emphasized by the popular media, current sex manuals, and the writings of certain sex "researchers." As a result, many females in our culture now have performance anxiety, which inevitably leads to sexual dysfunction (Masters and Johnson 1970). The latter often is related to the relentless pursuit of an orgasm, popularly referred to as "the big O," thus making sex an athletic contest of sorts. Strong demands for subjective sensual satisfactions often can negate reciprocal gratification and lead to inability to share pleasures with one another. These prevent the sexual union from being a truly fulfilling and rewarding experience. In such situations, females naturally seldom experience orgasmic responses despite the degree of male sexual prowess, superb technics, and acrobatic performances.

Some of the recent studies on human sexuality emphasizing positions, technics, and erotic zones as well as those measuring sexual experiences in terms of orgasm only reinforce the great coital myth, namely, that enjoyable sex interactions should always be accompanied by climaxes of one type or another. We

150

are not implying that women should be deprived of orgasm, rather we are disturbed by increasing numbers who, because they do not have orgasms of any type, think that they are "frigid" (a pejorative term) and cease to enjoy sex. Sexual responses are as variegated as the thumb print; the real question is how much the female likes her mate and whether she enjoys the sex act. Some mature women who have a happy marriage are nonorgasmic and yet derive considerable satisfaction from sexual congress with a loving mate. We all have seen marriages break down in spite of the female being fully orgasmic. Often she will remark "it's the only thing we had between us."

Thus, before any kind of treatment can be successful there should be an emotional commitment, a creative interchange, and mutuality of goals. These involve self-esteem, concern for and responsibility for the emotional needs, actions, and feelings of the partner as well as good communication between them. As mentioned in the preceding chapter, satisfying copulation on a long-term basis requires good communication. Presence of the above factors invariably leads to love in its most esthetic sense. We shall discuss the confusion and differences between love and sex below. Sexual intimacy is a unique and complicated state and cannot be developed to its fullest potential merely through mechanical sex alone or the degree of arousal per se.

CLASSIFICATION OF VARIOUS TYPES OF FRIGIDITY

We shall briefly discuss the classification of the various kinds of "frigidity." The term has been used to denote the degree of pleasurable sensitivity ranging from painful aversion to complete insensitivity. Personal attitudes range from desire to get it over with in a hurry to mounting excitement and hope for contact of long duration (Kroger 1962). These women have a great deal of anxiety and tension; some have the pelvic congestion-hyperemia syndrome. Pseudofrigidity involves aplasias, hypoplasias, organic lesions of the genitals, incorrect technics, and complete sexual ignorance. Postpartum frigidity is commonly noted in multiparae. There is a large number of so-called facultative cases, in which orgasm is possible with one partner and not another.

The psychoanalytic concept that the female who can only have clitoral orgasm rather than a vaginal one (Bergler and Kroger 1954) is immature and presumptively frigid is no longer accepted as valid. Subjective experiences are not related to personality, nor always to the site of stimulation (Glenn and Kaplan 1968). It has been postulated that the physiologic basis of different sites for origin of orgasmic sensations originate in the clitoris (Marmor 1954, Sherfey 1966, Masters and Johnson 1970). Though this may be true, we see many females who prefer vaginal orgasms over clitoral orgasms.

Masters and Johnson classify women who are frigid with all partners as having primary orgasmic dysfunction. Those unresponsive only with certain partners are classified as having secondary orgasmic dysfunction. Both may involve nonconsummation, vaginismus due to dyspareunia, and orgasmic incompetency. However, none of these classifications embraces all the relevant factors involved, thus making it difficult to evaluate the effectiveness of various therapies. Faulk (1973) compares nonconsummation to a phobic state and orgasmic inadequacy to a state of hysterical dissociation. This comparison theoretically indicates that better results would be obtained with hypnobehavioral therapy, desensitization, and retraining by sensory-imagery conditioning. This, too, has been our experience as we have long since given up the *classical* psychodynamic approach for treatment of frigidity (Kroger 1974).

THE INITIAL VISIT

In handling sexually inhibited patients, the following ten points are important.

1. They usually are extremely susceptible to chance remarks. Therefore, we say very little and seldom ask intimate questions or probe deeply into personal matters until good rapport is present.

2. We try to be warm, sympathetic, and reassuring because as soon as the patient senses that we are interested in solving her troubles, she will develop more confidence in us.

3. When taking the history, we try to avoid a dictatorial or know-it-all pontificating attitude. The patient has not come for a lesson in morality.

4. We do not make premature pronouncements such as "You are going to be all right." This can result in a hostile ex-patient as she wonders, "How can the therapist know this until he hears my whole story and finds out what's wrong with me?"

5. We always avoid such platitudinous remarks as, "A lot of people are worse off than you." These are fighting words to the sexually inhibited patient because now she really has to prove the validity of her inadequacy.

6. Before obtaining sexual information, one must be sure that he can discuss any type of sexual behavior objectively without overt signs of disgust, disapproval, or condemnation irrespective of what the patient says.

7. We find it almost always necessary to interview other members of the family with the couple's permission. Important are the kinds of interpersonal relationships within the family, friends, and members of the opposite sex. Not to be omitted are the patient's religious scruples and upbringing. All of this information provides clues for the *raison d'être* of the patient's sexual dysfunctions and brings them into sharp focus.

8. The problem often requires the couple to be treated as a unit. Conjoint interviewing is invariably more effective than a single dyadic situation, as there are three sides to every story.

9. Better data can be obtained if the room is soundproof, free from interruptions, and, most important, if the patient knows that the information revealed is confidential.

10. After the history is taken, we often ask "Is there anything else you would like to add?" Often pertinent data will readily be revealed.

CURRENT METHODS OF THERAPY

Before discussing our therapeutic approach we shall briefly discuss the pioneering work of Masters and Johnson (1966) and their treatment of orgasmic dysfunctions. In essence, their approach utilizes a relearning process for the partners. They tell one another precisely which erotic stimuli they enjoy and which are not satisfactory. This frees the partners from the taboos and anxieties that interfere with complete sexual gratification.

After detailed examination of the sexual make-up, problems, and causes, the couple are instructed to engage in "sensate focus" exercises through exploratory bodily contacts. The wife indicates exactly where and how her husband's touch affords the greatest pleasure. The genitals initially are deliberately *avoided*. This creates a nondemand situation during which the wife can enjoy physical contacts without developing performance anxiety. This follows the law of reverse effect described in Chapter 3. The therapist then gives a specific sequence of instructions to think and feel erotically, and throughout the subsequent therapy the couple discuss their respective progress with each of the two co-therapists, a male and female. This is done singly at first and then with all four together. The next phase consists of *genital* touching during which the wife continues to inform her mate of the zones she likes and dislikes to be stimulated. When couples are ready emotionally and physically, intercourse is advised with the wife in the female-superior position. The goal is exploration of her erotic responses rather than having an orgasm. Coitus is then tried in different positions until the optimum one is discovered. This trial and error experimentation is directed to mutual enjoyment. It is emphasized that sex cannot be willed or forced to fit preconceived notions. Masters and Johnson have a high percentage of cures as long as the partners cooperate. After treating 510 *selected* dysfunctional couples, a 5-year follow-up showed 80-per cent success with a relapse rate of only 5 per cent.

Kaplan (1974), utilizing a single-therapist approach, relieved about 70 per cent of orgasmic dysfunctions in *carefully screened patients who did not* have psychopathology. The data were not controlled and were based only on impressions. She warns that these technics offer no panacea, nor can they cure a deep-seated neurosis or a marriage that has failed. Her approach is more concerned with whether or not arousal occurs and whether orgasmic response is achieved.

The defenses the couple have built up against adequate sexual responses are also elicited. These usually are based on either hostility or performance anxiety, and they must be differentiated and resolved. The therapeutic goals are limited to relief of the orgasmic incompetency. Specific sexual experiences that the couple find enjoyable are suggested, and these are carried out when they are alone. Such experiences provide erotic stimulation and reassurance that a behavioral change will occur.

Sarrel and Sarrel (1974) recently reported a 90-per-cent success rate using the Masters-Johnson technics. They acknowledge that the significance of the fee, screening out and selecting applicants unlikely to respond, the couple's being treated away from home, and the treatment's specific and nonspecific stressors are important variables to be evaluated. Also, the double-dyadic or co-therapist model does not appear to be any more effective than a single sex therapist utilizing conjoint therapy. Other variables to be considered in the dual-sex team-therapy approach are the current avalanche of publicity accorded the method leading to a favorable mental set, the prestige suggestion resulting from the manner by which the referral is made, and the shrinelike transference aspects. Also, where group therapy is utilized the emotional contagion involved in group dynamics is a potent factor. Finally, because of the emphasis on orgasm, one might ask if the "pluralism of sexuality" has replaced love.

Another unique and very effective goal-limited approach is described in the preliminary report of Lo Piccolo and Lobitz (1972), who demonstrated that a program of directed masturbation could be very effective in primary orgasmic dysfunction (P.O.D.). They stress the normality of masturbation; that it can lead to a more intense orgasmic response and that the act itself with its associated vasocongestion enhances the capacity for future sexual connections. Their nine-step program of systematic desensitization consists of a sequence of specific masturbation-related activities assigned to the patient, who practices the procedures at home. These assignments range from brief visual exploration of her nude body to 45-minute sessions of manual stimulation of the genital area. The method is used in conjunction with a treatment program modeled after the procedures of Masters and Johnson. Lo Piccolo and Lobitz recognized that most individuals are negatively conditioned toward masturbation and that if these faulty attitudes are reversed, gratifying results ensue, particularly when the husband's cooperation can be elicited. The latter should always be advised what the spouse is doing, why and how she should masturbate. The crucial first orgasm could occur at any step of the program or even in response to nonmasturbatory stimulation.

Kohlenberg (1974), using similar technics, observed a successful outcome with P.O.D. He noted that as directed masturbation becomes an arousing experience and as sexually arousing locations were discovered, the sexual interaction improved as these were integrated into the conjoint relationship. The directed masturbation was used only as an adjunctive technic to a comprehensive counseling program which particularly emphasized communication. We have utilized directed masturbation combined with hypnobehavioral therapy with some modicum of success.

HYPNOBEHAVIORAL THERAPY

The following case is illustrative of our hypnobehavioral model:

"Bobbie Sue," aged 24, was born in a sort of *Tobacco Road* environment. At an early age nearly all male members of her family had intercourse with her. She stated, "Ever since I can remember, whenever a man came close to me, up went my legs." Rather than marry at 15, she ran away to a large metropolitan city and drifted into prostitution. At no time was she ever able, by any means, to have any type of orgasm, vaginal or clitoral. She abhorred sex and stated, "I'm completely numb down there."

After several years, she decided to "get out of the racket," and thought of marrying a well-to-do man who had been one of her "johns." She felt a great deal of affection—not love—for him because he represented respectability, kindness, and security. She was wholly unable to achieve any pleasurable response by either mouth-genital contacts or any type of sexual relationships even under the influence of bennies, pot, or liquor. Because of these circumstances, she felt it was not fair to marry him. Her fiance was aware of her past, but not of her extreme frigidity. She was an attractive and intelligent girl who, despite her limited formal education, maintained an outer veneer of sophistication.

She was taught hypnosis, autohypnosis, dehypnotization, and sensory imagery conditioning for warmth and cold, which she was able to achieve. However, she was unable to recall the slightest pleasurable response from any type of coital activity. Sexual relations only revived disgusting thoughts and feelings, which were to be expected because of her past. Had she at least had the slightest gratification from the vaginal, rectal, or clitoral zones, we might have utilized and transferred these sensations as we have been able to do in other intractable cases of frigidity.

It was sensed that under her worldly facade there was a frightened, immature, childlike person wholly incapable of really understanding love in a spiritual sense. Most marital breakdowns occur because of this lack of the noblest of human emotions.

She tearfully stated, "Every time I make love to my boy-friend, I have to fake a climax."

I said, "You mean every time you have sex—not love. There is a difference, you know."

"What do you mean, Doctor?"

"Well, there are roughly four types of love. There is the 'I love me' type, which is seen in the child. This is in reality self-love. The child says, 'This is my toy; give me this.' If he doesn't get it, he gets angry, hostile, and frustrated and cries or stomps off. There are adults who have never really emerged from this 'I love me' period of their sexual development. They are totally incapable of giving in any type of sustaining relationship. Naturally, from the start, such a selfish relationship is destined to failure.

"The next type is projected self-love: 'I love me—in you.' This, too, is 'I love me', as those people worship themselves in another person—for instance, in hero adulation. When the person realizes he is loved only for *who* he is, not for *what* he is, he turns cold. This type, too, cannot have any degree of durability. It is all incoming, not outgoing.

"The third type of love is characterized by romantic love, based chiefly upon sex. It is the same type of unrealistic, romantic love portrayed in movies, novels, and popular songs. After the initial thrill of the honeymoon, the chill sets in. The sexual ardor and intoxication then begin to wear off and the quarreling begins. Eventually these frustrated individuals discover that they have nothing in common except self-love. Since neither is willing to give to the other, neither receives.

"The last type of love, by far the rarest, may be noted in some old married couples celebrating their golden wedding anniversaries. They are just as much in love as when they first met. They did not enter this relationship thinking of what they were going to get, but rather what they were going to give to each other! Their sexual responses may have been weak at first, but increased in intensity as they developed respect, mutuality of interests, sacrifice, tolerance, and most important, the spiritual merger of one personality into another in a long-time affectional relationship.

"Briefly, we can say that sex is the passionate interest in another body, and love is the passionate interest in another personality! Just as whisky and soda are found together, so are love and sex found together, but they are separate ingredients.

"Now, Bobby Sue, where do you fit into these four groups?"

She remarked, "I guess mostly in the first one, and perhaps in the second one."

[We have found this differentiation of love useful in treating the majority of our sexual disturbances due to strong religious scruples—ecclesiogenic neuroses—(Kroger 1969), and in marital and sexual disorders.]

Bobby Sue fortunately was a somnambulist who went into deep hypnosis. Amnesia was engrafted for the intense revulsion she had toward previous sexual relationships. During autohypnosis, she began to feel erectile sensations of a mild nature in her nipples. Later she was given PHS to transfer these to the clitoral area by directed masturbation. She was advised to abstain from all sexual relationships. Sixteen sessions over an interval of 4 months were required before she noted pleasurable sexual responses in the genital area as the result of the sensory imagery conditioning.

She was asked to bring in a list of her aversive reactions with the most vexing ones at the top and the lesser ones at the bottom, until she could talk about sex, men, her fiance, and other situations which in the past had mobilized revulsion toward sexual activities. [We discussed this hierarchy of feelings under hypnosis as described by Wolpe (1958).] This desensitization procedure apparently helped, since with each successful imagogic experience a subtle change occurred in her thoughts of sexual activities. It was recommended that the affirmations to attain sexual gratification should be used under autohypnosis at least six times a day.

Her interests were channelled by PHS into reading fine books consistent with her intellectual stature. She became involved in art lessons and discovered she had considerable talent, and actually sold some paintings. The effects of such *symptom-substitution* helped diminish her guilt, tension, and anxiety. Through *symptom-transformation,* her aversions were transferred by appropriate PHS to behaviors such as loathing the idea of financially exploiting men, buying expensive clothes, jewelry, and other material things which the "gold-digger" pursues in the vain hope that such compensatory pursuits will alleviate her dissatisfactions. Developing her skills at art helped to shore up her weak ego and diminish her feelings of inferiority. Symptom-utilization was employed to allow her the type of sexual response *she desired* to achieve. All of these hypnotic technics increased her motivation and faith in the therapist. Thus far therapy had been directed strictly to the symptomatic level. The remaining sessions were used to make her more aware of her masochistic "injustice collecting." She realized that if she made the most of her disappointments and even pursued them as she had done in the past, there was no danger of running out of the raw materials of misery.

We find that many sexually inhibited patients, especially those with frigidity and impotence, are afflicted with the "pleasure-in-displeasure" syndrome— psychic masochism. It is almost a universal phenomenon. Psychic masochists are constantly creating situations wherein they are rejected and humiliated. Then, unaware that they have engineered their disappointment, they turn on their self-provoked "enemy" in righteous indignation. After each juicy defeat they revel in self-pity. They never seem to learn from the beating they are willing to take in disappointing life situations. As a result, they continue to commit the same offenses—a repetition-compulsion pattern. Such persons obviously are willing to pay a high rate of psychic interest on their original masochistic capital (Bergler and Kroger 1954).

Having a rich experience with psychic masochists, we had little trouble working through the basis for Bobby Sue's neurotic needs at hypnotic levels. She developed a more wholesome attitude toward males, and lost the desire to obtain revenge on them. She realized that giving of herself meant receiving pleasurable sexual responses. It was emphasized that sex was not a "mutual gratitude society" into which two people enter to negate their respective neuroses. Rather, it was all-important to enter the relationship on the basis of mature love.

This was not very difficult since she had developed a positive transference relationship toward the therapist, and it took little effort to "switch" this affection to her husband-to-be. As she improved, the amnesia for unpleasant past sexual experiences was "held on leash" until she could face her earlier and adult experiences with more equanimity.

The early milestones of her psychosexual development were so distorted, it was felt it would be hopeless to try to work through these areas. It was more feasible to rely on emphasizing positive and healthy aspects of her personality that had been brought out.

Bobby Sue married a year later and made a successful adjustment. She never conceived, and this undoubtedly allowed her to give undivided love to her husband.

In the above case we did not hesitate to use psychodynamic technics and concepts within the context of the hypnobehavioral model.

Ward (1975) notes that hypnoanalysis serves as a helpful modality in the treatment of frigidity. The pertinent psychodynamic factors of five patients are illustrative. The first, a young married woman who could not achieve an orgasm, responded after underlying guilt was brought out. The second patient complained that she was frigid, but was found to have an underlying immature personality disorder with a death fear. The third, a married woman of 34, complained of not being able to climax with her husband in intercourse; she was found to have a guilt syndrome that had started at age 5. The fourth patient stated that she was always depressed and felt bogged down. This young woman also had a guilt-punishment problem; she was punishing herself for adolescent sex with her brother. The fifth patient, an unmarried woman of 25, wanted to correct her sexual problems before marriage. She had a definite hate for and fear of men, and surgery had given her an escape through pain. Once the patient understood how her problems developed, she was then receptive to positive suggestion, which enabled her to permanently eradicate the symptoms.

THE PREORGASMIC FEMALE

The female who enjoys intercourse but is simply unable to achieve a climax is not termed frigid but "pre-orgasmic." In such cases the woman enjoys intercourse but is unable to have either a clitorial or vaginal orgasm as a function of her partner's thrusting inside her even though he may be able to bring her to climax manually or by cunnilingus. The following is a description of such a case.

F.L., aged 25, was an attractive, intelligent young woman who was unable to reach a climax with her husband. He was the only man she had ever had sex with. She had had one climax with him before they were married, but had not been sexually satisfied in the last 5 years. One source of worry to her was that intercourse would hurt her bladder. At the age of 19 she had chronic cystitis, and ever since said she could "feel" her bladder during intercourse.

She and her husband had been sleeping in night clothes and having sex in the dark. They were severely limiting their tactile and visual sensations. Also, they were not fully experiencing each other sensually. She was instructed to sleep nude and have intercourse by candlelight. Her husband was instructed to touch her breasts and clitoris as she had reported these areas to be particularly erogenous. Previously he had engaged in very little foreplay.

In structuring her sexual imagery, it was found that she was sexually aroused by hot water and pornographic movies and books. Her past pattern had been to think about her job and housework during intercourse. She was told to focus on sexually arousing thoughts during intercourse whether it be the erotic aspects of the present situation or the recall or creation of another sexually arousing condition. Sexual recall of an actual experience involved hypnotic reliving of her first and only successful sexual encounter with her husband. After considerable questioning by the therapist, a detailed description of the event was obtained and recounted back to the subject in hypnosis as follows:

"It is 5 years ago. You are parked in a car with your lover. You haven't seen him in a week and you have missed him very much. You have been driving 45 minutes and are now stopped on an isolated road in a wooded area. It's getting dark. Soft music is playing on the radio. The night is clear, the sky is filled with stars. You can smell the light fragrance of pine in the air. There is a gentle breeze. He looks into your eyes and says, 'I love you.' His voice is soft and low. He puts his lips to yours. They are warm and soft—feel his breathing. Feel the touch of his hand on your face, on your breasts, on your thighs. Your breathing is becoming heavy, feel the blood rushing to the surface of your skin. Your body feels warm and pulsating. He unbuttons your blouse, removes your bra, removes his shirt, holds his warm body against yours.''

"Feel the warmth and texture of his skin. He pulls down your skirt. You feel his hands slipping under your pants, massaging your thighs, rubbing your clitoris. Feel the heat, the pressure, the congestion. He lies upon you, unzipping his trousers. You can feel his penis, hot and throbbing against your clitoris. He penetrates. He thrusts. Every thrust he makes, you get warmer and warmer, every thrust he makes the pressure builds, every thrust he makes you get closer and closer. There is an explosion, a release of energy. Every muscle, every fiber in your body spasms and quivers. You are overwhelmed by an electrifying wave of emotion. Now he jerks, crys out, tenses, and releases his semen inside of you. You hold each other close, feel the body heat, the sweat, the smell of his hair, the touch of his skin. You have a complete sense of satisfaction, of total release. You gaze at the stars in each other's arms . . . you drift . . . you float . . . you dream.''

These scenes must be experienced using sensory recall of all five senses. They must be vivid. While it is easier to just tell the patient to make up her own scene (Kosbab 1974) she usually will not understand just how exact the imagery must be constructed. The therapist should therefore, at least for the first sexual image, help the patient in its construction and feed it back to her once before she practices recalling it on her own. Many females have reached multiple orgasms in hypnosis using vivid sexual imagery without any manual manipulation whatever.

The second form of sexual imagery used with F.L. was having her recall scenes from books which she found sexually stimulating. Throughout therapy, she read many erotic books and was able to come up with a new scene almost every week. [While the therapist's recounting and discussion of sexual images may be embarrassing to the patient at first, it serves to decondition her to topics of a sexual nature. Sexual inhibition is usually found in conditions of sexual inadequacy and it must be dealt with not by avoiding sexual topics but by gradually bringing them up and examining them. We have all read sexually erotic literary passages, so we need not describe one here.]

After several weeks of practice with the sexual imagery, the patient reported, "I felt like a woman this week. We made love three times and I felt close to coming about five times each session": Her sex drive was greatly improved and her imagery was very vivid. She stated, "Using hypnotic sexual imagery I induced a feeling of warmth, pressure, rapid beating of the heart, felt really excited—felt like I was going to climax in hypnosis—I come closer every time.''

She was next instructed to practice masturbating to climax so that she could benefit from the immediate hypnotic recall of an orgasm. The more recent the experience the easier it is to recall. She also began giving herself a direct autohypnotic suggestion, "It's all right, I won't get a bladder infection from intercourse.''

The next erotic image constituted the creation of a scene involving her husband. The scene was designed primarily by the patient and was as follows: "You are arriving at a large hotel in the mountains. It's freezing cold. You are shivering. You walk into the lobby. There is a blazing fire. Feel the warmth from the fire, smell the smoke from the burning pine logs. A bellboy approaches you (this is her husband) dressed in dark blue. He asks to take your bags. You follow him up the stairs to the right, feeling a strong physical attraction. Notice the way he moves, the sound of his voice. Every step you take you feel more and more sexually aroused. On the third floor he puts your bags down in your room, stands there looking at you. Your eyes meet; you want him; he comes closer to kiss you. You say, "Leave." He goes. You remove your coat. There is a warm fire. You sit in front of it, feeling its warmth—your body is very warm—tingling. Suddenly there is a knock on the door. Your heart pounds. You answer it; it's the bellboy. You ask, "What do you want?" He pleads, "Please let me in, I've wanted you from the moment I saw you."

He embraces you, you resist, but he overpowers you, pulling you down on the carpet in front of the fireplace. Feel his body heaving and sighing over yours. Feel his wet lips against yours. He takes off your clothes and penetrates your vagina. You feel him hard and pulsating inside you. A flood of heat rushes to your thighs. There is a rhythmic rise in pressure and he climaxes at the same time as you. You tear at his body and then lie silent looking into his eyes. He says, 'I love you.' You remain there together, with the warmth from the fire, the howling outside of the wind, the smell of the pine logs."

These scenes should be even further embellished with sensory descriptions of taste, smell, touch, color, and sound. Certain portions may need elaboration, and the therapist must pause appropriately during the description so that the subject has time to construct the image. The subject is always encouraged to add to the image to make it as vivid and real as possible. The images may also be taped for future use by the patient.

In addition to recalling or creating sexual images, it is very important that the subject focus during intercourse on the most sensually exciting aspects of intercourse. The hypnotic training in sensory recall makes the patient more aware of her present situation, giving her a heightened sensitivity and receptivity. During intercourse itself, she must focus on the touch of her partner's skin, the smell of his hair, the sound of his voice, the movements of his body, and other associated sensory inputs.

Also, any of the standard relaxing images may be used. For example, in Image I (beach scene), she meets a man on the beach, they go to the sand dune, make love, look at the sunset, and finally feel themselves as one with the universe. Most of these images are fine settings for a love affair. After practicing the beach scene with the added sexual imagery, F.L. reported feeling a tingling wave coming over her which she could feel all over her body.

Progress was being made in that she was now initiating sex more regularly. The male often feels rejected and unwanted if it is always he who makes the first sexual advances. He feels that he is the only one who wants sex and, therefore, may be inhibited during the sex act. His inhibition leads to his partner's feeling inhibited and thus not being satisfied.

F.L. next described a new sexual image that she was using. In it she is living in a new house and is out in the garden. She is wearing shorts and a low-necked blouse and is observed by the man next door. That night, this man (actually her husband) breaks into the house and rapes her in her sleep. She had mentioned before that she was most aroused when wakened from sleep. In addition to being a good image for eliciting sexual arousal in the patient it provided a clue as to why her sex drive was not as great as she wished. In her image she had made herself very appealing, but in reality she said she felt very unattractive due to a recent weight gain. This gain was not even noticed by the therapist but it was having a marked effect on the patient. It is quite common to find that if a person does not feel sexually attractive he will have less desire for sex; he represses his sexual urges rather than risk rejection. While her husband still found her attractive, she was rejecting herself as a sexually attractive person. She was thus instructed to begin dieting. Several of the technics described in the chapter on obesity were used.

Achieving orgasm is a function of the mind; no amount of physical stimulation will produce a climax if the sex partner is not thinking sexually arousing thoughts during intercourse. If one's mind is on things of a nonsexual nature, such as doing the gardening or when will the act be over, a climax will not be possible. The patient mentioned above rehearsed the recall of sexually arousing imagery and revivified it during intercourse. Concentration was directed to the feel of her husband's body against hers and the warmth of his caress rather than to her concern about whether she could climax or not. Focusing on the recall of erotic imagery and present sexual feelings prevents the occurence of any fear or anxiety-provoking thoughts. Once control over one's sexual imagery is attained, sexual functioning can be rewarding.

Time expansion was now added to the sexual image to prolong the feeling of sexual arousal. F.L. was told: "For every minute of friction you receive during the sex act, it will *seem like five minutes!* Thus, whenever she required prolonged contact and her husband had premature ejaculation, time was "lengthened" to give each of them greater satisfaction. [One also may employ hallucinated pseudo-orientation in time wherein sexually arousing fantasied material of an erotic nature can be suggested through posthypnotic suggestions so that the desired experiences will occur in the future. Naturally, these adjuncts must be combined with treatment of the overall relationship (Kroger 1963).]

It was also suggested at this time that she purchase a vibrator to enable her to achieve a vaginal climax so that she could work on the recall of this particular sensation. It took several weeks of getting used to the idea, but she purchased one. Later, she used the vibrator in conjunction with time expansion and sexual imagery to strengthen the imagery for when it would be used alone. Pairing the sensations from the vibrator with the sexual imagery associated with projected fantasies also increased her level of sexual arousal.

She next reported that she was becoming a much better sex partner and that intercourse was more stimulating. She described performing fellatio on her husband and swallowing the semen. She stated, "I felt part of him." As her prowess increased, however, she became more dissatisfied with her husband's performance. She stated, "He just lies there with his eyes closed . . . he can't stand to be touched . . . he's so ticklish . . . he makes no movements or noise. The only evidence I have that he is sexually excited is his erection." It was evident from this revelation that it was time for another talk with the husband. His wife's feelings were discussed and he agreed that he needed to be more responsive and allow himself to be touched. Half of the excitement of sexual arousal is feeling and caressing the other person. F.L. had also mentioned that he had been exerting too much pressure on her clitoris during manual manipulation and this was discussed with him.

F.L. was now having multiple orgasms with the vibrator and hypnotic sexual imagery. In addition, she had been persuaded to use a lubricant for lessening stinging sensations on penetration. It was interesting that she felt a stinging sensation and fear for her bladder only when her husband penetrated her, but not when she used the vibrator. This discrepancy was pointed out to her and after some probing it became evident that there was considerable hostility toward the husband. During her bladder infection 5 years ago, he had forced her to have intercourse against her will and she had blamed him for the condition's increasing severity. The stinging sensation in the bladder area decreased considerably after this discussion.

Next, the patient was instructed to use the vibrator to strengthen her sex drive before intercourse. The next step was using the vibrator during intercourse. She expected her husband to object, but to her surprise he was happy to comply. Watching her have multiple orgasms via the vibrator was very stimulating to him. She had now lost considerable weight and her libidinous drives increased. His sexual performance improved rapidly. Also, he was letting her touch him, and being verbally as well as physically responsive.

The patient reported being more sensitive after a climax from the vibrator. She was now having multiple orgasms. The following plan was devised: He would penetrate her, thrust for a couple of minutes, then withdraw. She would then insert the vibrator until she had one climax. He would then repenetrate, delaying his climax for a period of time reasonably long enough for her to reach a climax. Whether she climaxed from him or not, she would then reinsert the vibrator again, having another climax. It was hoped that seeing her climax again would energize the husband enough to attempt a second climax on his part. Up to this point he had never had more than one climax a night.

After several weeks of practice with this procedure she reported reaching orgasm as a function of his thrusting inside her after she had already climaxed once with the vibrator. At a later date the vibrator was deleted completely and she was still able to climax vaginally. However on occasion they continued using the vibrator because they liked it. (As long as there is something that arouses a person sexually, it should be used in the interest of the patient if it is beneficial.) To this date, nevertheless, the husband is still capable of but one climax a night.

The following is an example of a case where a rather unusual sexually arousing stimulus was used to attract a wife more to her husband.

M.W. was a very childlike, immature woman, aged 34, who complained that while she felt very loving toward her husband, she was pre-orgasmic. While doing Image III (garden scene), she reported feeling sexually aroused at the sight of herself nude by the pool. She then remembered several dreams of an erotic nature in which men were watching her nude or stripping. The more alluring she felt, the greater was her sex drive. In her next sexual image, she was told to imagine that men were watching her swim nude in a marble pool. She was then instructed to see herself nude having sex with her husband as if on a screen with an audience of men. She used this image during actual intercourse and was able to attain her first orgasm with her husband. Whether it is "normal" or not hardly seems relevant. What is relevant is that she is now being sexually satisfied by her husband.

VAGINISMUS

Vaginismus is an involuntary spasm or locking of the vaginal muscles during attempted intercourse. Mere examination or touch of the labia produces spasm and pain. In others, the tip of the examining finger cannot be inserted. The perineal muscles may constrict up to the vaginal fornices. Contractions of the adductor muscles of the thighs, the "pillars of virginity" are accompanied by arching of the back in the opisthotonos. The symptom may be either primary or secondary, of organic or psychogenic origin, or both. Though the cause is usually psychogenic, there are many physical factors responsible for vaginismus that always should be ruled out by a history and examination. These include congenital malformations of the vagina, introital damage or infection, retroversion of the uterus, pelvic tumor, polyps, cervictis, a tender episiotomy scar, kraurosis vulvae, a urethral caruncle, and other conditions.

There are many speculative theories, too numerous to mention, regarding the etiology of vaginismus (Kroger and Freed 1951). It often is a symptom of faulty psychosexual development. The vaginismus frequently may be associated with religious orthodoxy. The guilty fears usually evolve into a phobic reaction to penetration of the vagina by a foreign object. Psychogenic vaginismus also can be due to fear of pregnancy, especially in the presence of strong religious taboos against contraception. The vaginismus can be either a defense against intercourse or a way of showing hostility to the mate by passive resistance. The prognosis is ominous if the vaginismus is a reaction to an impotent husband or one suffering from premature ejaculation. Here repeated anticipation of orgasm and subsequent frustration leads to pelvic congestion and pain, resulting in an insidious onset of protective vaginismus. In such cases, therapy should be directed toward the husband. However, even though marital incompatibility is present, the vaginismus often is ignored by the partners.

Physically, the levators constrict the lower third of the vaginal barrel, totally preventing penetration. Attempts to penetrate set up an involuntary conditioned reflex. The severe vaginal spasm leads the patient to think she is too small. The husband of such females usually are timid and need assurance that they are not beasts. Their problems and attitudes should be restructured to restore confidence. A rigid hymen often is blamed as the culprit for vaginismus, but surgical defloration is seldom successful and often can worsen the condition.

There are three approaches to treatment. The first is education by sexual counseling for correction of faulty misconceptions. The second is behavior therapy for removal of the maladaptive behavior (J. P. Brady 1966). The behavior approach can be combined with a psychodynamic frame of reference as promulgated by Abraham (1956). The third is systematic desensitization or counterconditioning as described by Wolpe (1969) or hypnodesensitization as developed by Fuchs, et al. (1973). The latter approach described below involves the principles of deconditioning "in vivo" (actually using vaginal dilators of increasing size to penetrate) or "in vitro" (imagery or visualization of penetration by the penis) under hypnotic relaxation. We shall discuss this method below.

DYSPAREUNIA

Organic factors usually account for dyspareunia. Even a minimal somatic factor initiates a phobic reaction or negative attitude toward intercourse. If the painful intercourse persists after detection and therapy of the local cause, then psychological intervention is necessary. Common organic causes are the bruised remains of the hymenal ring, stenotic scars from injury to vaginal canal or a faulty episiotomy, clitoral adhesions, enlargement of base of the Bartholin glands and postmenopausal atrophy. Other causes are infections such as trichomoniasis and fungal vaginitis, sensitivity to intravaginal contraceptives, rubber prophylactics, and douching preparations. Insufficient lubrication due to lack of interest in the partner, fear of pregnancy, and sexual inadequacy have been implicated. It can occur in multiparae as well as in virgins. Pain at the back of the vagina may be due to acute cervicitis, endometriosis, parametritis and third degree retroflexion of the uterus. Occasionally the uterine contractions accompanying intense orgasm can cause dyspareunia. Though rare, some females who have orgasmic dysfunction use their lack of sexual desires to conceal an embarrassing somatic condition such as vulvovaginitis. Also, a few women with dyspareunia are not sexually cold. They can achieve orgasm from interfemoral intercourse, petting, and cunnilinguus. As in the case of vaginismus, a thorough gynecological examination is always mandatory before instituting psychotherapy.

THERAPY

Therapy depends on the nature of the emotional conflict. Most cases require joint psychotherapy for establishing a warm, giving, and loving relationship. Need for adequate preliminary foreplay is usually indicated to arouse the wife by erotic measures in order to obtain maximum lubrication and relaxation. Premature ejaculation and impotency are frequently present in the male. Sex for the female becomes repugnant, disgusting, and painful. One should advise the husband that haste makes waste. Many couples are naive and require education in the fundamental technics of coitus and preliminary sex play.

Adjunctive measures are lubricating jelly with 5-per-cent novocaine; a pillow below the buttocks facilitates penetration; flexion of the thighs on the abdomen often prevents spasm of the perineal and adductor muscles. Initially, penetration should be performed slowly and friction avoided until the vaginal canal relaxes. The latter is facilitated by endearing phrases, utmost tenderness in the sex act, and other manifestations of love.

In the simpler cases, superficial psychotherapy can be effectively utilized by the gynecologist. However, many women are resistant to even expert psychiatric therapy. Some present a myriad of presenting psychosomatic symptoms. Others blame their husbands (often rightly) and use numerous rationalizations for their refusal to have sexual relations. Because of the secondary gain values from the illness, some females maintain their symptom to avoid all sex contacts with their mate. Those who remain persistent virgins after marriage have deep-seated psychopathology. Many of this type are suicidal and psychotic.

HYPNOTHERAPY AND DESENSITIZATION

It is imperative to treat the interpersonal relationship between husband and wife, not only the symptom-complex. The authors have had a high recovery rate with hypnotic relaxation, and imagery conditioning accompanied by systematic desensitization. We remember three cases where the conjugal union was never consummated and which culminated in divorce. Another couple lived together for 40 years, and rather than face the problem, adopted three children.

Fuchs, et al. (1973) used hypnodesensitization under hypnosis according to "in vivo" and "in vitro" technics described above. Both require relaxation, which induces a feeling of safety so that the patient can be confronted with the lowest item on a hierarchy of anxiety-provoking stimuli. Each item is presented until eventually even the strongest of the anxiety-evoking stimuli fails to evoke any degree of anxiety in the patient. In the "in vitro" technic, the patient is asked to imagine the stimuli. In the "in vivo" technic, real stimuli such as graduated Hegar dilators substitute for the imaginary ones.

To augment the desensitization process, hypnosis was used not only for its relaxation effect, but also because the imagery and visualization of the suggested material becomes more vivid and realistic. The "in vitro" methods were used by the psychiatric department and the "in vivo" by the gynecology department; both were in contact with each other. The investigators emphasize that the first step should be done "in vitro." If not successful, then the "in vivo" technic should be used by gynecologists trained in medical hypnosis.

This chapter has presented some of the methodological technics and current developments in contemporary scientific hypnosis and behavioral modification with fantasy evocation for treating sexual dysfunctions. It is evident that systematic desensitization, imagery conditioning, and the various types of symptom manipulation are valuable procedures when utilized in a hypnobehavioral model.

We deliberately chose to describe the handling of several difficult cases of frigidity by hypnodesensitization and fantasy evocation. There are drawbacks—not all patients are amenable. It is hard work for the patient and therapist, and these methods are not a panacea. In proper hands, used wisely and judiciously, the methods described can benefit other patients with sexual dysfunctions, particularly those with dyspareunia and vaginismus. We hope that other investigators will validate, refine, and improve upon the various approaches described in this chapter.

REFERENCES

Abraham, H.: Contribution to the problem of female sexuality. Internat. J. Psychoanal., *37*:351, 1956.

Brady, J. P.: Brevital-relaxation treatment of frigidity. Behav. Res. Therap., *4*:71, 1966.

Bergler, E., and Kroger, W. S.: Kinseys' Myth of Female Sexuality. New York, Grune & Stratton, 1954.

Caplan, H. W., and Black, R. A.: Unrealistic sexual expectations. Medical Aspects of Human Sexuality, *8*:8, 1974.

Faulk, M.: "Frigidity" a critical review. Arch. of Sexual Behavior., *2*:257, 1973.

Fuchs, K. et al.: Hypno-desensitization therapy of vaginismus: Part I. "in vitro" method. Part II. "in vivo" method. Int. J. Clin Exp. Hypn., *20*:144, 1973.

Glenn, J., and Kaplan, E. H.: The types of orgasm in women. J. Psychoanal. Ass., *16*:549, 1968.

Kaplan, H.: New Sexual Therapy. New York, Quadrangle Press, 1974.

Kohlenberg, R. J.: Directed masturbation and the treatment of primary orgasmic dysfunction. Arch. Sexual Behavior., *3*:349, 1974.

Kosbab, F.: Imagery techniques in psychiatry. Arch. Gen. Psychiat., *31*:283, 1974.

Kroger, W. S.: Psychosomatic Obstetrics, Gynecology and Endocrinology, Springfield, Charles C Thomas, 1962.

————: Clinical and Experimental Hypnosis. Philadelphia, J. B. Lippincott, 1963.

————: Comprehensive approach to ecclesiogenic neurosis. J. Sex Research, *1*:2, 1969.

————: Hypno-Desensitization Therapy for Frigidity: The Role of Fantasy. Paper read before the Society for Scientific Study of Sex, San Diego, Ca. June 29, 1974.

Kroger, W. S., and Freed, S. C.: Psychosomatic Gynecology: Including Problems of Obstetrical Care. Philadelphia, W. B. Saunders, 1951.

Lo Piccolo, J., and Lobitz, W. C.: The role of masturbation in the treatment of orgasmic dysfunctions. Arch. Sexual Behavior., *2*:163, 1972.

Marmor, J.: Some considerations concerning orgasm in the female. Psychosom. Med., *6*:240, 1954.

Masters, W. H., and Johnson, V. E.: Human Sexual Response. Boston, Little, Brown, 1966.

————: Human Sexual Inadequacy. Boston, Little, Brown, 1970.

Sarrel, P. M., and Sarrel, L. J.: Medical Tribune, *15*:1, 1974.

Schultz, J. H., and Luthe, W.: Autogenic Training. New York, Grune & Stratton, 1959.

Sherfey, M. J.: The evolution and nature of female sexuality in relation to psychoanalytic theory. J. Am. Psychoanal. Ass., *14*:28, 1966.

Ward, W. O.: Successful treatment of frigidity through hypnosis. V. A. Med. Mon., *102:*223, 1975.
Wolpe, J.: Psychotherapy by Reciprocal Inhibition. Stanford, Stanford University Press, 1958.
————: Basic principles and practices of behavior therapy of neuroses. Am. J. Psychiat., *125:*1242, 1969.

SUGGESTED READINGS

Abraham H.: Contribution to the problem of female sexuality. Internat. J. Psychoanal. *37:*351, 1956.
Brady, J. P.: Brevital-relaxation treatment of frigidity. Behav. Res. Therap., *4:*71, 1966.
Conn, J. H.: Psychobiologic therapy. Maryland State Med. Jour. *8:*192, 1959.
Cooper, L. F. and Erickson, M. H.: Time Distortion in Hypnosis. Baltimore, Williams and Wilkins, 1954.
Deutsch, H.: Frigidity in Women. *In* Sutherland, J. D., and Kahn, M. M. R. (eds.): Neuroses and Character Types. Clinical Psychoanalytic Studies. London, Hogarth Press, 1947.
Frank, J. D.: Persuasion and Healing: A Comparative Study of Psychotherapy. Baltimore, Johns Hopkins Univ. Press, 1961.
Kroger, W. S.: The treatment of psychogynecic disorders by hypnoanalysis. Am. J. Obst. Gynec., *46:*1818, 1943.
————.: Psychosomatic aspects of frigidity and impotency. Int. Rec. of Med., *171:*469, 1958.
————: Frigidity: the emotional plague. J. Mind., *2:*150, 1964.
————.: Sensory Processing and Control in Higher Nervous Systems Functioning. *In* Sances, A. (ed.): Proceedings of the Symposium on Biomedical Engineering. Milwaukee, Marquette Univ. Press, 1966.
Kroger, W. S., and Bergler, E.: The dynamic significance of vaginal lubrication to frigidity. West. J. Surg. Obst. Gynec. *61:*711, 1953.
Kroger, W. S., and Freed, S. C.: Psychosomatic Aspects of Frigidity. J. A. M. A., *143:*56, 1950.
Madsen, C. H. and Ullmann, L. P.: Innovations in the desensitization of frigidity. Behav. Res. Ther., *5:*67, 1967.
Miller, G. A., Galanter, E., and Pribam, K. H.: Plans and the Structure of Behavior. New York, Holt Rinehart & Winston, 1960.
Rado, S.: Recent advances of psychoanalytical therapy in psychiatric treatment. Proc. Assoc. for Research in Nervous and Mental Disease., *31:*57, 1953.

13

Sexual Deviations

The term *sexually deviant* refers to any method of obtaining sexual satisfaction which is disapproved of by the community. Every social group has its approved and disapproved sexual patterns and its sexual deviates. Transvestism and male homosexuality were given formal sanction by the Plains Indian tribes who institutionalized these "perversions" in the form of the "berdache" the man who lived as a woman in all respects. In Imperial Germany, fetishism and flagellation had a very great appeal, as attested to by the work of Krafft-Ebing and Hirschfeld. Homosexuality, overt and latent, can be seen in many cultures and, in fact, in some is considered normal behavior. The American Psychiatric Association recently stated that homosexuality could not be considered perverse behavior. Marmor was among the first to promulgate this viewpoint. His cross-disciplinary studies (1965) provide penetrating insights into homosexuality—male and female.

If we adhere to the social definition of sexual deviancy and give the label "deviant" to any act which is disapproved of by the community we will find that sexual deviancy in our society is quite prevalent. In the case of sadism or masochism, the response is the giving or receiving of pain in order to attain sexual pleasure. Orgasm may be achieved with the complete absence of physical genital stimulation. Voyeurism (obtaining full sexual gratification from "peeping" or observing others, particularly in the nude or in the act of intercourse) and fetishism both involve activities which may be an aspect of sexual arousal in normal individuals but which become deviant when they displace the normal outcome of sexual arousal (sexual intercourse). Exhibitionism, which consists of exposing genitalia to others, may involve no sexual arousal in the individual who exposes himself. Transvestism (dressing in the clothes of the

168

opposite sex) appears to be of two types. The first type represents the extreme of fetishism in that touch of symbols and clothes associated with the opposite sex is not enough; the clothes must actually be worn before sexual arousal can be experienced. In the second kind of transvestism there is an attempt to take over the superficial aspects of the opposite sex role by wearing the appropriate clothes; the man wishes to be a woman but still retain his male genital organs. Behavior involving a deviant response is more "abnormal" than behavior involving a deviant object, particularly when men or women are forced to endure long periods without heterosexual contacts. Then it is "only natural" that they turn to homosexuality or masturbation for sexual outlets.

ETIOLOGIC FACTORS

Sexual identity and gender role are affected by more than chromosomes, hormones, or genetics. Money and Ehrhardt (1972) believe that it is a mistake to think that gender identity is so firmly fixed by nature prenatally that it is not open to options of developmental differentiation. They have advanced the "Adam principle," namely that nature decides that the sexually undifferentiated embryo, whatever its genetic sex, will differentiate as a female unless androgen is added. This occurs about the sixth week. Inasmuch as the testis, which supplies androgens, originates from neutral ambisexual gonadal tissues under instructions from the Y chromosome, the chain of command in the Y chromosome stimulates the testis to produce androgen.

Whenever the prenatal environment is alerted at a critical period at any point in this chain, masculine differentiation is prevented or arrested. As a result, the "Eve principle" takes over. Embryologists believe that all human tissue is female during the early weeks of gestation. Therefore, one might facetiously say that Adam was an Eve. With reference to postnatal differentiation of gender identity role, sex differences programmed after birth become incorporated as indelibly as those taking place before birth. Thus, importance of early postnatal experiences and child-rearing can produce markedly different outcomes. The critical period for sexual differentiation is around 18 months. If a boy is dressed as a girl from birth and plays with girl's toys it is highly possible that he could develop into a feminine male before hormonal puberty.

Gender roles are learned responses and therefore culturally determined. Gender identity is defined as the sameness or persistence of one's individuality as a male, female, or bisexual person. Therefore gender identity is the experience of gender role. It is also outmoded to pit genetic, biological, or instinctual responses against environmental, psychological or learned ones. The basic problem is to emphasize the interaction involved in psychosocial and hormonal interactions (Stollar 1973, Green 1974). Finally, our behavior is, in reality, programmed by psychosocial factors. Repeated reprogramming produces fairly stable gender roles.

Reinish (1974) stresses the important role of hormones during the critical period of brain differentiation and how they affect behavior. Phoenix et al. (1968) suggest that androgens can influence such behaviors as aggression, fighting, and dominance. Harris (1964) posits that differences in hormonal regulation during fetal development can organize undifferentiated neural tissues into either a "male" or "female" type of brain. The most frequently noted family pattern for homosexuals has included a close-binding, controlling mother and a detached, rejecting father. The majority of studies substantiating this finding have examined emotionally disturbed patients. When nonclinical homosexual and heterosexual groups were examined (Siegelman 1974), homosexuals and heterosexuals scoring low on neuroticism showed no significant family differences. The author concludes, "The overall results . . . cast serious doubt on the prevalent assumption that negative parental behavior, especially of mothers, plays a critical role in differentiating the backgrounds of homosexuals and heterosexuals." Evans (1969), Greenblatt (1966), Hooker (1969), and West (1959) came to similar conclusions. Siegelman's findings question the existence of *any* association between family relations and homosexuality versus heterosexuality. This is consistent with the belief of Hooker (1969) that "disturbed parental relations are neither necessary nor sufficient conditions for homosexuality to emerge."

ROLE OF LEARNING THEORY

Rather than assuming that a sexual deviation is the expression or result of some unresolved psychodynamic conflict, learning theory assumes that the deviation is the result of the learning of inappropriate responses. Since the problem results from learning rather than an unresolved conflict, treatment entails relearning rather than an attempt to bring to light and resolve the suspected conflict. Histories of sexual deviants are filled with instances of sexual stimulation in the presence of stimuli which subsequently come to elicit sexual arousal. In the development of "perversion" there seems to be a pairing of a sexually exciting stimulus (such as visual or tactile stimulation) with a neutral stimulus, followed by the response of sexual arousal. This example of classical conditioning also explains the arousal properties of sexual stimuli falling in the "normal" range. Most men are sexually aroused by seeing female breasts or genital organs even though there is nothing intrinsically arousing about such stimuli.

Rachman and Hodgson (1968) conditioned a form of sexual deviation in normal subjects, thus providing further and more powerful support for the learning theory hypothesis that sexual deviation is acquired. These authors conditioned five subjects to give sexual response (measured by a penile plethysmograph) to a photograph of a pair of knee-length boots (CS), and then the response was extinguished by repeated presentation of the CS alone. Another condition (backward conditioning in which the CS followed the UCS) was included as a control for the possibility of pseudo-conditioning. None of the subjects reached the criterion in this control condition. While this study does show that a fetish can be learned, it still of course does not prove that all fetishes are acquired in this manner.

TREATMENT

The authors believe that homosexuality can best be treated by associating sexual arousal with the sex to which the patient wishes to be attracted. Aversion therapy is useful in deconditioning deviant arousal but does not necessarily lead to preferred alternate patterns of arousal. It should, therefore, be used primarily in cases of fetishisms and other forms of deviant sexual behavior where the only objective is to decondition and not *re*condition a response. Also, technics often added to aversion therapy for the purpose of increasing heterosexual arousal such as aversion relief (Feldman and MacCulloch 1965), have not been demonstrated to be effective (Barlow 1972).

Several investigators have reported successful attempts to increase heterosexual arousal without aversion therapy (Huff 1970; Harbison, Quinn, and McAllister 1970; LoPiccolo 1971; Kraft 1967a, 1967b). In one case (Beech, Watts, and Pool 1971), a heterosexual pedophile was successfully treated by a classical conditioning technic in which pictures of very young, prepubertal girls (most attractive age group) were used as unconditioned stimuli (UCS) and were paired with pictures of progressively more mature girls. As pictures of the older, more mature girls became arousing, these in turn became the UCS and were paired with pictures of still older and more mature females and so on until responses had been conditioned to pictures of sexually mature females.

That sexual arousal can be learned has also been suggested by analogue research. Changes in GSR (Lovibond 1963) and heart rate (Wood and Obrist 1968) have been conditioned to tone and light using erotic pictures as UCS. McConaghy (1970) conditioned increases in penile response to geometric shapes using slides of females as the unconditioned stimulus in a group of heterosexuals, and slides of males in a group of homosexuals. Using slides and films with homosexual content as UCS, Herman, Barlow, and Agras (1974) increased heterosexual arousal in two out of three homosexuals.

HYPNOTIC IMAGERY

The hypnobehavioral model combines hypnosis with classical conditioning procedures to provide a fruitful method of increasing heterosexual arousal in homosexuals. According to Alexander (1967) it is relatively easy to extinguish conditioned associations and establish new ones in sexual deviants by hypnosis. Vivid hypnotic images with homosexual content serve as UCS. After developing powers of sensory recall through hypnotic procedures described earlier in this book, the patient is given erotic images in which members of both sexes are present. To increase the intensity of the UCS the patient is also instructed to masturbate to these images while in hypnosis. For example, a male homosexual may see himself walking in a moonlit garden such as the one in Image III. He is joined by a young man and woman who strip him and begin making love to him. Sexual arousal elicited by the male in the image (USC) is paired with the female (CS) in the image. After a sufficient number of hypnotic sessions the image or thought of a nude female will produce sexual arousal as a function of having been paired with arousal a given number of times.

As already emphasized, hypnotic imagery is very vivid and therefore a strong sexual arousal can be produced from erotic hypnotic images. The images must be tailored to the individual according to his preferences, and they can be arranged in a hierarchy. For example, in the first image, the subject can see himself making love to another male while a nude female simply watches from afar. In a second image the female may make love to the other male but not touch the subject. In a third image, the female caresses the patient, but the patient remains passive with respect to the female. A fifth image could include the patient's fondling both the other male and the female and finally penetrating the female while kissing the male. The next progression could have the patient making love to the female while a nude male watched. Finally the other man would be removed from the imagery entirely and the patient would see himself making love to a beautiful young woman in a garden on a midsummer's night. Once the image of the female alone is arousing to him, so will be the female in reality.

Recall of actual past pleasant sexual experiences can also be paired hypnotically with the image of a nude female. Once the homosexual begins having sexual relations with the opposite sex, he may at first need to use hypnotic images of homosexual content to maintain his sexual arousal during intercourse. The pairing of sexual arousal (however induced) with intercourse with a female will strengthen his attraction to her and decrease his inhibitions and fear of failure. Eventually there will be no need for any more pairings of hypnotic imagery of homosexual content, and the nude male will no longer constitute a UCS.

Actual relations with a female should also progress gradually, beginning with just talking to females, then platonic dating, holding hands, kissing, fondling with clothes on, stimulating erogenous zones under the clothing, kissing and cuddling in the nude, genital to genital contact and body friction without penetration, penetration and immediate withdrawal, penetration and insertion maintained for progressive periods of time without thrusting, penetration and thrusting for an increasing number of times, and finally penetration and thrusting to climax. This hierarchy is simply an example and it can be shortened or lengthened depending upon the individual needs of the patient. Hypnosis can potentiate the sensory imagery conditioning, and it has been used in deviant behavior (Alexander 1967).

The homosexual can be taught to control his blood flow and other vasomotor responses by the methods described in Chapters 11 and 12. Here we describe how the orgasm and sexual arousal of both the male and the female result from congestion of blood in the genital area. Recollection of a sensation of warmth in the genital area will produce sexual arousal, which can then be paired with an image of the opposite sex, or at a later stage, used during intercourse with the opposite sex. If sexual arousal (UCS) is paired a sufficient number of times with a given object, that object will come to elicit sexual arousal.

If all that is desired is to decondition sexual arousal to a given object without reconditioning that attraction to another object, then the object to be deconditioned can be associated in hypnotic imagery with negative sensations. For example, to decondition a slip fetish the patient could see himself in a hypnotic image such as the following:

You are sitting on a bed. Beside you is a silk slip. Feel it. Smell it. A dog enters the room and jumps on the bed. He urinates on the slip. Suck the dog urine from the material . . . a feeling of nausea coming over you . . . You throw up. Huge chunks of vomit are all over the slip. Smell the sour puke. You lick the vomit off the silk. You choke and heave again. Leave the room. As soon as you are out of sight, touch, and smell of the slip you feel fine! Take a big, deep breath of fresh air.

The pairing of negative hypnotic imagery with the thought of the slip will turn the patient off with respect to this article of apparel. It will also be noted that the act of resisting or not looking at the slip is reinforced by the relief of the nausea and a breath of fresh air.

Whether it is biologically, psychodynamically, socially, or multi-determined, the most important fact about a sexual preference is that it can be modified. Whether inborn or acquired, a behavior pattern can be changed. The origins of such behavior are therefore less important than the methods for breaking an undesirable habit.

REFERENCES

Alexander, L.: Psychotherapy of sexual deviation with the aid of hypnosis. Am. J. Clin. Hypn., 9:18, 1967.
Barlow, D. H.: The treatment of sexual deviation: towards a comprehensive behavioral approach. *In* K. S. Calhoun, H. E. Adams, & K. M. Mitchell (eds.): Innovative Treatment Methods in Psychopathology. New York, John Wiley & Sons, 1972.
Beech, H. R., Watts, F., and Poole, A. D.: Classical conditioning of sexual deviation: a preliminary note. Behav. Ther., 2:400, 1971.
Evans, R. B.: Childhood parental relationships of homosexual men. J. Consult. Clin. Psychol., 33:129, 1969.
Feldman, M. P. and MacCulloch, M. J.: The application of anticipatory avoidance learning to the treatment of homosexuality. 1. Theory, technique, and preliminary results. Behav. Res. Ther., 2:165, 1965.
Green, R.: Sexual Identity Conflict in children and adults. New York, Basic Books, 1974.

Greenblatt, D. R.: Semantic Differential Analysis of the "Triangular System" Hypothesis in "Adjusted" Overt Male Homosexuals. (Unpublished doctoral dissertation, University of California), 1966.

Harbison, J. J. M., Quinn, J. T., and McAllister, H.: The positive conditioning of heterosexual behavior. Paper presented at the Second Behavioural Modification Conference, Kilkenny, England, Sept., 1970.

Harris, G. W.: Sex hormones, brain develgpment and brain function. Endocrinology, *75:*627, 1964.

Herman, S. H., Barlow, D. H., and Agras, W. S.: An experimental analysis of classical conditioning as a method of increasing heterosexual arousal in homosexuals. Behav. Ther., *5:*33, 1974.

Hooker, E.: Parental relations and male homosexuality in patient and nonpatient samples. J. Consult. Clin. Psychol., *33:*140, 1969.

Huff, F. W.: The desensitization of a homosexual. Behav. Res. Ther., *8:*99, 1970.

Kraft, T.: A case of homosexuality treated by systematic desensitization. Amer. J. Psychother., *21:*815, 1967a.

————: Behavior therapy and the treatment of sexual perversions. Psychother. Psychosom., *15:*351, 1967b.

LoPiccolo, J.: Case study: systematic desensitization of homosexuality. Behav. Ther., *2:*394, 1971.

Lovibond, S.: Conceptual thinking, personality and conditioning. Brit. J. Soc. Clin. Psychol., *2:*100, 1963.

Marmor, J.: Sexual Inversion. New York, Basic Books, 1965.

McConaghy, N.: Penile response conditioning and its relationship to aversion therapy in homosexuals. Behav. Ther., *1:*213, 1970.

Money, J. and Ehrhardt, A.: Man and Woman, Boy and Girl. Baltimore, Johns Hopkins University Press, 1972.

Phoenix, G. H., Goy, R. W., and Resko, J. A.: Psychosexual differentiation as a function of androgenic stimulation. *In* Diamond, M. (ed.): Perspectives in Reproduction and Sexual Behavior. Bloomington, Indiana University Press, 1968.

Rachman, S. and Hodgson, R. J.: Experimentally-induced "sexual fetishism": replication and development. Psychol. Rec., *18:*25, 1968.

Reinisch, J.: Fetal hormones, the brain, and human sex differences: a heuristic, integrative review of the recent literature. Arch. Sex. Behav., *3:*51, 1974.

Siegelman, M.: Parental background of male homosexuals and heterosexuals. Arch. Sex. Behav., *3:*3, 1974.

Stollar, R. J.: Contemporary Sexual Behavior. Baltimore, Johns Hopkins Univ. Press, 1973.

West, D. J.: Parental figures in male homosexuality: a critical perspective. Behav. Ther., *5:*16, 1974.

Wood, D., and Obrist, P.: Minimal and maximal sensory intake and exercise as unconditioned stimuli in human heart-rate conditioning. J. Exp. Psychol., *76:*254, 1968.

SUGGESTED READINGS

Barlow, D. H.: Increasing heterosexual responsiveness in the treatment of sexual deviation: a review of the clinical and experimental literature. Behav. Ther., *4:*655, 1973.

Barlow, D. H., Leitenberg, H., and Agras, W. S.: Experimental control of sexual deviation through manipulation of the noxious scene in covert sensitization. J. Abnorm. Psych., *74:*596, 1969.

Canton-Dutari, A.: Combined intervention for controlling unwanted homosexual behavior. Arch. Sex. Behav., *3:*367, 1974.

Conn, J. H.: Hypnosynthesis: dynamic psychotherapy of the sex offender utilizing hypnotic techniques. J. Amer. Soc. Psychosom. Dent. Med., *15:*18, 1968.

Denholtz, M. S.: An extension of covert procedures in the treatment of male homosexuals. J. Behav. Ther. Exp. Psychiat., *4:*305, 1973.

Doerr, P., Kockott, G., Vogt, H. J., Pirke, K. M., and Dittmar, F.: Plasma testosterone, estradiol, and semen analysis in male homosexuals. Arch. Gen. Psychiat., *29:*829, 1973.

Evans, D. R.: Masturbatory fantasy and sexual deviation. Behav. Res. Ther., *6:*17, 1968.

Feldman, M. P.: Aversion therapy for sexual deviations: a critical review. Psychol. Bull., *65:*65, 1966.

Freund, K., Langevin, R., Cibiri, S., and Zajac, Y.: Heterosexual aversion in homosexual males. Brit. J. Psychiat., *122:*163, 1973.

Harbert, T. L., Burlow, D. H., Hersen, M. and Austin, J. B.: Measurement and modification of incestuous behavior: a case study. Psychol. Rep., *34:*79, 1974.

McConaghy, N. and Barr, R. F.: Classical, avoidance and backward conditioning treatments of homosexuality. Brit. J. Psychiat., *122:*151, 1973.

McCrady, R. E.: A forward fading technique for increasing heterosexual responsiveness in male homosexuals. J. Behav. Ther. Exp. Psychiat., *4:*257, 1973.

McSweeny, A. J.: Fingernail fetishism: report of a case treated with hypnosis. Amer. J. Clin. Hypn. *15:*139, 1972.

Pillard, R. C., Rose, R. M., and Sherwood, M.: Plasma testosterone levels in homosexual men. Arch. Sex. Behav., *3:*453, 1974.

Rooth, G.: Exhibitionism, sexual violence and paedophilia. Brit. J. Psychiat., *122:*705, 1973.

Rooth, F. G. and Marks, I. M.: Persistent exhibitionism: short-term response to aversion, self-regulation, and relaxation treatments. Arch. Sex. Behav., *3:*227, 1974.

Stoller, R. J., Marmor, J., Bieber, I., Gold, R., and Socarides, C. W.: A symposium: should homosexuality be in the APA nomenclature? Amer. J. Psychiat., *130:*1207, 1973.

Tanner, B. A.: Shock intensity and fear of shock in the modification of homosexual behavior in males by avoidance learning. Behav. Res. Ther., *11:*213, 1973.

————: A comparison of automated aversive conditioning and a waiting list control in the modification of homosexual behavior in males. Behav. Ther., *5:*29, 1974.

Tennent, G. Barncroft, J. and Cass, J.: The control of deviant sexual behavior by drugs: a double-blind controlled study of benperiodal, chlorpromazine, and placebo. Arch. Sex. Behav., *3:*261, 1974.

Wilson, G. T., and Davison, G. C.: Behavior therapy and homosexuality: a critical perspective. Behav. Ther., *5:*16, 1974.

PART FOUR

Removal of Habit Patterns

14

Alcoholism

ETIOLOGIC FACTORS

Chronic alcoholism often is a symptom of a deep-seated personality disorder usually selected to avoid intolerable life situations. There is no typical personality profile, but hostility, insecurity, and feelings of inadequacy are usually present. Alcoholics have a low frustration tolerance, increased sensitivity, and feelings of omnipotence characterized by the belief that "nothing can happen to me." Outwardly they present a confident appearance, which is usually a facade for their deep-seated dependency needs.

Some have little or no concern about the trouble caused by the habit. For instance, a binge, with its days of misery and sickness, often results in a lost job, a ruined career, and a broken marriage. The alcoholic is an "injustice collector" for whom the overt self-punishment fulfills a pleasurable need, as well as a rationalization for the inability to face reality. Seldom is he aware of his masochistic need to suffer.

Such individuals do not have the courage to commit suicide, but are, in reality, slowly destroying themselves by the noxious habit. To allay their tensions they retreat to a childlike behavior pattern, with a need for attention, pity, and love. By becoming inebriated, the alcoholic develops a greater capacity to give and receive attention. This maneuver temporarily increases his self-esteem and well-being.

In the typical history of the alcoholic there is a compulsive pattern represented by repeated incidents involving self-debasement, various types of sexual involvements, and defiance of authoritarian and other surrogate figures. When the demands for sympathy and attention are not met, more frequent

179

"binges" are usually necessary to provide a respite from the mounting tensions. Exhortations aimed either at shaming the individual into sobriety or pointing out the harmful medical sequelae are useless. Since the alcoholic seldom realizes the needs for his habit, he cannot control his drinking. Successful therapy requires that these needs must become evident to him. Intellectualizing or moralizing on the dire mental and physical dangers are utterly futile with the chronic alcoholic.

PRINCIPLES OF PSYCHOTHERAPY

The purpose of therapy is first to motivate the individual to stop drinking, then teach him how to adapt to his difficult problems rather than using regressive behavior patterns at the first sign of stress. Here a sympathetic, noncondemnatory attitude will make the patient feel that he is being treated like an adult, and this helps establish healthy motivation. Chronic drinkers are seldom motivated if their immaturity and strong dependency preclude admitting that they have a drinking problem.

Since most alcoholics are generally passive and dependent, the hypnotic relationship initially helps the patient in therapy at a time when he is most resistant. Later this dependency is dissolved and the needs for it and other reasons are worked through. Because of greater rapport with the therapist, the patient now is willing to trade his self-destructive tendencies and immature attitudes for healthier goals.

The chronic alcoholic who does not wish to be helped, or who is literally brought in by friends or relatives against his will, cannot be helped by any psychotherapeutic approach unless he is institutionalized for long-term psychotherapy. The prognosis is usually poor, as each recovery is only a "flight into health." His ardent protests that he is cured and his vows that he will never drink again are only rationalizations for the breaking off of therapy. Overcompliance merely follows the old adage, "If you can't lick them, join them." Follow-up studies indicate that severe cases are difficult to help, irrespective of the therapy employed. If the patient refuses to take Antabuse during the early phase of therapy, this indicates poor motivation and an uncertain prognosis.

BEHAVIOR MODIFICATION TECHNICS

The technics used in behavior therapy with alcoholics parallel those already described in the treatment of sexual deviations. Therefore, it will not be necessary to describe them in any great detail. The technics include classical aversive conditioning with drugs (Markovnikov 1934; Voegtlin 1940; Lemere, Voegtlin, Broz, O'Hollaren, and Tupper 1942; Kroger 1942; Shadel 1944; Kant 1944; Thimann 1949; Raymond 1964; Miller and Barlow 1973; Reusky 1973), classical aversive conditioning with paralysis (Sanderson et al. 1963; Campbell et al. 1964), instrumental escape conditioning with shock (Blake 1965), instrumental avoidance conditioning with shock (MacCulloch et al. 1966), aversive imagery technic (Anat 1966, 1967a, 1967b), relaxation aversion technic (Blake 1965), behavioral contracting (Miller 1972), and "in vivo" operant conditioning (Miller and Barlow 1973). The use of classical aversive conditioning with shock does not appear to have been successfully used in the treatment of alcoholism. Results from these methods are largely equivocal, and more research needs to be done to determine their efficacy.

HYPNOTIC TECHNICS

Hypnotic technics for treating alcoholism as reported in the literature are very similar to those reported by the behavior modifiers; there is an overlap between hypnotic and behavioral methods in the treatment of chronic alcoholism. Hypnotherapists also speak of conditioned reflex treatment by hypnosis and aversion treatment (Kroger 1942, Miller 1959, Smith-Morehouse 1969). Conditioned reflex treatment has been successful for some patients. In this approach the individual while under hypnosis is given a drink and an emetic is administered. An association between vomiting and drinking is produced by this method, but it is not helpful unless the patient is highly motivated or is seen immediately after a hangover. Relatively permanent recovery in carefully selected patients is obtained by reinforcing this technic through posthypnotic suggestions to vomit at the sight, taste, or smell of liquor. Under sensory-imagery conditioning, the patient recalls repeatedly the horrible nausea and the disgusting sensations produced by the emetic. Thus, the unpleasant memory is seldom forgotten, and the constant revivification of a repugnant experience dissuades him from drinking.

If a healthy relationship exists between therapist and the patient, the recovery forces will be mobilized. The desire to abstain is reinforced by appropriate posthypnotic suggestions. Motivation is increased by such other posthypnotic suggestions as the setting of a deadline for the daily or the weekly decrease in the quantity consumed, and the stressing of the health factor, and, above all, by the effect of the patient's self-esteem that has been enhanced by the permissiveness of the therapeutic regimen.

The key points in the conditioned reflex treatment under hypnosis, outlined by Kroger (1942), Miller (1959), Wolberg (1948), and others, are based on repeatedly emphasizing, under hypnosis, the deleterious effects of alcohol, the conditioned repugnance for alcoholic beverages, and the patient's ability to control his own behavior, and finally on establishing the emotional needs for the symptom. The self-destructive drives should be channeled into healthy outlets such as hobbies, sports, social activities, and other constructive endeavors.

After hypnosis and autohypnosis have been instituted, strong suggestions are given, such as, "Each time that you even think of drinking, you will develop a horrible disgust and taste for the liquor by associating it with the most horrible, repugnant smell and taste that you have ever experienced. After you have said this to yourself again and again, you will *really* begin to believe that a drink will smell and taste awful.'' Such autosuggestions are repeated continuously for reinforcement. After sobriety has been maintained, these can be made at longer intervals.

Wolberg (1948) has described a very interesting technic in which symptom-substitution is utilized. He informs the patient, ''Every time you crave a drink you will reach for a malted milk tablet and this will give you a sense of pleasure and relaxation.''

Another effective method is to open a bottle of whiskey while the patient is hypnotized and to assure him that the bottle has not been tampered with or opened. He is offered a drink and requested to hold it in his mouth for several minutes to get the full taste. Naturally, a burning sensation on his tongue is created. After the patient has finally swallowed the drink, he is asked how he liked it. His usual reply is, ''It tasted fine,'' whereupon the therapist informs the subject that he has been deceived: ''You have not been given whiskey but a mixture of lemon juice and ammonia.'' If hypnotized, the subject will exhibit marked revulsion and disgust.

If this is unsuccessful, the procedure is repeated and the chances are that the next time he will react in the expected manner. Before concluding the hypnotic session, the patient should be given a posthypnotic suggestion that any time he is offered a drink, these reactions will certainly occur. Even the thought or the smell of a drink will induce profound distaste.

A substitute habit should be suggested to trade down or take the place of the drinking. For instance, drinking nonalcoholic beverages satisfies the oral cravings. Whenever a deeply ingrained habit pattern is changed, it should be replaced by a more innocuous substitute habit. Tranquilizers or amphetamines can be employed during the ''weaning-off'' period.

Before terminating each session, suggestions should be made that the patient will feel very relaxed. Immediately after dehypnotization, he can be offered a drink to see how much disgust is produced. In selected subjects, this approach often produces a 60 to 70 per cent abstinence. Social drinking is discouraged. Suggestions to bolster self-confidence and overcome feelings of inadequacy can be given during hypnosis.

GROUP THERAPY

The success of Alcoholics Anonymous (A.A.) depends upon a powerful group identification factor, which makes the sufferer feel accepted, and his intense desire to please the leader of the group or the person assigned to him (his sponsor) is an additional factor. The group situation mobilizes the inherent competitiveness present in every individual and, through the strong support given by other members, the alcoholic's weak personality structure is bolstered. Finally, as a result of healthy motivation established by the emotional contagion, and alliance with a power greater than himself, the recovery forces of the individual are unleashed. Faith in a beneficent power means the difference between success and failure. The alcoholic has little or no reason to take issue with this new parental figure or to challenge his omnipotence. Through further friendly exhortations from former alcoholics, he often renounces his drinking habit. The authors have a high regard for A.A. Beahrs and Hill (1971) had good results with hypnosis and group psychotherapy.

Most problem drinkers are looking for a magical gesture and, because of their strong dependency strivings, attempt to "crawl into the lap" of the therapist. From the initial visit, they must be informed that this is a do-it-yourself program, that results are in direct proportion to the desire for recovery and the willingness to perfect their sensory-imagery conditioning technics. By using such measures the therapist cannot get out on a limb, nor lose face with the patient. It also is stressed that if the symptom returns, it can be controlled by autohypnosis; resistances are diminished whenever suggestions are self-originated. The therapist must not be too authoritative. To avoid criticalness, we state, "You will stop drinking as soon as you desire to, will you not? And it will be because you really want to do so down deep inside. I am only a friend who wishes to guide you as long as you need me." This obviates the therapist's being placed in the role of a dominating parental figure.

Results in small groups are often better than with individual hypnotherapy. In addition to hypnosis, the technics include free discussion and expression of feelings, re-education, reassurance, strong emotional support, and thorough explanations of the commonly encountered problems. There are many rationalizations that alcoholics use to explain their drinking. They must recognize that dishonesty with themselves and with others, omnipotence, impulsiveness, guilt, shame, and the inability to establish durable relationships are related to their drinking. The manner in which tensions are displaced, self-abuse, the striving for perfection and the need to manipulate others also should be pointed out. When a permissive approach is employed that is directed toward these needs, guilt, anxiety, insecurity, and fear can be resolved, especially if the individual identifies with strong members of the group. The stronger the identification, the more the alcoholic will emulate those whom he admires. The important factor in group as well as in individual psychotherapy is giving the patient the feeling that the therapist really understands the patient's problems and is willing and able to help him. The greater ability to concentrate speeds up any type of psychotherapy. When group hypnotherapy is combined with decreasing doses of Antabuse medication, maximal improvement occurs. Wallerstein (1958) obtained an improvement rate of 53 per cent with Antabuse, 36 per cent with group hypnotherapy, 26 per cent with milieu therapy, and 24 per cent with conditioned-reflex treatment.

Two-hour weekly sessions are held. Each one begins with a general discussion of alcoholism. Questions and answers pertaining to all aspects of drinking are conducted the first half hour. Then several former patients, who have been helped and who have returned to visit the group, relate their experiences. They usually state that initially they did not believe that this kind of approach would help them. Then, after observing improvement in other members, they were more motivated to obtain similar results. One or more grateful patients describe how they were taught hypnosis, autohypnosis, and how through sensory-imagery conditioning they finally developed a profound disgust for alcohol (technics outlined in the section below were used). Having a sufferer sincerely relate his feelings to the group develops a considerable amount of hope rapidly, especially for the neophyte or the unsophisticated or the skeptic.

Those volunteers who are successfully hypnotized are given the appropriate suggestions for producing disgust and a strong aversion for drinking. Since disgust to a specific taste and smell will vary from patient to patient, it is wise to let each one pick these. In successive sessions, the technics of autohypnosis and sensory-imagery are inculcated into each person. The incidence of success is much higher where autohypnosis is employed. With this approach, the patient realizes that he must achieve the results through his own efforts. This is highly motivating and contributes to his self-esteem.

The medical management of the chronic alcoholic is not within the scope of this presentation. It involves a knowledge of the effects of long-term consumption of alcoholic beverages, including metabolic factors. The rehabilitation of the chronic alcoholic is tedious and requires painstaking attention, patience, and a mixture of empathy and firmness. At all costs, the therapist must maintain a prestige position at all times.

IMPORTANCE OF AUTOHYPNOSIS

Before detailed construction of negative or positive imagery the patient is given several specific posthypnotic suggestions to be used in autohypnosis. It is not difficult for the alcoholic to practice autohypnosis. Frequently, however, he may procrastinate, saying, "I just don't feel up to it." Here a careful step-by-step explanation should be given, stressing that the autosuggestions so necessary for his recovery should be under his control. This factor is of the utmost importance for establishing healthy motivation. Under autohypnosis, the patient can suggest when he thinks he will be able to substitute a soft beverage for the liquor. Through use of these measures, direct symptom-removal is not employed. Instead, recovery is obtained by a weaning-off process in which the patient decides *how* and *when* to cut down on the number of drinks taken per day. It is also helpful to allow a choice of the type of beverage substitute that is to replace the liquor.

IMPORTANCE OF POSTHYPNOTIC SUGGESTIONS

Irrational fears of the patient that he will not be able to stop drinking can be reversed through posthypnotic suggestions directed to the possibility *that maybe he will stop too abruptly*. Other posthypnotic suggestions can be given to pick a date in the not-too-distant future when he will have reduced his drinks to one or two a day. It is suggested that he will be extremely worried about whether he is going to be taking one drink a day or three drinks a day by the chosen date. Such extraverbal suggestions produce overreaction, often with resultant improvement.

As in the treatment of obesity, posthypnotic suggestions are given that if the patient is in doubt about taking a drink, he will see the therapist in fantasy, shaking his head in disapproval. When all these technics are employed with supportive psychotherapy consisting of rapport, ventilation of problems, and skillful guidance, excellent results can be obtained in a high percentage of patients.

If a patient who apparently is doing well, relapses or "falls off the wagon," he is never censured or criticized. However, the question can be raised with him as to *what* the particular situation was for doing this and *why* he had to take ten drinks; perhaps he could have gotten by with four drinks, or two drinks, or perhaps one drink. Also, what was he thinking about before he began drinking? These and other problems are fully discussed. It is important to emphasize that with most chronic alcoholics, the ultimate therapeutic goal is total abstinence. The following verbalization is typical for the aversion treatment of alcoholism:

John, you are deeply relaxed. Listen to all my suggestions, as each one will be indelibly imprinted in your mind. You will not remember all these suggestions today, but eventually you *will* remember all of them. Each and every suggestion will be remembered over the coming weeks and months. If you really wish to stop drinking, think of the most disgusting, nauseating taste that you have ever had. Maybe a drink will taste like onions, rutabagas, parsnips, or whatever other food you dislike. That's right. You are beginning to taste something awful, are you not? ["Yes."] Did you say it's turnips; is that what you said? ["Yes."] Now, each time you even think of taking a drink, you are going to experience this taste of turnips . . . this vile, horrible taste of the turnips during the next few weeks and months. Each and every time you take a drink, you will associate it with the disgusting taste of turnips. Right now, this awful taste is getting more and more marked, is it not? ["Yes."].

Now, think of the most putrid smell that you've experienced. Take your time and try to think of the most horrible stench that you've ever smelled . . . Rotten eggs? Well, every time you hold a drink in your hand and smell it, you will think of rotten eggs . . . the horrible, violent, disgusting smell of rotten eggs. And each and every time you even think of taking a drink now, you are not only going to get the terrible taste of turnips but also the smell of rotten eggs. This may not make itself apparent until you have said this to yourself again and again, perhaps 50 or 100 times while under autohypnosis. Eventually you will associate this smell with the odor of liquor until you are sure that you really hate the sight, taste, and smell of a drink [sensory-imagery conditioning].

John, the next thing I'd like to have you do is to recollect how horrible you felt after you had a lot of drinks last Saturday night, just as if you were doing it all over again [age regression]. Remember the terrible feeling that you had in your stomach, and how you had to vomit? Recollect, if you will, that sickening feeling you had and how you trembled and shook all over and how weak you were, and the headache and the dizziness and all the other symptoms associated with your hangover. Recall all the details of that hangover and, if you really think about it, you will really become disgusted with drinking. Each and every time you even think of taking a drink, all of these positively awful tastes and smells will be etched in your mind. You can re-experience all of these sensations in a few minutes even though the hangover lasted for several hours.

I'm going to show you how this can be done by condensing (distorting) time. You know how when you're waiting for a traffic light to change. . . . it seems like 5 minutes when actually it has only taken one minute. Or, conversely, when you're chatting with an old friend and a cab is due in 20 minutes, it seems like 2 minutes. And so, during the next 2 minutes, you are going to be able to experience all of the unpleasant, disgusting sensations associated with a half hour of the hangover that you had last Sunday morning. Ten minutes of actual time will *seem* like 1 minute of time. So, therefore, in 2 minutes by the clock, you will be able to relive all of the disgusting feelings that you experienced in approximately one half hour. [Two minutes elapse, during which the individual screws up his mouth, begins to get sick and has a tendency to vomit.] Your time is now up. Wasn't that a horrible sensation? Now, each time when you have the desire to take a drink, you will re-experience the horrible sensations of that last hangover.

Remember, this is your problem. If you wish to drink, it is your privilege. Over the next few weeks, you might raise the question as to exactly how much you have the *need* to drink. Do you need to drink 80 per cent of the time, or 50 per cent, or 10 per cent? Maybe 5 or 10 per cent will fulfill your needs. I'm sure that once you realize the need to drink, you should be able to recognize the deep-seated feelings responsible for the habit. Don't press or try to think of these reasons, but just rest assured that some of the reasons will become apparent to you in the near future.

Now, John, perhaps you can step out of yourself, much as you would in a dream [depersonalization]. Look at yourself standing at a bar, uncertain, wobbling, making a fool of yourself. Take another good look at yourself. Are you not disgusted with the terrible smell of liquor on your breath? Observe the sloppiness of your clothes. When you are sober, you are always very neat. Are you not disappointed with what you see?" [depersonalization often can be very effective in creating a disgusting self-image].

Picture yourself at one of the drunken brawls where everybody is making a fool of himself. Is it not disgusting to see someone you respect sink lower and lower into utter insensibility and helplessness? I am interested in all your problems, and I want you to remember that any time you feel you need my help, regardless of where you are, I want you to please call me. If this is not possible, and if you are in doubt as to whether or not you should take that second or third drink, you will really see me standing beside you, shaking my head in disapproval [introjection of therapist].

And now you can come out of this very nice state of relaxation, can slowly open your eyes in the following manner: Number 1, say to yourself, "I will go deeper next time." Number 2, "I will follow all the suggestions that I am giving to *myself* to the best of my ability." Note that I said, *"I am giving to myself,"* rather than "those given by the doctor." Three, "I will open my eyes. I will feel supremely confident that *I* can lick my problems."

You will feel, John, that you were the one who did it. Remember that. You were the one who was able to *control your need to drink.* Remember, the degree of success you achieve will be in direct proportion to the amount of effort you put forth. Practice makes perfect! Think of a foul-smelling, evil-tasting sensation every time you crave a drink. If you do this again and again, *you will be able to break this vicious habit.*

You need not feel guilty if you "fall off" at any particular time. Progress is never in a straight line. It is characterized by a series of ups and downs. However, the long-term trend will be ever upward.

You have a very powerful tool that is only as good as you use it. Use it well, sharpen it, and it will cut to the core of your problem. The manner in which you use it can be very helpful in this regard. A tape of this discussion with you is being recorded. It would be a good idea if you played it on your tape-recorder every night. Then these suggestions will be deeply implanted again and again into your mind until they achieve a conditioned response. Whenever we hear a suggestion again and again, we eventually carry out the suggested act. You do have a great deal of confidence in yourself and you know that you can lick this problem in your own particular fashion.

IMAGERY CONDITIONING

Since the use of drugs and shocks is both unpleasant and difficult to control in terms of basic conditioning parameters such as intensity, duration, and clarity of onset and termination, we prefer to use the imagery technics described above in conjunction with hypnotic relaxation. The imagery may be either positive or negative. As alluded to earlier, when using an aversive imagery technic, the subject in hypnosis is given an unpleasant image involving a bad taste and smell combined with the real or imagined taste and smell of alcohol. The patient may use alcohol as a prop and actually taste and smell it during the recall of his unpleasant image or he may imagine the taste and smell of the alcohol in conjunction with the aversive image. Another variation is to have the patient in hypnosis, drink water which he imagines to be alcohol while he recalls an aversive sensation (Kroger 1942).

The negative image can be either the recall of a particularly bad experience or a created one. The therapist aids the subject in the construction of the image by asking him to remember any incidences he may have had involving a bad taste and smell. One woman recalled exposing rotten meat with maggots in it at a restaurant, another remembered the smell when her sick cat threw up on the radiator, another recalled the smell of a corpse he was asked to identify from a deer hunting accident. Once the aversive image is determined, the subject is asked to practice recalling it in conjunction with the recalled or actual taste and smell of liquor. The subject sees himself drinking in these images. For example, the woman who recalls smelling her cat throwing up on the radiator also pictures herself drinking at the time, even if this was not actually the case, so that the smell of cat vomit can be paired with the taste and smell of liquor.

An example of an aversive scene created for a subject is as follows:

You are riding in an airplane. Feel the motion of the plane. Look out the window. See the blue sky, the white clouds. You are drinking a whiskey sour. Taste it. Smell it, the strong taste and smell of alcohol. Suddenly the man next to you bends over and retches; smell the vomit. The sour smell of puke is all over you. There are chunks of vomit in your drink. Green slime is running down your glass. You take another gulp of the whiskey sour; chunks of vomit slosh together with the whiskey. Pieces of vomit catch in your throat. You keep drinking. A stronger feeling of nausea is coming over you with each gulp you take. Your stomach is distending from the alcohol. You are licking the slime from the rim of your glass. You retch . . . vomit and whiskey are all over, the plane is lurching, dipping like a roller coaster in turbulent weather. From this day forth, whenever you taste or smell alcohol you will think of vomit and nausea.

Images XVI (scuba), XVII (picnic), and XXII (hayloft), which involve recall of intoxication and euphoria from rum, beer, and hot brandy, may be modified to produce nausea rather than euphoria. During the nausea it is suggested to the patient that the pleasant image blurs from the effects of the liquor. The patient is then to see himself resisting further imbibing and the beautiful scene comes into focus again to reinforce the act of resistance or avoidance.

Alcoholism can also be treated using positive imagery. The subject is told to imagine himself in a situation such as his living room or a bar where he usually drinks. He structures the scene vividly using all five sense modalities. He then is told to imagine seeing a glass of whiskey sour. He walks over to it, smells it, then resists it, walking away. The moment he sees himself resisting or avoiding the liquor he reinforces the avoidance response by immediately recalling one of the pleasant, relaxing images. Avoidance is reinforced with relaxation.

The subject should also work at emotional as well as sensory recall so that he can turn on feelings of elation, sadness, disgust, or rage on cue. He sees himself resisting the liquor and immediately reinforces this resistance by the recall of the emotion of elation. Emotional recall has been studied in detail by the Russian dramatists, Stanislavsky and Boleshevsky. From the study of emotional recall under hypnosis has come the school of acting termed "method acting"—a form of role playing. The method actor feels the emotion of his character. He does not simulate the character, he *is* the character.

Emotional recall is accomplished in much the same way as sensory recall. The subject goes back to a specific point in time when he was experiencing a given emotion and recalls that experience with both the appropriate sensory and affective components. Recalling the funeral of a loved one can bring tears, just as recalling the moment someone said he loved you can bring back the feeling of joy that accompanied that event. The positive-imagery approach to alcoholic avoidance conditioning also changes the patient's self-concept. He sees himself as able to resist a drink; he sees himself doing what he wishes to accomplish, that is, refusing a drink.

Often, both positive and negative imagery are used together. The subject sees himself drinking the liquor, throwing up, approaching again, resisting, and immediately feeling a sense of elation, euphoria, and well-being. The suggestion is given that as soon as he is out of range of the taste and smell of the liquor he feels fantastic. The sense of well-being is potentiated by the contrast with the prior feeling of nausea. It is best to try the positive imagery technic alone first, as the unpleasantness associated with the aversive imagery causes some subjects to avoid practicing it. Positive reinforcement is always preferred to a negative approach if it can be implemented.

While a great deal of the research and clinical application in the treatment of alcoholism has involved aversive conditioning, it is hoped that future treatment strategies will make more use of positive reinforcement to modify this condition. We encourage students of the hypnobehavioral model to make full use of positive imagery as described in Chapter 10 in order to create pleasant feeling states to be used as reinforcers for the act of resistance.

REFERENCES

Anant, S. S.: The treatment of alcoholics by a verbal aversion technique: a case report. Manas, *13:*79, 1966.

————: A note on the treatment of alcoholics by a verbal aversion technique. Canad. Psychol., *8:*19, 1967a.

————: Treatment of alcoholics and drug addicts by verbal aversion technique. Paper read at the 7th Internat. Congress of Psychotherapy, Wiesbaden, 1967b.

Beahrs, J. O. and Hill, M. M.: Treatment of alcoholism by group-interaction psychotherapy under hypnosis. Am. J. Clin. Hypn., *14:*60, 1971.

Blake, B. G.: The application of behavior therapy to the treatment of alcoholism. Behav. Res. Ther., *3:*75, 1965.

Campbell, D., Sanderson, R. E. and Laverty, S. G.: Characteristics of a conditioned response in human subjects during extinction trials following a single traumatic conditioning trial. J. Abnorm. Soc. Psychol., *68:*627, 1964.

Kant, R.: The conditioned-reflex treatment in the light of our knowledge of alcohol addiction. Quart. J. Stud. Alcohol., *5:*371, 1944.

Kroger, W. S.: The conditioned reflex treatment of alcoholism. J.A.M.A., *120:*714, 1942.

Lemere, F.: The conditioned reflex treatment of chronic alcoholism: VIII. A review of six years' experience with this treatment of 1,526 patients. J.A.M.A., 120:269, 1942.

MacCulloch, M. J., Feldman, M. P., Orford, I. F. and MacCulloch, M. L.: Anticipatory avoidance learning in the treatment of alcoholism: a record of therapeutic failure. Behav. Res. Ther., *4:*187, 1966.

Markovnikov, A.: (Le traitment de l'alcoolisme au moyen de la suggestion et de la formation d'un reflexe conditionnel, provoque par une gorgee de spiriteu.). Sovet. Vrach. Gaz., *10:*807, 1934.

Miller, M. M.: Treatment of chronic alcoholism by hypnotic aversion. J.A.M.A., *171:*164, 1959.

Miller, P. M.: The use of behavioral contracting in the treatment of alcoholism: A case study. Behav. Ther., *3:*593, 1972.

Miller, P. M. and Barlow, D. H.: Behavioral approaches to the treatment of alcoholism. J. Nerv. Ment. Dis., *153:*10, 1973.

Raymond, M. J.: The treatment of addiction by aversion conditioning with apomorphine. Behav. Res. Ther., *1:*287, 1964.

Reusky, S.: Some laboratory paradigms for chemical aversion treatment of alcoholism. J. Behav. Ther. Exper. Psychiatry, *4:*15, 1973.

Sanderson, R. E., Campbell, D. and Laverty, S. G.: An investigation of a new aversive conditioning treatment for alcoholism. Quart. J. Stud. Alcohol., *24:*261, 1963.

Shadel, C. A.: Aversion treatment of alcohol addiction. Quart. J. Stud. Alcohol., *5:*216, 1944.

Smith-Moorhouse, P. M.: Hypnosis in the treatment of alcoholism. Brit. J. Addiction, *64:*47, 1969.

Thimann, J.: Conditioned reflex treatment of alcoholism: I. Its rationale and technic. New Eng. J. Med., *241:*368, 1949.

Voegtlin, W. L.: The treatment of alcoholism by establishing a conditioned reflex. Amer. J. Med. Sci., *199:*802, 1940.

Wallerstein, R. S.: Hospital Treatment of Alcoholism. New York, Basic Books, 1958.

Wolberg, L.: Medical Hypnosis. Vol. 1. New York, Grune & Stratton, 1948.

SUGGESTED READINGS

Bigelow, G., Cohen, M., Liebson, I. and Faillace, L. A.: Abstinence or moderation choice by alcoholics. Behav. Res. Ther., 1972, *10:*209, 1972.

Cautela, J. R.: The treatment of alcoholism by covert sensitization. Psychother. Theory Res. Pract., *7:*86, 1970.

Cheek, F. E., Franks, C. M., Laucius, J. and Burtle, V.: Behavior modification training for wives of alcoholics. Quart. J. Stud. Alcohol, *32:*456, 1971.

Hallam, R., Rachman, S. and Falkowski, W.: Subjective, attitudinal and physiological effects of electrical aversion therapy. Behav. Res. Ther., *10:*1, 1972.

Hunt, G. M. and Azrin, N. H.: A community-reinforcement approach to alcoholism. Behav. Res. Ther., *11:*91, 1973.

Langen, D.: Modern hypnotic treatment of various forms of addiction, in particular alcoholism. Brit. J. Addiction, *62:*77, 1967.

Miller, P. M. and Hersen, M. Quantitative changes in alcohol consumption as a function of electrical aversion conditioning. J. Clin. Psychol., *28:*590, 1972.

Mills, K. C., Sobell, M. B. and Schaefer, H. H.: Training social drinking as an alternative to abstinence for alcoholics. Behav. Ther., *2:*18, 1971.

Schaefer, H. H.: Twelve-month follow-up of behaviorally trained ex-alcoholic social drinkers. Behav. Ther., *3:*286, 1972.

Sobell, L. C. and Sobell, M. B.: A self-feedback technique to monitor drinking behavior in alcoholics. Behav. Res. Ther., *11:*237, 1973.

15

Excessive Smoking

Excessive smoking is one of the most common symptoms the hypnobehaviorist is asked to treat. Almost every chain smoker has at one time or another attempted to break the habit. He seldom realizes that this cannot be accomplished by will power, nor is he aware that it can be broken more readily through the use of his own imagination.

BEHAVIOR THERAPY

There have been many attempts by a behavioristic type of therapy to modify smoking habits. Koenig and Masters (1965) and Pyke et al. (1966) used a simple method of requiring the smoker to keep a tally of the number of cigarettes smoked. This method has been used by behavior therapists in conjunction with other methods. Whenever there is a behavior the frequency of which we wish to decrease, it is desirable to get a base rate so that we can evaluate progress. The pairing of shocks with various responses involved in smoking a cigarette has been used by several investigators (Koenig and Masters 1965, McGuire and Vallence 1964, Powell and Azrin 1968).

INSTRUMENTAL AVERSIVE ESCAPE AND RELIEF CONDITIONING

Wilde (1964) used a form of *instrumental aversive escape conditioning*. In his procedure a special apparatus blew an unpleasant mixture of cigarette smoke and hot air into the face of the smoker while he was smoking. When the smoker could no longer stand the situation, he would put out the cigarette. The act of extinguishing the cigarette was rewarded by a blast of fresh air (mixed with menthol on 50 per cent of the trials) so that the technic also involved *aversion-relief-conditioning*. Franks et al. (1966) developed an improved version of this apparatus. Greene (1964) used another technic within the same general framework. In a situation disguised as a task of music appreciation, a subject sat in a booth and listened to music while smoking. Whenever the subject drew on the cigarette, its glow activated a relay, which produced aversive white noise until the puff was completed. While Wilde (1964) reported encouraging results with 7 smokers, he later reported (Wilde 1965) that all of his "successes" had relapsed. The more favorable results reported by Franks et al. (1966) with the same technic must therefore be treated with caution until there is adequate follow-up data.

SYSTEMATIC DESENSITIZATION

Forms of systematic desensitization have also been used based on the assumption that smoking is a response to anxiety. Koenig and Masters (1965) required their subjects to visualize smoking scenes while in a relaxed state, the scenes being ranked from least to most productive of smoking behavior. They compared this method with classical aversive conditioning using shock and supportive counseling and found no difference in the effect of the three treatments, although all three were followed by a reduction in smoking behavior. Pyke et al. (1966) used a similar technic. They found that some of the smokers who significantly reduced their smoking during treatment were smoking *more* on follow-up. Working from the same assumption, Kraft and Al-Issa (1967) used systematic desensitization to reduce anxiety by relaxation to social situations in which smoking was likely to occur.

COVERT SENSITIZATION

Tooley and Pratt (1967) used *covert sensitization* as the preliminary step in their treatment procedure. They requested their smokers to imagine lighting up and smoking cigarettes in various situations that would lead to nausea. A variant of this procedure was used by Janis and Mann (1965) and Mann (1967). They required the subject to role-play an interview with a doctor involving unfavorable results of medical tests. A control subject listened to a similar interview, but did not role-play.

CONTINGENCY MANAGEMENT

The second step of Tooley and Pratt's (1967) treatment procedure involved *contingency management,* which is based on the *Premack principle* that the more probable response serves as a reinforcer for the less probable. For example, low-probability thoughts incompatible with smoking (e.g., I'll die of lung cancer if I continue to smoke) are reinforced by high-probability events (e.g., drinking coffee). The smoker contracts not to indulge in the high-probability behavior until he has thought of at least one low probability event. Tooley and Pratt call their third stage of treatment *contractual management*. In this stage the smoker contracts not to indulge in smoking in a specific situation. Nonsmoking contracts are gradually extended in an attempt to institute *environmental control* of smoking (Nolan 1968). Smoking behavior becomes attached to so many environmental stimuli that laboratory control of smoking is unlikely to maintain control over smoking outside the laboratory. Smoking behavior thus needs to be controlled in the real environment. A more detailed coverage of environmental control will be given in relation to the treatment of obesity.

MASSED PRACTICE

Only two studies have used *massed practice* in an attempt to produce satiation and conditioned inhibition. Resnick (1968) brought his smokers up to smoking four packs of cigarettes a day within 2 days of the commencement of treatment. Keutzer (1968) compared the effects of "coverant" control (this term is identical in meaning to the term "contingency management" as used by Tooley and Pratt, 1967), breath-holding (a particular form of covert sensitization), massed practice, placebo tablet, and no treatment. All four treatment conditions (including placebo) produced better results than no treatment but did not differ among each other.

HYPNOBEHAVIORAL MODEL

It must be admitted that the results of most of these approaches within the framework of behavior therapy technics have not thus far been very impressive. Used in the context of a hypnobehavioral model however, these *technics have proven to be very useful*. In conjunction with standard training in hypnotic induction and sensory recall, the patient is given images and suggestions related directly to smoking. As in the treatment of alcoholism, imagery involves the pairing of nauseous stimuli with smoking (covert sensitization), pairing of pleasant stimuli with the act of resisting a cigarette, or both combined in one image. In the treatment of smoking using systematic desensitization (Koenig and Masters 1965, Pyke et al. 1966), the act of smoking was paired with relaxation, which would only serve to reinforce the smoking behavior. The response of not smoking or resisting the cigarette must be paired with reinforcement or relaxation. Imaginal massed practice is often used in a type of covert sensitization model with hypnosis. Here the subject sees himself smoking past the point of satiation, bloating, feeling a distension in his stomach, and becoming nauseated from the taste and his overindulgence in smoking. In the massed-practice model, no other foul taste or smell is paired with the smell of the cigarette. The suggestion is simply made that as the subject continues to smoke one cigarette after another the cigarette taste itself will become foul and repugnant.

The role-playing model of Janis and Mann (1965), which is also a form of covert sensitization, is very effective in the hypnobehavioral model as is the concept of contractual management or environmental control. The following case illustrates the use of these technics in a hypnobehavioral model:

L.C., aged 63 and recently retired, came complaining he was smoking over two packs of cigarettes a day and had been a heavy smoker for the last 2 years. He was presently quite concerned about a constant irritation he felt in his throat. Although a medical examination had shown no cancer was present, his doctor had warned him about abusing the already sensitized lung and throat tissue. In addition to working on the smoking problem, therapy was directed at alleviating the boredom of retirement, and motivating him to get more exercise, sleep, and a proper diet. He presently was eating only once a day and sitting around the house. With so much time on his hands, he was constantly thinking of smoking. The excess time also made him nervous and the added tension produced more smoking. As mentioned before, anxiety mediates and exacerbates most bad habit patterns.

The patient was first taught hypnosis and self-hypnosis so that he could work at lowering his general level of anxiety. After a week of practice with hypnosis, patients generally report feeling much more relaxed and able to cope with their problems. He was also directed to chart or record every time he took a cigarette. Grids dividing the days into 15-minute segments were supplied and he was to put a slash mark in the appropriate box each time he smoked. Not only is a frequency count possible using this method but it enables the therapist to see whether there is any particular pattern to the smoking behavior, (i.e., does the patient smoke more on Thursdays, or evenings, or on the hour, etc.). If it is found that smoking is heavier at certain times than others, the subject should be questioned thoroughly about the conditions prevailing around these particular time periods. This questioning may lead to the uncovering of certain stimuli which are primary in eliciting the smoking behavior. One must always ask the question, "What variables or stimuli are more often present during smoking than during periods of not smoking?" The patient, when requested to chart, will very often say that he smokes all the time and there is no pattern. Do not listen to this; most people are not aware of their habit patterns until they are recorded.

In addition to revealing a smoking habit pattern and stimuli eliciting this habit, charting serves two other functions: (1) It gives the therapist a pre-treatment base rate so that he knows exactly the frequency of occurrence of the behavior he wishes to eliminate. Thereafter it gives him a periodic evaluation of progress. Criterion for cure is simple—no emission of the smoking behavior. This type of measurement makes possible a valid evaluation of psychotherapeutic methods. (2) The act of recording itself is somewhat aversive and may serve to decrease the unwanted behavior. Rather than record it each time, it may be easier just to not smoke the cigarette. We once had a patient exclaim when asked to chart, "Oh, but what if I don't smoke anymore then?" Also, knowing that the therapist will review his charting at the beginning of each session makes the patient less likely to transgress. He will in fact be held accountable for *every* cigarette he smoked that week. The patient can of course cheat and not record everything, but it is made very clear to him that this is only defeating himself. Usually, patients either record *every* cigarette or refuse to chart at all. We have never had a case where a chart was "fudged" to look good. Sometimes facing the full reality of the situation by charting is too depressing for the patient and he should not chart until he is making better progress. He is then reinforced by seeing the results on paper. Charting becomes very reinforcing for the patient once he is progressing, as it serves as a clear indication of his improvement. Rather than quitting "cold-turkey," the patient is usually given the suggestion to phase out smoking gradually. Records of smoking should show a gradual decrease in frequency of smoking behavior. The decrease can be monitored down to a decrease of as little as one cigarette a week using the charting technics.

L. C. was also given explicit instructions in environmental control. Ideally, no other activity should ever be paired with smoking. When the smoker smokes, he should be doing nothing else. He should not be talking, eating, reading, or watching television. The more activities (CS) he pairs with smoking (UCS) the more these activities will elicit smoking behavior. If for example, a person always smokes a cigarette when speaking on the telephone, soon the act of telephoning will lead to the subject's wanting a cigarette. It's a simple classical conditioning paradigm.

Not only the activities, but the physical settings associated with smoking must be limited. The patient should smoke only in one chair in one room of the house. If he associates smoking with all the rooms in his house, and his car, and his office, all of these environmental stimuli will come to elicit smoking behavior. In the beginning it is best to request that the patient phase out one activity and environmental space at a time in regard to conditions under which he will not smoke. In the case of L. C., he first agreed not to smoke while telephoning or while in his car. Throughout therapy, situations and activities in or during which he could smoke were finally narrowed down to sitting in a green chair in his den. Smoking behavior can be delimited along other dimensions, also, such as temporal ones. In this case the subject agrees to smoke only during given hours of the day.

In the beginning of treatment the whole world was associated with smoking; toward the end of therapy the subject's green chair was the only object associated with smoking. The desire to smoke was not reinforced in the presence of any other stimulus configuration than the green chair in his study. In conjunction with other technics which follow, even the association of smoking with the green chair was extinguished, and smoking was not elicited by any stimuli. Environmental control of this nature is also used with alcoholics and cases of obesity. It was not mentioned in the chapter on alcoholism, as drinking usually is much more situation-specific.

Contingency management is also used in the hypnobehavioral model. This term applies to the patient's ability to reinforce himself (self-reinforcement). Every time the patient resists a cigarette or makes a negative statement either to himself or out loud concerning smoking he reinforces himself. He may reinforce himself with a high probability behavior such as having a coke; he may simply say to himself, "Well done, that was good," and feel great; or he may flash on a pleasant image or happy experience, thus reinforcing himself with relaxation or emotional recall of elation. It is important that the patient pat himself on the back every time he resists a cigarette rather than saying, as most smokers do, "Yeah, I didn't smoke this time, but big deal, what about the pack I smoked this morning?" It is imperative that the patient's mood remain elevated, and he must repeatedly be told not to berate himself for smoking an extra cigarette. If he "kicks himself" for taking an additional cigarette, he will feel depressed. The depression will lead to anxiety and despondency, which will only lead to more smoking. It is a common pattern to see a person go just a little off his regimen and then "blow" the whole program. These binges are triggered by the patient's intrapunitiveness at waivering just a fraction off his given course to total abstinence. The patient is forewarned of this pattern so that he will recognize it when he feels himself slipping into it.

POSTHYPNOTIC SUGGESTIONS

In the first hypnotic session the patient is given specific posthypnotic suggestions, which are elaborated upon later in therapy. Often only one session of hypnosis is required (Dengrove, Nuland, and Wright 1970; Kline 1970; Spiegel 1970; Von Dedenroth 1968). Others as (Hall and Crasilneck 1970, Nuland and Field 1970, Johnson and Donoghue 1971, Wright 1970, Kroger 1967) describe more extensive hypnotherapy. The following is a sample verbalization of the posthypnotic suggestions of Kroger (1967), which the authors have used successfully on many smokers:

Place your favorite brand of cigarettes in a Band-Aid box. On one side paste a poison label with a skull-and-bones logo. On the other side, paste the outer side of a pack of your favorite brand. The association of the two will be obvious. Also wedge the top firmly so it's hard to open the box. [Frequent pairing of the poison label and cigarettes is better than pontificating on the dangers of smoking.] Next, use your imagination to curb your desire rather than your will. Therefore, each time you even think of smoking a cigarette, associate the pleasurable aroma and taste of a cigarette with the most horrible and awful smell and taste that you have ever experienced. Under autohypnosis you can convert your craving for a cigarette into an aversion. This will not happen immediately, but after you have given yourself a sufficient number of autosuggestions in this regard, you will notice that slowly and systematically you will have less and less desire for cigarettes. Also, smoke several cigarettes and notice the awful, foul taste in your mouth. Then rinse with your favorite mouthwash. Note how clean and fresh your mouth feels. Do you want to have a foul breath all the time?

Next, if you really wish to stop smoking, every time you puff on a cigarette, think of a cut-off or quitting date (Q.D.). Ask yourself, will I be successful and make it on the exact date, before or after the Q.D.? [This extraverbal approach in effect assures the patient of having a goal.]

You will agree that the best results are obtained if one has a goal. Hence, suggest smoking half as much during the next two weeks. Then cut down half as much again for the following two weeks until you are able to wean yourself from the habit. You can set a goal and an arbitrary number of cigarettes to be smoked daily according to your needs and at your own pace.

Since you are right-handed, would you mind *holding the cigarette in your left hand* and, instead of placing the cigarette in the right side of your mouth, which is customary for you, would you mind using the left hand for putting the cigarette in the left side of your mouth? You will, I am sure, find that if you follow these suggestions, you will be breaking up a well established reflex.

Would you mind holding the cigarette first between your thumb and little finger, then your thumb and ring finger, middle finger, or other fingers. By utilizing different combinations, you will soon find that smoking becomes rather inconvenient.

If you really are interested in giving up this habit, allow several cigarette butts to remain in the ashtray until they develop a very stale odor. Then sniff this odoriferous ashtray at least once every hour. If you do this, you will easily develop a distaste for cigarettes. May I suggest that another ashtray with stale butts be placed on your nightstand beside your bed just before retiring. When you no longer can bear the obnoxious smell, place the ashtray out in the hall, but do not empty the ashtray, as you should repeat this procedure the next night until every fresh cigarette reminds you of a stale one.

After your smoking is reduced, you might consider the possibility of trading down to a more innocuous habit. How about substituting a peppermint Lifesaver for each cigarette that you do not smoke? You will find that, whenever the tip of your tongue is put into the hole of the Lifesaver the same satisfaction will be obtained as if you had smoked a cigarette. If this is not feasible, you can use chewing gum or a dummy cigarette instead. You can hold the latter between your lips and imagine it's real.

In addition to the above suggestions, one can stress the health and other benefits related to abstinence. If the individual is a heavy smoker, his nails usually are discolored by nicotine. One can, with tongue in cheek, point out that this discoloration occurs in the bronchial tubes, too; that the inside of the bronchial tubes actually "stinks" like the stale cigarettes. It is emphasized that all these suggestions, if given by the patient to himself, afford a distinct possibility that the habit can be broken because of his own efforts. Furthermore, it should be emphasized that all credit for breaking the habit belongs to him, since he really did it through his imagination. The posthypnotic suggestions are useful for symptom-removal. About 40 per cent of patients relapse. Therefore, it is advisable to reinforce the suggestions at least every week.

When excessive chain smoking is a symptom of underlying tension, the needs for the nervous tension must be eliminated. When hypnosis was used for symptom-removal, the authors have never seen the slightest harm.

In the case of L.C., once he had learned these specific suggestions and was becoming adept at sensory recall, work was begun in the construction of an aversive image to be paired with the thought of smoking. The patient recounted an incident during which he was to sit up with his sick brother-in-law. In the middle of the night the man defecated all over the bed. The smell was horrendous. Covert densitization was then begun by having L.C. vividly recall that particular night, see himself smoking, smell and taste the cigarette, then smell the bowel movement, dip the cigarette into the feces, smoke it, throw up, roll the cigarette in the vomit, swallow it, taste the feces, vomit the cigarette from his mouth, and leave the room and cigarette behind. Immediately upon leaving the room and the smell of cigarette smoke, he was told he felt fine and that the taste and smell of cigarettes was gone, and a feeling of euphoria came over him. In this image a *relief stimulus* is used. The moment the subject makes an avoidance response to escape the taste and smell of the cigarette, he is reinforced by a feeling of well-being and the disappearance of the nauseous feeling. The termination of nausea is associated with the escape from the cigarette.

Any of the 25 standard images can be employed to reinforce the avoidance response. The patient is to place himself in one of these scenes smoking a cigarette. He is to concentrate on the taste and smell of it. The taste and smell grow stronger and stronger with each puff and the image is soon obscured by a cloud of stale yellow smoke. All other senses also dull. The moment he stops or avoids smoking, the cloud clears and the beautiful image reappears in all five sense modalities. If aversive conditioning is desired, Image V (desert) can be modified to pair the dry, parched, hot, tongue-thickening, throat-constricting sensations therein with the act of smoking. When the cigarette is put out, the freshwater sea appears and the thirst is quenched and taste freshened. Verbalizations such as "Every puff you take it gets hotter and hotter . . . every taste you take your throat gets drier and drier" are very effectively incorporated into this image to sensitize the smoker to cigarettes.

L.C. was also given, and told to practice, sessions of positive imagery alone. In these sessions he was simply told to see and smell a cigarette, approach it, then resist. The act of resisting was self-reinforced by pleasant emotional and/or sensory recall. No sense of nausea or repulsion is felt at any point in this technic. The subject sees himself as able to resist a cigarette and he feels good about it.

The next technic used was that of role playing a doctor-patient interview while the patient was in hypnosis. The instructions were as follows:

You have been bothered for a long time by an irritation in your throat. Although you have been warned to stop smoking, you have continued to do so. You have just completed a long series of medical tests and have come to the doctor's office for the results. You are standing in front of the doctor, who is seated at his desk. See the room, what color are the walls? What is the room temperature; is it stuffy; do you smell anything? What are you wearing? Do you hear any outside noises? Feel that sinking-feeling in your stomach. Your heart is pounding rapidly in anticipation of the results. The doctor speaks, "How have you been?" [The patient answers.] "I'm afraid I have some rather bad news for you. We must surgically remove your voice box. There is a cancerous pocket in the back of your throat that must be cut out." [Further statements may be made between patient and therapist in their respective roles before the subject is brought out of the hypnotic state. The following final posthypnotic suggestion is given.] At anytime hence that you feel the urge to take a cigarette, you will think of this scene and the terrible feeling it evoked in you.

It is common to use several technics on one case. In reference to L.C., the hypnotic technic using positive imagery alone seemed to be most beneficial. It was not given first because the patient had specifically asked for covert sensitization using aversive imagery. He was quite surprised to find that positive imagery worked better. After 15 sessions the patient was no longer smoking. Two years later he is still not smoking. Whenever he feels the urge, he induces the hypnosis, sees himself resisting the cigarette, and recalls a sense of elation. He finds it necessary to practice self-hypnosis on the average of twice a week, 10 minutes each session, in order to maintain his abstinence.

IMPORTANCE OF MOTIVATION AND REINFORCEMENT

We have not emphasized motivation as an important variable in the alleviation of the smoking habit. Nor have we pointed out that prepayment of a fee results in a higher recovery rate. Another important variable to be considered is long-term reinforcement at monthly intervals. Since we are dealing with a condition which has a high relapse rate, this is necessary in the chronic smoker. Hypnobehavioral therapy when combined with the aforementioned variables can "bind a patient in treatment" and yield a higher success rate.

REFERENCES

Dengrove, E., Nuland, W. and Wright, M. E.: A single-treatment method to stop smoking using ancillary self hypnosis: Discussions. Internat. J. Clin. Exp. Hypn., *18:*251, 1970.

Franks, C. M., Fried, R., and Ashem, B.: An improved apparatus for the aversive conditioning of cigarette smokers. Behav. Res. Ther., *4:*301, 1966.

Greene, R. J.: Modification of smoking behavior by free operant conditioning methods. Psychol. Rec., *14:*171, 1964.

Hall, J. A. and Crasilneck, H. B.: Development of a hypnotic technique for treating chronic cigarette smoking. Internat. J. Clin. Exp. Hypn., *18:*283, 1970.

Janis, I. L. and Mann, L.: Effectiveness of emotional role-playing in modifying smoking habits and attitudes. J. Exp. Res. Pers., *1:*84, 1965.

Johnston, E. and Donoghue, J. R.: Hypnosis and smoking: A review of the literature. Amer. J. Clin. Hypn., *13:*265, 1971.

Keutzer, C. S.: Behavior modification of smoking: the experimental investigation of diverse techniques. Behav. Res. Ther., *6:*137, 1968.

Koenig, K. P. and Masters, J.: Experimental treatment of habitual smoking. Behav. Res. Ther., *3:*235, 1965.

Kraft, T. and Al-Issa, I.: Desensitization and reduction in cigarette consumption. J. Psychol., *67:*323, 1967.

Kroger, W. S. and Libott, R. Y.: Thanks Doctor I've Stopped Smoking. Springfield, Charles C Thomas, 1967.

McGuire, R. J. and Vallance, M.: Aversion therapy by electric shock: a simple technique. Brit. Med. J., *1:*151, 1964.

Mann, L.: The effects of emotional role playing on desire to modify smoking habits. J. Exp. Soc. Psychol., *3:*334, 1967.

Nolan, J. D.: Self-control procedures in the modification of smoking behavior. J. Consult. Clin. Psychol., *32:*92, 1968.

Nuland, W. and Field, P. B.: Smoking and hypnosis: a systematic clinical approach. Internat. J. Clin. Exp. Hypn., *18:*290, 1970.

Powell, J. and Azrin, N.: The effects of shock as a punisher for cigarette smoking. J. Appl. Behav. Anal., *1:*63, 1968.

Pyke, S., Agnew, N.McK., and Kopperud, J.: Modification of an overlearned maladaptive response through a relearning programme: a pilot study on smoking. Behav. Res. Ther., *4:*196, 1966.

Resnick, J. H.: The control of smoking behavior by stimulus satiation. Behav. Res. Ther., *6:*113, 1968.

Spiegel, H.: A single-treatment method to stop smoking using ancillary self-hypnosis. Internat. J. Clin. Exp. Hypn., *18:*235, 1970.

Tooley, J. T. and Pratt, S.: An experimental procedure for the extinction of smoking behavior. Psychol. Rec., *17:*209, 1967.

Von Dedenroth, T. E.: The use of hypnosis in 1000 cases of "tobaccomaniacs." Amer. J. Clin. Hypn., *3:*194, 1968.

Wilde, C. J.: Behavior therapy for addicted cigarette smokers: a preliminary investigation. Behav. Res. Ther., *2:*107, 1964.

————: Correspondence. Behav. Res. Ther., *2:*313, 1965.

Wright, M. E.: A single-treatment method to stop smoking using ancillary self-hypnosis: Discussion. Internat. J. Clin. Exp. Hypn., *18:*261, 1970.

SUGGESTED READINGS

Kline, M.: The use of extended group hypnotherapy sessions in controlling cigarette habituation. Internat. J. Clin. Exp. Hypn., *18:*270, 1970.

Marston, A. R. and McFall, R. M.: Comparison of behavior modification approaches to smoking reduction. J. Consult. Clin. Psychol., *36:*153, 1971.

16

Insomnia

IMPORTANCE OF AUTOHYPNOSIS AND AUTORELAXATION

It is interesting that one of the first effects patients report from their practice of autohypnosis is that they are able to sleep much better. Hypnotic relaxation very easily merges into true sleep if properly directed. It appears that insomnia is a label describing the persistence of behaviors that are incompatible with sleep, such as worry and excessive rumination. Many patients suffering from insomnia report that their minds "race" when trying to sleep. They relive the whole day's activities and also worry about the events of tomorrow.

In a study in behavior therapy, Geer and Katkin (1966) cite a case involving a 29-year-old female insomniac helped by relaxation training. The subject was instructed to visualize going to bed, ruminating (she was worried over a broken engagement, her future, and her inability to sleep), and then relaxing.

Hypnosis effects improvement in acute cases of insomnia. Often a single session is effective in restoring the sleep cycle, particularly if autohypnosis has been taught on the initial visit. It can be suggested that the autohypnosis will merge with real sleep. The following posthypnotic suggestions are efficacious:

After you have established a deep state of autohypnosis, with each breath you will find yourself going *deeper* and *deeper relaxed.* And as your breathing gets *slower, deeper,* and more *regular,* you will find yourself going into a *deeper* and *deeper* state of *relaxation.* And as you relax *deeper,* you will find that you will become *drowsier* and *drowsier* until you get *sleepier* and *sleepier.*

POSTHYPNOTIC SUGGESTIONS

Chronic insomnia, however, is more difficult to treat. Many patients have deep-seated problems, and the symptom cannot be alleviated unless the patient is able to recognize and deal objectively with these problems. When the tensions are decreased, the insomnia can be controlled. Here, too, the imagination plays an important role. Patients are instructed that the harder they try to fall asleep, the less chance they will have of doing so; that lack of sleep seldom produces harm but that worry wreaks more havoc than lack of sleep. Following the law of reversed effect, the posthypnotic suggestions must be directed *toward the need to keep awake!* The harder they try to remain awake, the more likely they are to fall asleep. Adjunctive procedures such as regular hours for going to sleep, mild exercise to induce fatigue, hot drinks, and warm baths are helpful for promoting relaxation. Barbiturates and other drugs should not be removed at once but should be reduced gradually. Environmental factors such as noise also must be eradicated. The physiology and pathology of sleep disorders have been described by Kales (1969); the technics for sleep styles by Rechtschaffen and Kales (1968). More specifically, hypnosis can be directed to symptom-removal as follows:

At first you might consider the possibility of deliberately trying to keep awake; that is, do *not* try to fall asleep but, rather, imagine that you must stay awake as long as possible. Thus, you can imagine that you are a watchman or sentry; that it is necessary to continually screen all sounds you hear. You will notice that it will become increasingly difficult to deliberately stay awake, and that sleep will gradually come over you.

Next, sleep can be facilitated by the "theatre technic," that is, stepping out of yourself in slow motion (depersonalization). In a dream you can see yourself performing all sorts of tasks, can you not? Thus, during hypnosis you can also see yourself on a motion picture screen. You are lying in your bed. Now you are stepping out of yourself as if you were looking at a trick picture shot in which your other, depersonalized self is getting up slowly. In slow motion it is walking over to the other side of the room and sitting down in a comfortable chair alongside the bed. Now as your other self sees you lying there with your eyes closed, you can notice your breathing getting *slower, deeper,* and more *regular.* You also can notice the slow, rhythmic *rise* and *fall* of your chest, and the *calm, relaxed* expression on your face. And as you keep looking at this image of yourself, you will become *very, very relaxed. Very, very relaxed.* As long as you keep your arms and legs in a nice, comfortable position, you will find that every muscle is *relaxing* more and more, and with every *breath* you will find that every muscle is *relaxing* more and more, and with every *breath* you will get very *drousy.* And as you get *very, very drousy* you will find that even though your eyes remain tightly closed, you will get *sleepier* and *sleepier.* After you become *sleepier* and *sleepier,* the image of yourself will in slow motion get up from the chair and in still slower motion walk over to the bed, and your depersonalized self will then merge and become as one with your own real self.

TECHNICS FOR AUTOHYPNOSIS AND SCENE VISUALIZATION

Another excellent technic successful for resistant patients is the *doubling back*, or modified progressive relaxation, technic. This is somewhat similar to the technics used for self-hypnosis. The added advantages are the use of scene visualization for each zone of the body and the continual doubling back after each progressive step to relax each portion of the body. The repetitive relaxation scenes are induced again and again until the individual escapes by falling asleep. This is somewhat similar to the technic termed *escape-avoidance* by the behaviorists. The following is our technic verbatim:

If you wish to *stop remaining awake,* first fix your gaze on a spot on the ceiling above your forehead or a light coming in through the blinds, drapes, or shades. Suggest to yourself that your lids are getting *very, very heavy.* After they have become *very, very, very heavy,* you will let the lids gently *close* together. Then roll your eyeballs up into the back of your head for a few seconds to *seal* the eyelids *tighter, tighter,* and *tighter.* Now, let your eyeballs roll back down into normal position. Note how your eyelids are stuck *tighter* and *tighter* together. Next tell yourself that your toes, legs, feet, and thighs are getting *very, very heavy.* Imagine that they are just as *heavy* as they would be as if your legs were dangling over a pier while fishing. Or just as *heavy* and leaden as if you were walking for miles along a beach, and your feet were continually sinking into the soft, wet sand. Now after your legs up to your thighs have become very, very heavy, double back and repeat to yourself, "My eyes and legs (this includes the toes, legs, feet, and thighs) are *very, very heavy* and *relaxed."* Now suggest to yourself, "My arms are just as numb, *heavy* and *relaxed* as if I had fallen asleep on them." Now repeat, "My eyes, legs and arms are completely *relaxed."* Next, *relax* your trunk to the waist. Imagine that you have taken off a *very, very* tight belt or pair of swim trunks—you feel the entire area below the waistline relaxing, getting *deeper* and *deeper relaxed.* Now, double back and suggest to yourself "My eyes, legs, arms, and trunk are completely *relaxed."* Now relax your chest. Imagine that you have been swimming underwater and holding your breath as long as possible. Imagine how good it feels to come up out of the water and feel your chest wall *relax* after you start breathing again. Now suggest to yourself, "My eyes, legs, arms, trunk, and chest are completely *relaxed."* Finally, imagine that your head is completely *relaxed.* Just as *relaxed* as if you were taking a hot sauna bath or if you were in a hot steam room. Or you can imagine how your head feels after a cold breaks up and you can breathe easily again. Double back, suggesting to yourself, "My eyes, legs, arms, trunk, chest, and head are completely *relaxed.* I am completely relaxed *from my head to my toes."*

This technic can be used in one form or another and modified by the hyno-therapist. We have noted that the continual doubling back or repetition increases the likelihood of a response being attained if prior, invoked suggestions have resulted in desired responses. The individual is instructed to keep repeating this procedure several times during the night. Usually individuals become so fatigued by the mental gymnastics of this technic, particularly if it is repeated several times, that they readily fall asleep. The relaxing images thus become a means of misdirecting the patient's thoughts from those that are keeping him awake to those that will produce general relaxation leading to sleep. Worrisome thoughts are thus reciprocally inhibited, leading to the extinction of responses incompatible with sleep.

HYPNOBEHAVIORAL TECHNICS

In general, one must minimize the importance of sleep. Also, one must use strong suggestions that the hypnotic relaxation will eventuate in sleep, as it often does. Another technic utilizing the principle of paradoxical intention can also be used in conjunction with the charting technic. The patient is asked to record every time he wakes up. It is then determined at what time he usually wakes, and the alarm clock is set for that time. The directive is given that the patient must get up when the alarm goes off. Deliberately attempting to wake up at a premature time generally leads to the patient's sleeping straight through the signal.

The concept of environmental control is also very important in regard to insomnia. The bed should be a symbol for sleep; sleep should be the only response elicited by the bed. Therefore, no activities other than sleep should be paired with the bed, especially if the patient has a sleep problem. He should not read, smoke, eat, or watch television in his bed. If, for example, his mind is very active during the reading of a novel in bed, the bed after several pairings with intellectual activity, comes to elicit this activity without the book being present. Likewise it is best if sleeplessness and restlessness are not associated with the bed. It is advisable to get out of bed when you cannot sleep.

People who cannot sleep at night often nap in the day. This should definitely be avoided, as it interferes with the normal sleep pattern. Also, if a person does nap in the afternoon, it should be in his bed, not on a couch or easy chair. Only one object should be associated with sleep and that is the bed. The importance of not associating failure, such as sleeplessness, with a particular object is also illustrated in problems of a sexual nature. Several males have said that they are potent everywhere except in the bed. The bed has been associated with failure or impotence so many times that just its presence elicits feelings of impotence and sexual inadequacy.

The most common approach to achieving sleep is to induce hypnosis, recall a pleasant image or childhood memory, and let the mind free-associate. This method combined with either hypnotic or progressive relaxation and "misdirection of attention" will merge into sleep.

Punishing suggestions, such as reading a dictionary, legal documents or lease agreements often are effective in inducing sleep. If these technics fail, we suggest contractual management as follows: "Every night you cannot sleep, you must take every dish and utensil out of the kitchen cabinet, wash and dry each and every one of them, and you will return each to the proper drawer or shelf." This technic of behavioral management is highly effective for confirmed insomniacs.

STANDARDIZED IMAGES

Any of the standard relaxing images is conducive to sleep, and many end with the suggestion, "you drift, you float, you dream." Particularly effective for insomnia is Image III (garden) which, in effect, is a midsummer night's dream. Images II (mountain cabin), VII (farm), and XVI (thunder shower) are all also good, as they end with the subject's sleeping by a fireplace, in a field of clover, or in a large, canopied bed with heavy quilts. These images make it particularly easy for the subject to go directly from the hypnotic state into sleep, and they can be induced at bedtime.

REFERENCES

Geer, J. H. and Katkin, E. S.: Treatment of insomnia using a variant of systematic desensitization: a case report. J. Abnorm. Psychol., *71:*161, 1966.
Kales, A.: Sleep: Physiology and Pathology. Philadelphia, J. B. Lippincott, 1969.
Rechtschaffen, A. and Kales, A. (eds.): A Manual of Standardized Terminology, Techniques and Scoring System for Sleep Styles of Human Subjects. United States Public Health Service publication. Washington, D.C., 1968.

SUGGESTED READINGS

Boblitt, W. E.: Electrosleep as a sleep induction method. Psychiat. Forum, *1:*9, 1969.
Koegler, R. R., Hicks, S. M., and Barger, J.: Medical and psychiatric uses of electrosleep. Dis. Nerv. Syst., *32:*100, 1971.
Weiss, M. F.: The treatment of insomnia through the use of electrosleep: an EEG study. J. Nerv. Ment. Dis., *153:*108, 1973.

17

Narcotic Addiction

ETIOLOGIC FACTORS

Drug addiction involves many of the psychological factors that account for chronic alcoholism and obesity. In general, there are three types. In the first, the addict attempts to meet stressful situations with more equanimity through the use of drugs. In the second, individuals use drugs to give them a lift. In the third, the addict requires drugs to help to overcome depressive reactions due to characterologic disorders.

It is contended that an uncontrollable craving occurs in predisposed individuals even after a single exposure to a narcotic drug. Regardless of the method of addiction, drugs are utilized to provide the equivalent of sexual gratification, security, and self-esteem. The fact that the emotional needs are more important than the physiologic factors is noted in the response of the addict after withdrawal symptoms have ceased. Usually he will return to the use of whatever drug satisfied his emotional needs.

BEHAVIOR TECHNICS

Very little research on drug addiction has been done by behavior therapists. Raymond (1964) and Liberman (1968) used modified apomorphine technics with apparent success. Wolpe (1965) treated a physician addicted to Demerol by means of a portable shock apparatus, which the patient carried with him. Whenever the craving for the drug arose or whenever it was precipitated by external stimulation, the physician administered shocks to himself. While the patient relapsed after shock was discontinued, Wolpe suggests that regular booster treatment (self-administered) on a partial reinforcement basis might have prevented reinstatement of the craving.

O'Brien, Raynes, and Patch (1972) combined several behavioral treatment approaches to develop an effective and rapid treatment of heroin addiction. A classical aversive conditioning procedure using both an electric shock and verbal imaginal aversive stimulus (UCS) was used to extinguish the consummatory response of heroin use. A modified form of Jacobson's (1938) relaxation was used to overcome tension and to develop an alternate behavior as a substitute for drug-induced relaxation. Wolpe's (1958) systematic desensitization technic was used to treat anxiety that was cueing the consummatory response of heroin use.

Matefy (1973) used systematic desensitization to treat a client who for 5 months was experiencing spontaneous recurrences of LSD effects. Several imaginal anxiety hierarchies were constructed—all with interpersonal themes taken from real-life situations. The patient was taught to relax deeply and then to associate this deep relaxed state with images of increasingly more threatening situations. In time, the patient could visualize the most stressful scene in the series without anxiety. Besides the elimination of the target symptoms (flashback effects), additional desired changes occurred on both cognitive affective and behavioral levels.

Gotestam and Melin (1974) developed a covert extinction paradigm applied to four amphetamine addicts with long-term and heavy intravenous abuse of central nervous system stimulants. The technics included the imaginative presentation of the patient's injection ritual, repeated 15 times a day. Three of the addicts had not taken amphetamines during a 9-month follow-up period. Covert technics such as these, which make use of imagery, offer several advantages over alternative behavior modification procedures. First, they enable one to use more vivid situations (the complete addiction situation) compared to the simple items one could otherwise use in the ward (syringes, capsules, etc.); second, there are modest- or no equipment requirements; and third, experimenters using these methods have reported better patient participation and lower dropout rates.

PSYCHOTHERAPY

Addicts are usually immature, impulsive individuals who have a low frustration tolerance. They are irresponsible, with a limited ability to face reality and a distorted idea of social values. Many feel inadequate and inferior even though they present a facade of arrogance and confidence. They also manifest strong dependency strivings, but, instead of looking for assistance from healthy individuals, they seek other equally maladjusted persons. Therapy should be directed toward restoration of their self-confidence, elimination of despondency, induction of a sense of well-being or elation and, in some instances, simply toward maintenance of normal equilibrium. Most addicts find greater satisfaction in the immediate attainment of self-confidence by drugs and cannot tolerate the time-consuming work-and-reward process of secure individuals.

HYPNOTIC TECHNICS

The results with hypnosis in narcotic addiction, until recently, have been poor. Some addicts do better for awhile, but ultimately relapse. Many have conditioned pain-pattern syndromes that are well established, and it is difficult for such persons to give up the drug even temporarily. In our opinion, group hypnotherapy is more likely to achieve results, especially if it is employed in an institution where withdrawal symptoms can be handled and where the addict can be kept under strict supervision. Other adjuvant medical therapy, such as drugs for withdrawal symptoms, vitamins, occupational therapy, sedation, and a nutritious diet can be helpful. Vogel (1937), former chief of the U.S. Public Health Service at Lexington, stated that the most effective adjunctive therapy of addiction was by hypnotherapy.

AUTOHYPNOSIS

Autohypnosis is especially helpful for withstanding the disagreeable subjective sensations produced by withdrawal. Posthypnotic suggestions and deep relaxation help to reduce the intensity of the suffering, particularly the nervousness and the insomnia. Other posthypnotic suggestions, similar to those given to the alcoholic, help to reduce the craving for the drug. Hypersuggestibility tends to decrease with the withdrawal of drugs, and this factor, together with a weak personality structure, accounts for the poor results.

SENSORY IMAGERY CONDITIONING

In several refractory cases, the authors have suggested that the addict use sensory-imagery conditioning to imagine that he is giving himself an injection or taking a drug by mouth while under autohypnosis. When individuals can actually revivify the pleasurable effects afforded by the drug, withdrawal is accomplished more readily.

Newton (1976) used hypnorelaxation to relieve psychosomatic withdrawal symptoms in heroin addicts.* Three other procedures were devised to deal directly with behavior relating to the use of drugs. One procedure consisted of the hypnotized patient imagining himself using heroin and obtaining no effect from the fix. He was given posthypnotic suggestions to lead him to believe the drug trip was of no value to him. Another posthypnotic suggestion was given that he

---

* Personal communication.

remember this fantasied experience whenever the urge to fix occurred. A second procedure involved a hypnotic fantasy in which the patient's preparation for self-injection was paired with increasingly threatening stimuli such as rats, spiders, and snakes. These aversive stimuli disappeared when the addict imagined himself completely rejecting the proposed drug experience.

The final procedure dealt with hypnotically induced fantasies of the addict's imagining himself in situations that usually were resolved by injecting drugs. In these tenuous situations, the addicts imagined themselves declaring that they would not use heroin. This declaration during the imagery was immediately followed with a very rewarding and satisfying fantasy experience. The posthypnotic suggestion, in essence, was that whenever the patient found himself in these situations and had the urge to fix, he would declare to himself that he would not fix, imagining himself refusing the fix, and then rewarding himself with the satisfying sequence.

STANDARDIZED IMAGES

Many hypnotic effects are similar to those produced by drug states and can serve to substitute for the reinforcing sensations of the drug state once the patient has mastered them. Time distortion is particularly pronounced when one is under the influence of a drug, and it can be created by Images VI (space), VII (farm), XI (clock), and XII (blue bird). Dissociation and "out-of-body" experiences are also common with drugs and can be produced with Images I (beach), VIII (jungle), XVII (picnic), XVIII (Shangri-La), and XXII (hayloft). The effects of hallucinogenic drugs can be replicated in Image XX (volcano), where colors intensify and form distorts. A "rush" similar to that experienced from heroin is reported by some patients from practicing Image VI (space) and Image XXIV (mine). In the latter image, surges of hot and cold are felt shooting through the very marrow of the skeletal system.

In general, particular attention must be paid to the individual who has the addiction problem. Treatment by any method cannot be considered successful until the craving for a drug has been abolished permanently.

REFERENCES

Gotestam, D. G. and Melin, L.: Covert extinction of amphetamine addiction. Behav. Ther. *5:*90, 1974.

Jacobson, E.: Progressive Relaxation. Chicago, University of Chicago Press, 1938.

Liberman, R.: Aversive conditioning of drug addicts: a pilot study. Behav. Res. Ther., *5:*251, 1968.

Matefy, R. E.: Behavior therapy to extinguish spontaneous recurrences of LSD effects: A case study. J. Nerv. Ment. Dis., *156:*226, 1973.

O'Brien, J. S., Raynes, A. E., and Patch, V. D.: Treatment of heroin addiction with aversion therapy, relaxation training and systematic desensitization. Behav. Res. Ther., *10:*77, 1972.

Raymond, M. J.: The treatment of addiction by aversion conditioning with apomorphine. Behav. Res. Ther., *1:*287, 1964.

Vogel, V. H.: Suggestibility in narcotic addicts. Pub. Health Rep. Suppl., *16:*132, 1937.

Wolpe, J.: Psychotherapy by Reciprocal Inhibition. Stanford, Stanford University Press, 1958.

————: Conditioned inhibition of craving in drug addiction: A pilot experiment. Behav. Res. Ther., *2:*285, 1965.

SUGGESTED READINGS

Barber, T. X.: LSD, Marihuana, Yoga and Hypnosis. Chicago, Aldine, 1970.

Baumann, F.: Hypnosis and the adolescent drug abuser. Amer. J. Clin. Hypn. *13:*17, 1971.

Deissler, K. J.: Synanon—Its concepts and methods. Drug Dependence, NIMH, Issue #5, Oct. 1970.

Khantzian, E. J.: Opiate addiction: a critique of theory and some implications for treatment. Amer. J. Psychotherapy *28:*159, 1974.

Lesser, E.: Behavior therapy with a narcotics user: A case report. Behav. Res. Ther., *5:*251, 1967.

Liebson, I. and Bigelow, G.: A behavioral-pharmacological treatment of dually addicted patients. Behav. Res. Ther. *10:*403, 1972.

Renner, J. A. and Rubin, M. L.: Engaging heroin addicts in treatment. Amer. J. Psychiat., *130:*976, 1973.

Suinn, R. M. and Brittain, J.: The termination of an LSD "freak out" through the use of relaxation. J. Clin. Psychol., *26:*127, 1970.

Wikler, A.: Some implications of conditioning theory for problems of drug abuse. Behav. Sci., *16:*92, 1971.

18

Obesity

ETIOLOGIC FACTORS

Obesity is one of the most common problems brought to the therapist's attention. It is associated with and exacerbates many other problems such as sexual inadequacy, feelings of inferiority, and anxiety states. It also accounts for a high percentage of cardiovascular and degenerative diseases; therefore, its treatment will be discussed in detail. Numerous authors have discussed the importance of psychic factors in stimulating the drive to eat. This is particularly pronounced during the evening, and has been referred to as the "night-eating" syndrome.

It has been demonstrated that, in addition to the deeper psychological forces at work, the ordinary vicissitudes of daily living contribute to the desire to overeat and to the inability to diet. Thus, domestic upsets, fatigue, sexual problems, economic worries, and many other such common sources of tension interfere with the reduction of food intake. The treatment of overweight is much easier if tensions are eliminated. It has been noted that most of the patients who feel well as a result of reduced tension and frustration achieve successful weight reduction. Only those who are emotionally stable should undertake a drastic reducing regimen.

Tension and frustration often lead to excessive caloric intake and subsequent obesity. These reactions usually depend on early developmental patterns. For example, the hungry infant soon learns that frustration is relieved by the pleasurable experience of nursing, thumb-sucking, or playing with a rattle. Although these earlier tension-relieving mechanisms are repressed, the individual always "remembers" the route by which this gratification was once afforded.

211

Other oral methods for the relief of tension are chain-smoking, gum-chewing, and nail-biting. Insecure adults, when faced with frustration, resort to one of these tension-allaying outlets. This "return-to-the-breast" mechanism now involves the use of food to satisfy the oral cravings, since the bottle, the nipple, and the thumb are no longer acceptable. Contrarily, many individuals lose weight following stress.

Excessive food intake can also result from other causes. For instance, in certain "food addicts," overeating is often a substitute for suppressed hostile impulses. Since they cannot express anger toward those around them, they take it out on food, which is smashed to pieces. In homes where food is hard to get, the children eat everything available today, for tomorrow there may be no food. Many parents warn against wasting food, and also praise their children for being good eaters. Even after becoming wealthy, such individuals must "always clean the plate." Parental attitudes and other psychosocial factors determine one's eating habits. Thus, a child brought up on large, rich meals usually imitates the parents' eating habits. This tendency is often more responsible for obesity than hereditary factors.

Overeating due to tension may follow the death of a friend or a relative. Frequently, food is used as a substitute for love. For example, people who are alone and who feel unwanted and unloved substitute the pleasure of eating for affection. Their attitude is *As long as no one loves me, I will be good to myself.* Unwanted children often become obese. To relieve their guilt feelings, some mothers become overprotective and stuff the children with food as a proof of their love. Then, being concerned about their children's weight, they seek the physician's help. They refuse psychotherapy, however, because of their own emotional problems. Adult obesity is a sign of social prestige and a badge of wealth in many races, who overfeed a child to make it fat, not only because they think big babies are healthy babies but also because a plump baby is highly esteemed.

An occupation sometimes is the primary cause of obesity. In high-strung individuals such as actors, singers, or executives, eating may be used for relaxation. Conversely, people who lead a dull life eat more often than usual to relieve the monotony. This is commonly noted in housewives who raid the icebox between meals to lessen the drudgery of their work. There are many fat women who remain obese because their spouses prefer them fat; since these husbands usually have an inferiority complex, they feel more secure with plump, unattractive wives. Sterile women often use obesity as a symbol of the wish for pregnancy.

Persons with heightened sexual impulses often displace these drives by food intake and eat ravenously. Sooner or later this type of individual reacts toward eating with the same feelings as he or she had about sex—namely, shame, guilt and anxiety—and then more food is required to alleviate the tension. Many emotionally insecure individuals unconsciously believe that a heavy layer of body fat is a protective armor against a hostile world. For instance, the young girl, guilty over her sex drives, often retreats behind the "wall of obesity." By doing this, she now has a ready-made alibi for not being attractive to men. She can safely say, "I am so fat; no wonder boys are not interested in me."

Many young athletes enjoy eating large quantities of good food, but they do not gain weight when they are physically active. As they grow older and their lives become more sedentary, their caloric intake exceeds their energy requirements, yet their level of satiation is raised because of their previous eating habits. This type loses weight with difficulty.

The rationalizations proffered for overeating are many. Some of these are: *It runs in my family; it's my glands; others eat twice as much as I do.* However, the actual causal factors are hostility, anxiety, guilt, self-pity, self-punishment, and depression. These are usually found in combination and are often repressed from awareness.

BEHAVIOR MODIFICATION THERAPY

Behavior therapists have now begun to touch a wider range of abnormalities of behavior. Much recent work has been carried out on obesity (Bernard 1968, Cautela 1966, Foreyt and Kennedy 1971, Hall 1972, Harmatz and Lapuc 1968, Harris 1969, Horan and Johnson 1971, Mahoney 1974, Tilker and Meyer 1972, Stuart and Davis 1972, Manno and Marston 1972). Ferster et al. (1962) emphasize that obesity involves a classical instance of the short-term reinforcing effects of overeating's becoming paramount over the longer-term aversive consequences. Therapy in this area has involved essentially the teaching of self-control. Aversive facts about the ultimate consequences of overeating are attached to the eating behavior so that eating becomes an aversive stimulus itself. Self-control procedures are then reinforced because they reduce or terminate the aversive stimulus of eating. In order to make the patient an active participant, he is instructed in the caloric values of food, told to record food intake and weight loss, decrease the range of stimuli for eating responses, increase the chain of responses that precede food ingestion, and strengthen behaviors incompatible with food ingestion. Meyer and Crisp (1964) report success with one patient but not the other in their treatment of two cases of obesity. They used aversive treatment (shock) for approach to "temptation" food while the patients were on a 1000-calorie diet.

Penick et al. (1971) stress control by charting of the discriminatory stimuli that increased eating and such technics to slow down eating as counting each mouthful and placing utensils on the plate after every third mouthful until it is swallowed. They also use positive reinforcement with money as a reward along with negative reinforcement by "doctoring" favorite foods with castor oil or aversive tastes. Reinforcement for weight loss consists of a pound of pure fat hung in the refrigerator and cut into 16 pieces. For each pound lost or gained, the patient removed or replaced one ounce of fat. When all the fat was dissipated, the patient received a prize and lavish praise. Those treated with behavior therapy did better than a control group.

Stunkard (1975) stresses planned social intervention by behavior modification. The program consists of (1) description of behavior to be controlled; (2) control of stimuli that precedes eating; (3) development of technics to control eating; and (4) modification of the consequences of eating. Moderately obese patients can be taught to apply covert sensitization (Cautela 1967) to high-calorie foods, particularly pastries and candy. In this procedure the patient imagines nausea while visualizing eating interdicted foods. Here a pleasurable response is paired to an aversive stimulus, resulting in a decrease in response frequency. All patients are instructed to eat three regular meals daily (Cautela 1971). Covert extinction can be employed to potentiate the effects of covert sensitization. The patients imagine that they are behaving in a particular maladaptive manner (responding) but that the consequences (pleasures) are absent. For instance, they are instructed under hypnosis to imagine eating their favorite high-calorie foods, but the taste or flavors are nonexistent.

Covert reinforcement (Cautela 1970) can be applied to such high-protein, low-preference foods as cottage cheese, raw vegetables and lean meats. The assumption here is that response probability is increased when followed immediately after by a reinforcing stimulus. Patients are instructed to imagine eating high-protein foods (favorable response) followed by a highly pleasurable scene (reinforcer) taken from the reinforcement survey schedule. In good hypnotic subjects, negative and positive hallucinatory experiences can be suggested (Cautela and Kastenbaum 1967).

HYPNOBEHAVIORAL MODEL

In the hypnobehavioral model, the preliminary discussion conducted before the induction of hypnosis is as follows:

First, it is axiomatic that you cannot lose weight unless you take in fewer calories; this means that you will have to follow a diet. All diets are good, but they are only as good as the way they are followed. You will be helped to avoid fattening food through various techniques. Please be assured that you will not be hungry and that you will be able to eat an adequate amount of nutritious and healthful foods. Diets, as you know, can actually mean eating *more* food, but of the right type.

Second, you will be given training in hypnosis and autohypnosis, wherein you will give yourself appropriate autosuggestions. The degree of success will be in direct proportion to the amount of effort you put forth in the practice sessions. If you practice autohypnosis faithfully, you can expect better results. You additionally will be helped to understand what your *need to overeat* represents. You will also be taught how you can face your problems on a more adult level instead of putting food in your mouth to allay anxiety-provoking tensions in the same manner you once used a rattle, a nipple, or a bottle.

When the patient is put on an appropriate diet, he must not only eat the right foods, he must eat them on the proper schedule. Meals should be eaten three times a day with no snacking between. They should be eaten at the same time every day. Hunger is felt according to when the patient is used to eating; if he eats at 9 am, 12 am, and 6 pm every day, his stomach will be conditioned to produce hunger pangs at this time. If, however, food is consumed at inconsistent times from day to day, a production of almost continual hunger pangs will ensue. Many patients report being particularly hungry at night before bed. They have programmed this hunger by continually eating at this time. They find that once they stop reinforcing the feeling of hunger with food at this time, they no longer feel hungry before bed. Not only must the patient not eat more than three times a day, he should not eat less. Meals should not be skipped, as this throws the body's signaling system for hunger off balance. Breakfast is especially important, and it is often seen that dieters skip this meal. If the dieter is still not losing weight once he is eating the right foods at the right time, technics are used to reduce the magnitude of his food intake.

From the beginning, each patient is told to chart his eating behavior and weight loss. He is to record exactly what he eats, the quantity, time of day, and place. He is to record this *before* he eats it. This may discourage his eating of the inappropriate food altogether, and it guarantees an accurate recording. If the individual waits until after the meal or the end of the day to record food consumption, much will be forgotten. This method also insures some immediately aversive consequences of the approach to eating responses. One link in the chain of responses leading to ingestion is now recording the food to be eaten. Recording of this food is a negative experience for a dieter. The approach to food is thus punished immediately before it ends in consummatory behavior. The written name of a forbidden food is definitely a negative secondary reinforcer. Merely going over this list can elicit strong feelings of depression in the patient.

Environmental control is very important in a program for weight loss. Eating must be attached to as few other stimuli as possible. It is very common to find people who eat every meal while watching television. We are started in this practice at a very young age when we are given popcorn at the theatre. Eating must occur only at the table and not in conjunction with any other activity except perhaps a pleasant dinner conversation. Snacking while on the telephone, in bed, at the pool, or in front of the fireplace should be avoided. The more situations that are associated with eating, the more situations that will come to elicit this behavior.

POSTHYPNOTIC SUGGESTIONS

Before strengthening behaviors incompatible with food ingestion, specific posthypnotic suggestions in reference to weight control are given (Kroger 1970a, 1970b). These suggestions after hypnotization have been found applicable to most patients:

If you really wish to lose weight, you will roll the food from the front of the tongue to the back of the tongue and from side to side in order to obtain the last ounce of satisfaction and the "most mileage" out of each morsel and each drop that you eat. By doing this you will more readily satisfy the thousands of taste cells that are located all over your tongue (there is an appetite center located in the hypothalamus), and, as a result, less food will be required and your caloric intake will be immeasurably curtailed.

Second, you will "think thin," that is, you will keep an image uppermost in your mind of how you once looked when you were thin. Perhaps you have a picture of yourself when you weighed less. If so, place this in a prominent position so that you will be continually reminded of the way you once looked. There is considerable basis for this suggestion. You undoubtedly are aware that, if a woman imagines or thinks that she is pregnant, her body will develop the contour of a pregnant woman; her breasts will enlarge and she may, in many instances, stop menstruating. Also, you may have at one time experienced a great deal of inner turmoil and lost weight in spite of the fact that you ate excessively. Cannot a frustrated lover also "pine away" for the beloved?

Third, you might like to think of the most horrible, nauseating, and repugnant smell that you have ever experienced. Perhaps it might be the vile odor of rotten eggs. In the future, whenever you desire to eat something that is not on your diet, you will immediately associate this disagreeable smell with it. Also, you might like to think of the most awful and disgusting taste that you may have had in the past. This, too, can be linked with fattening foods even when you merely think of them.

Finally, for this session, remember that you cannot will yourself to lose weight. The harder you try, the less chance you have to accomplish your aims. So relax—don't press. The next suggestion is to motivate you. Would you mind purchasing the most beautiful dress that you can afford, hang it up in your bedroom where you can see it every morning and imagine yourself getting into it within a relatively short time. You can speculate how soon this will be. Now this is important! The dress you buy should be at least one or two sizes too small for you.

The four suggestions above are given after the operator is certain that hypnosis has been induced. Following dehypnotization, the rationale for these suggestions may be discussed if the patient is inquisitive about them. There is no question that there is a close association between the thousands of taste buds and the impressions that they convey to the higher brain centers for interpretation.

The "think thin" suggestion, to a degree, makes use of the alteration in body image secondary to strong emotional stimuli. It is well recognized that emotions can alter metabolic and endocrine activities to produce weight gain. This has been illustrated vividly in phantom pregnancy or pseudocyesis. If the autonomic nervous system can "trick" endocrine activities and bodily processes into responding with a weight gain to expressed or unexpressed wishes regarding pregnancy, then it is conceivable that these same pathways can produce loss of weight. The opposite side of the coin is to pair the altered body image (leanness) with the instruction that the patient "see" himself in the near future on a scale with the pointer set at the desired weight goal. At this time the therapist can give verbal approval for the imagined weight loss. This is similar to hypnotic age progression or pseudo-orientation in time. The imaginal reinforcement leads to the actual response. In this case the reinforcement is delivered before the response.

The association of fattening foods with disagreeable tastes and odors to produce an aversion is based on classical conditioning methods. Since the organs of taste and smell are distinct, the impulses from each reach the cortex by different pathways. However, the two senses are closely associated psychophysiologically. They should be designated as chemical senses because chemical rather than physical stimuli act on the receptors in the higher centers. The most important aspect of flavor is due to the sense of smell rather than of taste. Olfaction is sensitive to small changes because it is capable of ascertaining the location of the source of a smell. In addition to these chemical sensations, smoothness and roughness, temperature, and pressure sensations originating in the mouth contribute to taste impressions. Zeigler (1973) postulates that the trigeminal system, which carries information about touch and temperature from the mouth, constitutes a link in a "feeling circuit" that controls hunger.

However, in man the sense of smell remains closely associated with the motivation of the individual to eat. The close association of the limbic system (cortical areas, nuclei and fiber tracts phylogenetically associated with the sense of smell) with the emotions is now generally accepted. Perhaps no sense is more provocative of moods and memories than that of smell, and so the smell of food may enhance or diminish the appetite. The close association of taste and smell with feeling states is further reflected in the words that we use to express our reactions to things; we speak of a "sweet" girl, a "salty" character and "sour" grapes. In particular, we use the idea of taste to express our feelings.

The fourth suggestion has a twofold meaning. First, it is highly motivating, as it stresses the value of a nice figure by indirection or extraverbal suggestions. This approach does not mobilize a critical attitude. It makes full use of the imagination. One must be careful to suggest that not all these affirmations or aids will be utilized immediately but that continual repetition through autohypnosis eventually will enable the overweight person to respond to these autosuggestions. If the subject has had some modicum of success, the following verbalization is used on subsequent visits:

You will, if you really wish to lose more weight, consider the following suggestions: Do not plan on more than a 6- to 8-pound weight loss per month, but set a deadline for this weight loss. You will try harder when you have to meet a deadline. Wonder whether you will reach your objective before or after the deadline date. Another helpful suggestion is: "Could you overeat enough to lose 2 pounds per week?"

The desire to eat results when the appetite center in the brain is stimulated, whereas hunger is brought on by contractions of the stomach. If you wish temporarily to delay eating your next meal for several hours, all you have to do is to employ glove anesthesia over the pit of the stomach in order to "knock out" the hunger contractions that are initiated in this area. Another suggestion that might appeal to you, especially if you are interested in having a trim figure, is to think of your ultimate goal in terms of the actual weight desired. Let us assumed, for instance, that you would like to get down to 130. This will be what I call a "food stamp" suggestion, that is, every time you even think of eating something you are not supposed to, you will see the number 130 in blue encircled by a blue ring, much as the price of an item is stamped on the food can in a grocery store. You will give yourself this suggestion particularly at night if you get extremely hungry before retiring.

Finally, if you find that you have exceeded the required food intake and you are still hungry, you can place yourself in hypnosis and *imagine* that you are eating enough pleasurable food to satisfy yourself.

During subsequent visits the patient is asked to repeat the affirmations until they are remembered, and also for reinforcement. New suggestions to reduce caloric intake can be incorporated with the old. These consist of strengthening the patient's desire for weight loss by stressing the health, the social facility, and the beneficial appearance of a trim figure; these act to reinforce the patient's own specific reasons for losing weight. Posthypnotic suggestions may be given to eliminate eating between meals, nibbling, and munching on such items as peanuts while watching television. For those who have a full social life, suggestions can be given to resist inordinate demands for eating and drinking. Suggestions for a specific type of diet, such as one high in protein but low in fats, carbohydrates, and sodium, may be employed at hypnotic levels. Likewise, suggestions at hypnotic levels may be given to induce proper alimentary functions.

Some of the above suggestions have a psychophysiologic basis. In addition to a feeling circuit discussed above, there are hypothalamic centers mediating hunger and satiety. They have not only separate anatomic locations but also different behavioral consequences. Appropriate lesions made in these brain areas in experimental animals result in bulemia, and they eat ravenously. Either a decreased satiability or an increased hunger drive may account for obesity.

It has been established that one of the principle physiologic centers for initiating hunger contractions is just below the xiphoid process in the region of the epigastrium. Glove anesthesia and even pressure to this area minimizes snacking. This may explain why the old adage, "Tighten up your belt a notch," has been thought to assuage hunger.

The "deadline" suggestion is employed only to increase further motivation. This applies also to the "food stamp" suggestion. Many of the other suggestions are based upon stimulating both the taste and visual senses. The visual sense enhances the appetite at the expense of taste and smell. The tongue and the connecting brain centers are continually stimulated by the reciprocal feedback connections. No wonder one unidentified wit said, "One tongue may have three times as many taste buds as another and the empire of taste also has its blind men and deaf mutes."

Hypnoanalytic technics to elicit the needs for overeating are sometimes required. A strong rapport, a noncondemnatory attitude and encouragement when failure occurs facilitate psychotherapy. When permissive technics are employed and it is emphasized that it is a "do-it-yourself program," dependency is avoided.

GROUP HYPNOSIS

Group hypnosis for obesity can be even more rewarding than individual sessions. The authors see four to five patients for 1 hour, at first weekly and then biweekly. The patients first learn autohypnosis and how to modify their eating habits. The use of psychotherapy is helpful in maintaining the optimal weight after it is reached. About 40 per cent relapse and require periodic reinforcement to prevent further weight gain.

IMAGERY CONDITIONING

The patient's general level of anxiety is lowered as a function of his practicing the autohypnosis and appropriate relaxing images. The patient's greater sense of relaxation, combined with the suggestions and information described in the preceding paragraphs, leads to weight loss. If at this point in treatment the patient is still indulging in nondietetic foods, specific imagery is tailored to sensitize the patient to these foods so that he will no longer crave them. Positive imagery is first used. For example, the subject sees himself going to the doughnut box, sniffing the doughnut, replacing it, and walking away. He reinforces the response of walking away or resisting temptation by immediately recalling a sense of elation or relaxation, or an image of himself as thin. After several conditioning trials of this type at home, patients have stated that they have looked at various foods used in this paradigm and could not conceive of actually eating them. The patient can use this procedure with any food and at any time he feels tempted.

If the positive imagery alone does not produce rapid-enough results, specific negative images involving bad tastes and smells are paired with the recall of foods to be negatively conditioned. Preferably the patient recalls aversive experiences from his own life to pair with the food. For example, one female patient recalled an incident that occurred 30 years ago in her childhood. Her grandmother was going to show her the wonders of creation by opening a fertilized chicken egg. When the egg was broken the smell of rot was overwhelming. The egg contained a putrefying embryo covered with thick, clotted blood. The child was requested to bury it. The patient paired the recall of this scene with eating chocolate and never went near chocolate again. In the sensitization image, the patient sees herself eating chocolate while the egg is opened. It should be pointed out that sensitizing a subject to chocolate candy also generalizes to all things with chocolate taste such as chocolate pie, cake, and cookies. Bread and chocolate are probably the two most common objects of food sensitization.

It is even better if the situation recalled involves food. One man recalled throwing up greasy spoiled chicken his mother had served him when a child. Another man remembered being sea sick on a ship during the second World War while a friend of his ate biscuits next to him. One woman recalled finding maggots in a sandwich she was eating.

STANDARDIZED IMAGES

Image III (garden) is very important, as it develops the patient's facility for recall of taste and smell, which is paramount for covert or imaginal sensitization to be effective. Image IV, which incorporates glove anesthesia can be used to "freeze" the hunger pangs by having the patient transfer numbness from his hand to his stomach. It is assumed that if a subject can intensify a feeling he can likewise reduce the intensity of the same feeling. If the patient can be taught to induce hunger he can then also eliminate it. Images VII (farm), X (Arctic), XII (bluebird), XV (mansion), XVIII (Shangri La), and XXI (cantina) all include food and the suggestion for hunger. They can be used effectively to enable the patient to gain control over the hunger drive. They can also be used to sensitize the patient to food by pairing a noxious stimulus with the eating of food or a pleasant stimulus with the avoidance of it.

SPECIALIZED HYPNOBEHAVIORAL TECHNICS

The sensitization need not always be completely covert or imaginal, it may also be completely or partially "in vivo." An example of complete "in vivo" hypnotic sensitization involved a girl who brought a taco and a seaweed pill to overcome her desire for tacos. She hated the smell of seaweed. In hypnosis she was instructed to smell and then eat the taco while smelling the seaweed pill, which had been moistened to increase its potency. She was given the suggestion that from that day forth whenever she smelled or tasted a taco she would also recall the smell of the seaweed, and the concomitant aversive feeling it elicited.

In partial "in-vivo" sensitization, either the negative stimulus is real or the stimulus to be conditioned is real. In an example of the first method, a woman brought an old smelly sock from her husband, who was suffering from a foot disease, and sniffed it while imagining she was eating chocolate brownies. Craving for chocolate ended almost immediately. In an example of the latter method, a patient ate potato chips while imagining that a sewer line broke and covered him with rotting dead fish and rattlesnakes. These technics can be used to sensitize a patient to any object or stimulus he wishes to avoid whether it be cigarettes, alcohol, food, the racetrack, or prostitutes.

Time distortion can also be used in the treatment of obesity. The subject is told to induce a sense of time expansion while he is eating so that he will not eat so long. If it seems as if he has been eating an hour when in fact he has only been eating 5 minutes, the patient will spend much less actual time engaged in eating. In addition, the feeling of satisfaction or fullness derived from eating can be prolonged through time expansion. If a dietetic meal only satisfies the patient for an hour of actual time, during time expansion he can make himself feel as if he had been satisfied for 5 hours. If the subject continues eating even though it seems as if he has been eating a very long time, he will feel he has eaten much too much and develop a sense of nausea. Once the subject feels hungry again, he can use time concentration to make the intervals between meals seem very short and easy to endure.

As stated earlier, it is important for the patient to think of himself as thin. Seeing himself thin provides a strong incentive for weight loss. This self-image is reinforced by having the patient see himself in perfect physical form while in the standard relaxing images. For example, in Image III (garden scene) a woman sees herself disrobing in the moonlight before a marble pool. She sees her reflection in the water. She is thin and beautiful. She *feels* light; she verily glides as she walks. It is also beneficial to put into these scenes people who are admiring the subject for her beauty, her trim figure. Also, Image VIII (jungle scene) is a good one for weight control. Here the subject feels himself shrinking, getting smaller and smaller. He thinks of himself as able to decrease in size.

Appropriate food images for sensitization also can be incorporated into any of the standard relaxing images. For example, the dizziness and possible nausea experienced in Image VII (space scene) can be paired with eating by having the patient imagine himself eating a specific food in bed before the room starts spinning. It is very important that the subject continue practicing hypnosis and sensory recall throughout treatment. It has been our observation that when the discipline of practicing self-hypnosis goes, so does the discipline of staying on the diet. Patients must continually be supported by being informed to expect that they will fall off their diets once in awhile. It is most important that they not punish themselves at this time with self-deprecation. This only leads to depression and further loss of control. On the other hand, some patients don't appear able to handle success. They actually reward themselves for a weight loss by going out and eating their favorite foods. One female patient said she could not understand it; her husband told her that her face looked thinner, so she went out and ate like a horse. Information concerning this behavioral pattern should be given patients so that they can recognize and curb the behavior if it manifests itself. Also, many patients become discouraged because they maintain a rigid diet but don't lose any weight at first. In this case, it must be explained to them that their bodies are still retaining water—they have probably lost the actual fat or adipose tissue, but this is not indicated on the scale because the body tissue is still retaining water for as much as 2 to 3 weeks longer.

If weight loss is still not rapid enough once the proper foods are being eaten on a regular schedule, then the *amount* of the proper foods eaten must be cut down. One simply cannot eat all he wants of a given food and expect to lose weight if he is accumulating more calories than are being expended. While the therapist can instruct the patient to serve himself smaller portions or see himself in hypnosis serving himself smaller portions, this seldom works. The best method is to instruct the subject both at a normal level of awareness and in hypnosis, to leave food on his plate. As noted earlier, this dictum goes against most childhood training to eat everything and to think of the starving children of India. In a purely positive image, the subject sees himself eating, finishes half the meal, gets up to leave the plate with food on it, and feels fantastic.

A variation of this scene, using negative recall, involves the subject's seeing himself at the table eating with the following hypnotic instruction:

Every bite you take your stomach grows larger and larger. Feel the distension in your stomach muscles. Feel the pulling, the bloating. You continue to shovel the food in, mouthful after mouthful. Every gulp you get sicker and sicker to your stomach; you feel like throwing up. Your meal is but half finished. You get up. You leave the table. You feel fantastic. The nausea is gone. You are light as a feather.

In this type of imagery, the subject always feels fantastic as soon as he is out of the sight, smell, and taste of the food. The cessation of nausea serves as a relief stimulus for reinforcing the response of leaving the table. Also, in reality, when the subject resists food he should reinforce this resistance by recalling a pleasant hypnotic image and telling himself, "well done." As the patient becomes proficient in self-hypnosis he can recall the hypnotic state and appropriate image in the time it takes to blink an eye. The process of self-reward for appropriate response has been called many things, including contractual management, self-reinforcement, and self-endorsement. The latter is a term used by the movement called Recovery Inc., which has thousands of converts, and it is an integral part of their method of therapy.

REFERENCES

Bernard, J. L.: Rapid treatment of gross obestiy by operant techniques. Psychol. Rep., *23:*663, 1968.

Cautela, J. R.: Treatment of compulsive behavior by covert sensitization. Psychol. Rec. *16:*33, 1966.

———: Covert sensitization. Psychol. Rep., *20:*459, 1967.

———: Covert reinforcement. Behav. Ther. *1:*33–50, 1970.

———: Covert extinction. Behav. Ther. *2:*192, 1971.

Cautela, J. R. and Kastenbaum, R. A.: Reinforcement survey schedule for use in therapy, training and research. Psychol. Rep., *20:*1115, 1967.

Ferster, C. B., Nurnberger, J. I., and Levitt, E. E.: The control of eating. J. Mathetics, *1:*87, 1962.

Foreyt, J. P. and Kennedy, W. A.: Treatment of overweight by aversion therapy. Behav. Res. Ther., *9:*29, 1971.

Hall, S. M.: Self-control and therapist control in the behavioral treatment of overweight women. Behav. Res. Ther. *10:*59, 1972.

Harmatz, M. G., and Lapuc, P.: Behavior modification of overating in a psychiatric population. J. Consult. Clin. Psychol., *32:*583, 1968.

Harris, M. B.: Self-directed program for weight control: A pilot study. J. Abnorm. Psychol., *74:*63, 1969.

Horan, J. J. and Johnson, R. G.: Coverant conditioning through a self-management application of the Premack Principle: Its effects on weight reduction. J. Behav. Ther. Exp. Psych. *2:*243, 1971.

Kroger, W. S.: Systems approach for understanding obesity: Management by behavior modification through hypnosis. Psychiat. Opin., *7:*7, 1970a.

———: Comprehensive management of obesity. Am. J. Clin. Hypn., *12:*165, 1970b.

Mahoney, M.: Self-reward and self-monitoring techniques for weight control. Behav. Ther. *5:*48, 1974.

Manno, B. and Marston, A. R.: Weight reduction as a function of negative convert reinforcement (sensitization) versus positive covert reinforcement. Behav. Res. Ther., *2:*143, 1972.

Meyer, V. and Crisp, A. H.: Aversion therapy in two cases of obesity. Behav. Res. Ther., *2:*143, 1964.

Penick, S. B., Filion, R., Fox, S., and Stunkard, A. J.: Behavior modification in the treatment of obesity. Psychosomatic Med., *33:*49, 1971.

Stuart, R. B., and Davis, B.: Slim Chance in a Fat World: Behavioral Control of Obesity. Champaign, Research Press, 1972.

Stunkard, A. J.: From explanation to action in psychosomatic medicine: The case of obesity Psychosom. Med., *37:*192, 1975.

Tilker, H. A. and Meyer, R. G.: The use of covert sensitization and hypnotic procedures in the treatment of an overweight person. Amer. J. Clin. Hypn., *15:*15, 1972.

Zeigler, H. P.: Trigeminal deafferentiation and feeding in the pigeon: sensorimotor and motivational effects. Science, *182:*1155, 1973.

19

Enuresis and Encopresis

ENURESIS

Conditioning Technics

Use of conditioning methods in the treatment of enuresis was begun quite early (Pfaundler 1904, Genouville 1908) although credit is usually given to Mowrer and Mowrer (1938) for providing a rational theory for the method. Mowrer and Mowrer (1938) used a classical conditioning theory and the "bell method." They state, "If some arrangement could be provided so that the sleeping child would be awakened *just after the onset of urination,* and only at this time, the resulting association of bladder distention and the response of awakening and inhibiting further urination should provide precisely the form of training which would seem to be most specifically appropriate" (Mowrer and Mowrer 1938, p. 445).

Three stages in the acquisition of bladder control are distinguished. Stage I is the pretraining stage in which detrusor tension (US) exceeds a given threshold and involuntary urination (UR) occurs without the child's waking. In stage II the child is trained to awaken immediately after the onset of micturition. The process involves two unconditioned stimuli and three unconditioned responses. Threshold detrusor tension (US_1) produces micturition (UR_1), which in turn rings the bell. Mowrer constructed an apparatus for applying this technic which has been modified for much greater efficiency and simplicity (Davidson and Douglass 1950, Coote 1965, Freyman 1963). The bell (US_2) wakes the child and produces two unconditioned responses (UR_2, waking, and UR_3, inhibition of micturition). Threshold detrusor tension also serves as a CS for waking (CR_1) and inhibition of micturition (CR_2), which theoretically should condition

225

waking and inhibition of micturition to increasing detrusor contractions. In stage III, the child is wakened by increased detrusor contractions before the bell rings and therefore before wetting occurs. In the last stage there is a continuation of inhibitory control (sphincter contraction to increasing bladder pressure) but also the inhibition of the waking response so that the child sleeps through the night, remaining dry.

A supposedly different method based on electric shock was developed by Crosby (1950). Crosby contends that in most cases of enuresis, wetting occurs not as an unconditioned reflex but rather as a conditioned response. He states that his treatment is aimed, "at extinguishing any conditioned responses which initiate micturition" (Crosby 1950, p. 538). In Crosby's technic, stimulating electrodes are attached to the loin region and when urine is voided, the contact electrodes result in the delivery of an electric shock to the loin of the child, sufficient to wake him.

Lovibond (1963, 1964) reformulated the theory in terms of instrumental avoidance conditioning together with the elaboration of a modified method of treatment involving an instrument that permitted escape from the aversive stimulus (the bell). He devised a twin signal apparatus in which a loud 1-second hooter occurs on initial wetting followed by a minute of silence. A buzzer then sounds until switched off. The first auditory stimulus lasts slightly longer than the latency response of the sphincter contraction plus its duration. Therefore, sphincter contraction to the hooter would be followed immediately by cessation of the hooter and provide escape from the aversive stimulation of the buzzer or bell. Lovibond (1964) compared the CR apparatus of Mowrer, Crosby, and Lovibond and suggested there was no important difference between the three instruments when used in the standard way.

Young (1964) described a "staggered-awakening" procedure in which 58 enuretic children were wakened at different times each night for 4 weeks at fixed but arbitrary times (i.e., unrelated to the time of wetting) and found 67 per cent were improved on follow-up. Several authors (Muellner 1960) have trained children to increase bladder control and capacity through the ingestion of increased amounts of fluid on the assumption that the increased control would generalize to sleep. They reported good results.

A conditioning treatment involving an enuresis alarm has been described by Young (1965) and Turner, Young, and Rachman (1970). The alarm utilizes a powerful buzzer triggered at the commencement of wetting through the completion by urine of an electrical circuit through a pair of gauze mats beneath the sleeping child. The child is to switch the buzzer off himself before completing urination in the toilet. A procedure of overlearning was later combined with this treatment to reduce relapse rate (Young and Morgan 1972). In overlearning the child is instructed to drink two pints of liquid in the last hour before retiring as a means of strengthening the resistance of the learned response to extinction. Ideally a CR apparatus should be used in conjunction with hypnotherapy so that abstinence can be eventually maintained without the apparatus.

HYPNOTHERAPY

Before instituting hypnotherapy, the presence of physical problems such as kidney infections, hypercontractility, such urethral abnormalities as meatal stenosis, destrusor hypertrophy, and bladder involvements and diseases of the nervous system must be eliminated. Yet, evidence of a neurologic defect is rarely found (Dorfman, Bailey and Smith 1969). Treatment is not simple, and various combinations of therapy such as re-education and psychotherapy often must be used together. Parents must not humiliate, punish, or use the child for the displacement of their own tensions. Hypnotherapy has been used successfully by numerous investigators (Braithwaite 1950, Gilbert 1957, Koster 1954, Solovey and Milechnin 1959, Van Pelt 1950). The following illustrates the hypnobehavioral approach:

The child usually is brought in for the initial visit against his will. Therefore, a friendly relationship must be established immediately. The following ruse is often effective. In mock anger, the mother is asked, "Why did you bring Johnny in on such a beautiful day?" Without waiting for her reply, the therapist remarks, "Isn't that right, Johnny?" Wide-eyed, he now sees in the therapist a new-found friend. (The mother has been apprised of these tactics prior to the first appointment.)

Then he is told, "Johnny, you have a perfect right to wet the bed as often as you please, and it is also your privilege to stop wetting the bed whenever you feel like it." After listening carefully to his views, one can ask him, "How would you like to play a little game where you can relax and imagine seeing your favorite television program?" Invariably, Johnny will agree, because of the good rapport that has been established. Visual-imagery technics are used to induce hypnosis.

After hypnosis is achieved, the child is asked, "Do you enjoy wetting the bed?" If a negative response is elicited, the following questions are asked. "How many of your classmates wet their beds?" By indirection, this makes him feel unusual and helps to establish the motivation for a change. "If you slept overnight at a friend's house who did not wet his bed, and had an accident, how would you feel?" If he agrees that this would be embarrassing, he is asked, "Would you like to be helped to avoid this situation in the future?"

These questions focus his attention on the fact that he has a problem, and yet he has not been made to feel guilty. They also reveal his personality structure and, hence, the most appropriate therapeutic route. With an aggressive child, a permissive approach is used in order not to identify the therapist with the parents. The therapist can also point out, providing the child is mature enough, that he is harming himself more than his parents. If the child is passive and dependent, he can be encouraged to assert himself the way others of his age group do, by allowing him to vent his resentments on the therapist, and later, channel his aggression into more constructive outlets.

The usual posthypnotic suggestions for symptom-removal are presented briefly as follows: "Would you try holding your water (urine) as long as possible during the day?" (This increases the bladder capacity.) "Also, perhaps you might be interested to see how well you can start and stop the passing of your water." (This invites his participation.) "Maybe you will gain better control than your friends. If you concentrate on what it feels like to pass your water during the day, you will have little or no trouble feeling this identical sensation even when you are sound asleep. And after you have gone to the toilet, you will return to your bed and immediately fall asleep." The child should be given positive suggestions that, when he gets out of bed to urinate during the night, the time intervals between trips to the toilet will be increased until he can sleep through the night without urinating.

Under hypnosis, he is taught how to contract the diaphragm and simultaneously relax the pubococcygeus musles; the downward push on the vesical neck stimulates contraction of the detrusors and opens the internal sphincter, which leads to urination. Rehearsal of the act of urination should be repeated several times during each session. Under autohypnosis he can rehearse or have a "dry run" of all the accompanying sensations of micturition, and thus speed up bladder control.

The next step is to reverse the child's fears about the bed-wetting. The youngster is asked, while under hypnosis, "Would you be interested in how much of your bed can remain dry?" This shifts his attention from himself to the bed. It can be suggested that since he controls his own bladder functioning, he can have a dry bed if he wants it badly enough. The word "wet" is never used! The mother also is instructed always to speak in terms of a "dry bed." She can remark, "My goodness, your bed was three quarters dry!" or "Last night it was all dry!" If this positive approach is used over a period of time, the idea of a "dry bed" will be indelibly imprinted on the child's mind. Convincing the child that a dry bed is a sign of maturity is in itself often therapeutic.

Therapy is facilitated, in some instances, by establishing a time limit for when the bed will be dry. Most effective are posthypnotic suggestions such as, "Johnny, you can set a time when you will be able to have full bladder control." If he names a date, this goal can be strengthened by saying, "You can be very proud if you reach your goal beforehand." This, of course, implies that bladder control will be developed (extraverbal suggestion). A child can be hypnotically conditioned to derive pride in the achievement of establishing bladder control. These suggestions may be repeated as necessary to effect a conditioned response. Any reason for failure should be analyzed.

The urine also can be measured every morning, a larger amount indicating increased bladder capacity. It is very helpful, too, to give a reward for achieving a goal within a certain period. A calendar used to mark off the nights on which the bed was dry helps to add to the sense of achievement. Drugs to reduce the depth of sleep, amphetamines, atropine, and such procedures as fluid restriction have only a placebo effect. However, if parents and child are convinced of their utility, they may be employed.

The parents are instructed not to scold or chastise the child over a wet bed. Humiliation and ridicule only serve to compound the problem. The entire family should look upon the child's progress in overcoming his difficulty as an important event, and he should be praised for each small victory. He should likewise be encouraged to overcome a sense of defeat if the bed is wet on occasions. Often the problem is intensified if the child cannot communicate effectively with his parents. The insecurity, the inadequacy, and the tensions present in the mother, therefore, must be corrected. She can be advised to read a bedtime story in a soft and soothing manner and to emphasize her love for the child. Other members of the family who need help for their own tensions often must be treated as part of the total therapy. The following case illustrates the authors' approach:

> Simon B., a 12-year-old boy, was a chronic bed-wetter. In addition to poor grades in school, he had poor relationships with playmates, superiors, and relatives. The bed-wetting began soon after the adoption of a sister when he was four.
>
> He was hypnotized readily in the first session. During the second session, he was taught autohypnosis. It was also suggested that he practice inducing self-hypnosis frequently; that the more he practiced, the more proficient he would become. On the third visit, a week later, he readily induced self-hypnosis, and related how his mother continually "rode" him, that he was unwilling to accept any of his mother's suggestions because she favored his adopted sister. During subsequent sessions, he stated that he was looking for ways to get even with his parents and that perhaps the bed-wetting pattern was being maintained for this purpose.
>
> At this time, Simon's mother was interviewed. She said that Simon had always wanted a baby sister; he knew that she was adopted. She thought that perhaps because of her own perfectionistic attitudes and demands she had pushed Simon too rapidly. In addition, she was not getting along too well with her husband and wondered if she might not be displacing her tensions to Simon. Simon and his sister were constantly fighting, and this, too, made her nervous. For some reason, she always protected the little girl. One day, in a fit of anger, Simon remarked, "Pretty smart girl we've got here." After this, she noted that Simon was becoming increasingly argumentative and sulky. During the next few sessions, other ambivalent attitudes toward his mother were brought out. He angrily remarked, "The tone of my mother's voice annoys me. She never even lets me finish what I have to say."
>
> Other areas of insecurity were explored. During the next three sessions, at weekly intervals, he was given posthypnotic suggestions to maintain a full bladder until the last possible moment; to remember the sensations accompanying a full bladder, and to re-experience these sensations even during the deepest sleep. It was emphasized that all sensations accompanying a full bladder would be "telephoned" to his brain and would wake him up; that if he wished, he would then awaken and go to the toilet, empty his bladder, and promptly return to his bed and fall asleep. Simon reported at the next session that during sleep his bladder "felt like a big balloon," and that he awakened, was able to pass his water and again immediately fall asleep. It was now suggested that under no circum-

stances would the symptom be given up until he was willing to yield it, and that this would occur through autohypnosis and in full accordance with his wishes.

The mother was also instructed never to mention the word *wet* but always to speak in terms of a dry bed. She was advised particularly to watch the tone of her voice when speaking to Simon. In several sessions, at nonhypnotic levels, it was made evident to her that she should love the boy for himself rather than for his intellectual accomplishments. She was advised not to vent her ire on him; this would curb his rebellious attitudes. Through the combined use of hypnosis directed toward symptom-removal, and psychotherapy for the mother, Simon overcame his bed-wetting pattern within three months from the time he began therapy.

Another interesting case was that of a 10-year-old boy who presented a problem of generalized irritability and enuresis. All efforts to cure the bed-wetting had been unsuccessful. Although outwardly diffident and hesitant, the boy was an alert and co-operative patient who was easily hypnotized by a visual-imagery technic. Intellectually, he manifested a sophistication and an awareness of adult values beyond his years.

The history revealed a feeling of guilt over masturbation and that his behavioral problems originated in the home, primarily from the father, who, the boy stated, "never spends any time with me." He, too, readily admitted that he wet his bed to get even with his parent, saying, "What other way is there to get even with my dad?"

Hypnotherapy was directed at both the symptom and the characterological level. The same posthypnotic suggestions were employed as in Simon's case. During subsequent sessions, it was pointed out that he had a continual need to assert himself but was inhibited by his inadequate concept of himself. He also felt compelled to adhere to the high standards set up by his strict father. He viewed his parent's concern and attention as a burden, yet he feared his father's authority and loss of support. Additionally, he showed increasing concern, guilt, and anxiety over masturbation, which was allayed by re-education and reassurance that it was not a wicked act.

The enuresis improved after the father began to spend more time with him, and when the boy was made aware that the enuresis served as an outlet for his growing aggression toward his father and for his increased sense of shame. As a result, his confidence and self-esteem were increased, and a complete cure was established after the father relaxed his ambitions and high standards for the boy. Sixteen sessions were required to effect these results.

STANDARDIZED IMAGES FOR ENURESIS

The images described in Chapter 10 are used to reduce the high level of anxiety typically found in the enuretic. Of particular impact are Images V (desert), XII (lake), XIV (thunder shower), XX (volcano), and XXII (sand pit), which deal with recall of pressure in the genital area. The enuretic is not sensitive enough to the pressure exerted by a full bladder to wake before wetting. He must therefore be trained to lower his sensory threshold to pressure in the genital area. It is possible to develop finer discrimination and lower thresholds in any sense modality simply by directing more attention to it. We are all familiar with the acute hearing of the blind man, the fine color discrimination of the artist, the sensitive taste and smell of the wine taster and gourmet cook, and the precise touch of the sculptor. These are all examples of how specific senses can be further developed through training and concentration. The enuretic is trained to develop greater sensitivity to pressure in the bladder.

ENCOPRESIS

Behavior Modification

Warson et al. (1954) define encopresis as a "disturbance in regulation of bowel evacuation." Unfortunately, virtually nothing is known of how voluntary initiation of defecation or its inhibition is achieved. Neale (1963) stressed the retentive aspect of encopresis and considered that the initiation of the reflex was disrupted by fear following punishment. His technic used a graded series of reward-training for expulsion at the appropriate time in the right place. Children were first placed on the toilet four times daily with variable rewards for appropriate performances. Then a shift was made from experimenter-control to self-control. The subject was told to take himself to the toilet and was rewarded for doing so. Of the four subjects, three achieved control. In the one case of failure, Neale posited that a full rectum produced pleasurable sensations that were stronger than the pleasure produced by reward for evacuation. Other authors have also applied systematic retraining schedules using operant conditioning technics (Gelber and Meyei 1965, Keehn 1965, Peterson and London 1964). Simple play therapy also has been successfully used to treat encopresis (Sousa and Abuchaim 1975).

STANDARDIZED IMAGES FOR ENCOPRESIS

Like enuresis, encopresis is largely mediated by anxiety and is ameliorated by relaxation training. Image XX (volcano) is particularly effective in giving the encopretic control over his bowels. Hypnotic direction of attention to the excretory function in this image leads to one's gaining a finer discrimination and sensitivity to the workings of this system and thus more control over it.

REFERENCES

Braithwaite, J. V.: Enuresis in childhood. Practitioner, *165:*273, 1950.
Coote, M. A.: Apparatus for conditioning treatment of enuresis. Behav. Res. Ther., *2:*233, 1965.
Crosby, N. D.: Essential enuresis: successful treatment based on physiological concepts. Med. J. 'Austr., *2:*533, 1950.
Davidson, J. R. and Douglass, E.: Nocturnal enuresis: a special approach to treatment. Brit. Med. J., *1:*1345, 1950.

Dorfman, L. E., Bailey, J., and Smith, J. P.: Sub-clinical neurogenic bladder in children. J. Urol., *101:*48, 1969.

Freyman, R.: Follow-up study of enuresis treated with a bell apparatus. J. Child Psychol. Psychiat., *4:*199, 1963.

Gelber, H. and Meyer, V.: Behavior therapy and encopresis: the complexities involved in treatment. Behav. Res. Ther., *2:*227, 1965.

Genouville, F.: Incontinence d'urine. L'Assoc. Franc. d'Urol., *12:*97, 1908.

Gilbert, S. F.: Juvenile enuresis: hypnotherapy in children. Brit. J. Med. Hypn., *8:*43, 1957.

Keehn, J. D.: Brief case-report: reinforcement therapy of incontinence. Behav. Res. Ther., *2:*239, 1965.

Koster, S.: Hypnosis in children as a method of curing enuresis and related conditions. Brit. J. Med. Hypn., *5:*32, 1954.

Lovibond, S. H.: The mechanism of conditioning treatment of enuresis. Behav. Res. Ther., *1:*17, 1963.

————: Conditioning and Enuresis. Oxford, Pergamon, 1964.

Mowrer, O. H. and Mowrer, W. A.: Enuresis: a method for its study and treatment. Amer. J. Orthopsychiat., *8:*436, 1938.

Muellner, S. R.: Development of urinary control in children: a new concept in cause, prevention and treatment of primary enuresis. J. Urol., *84:*714, 1960.

Neale, D. H.: Behavior therapy and encopresis in children. Behav. Res. Ther., *1:*139, 1963.

Peterson, D. R. and London, P.: Neobehavioristic psychotherapy; quasi hypnotic suggestion and multiple reinforcement in the treatment of a case of postinfantile dyscopresis. Psychol. Rec., *14:*469, 1964.

Pfaundler, M.: Demonstration eines Apparatus zur Selstättigen Singalisierung Stattgehabter Bettnässung. Verhandl. der Gesellsch. für Kinderhlk., *21:*219, 1904.

Solovey, G. and Milechnin, A.: Concerning the treatment of enuresis. Amer. J. Clin. Hypn., *2:*22, 1959.

Sousa, P. L. and Abuchaim, S. R.: Quoted in Clinical Psychiatry News, *3:*5, 1975.

Turner, R. K., Young, G. C., and Rachman. S.: Treatment of nocturnal enuresis by conditioning techniques. Behav. Res. Ther., *8:*367, 1970.

Van Pelt, S. J.: Hypnotism and the Power Within. London, Skeffington, 1950.

Warson, S. R. et al.: The dynamics of encorpresis. Amer. J. Orthopsychiat., *24:*402, 1954.

Young, G. C.: A "staggered-wakening" procedure in the treatment of enuresis. Med. Offr., *111:*143, 1964.

————: Conditioning treatment of enuresis. Develop. Med. Child. Neurol., *7:*557, 1965.

Young, G. C. and Morgan, R. T.: Overlearning in the conditioning treatment of enuresis. Behav. Res. Ther., *10:*147, 1972.

SUGGESTED READINGS

Baker, B. L.: Symptom treatment and symptom substitution in enuresis. J. Abnorm. Psychol., *74:*42, 1969.

Lovibond, S. H.: Critique of Turner, Young & Rachman's conditioning treatment of enuresis. Behav. Res. Ther., *10:*287, 1972.

Morgan, R. T. and Young, G. C.: The treatment of enuresis: Merits of conditioning methods. Community Med., *128:*119, 1972.

20

Stuttering

Stuttering in young children, adolescents or adults is often difficult to treat by any method, including hypnosis. There are some interesting references to hypnosis in speech therapy and clinical audiology (Ambrose and Newbold 1956, Solovey and Milechnin 1959, Wolberg 1948, McCord 1955, Rosen 1953). Silber (1973) describes utilizing fairy tales, folklore, and symbols in conjunction with hypnosis to treat stuttering in children. He reports a case in which a 9½-year-old girl who had been stuttering for 2½ years was told that when she closed her eyes, she would accompany the therapist through the "corridor of the inner realms of the imagination directly to fairyland." Environmental change was magically produced through this simple procedure. The patient was led through hallucinated gardens, blooming profusely with gorgeous flowers. In a secluded spot, the therapist pointed out the sleeping beauty (the patient) who was just being awakened out of the witch's spell (stuttering) by a kiss from her dazzling young prince (the therapist).

After this session, stuttering stopped almost completely until the patient was confronted in the fantasy by her father, who was the prime source of the child's anxiety. In the next session, the child was told that no one could follow her into Fairyland without her permission. This enabled her to dissociate herself from her father's presence and once again relax. Silber suggests that "psychic factors mediate disturbances of verbalization by interfering with the meshing of feedback mechanisms which fail to integrate phonation and the auditory awareness of speech" (p. 282).

ETIOLOGIC FACTORS

Adoption of a model that regards stuttering as caused by a fault in the feedback control system for speech does not rule out the possibility that stuttering can be an anxiety-reducing response. Anxiety may produce a defect in the feedback control system. Therefore, an attack on any point in the chain of events which represents stuttering may be therapeutically beneficial. The hypnobehavioral model emphasizes the reduction of anxiety that may be contributing to the breakdown of the feedback control system for speech.

A moderate or severe stutterer ordinarily requires an intensive evaluation of what is taking place between himself and his hearers. Ordinarily, there is a great deal of repressed hostility, the expression of which is masked. The stutterer feels insecure around other persons, and is unable to express his feelings since he is always on guard.

In children, the anticipation of stuttering brings it about by setting up a conditioned pattern. The attempt to defeat this anticipation and to control it, and the resulting heightened tension, lead to further hesitation and disruption of speech. Thus, the stutterer believes that he is going to stutter, and that he must not stutter. He is controlled by these ambivalent thoughts, which have become entrenched through repeated reinforcement in speech situations, often since he first started to talk. He now finds it impossible to eliminate them by will alone.

SYMPTOMS

The stutterer often develops auxiliary symptoms that are a misguided effort to overcome his speech defect. He blinks his eyes, stamps his foot, or pounds his fists in order to overcome the blocking. He develops these reactions to avoid becoming aware of certain words and sounds. He then substitutes other words or sounds in a vain attempt to hide his stuttering. These attempts invariably lead to more symptoms. The individual who starts out by stuttering and finds that, initially at least, he stutters less when he lifts his head, will begin to lift his head more and more until he develops a real spasm. And this spasm can often become more disabling than the initial stuttering symptom that he is trying to overcome by this mechanism.

Most stutterers are, of course, very reluctant to deal with the symptom itself. The stutterer is so ashamed and overwrought that he is unable to cope with it directly. Because stuttering is not a uniform phenomenon, its severity is more or less dependent upon the environmental situation. Therefore, one must elicit situations that the individual fears or emotional expressions in relation to other people that he finds impossible to make freely. Under hypnosis, the symptom is much more amenable to a direct attack, as he can rehearse speech situations particularly dreaded by him, especially in relation to those who upset him.

BEHAVIOR MODIFICATION TECHNICS

Several behavior therapy technics have also been applied to the treatment of stuttering. Feedback control of stuttering has been found to be very effective (Cherry and Sayers 1956, Maclaren 1956, Meyer and Mair 1963, Kondas 1967, Kelham and McHale 1966). In a feedback control method (shadowing), the stutterer speaks aloud as closely as possible after another speaker who is reading from a prose passage that the stutterer does not see. Striking results are also obtained if a tape recording or a speaker's voice on the radio is shadowed. More simply, stuttering may be eliminated by means of simultanous reading, in which the stutterer and another person read from the same book.

Masking by means of white noise, which prevents the speaker from hearing his own voice has also been found a beneficial technic to be used with stutterers. Cherry and Sayers (1956) showed that stuttering is substantially reduced if the stutterer is prevented from hearing the low-frequency components (which are mainly bone-conducted) of his own voice while speaking. Elimination of air-conducted feedback alone did not affect stuttering. Maraist and Hutton (1957) showed that stuttering decreased as a function of increase in intensity of masking white noise. Although criticized on technical grounds by Yates (1963) and Webster and Lubker (1968), a study was done by Sutton and Chase (1961) which concluded that white noise did not produce its effect by preventing the speaker from listening to his own voice. Although a high level of intensity of white noise is required to completely attenuate bone-conducted feedback, two portable masking instruments have been reported (Parker and Christopherson 1963, Trotter and Lesch 1967).

Another method is that of negative practice in which stutterers are required to stutter words deliberately (Fishman 1937, Case 1960). Adaptation definitely takes place with the method of massed practice in which the same passage is read repeatedly (Donohue 1955, Johnson and Knott 1937, E. L. Jones 1955, Tate and Cullinan 1962, Tate et al. 1961, Rousey 1958). Imposition of rhythm on speech may attenuate stuttering to a very significant degree (Johnson and Rosen 1937, Van Dantzig 1940, Meyer and Mair 1963). Rhythmic speech may be accomplished by speaking in time with arm swinging, reading in a sing-song voice, or finger tapping. A more recent development has been the introduction of a technic termed syllable-timed or ST speech in which speech output is evenly produced with clear separation between each speech unit, yet with smooth enunciation (Holgate and Andrews 1966, Brandon and Harris 1967, Horan 1968). In reference to these technics, Yates (1970, p. 124,) states:

> Why ST or metronome-controlled speech should reduce stuttering so dramatically is by no means clear as yet. It is possible that, by reducing the length of the speech units and increasing the length of the interval between them, feedback from each speech unit falls entirely within the interval between speech units. The effect would then be the same as that achieved by white noise—the feedback

would be irrelevant to the output and the stutterer would be speaking, in effect, without airborne and bone-conducted feedback.

Success has also been reported using operant technics (Goldiamond 1965, Rickard and Mundy 1965, Martin and Siegel 1966a, 1966b, Quist and Martin 1967, Haroldson et al. 1968, Shames et al. 1969, Lanyon 1969, Webster 1970). Martin (1968) concluded that a fixed interval schedule of response-contingent verbal reinforcement of fluency did not occasion any appreciable reduction in the frequency of stuttering. Gross (1968) investigated the effects of response-contingent punishment of dysfluency, reinforcement of fluency, and a combined procedure of reinforcement of fluency and punishment of dysfluency. She concluded that these three contingencies were all equally effective in reducing the frequency of dysfluencies in the oral reading of stutterers. Siegel (1970), in an extensive review of research concerning punishment of the dysfluencies of both stutterers and normally fluent subjects, states: ''. . . stutterings and normal dysfluencies were consistently decreased when the stimuli were made contingent on the response.'' Moore and Ritterman (1973), using two punishment contingencies and one punishment and reinforcement combined contingency, under a procedure of stimulus control, indicated all three conditions to be equally effective in the reduction of stuttering frequency.

Brutten and Shoemaker (1968) argue that systematic desensitization should be used to reduce anxiety associated with stuttering, while technics such as those described above may be appropriate for treating the stutter itself. Rosenthal (1968) successfully treated a severe stutterer using systematic desensitization applied to situations in which stuttering occurred. Boudreau and Jeffrey (1973) successfully modified stuttering in eight male subjects treated by ten sessions of systematic desensitization. In the desensitization procedure, the subject, while relaxed, is asked first to imagine the least anxiety-provoking situation and then speak out loud in a manner appropriate to the imagined scene. Subjects were exhorted to practice at home. Masson, Kovitz, and Muir (1972) compared three relaxing methods for relief of stuttering. Their study included autogenic training, suggestive therapy with group hypnosis, and systematic desensitization. Their study showed that to some extent all three methods were effective. Major change occurred when there were consistent increases in expressed assertiveness, effectiveness, and sociability.

Autogenic training was the most effective approach for decreasing the stuttering in reading. Systematic desensitization was more effective for speech. The authors note that had the experiment been continued longer than two months, the improvement in self-concept might have had an effect on the speech itself. Had these technics been combined with imagery conditioning, we believe the hypnotically treated group would have performed best.

HYPNOTHERAPY

Hypnoanalysis is an excellent method for investigating the particular situations and stimulus patterns that produced the stuttering. It enables the patient to understand the need for the avoidance reaction, to rehearse it, and to work it through to help release the specific tensions that arise in his oral musculature during the act of speaking. Exploration through hypnotic age regression in good subjects often helps to pinpoint specific episodes that brought about these inhibitory patterns. However, Cooper (1973) believes that psychotherapy and hypnosis are not effective for most voice disorders.

Successful therapy must be directed to all the accompanying symptoms. The subject is shown that during hypnosis, he can speak in a manner that is more satisfactory both to himself and to his listeners. Stutterers are surprised that they can speak without the involuntary head motions, the foot stamping, the finger snapping, or whatever other muscular manifestation they employ.

Shadowing with a tape recorder often can be used to good advantage with hypnotherapy. Stutterers are almost always free of symptoms when their ears are plugged, when they are reading from a prepared text, when they are speaking in unison with someone else, or when alone. It is helpful to have the individual speak into the tape recorder when alone. Then he listens to himself while under hypnorelaxation, and reads the same passage in unison with his tape-recorded verbalization. The resulting good fluent speech encourages him to identify with a person who obviously is able to speak normally and gives him confidence.

This procedure is accomplished best by a permissive approach, judiciously utilizing posthypnotic suggestions. Suggesting that the subject is never going to stutter is seldom effective, it works for only a short time. As a result, the patient becomes disheartened and loses confidence not only in the therapist but also in hypnotherapy.

Posthypnotic suggestions and autohypnosis can be limited to specific situations; for example, comfort and ease can be induced in the child who dreads speaking in class by remarking, "Under self-hypnosis you will imagine that you feel relaxed and more comfortable in class, and if you can see yourself talking without difficulty in your imagination, you will find it easier to talk." If each situation is approached through sensory-imagery conditioning, there is a good chance that, to a degree, the vicious fear-reaction cycle can ultimately be reversed. The following selected case is illustrative of the authors' technic:

A 12-year-old child was taught hypnosis and autohypnosis in one 50-minute session. He was a hissing stutterer who took about half a minute to say one word. Yet, under hypnosis, he said, "Around the rugged rock the ragged rascal ran" and other tongue twisters, all in one breath, without any hesitation whatsoever. This indicated that a psychological approach would be helpful.

His speech difficulty began at age 2. Since he had received intensive psychotherapy, it was decided that the best course was to break up the reflex at one level or another. During the next session, he spoke under hypnosis into a tape recorder without difficulty. It was suggested: "If, under autohypnosis, you listen enough to yourself, you will become accustomed to the sound of your own voice speaking normally. After all, when we hear a tune played over and over again, do we not hum the tune exactly the way we heard it?" Such measures establish a healthy pattern, so that the stutterer has a firm foundation upon which to build a more natural and normal type of speech. At first, if he wishes, he can hum a tune, then sing words, and later speak short sentences. The first tapes can be compared with later ones; the resultant improvement instills confidence.

During the third hypnotic session, it was suggested that perhaps the blocking of the muscles involved in speaking might be transferred to another portion of the body. It was pointed out that the subject had no control over the gestures and the spasms that usually accompanied his stuttering; that nature's first line of defense could be employed in a constructive manner by giving him something that he could control. A twitching of one of the fingers of either the right or the left hand was suggested. Under hypnosis, he was asked, "Which finger would you like to twitch; would it be the little finger on the left hand, or perhaps the little finger on the right hand, or even the thumb on the left hand?" The fact that he was given a choice led him to believe that he was acting under his own volition. The posthypnotic suggestion was given, "Each time you feel that you are going to stutter, you can control it by twitching your finger. And you can, if you feel embarrassed, do this with your hand closed. In this way no one will see it."

The transfer of the blocking from the muscles of the speech to the muscles of the finger is a trading down, or an attempt to siphon off the energy with which the original symptom is invested. Furthermore, the finger-twitch takes the place of stuttering in fulfilling the need for a symptom. Symptom-transformation of this type does not remove the symptom all at once but, rather, substitutes a weak conditioned-response for a noxious or well-entrenched one. In this case, the child made progressively more use of the finger twitch for several weeks. At this point, the twitch could be either increased or decreased. If it can be increased (symptom-intensification), obviously it can be decreased. The child was eventually weaned from the finger-twitch by posthypnotic suggestions directed toward increasing and diminishing it. During this period, considerable improvement in his speech difficulty was manifested.

Under hypnosis, he was next taught "loose contact." Most stutterers have difficulty only with the first letter or two of any word on which they block. Therefore, it is advisable to reverse the emphasis by suggesting, "You are going to worry about the last syllables. For example, if you have trouble saying the word *democratic* and you find yourself saying, "de-, de-, de-," become more interested in the "mo-cra-tic" portion, and you will notice that if you direct your attention to the bulk of the word, you will easily slide over the first two or three letters."

In the case just described, the child had considerable resentment toward the father, who was too busy to spend an appreciable amount of time with him. In another case a similar factor was elicited. In both instances the parents were interviewed and these problems were discussed. Both boys were completely cured of their stuttering after attending the authors' group hypnosis speech-training program. In many instances, such patients must be prepared for a relapse. Rather than regarding this as a failure, they should be asked to describe the factors that produced the relapse. Patients are urged to return at monthly or bimonthly intervals for reinforcement suggestions. For further amplification of many of the above technics and those to be described below in conjunction with hypnotherapy the reader is referred to Kroger (1963).

Other posthypnotic suggestions are commonly employed, such as, "If possible, try looking at the face of the person to whom you are speaking.'' Most stutterers look down or away in shame. It is emphasized that they should maintain a steady gaze at all times; that, just as they need not be ashamed of speaking rapidly, they likewise should not feel embarrassed if they speak slowly. Reading backward and forward again and again helps to slow rapid speech, and also favorably conditions the auditory centers to adopt normal speech patterns. Other posthypnotic suggestions are directed toward improvement in vocalization and articulation.

Another feasible approach, as described above, is the use of sensory-imagery conditioning under autohypnosis. In this technic, the individual imagines that he is speaking normally. Just as we have a ''mind's eye,'' we have a ''mind's ear.'' During hypnosis, the subject is asked to ''listen'' to his own voice, and to ''hear'' himself talking on a wide variety of subjects, without hesitation, blocking, or difficulty of any type. After he begins to think that he can ''speak'' normally, he finds it much easier to speak at nonhypnotic levels.

It is easier to recognize the basic speech patterns than to direct treatment primarily to the cause of the speech disorder. As fluency improves, the stuttering will diminish, particularly if training is directed to sensory functions rather than to motor ones. The thinking processes involved in speech are more important than the talking processes. Thus, as the ear-training establishes a good mental pattern of speech, talking becomes ''thinking out loud.'' As a result, the autonomic portion of the brain transmits impulses to the mouth; the words ''say themselves.''

> Sensory-imagery conditioning was most efficacious in the case of a 16-year-old boy with hysterical aphonia who had not spoken for 2 years because of profound guilt over masturbation. The therapeutic goals were directed toward symptom-removal and toward helping him to solve some of his adolescent problems, which consisted of withdrawal tendencies and anxiety over suppressed rage toward his parents. They were advised of their faulty attitudes. Posthypnotic suggestions were employed also to redirect his aggressive needs along healthy outlets such as taking a paper route, using the money to go out with girls, and thus improving his self-esteem. Eighteen sessions at weekly intervals were required. Such brief hypnotherapy effected a healthier personality integration.

Since stuttering often begins early, there is no use exhuming a great deal of memorial data, nor is it helpful to search for early traumata by questioning about events before the age of 4 or 5 years. Attempting this generally yields diminishing returns. Johnson (1959) states: ''Considerable research to date provides no appreciable support for the hypothesis that stuttering is characteristically associated with or symptomatic of severe emotional disturbance or neuroses in a clinically significant sense.'' In this regard, he states that speech training often does more harm than good, as it emphasizes the use of the will rather than the imagination. The stutterer becomes more conscious of his speech difficulty, and thus it becomes intensified.

Another valuable approach is to suggest that the stutterer speak out loud as often as necessary when he is alone. A 15-minute session daily is suggested. Through posthypnotic suggestions, the duration can be decreased by 1 minute daily, and then 1 minute every other day, every third day, etc., until he is weaned from the symptom. It is surprising that when a stutterer deliberately tries to stutter, he is unable to do so. By reversing his fears, one can break up the reflex. Through hearing his own voice speaking normally, the stutterer gains confidence in his ability.

GROUP HYPNOTHERAPY

Group hypnotherapy is ideal for the stutterer, as group dynamics involving emotional contagion, inherent competitiveness, and desire to please the therapist operate with beneficial effects. Most stutterers then feel that they are all in the same boat; they do not hesitate to speak before other members. It also is surprising how quickly they perceive another individual's mistakes and make constructive suggestions for improved speech. This increases the stutterer's self-esteem and confidence and motivates him toward further therapy.

CORRECTION OF FAULTY ATTITUDES

Faulty parental attitudes can arouse tensions in a child and lead to stuttering. Many parents are worriers and perfectionists. They react to their child's nonfluent speech with concern or impatience. By correcting him, they make the child conscious that his speech is unacceptable. He responds by talking less and less, with the growing fear of failure—until he is speaking with the fear and stress of a stutterer. Hence, parents should allow the child to develop at his own pace, and his speech should not be judged by adult standards.

If a child gets past the age of 3 or 4 years without being classified as a stutterer, the chances are that he will never stutter unless he runs into the same problem with listeners when he enters school. There are approximately two-and-one-half times as many male stutterers as female. One possible explanation of this is that mothers are less likely to be critical of the speech of girls than of boys.

ADJUVANT METHODS AND HYPNOTHERAPY

Marchesi (1960) cured 75 to 80 per cent of 98 cases of stammering by hypnotherapy directed toward symptom-removal even though antecedent emotional tensions and traumas apparently were causative factors. Stammering developed as an imitative reflex; removal from the person who caused it was all that was necessary. The condition also may be due to an accident, with personal involvement or as a witness.

The specific treatment began with a study of the vital capacity of the lungs, as breathing exercises are employed with hypnotherapy. The breathing is chosen as the starting-point because the arrhythmic respiration, upon which the stammering is based, is restored to a more normal rhythm. More importantly, as a result of the rhythmic breathing, the emotional aspect of the stammering is now separated from the association with the abnormal breathing. Hypnotherapy is continuously maintained—on the average, two sessions weekly for about 1 month. The breathing exercises are prescribed in the office for use during hypnorelaxation there as well as at home. Concentration is directed to the character of the breathing as well as to subjective thoughts. However, the patient is informed that he should not try to concentrate too hard, as failure is inevitable. At the beginning, he is apprised that progress will not be upward, that relapses can be expected.

Marchesi stresses a nondirective hypnotic approach, which leads to very deep hypnotization because criticalness is not developed. This provides considerable self-satisfaction because the patient gets the impression that the operator needs his help. Objectivity and the self-realization that hypnosis produces psychophysiologic alterations enhances the expectancy level of the patient. By the second week, the patient is able to develop numbness and lightness of the extremities, and is able to breathe so that the rhythm is undisturbed by any type of noise. After this the breathing becomes smooth in type.

The stammering is attacked by asking the patient to spell out words that caused difficulty in the past. Success in doing this leads to a more positive attitude. The patient who does not respond is asked to speak under those emotional conditions which formerly caused the stammering. Attention is directed to spasmodic contractions of the diaphragm and the glottis, and to the character of the breathing. Errors are pointed out, and under hypnosis the patient is asked to breath as taught, to spell words without any hesitations, and to note the differences in speech when these functions are correctly performed. This, too, adds to his confidence. In the failure group, 15 per cent did not respond due to insufficient attention by the therapist. About 5 per cent did not have the necessary intelligence to participate in the program.

STANDARDIZED IMAGES

With a slight modification, the images described in Chapter 10 can be used to desensitize stutterers. The patient is instructed to see himself talking and singing while experiencing the deep relaxation generated by these images. The dialogue is worked out beforehand so that no anxiety will be produced in trying to figure out what to say or sing once hypnotic practice is begun. A familiar poem or lyrics to a popular song are good material with which to begin.

Rhythmic and syllable-timed speech can be facilitated by greater breath control. The suggestion, "Every breath you take, you go *deeper* and *deeper re-*

laxed" is given in every induction and promotes this control. Images that pair breathing and relaxation with other physical phenomena are particularly effective in training the stutterer to pace or pair proper breathing with speaking. These images include I (beach) "As the sun goes lower and lower, you go deeper and deeper relaxed."), III (garden) ("You begin to descend the stairs . . . every step you take, you go deeper and deeper relaxed."), and V (desert) ("Every breath you take the sky gets bluer and bluer, every breath you take, it gets warmer and warmer."). The four images for time distortion (VI, VII, XI, XII) are also used effectively to help the stutterer gain proper timing. Time control is important to keep the stutterer in the "now." Expectation or "intent" to speak often produces anxiety and blocks speech.

REFERENCES

Ambrose, G. and Newbold, G.: Handbook of Clinical Hypnosis. London, Bailliere, Tindall and Cox, 1956.

Boudreau, L. A. and Jeffrey. C. J.: Stuttering treated by desensitization. J. Behav. Ther. Exp. Psychiat., *4:*209, 1973.

Brandon, S. and Harris, M.: Stammering: an experimental treatment programme using syllable-timed speech. Brit. J. Discord. Commun., *2:*64, 1967.

Brutten, E. J. and Shoemaker, D. J.: The Modification of Stuttering. Englewood Cliffs, Prentice Hall, 1968.

Case, H. W.: Therapeutic methods in stuttering and speech blocking. *In* Eysenck, H. J. (ed.): Behavior Therapy and the Neuroses. Oxford, Pergamon, 1960.

Cherry, C. and Sayers, B. McA.: Experiments upon the total inhibition of stammering by external control and some clinical results. J. Psychosom. Res., *1:*233, 1956.

Cooper, M.: Modern Techniques of Vocal Rehabilitation. Springfield, Ill., Charles C Thomas, 1973.

Donohue, I. R.: Stuttering adaptation during three hours of continuous oral reading. *In* Johnson, W. (ed.): Stuttering in Children and Adults. Minneapolis, Univ. Minnesota Press, 1955.

Fishman, H. C.: A study of the efficiency of negative practice as a corrective for stammering. J. Speech Dis., *2:*67, 1937.

Goldiamond, I.: Stuttering and fluency as manipulatable operant response classes. *In* Krasner, L. and Ullmann, L. P. (eds.): Research in Behavior Modification. New York, Holt, Rinehart & Winston, 1965.

Gross, M. S.: A study of the effects of punishment and reinforcement on dysfluencies of stutterers (unpublished doctoral dissertation). Chicago, Northwestern Univ., 1968.

Haroldson, S. K., Martin, R. R., and Starr, C. D.: Time-out as a punishment for stuttering. Speech Hear. Res., *11:*560, 1968.

Holgate, D. and Andrews, J. G..: The use of syllable-timed speech and group psychotherapy in the treatment of adult stutterers. J. Austr. Coll. Speech Ther., *16:*36, 1966.

Horan, M. C.: An improved device for inducing rhythmic speech in stutterers. Austr. Psychol., *3:*19, 1968.

Johnson, W.: Problems of impaired speech and language. J. Amer. Med. Assoc., *170:*148, 1959.

Johnson, W. and Knott, J.: Studies in the psychology of stuttering: I. The distribution of moments of stuttering in successive readings of the same material. J. Speech Dis., *2:*17, 1937.

Johnson, W. and Rosen, L.: Studies in the psychology of stuttering: VII. Effect of certain changes in speech pattern upon frequency of stuttering. J. Speech Dis., *2:*105, 1937.

Jones, E. L.: Explorations of experimental extinction and spontaneous recovery in stuttering. *In* Johnson, W. (ed.): Stuttering in Children and Adults. Minneapolis, Univ. Minnesota Press, 1955.

Kelham, R. and McHale, A.: The application of learning theory to the treatment of stammering. Brit. J. Disord. Commun., *1:*114, 1966.

Kondas, O.: The treatment of stammering in children by the shadowing method. Behav. Res. Ther., *5:*325, 1967.

Kroger, W. S.: Clinical and Experimental Hypnosis. Philadelphia, J. B. Lippincott, 1963.

Lanyon, R. I.: The relationship of adaptation and consistency to improvement in stuttering therapy. J. Speech Hear. Res., *8:*263, 1965.

————: Behavior change in stuttering through systematic desensitization. J. Speech Hear. Disord., *34:*253, 1969.

Maclaren, J.: The treatment of stammering by the Cherry-Sayers method: clinical impressions (1956). *In* Eysenck, H. J. (ed.): Behavior Therapy and the Neuroses. Oxford, Pergamon, 1960.

McCord, H.: Hypnotherapy and stuttering. J. Clin. Exp. Hypn., *3:*40, 1955.

Maraist, J. A. and Hutton, C.: Effects of auditory masking upon the speech of stutterers. J. Speech Hear. Dis., *22:*457, 1957.

Marchesi, C.: Hypnotic Treatment of Stammering. Paper read at Pan American Medical Assn. Meeting, May 5, 1960.

Martin, R. R.: The experimental manipulation of stuttering behaviors. *In* Sloane, H. N. Jr. and MacAulay B. D. (eds.): Operant Procedures in Remedial Speech and Language. Boston, Houghton Mifflin, 1968.

Martin, R. R. and Siegel, G.: The effects of response-contingent shock on stuttering. J. Speech Hearing Res., *9:*340, 1966.

————: The effects of simultaneously punishing stuttering and rewarding fluency. J. Speech Hearing Res., *9:*466, 1966.

Masson, L. J., Kovitz, D. M., and Muir, L.: A comparative study of the treatment of stuttering by 3 relaxing methods. Brit. J. Clin. Hypn., *3:*34, 1972.

Meyer, V. and Mair, J. M. A new technique to control stammering: a preliminary report. Behav. Res. Ther., *1:*251, 1963.

Moore, W. H. and Ritterman, S. I.: The effects of response contingent reinforcement and response contingent punishment upon the frequency of stuttered verbal behavior. Behav. Res. Ther., *11:*43, 1973.

Parker, C. S. and Christopherson, F.: Electronic aid in the treatment of stammering. Med. Electron. Biol. Engin., *1:*121, 1963.

Quist, R. W. and Martin, R. R.: The effects of response contingent verbal punishment on stuttering. J. Speech Hearing Res., *10:*795, 1967.

Rickard, H. C. and Mundy, M. B.: Direct manipulation of stuttering behavior: an experimental-clinical approach. *In* Ullmann, L. P. and Krasner, L. (eds.): Case Studies in Behavior Modification. New York, Holt, Rinehart and Winston, 1965.

Rosen, H.: Hypnotherapy in Clinical Psychiatry. New York, Julian, 1953.

Rosenthal, T. L.: Severe stuttering and maladjustment treated by desensitization and social influence. Behav. Res. Ther., *6:*125, 1968.

Rousey, C.: Stuttering severity during prolonged spontaneous speech. J. Speech Hear. Res., *1:*40, 1958.

Shames, G. H., Egolf, D. B., and Rhodes, R. C.: Experimental programs in stuttering therapy. J. Speech Hearing Dis., *34:*30, 1969.

Siegel, G. M.: Punishment, stuttering and disfluency. J. Speech Hearing Res., *13:*677, 1970.

Silber, S.: Fairy tales and symbols in hypnotherapy of children with certain speech disorders. Internat. J. Clin. Exp. Hypn., *21:*272, 1973.

Solovey, G. and Milechnin, A.: Concerning the nature and treatment of stuttering. Brit. J. Med. Hypn., *10:*2, 1959.

Sutton, S. and Chase, R. A.: White noise and stuttering. J. Speech Hear. Res., *4:*72, 1961.

Tate, M. W. and Cullinan, W. L.: Measurement of consistency of stuttering. J. Speech Hear. Res., *5:*272, 1962.

Tate, M. W., Cullinan, W. L., and Ahlstrand, A.: Measurement of adaptation in stuttering. J. Speech Hear. Res., *4:*322, 1961.

Trotter, W. D. and Lesch, M.: Personal experiences with stutter-aid. J. Speech Hear. Dis., *32:*270, 1967.

Van Dantzig, M.: Syllable tapping: a new method for the help of stammerers. J. Speech Dis., *5:*127, 1940.

Webster, M. L.: A clinical report of the measured effectiveness of certain desensitization techniques with stutterers. J. Speech Hear. Dis., *35:*369, 1970.

Webster, R. L. and Lubker, B. B.: Masking of auditory feedback in stutterer's speech. J. Speech Hear. Res., *11:*221, 1968.

Wolberg, L.: Medical Hypnosis. New York, Grune & Stratton, 1948.

Yates, A. J.: Recent empirical and theoretical approaches to the experimental manipulation of speech in normal subjects and in stammerers. Behav. Res. Ther., *1:*95, 1963.

————: Behavior Therapy. John Wiley and Sons, 1970

SUGGESTED READINGS

Brady, J. P.: A behavioral approach to the treatment of stuttering. Am. J. Psychiat., *125:*843, 1968.

Chase, R. A.: An information-flow model of the organization of motor activity: I. Transduction, transmission, and central control of sensory information. J. Nerv. Ment. Dis., *140:*239, 1965.

————: An information-flow model of the organization of motor activity. II. Sampling, central processing, and utilization of sensory information. J. Nerv. Ment. Dis., *140:*334, 1965.

Gray, B. B. and Brutten, E. J.: The relationship between anxiety, fatigue and spontaneous recovery in stuttering. Behav. Res. Ther., *2:*251, 1965.

Hedge, M. V. Stuttering, neuroticism and extraversion. Behav. Res. Ther., *10:*395, 1972.

21

Tics

Tics or habit spasms may involve all sorts of facial or bodily movements. They occur usually in hyperkinetic, sensitive, and nervous children. Other extenuating factors, such as familial traits and mannerisms, quarreling parents, an insecure mother who continually screams at the child, or physical defects, contribute to the child's unhappiness and tensions. Anxiety over poor grades, lack of interests, fright, and identification with children who display similar involvements are other causes.

BEHAVIOR MODIFICATION THERAPY

Most of the research on tics in behavior therapy deals with the method of massed practice (Yates 1958, Jones 1960, Rafi 1962, Walton 1961 and 1964, Lazarus 1960, Clark 1966, Feldman and Werry 1966). All the above studies except the last, showed the method to be successful. Massed practice is based on the Hullian theory that rapid repeated performance of the tic will build up reactive inhibition or the incompatible habit of not performing the tic. The habit of not responding will be associated with drive-reduction resulting from the dissipation of reactive inhibition and so will be reinforced. In the study by Feldman and Werry (1966), however, it was found that both voluntary and involuntary evocation of the tic *increased* significantly and an old tic reappeared as a function of massed practice.

Treatment based on operant conditioning has been very limited. Barrett (1962) used cessation of music or the initiation of white noise following a tic as contingent instatement of aversive stimulation and found the movement to be significantly affected. Rafi (1962) produced a significant reduction in evocation of foot tapping using a buzzer as a contingent aversive stimulus. Massed practice had previously been unsuccessful with this patient. We have found that some tics are suggestive in origin as in the following case:

HYPNOTHERAPY

A 7-year-old child had developed an incessant twisting of the lips inwardly, accompanied by raising her eyebrows and pushing her chin downward. She had been a bed-wetter and a thumb-sucker, and was the most insecure of four small children. The father was overly concerned with the position of the girl's teeth and constantly admonished her that she would have "buck teeth" if she sucked her thumb. Involuntarily, the child began to pull the upper lip over and under the upper teeth in a futile attempt to push them back. Under a medium stage of hypnosis, it was suggested, "Your teeth are fine; the next set of teeth will grow in right. Don't worry about them." Even a light or hypnoidal stage is often very efficacious. In this case, reassurance under hypnosis and reduction of the father's undue concern were sufficient to allay the child's tensions. As a result, the tic disappeared without further probing.

Another illustrative case is the following:

A 13-year-old boy who was failing in school had had a blinking tic of the eyelids for 3 years. The constant blinking was accompanied by a severe conjunctivitis. He had been treated unsuccessfully by psychodynamic psychotherapy. His father was a physician and wanted the boy to follow in his footsteps. However, the boy was more interested in mechanical hobbies such as radio and electronic devices. It was apparent that the frustrated father was attempting to live out his life in the son.

Under hypnosis it was suggested, "Would you mind twitching the forefinger of your right hand several times a minute? This will take the tension off your lids." Four sessions were required for reinforcement of this suggestion under autohypnosis before the blinking tic of the lids was transferred to a finger-twitch. During the next six sessions, the finger-twitch was reduced in frequency until it, too, subsided. The father's faulty attitudes were discussed, and he decided not to push the boy.

Such symptom-transformation is usually successful because it is much easier to remove a recently established conditioned reflex than a long-standing one. When the new reflex is manifested, the intensity of it can slowly and gradually be reduced. By such measures one can be fairly certain of a successful outcome. If psychological guidance is combined with conditioning under autohypnosis and proper posthypnotic suggestions, better results can be obtained.

Tics, like other maladaptive defenses against anxiety, tend to decrease in frequency when the anxiety level is lowered. The practice and learning of hypnotic relaxation alone often will reduce the general anxiety level of the subject and lead to a diminution of his tic behavior.

T.K. was a very tense, fidgety 10-year-old boy with a vocal tic. He would make high pitched snorting sounds mainly while talking. His classmates made fun of him, calling him "kooky" and it was difficult for him to verbally participate in class discussions. He was under pressure to get good grades and was in competition with his 12-year-old sister. His mother stated that the sister was not actually brighter than the patient but was much more mature and could present a better front. In addition to the tic, T.K. was acting out some of his frustration by getting into fights on the playground and was in danger of expulsion.

The patient was first taught self-hypnosis. Children make excellent hypnotic subjects, as they have vivid imaginations. After his first session in hypnosis he reported, "I feel funny . . . heavy on my whole body." In the first few hypnotic sessions, the tics were absent during hypnosis but showed a temporary increase in frequency immediately after the session. A temporary increase in an anxiety-mediated behavior is often seen after the initial hypnotic sessions if the subject is extremely tense. It takes time for the anxiety-ridden subject to become comfortable with feeling relaxed. Relaxation is often interpreted by the anxious individual as a state of vulnerability in which he is defenseless. They mistake tension for alertness and a necessary condition for protection. Defenses are actually stronger and sensations more acute when the subject is relaxed than when he is tense. It takes time and careful coaching by the therapist to get the patient to allow himself to feel relaxed, even for a brief period. Once he allows himself this experience of relaxation without any harmful consequences, he is more willing to let himself relax for longer periods of time. After a month of practice in hypnotic relaxation, T.K.'s tics had reduced by 50 per cent and there had been no further behavior problems at school.

T.K. often stated that he was unaware that he had a tic and that he was not actually certain what the behavior was that we were trying to reduce even though his mother and I would parrot the undesired sound back to him. His fifth session was recorded on tape. The tape was played back and each time the tic was uttered the therapist tapped on the desk with a pencil. The patient was amazed and embarrassed at what he really sounded like and the tic further decreased in frequency. An audio or video tape is very effective in making the ticquer aware of the target behavior to be eliminated. The actual revelation on tape is often quite traumatic however, and for this reason sessions are not taped until a therapeutic relationship has been established.

Next T.K. was informed that whenever he had the verble tic the therapist would tap the desk with his pencil. The verbal interchange was to continue uninterrupted by the pencil tap. A timer was also introduced at this period. The first timer was a 1-minute hour glass. Whenever a minute of verbal interchange elapsed without a tap (tic), the subject was given a poker chip. If the subject tiqued within one minute, the timer was reset, that is the hour glass was turned back over. It is good to have the timer in view of the subject during initial sessions as the response of "not responding" is very voluntary at first and the subject can more easily hold off a tic if he can see he has only a few more seconds to go before his reinforcement. An exchange system for the poker chips was worked out prior to the introduction of this procedure. It was decided that 200 chips was worth a new record album.

When the subject was able to go 5 consecutive minutes without a tic, the interval of time for which not responding or ticing was to be reinforced was extended to 3 minutes, then 5 minutes, then 10 minutes, and finally 30 minutes. It was explained that increasing the contingency for reward was a good sign, and showed much progress on his part. There was, therefore, no actual resistance at having to do more work for the same reward when the contingencies were

changed. After 20 sessions the tic was gone. T.K. was encouraged to keep practicing the hypnotic relaxation with recall of the standard images for daily 5-
minute sessions in order to maintain his relaxation. It has been over a year since
this patient was last seen and his mother reports the tic has not returned.

HYPNOBEHAVIORAL THERAPY

Wickramasekera (1974) treated a case of blepharospasm (severe eye-blink
tic). The blepharospasm apparently did not respond to analytic psychotherapy,
which had previously been attempted. The dynamics and etiology of the symptoms seemed clear to the previous therapist, present therapist, and to the patient. Combining hypnosis and behavior therapy appeared to have been the critical therapeutic intervention.

REFERENCES

Barrett, B. H.: Reduction in rate of multiple tics by free operant conditioning methods.
J. Nerv. Ment. Dis., *135:*187, 1962.
Clark, D. F.: Behavior therapy of Gilles de la Tourette's syndrome. Brit. J. Psychiat,
*112:*771, 1966.
Feldman, R. B. and Werry, J. S.: An unsuccessful attempt to treat a tiqueur by massed
practice. Behav. Res. Ther., *4:*11, 1966.
Jones, H. G.: Continuation of Yates' treatment of a tiqueur. *In* Eysenck, H. J. (ed.): Be-
havior Therapy and the Neuroses. Oxford, Pergamon, 1960.
Lazarus, A. A.: Objective psychotherapy in the treatment of dysphemia. J. South Afri-
can Logopedic Soc., *6:*8, 1960.
Rafi, A. A.: Learning theory and the treatment of tics. J. Psychosom. Res., *6:*71, 1962.
Walton, D.: Experimental psychology and the treatment of a tiqueur. J. Child Psychol.
Psychiat., *2:*148, 1961.
————: Massed practice and simultaneous reduction in drive level—further evidence of
the efficacy of this approach to the treatment of tics. *In* Eysenck, H. J. (ed.): Experi-
ments in Behavior Therapy. London, Pregamon, 1964.
Wickramasekera, I.: Hypnosis and broad-spectrum behavior therapy for blepharospasm:
A case study. Int. J. Clin. Hypn., *22:*201, 1974.
Yates, A. J.: The application of learning theory to the treatment of tics. J. Abnorm.
Soc. Psychol., *56:*175, 1958.

SUGGESTED READINGS

Fernando, S. J.: Gilles de la Tourette's syndrome. Brit. J. Psychiat. *114:*123, 1968.
Prabhakaran, N.: A case of Gilles de la Tourette's syndrome, with some observations on
aetiology and treatment. Brit J. Psychiat., *116:*539, 1970.
Sand, P. L. and Carlson, C.: Failure to establish control over tics in the Gilles de la
Tourette syndrome with behavior therapy techniques. Brit. J. Psychiat., *122:*665,
1973.
Yates, A. J.: Behaviour Therapy. New York, John Wiley & Sons, 1970.

PART FIVE

Neuroses and Psychoses

22

Phobias

BEHAVIOR MODIFICATION THERAPY

There are literally hundreds if not thousands of articles and studies regarding the treatment of a phobia by behavior therapy. In fact, it was once believed that behavior modification was useful only for this particular patient population. Most of the technics now employed under the rubric of behavior therapy were applied in one form or another over 40 years ago, almost entirely in attempts to treat children's fears. Watson and Rayner (1920) suggested four ways in which the conditioned fear response might be eliminated. The first involved repeated presentation of the feared object, with the expectation that this procedure would lead to habituation. The remaining three technics involved reciprocal inhibition. Responses incompatible with anxiety were produced by stimulating erogenous zones, feeding, and building up constructive activities around the feared object such as manipulating it with the hands.

The common method of treatment today is systematic desensitization, involving training in relaxation, the construction of anxiety hierarchies, and pairing each anxiety-eliciting step with a response incompatible with anxiety and thus counterconditioning the anxiety-eliciting stimulus. Relaxation is the most common "incompatible response" although sexual arousal and eating may also be used. Here, of course, there is a danger that we may condition anxiety to sex or eating and the cure will be worse than the disease. The desensitization procedure may be carried out in the absence of the real feared object by imagining the objects or it can be carried out by direct exposure (on a generalization gradient) to real objects. Wolpe (1961) has argued that the reduction in anxiety generated by imaginal or covert desensitization will generalize to real situations

251

almost completely. As mentioned in Chapter 9, we have found relaxation produced via our hypnotic induction method to be much deeper than that produced via the technics described by Wolpe (1958). Another form of effective desensitization is "flooding" or "implosion" therapy in which the phobic situation is intensified. However, Morganstern (1973) concludes that there is no convincing evidence of the effectiveness of these procedures. Nor are the technics superior to standard desensitization. Not only does the theoretical basis of implosive therapy appear to be unsupported, it raises serious ethical questions in regard to the desirability of its clinical use. Some patients may be overwhelmed by the intensity of the fear-eliciting stimuli. The following case illustrates the use of the hypnobehavioral model in the treatment of a phobic:

> Mrs. L.E. was an attractive young English woman, age 25, who complained of an acute case of claustrophobia. She panicked in any situation where she felt a sense of being trapped. She always needed the security of being near an exit. Fear was particularly great in elevators, theaters, automobiles on the freeway and airplanes. Plane flights were especially traumatic. When the plane doors closed she would tell herself, "I can't get out," which led to panic. She particularly enjoyed traveling and her therapeutic objective was to make a long trans-Atlantic flight.
>
> The phobia had begun on such a flight one year prior when she and her new husband were traveling to London to attend the funeral of his father. She had been nervous on this flight as she had never met her husband's relatives and worried about what they might think of her. Her tension associated with the 12-hour flight initiated the subsequent conditioning of fear to closed, trapped situations. This was explained to her and she was then informed that just as her fear of planes was conditioned by pairing a state of high anxiety over a long period of time (12 hours) with the closed plane compartment, the fear would be deconditioned by pairing the plane compartment with a response incompatible to anxiety, namely relaxation. She accepted the rationale for the conditioning paradigm. There were also other sources of tension in her life. Her spouse was overly dependent upon his mother. She stated that he and his brothers were like little girls when around their mother. In addition she felt uncomfortable adjusting to the United States. The people were "cold" compared to the Europeans.
>
> Most phobics have high levels of anxiety and are generally nervous people. Hypnosis in conjunction with imaginal recall of relaxing scenes was begun immediately. Once the patient began practicing autohypnosis she reported feeling tremendously more relaxed in all situations. She was no longer bothered by her mother-in-law, and her husband's faults seemed minor. After doing Image III (garden scene) she stated, "It gave me great peace of mind to know I had the power of concentration to lie here on the couch and smell a lemon or an orange without one being present." It is often the case that as patients gain control over their powers of concentration and physical functioning they feel much more in control and confident in general.
>
> An image specific to her problem was then constructed in which she was to see herself sitting in a theatre, thoroughly calm, viewing a play. After practicing this image for 2 weeks she was able to attend the theatre, sit through an entire play, and feel no anxiety.
>
> At this point a hierarchy was constructed directed toward alleviating her fear of flying. The initial hierarchy was as follows: "1. You are checking in at the desk

in the airport. 2. You are riding the escalator to the second floor. 3. You walk around the terminal for 20 minutes. 4. The intercom announces boarding time. 5. You board the plane. 6. You fasten your seat belt. 7. Look out the window. 8. You see them close the doors. 9. The announcement comes, 'We'll be taking off in a few minutes.' 10. You sit, waiting for take-off for 10 minutes. 11. The plane takes off. 12. You ride 5 minutes, the plane lands, and the doors open immediately.''

It is imperative that this hierarchy be taken one step at a time and that the patient not look ahead during any one of the steps. For example, if during Step 2 the subject is thinking of boarding the plane while seeing herself on the escalator, she has already jumped ahead 2 steps and is defeating the purpose of the hierarchy. When she is riding the escalator, she is to be thinking of nothing but the escalator or a pleasant image. This holds true when in reality the patient makes the flight; she is to take one step at a time. Several technics are used to prevent future steps from creeping into current stages in the hierarchy. The patient is first instructed to go through the hierarchy with the mental set that she is not going to take the flight. At Step 9 therefore, she gets off the plane; she is merely seeing her husband off. Also, it will be noted that the last step in the initial hierarchy involves only a 5-minute flight. Flight duration was increased and other steps added as the patient became more comfortable with the chain of responses leading up to sitting through a 12-hour flight.

In the actual counterconditioning procedure, L.E. was put into hypnotic relaxation. The first step in the hierarchy was then described in vivid detail, "You are at the airport. It is a beautiful day. The sky is deep blue, the sun a blazing yellow. Feel the warmth of the sun against your face, feel its heat against your skin. Smell the clean crisp air; it smells like autumn. Hear the planes taking off. You feel fantastic, perfectly calm, and at peace with the world. You walk up to the desk to check in. Your steps are brisk, your gait assured. Hear the sharp echo of your footsteps.'' The therapist continues describing the hierarchical steps in detail using all five sense modalities. Repeated reference is made to the subject's feeling and appearance of being calm, cool, and collected. The subject has been instructed beforehand that if at any point in this description she experiences the *least* bit of anxiety, she is to lift her right index finger. This is a cue for the therapist to switch off the desensitization image and switch on a relaxing image. The subject is taken completely through the relaxing image and is not returned to the airport image until next session. [A variation of this procedure often used in behavior therapy is to switch back and forth between anxiety-eliciting and relaxation-producing images in one therapy session. This is not a sound procedure, however, as the relaxation image soon comes to be a cue for the anxiety-eliciting image if it repeatedly precedes it. The relaxing image itself could thus become a negative secondary reinforcer using this procedure.]

It is mandatory that the moment the subject experiences any anxiety in conjunction with the hierarchy, she switch it off by recalling relaxation. Otherwise she will be conditioning more anxiety to the hierarchy. L.E. was then instructed to role-rehearse this hierarchy in hypnosis five times a day at home. She was to imagine it as far as she could before experiencing anxiety, and then to recall a relaxing image. Soon, the onset of anxiety became a cue for relaxation, so that at any time the patient began to feel anxious, relaxation ensued. What was voluntarily programmed in the beginning became reflexive. The patient was told to proceed along the hierarchy very slowly. She spent as much as 3 weeks on some of the more difficult steps. The subject begins at the beginning of the hierarchy each session, reviewing steps that have already been desensitized. It is felt that this is a more thorough method than starting each session one step before the step which last elicited anxiety, although in cases where little time is available, the latter procedure may prove acceptable.

At this point in her therapy, L.E. experienced a traumatic incident. She was dining out with her husband, and when they tried to leave, the front door had been barred. The restaurant was closing and customers were exiting through a side door. She felt a surge of panic and had to be helped out. This incident depressed her and she felt she had relapsed. She was reassured that this was an isolated incident, and not related to her future ability to fly. It was an *unexpected* event for which she had no preparation. She had made considerable mental preparations for making the plane flight. To amplify on these thoughts, she was told to imagine herself in this particular restaurant around closing time. In addition to relaxation, the incompatible response of humor or laughter was paired with the image. Injecting humor into previously fearful scenes has proven most effective with many patients. The image was as follows: "You are sitting in the same restaurant. It is closing time. See the counter, the waiters. Your back is to the door. They are giving the food away. It's so bad no one will pay to eat it. You get up and begin dancing to modern jazz around the tables, throwing grapes to the customers. The customers join you in a circle dancing and singing through the kitchen." The patient found the scene terribly amusing, practiced it, went back to the same restaurant, encountered the barred door, and experienced no fear. She was prepared this time. In time, enough control develops so that even unexpected events do not lead to panic. As more and more individual stimuli are deconditioned, there is greater generalization to other situations.

Humorous imagery was now injected into the airplane hierarchy. The patient was instructed to see herself singing *Wunderbar* on boarding and then during take off, dancing down the aisles in a fantastic sort of ballet. After practicing this imagery she went through the entire hierarchy without experiencing anxiety. At this time she desired to make a 1-hour flight to San Francisco. Instructions were given to induce hypnosis and relaxing imagery on boarding and to maintain the anxiety-free relaxation during the trip. She did this successfully.

Time concentration was then incorporated into the hierarchy whereby she saw herself on a 12-hour flight in which 12 minutes seemed like 1 minute. The whole flight seemed to have taken only an hour. She had already successfully made a one hour flight and felt ready for the trip to London. She made the trip, inducing time concentration during flight, and experienced little, if any, anxiety.

STANDARDIZED IMAGES

Any image that is relaxing to the patient is useful in counterconditioning the phobic. In cases of claustrophobia we have found that images of wide-open spaces such as I (beach), VI (space), and XVIII (Shangri La) are especially pleasing. Images inducing dissociation (I, beach; VIII, jungle; XVII, picnic; and XXII, hayloft) are beneficial in helping the patient to mentally and emotionally remove or detach himself from a fearful situation that would become overwhelming were he to direct his attention to it. From the practice of these images the patient develops the facility to dissociate. He is instructed to use this ability whenever he is in a fearful situation. At this time he may actually recall a particular image to redirect his attention or simply recall the feeling of dissociation (detachment, floating) once he has learned the technic via these images.

OTHER BEHAVIORAL TECHNICS

The procedure of massed practice by repeatedly exposing the feared object to the patient for many trials each session has also been used in desensitization. Theoretically, repeated exposure was supposed to produce stimulus overload, or inhibition of the fear response to the feared object. Combining this method with reciprocal inhibition has proven very effective. The following case illustrates its use:

Mrs. H., aged 41, had been fearful of words having a homosexual connotation since she was 18. She was afraid that if she heard one of these words, she would overreact to it. She also felt that others would note her overreaction to this particular word, and thus think she was "queer." As a result, she was continually on guard and tense waiting for such words to be spoken. There were no reasons based on our behavior analysis to believe she had any homosexual tendencies. She was happily married with two teenage daughters.

A list of feared words was first compiled. It included words such as "fruit," "faggot," "lesbian," and "pervert." Hypnosis was induced and these words were repeated 50 times each per session by the therapist. The patient was then instructed to repeat these words out loud during hypnosis to the therapist and while practicing at home. After four sessions, the words no longer produced any anxiety.

HYPNOBEHAVIORAL THERAPY

Phobias related to impotence and frigidity are covered in those chapters. However, one case of sexual inadequacy will be discussed in this chapter as it involved a fear extending to areas other than the sexual. The fear was of being penetrated. The patient feared not only vaginal penetration but anal as well. She could not endure enemas, intercourse or undergo a gynecological examination. She could not even put her own finger into her vagina.

Mrs. M. was a very pleasant 41-year-old virgin. She had been married twice, once to a homosexual for 6 months, and presently to a virile man whom she loved very much. They had been married 10 years and had never had intercourse. She felt sexually aroused during foreplay but felt an urge to vomit whenever he touched her genital area. She stated, "The idea of my husband even inserting his finger into my vagina makes me want to throw up." She was very confused and anxious with reference to most sexual technics calling herself a "dumb, weird, frustrated old bag."

In hypnosis, she first imagined herself penetrating her vagina with her finger, going deeper each image. She was then able to insert her own lubricated finger into her vagina. Next, she imagined her husband merely holding his finger next to her vagina, then gradually penetrating with his finger. Finally she imagined having genital to genital contact and graduated degrees of penetration with her husband. Once she was able to imaginally experience penetration without fear or nausea she was able to experience actual penetration. She subsequently became orgasmic.

Desensitization in hypnosis need not be completely covert or imaginal. "In vivo" desensitization is also aided by hypnosis, which potentiates conditioning. An example of partial "in vivo" desensitization where the UCS was real and the CS was imaginal or recalled ("in vitro") was given in the chapter on sexual inadequacy. Here, an impotent subject paired masturbation (USC) with the thought (CS) of having intercourse with his girlfriend. The following case illustrates the use of "in vivo" desensitization in conjunction with hypnosis in the treatment of a phobic:

> Mrs. N., aged 58, had a multitude of complaints. She was lonesome, depressed, suicidal, nonorgasmic, and hypochondrical. In addition, she had a chronic fear of choking, which had started at 17. The choking phobia limited her diet and prevented her from dating. She feared she would be served something she could not eat and would be considered "crazy" or inferior. She chewed her food excessively until it was almost liquified before swallowing. She had been in therapy of one kind or another the past 30 years and was presently making daily visits to a Suicide Prevention Center and various day treatment centers. She could not be alone. On arising, the mere thought of eating depressed her, making it difficult to get up in the morning.
>
> Hypnotic relaxation training and sensory recall were initiated to reduce her anxiety level. She was instructed to chart her food intake to determine what foods she could eat. A hierarchy of foods was constructed in order of their progressive difficulty of eating. She was then instructed to see herself eating these foods in the context of the standard relaxing images described in this book. For example, she imagined herself eating chocolate cookies under the willow tree by the river bank in Image XII (bluebird scene). During the imagery, she always saw herself as calm, chewing at a regular rate. She was then instructed to induce self-hypnosis at home and eat in the hypnotic state, which constituted "self-in vivo desensitization."
>
> She was then requested to bring foods into the office that were increasingly difficult for her to eat. She first brought a banana. The therapist induced hypnosis, began description of the beach scene, then had the patient eat the banana in the office while imagining eating it in the scene. While the patient was actually eating, the therapist continued to vividly describe the scene imagery to maintain relaxation and misdirect attention from her fear of swallowing. Mrs. N. had reported earlier that she could think of nothing else but the act of eating while she was partaking of food. She could not even carry on a conversation during a meal and needed to be completely alone so that her total attention could be directed to chewing and swallowing. Description of the scene imagery was to direct her attention from ingestion while eating. Mrs. N. continued to bring food—a cheese sandwich, whitefish sandwich, an apple—until she reported having little difficulty with these foods. She was also chewing less. New foods were added to her diet and she began to go out more frequently. Subsequently her depression lessened and as a result she developed more self-esteem and confidence. She also felt warmer toward her husband.

Used intelligently, the hypnobehavioral model can be used successfully to treat phobic reactions ordinarily refractory to conventional psychotherapies.

REFERENCES

Morganstern, K. P.: Implosive therapy and flooding procedures: A critical review. Psych. Bull., *79:*318, 1973.

Watson, J. B. and Rayner, R.: Conditioned emotional reactions. J. Exp. Psychol., *3:*1, 1920.

Wolpe, J.: Psychotherapy by Reciprocal Inhibition. Stanford, Stanford Univ. Press, 1958.

———: The systematic desensitization treatment of neuroses. J. Nerv. Ment. Dis., *132:*189, 1961.

SUGGESTED READINGS

Brough, D. I., Yorkston, N., and Stafford-Clark, D.: A case of wasp phobia treated by systematic desensitization under light hypnosis. Guy's Hospital Rep., *114:*319, 1965.

Hain, J. D., Butcher, R. H. G. and Stevenson, I.: Systematic desensitization therapy: an analysis of results in twenty-seven patients. Brit. J. Psychiat., *112:*295, 1966.

Hoenig, J. and Reed, G. F.: The objective assessment of desensitization. Brit. J. Psychiat., *112:*1279, 1966.

Krapfl, J., and Nawas, M.: Differential ordering of stimulus presentation in systematic desensitization. J. Abnorm. Psychol., *75:*333, 1970.

Leitenberg, H. and Callahan, E. J.: Reinforced practice and reduction of different kinds of fears in adults and children. Behav. Res. Ther., *11:*11, 1973.

MacKenzie, K. R.: The eclectic approach to the treatment of phobias. Amer. J. Psychiat., *130:*1103, 1973.

Marks, I. M.: Fears and Phobias. New York, Academic Press, 1969.

Nawas, M., Fishman, S., and Pucel, J. A.: Standardized desensitization program applicable to group and individual treatments. Behav. Res. Ther., *8:*49, 1971.

Orwin, A.: Augmented respiratory relief: a new use for CO_2 therapy in the treatment of phobic conditions: A preliminary report on two cases (abstract). Br. J. Psychiat., *122:*163, 1973.

Scrignar, C. B., Swanson, W. C., and Bloom, W. A.: Use of systematic desensitization in the treatment of airplane phobic patients. Behav. Res. Ther., *11:*129, 1973.

Snaith, R. P.: A clinical investigation of phobias: Part I. A critical examination of the existing literature. Brit. J. Psychiat., *114:*673, 1968.

Suinn, R., Jorgensen, G., Stewart, S., and McGuirk, F.: Fears as attitudes: Experimental reduction of fear through reinforcement. J. Abnorm. Psychol., *78:*272, 1971.

23

Delinquency and Disciplinary Problems

DELINQUENCY

The literature on delinquency, psychopathy, and criminality is immense. Since we are primarily concerned with behavior and not the question of whether there is a "delinquent personality," a "psychopathic personality," or a "criminal personality," we shall refer to all behavior subsumed under these headings as "disciplinary problems." The delinquent act naturally differs from culture to culture. Whether an act is criminal is also culturally defined. The concept of the psychopathic personality is also open to debate. Craft (1966) stated that two primary features characterize the psychopath: a lack of emotional responsiveness in situations in which this would be called forth in normal persons, and an irresistible tendency to act on impulse. Secondary characteristics derived from these primary characteristics are: lack of guilt following antisocial behavior, failure to be influenced by punishment or aversive consequences of antisocial behavior, and a lack of positive drive or motivation.

Theories on Delinquency

There have been four basic theories to explain delinquency and psychopathy: 1. The biological approach relied mainly on studies of the criminal record of identical twins (Lange 1931). The reader should also familiarize himself with the biological research on aggression if he wishes to be knowledgeable about this model. Avis (1974) gives an excellent review on the neuropharmacology of aggression. 2. The dynamic approach (Healy and Bronner 1926, Aichhorn 1935, Lindner 1944) argued essentially that disciplinary problems represent symptoms of underlying conflict. Delinquency manifests itself as a function of the interaction of unsatisfied inner drives with opportunities provided by the culture to indulge in substitute activities that offer at least partial satisfaction of these inner drives. 3. The sociological approach (Cohen 1956) states that delinquent behavior should be treated as a form of learned behavior generated in, and representative of, a particular kind of culture. In America the frame of reference for the majority is derived from the Protestant ethic, which stresses material achievement. The Negro and working-class child start the race for achievement at a definite disadvantage. This problem is dealt with in the delinquent subculture by providing criteria of status which these people can meet. The subcultural solution does not always involve criminal behavior, as has been strikingly illustrated in recent years by the development of other subcultural solutions such as those of the beatniks and hippies. 4. The behavioral approach (Mowrer 1950, Eysenck 1957, Trasler 1962) describes a general theory of socialization. This theory makes a basic distinction between the learning of skilled forms of behavior, such as walking, and the learning of values. The learning of values or socialization involves training in conformity to certain rules of behavior laid down by society as necessary to its own preservation, rules which often conflict with the child's natural urges. Such training is basically mediated by the technic of passive avoidance training in which conditioned fear (anxiety) is aroused by the initial approach to or performance of the undesirable act.

Conditioned fear is produced by two basic training technics, physical punishment and withdrawal of parental approval or love. If there is no love between the parent and child, the latter form of training has little validity, and all such training must be in the form of physical punishment. If socially approved behavior is to be self-regulated and "conscience" developed, the stimuli producing conditioned fear must become internalized (Eysenck 1960). This theory, therefore, implies that there is a constitutionally determined capacity for socialization determined by the capacity for acquiring conditioned fear responses. There have been several studies of the "conditionability" of psychopaths. Hare (1965a) postulated that, "the gradient of avoidance tendencies is steeper and of lower height for the psychopath than for the normal person (p. 16)," and from this model he inferred that psychopaths show less generalization of avoidance responses, are influenced by immediate punishment but not by threat of punishment, and show increased deficiency of learning as the onset of the punishing stimulus is more and more delayed. The results obtained by Hare in a long series of studies (Hare 1965b, 1965c, 1965d, 1966, 1968a, 1968b) and other researchers (Bernard and Eisenham 1967, Bryan and Kapche 1967, Hetherington and Klinger 1964, Johns and Quay 1962, Schacter and Latane 1964, Persons and Bruning 1966) lead to only two clear conclusions: (1) Psychopaths do not appear to be defective in the acquisition of ordinary skills; (2) Psychopaths do appear to be less influenced by the threat of punishment, particularly if it is to occur at some time (definite or indefinite) in the future.

Delinquents have been consistently discriminated from nondelinquents in terms of two variables that appear to be related to extraversion: 1. Little future-time orientation—that delinquents are more present-oriented in time has been verified by a number of experimental studies of future-time orientation (Barndt and Johnson 1955; Siegman 1961; Davids, Kidder, and Reich 1962; Stein, Sarbin, and Kulik 1968) 2. Greater impulsivity—a fairly consistent pattern appears to emerge of the delinquent as being relatively unsocialized, extraverted, neurotic, and impulsive (Rankin and Wikoff 1964, Kelly and Veldman 1964).

Behavior Modification Therapy

Until recently, the application of behavior therapy to the treatment of delinquency has been mainly at a theoretical level (Jones 1965, Gelder 1965). Recently, treatment involving social isolation (time-out) or loss of tokens for behaviors labeled unacceptable, together with token awards for acceptable behavior, has proven effective in modifying deviant behavior (Burchard and Tyler 1965, Burchard 1967, Tyler and Brown 1967). Clements and McKee (1968) successfully made use of the Premack principle by reinforcing prison inmates with favored recreational activities for increased output.

Kellam (1969) reports an ingenious method of treating shoplifting by aversion to a film. A 10-minute film was made depicting a 48-year-old female patient entering a shop and commencing to shoplift. After each theft (the film showed 19 thefts in all), during the secretion of the articles stolen, a shot of 8-frames' length (⅓ sec. at 24 frames per sec.) of a disapproving face was inserted. The film was then shown to the patient while shock was administered to the left forearm near the wrist and elbow to coincide with the showing of the face during the theft (VR3 schedule). After 5 weeks and forty showings, she had a generalized fear of shops accompanied by a strong sensation of being watched whenever she entered a shop. She noticed she was avoiding large shops in favor of small ones and had to avoid going past the shop used in the film. At this stage she was discharged. At follow-up 3 months later, she was able to shop but avoided it if she could. She felt anxious when she entered shops and had an urge to steal. This urge had resulted in anxiety, tension in the left arm, and an overwhelming memory of seeing the film, especially the faces which "loomed before her eyes." Everyone in the shop seemed to turn to look at her and the urge to steal disappeared. She felt that but for this reaction she would inevitably have stolen each time. Nir and Culter (1973) describe a more global application of therapy in a collaborative program between an adolescent psychiatric clinic and a juvenile court.

DISCIPLINARY PROBLEMS

Etiologic Factors

The behavior pattern of the child is laid down from the first few weeks of life. Recently it was shown that if newborn monkeys were taken away from their mothers and nursed on a wire surrogate "monkey," these monkeys, deprived of warmth, became asocial, detached, quarrelsome, nervous, and, in short, psychoneurotic adults. When a control group was nursed on a soft, cuddly teddy bear "monkey," they grew up to be warm, gregarious, mature adults, normal in every respect. It was also found that leaving the monkeys on the wire "mother" for only a week and then transferring them to the teddy bear monkey did not reverse the harmful patterns that were laid down. This ingenious experiment indicates that personality is molded early in life (Harlow et al. 1972). Prescott (1975) attributes these effects to somatosensory deprivation.

The developing personality, in order to mature into a healthy one, must as Freud pointed out, pass through the early developmental mileposts of infantile sexuality. If an individual is unable to adapt to a more mature orientation, he will do one of two things: he will either retreat to a previous stage of development or remain at the latest one. This is analogous to the soldier who finds that the pillbox that he is attempting to attack is too heavily fortified, and so he retreats back to his slit trench where he once knew safety. Immature, frustrated individuals who are insecure hate to leave the slit trench of childhood and remain fixated at earlier levels of development.

To encourage growth of the personality, parents, particularly the mother, of necessity, have to walk a tightrope; they must give the child an equal amount of love and of discipline. However, children must not be reared as if they were mass-produced; each child needs to have his own particular needs, wishes, and feelings satisfied in his own particular manner. Therefore, mothers especially must make their children feel that they are loved for themselves and not for their accomplishments. If he is given a considerable amount of love, the child will be willing to abandon his hostility and reciprocate with compliance and the giving up of earlier patterns of behavior. "Smother love" is not "mother love," and mothers must be careful not to be oversolicitous toward the child. This will only make him more dependent and less likely to mature in a healthy fashion.

Parents should also remember that unruly behavior, rebellion, and delinquency of any type are often used as attention-getting devices—the child uses these mechanisms to invite interest on the part of the parents. This type of behavior is often seen in the chronically ill child, who uses complaints as a means of gaining sympathy and attention. It is important to ascertain whether or not parents are taking out their own frustrations on a child as a means of acting out their own neurotic needs. Other parents live out their own thwarted ambitions through the child (appersonation)—the stage mother is a typical example. Still others make unreasonable demands that the child is unable to fulfill, and, as a result, he retreats to earlier levels of behavior where he once had security. He then develops many of the harmful sequelae described in this book.

EVALUATING PROBLEM BEHAVIOR

A big problem in evaluating the emotional behavior of a child is that the same symptom may signify different levels of disturbance in different children. There are criteria for evaluating the seriousness of a child's behavioral difficulty that can be helpful in determining whether or not a child needs hypnobehavioral treatment. Whether the conflicts are internal or external is an important criterion. Problems created by the environment are much easier to deal with than internal conflicts.

Another criterion is whether the disturbance is limited or affects most aspects of the child's development. Does the child have difficulty getting along with his mother only, or does he have difficulty in other interpersonal relationships? Most normal adolescents are in a constant state of turmoil. In fact, the adolescent who is not struggling to conquer his impulses and to achieve independence is the one who may eventually need psychological care. However, the particular type of emotional disturbance that develops depends on the parental behavior, the degree of the child's exposure, and the response of the parents and others to his psychological disorder. The length of time that the disturbance has been present also is important. One present for a month will clear up more readily than a symptom present for years. Robins (1966) carefully followed adolescents into adulthood. His studies show how the child who will eventually be disturbed can be identified by the number of antisocial symptoms in adolescence, the family history of sociopathy or alcoholism, and lax or inconsistent home discipline.

School problems can be treated in the incipient stage by posthypnotic suggestions directed to increasing the child's interest in his studies. If this approach is not successful, arrangements can be made for the mother to sit in class with the child for gradually diminishing periods of time. If the classroom, schoolmates, or teachers are disturbing factors, these should be discussed at either hypnotic or nonhypnotic levels.

Eating problems appearing early in life usually represent hostility toward parents. When eating becomes a means of expressing pleasure or displeasure, hunger ceases to dictate the amount of the food intake; a vicious cycle is established, the origin of which is eventually forgotten. In this situation, the mother needs greater confidence in her ability as a parent. She must recognize that the child's own physiology will ensure an adequate dietary intake as long as she does not fuss about his eating habits.

Dawdling is probably normal in preschool children and it, too, denotes resentment of the nagging parent. Fear of punishment or loss of love causes the child to choose this pattern rather than one of overt rebellion. Therapy should be directed against parental overreaction, but the longer dawdling has existed the more time and support will be required to help parents guide their child through this phase of adjustment.

Rebellious or delinquent behavior suggests that the child is angry and has such a poor relationship with his parents that he fears neither punishment nor loss of love. At other times, rebellion occurs when the child feels omnipotent as a result of lacking parental control. Thus, the parents require guidance regarding the need for parental unity in providing realistic, consistent demands on the child, combined with continuing love and acceptance.

Sadistic and destructive behavior gives pleasure to most 2- or 3-year-old youngsters, as they seek and even enjoy punishment for their misdeeds. Parents should recognize this as an attention-getting device, and increase approval, and decrease rejection and punishment. If the syndrome is noted too late, psychotherapy will be required when the child is older.

HYPNOTHERAPY

Ambrose (1951) employed hypnotherapy in a child guidance clinic and reported cures or improvement in phobias, nightmares, chronic anxiety states, and other psychosomatic disorders. Symptomatic cure was established in over 60 per cent of the cases. In investigations (1951, 1953), he demonstrated how hypnosis could speed up psychotherapy, compared with more time-consuming methods. Hypnotherapy was utilized primarily to relieve tension, and positive suggestions were stressed along with reeducation and supportive therapy for both parents and children. Symptom-removal by direct authoritative suggestion is seldom effective (Solovey and Milechnin 1955).

Hypnotherapy has been employed effectively in juvenile delinquency (Ambrose 1952, Gilbert 1954). Relaxation alone, under hypnosis, relieved the significant tensions (Gilbert 1954). Behavioral problems such as stealing, truancy, sex offences, and lying were helped in patients who were followed for 1 to 6 years.

Ambrose and Newbold (1956) have an excellent chapter devoted exclusively to the use of hypnotherapy in delinquency. Hypnosis was used to allow children to vent their fears and, together with re-education, this helped a high percentage of delinquents. Parents were also treated to correct aggravating factors. When they saw the improvement in their children through hypnosis, the parents became even more cooperative. In some cases, abreaction, regression, and revivification were used to relive actual traumatic episodes. The protective value of hypnosis, as well as its corrective features, was emphasized.

Mellor (1960) cured 13 of 14 hardened juvenile delinquents, who were refractory toward all types of therapy, in an average of 6 sessions. He made use of communication with the "unconscious" by technics involving finger- or hand-levitation to produce answers establishing the authenticity of traumatic or emotional causative factors. This technic (finger signaling) rapidly eliminated emotional blocks and avoided anger and defiance. In several cases the benefits occurred during the first session. It is likely that the finger signaling here acts as a "magical gesture," fitting in with the subject's inordinate need for security, attention, and love. This, together with a permissive and noncritical approach, was very valuable for the juvenile delinquent.

Weitzenhoffer (1960) questioned the validity of eliciting the so-called "wisdom" of the "unconscious" by ideomotor finger signaling. He believes that there is little justification for assuming that some sort of psychic entity, "the unconscious," has been communicated with or is responsible for the observed phenomena. Nevertheless, Mellor's brief pilot study indicates that the method established good motivation for self-improvement. Regression, revivification, and cathartic recall aided recognition and understanding of the underlying reasons for the tensions. Mellor thinks that, during hypnosis, subjects overcome their difficulties by developing insight and learning better ways of responding to their tensions.

The following patient with a behavior problem was helped in five sessions of hypnotherapy:

> G. E., a 13-year-old boy, had run away from school, was continually at odds with his parents, and was always making inordinate demands on his family for a motorcycle, a hot-rod auto, etc. He had been suspended from two schools because of obscene language, insubordination, and poor grades.
>
> Through hypnosis, a good rapport was readily established and was used to express some of his hostile attitudes toward his parents. He and his younger sister were adopted. He realized that he needed his parents' support, yet he felt a considerable amount of hostile dependence toward them. This attitude was projected to teachers and other surrogate parent-figures.
>
> His parents, who had adamantly refused to let him go out with girls, were advised to let him go steady with a girl of his own age. Posthypnotic suggestions were utilized to improve his concentration, especially for spelling and reading. His grades improved. The nature of his rebellious attitudes and attempts to retaliate for excessively strict supervision was also worked through by re-education, enabling him to make a satisfactory adjustment. Hypnosis here speeded up the psychotherapeutic process.

DISCUSSION OF PROBLEM BEHAVIOR

As stated earlier, these authors see no utility in making a dichotomy between "criminal," "delinquent," and "psychopathic" behavior. That lack of capacity for negative conditioning leads one to psychopathy is doubtful. The "psychopath's" decreased regard for threatened future punishment may be a defense developed to deal with his environment. He engages in deviant acts *first* and then develops the capacity to deny the possibility of punishment so that he can cope with his deviant way of life. Certainly sociological factors interact to determine reinforcement contingencies. Also, the more difficult it is for a person to obtain a reward through approved means, the greater the probability that he will resort to deviant means. The concept of the "bad seed" seems most fatalistic. Even if one could inherit tendencies toward specific forms of deviant behavior, as the behavior geneticists argue, these tendencies are still modifiable. Even inherited characteristics are subject to change.

Delinquent behavior must be taken simply for what it is—a segment of behavior that is not considered appropriate by someone else. The subject is not obeying the rules, someone else is not able to properly control or discipline the subject. Problems referred to in this chapter are not concerned with problems in self-discipline but in disciplining someone else. The person who deviates without voluntary control, such as the kleptomaniac, is considered in the chapter on compulsions. There the problem is one of self-discipline. It is when the subject *chooses* to deviate that we have what is commonly called a disciplinary problem or delinquency or psychopathy. The choice may be motivated out of poverty, sibling rivalry, lack of love, and other factors, but it is still a choice.

BEHAVIOR MODIFICATION OF DISCIPLINARY PROBLEMS

Discipline problems with children are most easy to handle because the disciplinarians (parents, teachers) are present a good deal of the time and can exercise control over contingencies for various target behaviors. It is most important that the problem behavior be clearly defined. Complaints about a child such as, "he has a bad attitude" or "he's too messy" are much too vague to be dealt with. What specific behaviors are labeled by his parents as a "bad attitude"? Is he late for dinner? Does he swear? Does he make faces at his parents? What is meant by "messy"? Does he leave his pajamas on the floor, eat with his mouth open, leave his books open?

Blanchard and Johnson (1973) treated behavior-problem students by operant classroom control procedures. They recorded the frequency of the target behaviors of the subjects in which the operant procedures were applied. Significant improvement resulted from the contingent administration of tangible rewards and punishments. The experiment was designed to control effects of emotional variables.

It is best to start with one piece of behavior and zero in on the target rather than try to change the whole child at once. Say, for example, that the parent's complaint is that his child "won't do what he's told" (a common complaint). What specific things is he told to do that he does not do? A list of several items is then compiled. One item may be that the child is never home on time. The time he is expected must then be determined, say 4 o'clock, and the parent is asked, "Have you told your child specifically that he is to be home by 4:00?" It is amazing how many times the parent never directly tells the child what is expected of him. It is also discussed with the parent whether he thinks his expectations are reasonable. Often the parent does not consider the age of the child and what he was like when that age. A direct question like, "When you were 12, did you have to be home by 4:00?" may reveal the unreasonability of the parent's demand.

Once the expectation or desired behavior is clearly defined and established as reasonable by the parent (it does not matter whether the therapist considers it reasonable; it is the parent who has labeled the behavior "deviant" and thus a problem for discipline), the parent is told to chart this specific behavior. A paper is placed on the wall at home in view of the child with spaces drawn for each day of the week. When the child is home before 4 o'clock, an X is marked in the appropriate space. This procedure is explained to the child with the parent present, and an exchange system is worked out whereby a certain number of X's for a certain prize is established a priori. Any ambiguity in the procedure will lead to its failure. This form of token system is very effective, and its progress is discussed with both parent and child in future sessions. Once discipline or control is established by the parent over one type of behavior, other behaviors are much more easily controlled.

Therapy is also directed at improving the relationship between parent and child. As mentioned earlier, withdrawal or giving of love is a powerful reinforcer. The parent who does not have this reinforcer to give or withdraw is severely hampered in his ability to control the child and must rely solely on physical means of reinforcement. Also, if the parent doles out reinforcement inconsistently, this can cause severe forms of problematic behavior to develop in the child. A behavior for which the child is sometimes punished and sometimes reinforced is very resistant to extinction. It will be remembered that intermittent reinforcements lead to the most durable behavior pattern.

> We recall one mother who complained her little girl was "unmanageable." She described an incident in which the child had completely covered herself with her mother's lipstick. The mother was in a vile mood and had beat the child with a hose. Two sessions later, however, the same mother recounted a similar incident in which the child had gotten into her make-up. On this occasion, however, she thought it terribly cute of the girl to play adult and had laughed. Here was the same piece of behavior, punished one time and reinforced the other. The reinforcement contingencies were not dependent on the child's behavior, but on the mother's mood. It is asking too much to expect a child to discriminate the proper mood for the proper behavior.

While a negative reinforcer such as sitting in the corner (time-out) may be used in the home, it is generally more enforceable in a classroom situation where the teacher is always present. Although it is sometimes necessary to isolate problem children from others so that they will not be disruptive, more long-term modification of behavior is usually obtained using a positive means of manipulation. If the problem occurs at school, the therapist must work with the teacher. One brief phone call will usually suffice to determine the specific target behavior and work out a reinforcement procedure the teacher can practically use. School problems usually consist of not studying, fidgeting in the seat, talking to other children, talking without being called on, and hitting other children.

Once again, use can be made of a timer set in front of the child. Whenever a certain amount of time lapses in which the undesired behavior has not been emitted, the child is given a token. For example, if the child sits 10 minutes without talking out of turn, he is rewarded with a token. An exchange system for the token is always worked out beforehand so that the child knows exactly what he is working for. The child is required to go for longer and longer periods of good behavior before reinforcement as time progresses.

Later, the child may be moved from a fixed to a variable schedule and the timer is not used. Every so often the teacher simply gives the child a token, provided of course he is behaving. Misbehavior at this point leads to his having to forfeit a token rather than having his timer reset. It is very effective to put a whole classroom on a token system. Rewarding the desired behavior is much more effective than punishing the undesired behavior. Using simply verbal reinforcement the teacher will say things such as, "I like the way Johnny is sitting quietly in his seat," or "It's very nice the way Rosie hasn't talked to anybody next to her." Verbal reinforcements such as these are given at least once every 5 minutes throughout the class day. If verbal reinforcement is disruptive or not strong enough, the entire class may be put on a token system with a standard exchange for prizes worked out. As timers for each pupil in a larger class are too tedious for one person to handle, an intermittent schedule is used. Every so often the teacher goes around the room giving each pupil who behaves well a token. She may possibly whisper to him some particularly good behavior the pupil is exhibiting when she gives him the token. If a pupil acts up, he must forfeit a token and miss a reinforcement.

As children grow into adolescence they spend less time with the same teacher and less time with their parents. Contingencies thus become more difficult for the disciplinarian to manage. Once young adults graduate and leave home, discipline is left largely to the police with whom the subject has little if any contact until he is punished. There is little opportunity to receive positive reinforcement from the police. Punishment, however, has proven miserably ineffective as a deterrent to crime. Prison, which is the time-out at its extreme, falls far short of its purpose as a tool for discipline. When people are not rewarded enough for appropriate forms of behavior, they resort to inappropriate ones. The adult who constitutes a discipline problem to the police is much more difficult to control than the juvenile. The reinforcers maintaining his deviant behavior must be uncovered and the contingencies modified. He then must be led to find reinforcement through alternative, more acceptable activities.

A "Clockwork Orange" type of aversive conditioning to criminal acts that the subject is forced to view merits some consideration. It is, however, doubtful that this method would be efficacious, in that there is an almost infinite number of acts which could be considered illegal. While it is plausible that a subject could be sensitized to one act much as is the cigarette smoker sensitized to the cigarette, there would be little generalization to other acts also considered criminal.

A spouse may also constitute a disciplinary problem to his mate. Many a patient comes in stating that he or she is there because his or her husband or wife said he or she needed help. The wife may complain that her husband never lets her talk in company or the husband may complain that his wife rejects him sexually too often. These target behaviors can be charted by the complaining spouse, who is serving as the disciplinarian. An exchange system can also be worked out. The reward is often a time-out from the mate.

These problems lend themselves admirably to hypnobehavioral therapy. Since the target behaviors require change, operant conditioning is the method of choice. Such an approach works best if the rewards and punishments are monitored by an external agent. This can be best done on an inpatient basis, but can also be administered by parents and other significant or surrogate figures.

REFERENCES

Aichhorn, A.: Wayward Youth. New York, Viking, 1935.

Ambrose, G.: The value of hypnotic suggestion in the anxiety reactions of children. Brit. J. Med. Hypn., *2:*20, 1951.

————: Hypnotherapy in the treatment of the delinquent child: I. The intelligent delinquent. Brit. J. Med. Hypn., *3:*56, 1952.

————: Positive hypnotherapy versus negative psychotherapy in child psychiatry. Brit. J. Med. Hypn.,*4:*26, 1953.

Ambrose, G., and Newbold, G.: Handbook of Clinical Hypnosis. London, Baillière, Tindall and Cox, 1956.

Avis, H. H.: The neuropharmacology of aggression: A critical review. Psychol. Bull., *81:*47, 1974.

Barndt, R. J. and Johnson, D. M.: Time orientation in delinquents. J. Abnorm. Soc. Psychol., *51:*343, 1955.

Bernard, J. L. and Eisenman, R.: Verbal conditioning in sociopaths with social and monetary reinforcement. J. Person. Soc. Psychol., *6:*203, 1967.

Blanchard, E. B. and Johnson, R. A.: Generalization of operant classroom procedures. Behav. Therap., *4:*219–229, 1973.

Bryan, J. H. and Kapche, R.: Psychopathy and verbal conditioning. J. Abnorm. Psychol., *72:*71, 1967.

Burchard, J. D.: Systematic socialization: a programmed environment for the habilitation of antisocial retardates. Psychol. Rec.,*17:*461, 1967.

Burchard, J. and Tyler, V.: The modification of delinquent behavior through operant conditioning. Behav. Res. Ther., *2:*245, 1965.

Clements, C. B. and McKee, J. M.: Programmed instruction for institutionalized offenders: contingency management and performance contracts. Psychol. Rep., *22:*957, 1968.

Cohen, A. K.: Delinquent Boys. London, Routledge and Kegan Paul, 1956.

Craft, M.: Psychopathic Disorders and Their Assessment. London, Pergamon, 1966.

Davids, A., Kidder, C., and Reich, M.: Time orientation in male and female juvenile delinquents. J. Abnorm. Soc. Psychol., *64:*239, 1962.

Eysenck, H. J.: The Dynamics of Anxiety and Hysteria. London, Routledge and Kegan Paul, 1957.

————: The development of moral values in children: the contribution of learning theory. Brit. J. Educ. Psychol., *30:*11, 1960.

Gelder, M.: Behavior and aversion therapy in the treatment of delinquency. II. Can behavior therapy contribute to the treatment of delinquency? Brit. J. Criminol., *5:*365, 1965.

Gilbert, S. F.: Hypnotherapy in children. Brit. J. Med. Hypn., *6:*36, 1954.

Hare, R. D.: A conflict and learning theory analysis of psychopathic behavior. J. Res. in Crime and Delinq., *2:*12, 1965.

————: Psychopathy, fear arousal and anticipated pain. Psychol. Rep., *16:*499, 1965.

————: Acquisition and generalization of a conditioned fear response in psychopathic and nonpsychopathic criminals. J. Psychol., *59:*367, 1965.

————: Temporal gradient of fear arousal in psychopaths. J. Abnorm. Psychol., *70:*442, 1965.

————: Psychopathy and choice of immediate versus delayed punishment. J. Abnorm. Psychol., 1966. *71:*25, 1966.

————: Psychopathy, autonomic functioning, and the orienting response. J. Abnorm. Psychol. Monogr. Suppl., *73:*1, 1968.

————: Detection threshold for electric shock in psychopaths. J. Abnorm. Psychol., *73:*268, 1968.

Harlow, H. F., Gluck J. P. and Suomi, S. J.: Generalization of behavioral data between human and non-human animals. Am. Psychologist, *27:*709, 1972.

Healy, W. and Bronner, A. L.: Delinquents and Criminals: Their Making and Unmaking. New York, Macmillan, 1926.

Hetherington, E. M. and Klinger, E.: Psychopathy and punishment. J. Abnorm. Soc. Psychol., *69:*113, 1964.

Johns, J. H. and Quay, H. C.: The effect of social reward on verbal conditioning in psychopathic and neurotic military offenders. J. Consult. Psychol., *26:*217, 1962.

Jones, H. G.: Behavior and aversion therapy in the treatment of delinquency: I. The techniques of behavior therapy and delinquent behavior. Brit. J. Criminol., *5:*355, 1965.

Kellam, A. M.: Shop lifting treated by aversion to a film. Behav. Res. Ther., *7:*125, 1969.

Kelly, F. J. and Veldman, D. J.: Delinquency and school drop-out behavior as a function of impulsivity and nondominant values. J. Abnorm. Soc. Psychol., *69:*190, 1964.

Lange, J.: Crime as Destiny. London, Allen and Unwin, 1931.

Lindner, R. M.: Rebel Without a Cause. New York, Grune and Stratton, 1944.

Mellor, N. H.: Hypnosis in juvenile delinquency. Read before 35th Pan-American Med. Assn. Meeting, May 4, 1960.

Mowrer, O. H.: Learning Theory and Personality Dynamics. New York, Ronald Press, 1950.

Nir, Y. and Cutler, R.: The therapeutic utilization of the juvenile court. Amer. J. Psychiat., *130:*1112, 1973.

Persons, R. W. and Bruning, J. L.: Instrumental learning with sociopaths: a test of clinical theory. J. Abnorm. Psychol., *71:*165, 1966.

Prescott, J. W.: Body pleasure and the origins of violence. The Futurist, April, 1975.

Rankin, R. J. and Wikoff, R. L.: The IES Arrow Dot performance of delinquents and nondelinquents. Percept. Motor Skills, *18:*207, 1964.

Robins, E.: Antisocial and dyssocial personality disorders. *In* Freedman, A. M., and Kaplan, H. I. (eds.) Comprehensive Textbook of Psychiatry. Baltimore, Williams & Wilkins, 1967.

Schachter, S. and Latane, B.: Crime, cognition, and the autonomic nervous system. *In* Levine, D. (ed.): Nebraska Symposium on Motivation. Lincoln, Univ. Nebraska Press, 1964.

Siegman, A. W.: The relationship between future time perspective, time estimation, and impulse control in a group of young offenders and in a control group. J. Consult. Psychol., *25:*470, 1961.

Solovey, G., and Milechnin, A.: Conduct problems in children and hypnosis. Dis. Nerv. System, *16:*249, 1955.

Stein, K. B., Sarbin, T. R., and Kulik, J. A.: Future time perspective: its relation to the socialization process and the delinquent role. J. Consult. Clin. Psychol., *32:*257, 1968.

Trasler, G.: The Explanation of Criminality. London, Routledge and Kegan Paul, 1962.

Tyler, V. O. and Brown, G. D.: The use of swift, brief isolation as a group control device for institutionalized delinquents. Behav. Res. Ther., *5:*1, 1967.

Weitzenhoffer, A.: Reflections upon certain specific and current "uses of the unconscious" in clinical hypnosis. Internat. J. Clin. Exp. Hypn., *8:*165, 1960.

SUGGESTED READINGS

Berkowitz, B. P., and Graziano, A. M.: Training parents as behavior therapists: a review. Behav. Res. Ther., *10:*297, 1972.

Graziano, A. M. (ed.): Behavior Therapy with Children, New York, Aldine-Atherton, 1971.

Wallace, C. J., Teigen, J. R., Liberman, R. P., and Baker, V.: Destructive behavior treated by contingency contracts and assertive training: a case study. J. Behav. Ther. Exp. Psychiat., *4:*273, 1973.

Wetzel, R.: Use of behavioral techniques in a case of compulsive stealing. J. Consult. Psychol., *30:*367, 1966.

24

Obsessive-Compulsive Disorders

DEFINITIONS

The term *obsession* usually refers to persistent, repetitive, and unwelcome trains of thought. *Compulsion* refers to impulsions to perform repetitive acts or rituals that may involve complex sequences of acts, or to the acts themselves. The question of whether obsessive thoughts precede and determine the occurrence of compulsive rituals has not been resolved.

BEHAVIOR MODIFICATION THERAPY

These disorders have recently become treatable by newer psychological technics (Marks 1973). Compulsive rituals have responded to modeling with "in vivo" exposure coupled with flooding or response prevention. This response-prevention method involves the therapist's bringing the patient into prolonged contact with the stimuli that trigger his compulsive rituals and asking the patient to refrain from carrying out rituals thereafter. The therapist first demonstrates such contact before the patient undertakes it. Obsessive thoughts have been successfully treated by a variety of uncontrolled methods. In "thought stopping," the patient is asked to induce his obsessive thought and then stop it by shouting "Stop" first aloud and then subvocally. When using the method of flooding, the patient is asked to imagine scenes concerning his obsessive thoughts for an hour or more while the therapist describes them at length. This technic works better under hypnosis (hypnotic flooding); strong affective responses are provoked, and it is less time-consuming.

Walton (1960) and Walton and Mather (1963) have contributed some very important studies of the behavioral treatment of obsessive behaviors. Walton proposed that obsessions, during the early stages of the disorder, represented examples of drive-reducing conditioned avoidance responses. In the later stages of the disorder, these responses would be evoked by a wide range of stimuli in addition to the anxiety that originally elicited them. He thus predicted that in the early stages of the disorder, the obsessional behavior could not be directly removed. It would be necessary to desensitize the patient to the anxiety-eliciting stimuli. The obsessional behavior would then disappear as there would be no anxiety to evoke it. In the case of long-standing obsessions, a direct attack on the obsessional behavior itself might be at least partially successful, since the behavior has become, to some degree, detached from the anxiety that originally maintained it. Removing the anxiety would not, however, completely eliminate the obsessional behavior.

Walton and Mather (1963) constructed hierarchies of the stimuli that currently evoked the ritualistic behavior. In one case the patient had a compulsion for cleaning a doorknob. She was instructed to touch the door handle after it had been cleaned with a cloth that had been washed in hot water; then to touch it after it had been wiped with a hot, damp cloth; and so on up the hierarchy. She was progressively prevented from carrying out the ritual, while at the same time being progressively required to touch a knob that, in her eyes, was getting less and less clean.

While it is generally considered that preventing the obsessional patient from performing his rituals will induce severe anxiety, Meyer (1966) prevented his two patients from performing their obsessional rituals while at the same time making them perform actions *inconsistent* with the ritualistic activities. The patient with compulsive washing behavior was made to handle doorknobs without being given the opportunity of washing her hands or cleaning the objects. The patients were actually being required to reality-test for the belief that not performing the compulsion (such as touching certain "unclean" objects) would be followed by disastrous consequences (such as contamination or disease). When nothing disastrous does happen, the behavior should extinguish.

Haslam (1965) used Watson's original desensitization technic to treat a 25-year-old woman with a phobia about broken glass which had led to obsessional rituals. He introduced broken glass objects by stages in a feeding situation while she was very hungry. The obsessions and compulsion disappeared in conjunction with the dissipation of the fear about broken glass. Kushner and Sandler (1966) successfully associated shock with six specific suicidal images in a 48-year-old man with daily suicidal ruminations. Wolpe (1958) used assertion therapy, shock (for food-imagining in a case of obsessional eating), and hypnosis with countersuggestion. Lazarus (1958), Bevan (1960), Thorpe et al. (1964), and Solyom and Kinstone (1973) used aversion-relief therapy. Boulougouris and Bassiakos (1973) demonstrated the successful outcome of flooding with three patients with obsessional rituals. Much emphasis was given to long, combined fantasy-practice sessions lasting up to 3 hours and given each day.

The authors have generally found that in obsessions of recent onset it is usually sufficient merely to reduce the subject's general anxiety level via hypnotic relaxation in order to eliminate the obsession. The obsessional behavior disappears, as there is no anxiety to evoke it. In cases of long-standing obsessional behavior not only is it necessary to reduce the general anxiety, but the undesired thought or behavior must be dealt with specifically. The following is a case concerning a compulsion of relatively recent onset in which simple hypnotic relaxation without any attention to the specific undesirable behavior lead to complete cessation of the compulsion in one 50-minute session:

J.R. was an attractive 16-year-old girl who came with the presenting problem of trichotillomania (hair pulling). Hair loss had begun 2 years before and she had seen several physicians in both Los Angeles and New York. She had been treated with ultraviolet radiation, thyroid tablets, Aristocort, and Bellergal to reduce tension. None of these treatments had been successful, and at this point the patient was forced to wear a wig, as she was completely bald.

She reported that she pulled her hair when she felt tense and often was not even conscious of doing so. Hair pulling occurred only when she was alone and no one, therefore, had ever seen her indulge in this behavior. It had taken her parents 2 years to connect the hair pulling with the balding. J.R. was a junior in highschool. She had an older brother age 25, married and in college, and an older sister, age 31, living in New York. She was well adjusted in all other respects and was not under any unusual or extreme pressures.

In her first session it was explained to her that the hair pulling was anxiety-mediated. Through hynoptic relaxation she was to reduce the tension so that the hair pulling behavior would not be elicited. Later mastery of self-hypnosis would enable her to immediately induce a state of deep relaxation whenever she felt anxiety coming on—anxiety would become a cue for relaxation. She was also instructed to record the time of day whenever she indulged in the hair-pulling behavior.

On her second visit she stated that she had not once touched her head in order to pull her hair. The hair pulling never returned. The hypnotic relaxation and reassurance from the first session was sufficient to lower her anxiety to a level where it no longer elicited this behavior. Hypnorelaxation was continued on a weekly basis, however, to ensure that the absence of hair pulling would be maintained. Also the patient had complained of occasional nail biting and eyelash pulling. Although these latter two behaviors had decreased in frequency over the past week they returned occasionally. The patient was taught self-hypnosis the second session.

On the third visit she reported that her best friend had said that she had never seen her so relaxed before. The nail biting and eyelash pulling had disappeared. Had the relaxing images alone not completely eradicated the compulsion, she would have been given images more directly related to the problem, such as seeing herself calmly studying and not touching her hair (seeing herself in a hypnotic image doing what she wants to be able to do in reality) or seeing herself putting her fingers to her head, almost touching the hair, and then putting her hand at rest again. This imaginal act of resistance would be immediately reinforced by the emotional recall of elation or the sensory recall of relaxation. As stated earlier, elation can be experienced under hypnosis by vividly recalling a happy past experience, and relaxation is induced by recalling one of the standard pleasant relaxing images. On two occasions the nail biting and eyelash pulling returned for brief intervals, but the hair pulling never manifested itself again after the first therapeutic session.

Taylor (1963) has reported a remarkable case using a simple technic whereby a female with a 30-year history of trichopilomania (pulling out the hairs of the eyebrows) was cured in 10 days of treatment. Taylor first instructed the patient to inhibit the *first* movement in the chain of events leading to the plucking of hair by consciously inhibiting her hand from moving while at the same time saying "No, stay where you are" or words to that effect. In the second stage, the patient deliberately put her hand to her brow until the impulse came and then removed her hand. A 3- and seven-month follow-up visit showed a perfect set of eyebrows.

Unfortunately, most obsessive compulsive disorders take much longer to modify than the two cases mentioned above. The following is illustrative of a compulsion of long duration (35 years) which took considerable hypnotic relaxation and specific imagery to ameliorate:

> Mrs. K. was a 51-year old woman who complained of shyness, inferiority, and an obsessive thought that she would lose her self-control and expose herself. She was bothered by a recurring fantasy of running out of the bathroom, her skirt held high over her face, showing her genital area. The fantasy made her feel very guilty and unworthy.
>
> The patient had a long history of previous therapy and analysis with many therapists. As a result of her analysis she had come to the belief that the problem had originated when at the age of 8 she had exposed herself to her 12-year-old brother. She came from a large family and received little attention. This exposure had excited her brother and for the first time in her life she felt she had a means of controlling other people to get their attention. She also experienced a great deal of guilt from this desire to show her private parts. In adolescence she would often wear full skirts without underpants. She recalled one incident in a boat with two boys when the wind blew her skirt up, exposing her vagina for a second. She saw one of the boys looking, but nothing was said. However she felt much guilt over the incident.
>
> It was not until her late twenties that the obsessive fantasy of exposing herself began to manifest itself. She read somewhere that a man can tell the size of a woman's vagina by the size of her mouth. She generalized her sexuality to her mouth and stated that she would talk incessantly. She stated, "I open my mouth instead of exposing myself; my mouth became my body." She then developed a need to shock people orally rather than vaginally and would say shocking things; she would rather expose her mouth than her vagina. She developed considerable facial tension around the mouth, began grinding her teeth, and could not look people squarely in the face. She felt "defective" and wore dark glasses to partially mask her defect.
>
> The patient had two children, a girl aged 11, and a boy, aged 8, about whom she was extremely worried. She was so inhibited that until recently she was not able to even smile at them. She feared they were not getting appropriate feedback

about who they were. Her daughter was withdrawn and was described as having a "frozen face." The children reminded her of her own hated brothers and sisters. She hated them for their demands upon her and she felt trapped. The first child was born when she was 40, and she was not prepared at that age to begin motherhood. She stated she only had them as an excuse to stay home so that she would not have to go out and face the world. She presently also had much hostility toward her husband and avoided him sexually. She felt he did not try hard enough to please her.

Although a very intelligent and well-read woman, Mrs. K. was presently working as a domestic because she had trouble looking people in the face. She also enjoyed the shock value of carrying on very intelligent conversations with people and then informing them she was a domestic. They were always very surprised and reinforced her by asking what a bright woman like herself was doing in such an occupation. In the long run, however, working as a domestic had led to even greater feelings of inferiority and she felt her life had been a failure.

Using the standard hypnotic imagery in sequence as described in Chapter 10, Mrs. K. was able to reach such a deep state of relaxation that her facial muscles became very relaxed and she could control the muscular tension around the mouth and eyes when talking to people. After five sessions with standard relaxing images, Mrs. K. was given an image specifically tailored for her obsessional thoughts of exposing herself. In this case the thought never led to the deed; Mrs. K. had never once in her life actually run out of the house with her skirt above her head. It would therefore be pointless to have her hypnotically imagine doing what it was she wanted to do (*not* exposing herself in given situations) when in reality she actually was not engaging in this behavior anyway. In cases where there is merely the obsessional thought without the compulsive act, the patient is desensitized to the thought by imagining it in hypnosis. The thought is obsessional only because it produces anxiety. Recollection of the obsessional thought is aversive and punishing. Once the thought is no longer frightening or anxiety-eliciting, it ceases to manifest itself. The pairing of the obsessional thought with hypnotic relaxation deconditions the patient of the ability for that specific thought to elicit anxiety.

Mrs. K. was given a very detailed image using all five sensory modalities in which she was to see herself running out of the bathroom holding her skirt over her face and exposing her genital area to other people in the house who showed no reaction. She practiced this image five times a day in 5-minute sessions at home for five weeks. As the practice progressed, she reported being less and less upset by the thoughts. By the end of the fifth week, the obsessional thoughts had ceased to appear. She was then instructed to practice this image, pairing relaxation with the obsessive thought, once a week for 5 minute sessions in order to maintain the counterconditioning. The thought has not returned since it disappeared over 2 years ago.

Mrs. K.'s life-style changed dramatically as a function of the elimination of the facial tension and obsessional thoughts. She began selling vitamins door-to-door and had little trouble meeting people. She was more relaxed in general and reported her husband as kiddingly saying, "You haven't been a bitch for a long time." She was no longer denying him sex, and they were having intercourse on the average of twice a week. Much of the hostility she had had toward him was displaced, a function of her own feelings of inadequacy. She was able to cope much better with her children and felt a considerable lessening of guilt concerning their upbringing. She stated that at last she was feeling in command of herself.

However, one problem still remained. She was guilty over all the attention she was getting as a "new woman." She had always suffered guilt when attended to and felt anything she did to gain approval was "exhibitionistic." Even such minor things as complimenting other people, smiling at her husband, or wearing lipstick made her feel guilty. These actions were a means of calling attention to herself and thus showing off or exhibiting herself. The fear of sexual exhibition had generalized to all acts that in any way could be construed as exhibitionistic. Even though the fear of sexual exhibitionism had been alleviated, the fear of exhibitionism in other forms still remained.

A second image was therefore devised to desensitize the patient to positive attention concerning her physical state. In hypnosis she was instructed to see herself running nude in an open field while onlookers admired her for her physical beauty. Hypnotic relaxation paired with imagery of being complemented led to the patient's being able to accept her attractiveness without feeling guilty.

The patient was then given a third image in which she was to see herself carrying on a conversation with a woman her own age. The woman was to tell her that she thought the patient was intelligent, warm, and attractive. The patient was to then say good things about herself and feel calm and confident, not embarrassed or ashamed at building herself up to others. After 3 weeks of practice with this image, the patient reported, "I've never felt as free as I do at this point. I've nothing left to hide." This was exactly right. The hypnotic imagery had brought out into the open and deconditioned all the fears that the patient had spent so many years and so much psychic energy trying to conceal. Mrs. K. was now selling tapes rather than vitamin pills. She was also attending classes in hypnosis and teaching Yoga to housewives. Her face had totally relaxed and she looked at least 10 years younger.

IMPORTANCE OF IMAGERY CONDITIONING

The images described in Chapter 10 can be successfully used in a "thought stopping" type of therapy. Not only does relaxation and hypnotic depth increase as one progressively practices these images, so does the vividness and rapidity with which they can be recalled. Rather than saying, "Stop" each time an unwelcome train of thought comes to mind, the patient is instructed to flash on to one of these images (usually the one he is practicing at the time). This not only breaks the negative, harmful train of thought; it changes its "valence" through association with positive imagery and serves to countercondition the negative cognition. The following illustrates a case in which specific imagery was devised to treat a patient suffering from both obsessional thoughts and compulsive acts:

> J.L. was a 30-year-old male who had been in treatment over 6 years with various therapists for a compulsion to look at men's zippers. He was afraid that men would see him looking at their flies and think him homosexual. Although he was not attracted sexually to men, he worried continually about being thought homosexual. He had received some teasing to this effect in the army and at a job, but it had now been over 6 years since he had been teased. He had withdrawn completely. He had not worked in 5 years. He lived alone in an apartment and ruminated over his fears. A secondary fear was that he might blink at a male and that it would be mistaken for a wink.
>
> J.L. was rendered completely nonfunctional by this compulsion. He wanted to

obtain a college education but was afraid to go to class for fear he would look at the flies of the males in the class and be called a "queer." The patient was also very overweight. Although he had gone from 340 to 240 pounds, he still had to lose more weight. He had not dated a woman in 8 years and had severe sexual frustration. Much of his time was spent fantasizing about intercourse with females. His only activities included watching television and reading. He no longer went to bars because he thought that always being alone would label him as a homosexual.

After five sessions in which hypnosis was taught and adequate information obtained, a hierarchy was constructed. The hierarchy consisted of a series of traumatic incidents that had led to the conditioning of the zipper compulsion. The items were arranged chronologically and the patient was instructed to hypnotically recall each incident. At any point in this recall that he experienced anxiety, he was to switch on a given standard relaxation image and not return to the hierarchy until his next hypnotic session. The patient was to engage in this countercondi-tioning procedure five times a day for 5- to 10-minute sessions. He was to go at his own rate along the hierarchy, with some items taking much longer to decondi-tion than others. When he could completely recall one item without experiencing any anxiety, he was ready to go on to the next item. The patient had spent many years building his anxiety by recalling these past painful incidents. He was now going to pair this recall with relaxation so that these memories would no longer be painful or anxiety-producing. When memories of the past no longer elicited inca-pacitating anxiety, the present could be dealt with.

The following is the hierarchy constructed for J.L. Each item was an actual ex-perience recounted by the patient. The reader must realize that the construction of the hierarchy requires an ingenious meticulousness to details. This includes speaking the patient's language. The more realism employed, the better the re-sults. As usual, the image was to be vivid and hypnotically experienced with all five senses. Sensory details are omitted here, as the reader should be familiar with this phase of the therapy by now. It is apparent from the images how the compul-sion was formed.

(1) You are 13 years old. You are masturbating with a friend. He wants to "blow" you, but you resist. He puts his mouth on your fly. He ejaculates. (2) You are 14. You are masturbating under the blankets in your bedroom. The dark room is suddenly illuminated by the door opening. Your mother is stand-ing there. She knows what you are doing. (3) You are in basic training. Some-one had urinated in the foxhole and the officer is questioning the men. He asks, "Who urinated in the foxhole?" There is a pause. Then the lieutenant states, "I think you did it, J.L." (4) You are overseas in the Army. You tried to pick up a girl while on leave and were not successful. You are back in your bar-racks in bed. To ease the sexual tension you begin to masturbate. Suddenly, you look up and see one of the guys in the bunk above you observing your be-havior. He says nothing. You sleep. It's morning. The guy razzes you about what he saw last night. (5) It is one week later. A guy in your division, the S4 division, has been turned in for "blowing" two other guys. You are standing in the chowline. You overhear two guys behind you say, "Everybody in the S4 division is queer." (6) It's two weeks later. You are alone in your office with another guy. You turn around and notice his fly is down. You say, "Your fly is down." He replies, "Only a cocksucker would notice that." (7) It is two months later. You have transferred divisions. You are watching two guys playing poker on a footlocker. One of your friends is in his underwear and you are looking at

his pubic hair. Suddenly you see that your friend notices where your gaze is directed. You are not sexually attracted to him. You just happened to be looking at his genital area. A minute later he puts a towel over his underpants. Then he whispers to one of the other guys, "I think he wants to suck my dick." It should be noted that at the time before Item 8 transpired the patient had had no compulsion concerning zippers. He was fearful of being labeled homosexual, but it was not until the occurrence of the incident described in Item 8 that the zipper began to become an eliciter of anxiety. (8) You are in line in the mess hall. The guy ahead of you turns around and puts his hand on his fly. He says, "Are you a cocksucker? (9) You are on the field. The sargeant looks at you and says, "Someday I want to talk to you confidentially about something J.L." (10) You are out of the Army on your first job at a magazine company. You are lifting a heavy box of merchandise and sigh loudly. The worker next to you says, "I hear you blow hard." (11) Two months later you are loading magazines. You blink. The guy next to you winks back. (12) It is one month later. You are at work. You notice that the guy next to you has his fly down. You stare at it. (13) It is the next day. You are at work. The boss comes in. He stands in front of you and exposes the material over his zipper. Two guys walk by you and one mutters, "I hate cocksuckers."

Two weeks after the incident described in Item 13, J.L. quit his job due to the fear engendered by his zipper compulsion. Although it had been over 5 years, he had never again sought employment. It took J.L. 8 weeks to desensitize himself to the items in this hierarchy. It was now time to deal with the present. J.L. had been discussing returning to college. He wanted a degree in business administration but had such deep feelings of inferiority that he could not imagine himself with a degree. He was also still terrified that he would be overwhelmed by anxiety from the men's zippers he would encounter in class. He was thus given a new image. He was instructed to see himself sitting in a classroom with a semicircle seating arrangement. As in the preceding case he was instructed to see himself doing what he feared he would do. He was to see himself staring at the flies of the guys in the room. The guys were to notice his staring but not really give a damn. Since it was not the act itself that was terrifying (as is the case when the compulsion is to do violence of some sort) but rather the reaction to the act that frightened the patient, he was to imagine committing the act but receiving no reaction for having done so. Since the act is paired with relaxation, and no negative consequences ensue in the scene as a function of its having been committed, the act or thought of performing the act no longer elicits anxiety. When the thought or act of looking at a zipper no longer elicits anxiety, the patient loses his desire to look at a zipper. J.L. did not look at zippers because he thought zippers beautiful. He looked at them because he was preoccupied with the fear they elicited and thus overattended to them. After 3 weeks with this image, a zipper no longer elicited anxiety. One month later he moved from his apartment and enrolled in school. Throughout therapy he had been dieting and had lost an additional 50 pounds. He experienced no further compulsions.

CHILDHOOD OBSESSIVE-COMPULSIVE DISORDERS

Obsessive-compulsive disorders are often found in children in the form of nail-biting or thumb-sucking. Reducing the child's anxiety level through hypnotic relaxation and finding possible sources of tension in the child's life which can be eliminated usually lead to the end of these problem behaviors. Nail-biting is generally indicative of insecurity and anxiety. Therefore, therapy must also be directed to the causes of the child's tensions, which usually involve the parents. The latter must be cautioned against evincing displeasure over the habit, as this only mobilizes more guilt and frustration and serves to perpetuate the vicious cycle.

HYPNOTHERAPY

Hypnotherapy can be employed for direct symptom-removal of nail-biting; at least the conditioned pattern can be interrupted until the emotional needs are elicited, as the following case illustrates:

A child of 9, who had an older and a younger sister, began to bite her nails following the birth of the younger one. Utilizing permissive technics, posthypnotic suggestions were employed as follows: "Would you like to stop biting your nails by your own efforts? Then, perhaps, you might be willing to bite one nail on each hand *five times as much* as you do ordinarily. Which one would you like to choose?" If the forefinger on each hand is chosen, one can remark, "Let's make the nail-biting more interesting. Maybe you would like to start biting the nail from left to right or would you rather bite it from right to left? Or perhaps you can start on the left side of your mouth first, using one bite from each tooth in succession across the mouth, and then doubling back to the side where you started. You will find it fun to repeat this at least 3 times. If you still think you are not satisfied, turn the nail upside down and repeat the same procedure." This makes the nail-biting so complicated that it becomes a chore.

As soon as the other nails began to grow, the child was praised for following instructions: "Aren't you really proud that the other four nails on each hand are as good-looking as those of your girl friends? Haven't any of your schoolmates noticed the other nice-looking nails?" Under hypnosis, it was suggested, "You can increase or decrease biting the nail you selected to the degree that you think necessary." Such a suggestion is designed to make the nail-biting a routine and boring task against which the patient will rebel just as she did against parental admonitions not to bite the nails. This reaction follows the law of reversed effect.

Four more sessions were required to "wean" the child from biting the one nail. During this period, the procedure was continually made more complex until the child's natural resistance to regimentation made the nail-biting non-rewarding in terms of her oral satisfactions. At this point, she described her jealousy of her parents' attention to her baby sister.

Therapy was now directed toward the emotional needs for the nail-biting. She was asked whether it was her desire to stop the habit or whether it was the wish of her parents that she do so. In order to determine how much of the habit the patient needs to maintain equilibrium, it is necessary to evaluate the strength of the desire to stop as opposed to the degree of oral satisfaction obtained. At a subsequent session, the child was asked to see herself as a little baby, and it was pointed out that is was perfectly natural for her at this earlier age to put a rattle or a thumb in her mouth. She readily agreed to this and stated, "I guess I was trying to be a little baby all the time, wasn't I?"

The parents were instructed to pay equal attention to all the children, to ignore the nail-biting and not to punish the girl if the habit returned. Further psychotherapy directed toward the parents, and permissive technics oriented around the patient's emotional needs were employed for reinforcement. This enabled the patient to break the habit in several months.

FURTHER APPLICATIONS

Excessively dominating parents or those who delegate the care of their youngsters to servants often need psychotherapy more than the child who is made insecure by such factors. Children who are unresponsive to permissive technics can be conditioned by a more direct approach: "Whenever you bite your nails, you will get a very bitter taste in your mouth; you will feel sick to your stomach." Also, hypnotic imagery can be employed in which the child sees himself biting his nails in conjunction with a bad taste and smell such as vomit on his nails which he is licking off when he bites the nail. Weekly reinforcements under hypnosis are necessary to break the habit. In general, however, a permissive approach is more successful.

Most infants suck the thumb, but the maneuver becomes more marked when a baby is weaned too soon. This results in an inner need for more sucking activities and, unless he gets more food, he may suck his thumb or even his whole hand. Not all children are alike, and the process of weaning cannot be governed by a timetable. Thumb-sucking at this early stage of development is not harmful even though vigorously performed. The baby teeth may be distorted, but the effects are temporary, provided that the youngster discontinues the habit before the permanent set erupts.

Interference only intensifies the symptom and makes the child rebellious. Thumb-sucking usually is gradually stopped by the age of 4. Some children return to it as a consolation when bored, tired, sleepy, or hungry. Others revert when lonely, tense, or upset because a younger brother or sister is getting more attention. If the youngster is made to feel important, loved, and secure, the habit disappears completely.

But something must be done if the child persists in sucking the thumb after the fourth birthday. Elbow-splints, mitts, rings and horrible-tasting concoctions are valueless. Little is accomplished through nagging, shaming, bribing, teasing, or punishing an already unhappy child. Parents should make it a point to fuss over the child, and it will help if other children in the family, relatives, and friends will do the same, or at least make no mention of the habit. Adequate rest and play outlets should be encouraged.

Eventually most children give up the habit, as by age 5 they are capable of self-discipline and can be taught to help themselves. But if the problem has been mishandled, the youngster may switch to nail-biting. Hypnotherapy can be very helpful in thumb-sucking and is employed in a fashion similar to that used for nail-biting.

GAMBLING

Another form of compulsive behavior is gambling. Barker and Miller (1966a) required a patient "hooked" on slot machines to gamble continuously on the machine for 3 hours at a time while receiving a minimum of 150 severe

70-volt shocks to the forearm. After 12 hours and 672 shocks, treatment was ended. A 2-month follow-up showed that he had not resumed the habit. In a second study by Barker and Miller (1966b) color films were made of the behavior of a subject who bet excessively on the races. Films were made of behavior both at the betting window and at home with wife and family. Tape recordings were also made of the sounds of activity at the betting windows and his wife describing the bad effects of his gambling on her and the children. With 10 days of hospitalization in which the patient received 450 shocks to the wrist while watching the betting-window film and listening to the betting-window tape recording, he had not resumed gambling 2 months after treatment. During treatment he had also watched the film and listened to the tape recording of his wife while receiving no shock.

Goorney (1968) stresses that it is important to treat the maladaptive behavior in all its possible forms (both overt and covert) and at all stages of the manifestation. Taking a patient with a 13-year history of periodic gambling, Goorney divided the behaviors involved in the subject's gambling activities into several stages such as selecting and recording bets from the morning newspapers, thinking about the selected names, races, odds, and possible winnings before the race began, listening to the race results on the radio, and watching the races subsequently on television. Shocks were provided to the upper arms during 10-minute sessions. After 9 days of treatment involving 45 sessions and 675 shocks the patient reported increasing reluctance to think about racing or make selections from the newspaper. Gambling had still not been resumed in a 12-month follow-up.

HYPNOTIC IMAGERY CONDITIONING

We have found hypnotic imagery employing negative imagery and a relief stimulus to be very effective in the treatment of chronic gamblers. The following illustrates how these technics may be used in such cases:

M. F. was a 35-year-old man who complained of smoking too much, overeating, and gambling. While all three disorders were treated concomitantly, only the gambling will be dealt with in detail here. The patient stated he had a compulsion to play cards and bet at the track. He had great feelings of inferiority stemming back from childhood. He had always been overweight and the neighborhood kids had called him "lard-ass." His mother had been overprotective and force-fed him. Gambling had become a means of bolstering his ego and making himself feel important when he was winning. In other areas he was always a failure. He had had no sex with his wife in over 1½ years and he was a premature ejaculator. She was too filled with hostility toward him for his excessive gambling to allow him to touch her.

The patient had been in psychoanalytic therapy for 10 years. He stated that he believed the gambling had evolved from an incident which had occurred when he was 3½ years old. At this early age he had fallen off a stool while holding a knife and accidentally cut his 7-year-old brother's ear. He was considerably guilt-ridden and never sure just how "accidental" the fall had been. The patient was assured that even if this incident were responsible for the present gambling, the disorder would still have to be tackled directly.

After training in hypnosis and sensory recall using several standard relaxing images the patient was given two images specific to card playing and the race track. Since the patient was also being treated for obesity and cigarette smoking, the images killed three birds with one stone in that they incorporated spoiled food and stale cigarette smoke as the aversive stimuli to be paired with the act of gambling. The first image went as follows:

You are sitting at a card table with your friends over at Karl's house. It is mid-July and 2 p.m. The room is stifling hot. You are holding eight cards in your hand. Cigarette smoke in the room has become thick, yellow, and stale. Smell the smoke. There is no ventilation. Next to you on the table in a blue dish are chocolates which have spoiled from sitting too long in the sun. They are a mottled light tan. Next to them is a white dish of ice cream with specks of fly shit in it (these last two items were picked by the subject a priori as being particularly nauseating to him).

The room is becoming warmer and warmer with every breath you take. You take one of the cards and dip it in the spoiled, rotten chocolate. You lick the thick, diseased chocolate off the card, a wave of nausea coming over you. You continue to successively dip the other seven cards in the chocolate, licking each one off in turn. The nausea grows in intensity. Your stomach muscles are beginning to distend. Feel the pressure. You wash down the chocolate, which has stuck in your throat, by drinking the dish of warm, melted ice cream. See the specks of fly shit floating on the scummy, creamy surface and then running into your mouth and down your throat. Feel the shit on your tongue and against your teeth. You begin to gag. You retch vomit all over the cards. There are big lumps of vomit on the Ace of hearts. Green slime with shit floating in it is covering the 2 and 3 of spades. The Queen and Jack of diamonds are floating in a pool of puke. Smell the sour aroma of vomit and stale cigarette smoke. You lick the slime and vomit off the 7 of clubs, and then every other card in turn. Next you stand up and leave the room. The moment you are out of sight of the cards, cigarettes, and chocolate you feel fine. You feel fantastic.

One of the standard relaxing images is then described in detail to further reinforce the act of leaving the gambling situation. The image for the races went as follows:

You are at the race track. It is a beautiful summer day. The sky is a deep blue. You have next to you a box of chocolates. You are smoking a cigarette. Smell the smoke. The race begins. The horses are off! You take a bite of chocolate. It is spoiled from the sun and is rotten. It makes you sick to your stomach, a wave of nausea is coming over you. You are watching intently the horse on which you have bet. With each stride he makes you get sicker and sicker to your stomach. With each stride he makes you take a deeper and deeper drag on your cigarette. With each stride he makes you gulp another piece of chocolate. The horses seem to go round and round and round (the therapist says round and round several times, picking up speed toward the end) until the whole track is spinning. You feel like retching. Your horse comes in first! You throw up. There is vomit everywhere, the sour smell of puke, rotten chocolate, and stale cigarette smoke. The whole track appears to be wavering and undulating.

You leave the track. The moment you are out of the grand stand you feel fantastic. Breathe the fresh air!

Once again, a standard relaxing image is now described to further reinforce the act of leaving the track.

After 2 weeks of practice (five 5-minute sessions a day) with these two images, the patient reported he no longer had a compulsion to play cards. He had succumbed to a temptation to go to the track, but stated that when the race began he had become nauseated and had gone home. A 1-year follow-up showed that the patient neither gambled at cards nor bet at the track during this period. He was still rehearsing these images once a week to maintain his aversion for these two activities.

These disorders are especially amenable to hypnobehavioral therapy. This is not surprising, since redirection of attention and concurrent positive reconditioning are the important vectors in this type of therapy. We have presented several illustrative case histories that demonstrate the utility of the hypnobehavioral model.

REFERENCES

Barker, J. C. and Miller, M. E.: Aversion therapy for compulsive gambling. Lancet, *1:*491, 1966.
————: Aversion therapy for compulsive gambling. Brit. Med. J., *2:*115, 1966.
Bevan, J. R.: Learning theory applied to the treatment of a patient with obsessional ruminations. *In* Eysenck, H. J. (ed.): Behavior Therapy and the Neuroses. Oxford, Pergamon, 1960.
Boulougouris, J. C. and Bassiakos, L.: Prolonged flooding in cases with obsessive-compulsive neurosis. Behav. Res. Ther., *11:*227, 1973.
Goorney, A. B.: Treatment of a compulsive horse race gambler by aversion therapy. Brit. J. Psychiat., *114:*329, 1968.
Haslam, M. T.: The treatment of an obsessional patient by reciprocal inhibition. Behav. Res. Ther., *2:*213, 1965.
Kushner, M. and Sandler, J.: Aversion therapy and the concept of punishment. Behav. Res. Ther., *4:*179, 1966.
Lazarus, A. A.: New methods in psychotherapy: a case study. S. Afr. Med. J., *33:*660, 1958.
Marks, I. M.: New approaches to the treatment of obsessive-compulsive disorders. J. Nerv. Ment. Dis., *156:*420, 1973.
Meyer, V.: Modification of expectations in cases with obsessional rituals. Behav. Res. Ther., *4:*273, 1966.
Solyom, L. and Kingstone, E.: An obsessive neurosis following morning glory seed ingestion treated by aversion relief. J. Behav. Ther. Exp. Psychiat., *4:*293, 1973.
Taylor, J. G.: A behavioral interpretation of obsessive-compulsive neurosis. Behav. Res. Ther., *1:*237, 1963.
Thorpe, J. G., Schmidt, E., Brown, P. T., and Castell, D.: Aversion-relief therapy: a new method for general application. Behav. Res. Ther., *2:*71, 1964.
Walton, D.: The relevance of learning theory to the treatment of an obsessive-compulsive state. *In* Eysenck, H. J. (ed.): Behavior Therapy and the Neuroses. Oxford, Pergamon, 1960.

284   *Obsessive-Compulsive Disorders*

Walton, D. and Mather, M. D.: The application of learning principles to the treatment of obsessive-compulsive states in the acute and chronic phases of illness. Behav. Res. Ther., *1:*163, 1963.
Wolpe, J.: Psychotherapy by Reciprocal Inhibition. Stanford, Stanford Univ. Press, 1958.

SUGGESTED READINGS

Grimshaw, L.: The outcome of obsessional disorder: a follow-up study of 100 cases. Brit. J. Psychiat., *111:*1051, 1965.
Hodgson, R. J. and Rachman, S.: The effects of contamination and washing in obsessional patients. Behav. Res. Ther., *10:*111, 1972.
Hodgson, R., Rachman, S., and Marks, I. M.: The treatment of chronic obsessive-compulsive neurosis: follow-up and further findings. Behav. Res. Ther., *10:*181, 1972.
Kuma, K. and Wilkinson, J. C.: Thought stopping: a useful treatment for phobias of "internal stimuli." Brit. J. Psychiat., *119:*305, 1971.
Lait, V. S.: A case of recurrent vomiting. Amer. J. Clin. Hypn., *14:*196, 1972.
Levy, R. and Meyer, V.: Ritual prevention in obsessional patients. Proc. R. Soc. Med., *64:*1115, 1971.
McNamara, J. R.: The use of self-monitoring techniques to treat nailbiting. Behav. Res. Ther., *10:*193, 1972.
Marks, I. M.: The current status of behavioral psychotherapy: theory and practice. Am. J. Psychiat., *133:*253–261, 1976.
Salzman, L.: The Obsessive Personality. New York, Science House, 1968.
Solyom, L., Garza-Perez, J., Ledwidge, B. J., and Solyom, G.: Paradoxical intention in the treatment of obsessive thoughts: a pilot study. Compr. Psychiat., *13:*291, 1972.
Yamagami, T.: The treatment of an obsessive by thought stopping. J. Behav. Ther. Exp. Psychiat., *2:*133, 1971.

25

Anorexia Nervosa

SYMPTOMS

The chief symptoms of anorexia nervosa are weight loss of a progressive and severe nature following a refusal to eat, and amenorrhea. Theander (1970) of Sweden, Selvini (1963) of Italy, and Dally (1969) of England have published large surveys of patients with anorexia nervosa. In the United States, Halmi (1974) made a comprehensive chart study of numerous clinical and demographic features in 94 patients with anorexia nervosa. Unlike other large series, this survey included the pediatric age group. Findings showed a significantly greater maternal and paternal age at time of the patient's birth and a greater incidence of both low and high birth weights compared with the general population. A high occurrence of death wishes associated with feeding was present. Anxiety and obsessive-compulsive traits were frequent premorbid symptoms. Characteristic behavior noted during the course of the illness was described.

Untreated cases have a high mortality. The condition occurs in very high-strung individuals, chiefly women. It must be distinguished from hypothalamic-pituitary dysfunction, in which pubic and axillary hair is lost. Hospitalization is often indicated in such cases, as it removes the individual from the stimuli eliciting the disorder and it enables the eating behavior of the patient to be brought under strict supervision.

BEHAVIOR MODIFICATION THERAPY

Bachrach, Erwin, and Mohr (1965) have contributed the most striking behavioristic study of the treatment of this disorder. Using strict operant control of

285

the contingencies following eating and non-eating behavior they were able to increase the weight of a hospitalized 37-year-old female with a 20-year history of anorexia from 47 pounds to 66 pounds on discharge. When last seen the patient weighed 88 pounds, was well and fully employed. Treatment involved placing the patient in a bare room where reinforcements such as television, visits, and other amenities were first made contingent on eating and later on weight gain. Close policing of contingencies and timing of sequences were crucial to the success of this study. Leitenberg, Agras, and Thomson (1968) carried out a similar study successfully using an operant conditioning program with two cases of anorexia nervosa.

Hallsten (1965) was not able to replicate the success obtained by Bachrach et al. (1965) using operant conditioning technics in the case of a 12-year-old girl. This may be due to his not controlling the eating situation as firmly or successfully as Bachrach et al. Hallsten was, however, able to produce a rapid and lasting weight gain using systematic desensitization in which he reduced the anxiety presumed to be motivating the anorexia. Garfinkel, Kline, and Stancer (1973) describe a successful operant conditioning program using a variety of reinforcers that were individualized for five hospitalized female anorexia nervosa patients, resulting in rapid weight gain to premorbid levels. Specific daily weight minimums were set. Special rewards included physical activity, socializing off the wards, overnight and weekend passes, and progressive privileges on the ward. Halmi et al. (1975) used behavioral therapy (reward contingent on weight gain) to successfully treat eight hospitalized patients with anorexia nervosa.

DISADVANTAGES OF BEHAVIOR MODIFICATION

Bruch (1973, 1974) warns that behavior modification therapy in a hospital setting, even though it may be successful in that there is a weight gain, "must be looked upon as potentially damaging and perilous. . . . In the non-pampering hospital setting, continued weight gain offers the only escape." She states that patients who feel "tricked into relinquishing control over their bodies and their lives" only develop inner turmoil. She further cautions that the possibility of a schizophrenic core should not be overlooked, "although not all patients with primary anorexia nervosa are overtly schizophrenic or ever progress to that state of disorganization."

HYPNOTHERAPY

The authors use hypnotherapy to reduce the anxiety motivating the anorexia and to keep the patient relaxed in bed. The appetite can be increased through posthypnotic suggestions associating food with pleasant memories. Concomitantly, feelings of aggression, disgust, and hostility should be ventilated. The value of any type of therapy in this condition is based on the rapport fostered by the hypnotic relationship.

STANDARD IMAGES

Images involving the ingestion of savory, delicious food (III, garden; VII, farm; X, Arctic; XII, bluebird; XV, mansion; XVIII, Shangri-La; XXI, cantina) can be used to induce hunger in the anorexic patient. Also this type of patient often states that he always feels full, as if he had just eaten. The hypnotic recall of the sensation of lightness or emptiness in the stomach is therefore beneficial in giving these patients better reality contact so that they will accurately perceive an empty stomach as empty. Images XVIII (Shangri-La), XIX (chalk cliffs), and XXI (cantina) employ the recall of the sensation of lightness in the digestive system.

DISCUSSION

In two cases recently seen by the authors, one patient lived and one died. Posthypnotic suggestion of an increase in appetite were accepted by one patient, and there was a subsequent weight gain. This patient, who came in regularly, faced the problems contributing to her depressive reactions. The patient who died of malnutrition did not come in regularly. She had profound guilt feelings and remorse because she had driven her daughter away from home. The daughter became a prostitute, and the mother never forgave herself and masochistically developed an intense need to punish herself.

There was only one reference, Crasilneck and Hall (1975), to the treatment of anorexia nervosa by hypnosis in the literature. This is surprising, since we consider the maladaptive behavior as one that is produced by autosuggestions that stimulate the same kind of responses that one would attain through posthypnotic suggestions. If patients can be taught how to reverse the negative, harmful, inappropriate autosuggestions that have produced the anorexia, dissolution of the behavior will occur. One way of potentiating these autosuggestions is through the use of fantasy evocation and the use of images that we have recommended as being most effective for this refractory condition.

Our clinical approach on a small sample seen over the past 10 years indicates that the most significant changes occurred when the patients received hypnotherapy on an outpatient basis. This is an obvious advantage over most behavior therapy, which relies on inpatient hospitalization.

REFERENCES

Bachrach, A. J., Erwin, W. J., and Mohr, J. P.: The control of eating behavior in an anorexic by operant conditioning techniques. *In* Ullmann, L. P. and Krasner, L. (eds.): Case Studies in Behavior Modification. New York, Holt, Rinehart & Winston, 1965.

Bruch, H.: Eating Disorders: Obesity, Anorexia Nervosa and the Person Within, New York, Basic Books, 1973.

————: Learning Psychotherapy: Rationale and Ground Rules, Cambridge, Harvard University Press, 1974.

Crasilneck, H. B. and Hall, J. A.: Clinical Hypnosis: Principles and Applications. New York, Grune and Stratton, 1975.

Dally, P.: Anorexia Nervosa. New York, Grune and Stratton, 1969.

Garfinkel, P. E., Kline, S. A., and Stancer, H.: Treatment of anorexia nervosa using operant conditioning techniques. J. Nerv. Ment. Dis., *157:*428, 1973.

Hallsten, E. A.: Adolescent anorexia nervosa treated by desensitization. Behav. Res. Ther., *3:*87, 1965.

Halmi, K. A.: Anorexia nervosa: demographic and clinical features in 94 cases. Psychosom. Med., *36:*18, 1974.

Halmi, K. A., Powers, P. and Cunningham, S.: Treatment of anorexia nervosa with behavior modification. Arch. Gen. Psychi., *32:*93, 1975.

Leitenberg, H., Agras, W. S., and Thomson, L. E.: A sequential analysis of the effect of selective positive reinforcement in modifying anorexia nervosa. Behav. Res. Ther., *6:*211, 1968.

Selvini, P.: L'Anoressia Mentale, Milano, 1963.

Theander, S.: Anorexia nervosa. Acta Psychiat. Scand. Suppl., *214:*1, 1970.

SUGGESTED READINGS

Barber, T. X.: "Hypnotic" phenomena: a critique of experimental methods. *In* Gordon, J. E. (ed.): Handbook of Clinical and Experimental Hypnosis. New York, Macmillan, 1967.

Barcai, A.: Family therapy in the treatment of anorexia nervosa. Amer. J. Psychiat., *128:*286, 1971.

Blinder, B. J., Freeman, D. M. A., and Stunkard, A. J.: Behavior therapy of anorexia nervosa: Effectiveness of activity as a reinforcer of weight gain. Amer. J. Psychiat., *126:*1093, 1970.

Brady, P. J. and Rieger, W.: Behavioral treatment of anorexia nervosa. *In* Proceedings of the International Symposium on Behavior Modification (Minneapolis, Minn., Oct. 4–6, 1972). New York, Appleton-Century-Crofts, 1974.

Bruch, H.: Changing approaches to anorexia nervosa. Internat. Psychiat. Clinics, *7:*3, 1970.

Stunkard, A.: New therapies for the eating disorders. Arch. Gen. Psychiat., *26:*391, 1972.

26

Conversion Hysteria

CLASSIFICATION

There is much dispute at the present as to the classification of conversion hysteria. While there is considerable agreement that patients can be classified as presenting a "hysterical personality" profile, the general consensus of opinion is that no significant correlation exists between conversion hysteria and a hysterical personality structure (Chodoff and Lyons 1958; Ziegler and Imboden 1962; Slater 1961, 1965). Hysterical reactions are always anxiety-mediated.

ETIOLOGIC FACTORS

Anxiety is a universal response to hidden tension. It becomes pathologic when fears are experienced without provocation or awareness. When these fears cannot be handled, then even minor stresses lead to emotional disturbances. These are chiefly insecurity, lack of self-esteem, inadequacy, inability to relate to others or to express pent-up feelings, and inordinate demands for attention. A typical example of an acute anxiety reaction is a person's being thrown into panic when some friend has suffered a heart attack or a nervous breakdown or has developed cancer. Such symptoms can be corrected by adequate reassurance, wise counseling and strong countersuggestions. Repressed anxiety, on the other hand, is usually due to a painful emotion that cannot be expressed directly. Instead, the associations with the original conflict are blocked from awareness by a secondary or defensive symptom which generally prevents further personality decompensation. These defensive symptoms constitute the bulk of the symptomatology.

MECHANISMS

There are roughly three types of anxiety reactions that are based on indirect expression. These can be classified as follows. Physiologic conversions are characterized by changes in smooth muscle, organ and glandular functions, and as mentioned above, lead to psychophysiologic or psychosomatic illnesses, fatigue states, and debilitated conditions. These disorders have a logical evolution, their history can be recalled, and they are subject to educational correction by psychotherapy, including hypnosis. The second type includes hysterical reactions such as the functional paralysis of a limb. The disorder has a logical development and an onset that can be recalled, but it is difficult to correct. In hysterical conversions, the fright leads to expectation of anxiety in similar situations. The condition can be relieved after it is deconditioned or re-experienced without anxiety. That is why the driver, following an automobile accident, should immediately get behind the wheel to prevent mobilization of fear and chronic anxiety; the lack of fear leads to the rebuilding of self-confidence. Hypnosis is almost specific in these disorders. The third type includes psychological conversions, in which the effects of anxiety are converted through many devious pathways into psychological symptoms and reactions. These include phobias, dissociation reactions, depressions, hypochondriases, obsessions and compulsions, and certain character and personality disorders, as well as the regressive behavior and symptoms associated with the psychoses.

These last-named disorders might be termed "logic-proof"; their genesis cannot be recalled, their history is rationalized, and the symptoms cannot be educated away. They are relieved, but with difficulty, by re-evaluation of the patient's needs and by positive conditioning. The second and the third types, to some degree, parallel the effects of posthypnotic suggestions. There are many combinations of these disorders. It is useless to elaborate on the specific characteristics of each one, as was stated, because of the overlapping mechanisms common to all.

DIFFERENTIAL DIAGNOSIS

Neurotic illness is one of the most insidious of all human afflictions and the end product of an emotional illness which evolved so imperceptibly that no one, least of all the patient, recognizes it. To assume that the symptoms are functional without first being able to recognize and understand positive signs of the psychogenic disorder beclouds the issue, dulls the therapist's acumen, and exposes him to the dangers of committing serious clinical errors. Even the most severe psychoses that appear with dramatic suddenness have a long history of gradual development. The therapist will be better equipped to diagnose the manifestations of long-standing emotional difficulties if he has had training in the fundamental principles of psychiatry. Therefore, it cannot be emphasized too strongly again that it is always necessary to rule out a physical basis: after a thorough physical examination, the need for certain laboratory tests can be suggested tactfully. The resultant discussion may reveal the fears, such as of heart trouble, cancer, and tuberculosis. Negative tests are of distinct psychotherapeutic value. The physical and the laboratory examinations thus help to establish rapport, as the patient now feels that he is a collaborator. If all the findings are negative, the patient can be informed that there is no sign of physical disease and that his presenting complaints are on a psychological basis.

HYSTERICAL BLINDNESS

Hysterical blindness is a conversion reaction to unpleasant circumstances that stimulate inner conflicts. Clinically, the condition resembles genuine blindness except that remissions and exacerbations may occur spontaneously. An individual with functional blindness will react to light with pupillary contraction (Dorcus 1937). Hysterical blindness has been found to have no effect on the appearance or the disappearance of the alpha pattern in EEG records (Lundholm and Lowenbach 1942, 1943). On the other hand, alpha activity has been recorded in hysterically blind individuals only when their eyes were shut (Loomis, Harvey, and Hobart 1936). These contradictory studies indicate that physiologic changes associated with artificially induced hypnotic phenomena and conversion reactions are not as clear-cut as those noted for well-established organic disorders.

HYPNOBEHAVIORAL TECHNICS

Some interesting behavioristic technics have been described in the treatment of functional blindness by Brady and Lind (1961). Considerable controversy was generated by their experiment, and later Grosz and Zimmerman (1965) criticized these researchers for failing to raise the issue of malingering as opposed to functional or hysterical blindness. The technics of Zimmerman and Grosz (1966) represented a marked advance from the technics used by Brady and Lind in the treatment of a case of hysterical total blindness. A report by Wilkins and Field (1968) and a previous discussion by Erickson (1954) dealt with the hypnotic treatment of hysterical blindness. Greenleaf (1971) discusses the successful hypnotic treatment of a person suffering from hysterical blindness. Wolberg (1948) reported the following case:

> A 27-year-old newly married woman had had several brief attacks of total blindness before and after her marriage. Using hypnotic age-regression, it was discovered that the symptom reinforced the repression of a traumatic episode in which she had seen a man killed in a train wreck. Killing had been equated with hostility toward her mother. In repressing the traumatic event, she denied her aggression toward her mother. Her hostility stemmed from strong dependency

strivings and inability to have a closer relationship with her father. Her husband's coldness reactivated these feelings of rejection, thus mobilizing her hostility and aggression toward her mother, which was linked with the killing fantasy that this entailed. Her blindness was a desperate attempt to deny the existence of her murderous impulses.

The authors have seen several cases of hysterical blindness.

The wife of a colleague developed blindness when she inadvertently saw her husband kissing his secretary. Their marriage had been very unstable for years, characterized by frequent arguments and separations. The cause for the symptoms obviously was an attempt to repress the humiliation produced by the unfaithfulness of her husband. Direct hypnotic suggestion promptly "restored" her vision, and she was advised to face her life situation, and decide whether or not she wished to seek a divorce. While she was making this important decision, her husband died. No other symptoms referable to the eyes occurred.

HYSTERICAL DEAFNESS

As in the case of functional blindness, the behavioristic approach to functional deafness has been almost entirely laboratory based and not primarily with therapeutic intent. It is clear, however, that conditioning technics similar to the ones used with functional blindness can be of value in relation to disorders of hearing (Malmo, Davis, and Barza 1952; Malmo, Boag, and Raginsky 1954; Barraclough 1966; Reed 1961).

Hysterical and hypnotically induced deafness are similar in that there is no hearing loss. However, the reaction to strong auditory stimulation is significantly less in hysterical deafness. Electromyographic studies of hysterical and hypnotically induced deafness have been made, and the similarities and the differences in these two conditions have been elucidated. The findings corroborated those of Kline (1954), who concluded from the study of delayed speech feedback that hypnotically induced deafness appeared to represent a valid alteration of hearing function but not a state akin to organic deafness.

Abnormal audiometric readings are indicative of hysterical deafness. This type must be differentiated from organic deafness. A simple test would be to make an unexpected loud noise. If a startle reaction occurred, it would indicate that hearing was unimpaired. According to Kodman and Pattie (1958), quantitative hearing tests should be made, rather than relying on subjective reports in diagnosing cases of psychological deafness. There are several methods to measure auditory sensitivity: pure-tone audiometry (air and bone conduction thresholds), speech audiometry (speech perception thresholds and speech discrimination) and the psychogalvanic skin response (in which a conditioned skin response is set up to tonal stimuli). These investigators made hearing tests on children who showed functional hearing losses. Although their hearing was apparently normal, they complained of an inability to hear, particularly in home and classroom situations. Laboratory tests made before and after hypnotherapy indicated that improvement was brought about in every case except one. In some cases the hearing loss inexplicably involved only one ear.

HYPNOTHERAPY

Kodman and Pattie (1958) used the following suggestions while the patient was lightly hypnotized: (1) he might think that there was something wrong with his ears, but actually nothing was wrong; (2) his troubles might come from not listening well, and listening was an important part of hearing and understanding; (3) in the future he would hear and listen much better. They used no challenges except that the patient would find it difficult to open his eyes. A similar approach is described by Hurst (1943), who used strong persuasion to make patients listen more attentively.

Others have described hypnotic technics that were used to re-educate and improve hearing acuity (Malmo, Boaz, and Raginsky, 1954). It is concluded from their clinical observations that hypnotherapy can be effective for abnormal hearing difficulties that are believed to be psychogenic in origin. Symptom-substitution was not utilized in any of the series. The hearing behavior improved in nearly all cases.

MISCELLANEOUS DISORDERS

Other disorders such as functional analgesia, astereognosis, anesthesia, and paralysis of motor function also respond to behavioristic technics. Sears and Cohen (1933) reported a series of careful experimental studies of a 45-year-old female with three functional deficits in the left hand: analgesia to superficial and deep pain; astereognosis (inability to identify objects by manual examination without sight); and anesthesia to superficial touch. Hilgard and Marquis (1940) demonstrated sensitivity to the paralyzed hand of a schoolteacher by presenting shock as a *conditioned* stimulus to that hand while presenting shock as an *unconditioned* stimulus to the normal hand. If sensitivity were present, shock to the paralyzed hand would serve as a signal for an unconditioned response by the normal hand. Sensitivity gradually returned completely to the paralyzed hand although there was little evidence of conditioning.

Hysterical paralysis in the male often dramatically responds to a single hypnotic session if it is suggested that potency will be lost by maintaining the "paralysis".

REFERENCES

Barraclough, B. M.: A method of testing hearing based on operant conditioning. Behav. Res. Ther., *4:*237, 1966.
Brady, J. and Lind, D. L.: Experimental analysis of hysterical blindness. Arch. Gen. Psychiat., *4:*331, 1961.

Chodoff, P. and Lyons, H.: Hysteria, the hysterical personality and "hysterical" conversion. Amer. J. Psychiat., *114:*734, 1958.

Dorcus, R. M.: Modification by suggestion of some vestibular and visual responses. Amer. J. Psychol., *49:*82, 1937.

Erickson, M. H.: Special techniques of brief hypnotherapy. J. Clin. Exp. Hypn., *2:*109, 1954.

Greenleaf, E.: The red house: hypnotherapy of hysterical blindness. Amer. J. Clin. Hypn., *13:*155, 1971.

Grosz, H. J. and Zimmerman, J.: Experimental analysis of hysterical blindness: a follow-up report and new experimental data. Arch. Gen. Psychiat., *13:*255, 1965.

Hilgard, E. R. and Marquis, D. G.: Conditioning and Learning. New York, Appleton-Century-Crofts, 1940.

Hurst, A.: (quoted by Guild, J.) Medical Diseases of War, ed. 3, Baltimore, Williams and Wilkins, 1943.

Kline, M. B., Guze, H., and Haggerty, A. D. An experimental study of the nature of hypnotic deafness: effects of delayed speech feedback. J. Clin. Exp. Hypn., *2:*145, 1954.

Kodman, F. and Pattie, F. A.: Hypnotherapy of psychogenic hearing loss in children. Amer. J. Clin. Hypn., *1:*9, 1958.

Loomis, A. L., Harvey, E. N., and Hobart, G. A.: Brain potentials during hypnosis. Science, *83:*239, 1936.

Lundholm, H. and Lowenbach, H.: Hypnosis and the alpha activity of the electroencephalogram. Character and Person., *11:*145, 1942–1943.

MacLean, P. D.: Limbic system ("visceral brain") in relation to central gray and reticulum of brain stem: evidence of interdependence in emotional processes, Psychosom. Med., *17:*355–366, 1955.

Malmo, R. B., Boag, T. J., and Raginsky, B. B.: Electromyographic study of hypnotic deafness. J. Clin. Exp. Hypn., *2:*305, 1954.

Malmo, R. B., Davis, J. F., and Barza, S.: Total hysterical deafness: an experimental case study. J. Pers., *21:*188, 1952.

Miller, N. E.: Learning of visceral and glandular responses. Science, *163:*434, 1969.

Parry-Jones, W. L., Santer-Weststrate, H. C., and Crawley, R. C.: Behaviour therapy in a case of hysterical blindness. Behav. Res. Ther., *8:*79, 1970.

Reed, G. F.: Psychogenic deafness, perceptual defense, and personality variables in children. J. Abnorm. Soc. Psychol., *63:*663, 1961.

Sears, R. R. and Cohen, L. H.: Hysterical anaesthesia, analgesia and astereognosis. Arch. Neurol. Psychiat., *29:*260, 1933.

Selye, H.: The General Adaptation Syndrome. J. Clin. Endocrinology, *6:*117, 1946.

Slater, E. The thirty-fifth Maudsley lecture: "Hysteria 311." J. Ment. Sci., *107:*359, 1961.

Slater, E.: Diagnosis of hysteria. Brit. Med. J., *1:*1395, 1965.

Wilkins, L. G. and Field, P. B.: Helpless under attack: hypnotic abreaction in hysterical loss of vision. Amer. J. Clin. Hypn., *10:*271, 1968.

Wolberg, L. R.: Medical Hypnosis. vol. I, p. 227. New York, Grune and Stratton, 1948.

Ziegler, F. J. and Imboden, J. B.: Contemporary conversion reactions: II. a conceptual model. Arch. Gen. Psychiat., *6:*279, 1962.

Zimmerman, J. and Grosz, H. J.: "Visual" performance of a functionally blind person. Behav. Res. Ther., *4:*119, 1966.

SUGGESTED READINGS

Brierley, H.: The treatment of hysterical spasmodic torticollis by behaviour therapy. Behav. Res. Ther., *5:*139, 1967.

Cooper, A. J.: Conditioning therapy in hysterical retention of urine. Brit. J. Psychiat., *111:*575, 1965.

Gray, B. B., England, G., and Mahoney, J. L.: Treatment of benign vocal nodules by reciprocal inhibition. Behav. Res. Ther., *3:*187, 1965.

Lader, M. and Sartorius, N.: Anxiety in patients with hysterical conversion symptoms. J. Neurol. Neurosurg. Psychiat., *31:*490, 1968.

Lewis, W. C. and Berman, M.: Studies of conversion hysteria. Arch. Gen. Psychiat., *13:*275, 1965.

27

Depression

BEHAVIOR MODIFICATION THERAPY

Depression is a disorder scarcely touched upon in behavior therapy thus far. Lazarus (1968) discusses some technics in the treatment of depression which are largely in the exploratory stages. He calls his first technic time projection with positive reinforcement. It involves imagining future activities that produce positive reinforcement. A second technic involves affective expression in an attempt to inhibit the depressive responses. Another technic uses sensory deprivation on the assumption that following a period of such deprivation, almost any stimulus will be reinforcing. A behaviorally oriented research program on depression was described by Lewinsohn (1973). A key assumption of the behavioral theory of depression is that a low rate of response-contingent positive reinforcement constitutes a critical antecedent condition for the occurrence of depression. The theory requires that the onset of depression be accompanied by a reduction in positive reinforcement, that intensity of depression vary inversely to the rate of positive reinforcement, and that improvement be accompanied by an increase in positive reinforcement.

The results of an earlier study (Lewinsohn and Libet 1972), which was designed to test the general hypothesis that intensity of depression is a function of the amount of positive reinforcement, were interpreted as consistent with the behavioral theory of depression. Specifically, a fairly substantial and statistically significant association between mood level and the number of pleasant activities engaged in was demonstrated. Also, a significantly larger number of activities was found to be associated with mood for depressed and for non-depressed psychiatric patients than for normal control subjects. In addition, 24 specific activities and events were identified that were associated with mood for more than 10 per cent of the sample.

Lewinsohn and Graf (1973) examined the relationship between engaging in pleasant activities and mood as a function of age, sex, and diagnostic group. Ninety male and female subjects, evenly divided into three age groups (18–29, 30–49, 50 and over) and three diagnostic groups (depressed, nondepressed psychiatric, and normal controls) completed activity schedules and mood ratings for 30 consecutive days. Results indicated that depressed subjects engaged in fewer pleasant activities. The procedure involved in this study is designed to provide a method for identifying specific activities that may be efficacious in counteracting depression.

Depression is characterized by an extensive lowering of the patient's energy level and ability to be reinforced. Other signs are loss of weight, libido, appetite, and early awakening. Fatigue and constipation are present. The depressed patient often says that he just does not care about anything anymore, that nothing means anything to him. In other words, nothing is reinforcing to him anymore. Finding a reinforcer for a depressed patient is a very difficult task. While the method of sensory deprivation used by Lazarus (1968) to enhance the stimulus value of various reinforcers may be effective, it is difficult to control the patient's environment to the extent necessary to insure a rigid deprivation schedule. Hospitalization or institutionalization is needed to adequately apply this technic.

The technic described by Lazarus using affective expression to inhibit depressive responses is very similar in philosophy to Kelly's statement that "you are what you do." If the patient can be made to *act* as if he is happy these "happy" responses will inhibit or replace the depressive responses. The patient is, therefore, encouraged to smile, laugh, go out, and talk with animation even though he does not *feel* like it. He is to play the role of a happy person. After the behavioral changes come the attitudinal changes. In time the role of a happy individual will become the natural behavior of the patient. We have all heard stories of the actress who becomes like the characters she portrays. If you play at a part long enough you become that character. If the depressed patient acts not depressed long enough the nondepressive behavior will become natural to him.

Unfortunately, it is very difficult for the patient to even act the part of a happy individual, because his energy level is so low. Therapy must therefore first of all be directed at raising his energy level. Wolpe and Lazarus (1966) view reactive depression as a consequence of anxiety that is intense and prolonged. When the patient can no longer tolerate the anxiety he is experiencing, he "crashes." It is our belief that all forms of depression are a reaction to anxiety. Depressive behavior is the patient's means of coping with overwhelming anxiety. It is pointless and confusing to attempt to differentiate and label different types of depressive states such as neurotic versus psychotic or endogenous versus exogenous depression. There are as many different types of depression as there are stimuli that elicit anxiety. A person may have long-standing or "functional" depression stemming from many painful childhood episodes of parental rejection or he may have a "reactive" depression stemming from a particular traumatic incident such as the death of a loved one. In any case the depressive behavior with its lack of affect and low energy level is the same; an infinite number of causes may produce the same result.

Preliminary studies by Falloon, et al. (1975) using a multi-modal approach suggested a program where each type of depressive behavior was countered by a specific procedure of either operant shaping or modeling. They found that simple behavioral technics often may be effective in modification of depressive behavior.

HYPNOBEHAVIORAL THERAPY

Abrams (1964) also views depression as a defense against or response to anxiety and states, "Hypnosis can be a valuable adjunctive measure in the treatment process." Once the anxiety is removed, there is no longer a *need* for the defense, or anything to respond to with depression. There are two ways to eliminate this anxiety. First, through psychotherapy the anxiety-eliciting stimuli are located. These stimuli are then eliminated or modified, or the subject's reaction to them is changed. For example, if the source of anxiety is a dominating mother who is not letting the patient lead his own life, the mother-stimulus can be eliminated as an elicitor of anxiety by breaking the tie and moving away from her. On the other hand, the mother-stimulus may be modified by instructing the patient to deal with her more assertively and not reinforce her dominance by complying. A third alternative is to allow the mother-stimulus to remain present and unchanged but change the patient's reaction to her mother. Then the patient is no longer bothered by her and she loses her ability to elicit anxiety. This can be done by counterconditioning in which the mother is hypnotically imagined engaging in several of the behaviors which irritate the patient, such as giving orders. By pairing hypnotic relaxation with the image of a directive mother, the mother's directiveness soon loses its ability to produce anxiety.

Second, it is possible to reduce a patient's general anxiety level without locating any of the sources of the anxiety. Often the source is difficult to pinpoint, or there are so many sources it is not feasible to deal with each one in turn. Training and practice in hypnotic relaxation using sensory recall to deepen the hypnotic state will lower the patient's general anxiety level. It is much easier to get the depressed patient to practice hypnotic recall of pleasant images than it is to get him to "role play" nondepressive behavior because the relaxation produced from the recall is immediately and intrinsically rewarding, while the secondary rewarding attitude change coming from role playing does not occur for quite some time after role playing has begun. When the anxiety level lowers, the depression will begin to lift and the energy level will rise. More stimuli will be reinforcing and the patient can then begin being reinforced for nondepressive behaviors such as smiling, animated talking, and engaging in social activities. It is also important that the patient not be reinforced at this time for emitting any responses that could be considered to be of a depressive nature. Complaints of not wanting to do anything or not giving a damn should be ignored while statements concerning a feeling of improvement or increased energy on the patient's part should be vigorously reinforced.

Once the patient begins coming out of his depression, it is important to engage him in activities that are intrinsically rewarding. The increased energy must be directed to enjoyable and constructive activities or the patient will begin ruminating again and not be able to cope with his free time. Structure is very important, and it is up to the therapist to direct the patient in adequately filling his time. Hypnotic time projection is a good technic to use. The subject is given images in which he sees himself engaging in specific activities that prove very rewarding in the image. After 1 or 2 weeks of hypnotically imagining himself in a given activity, the patient usually pursues the activity in reality. Rosen (1955) used age regression to forestall suicide in depression.

The following is an example of a case in which the anxiety-eliciting stimuli could be isolated and dealt with in the three ways described above:

J.K. was an extremely withdrawn, depressed, and anxious 23-year-old male. He described having one to six "panic attacks" a day accompanied by diarrhea; his heart would pound, his hands shake, and his palms sweat. The nervousness had begun in ninth grade due to fear of taking examinations even though he was a B student. He had many friends and had not been a nervous child. Depression and anxiety increased yearly, and he dropped out of junior college as he could not take the pressures. He never dated.

Currently he was living with his parents and two brothers, ages 20 and 11. He had no friends and never left the house. He was particularly sensitive to loud noises and could not tolerate the sounds of cats, his parent's fighting, or his younger brother's friends. People in general were avoided. The patient was also having difficulty sleeping. The past 8 years had been spent in various types of psychotherapy, and the patient had had five different therapists. He evidenced much intellectualization and hostility when discussing his problem and was very directive as to what given modes of treatment should and should not be used with him.

The insomnia was cured by eliminating the anxiety-producing stimuli of noise via ear plugs. Also the street noises were avoided by instructing the patient to switch rooms with his brother who slept in the back of the house. The brother was not even cognizant of the noise level to which J.K. had become sensitized. The stimuli of his brother's noisy friends were modified by having J.K. instruct them repeatedly to keep their voices down. The patient had little difficulty asserting himself in this manner. Also, his parents were called in for a session and informed how anxiety-producing their arguing was to their son. Their behavior thus also was modified.

In order to cope with the environmental stimuli at home which could neither be eliminated nor modified, J.K. was trained in hypnosis and sensory recall to lower his general anxiety level. The patient soon began feeling more relaxed. Complaints were no longer attended to and positive statements and actions were reinforced. He was told to smile, laugh, and talk at home even if he did not *feel* like it. Therapy was then directed to getting him out of the house for even brief intervals. He was to chart the amount of time each day spent away from home regardless of where he went. An exchange system was worked out whereby so much time away from home was worth a given reward. Even though J.K. was 23, his only source of support came from his parents and they could thus successfully incorporate such a system of rewards. As he became more at ease and spent more time away from the house, J.K. began considering part-time work. He made the statement, "Nervous people work too," which showed he was no longer using his anxiety as a cop-out to avoid people. He was getting less and less secondary gain from his condition.

Although still subject to occasional moments of panic and anxiety, J.K. got a part-time job. This took his mind off the continual rumination he had been indulging in for many years. He began to feel even better. His eventual goal was to return to school, and he was given time projection images in which he saw himself sitting totally relaxed in a classroom, happily socializing with the teacher and other students. The hypnotic relaxation associated with these images served to desensitize J.K. to the thought of going back to school and being with people. Four months after this imagery was begun, the patient returned to classes. A one-year follow-up showed that he was still in school, receiving good grades, and living with some other young men in an apartment off campus.

In some cases of depression, the source of anxiety is evident and singular. Separation anxiety due to the death of a loved one, divorce, or an unrequited love affair is a common cause of depression. The following is such a case:

M.W. was a 55-year-old woman who was suffering severe depression due to an unrequited love for her ex-husband. She had married him 25 years ago and had a son now aged 23. After 9 years of marriage during which he cheated on her and was negligent of the child, the marriage was terminated. Five years later she ran into him and they began seeing one another. He had now become a financial success. She was extremely jealous of his money and good times, since they had experienced only extreme poverty when married. She was still very attracted to him physically and would have intercourse when asked. He was the only man she had ever been intimate with. He continued to date other women however and M.W. felt she was being used. She would wait weeks for him to phone and when they did go out, he showed off to other women. This type of relationship continued to the present, and was causing her considerable anguish.

The patient first had to decide what kind of relationship she wanted with this man. She stated she did not wish to remarry him and that it appeared that he did not want to marry her. She had spent over 20 years trying to modify his behavior toward her to no avail. She could not expect to forget him, however, until she *decided* to forget him. Once this decision was made, therapy proceeded quite rapidly.

Hypnosis was then instituted to reduce her separation anxiety, as she had decided not to see him again. In the first hypnotic session, the "winding down" due to the relaxation unleashed a deluge of tears and she cried for over 30 minutes. The following five sessions all led to outbursts of tears after 5 to 10 minutes of hypnotic relaxation, and these lasted the remainder of the hour. After the release of all this emotion, which had been held back so many years, the patient was able to deal with the situation much more objectively. She discussed dating other men and doing things to improve herself, such as taking dancing lessons.

In the sixth session, the patient began crying for her mother while in hypnosis. She was asked where her mother was. For the first time it was revealed that her mother and father had died a short interval apart a year ago. The patient had been very close to both parents and experienced considerable guilt from their deaths because she felt that if she had money she could have gotten them better medical attention. This loss had been so painful she had refused to let it become conscious until her defenses were let down while hypnorelaxed. After much crying and two more sessions discussing her parent's death, M.W. was able to deal with the loss and recognize it for what it was. Much of the guilt was gone, and the depression associated with it was lifting.

By her tenth visit, the patient was able to induce and maintain the hypnotic state without breaking into tears. Much of the sorrow had been expressed and thus released. The series of standard relaxing images was then begun to deepen the relaxation. The patient soon began saying that she felt less tired in general and was thinking less of her ex-husband, or "the bastard" as she referred to him. She had not seen him in several weeks. She was able to effectively turn off longing thoughts of him by hypnotically recalling the bad experiences she had had with him whenever these thoughts came to mind. She was now much more relaxed, but was still leading the life of a recluse and periodically thinking she still loved her ex-husband.

In order to finally resolve her feelings toward him, two images were devised. In the first image, the patient was to imagine his begging her to come back. The therapist played the role of the husband during the hypnotic session. In a situation such as this, in which her husband wanted her, she refused him. It was pointed out to her later that she only wanted him because she could not have him. She did not love him. In the second image, M.W. was to see herself dancing with another very attractive man. She was then to see her husband approach her on the floor and request a dance. She was to role-play her response in hypnosis with the therapist as her husband. When the therapist said, "May I have this dance?" the patient replied, "Drop dead!" After being brought out of the hypnotic state, the patient realized that her love for this man had died many years ago. She said she only wanted him out of fear she could not get someone else. When she imagined herself with someone else, she realized how little feeling she really had for her ex-husband. After this, the patient began dating other men and leading a normal, socially active life. She was no longer troubled by thoughts of her ex-husband, and her depression was gone.

In many cases of depression, the anxiety is more free-floating, in that it is difficult to specify any particular sources of tension. Through the years a multitude of stimuli have, through association with the depressed state, come to be elicitors of anxiety and depression. As stated before, although helpful, it is not necessary to locate specific sources of anxiety in order to alleviate depression. Lowering the patient's general anxiety level and teaching him to cope with the onset of anxiety in everyday situations regardless of their source will lead to a lifting of the depression. The following is an example of such a case:

D.B. was a 48-year-old black male complaining of depression, migraine (on the left side accompanied by an aura and vomiting), and insomnia. He was suicidal, having first attempted to kill himself at the age of 18 by slashing his wrists. D.B. was also subject to anxiety attacks in which he shook uncontrollably and was not able to use his hands. Over the past 15 years he had seen six psychiatrists and tried all the anti-depressants available. One year prior to his coming to see us, he had been hospitalized in a psychiatric unit for 1 month for hallucinations and anorexia. The hallucinations were of short duration and never reappeared.

The patient bordered on paranoia because of a long history of persecution for being black and also for being homosexual. He had enjoyed heterosexuality until his later 20s, at which time he was "turned on" to homosexuality exclusively. D.B. recounted several incidents of persecution in the Army because of his color and sexual preference. Racial prejudice was encountered mostly, however, in the school systems where he had been a teacher. After the Army, the patient received a B.A. in French at the University of Paris. He loved France but returned to the United States to obtain his master's degree. While totally accepted abroad, he was looked down upon in the states for being black. After much conflict with his teachers, he finished his course requirements, but his thesis was rejected and he tried again and failed again at another school. He gave up trying to gain the M.A. and taught for 15 years in the public school system, always in a disadvantaged area where the students were unruly and disinterested in the subject. The patient was positive that his failing to get the M.A. or a job in a better school district was due to racial discrimination. He had, however, been criticized on personal mannerisms such as using his hands too much and may have appeared too effeminate to suit the school board.

A year ago the patient gave up teaching and began working for a family, cooking, washing dishes, and ironing. He held this job at the time he came for treatment and had no desire to return to teaching. This was all he could handle at present, he stated. D.B. said he could not relate to people and was a loner; people didn't like him. He deliberately avoided all social contact and would read and watch television in his free time. He had not had any sexual relations in 3 years and reported he was too weary to seek them.

The first therapeutic goal was to direct the patient into a more meaningful job in order to raise his confidence and self-esteem. Hypnosis was instituted in order to reduce his anxiety level, and after several sessions the patient reported that he usually felt very good for 2 or 3 days after the weekly session, and then the depression would come back. The patient was not able financially to handle more than one session a week. Self-hypnosis was then taught and the patient was instructed to practice induction of the hypnotic state and sensory recall of relaxation-producing images for 5-minute sessions 5 times a day in order to stave off the anxiety and ensuing depression. Four weeks and four images later, the patient reported that he was no longer having episodes of shaking or anxiety attacks.

At this point in therapy, D.B. reported that he was to be interviewed for a high-school teaching job. He was terrified of the interview situation. After questioning by the therapist to pinpoint the exact elements of the interview which were eliciting anxiety in the patient, it was found that he feared three possible questions: (1) "Why did you quit your last job?" (2) "How do you teach?" (3) "How do you discipline?" Each question was discussed at length with the patient until he felt comfortable with his answers and had even done some research on current methods in teaching and discipline. The interview was then role-played in hypnosis, combining rehearsal with desensitization. The patient went to the interview and reported feeling at ease but did not take the job, as he felt the teaching load too heavy.

Next, a teaching job at the college level came up for consideration. The patient was seeking to teach at this level, as the pressure from disciplining and over-crowding would be neglible compared to the patient's past teaching experiences. Once again he hypnotically practiced role-playing the interview situation. At the last moment, however, the patient decided he did not want to teach anyone and did not make the interview, telling the school that he was ill. He had wanted this job more than the last one, and the pressure to succeed had been greater than he could handle. After a "pep talk" and two more sessions of role-playing and hyp-notic relaxation, the patient rescheduled the interview and made it this time. He got the job, which consisted of teaching college French half-time while during the other half carrying credits to complete his master's degree. D.B. stated he had "calmed down a lot" and felt up to the job. He terminated therapy as his new work was in another town. Although his social life at this time was still nil, he was no longer depressed or suicidal. It was hoped that the improved self-image gained from a more fulfilling job would inspire confidence to improve his social relationships.

STANDARDIZED IMAGES

Since the onset of depression is accompanied by a reduction of positive rein-forcement, it is necessary to increase the amount of positive feelings the patient is experiencing. All 25 images described in Chapter 10 are designed to increase one's ability for pleasure in all five senses. The practice of these images is a reinforcing experience. Imagery involving pleasant activities (IX, pool; XIII, lake; XVI, scuba; XXV, autumn) are helpful in getting the patient to remember the joy he experienced from other similar activities. Positive emotional recall of these activities will motivate the subject to engage in them again. A patient often is heard to say after such imagery that he had forgotten how much he used to enjoy swimming, boating, diving, or whatever activity was described in the image.

The hypnotic induction of a deprivation state can also be used to enhance a reinforcing part of an image. This is particularly useful in cases of depression in which the patient appears apathetic to all sources of stimuli. In Image V (desert), thirst is induced hypnotically so that drinking of the clear liquid of the freshwater sea later in the image is more reinforcing. In Image VII (farm), the suggestion is given for hunger so that the eating of the blueberry muffins will be more reinforcing. Thirst, hunger, or both are also induced in Image IX (pool), X (Arctic), XV (mansion), XVII (picnic), and XVIII (Shangri-La) so that drinking or eating later in the image will be more reinforcing.

Hypnotic induction of sexual arousal, as in Image XXI (cantina), can be useful in dispelling the apathy so prevalent in depressed states. Intensification of any drive is incompatible with apathy. Finally, age regression, as described in Image XXV, is used to regress the patient back to a happier point in time so that he can once again experience and gain control over the experiencing of appropriate positive affects.

At present the treatment of depression is dominated by pharmacological agents. Many antidepressant drugs are helpful. The behavioral model has just recently been introduced. Even though hypnosis has been advocated for many years, we are among the first to espouse the integration of both disciplines in the treatment of this disorder.

REFERENCES

Abrams, S.: Implications of learning theory in treatment of depression by employing hypnosis as an adjunctive technique. Amer. J. Clin. Hypn., *6:*313, 1964.

Falloon, I. R. et al.: Therapy of depression: behavioral approach. Psychotherp. Psychosom. *25:*69, 1975.

Lazarus, A. A.: Learning theory and the treatment of depression. Behav. Res. Ther., *6:*83, 1968.

Lewinsohn, P. M.: Clinical and theoretical aspects of depression. *In* K. S. Calhoun, H. E. Adams, and K. M. Mitchell (eds.): Innovative Treatment Methods in Psychotherapy. New York, John Wiley and Sons, 1973.

Lewinsohn, P. M. and Graf, M.: Pleasant activities and depression. J. Consult. Clin. Psychol., *41:*261, 1973.

Lewinsohn, P. M., and Libet, J.: Pleasant events, activity schedules, and depression. J. Abnorm. Psychol., *79:*291, 1972.

Rosen, H.: Regression hypnotically induced as an emergency measure in a suicidally depressed patient. J. Clin. Exper. Hypn., *3:*58–70, 1955.

Wolpe, J. and Lazarus, A. A.: Behavior Therapy Techniques: A Guide to the Treatment of Neuroses. New York, Pergamon, 1966.

SUGGESTED READINGS

Dryden, S. C.: Hypnosis as an approach to the depressed patient. Amer. J. Clin. Hypn., *9:*135, 1966.

Hodge, J. R.: Hypnosis as a deterrent to suicide. Amer. J. Clin. Hypn., *15:*20, 1972.

28

Schizophrenia

This chapter will present experimental evidence that schizophrenics can be conditioned, and can, therefore, be influenced by suggestion, hypnosis, or both. Hence, hypnotherapy can be combined with behavior modification in the treatment of schizophrenia. It can also potentiate chemotherapy. The psychopharmacological approach will be omitted, as it has been amply discussed in the literature. Rather, we shall review the pertinent literature on behavior modification and hypnosis in detail, since it has been presumed by many that schizophrenics can neither learn nor be hypnotized.

ETIOLOGIC FACTORS

The person labeled as schizophrenic is characterized by poor reality testing. The term is a catchall for all types of thought disorders and bizarre behaviors. However, there are highly discriminating symptoms that readily facilitate the diagnosis in this disorder. Wing and Nixon (1975) have shown that a specific constellation of symptoms are characteristic—the nuclear syndrome. Their method of computer diagnosis was accurate in over 90 per cent of cases.

Considerable controversy as to its etiology exists (Jordan 1974; Shein 1974; Harrow, Bromet, and Quinlan 1974). Work in this area is so diffuse and immense, one can only cursorily cover the topic. Cancro (1974) in his annual review discussed the family theory, the "biochemical vulnerability" hypothesis, role of early perceptual-social deprivation, heredity, stress, environmental, and psychosocial factors.

Research on the motivational aspects of schizophrenia support the physiological stress theory proposed by Venables (1963a,b,c) and Venables and

Wing (1962). Lang and Buss (1965) thoroughly reviewed an extensive body of empirical evidence in regard to motivation and concluded that most autonomic functions are characterized by such reduced responsivity as deterioration of associational or psychomotor control. However, activity was increased in the cardiovascular and musculoskeletal systems, which could be positively correlated with symptoms of withdrawal and other manifestations of clinical exacerbation.

CONDITIONABILITY

A relevant question in this disorder is whether or not schizophrenics can be taught adequate coping mechanisms for developing more adaptive behaviors. This is important inasmuch as psychological deficits exist in various areas of perception, psychomotor performance, learning, motivation, and cognitive behavior involving concept formation, particularly in those dealing with language (Yates 1966a, Buss and Lang 1965, Lang and Buss 1965, Payne 1960, Silverman 1964, Johannsen 1964). That schizophrenics can be taught is born out by Yates (1970), who argues that under appropriate conditions higher level cortical processes are basically unimpaired, but that the failure to function adequately is due to deficits at lower levels of neural integration.

Studies relating to learning shed more light on the question of whether schizophrenics are conditionable. O'Connor and Rawnsley (1959) and Howe (1958) found little difference between schizophrenics and control subjects in reference to conditionability. However, Spence and Taylor (1953) and Taylor and Spence (1954) purport to have demonstrated that schizophrenics condition more readily than other psychiatric groups. There is no doubt that schizophrenics learn, but most evidence indicates that they learn more slowly than nonpsychotics (King 1954, Huston and Shakow 1948, 1949). Garmezy (1952) and Mednick (1955) have also alleged that under certain conditions, schizophrenics show a flattened generalization curve, that is, they have impaired discriminatory capacity.

In reference to the cognitive behavior of schizophrenics, Payne (1960) posited that they are able to form new concepts. Carson (1962), Hall (1962), Kew (1963), and Whitman (1963) found that the concepts they formed were similar to those of normal subjects. In a study on mediational processes, Moran, Mefferd, and Kimble (1964) clearly showed that schizophrenics and normal subjects share a common associative structure. Support for this interpretation has come from studies by Lang and Luoto (1962) and Spence and Lair (1964).

Chapman and McGhie (1962) have shown that schizophrenics could perform tasks as well as normals as long as distraction was not present. However, when attention had to be selective, especially when competing sensory channels were involved, performance tended to deteriorate. Also, the capacity for temporal integration, especially in the *perception* of speech, breaks down in schizophrenia

(Chapman and McGhie 1964). Building on the "filter theory" that there is a limit to the amount of information that can be processed in a given unit of time (Broadbent 1958), Yates (1966b) deduced, "If the subject is under continuous pressure to respond, the highest cortical processes will be adversely affected and ultimately the efficiency of the response process will deteriorate, with the appearance of language disturbance and other indices of 'thought disorder.' "

Such disturbances lead to social withdrawal, manifested in its most extreme stage as catatonia, and may thus be a protective mechanism against excessive stimulation. Evidence of this was shown in studies by McReynolds (1963) and Sidle, Acker, and McReynolds (1963) indicating that schizophrenics inhibit the input of novel stimulation. This finding is in line with the role of protective inhibition in schizophrenia (Lynn 1963). Usdansky and Chapman (1960) have produced quasi-schizophrenic responses in normals under increased rates of stimulus presentation. Kroger (1963) has pointed out that catalepsy induced by hypnosis is the other side of the coin of catatonia, particularly flexibilitas cerea. He also notes that amnesia and negative and positive hallucinations induced by hypnosis afford an artificial model for the study of schizophrenia in almost pure "culture." Although, as mentioned, schizophrenics are conditionable or can learn, learning does not necessarily imply a change in behavior. While these patients acquire new response patterns when positive reinforcement is contingent upon the emission of a novel response (Peters and Jenkins 1954, Mednick and Lindsley 1958, King et al. 1957, Bullock and Brunt 1959, Bullock 1960, Hutchinson and Azrin 1961, Beech and Adler 1963, Ullman et al. 1964), it is generally agreed that schizophrenics do not respond to positive reinforcers in the same manner as normal subjects. Positive verbal reinforcement has proven particularly unsuccessful in several studies (Cohen and Cohen 1960, Slechta et al. 1963, Bryan and Lichtenstein 1964, Ebner 1965).

Punishment in the form of verbal censure following an incorrect response has been found to facilitate learning more than verbal praise following a correct response (Buss and Buss 1956, Buss et al. 1954, 1956). Olson (1958), Losen (1961), and Johannsen (1962) also found such punishment as verbal criticism to be more effective than such reward as verbal praise. There is also strong evidence (Pascal and Swensen 1952, Cohen 1956, Rosenbaum et al. 1957, Cavanaugh 1958, Lang 1959) that a contingent aversive stimulus terminated by an appropriate response (escape training) facilitates emission of that response compared with a control condition. Cavanaugh et al. (1960) demonstrated that schizophrenics learn to emit responses faster, provided they prevent the appearance of a noxious stimulus in the form of verbal censure which will otherwise occur (avoidance training).

Comprehensive reviews on reinforcement experiments carried out on schizophrenics (Buss and Lang 1965, Johannsen 1964, Lang and Buss 1965, and Silverman 1963) suggest that contingent aversive stimulation is more effective than contingent positive stimulation in changing the behavior of the schizophrenic. Aversive stimulation appears to be particularly effective when it provides information about the incorrect and correct responses required.

BEHAVIOR THERAPY

Behavior therapy with schizophrenics deals primarily with the reinstatement or elimination of specific behaviors and does not concern itself with the "schizophrenic personality." Isaacs et al. (1960) reinstated verbal behavior in two mute catatonic males who had not emitted verbal responses in over 14 years by the use of a successive approximation technic involving several primary reinforcers such as candy. Reinstatement of minimal vocal behavior led to the spontaneous reinstatement of other verbal behaviors not treated directly. Mute catatonic patients are physically able to speak and are aware of what is going on around them. They appear, however, to be suffering from a massive degree of inhibition. Any break through the inhibition may lead to spontaneous reinstatement of whole areas of adaptive behavior. Sherman (1965) confirmed the validity of these technics by applying shaping, reinforced imitation of nonverbal behaviors that generalized to verbal behaviors, and fading to three schizophrenics hospitalized from 20 to 45 years and with 16 to 43 years' history of mutism.

Much of the ward behavior of psychotic patients is maintained by reinforcement received for it in the form of attention from ward personnel. Allyon and Haughton (1964) were able to demonstrate operant control over psychotic speech in a female schizophrenic by respectively vocally acknowledging and ignoring appropriate and inappropriate speech. Rickard et al. (1960) were able to increase rational speech in a 60-year-old male with delusional speech by reinforcing rational speech by nodding and smiling, while delusional speech was punished by being ignored. A follow-up study conducted 2 years later by Rickard and Dinoff (1962) further demonstrated that psychotic speech can be manipulated by the reaction of the listener.

While withdrawal of attention appears to be the most common form of punishment used for modifying schizophrenic behavior, other technics have also been employed. Ayllon and Michael (1959) describe the case of a schizophrenic female who refused to eat unless spoon-fed. It was noticed that this patient was extremely concerned to keep her clothing neat and clean. Spoon feeding was continued, but the nurse was instructed to become careless and allow food to spill onto the patient's dress. After eight weeks of treatment, spoon feeding was completely discontinued and the patient fed herself. The same authors also reported a case in which magazine hoarding was significantly reduced in a patient by flooding him with magazines (stimulus satiation). Allyon (1963) describes the successful treatment of towel hoarding using a similar flooding procedure.

Group studies involving token economy wards where the patients must work for tokens that can be exchanged for certain privileges or material rewards have proven very effective in modifying the behavior of schizophrenic populations. For a more detailed description of these "controlled environments," the reader is referred to the reviews by Krasner (1968) and Liberman (1972) on the work of token economy programs. Cohen et al. (1972) showed that introducing tokens contingent on the patient's behavior from the beginning had no disadvantage compared with having a pre-period in which the patients learn to exchange the tokens and thereby establish their value as generalized reinforcers. Also, having the tokens contingent on one's behavior seemed to heighten their subjective value over and above the pleasurable experience of exchanging them for primary reinforcers.

Ayllon and Haughton (1962) demonstrated that the eating behavior of schizophrenics can be controlled solely by food as a reinforcer. Entry to the dining room for 32 female patients was made contingent upon arrival within 30 minutes after the announcement of meal time. This time limit was progressively reduced to 5 minutes. All of the usual methods of coaxing, reminding, exhorting, and spoon or tube feeding were discontinued, and the nurses were kept away from the patients at mealtime to prevent social reinforcement (attention) from being given. None of the patients, some of whom went for long periods without food in the first part of the experiment, suffered any medical handicap as a result of treatment. This study indicates that severe psychotics can learn to make social responses to obtain reinforcers and that new social behavior may reinstate verbal behavior. Regardless of how bizarre these patients' behavior appeared, they were not actually "out of reality contact" and would respond to contingencies.

In other studies, Ayllon and Azrin (1965) clearly showed that secondary reinforcers can significantly control behavior in a schizophrenic population. Here patients worked for tokens that could be exchanged for primary or, at least, more significant reinforcers, namely, privacy (selection of particular room for sleeping, personal chair, etc.,); leave from the ward (walk in hospital grounds, trip to town, etc.); social interaction with staff (private audience with ward psychologist or social worker); devotional opportunities; recreational opportunities (movie on ward, exclusive use of radio); shopping items (food, toilet requisites, clothing). Similar encouraging results have been reported by Schaefer (1966) and Atthowe and Krasner (1968). In all of these studies, there remains the problem of generalization of behavior from hospital ward to real life or even from given personnel who have been the reinforcing agents to other personnel within the hospital itself. Suggestions have been made for intermediate wards that more closely approximate real-life conditions as well as training of the relatives of the patient so that inadvertent reinforcing of the largely extinguished abnormal behavior will not reinstate it. In general, it can be concluded that quite complex behavior (including *social* behavior) can be manipulated in the schizophrenic through use of reinforcement contingencies. Since hypnosis facilitates motivation, it can be used to enhance the reward value of the token in such systems. This should provide a fertile field for further research.

HYPNOTIZABILITY

To effectively apply the hypnobehavioral model to the treatment of the schizophrenic, we must have concrete evidence that such a patient is both conditionable and hypnotizable. The research cited above overwhelmingly shows that schizophrenics are definitely conditionable. That leaves one question left to answer: is the schizophrenic capable of being hypnotized? Studies designed to evaluate the hypnotic susceptibility of chronic psychotic patients have produced conflicting results. In a pilot study using the standardized induction and measurement procedures of the Stanford Hypnotic Suggestibility Scale, Vingoe and Kramer (1966), Hilgard (1965), Kramer and Brennan (1964), and Gordon (1973) reported that chronic psychotics are just as readily hypnotizable as normal subjects. Barber, Karacan, and Calverley (1964), however, presented a different picture. The results of this study indicated that chronic schizophrenics are generally difficult to hypnotize. These conflicting data may be resolved by studying the skills and technics of the hypnotherapist. Also important is the degree of motivation. Lavoie, Sabourin, and Langlois (1973) evaluated the nature and extent of hypnotic susceptibility for a random sample of chronic psychotics. They found that the susceptibility of most patients tended to cluster around a medium level of hypnotic susceptibility.

One fact is clear in all the research. Whether they are less, equally, or more hypnotizable than normals, schizophrenics definitely *are* hypnotizable. Authors using hypnotherapy successfully with schizophrenics are Wolberg (1948), Bowers (1961), Abrams (1963, 1964), Beaudet (1963), Scott (1966), Biddle (1967), Shibata and Kuwahara (1967), Shibata and Motoda (1967a,b, 1968), Shibata (1968), and Worpell (1973). In using the hypnobehavioral model to treat schizophrenia two primary stratagems are employed: 1. Appropriate behavior is reinforced. 2. The anxiety responsible for the schizophrenic break is reduced via hypnosis. It should also be noted at this point that as the anxiety level is reduced, "selective" attention develops in hypnosis that serves to correct the schizophrenic's "disturbed" attention. As a result, power to focus and attend to one stimulus is increased.

In order to carry out the first stratagem, the therapist must find a reinforcer, which admittedly is very difficult for a schizophrenic since he does not respond to positive social reinforcement. In a closed ward, contingencies and exchange systems can be enforced much in the same way they were in the literature discussed on the token economy wards. On an outpatient basis, however, it is hard to find a goal that the patient will work for. His basic needs are usually being met, and this is all he cares about. While the most common types of reinforcers used in the research have related to the two basic drives of hunger and thirst, the present authors have devised some reinforcers relating to the third basic drive, sex. We have found that male schizophrenics will work for tokens that can be exchanged for viewing slides or pictures of nude females.

From the physiological stress theory of Venables (1963 a,b,c) and Venables and Wing (1962), it can be seen that it is paramount to reduce the anxiety that is so incapacitating to the schizophrenic. Hypnosis and sensory recall with standard relaxing images is begun immediately to induce relaxation and alleviate the stimulus or input overload. While a number of therapists have reported using hypnotherapy successfully with schizophrenics, some authors have specified without documentation that not only is this treatment ineffective with schizophrenics, it can be quite dangerous (Lindner 1956, 1952). Other findings are in disagreement with this. Wolberg (1948) states:

> Hypnosis may be employed as an adjunct in the treatment of schizophrenia and, if adroitly used, is of value in a certain number of cases. A great deal of misinformation exists regarding the possible harmful effect of hypnosis on schizophrenics and schizoid individuals.

This conclusion was further corroborated by Gill and Brennan (1961).

In the past, hypnotherapy has been employed essentially as an uncovering device to hasten the development of insight, thereby reducing anxiety and promoting symptom-removal and correction. Abrams (1963), in citing a case of successful hypnotherapy with a schizophrenic patient, states:

> Hypnosis very definitely reduced resistances and allowed the patient to discuss areas that were too traumatic to deal with at a conscious level. Repressed memories and feelings were recalled and in most instances could be worked through. When direct questions failed, he used visualization and dream technics such as, ''Have a dream which will express your feelings,'' or ''When you look at the wall you will see a world that relates to your feeling.''

Comparable technics have been reported by Erickson (1948, 1958).

Abrams (1963) believes that the loosening of inhibitions and uncovering of repressed material via hypnosis leads to insight and a consequential reduction in anxiety. It is also true that anxiety can be reduced directly via hypnosis with or without this insight. Relaxation training and anxiety reduction can be begun immediately; achieving insight can take a lifetime or even may never develop. Many have feared that, in psychotics, if the symptom (anxiety) is removed without also removing the ''cause,'' another symptom will manifest itself as a replacement. There is no evidence that this will occur. The same criticisms are never leveled for use of antipsychotic drugs, which merely constitutes an acceptable form of symptomatic therapy.

STANDARDIZED IMAGES

In addition to reducing anxiety and developing concentration in the schizophrenic, some of the images described in Chapter 10 may serve other functions in the treatment of schizophrenia. We have found that, in schizophrenics, the more bizarre imagery can elicit a better response and greater attention span. The schizophrenic state appears to *feel* very much like many drug states in which time is distorted, colors intensify, and perspective alters. Training in the recall of these bizarre feeling states enables the patient to gain control over and *direct* these states. This is not to encourage "flights from reality" but to develop control over them. We must first begin with a feeling that the schizophrenic can identify with and then phase into and shape more appropriate sensation and cognition.

Images VI, VII, XI, and XII, teaching time control, are very important for regulating information processing and short-term memory. Images VIII (jungle), XX (volcano), XXII (hayloft), and XXIV (mine), with their elements of dissociation, quasi-narcotic feeling states, perceptual distortion, and bizarre content are most readily absorbed by the schizophrenic patient. Once the therapist has established a hypnotic rapport, he can then give the patient more realistic imagery and alter his perceptual processing closer to a normal range.

At present schizophrenia is largely a descriptive overlapping of many syndromes. Numerous etiologic factors have been posited. Thus far the therapy consists mainly of psychopharmacological methods. Only recently have the technics of behavior therapy and hypnosis been employed to help these patients. Though the schizophrenic poses a challenge to present-day methods of psychotherapy, the hypnobehavioral approach affords great promise in the management of this disorder.

REFERENCES

Abrams, S.: Short-term hypnotherapy in a schizophrenic patient. Amer. J. Clin. Hypn., *5:*237, 1963.
————: The use of hypnotic techniques with psychotics. Amer. J. Psychotherapy, *18:*79, 1964.
Atthowe, J. M. and Krasner, L.: Preliminary report on the application of contingent reinforcement procedures (token economy) on a "chronic" psychiatric ward. J. Abnorm. Psychol., *73:*37, 1968.
Ayllon, T.: Intensive treatment of psychotic behavior by stimulus satiation and food reinforcement. Behav. Res. Ther., *1:*53, 1963.
Ayllon, T. and Azrin, N.: The measurement and reinforcement of behavior of psychotics. J. Exp. Anal. Behav., *8:*357, 1965.
Ayllon, T. and Haughton, E.: Control of the behavior of schizophrenic patients by food. J. Exp. Anal. Behav., *5:*343, 1962.

————: Modification of symptomatic verbal behavior of mental patients. Behav. Res. Ther., *2:*87, 1964.

Ayllon, T. and Michael, J.: The psychiatric nurse as a behavioral engineer. J. Exper. Anal. Behav., *2:*323, 1959.

Barber, T. X., Karacan, I., and Calverley, D.: "Hypnotizability" and suggestibility in chronic schizophrenics. Arch. Gen. Psychiat., *11:*439, 1964.

Beaudet, S. C.: Hypnosis in a schizophrenic obstetrical patient. Amer. J. Clin. Hypn., *6:*11, 1963.

Beech, H. R. and Adler, F.: Some aspects of verbal conditioning in psychiatric patients. Behav. Res. Ther., *1:*273, 1963.

Biddle, W. E.: Hypnosis in the Psychosis. Springfield. Charles C Thomas, 1967.

Bowers, M. K.: Theoretical considerations in the use of hypnosis in treatment of schizophrenia. Internat. J. Clin. Exp. Hypn., *9:*39, 1961.

Broadbent, D. E.: Perception and Communication. Oxford, Pergamon, 1958.

Bryan, J. H. and Lichtenstein, E.: Failure to verbally condition socially desirable speech. Psychol. Rep., *14:*141, 1964.

Bullock, D. H.: Performance of psychiatric patients in a brief operant discrimination test. Psychol. Rec., *10:*83, 1960.

Bullock, D. H. and Brunt, M. Y.: The testability of psychiatric patients in an operant conditioning situation. Psychol. Rec., *9:*165, 1959.

Buss, A. H., Braden, W., Orgel, A., and Buss, E. H.: Acquisition and extinction with different verbal reinforcement combinations. J. Exp. Psychol., *52:*280, 1956.

Buss, A. H. and Buss, E. H.: The effect of verbal reinforcement combinations on conceptual learning. J. Exp. Psychol., *52:*283, 1956.

Buss, A. H. and Lang, P. J.: Psychological deficit in schizophrenia: I. Affect, reinforcement, and concept attainment. J. Abnorm. Psychol., *70:*2, 1965.

Buss, A. H., Wiener, M., and Buss, E. H.: Stimulus generalization as a function of verbal reinforcement combinations. J. Exp. Psychol., *48:*433, 1954.

Cancro, R.: The rehabilitation of chronic schizophrenics: genetic and environmental considerations. Int. J. Social Psychiat., *20:*68, 1974.

Carson, R. C.: Proverb interpretation in acutely schizophrenic patients. J. Nerv. Ment. Dis., *135:*556, 1962.

Cavanaugh, D. K.: Improvement in the performance of schizophrenics on concept formation tests as a function of motivational change. J. Abnorm. Soc. Psychol., *57:*8, 1958.

Cavanaugh, D., Cohen, W., and Lang, P. J.: The effect of "social censure" and "social approval" on the psychomotor performance of schizophrenics. J. Abnorm. Soc. Psychol., *60:*213, 1960.

Chapman, J. and McGhie, A.: A comparative study of disordered attention in schizophrenia. J. Ment. Sci., *108:*487, 1962.

————: Echopraxia in schizophrenia. Brit. J. Psychiat., *110:*365, 1964.

Cohen, B. D.: Motivation and performance in schizophrenia. J. Abnorm. Soc. Psychol., *52:*186, 1956.

Cohen, E. and Cohen, B. D.: Verbal reinforcement in schizophrenia. J. Abnorm. Soc. Psychol., *6:*443, 1960.

Cohen, R., Florin, I. Grusche, G., Meyer-Osterkamp, S., and Sell, H.: The introduction of a token economy in a psychiatric ward with extremely withdrawn chronic schizophrenics. Behav. Res. Ther., *10:*69, 1972.

Das, J. P.: Hypnosis, verbal satiation, vigilance and personality factors: A correlational study. J. Abnorm. Soc. Psychol., *68:*72, 1964.

Ebner, E.: Verbal conditioning in schizophrenia as a function of degree of social interaction. J. Pers. Soc. Psychol., *1:*528, 1965.

Erickson, M. H.: Hypnotic psychotherapy. Medical Clinics of North America, *32:* 571–583, 1948.

————: Deep hypnosis and its induction. *In* L. M. LeCron, (ed.): Experimental Hypnosis. New York, Macmillan, 1958.

Garmezy, N.: Stimulus differentiation by schizophrenic and normal subjects under conditions of reward and punishment. J. Pers., *20:*253, 1952.

Gill, M. M. and Brenman, M.: Hypnosis and Related States. New York, International Universities Press, 1961.

Gordon, M. C.: Suggestibility of chronic schizophrenic and normal males matched for age. Internat. J. Clin. Exp. Hypn., *21:*284, 1973.

Hall, G. C.: Conceptual attainment in schizophrenics and nonpsychotics as a function of task structure. J. Psychol., *53:*3, 1962.

Harrow, M., Bromet, E., and Quinlan, D.: Predictors of posthospital adjustment in schizophrenia: thought disorders and schizophrenic diagnosis. J. Nerv. Ment. Dis., *158:*25, 1974.

Hilgard, E. R.: Hypnotic Susceptibility. New York, Harcourt, Brace, and World, 1965.

————: Posthypnotic amnesia: experiments and theory. Internat. J. Clin. Exp. Hypn., *14:*104, 1966.

Howe, E. S.: GSR conditioning in anxiety states, normals, and chronic functional schizophrenic subjects. J. Abnorm. Soc. Psychol., *56:*183, 1958.

Huston, P. E. and Shakow, D.: Learning in schizophrenia: I. Pursuit learning. J. Pers., *17:*52, 1948.

————: Learning capacity in schizophrenia. Amer. J. Psychiat., *105:*881, 1949.

Hutchinson, R. R. and Azrin, N. H.: Conditioning of mental hospital patients to fixed-ratio schedules of reinforcement. J. Exp. Anal. Behav., *4:*87, 1961.

Isaacs, W., Thomas, J. and Goldiamond, I.: Application of operant conditioning to reinstate verbal behavior in psychotics. J. Speech Hearing Dis., *25:*8, 1960.

Johannsen, W. J.: Effect of reward and punishment on motor learning by chronic schizophrenics and normals. J. Clin. Psychol., *18:*204, 1962.

————: Motivation in schizophrenic performance: a review, (Monogr. Suppl., 6-VI5). Psychol. Rep., *15:*839, 1964.

Jordan, L. S.: Elecrodermal activity in schizophrenics: further considerations. Psychol. Bull., *81:*85, 1974.

Kew, J. K.: A comparison of thought processes in various nosological groups. J. Clin. Psychol., *19:*162, 1963.

King, G. F., Merrell, D., Lovinger, E., and Denny, M.: Operant motor behavior in acute schizophrenics. J. Personality, *25:*317, 1957.

King, H. E.: Psychomotor Aspects of Mental Disease. Cambridge, Harvard Univ. Press, 1954.

Kramer, E., and Brennan, E. P.: Hypnotic susceptibility of schizophrenic patients. J. Abnorm. Soc. Psychol., *69:*657, 1964.

Krasner, L.: Assessment of token economy programs in psychiatric hospitals. *In* Ciba Foundation Symposium: the Role of Learning in Psychotherapy. London, Churchill, 1968.

Kroger, W. S.: Clinical and Experimental Hypnosis. Philadelphia, J. B. Lippincott, 1963.

Lang, P. J.: The effect of aversive stimuli on reaction time in schizophrenia. J. Abnorm. Soc. Psychol., *59:*263, 1959.

Lang, P. J. and Luoto, K.: Mediation and associative facilitation in neurotic, psychotic, and normal subjects. J. Abnorm. Soc. Psychol., *64:*113, 1962.

Lang, P. J. and Buss, A. H.: Psychological deficit in schizophrenia: II. Interference and activation. J. Abnorm. Psychol., *70:*77, 1965.

Lavoie, G., Sabourin, M., and Langlois, J.: Hypnotic susceptibility, amnesia, and IQ in chronic schizophrenia. Internat. J. Clin. Exp. Hypn., *21:*157, 1973.

Liberman, R. P.: Behavior modification of Schizophrenia: A review. Schizophrenia Bull., *6:*37, 1972.

Lindner, R. M.: Hypnoanalysis as a psychotherapeutic technique. *In* G. Bychowski and J. L. Despert (ed.): Specialized Techniques in Psychotherapy. New York, Basic Books, 1952.

Lindner, H.: Hypnoanalysis: methods and techniques. *In* R. M. Dorcus (ed.): Hypnosis and its Therapeutic Applications. New York, McGraw-Hill, 1956.

Losen, S. M.: The differential effect of censure on the problem solving behavior of schizophrenics and normal subjects. J. Pers., *29:*258, 1961.

Lynn, R.: Russian theory and research on schizophrenia. Psychol. Bull., *60:*486, 1963.

McGhie, A.: Pathology of Attention. Baltimore, Penguin Books, 1969.

McGhie, A. and Chapman, J.: Disorders of attention and perception in early schizophrenia. Brit. J. Med. Psychol., *34:*103, 1961.

McReynolds, P.: Reactions to novel and familiar stimuli as a function of schizophrenic withdrawal. Percept. Mot. Skills, *16:*847, 1963.

Mednick, M. T. and Lindsley, O. R.: Some clinical correlates of operant behavior. J. Abnorm. Soc. Psychol., *57:*13, 1958.

Mednick, S. A.: Distortions in the gradient of stimulus generalization related to cortical brain damage and schizophrenia. J. Abnorm. Soc. Psychol., *51:*536, 1955.

Mitchell, M. B.: Hypnotizability and distractibility. Amer. J. Clin. Hypn., *13:*35, 1970.

Moran, L. J., Mefferd, R. B. and Kimble, J. P.: Idiodynamic sets in word association. Psychol. Monogr., *78:*22, 1964.

O'Connor, N. and Rawnsley, K.: Two types of conditioning in psychotics and normals. J. Abnorm. Soc. Psychol., *58:*157, 1959.

Olson, G. W.: Failure and subsequent performance of schizophrenics. J. Abnorm. Soc. Psychol., *57:*310, 1958.

Pascal, C. and Swensen, G.: Learning in mentally ill patients under unusual motivation. J. Pers., *21:*250, 1952.

Payne, R. W.: Cognitive abnormalities, *In* Eysenck, H. J. (ed.): Handbook of Abnormal Psychology. pp. 193–261. London, Pitman, 1960.

————: Disorders of thinking. *In* C. G. Costello (ed.): Symptoms of Psychopathology: a Handbook. pp. 49–94. New York, John Wiley and Sons, 1970.

Peters, H. N. and Jenkins, R. L.: Improvement of chronic schizophrenic patients with guided problem-solving, motivated by hunger. Psychiat. Quart. Suppl., *28:*84, 1954.

Rapaport, D. (ed.): Organization and Pathology of Thought. New York, Columbia Univ. Press, 1951.

Rapaport, D., Gill, M. M., and Schafer, R.: Diagnostic Psychological Testing: The Theory, Statistical Evaluation, and Diagnostic Application of a Battery of Tests. 2 vols. Chicago, Year Book Publishers, 1945–46.

Rickard, H. C., Digman, P. J., and Horner, R. F.: Verbal manipulation in psychotherapeutic relationship. J. Clin. Psychol., *16:*364, 1960.

Rickard, H. C. and Dinoff, M.: A follow-up note on "verbal manipulation in a psychotherapeutic relationship." Psychol. Rep., *11:*506, 1962.

Roberts, M. J. Attention and cognitive controls as related to individual differences in hypnotic susceptibility. (Unpublished doctoral dissertation, Stanford University), 1964.

Rosenbaum, G., Mackavey, W. R. and Grisell, J. L.: Effects of biological and social motivation on schizophrenic reaction time. J. Abnorm. Soc. Psychol., *54:*364, 1957.

Schaefer, H. H.: Investigations on operant conditioning procedures in a mental hospital. *In* Fisher, J. and Harris, R. E. (eds.): Reinforcement Theory in Psychological Treatment—a Symposium. pp. 25–39. California Mental Health Res. Monogr., *8:* 1966.

Scott, E. M.: Group therapy for schizophrenic alcoholics in a state-operated outpatient clinic: With hypnosis as an integrated adjunct. Internat. J. Clin. Exp. Hypn., *3:*232, 1966.

Shakow, D.: Psychological deficit in schizophrenia. Behav. Sci., *8:*275, 1963.

Shein, H. M.: Loneliness and interpersonal isolation: focus for therapy with schizophrenic patients. Amer. J. Psychotherapy, *28:*95, 1974.

Sherman, J. A.: Use of reinforcement and imitation to reinstate verbal behavior in mute psychotics. J. Abnorm. Psychol., *70:*155, 1965.

Shibata, J. I.: Limits of applications of autogenic training to schizophrenia and selection of the patients. Amer. J. Clin. Hypn., *11:*99, 1968.

Shibata, J. I. and Kuwahara, M.: Electroencephalographic studies of schizophrenic patients treated with autogenic training. Amer. J. Clin. Hypn., *10:*25–29, 1967.

Shibata, J. I. and Motoda, K.: The application of autogenic training to a group of schizophrenic patients. Amer. J. Clin. Hypn., *10:*15, 1967.

———: Clinical evaluation with psychological tests of schizophrenic patients treated with autogenic training. Amer. J. Clin. Hypn.,*10:*20, 1967.

———: A study of autogenic discharges in schizophrenic patients. Amer. J. Clin. Hypn., *10:*249, 1968.

Sidle, A., Acker, M., and McReynolds, P.: "Stimulus-seeking" behavior in schizophrenics and nonschizophrenics. Percept. Mot. Skills, *17:*811, 1963.

Silverman, J.: Psychological deficit reduction in schizophrenia through response-contingent noxious reinforcement. Psychol. Rep., (Monogr. Suppl., 2-V13). *13:*187, 1963.

———: The problem of attention in research and theory in schizophrenia. Psychol. Rev., *71:*352, 1964.

Slechta, J., Gwynn, W., and Peoples, C.: Verbal conditioning of schizophrenics and normals in a situation resembling psychotherapy. J. Consult. Psychol., *27:*223, 1963.

Spence, J. A. and Lair, C. V.: Associative interrference in the verbal learning performance of schizophrenics and normals. J. Abnorm. Soc. Psychol., *68:*204, 1964.

Spence, K. W. and Taylor, J. A.: The relation of conditioned response strength to anxiety in normal, neurotic, and psychotic subjects. J. Exp. Psychol., *45:*265, 1953.

Taylor, J. A. and Spence, K. W.: Conditioning level in the behavior disorders. J. Abnorm. Soc. Psychol., *49:*497, 1954.

Ullmann, L. P., Krasner, L., and Edinger, R. L.: Verbal conditioning of common associations in long-term schizophrenic patients. Behav. Res. Ther., *2:*15, 1964.

Usdansky, G. and Chapman, L. J.: Schizophrenic-like responses in normal subjects under time pressure. J. Abnorm. Soc. Psychol., *60:*143, 1960.

Venables, P. H.: Changes due to noise in the threshold of fusion of paired light flashes in schizophrenics and normals. Brit. J. Soc. Clin. Psychol., *2:*194, 1963.

———: Selectivity of attention, withdrawal, and cortical activation. Arch. Gen. Psychiat., *9:*74, 1963.

———: The relationship between level of skin potential and fusion of paired light flashes in schizophrenic and normal subjects. J. Psychiat. Res., *1:*79, 1963.

Venables, P. H. and Wing, J. K.: Level of arousal and the subclassification of schizophrenia. Arch. Gen. Psychiat., *7:*114, 1962.

Vingoe, F. J. and Kramer, E.: Hypnotic susceptibility of hospitalized psychotic patients: a pilot study. Internat, J. Clin. Exp. Hypn., *14:*47, 1966.

Whitman, J. R.: Learning from social and nonsocial cues in schizophrenia. J. Gen. Psychol., *68:*307, 1963.

Wing, J., and Nixon, J.: Discriminating symptoms in schizophrenia. Arch. Gen. Psychiat., *32:*853, 1975.

Wolberg, L. R.: Medical Hypnosis, Vol. I Principles of Hypnotherapy. New York, Grune and Stratton, 1948.

Worpell, D. F.: Hypnotherapy with a hallucinating schizophrenic. Amer. J. Clin. Hypn., *16:*134, 1973.

Yates, A. J.: Psychological deficit. Ann. Rev. Psychol., *17:*111, 1966.

————: Data-processing levels and thought disorder in schizophrenia. Austr. J. Psychol., *18:*103, 1966.

————: Behavior Therapy. pp. 273–303, New York, John Wiley & Sons, 1970.

SUGGESTED READINGS

Agras, W. S.: Behavior therapy in the management of chronic schizophrenia. Amer. J. Psychiat., *124:*240, 1967.

Arieti, S.: An overview of schizophrenia from a predominantly psychological approach. Amer. J. Psychiat., *131:*241, 1974.

Bateson, G., Jackson, D. D., Haley, J., and Weakland, J.: Toward a theory of schizophrenia. Behav. Sci., *1:*251, 1956.

Depue, R. A., and Fowles, D. C.: Electrodermal activity as an index of arousal in schizophrenics. Psychol. Bull., *79:*233, 1973.

Eysenck, H. J.: Cyclothymia and schizothymia as a dimension of personality: I. Historical review. J. Pers., *19:*123, 1950.

————: Schizothymia-cyclothymia as a dimension of personality: II. Experimental. J. Pers., *20:*345, 1952.

————: Classification and the problem of diagnosis. *In* Eysenck, H. J. (ed.): Handbook of Abnormal Psychology. London, Pitman, 1960.

Eysenck, S. B.: Neurosis and psychosis: an experimental analysis. J. Ment. Sci., *102:*517, 1956.

Freedman, A. M., Kaplan, H. I. and Sadock, B. J.: Comprehensive Textbook of Psychiatry. Baltimore, Williams and Wilkins, *2:*972–974, 1975.

Green, J. T.: Hypnotizability of hospitalized psychotics. Int. J. Clin. Exper. Hypn., *17:*103–108, 1969.

Heath, R. G.: Schizophrenia: Evidence of a pathologic immune mechanism. *In* Siva Sankar, D. V. (ed.): Schizophrenia: Current Concepts and Research. Hicksville, PJD, 1969.

Friedman, J., and Kleep, W.: Hypnotizability of newly admitted psychotic patients. J. Psychosomatics *4:*95–98, 1963.

Hoffer, A., and Osmond, H.: The adrenochrome model and schizophrenia. J. Nerv. Ment. Dis., *128:*18, 1959.

Kallmann, F. J.: The genetic theory of schizophrenia: An analysis of 691 schizophrenic twin index families. Amer. J. Psychiat., *103:*309, 1946.

Ludwig, A. M. and Stark, L. H.: Schizophrenia, sensory deprivation, and sensory overload. J. Nerv. Ment. Dis., *156:*210, 1973.

Polak, P. R., Mountain, N. E., and Erncle, R. N.: Hypnotizability and prediction of hypnotizability in hospitalized psychotic patients. Int. J. Clin. Hypn., *12:*252–257, 1954.

Reid, A. A.: Disease or syndrome? Arch. Gen. Psychiat., *28:*847–862, June, 1973.

29

Mental Deficiency and Organic Brain Syndrome

DEFINITIONS

Mental retardation is a syndrome; that is, a constellation of symptoms. According to Tarjan and Keeran (1974), the most commonly used clinical definitions include the following requirements: (1) a significant impairment in intellectual performance: (2) a similar impairment in general adaptation; (3) the concurrent presence of the two; and (4) an onset of the clinical manifestations before mental maturity, namely before the 17th year of life. Intellectual performance can be measured and results have usually been expressed in the IQ score obtained on one of several commonly used psychometric tests. It is generally agreed by clinicians that mental retardation should not be diagnosed unless the IQ is at least two standard deviations below the mean, that is, below 70.

ETIOLOGIC FACTORS

The causes of mental retardation are legion. In only about 20 to 25 per cent of all mentally retarded individuals can one find a definitive biological etiologic factor. Valente and Tarjan (1974) report that especially rapid strides have been made in the investigation of infectious diseases (rubella, rubeola), metabolic disorders (Tay-Sachs disease) and chromosomal disorders (Down's syndrome). Unfortunately, these advances involve diseases that cause but a small fraction of the total. The majority of mentally retarded individuals are in the mildly retarded range, and among these, socioeconomic, nutritional, and environmental factors play a major role.

319

TREATMENT

Many treatment methods have been utilized in working with both the mentally retarded themselves and with their parents. Treatments include drugs, psychotherapy, behavior modification, and special education, as well as various community interventions. In reference to chemotherapy, Simmons, Tymchuk, and Valente (1974, p. 52) state: "Drugs do not seem to affect the intellect directly, but have their greatest effects in controlling certain target symptoms such as seizures, hyperactivity, and psychotic behavior. Whatever influence drugs have on intellect seems primarily related to the reduction of events that interfere with intellectual functions." In general, traditional psychotherapeutic technics are aimed at higher-level and more complex behavior operations; whereas behavior modification has been more effective in training the retarded at the level of functional skills. Generally, traditional psychotherapeutic intervention with retarded persons does not aim to cure or alleviate the basic system of poor intelligence, although historically this might have been a primary aim. Rather, the aim of traditional psychotherapy has been to emphasize improvement in behavior, in emotional adjustment, and in achieving a realistic self-appraisal.

ROLE OF OPERANT CONDITIONING

In recent years, operant technics have been shown to be remarkably effective in the elimination of maladaptive behaviors and in the acquisition of more adaptive behaviors such as self-help, social, and academic skills. These technics have been described in detail in this chapter because when used in conjunction with hypnosis, conditioning is facilitated. In contrast to the more global criteria for change used by traditional psychotherapies, the operant approach demands: (1) a precise definition of behaviors to be changed; (2) the use of clearly defined intervention strategies; (3) the establishment of baselines against which to measure change; (4) the contingent management of reward and punishment; and (5) the use of reliable measurement technics.

BEHAVIOR MODIFICATION TECHNICS

Behavior modification offers a systematic way of accomplishing the things that the parents do as a matter of course in disciplining their child. While parents may attempt to teach their retarded child to eat or dress himself properly by using rewards or punishment, this training is often inconsistent and the behaviors too broadly defined to permit adequate assessment of change. A global behavior such as successful eating can be "shaped" by breaking down and reinforcing smaller acts (holding a spoon, pushing spoon into food, bringing spoon to mouth, inserting spoon), each of which is a component of the larger act of eating. Although behavior modification focuses heavily on positive reinforcement, aversive control is also effective in getting rid of inappropriate behaviors, especially by removal of attention or removal of the child from the environment in which he performs the inappropriate behavior (time-out).

"Token economics" has been used for the training of groups of the mentally retarded (Ayllon and Azrin 1968; Ball 1969; Lent, Le Blanc, and Spradlin 1970; Tymchuk 1971), and in special education classrooms for decreasing disruptive behavior, increasing study behavior, and improving academic performance. Axelrod (1971) and O'Leary and Drabman (1971) conclude that effectiveness of the program is related to the changing of the reinforcement system within the classroom from one that depends on infrequent and delayed administration of reinforcers (such as grades) to one that used immediate, often concrete and individual reinforcers, such as tokens, in a rich reinforcement schedule.

Over the past 15 years, learning theory and principles of reinforcement have produced a revolution in the approach to and the understanding of mental deficiency. The pessimistic views, which have been so widely and for so long entertained regarding the ineducability of the mental defective are unwarranted (Ross and Ross 1973). Yates (1970) states:

> One of the most important contributions within the operant framework relates to the assumption that defective performance should never be taken to indicate inability of the subject to acquire the particular response pattern in question. Rather, *failure on the part of the mental defective in a particular task should be taken as an indication that the experimentor has failed to analyze the task sufficiently, precisely, and discriminatively.*

Friedlander et al. (1967) showed that the amount and variety of responding that can be obtained from severely retarded (vegetative) children is much greater than had formerly been supposed. For a review of the empirical work carried out in the operant framework, the reader is referred to Spradlin and Giradeau (1966).

MODIFIABILITY

Research in behavior therapy with mental defectives will be considered in the following three areas: the modifiability of the behavior of severely and profoundly retarded persons; the educability of high-grade defectives; and the trainability and employability of both low-grade and high-grade defectives. Fuller (1949) described successful conditioning and extinction responses, using reinforcement technics. Similar findings have been reported more recently by Rice and McDaniel (1966) and by Rice et al. (1967).

Whitney and Barnard (1966) used successive approximation technics, with food reinforcement for appropriate responses and withdrawal of food reinforcement for inappropriate responses (such as knocking over food). Similarly dramatic results with operant procedures in eating problems were reported by Zeiler and Jervey (1968). Butterfield and Parson (1973) taught a moderately retarded 8-year-old mongoloid child to chew solid food. A series of steps was used to teach the child to chew his food. They included (1) removing attention for non-chewing behavior (2) having a model demonstrate chewing behavior (3) reinforcing the model with the subject's favorite food (4) reinforcing successive approximations to chewing and (5) attenuating the reinforcement schedule.

A great deal of work has also been accomplished in relation to the problem of toilet training (Baumeister and Klosowski 1965, Bensberg et al. 1965, Giles and Wolf 1966, Kimbrell et al. 1967, Marshall 1966, Miron 1966, Wayne and Melnyr 1973). Much of this work was derived from the theoretical model proposed by Ellis (1963), which involves *situational* training, that is, teaching the person to eliminate at the right time in the right place. Dayan (1964) treated 25 severe mental defectives (IQ 30 or below) by placing them on the toilet every two hours, with verbal praise as the reward for elimination and withdrawal of attention as the consequence of failure to eliminate. Hundziak et al. (1965) produced a significant increase in the use of toilet facilities for both urination and defecation in a group of severely retarded boys by using operant reward training with the reinforcers being candy, a light, and a tone.

Lovaas, Freitag, Gold, and Kassorla (1965) explored use of electric shock for self-destructive behavior. Lovaas, Shaffer, and Simmons (1965) found it to be effective in reducing self-destructive behavior. However, since the use of electric shock for the control of human behavior appears to be controversial (Lucero, Vail, and Scherber 1968) although clearly effective, alternative approaches are worthy of exploring.

Saposnek and Watson (1974) used a rage-reduction technic (Zaslow and Breger 1969, Saposnek 1972) for dealing with the problem of self-destructive behavior. In an autistic and retarded child, cure resulted from (1) first inducing and/or confronting "rage," or tantrum-like behavior (screaming and flailing of arms and legs) by means of physical restraint, for the purpose of (2) shaping hand-slapping, which is a response that is incompatible with head-slapping.

Webster and Azrin (1975) describe a method for inhibiting agitative-disruptive behavior of retardates by "required relaxation." Over-corrective practice in relaxation was given to each of eight adult retardates for their disruptions. The agitated resident was required to spend a fixed period of time in relaxation in his own bed upon each occurrence of agitation. This overcorrective relaxation resulted in a rapid, enduring and almost complete reduction in such behavior as self-injury, threats, physical aggression, screaming, crying, cursing, and tantrums. Ward attendants strongly preferred the required relaxation procedure to the time-out technic and other inhibition procedures they had used.

Foxx and Azrin (1972) developed a method they called "restitution" for successfully eliminating aggressive-disruptive behavior of retarded and brain-damaged patients. This procedure provided disruptive offenders with re-education, removal of the reinforcement for the offense, time-out from general positive reinforcement, and an effort requirement. The offender was required by instructions or physical guidance to overcorrect the general psychological and physical disturbance created by the offense.

Hamilton, et al., (1967) treated various disruptive behaviors (head and back banging, continuous breaking of windows with the head, undressing repeatedly, and assaultive behavior against other patients) by a time-out procedure. Most of these behaviors were being maintained by the attention they evoked from ward personnel. Henriksen and Doughty (1967) eliminated 5 types of undesirable mealtime behaviors (eating too fast, eating with the hands, stealing food from other patient's trays, hitting other patients at the meal table, and throwing food trays or spilling food deliberately) in four patients using the following procedure:

> The patients were isolated at a table where two aides were stationed, each at a corner of the table. The aides were to interrupt the undesirable behavior as soon as it began and *before* it was completed, together with a verbal and facial expression of disapproval and a positive response if a proper eating response was made. The aides were faded out as training progressed by gradually increasing their physical distance from the table and by the return of the children to the normal dining-room situation.

Wiesen and Watson (1967) eliminated continuous attention-seeking behavior using time-out for interference with adults and positive reinforcement for social interaction with other children. The reinforcement (candy) was provided by the child who was interacted with, this child being rewarded for his action at a later date. Considerable success has also been achieved in training self-care behavior using successive approximation technics (Mazik and Macnamara 1967, Minge and Ball 1967).

Lazarus and Abramovitz (1962) successfully employed "emotive imagery" with a variety of phobic children. In this procedure, considered by them to be a variant of systematic desensitization (Wolpe 1958), children are asked to imagine stories that engender a highly positive affective response. The feared events are then gradually woven into the story in accordance with a previously established anxiety hierarchy. Related procedures can be found in reports by Lazarus, Davison, and Polefka (1965), Obler and Terwilliger (1970), and Guralnick (1973).

EDUCABILITY

The educability of high-grade defectives has been successfully demonstrated in many studies. Greene (1966) has exhaustively reviewed the unpublished as well as the published work. Programmed instruction technics to teach the basic skills of reading, writing, spelling, and arithmetic are rapidly evolving (Bannatyne 1974). Bijou et al. (1966) reviews and outlines the procedures and problems involved in developing instructional materials and their use with mental defectives. Hewett et al. (1967) derived a teaching-machine approach together with individual teacher instruction in a reading program for brain-damaged, retarded, and disturbed children. Drabman and Spitalnik (1973) trained a retarded child as a behavioral teaching assistant. In this study, Hector, a 14-year-old boy with an IQ of 42, distributed candy reinforcers to the best-behaved pupils in a class for the severely retarded. Hector's appropriate behavior increased when he was reinforced for serving as a helper, and the target children behaved more acceptably through the behavior modification program even though the reinforcers were delivered by a peer.

TRAINABILITY

Defectives are not only more modifiable and educable than previously believed, they are also trainable or employable. This is borne out by the fact that most defectives are never institutionalized. When left to their own devices, they often can function in society. Studies carried out by Tizard and O'Connor (1952), O'Connor and Tizard (1956), and Loos and Tizard (1955) specified precisely the reasons for the previous failures in attempts to train defectives. O'Connor and Tizard (1956) state, ''At least two-thirds and probably four-fifths of those who might on IQ score be classed as feebleminded can live in financial and social independence under present economic circumstances'' (p. 130).

ORGANIC BRAIN SYNDROME

All treatment methods discussed in this chapter also apply to what clinicians have called brain disorders involving defects of the cerebral cortex and central nervous system, or ''organic brain syndromes.'' Whether the damaged or impaired tissue is a result of infections (meningitis, pneumonia, syphilis), ingestion of toxic substances (drugs, poisons, alcohol), trauma (head injury due to accidents, war, surgery), circulatory disturbance (arterial hypertension, cerebral embolism), convulsive disorder, metabolic disturbance, cancer, aging, poor nutrition, degenerative disease (such as Huntington's chorea, Parkinson's disease, Alzheimer's disease and Pick's disease), or genetic defect, after physical treatment has taken place, the therapist must train the individual to make the most of his abilities even if these abilities are genuinely reduced. Psychotherapy involves modifying the behavior; the etiology of the deficiency or organic impairment is superfluous at this point. Treatment is a function of the behavior manifested, not of its cause.

HYPNOTHERAPY

McCord (1956, 1956–1957) finds that mentally retarded children are readily hypnotized; good intelligence is not an important requisite for hypnotizability. Rather, these children are uneducated and really have never been taught how to learn; IQ tests are not indicative of their learning capacity; and many generalizations about "intelligence" do not apply to the mentally retarded child. Hypnosis, by increasing motivation, convinces the child that he can learn more than was anticipated; thus, the child's self-concept is altered and healthier attitudes are developed. Erickson (1963) describes therapeutic gains in a case of organic brain damage using hypnotically oriented psychotherapy. Eliseo (1974) reports 3 examples of hypnosis in the treatment of organic brain damage (brain psychoses) using hypnotically oriented psychotherapy. Short-term hypnotherapy using a direct authoritative approach resulted in better orientation to time and place, less confusion, some pain relief, and ability to achieve a level of self-hypnosis for two patients with cerebral cancer. The other patient, who had an undetermined organic psychosis, benefited from an indirect technic that avoided direct suggestion and emphasized the patient's control of her thinking and bodily reactions. She was able to control anxiety and delusional thinking. It has been our experience that hypnosis can prove very beneficial in the treatment of the mental defective, since it increases his ability to concentrate and to perform both simple and complex tasks through selective attention and lengthening of the attention span. Kroger (1963) noted this in treating cerebral palsy patients; they each had a low IQ. Barber (1960) and Leuba (1960) have suggested that hypnotic phenomena largely depend on the subject's ability to be selectively attentive. Selective attention in listening is defined by Moray (1969) as, "the ability of a listener, whether human or animal, to process only part of the information which he receives, and to ignore the rest." Barber (1960) suggests, "during an hypnotic experiment, the 'good' subject carries out a unique type of behavior; he becomes and remains selectively attentive, thinking about and responsive to cues emanating from the hypnotist (and concomitantly becomes and remains selectively inattentive, not-thinking-about, and unresponsive to other symbolic or concrete stimuli)." There has been much debate in hypnosis literature as to whether the hypnotic induction produces a condition of "diffuse" attention or "selective" attention. Krippner and Bindler (1974) conclude, "either condition can be produced, depending on the set, level of arousal, individual differences, type of task to be performed, type of instructions, etc." The selective attention produced by hypnosis has also proven beneficial in the treatment of the "disturbed" attention of schizophrenics. The following cases illustrate the authors' use of hypnosis with the mentally retarded:

A mentally retarded boy of 12 showed improvement in learning after instruction in autohypnosis. After reading a page, he induced self-hypnosis to "see" an after-image of what he had read. This enabled him to develop a "photographic mind,'' and with repeated posthypnotic suggestions his learning subsequently improved.

A 14-year-old boy was trained to utilize time distortion for speeding up his learning ability. This resulted in an observable increase in learning. Here, too, autohypnosis was employed. His mother had divorced her husband when the child was 6. She continually berated the boy so that he had never really been encouraged to study. The psychometric evaluation indicated a lack of confidence in himself rather than a marked learning deficit.

McCord (1956) reported on a series of "mongoloid-type" subjects with IQs under 40. In addition to bringing about increased motivation to learn, vocational motivation, and a lengthening of the attention span, hypnosis was believed to be of possible help in controlling perseverative excitement, including relaxation and relief of insomnia (McCord 1956–1957).

Uhr's (1958) excellent review of the effects of hypnosis on learning indicates that the results are inconclusive. However, the clinical observations overwhelmingly show definite and possibly striking improvements in learning. Other experiments indicate an improvement in learning from 2 to 40 per cent when time distortion (specifically, time condensation) was employed. The consensus of opinion from Uhr's studies indicates that "suggestion" or "motivation" or "attention" may well prove to be the crucial variable, with the hypnosis merely potentiating these factors. This view is in keeping with what is known about hypnosis.

We have found that retardates respond particularly well to sensory-imagery technics as a means of inducing and deepening the hypnotic state. As with children, images as described in Chapter 10 serve to catch and maintain their attention, whereas other inductions such as counting and instruction for progressive relaxation do not involve them sufficiently. Once their attention is directed, it can be developed and lengthened to increase their intellectual performance and general adaptation. In conclusion, as Ullman and Krasner (1969) point out,

> A first crucial point is that while genetic and physiological endowment may set limits on ultimate repertoires and speed of acquisition, the retarded individual is responsive to the environment and may be taught, whether his difficulty is physiological or environmental or both. . . . The point to be made is that a defect, even the most severe, does not rule out response to the environment and the alteration of behavior through training (p. 567).

REFERENCES

Allen, K. E. and Harris, R. R.: Elimination of a child's excessive scratching by training the mother in reinforcement procedures. Behav. Res. Ther., *4:*79, 1966.

Axelrod, S.: Token reinforcement programs in special classes. Except. Child., *37:*371, 1971.

Ayllon, T. and Azrin, N. H.: The Token Economy: a Motivational System for Therapy and Rehabilitation. New York, Appleton-Century-Crofts, 1968.

Ball, T.: The establishment and administration of an operant conditioning program in a state hospital for the retarded. Calif. Ment. Health Res. Symp., Dept. of Mental Hygiene, No. 4, 1969.

Baller, W. R.: A study of the present social status of a group of adults who, when they were in elementary schools, were classified as mentally deficient. Genet. Psychol. Monogr., *18:*165, 1936.

Baller, W. R., Charles, D., and Miller, E. L.: Mid-life attainment of the mentally retarded: a longitudinal study. Genet. Psychol. Monogr., *75:*235, 1967.

Bannatyne, A.: Programs, materials, and techniques. J. Learning Disabilities., *7:*1, 1974.

Barber, T. X.: The necessary and sufficient conditions for hypnotic behavior. Amer. J. Clin. Hypn. *3:*31, 1960.

Baumeister, A. and Klosowski, R.: An attempt to group toilet train severely retarded patients. Ment. Retard., *3:*24, 1965.

Bensberg, G. J., Colwell, C. N., and Cassel, R. H.: Teaching the profoundly retarded self-help activities by behavior shaping techniques. Amer. J. Ment. Defic., *69:*674, 1965.

Berkson, G.: Stereotyped movements of mental defectives: VI. No effect of amphetamine or a barbiturate. Percept. Motor Skills, *21:*698, 1965.

Bijou, S. W., Birnbrauer, J. S., Kidder, J. D., and Tague, C.: Programmed instruction as an approach to teaching of reading, writing and arithmetic in retarded children. Psychol. Rec., *16:*505, 1966.

Butterfield, W. H. and Parson, R.: Modeling and shaping by parents to develop chewing behavior in their retarded child. J. Behav. Ther. Exp. Psychiat., *4:*285, 1973.

Charles, D. C.: Abilities and accomplishments of persons earlier judged to be mentally defective. Genet. Psychol. Monogr., *47:*3, 1953.

Dayan, M.: Toilet training retarded children in a state residential institution. *2:*116, 1964.

Drabman, R. and Spitalnik, R.: Training a retarded child as a behavioral teaching assistant. J. Behav. Ther. Exp. Psychiat., *4:*269, 1973.

Eliseo, T. S.: Three examples of hypnosis in the treatment of organic brain syndrome with psychosis. Internat. J. Clin. Exp. Hypn., *22:*9, 1974.

Ellis, N. R.: Toilet training the severely defective patient: an S-R reinforcement analysis. Amer. J. Ment. Defic., *68:*98, 1963.

Erickson, M. H.: Hypnotically oriented psychotherapy in organic brain damage. Amer. J. Clin. Hypn., *6:*92, 1963.

Ferster, C. B.: Positive reinforcement and behavioral deficits of autistic children. Child Development, *32:*437, 1961.

Foxx, R. M. and Azrin, N. H.: Restitution: a method of eliminating aggressive-disruptive behavior of retarded and brain damaged patients. Behav. Res. Ther., *10:*15, 1972.

Friedlander, B. Z., McCarthy, J. J. and Soforenko, A. Z.: Automated psychological evaluation with severely retarded institutionalized infants. Amer. J. Ment. Defic., *71:*909, 1967.

Fuller, P. R.: Operant conditioning of vegetative human organism. Amer. J. Psychol., *62:*587, 1949.

Giles, D. K. and Wolf, M. M.: Toilet training institutionalized severe retardates: an application of operant behavior modification techniques. Amer. J. Ment. Defic., *70:*766, 1966.

Greene, F. M.: Programmed instruction techniques for the mentally retarded. Internat. Rev. Res. Ment. Retard., *2:*209, 1966.

Guralnick, M. J.: Behavior therapy with an acrophobic mentally retarded young adult. J. Behav. Ther. Exp. Psychiat., *4:*263, 1973.

Hamilton, J., Stephens, L., Allen, P.: Controlling aggressive and destructive behavior in severely retarded institutionalized residents. Amer. J. Ment. Defic., *71:*852, 1967.

Henriksen, K. and Doughty, R.: Decelerating undesired mealtime behavior in a group of profoundly retarded boys. Amer. J. Ment. Defic., *72:*40, 1967.

Hewett, F. M., Mayhew, D., and Rabb, E.: An experimental reading program for neurologically impaired, mentally retarded, and severely emotionally disturbed children. Amer. J. Orthopsychiat., *37:*35, 1967.

Hundziak, M., Maurer, R. A., and Watson, L. S.: Operant conditioning in toilet training of severely mentally retarded boys. Amer. J. Ment. Defic.,*2* 70:120, 1965.

Kimbrel, D. L., Luckey, R. E., Barbuto, P. F., and Love, J. G.: Operation dry pants: and intensive habit-training program for severely and profoundly retarded. Mental Retardation, *5:*32, 1967.

Krippner, S. and Bindler, P. R.: Hypnosis and attention: a review. Amer. J. Clin. Hypn., *16:*166, 1974.

Kroger, W. S.: Clinical and Experimental Hypnosis. Philadelphia, J. B. Lippincott, 1963.

Lazarus, A. A. and Abramovitz, A.: The use of "emotive imagery" in the treatment of children's phobias. J. Ment. Sci., *8:*191, 1962.

Lazarus, A. A., Davison, G. C., and Polefka, D. A.: Classical and operant factors in the treatment of a school phobia. J. Abnorm. Psychol., *70:*225, 1965.

Lent, J., LeBlanc, J., and Spradlin, J.: Designing a rehabilitative culture for moderately retarded adolescent girls. *In* Ulrich R., Stachnik T., and Mobry J. (eds.): Control of Human Behavior, Vol. II. Glenview, Ill., Scott, Foreman, 1970.

Leuba, C.: Theories of hypnosis: a critique and a proposal. Amer. J. Clin, Hypn., *3:*43, 1960.

Loos, F. M. and Tizard, J.: The employability of adult imbeciles in a hospital workshop. Amer. J. Ment. Defic., *59:*395, 1955.

Lovaas, O. I., Freitag,, G., Gold, V. J., and Kassorla, I. C.: Experimental studies in childhood schizophrenia: analysis of self-destructive behavior. J. Exp. Child Psychol., *2:*67, 1965.

Lovaas, O. I., Schaffer, B., and Simmons, J. Q.: Building social behavior in autistic children by use of electric shock. J. Exp. Res. Pers., *1:*99, 1965.

Lucero, R. J., Vail, D. J., and Scherber, J.: Regulating operant-conditioning programs. Hosp. Community Psychiat., *19:*53, 1968.

Marshall, G. R.: Toilet training of an autistic eight-year-old through conditioning therapy: a case report. Behav. Res. Ther., *4:*242, 1966.

Mazik, K. and Macnamara, R.: Operant conditioning at the training school. Training School Bull., *63:*153, 1967.

McCord, H.: The hypnotizability of the mongoloid-type child. J. Clin. Exp. Hypn., *4:*19, 1956.

———: Hypnotizing the mentally retarded child. Brit. J. Med. Hypn., *8:*17, 1956–57.

Minge, M. R. and Ball, T. S.: Teaching of self-help skills to profoundly retarded patients. Amer. J. Ment. Defic., *71:*864, 1967.

Miron, N. B.: Behavior shaping and group nursing with severely retarded patients. *In* Fisher, J. and Harris, R. E. (eds.): Reinforcement Theory in Psychological Treatment—A symposium. California Mental Health Res. Monogr., *8:*1, 1966.

Moray, N.: Listening and Attention. Middlesex, England, Penguin Books, 1969.

Obler, M. and Terwilliger, R. F.: Pilot study of the effectiveness of systematic desensitization with neurologically impaired children with phobic disorders. J. Consult. Clin. Psychol., *34:*314, 1970.

O'Connor, N. and Tizard, J.: The Social Problem of Mental Deficiency. London, Pergamon, 1956.

O'Leary, K. and Drabman, R.: Token reinforcement programs in the classroom: a review. Psychol. Bull., *75:*379, 1971.

Peterson, R. F. and Peterson, L. R.: The use of positive reinforcement in the control of self-destructive behavior in a retarded boy. J. Exp. Child Psychol., *6:*351, 1968.

Rice, H. K. and McDaniel, M. W.: Operant behavior in vegetative patients. Psychol. Rec., *16:*279, 1966.

Rice, H. H., McDaniel, M. W., Stallings, V. D., and Gatz, M. J.: Operant behavior in vegetative patients: II. Psychol. Rec., *17:*449, 1967.

Ross, D. M. and Ross, S.: Storage and utilization of previously formulated mediators in educable mentally retarded children. J. Educat. Psychol., *65:*205, 1973.

Rudy, L. H., Himwich, H. E., and Rinaldi, F.: A clinical evaluation of psychopharmacological agents in the management of disturbed mentally defective patients. Amer. J. Ment. Defic., *62:*855, 1958.

Saposnek, D. T.: An experimental study of rage-reduction treatment of autistic children. Child Psychiat. Human Devel., *3:*50, 1972.

Saposnek, D. T., and Watson, L. S., Jr.: The elimination of the self-destructive behavior of a psychotic child: a case study. Behav. Ther., *5:*79, 1974.

Simmons, J. Q., Tymchuk, A. J., and Valente, M.: Treatment and care of the mentally retarded. Psychiat. Annals, *4:*38, 1974.

Spradlin, J. E. and Giradeau, F. L.: The behavior of moderately and severely retarded persons. Internat. Rev. Res. Ment. Retard., *1:*257, 1966.

Tarjan, G. and Keeran, C. B.: An overview of mental retardation. Psychiat. Annals, *4:*6, 1974.

Tizard, J. and O'Connor, N.: The occupational adaptation of high-grade mental defectives. Lancet, *2:*620, 1952.

Tymchuk, A.: Token economy and motivating environment for mildly retarded adolescent boys. Men. Retard., *2:*8, 1971.

Uhr, L.: Learning under hypnosis: what do we know? What should we know? J. Clin. Exp. Hypn., *6:*121, 1958.

Ullmann, L. P., and Krasner, L.: A Psychological Approach to Abnormal Behavior. Englewood Cliffs, Prentice-Hall, 1969.

Valente, M. and Tarjan, G.: Etiologic factors in mental retardation. Psychiat. Annals, *4:*22, 1974.

Wayne, M. F. and Melnyr, W. T.: Toilet training of a blind retarded boy by operant conditioning. J. Behav. Ther. Exp. Psychiat., *4:*267, 1973.

Webster, D. R. and Azrin, N. H.: Required relaxation: a method of inhibiting agitative-disruptive behavior of retardates. Behav. Res. Ther., *11:*67, 1973.

Whitney, L. R. and Barnard, K. E.: Implications of operant learning theory for nursing care of the retarded child. Ment. Retard., *4:*26, 1966.

Wiessen, A. E. and Watson, E.: Elimination of attention seeking behavior in a retarded child. Amer. J. Ment. Defic., *72:*50, 1967.

Wolf, M., Risley, T., and Mees, H.: Application of operant conditioning procedures to the behavior problems of an autistic child. Behav. Res. Ther., *1:*305, 1964.

Wolpe, J.: Psychotherapy by Reciprocal Inhibition. Stanford, Stanford University Press, 1958.

Yates, A. J.: Behavior Therapy. New York, John Wiley & Sons, 1970.

Zaslow, R. W. and Breger, L.: A theory and treatment of autism. *In* Breger L. (ed.): Clinical-Cognitive Psychology: Models and Integration. pp. 246–291. Englewood Cliffs, Prentice-Hall, 1969.

Zeiler, M. D. and Jervey, S. S.: Development of behavior: self-feeding. J. Consult. Clin. Psychol., *32:*164, 1968.

SUGGESTED READINGS

Astrup, C., Sersen, E. A., and Wortis, J.: Conditional reflex studies in mental retardation: a review. Amer. J. Ment. Defic., *71:*513, 1967.

Belmont, J. M.: Long-term memory in mental retardation. Internat. Rev. Res. Ment. Retard., *1:*219, 1966.

Crandall, B. F.: Genetic counseling and mental retardation. Psychiatric Annals, *4:*70, 1974.

Drabman, R., Spitalnik, R., Hugamen, M., and Van Witsen, B.: The five-two program: an integrated approach to treating severely disturbed children. Hosp. Community Psychiat., *24:*33, 1973.

Erickson, M. H.: Hypnotically oriented psychotherapy in organic brain disease: an addendum. Amer. J. Clin. Hypn., *6:*361, 1964.

Feldshuh, B., Sillen, J., Parker, B., and Frosch, W.: The nonpsychotic organic brain syndrome. Amer. J. Psychiat., *130:*1026, 1973.

Fraas, L. A. Intentional and incidental learning: a developmental and comparative approach. J. Ment. Deficiency Res., *17:*129, 1973.

Gardner, W.: Behavior Modification in Mental Retardation. New York, Aldine-Atherton, 1971.

Heath, E. S., Stratas, N. E., and Davis, D. F.: Hypnotizability in senile and arteriosclerotic chronic brain syndromes. Dis. Nerv. Syst., *23:*23–24, 1962.

Jacobson, L. J., Bernal, G., and Lopez, G. N.: Effects of behavioral training on the functioning of a profoundly retarded microcephalic teenager with cerebral palsy and without language or verbal comprehension. Behav. Res. Ther., *11:*143, 1973.

Martin, J. A. and Iagulli, D. M.: Elimination of middle-of-the-night tantrums in a blind, retarded child. Behav. Ther., *5:*420, 1974.

Ribes-Inestra, E., Duran, L., Evans, B., Felix, G., Rivera, G., and Sanchez, S.: An experimental evaluation of tokens as conditioned reinforcers in retarded children. Behav. Res. Ther., *11:*125, 1973.

Ross, L. E.: Classical conditioning and discrimination learning research with the mentally retarded. Internat. Rev. Res. Ment. Retard., *1:*21, 1966.

Rubin, B. K. and Stolz, S. B.: Generalization of self-referent speech established in a retarded adolescent by operant procedures. Behav. Ther., *5:*93, 1974.

Sternlicht, M. and Wanderer, Z. W.: Hypnotic susceptibility and mental deficiency. Int. J. Clin. Exper. Hypn., *11:*104–111, 1963.

Surratt, P., Azrin, H. H., and Sulzer, B.: Maintenance of appropriate eating behavior with profoundly retarded adults. J. Appl. Behav. Anal., 1972.

Young, J. A. and Wincze, J. P.: The effects of the reinforcement of compatible and incompatible alternative behaviors on the self-injurious and related behaviors of a profoundly retarded female adult. Behav. Ther., *5:*614, 1974.

PART SIX

Psychosomatic Disorders

30

Asthma and Allergy

ETIOLOGIC FACTORS

There is extensive literature on the psychogenic aspects of asthma (Dunbar 1938, French and Alexander 1941, Vaughan 1939). Characteristically, these patients suppress intense emotions that involve threats to their dependent relationships or deprivation and insecurity induced by conflicts. As children, they are anxiety-ridden, lacking in confidence, and dependent to an extreme degree. The literature on bronchial asthma is extensive, and behavior therapists have barely scratched its surface. Freeman et al. (1964) provide a very thorough review of the psychological literature on allergic disorders, including bronchial asthma. Edwards (1964) has reviewed the effects of hypnosis on asthma. Search for the "asthmatic personality" has been generally unfruitful, so attention in this chapter is directed to the question of whether asthma can reasonably be conceptualized, in part at least, as a conditioned response.

Models of asthma as a conditioned response have been proposed by Turnbull (1962) and Moore (1965). That conditioning does play a role in bronchial asthma has been shown in studies by Dekker and Groen (1956) and Dekker, Pelser, and Groen (1957). Dekker and Groen (1956) stress the frequent relationship between the onset of asthma and a traumatic experience. Dekker et al. (1957) conditioned an asthmatic attack directly in 2 subjects by pairing neutral stimuli (neutral solvent, oxygen) with inhalation of nebulized allergens to which the subjects were known to be highly sensitive. Conditioning occurred both to the postulated neutral stimuli and to the sight and feel of the glass tube.

BEHAVIOR MODIFICATION TECHNICS

Deconditioning or treatment of asthma has been reported by Walton (1960) using covert systematic desensitization in the form of assertive training in social situations that precipitated the attacks. In a case in which the precipitating situations appeared more diffuse, Cooper (1964) used relaxation training coupled with desensitization, beginning with relaxation alone and then gradually introducing suggestions of anxiety and panic. Moore (1965), by using hierarchies related to an asthmatic attack, an allergic attack, and a psychological stress situation, concluded that desensitization combined with relaxation is effective in reducing breathing difficulties in bronchial asthma. Lyons et al. (1968) report that they were able to induce asthma in 19 of 40 patients suffering from respiratory disease by deliberately tricking them into believing that they had been breathing such allergenic agents as dust, pollen, or animal dander. These patients actually had breathed air containing non-irritating salt water mist, yet they reacted as if the allergens had been present. When the patients who developed asthma were then led to believe that they were to be given a remedy for asthma, which in fact was the same salt water mist, the condition of all the patients improved, indicating that beneficial effects might be just as much associated with a state of mind as might be the disease itself. Cautela (1968) successfully used behavior therapy on older patients with asthma and other lung conditions.

While all the studies described above used covert desensitization, Herxheimer and Prior (1952) describe a method they call hyposensitization, which includes an overt paradigm that can be used in the treatment of asthma:

> When the patient had been accustomed to breathing with the spirometer and to recording a stable vital capacity, he received through the breathing circuit for an arbitrary short period the aerosolized allergen extract to which, according to his history or to his skin tests, he was suspected to be sensitive. If no attack occurred, the inhalation time for the next test was increased by 50 per cent 3 to 7 days later. If a mild attack developed, the inhalation time of the next occasion was increased by 20 to 30 per cent. If the attack was moderate or severe, the inhalation time was dramatically reduced at the next sitting; this was repeated until either no attack or a mild attack was produced (Herxheimer and Prior 1952, p. 190).

This technic parallels Wolpe's systematic desensitization technic, except that it involves "real" and not "imaginary" desensitization. A fivefold increase in tolerance was shown by 27 per cent of the patients (N=27). They could tolerate five times the shortest inhalation time that had formerly caused an attack without having one. These patients remained symptom-free in spite of exposure to the allergen. About 27 per cent more showed increased tolerance and relative freedom from attacks. Beware of accidental hypersensitization by overexposure when using this technic.

HYPNOTHERAPY

The British Tuberculosis Association (1968) compared hypnosis with the teaching of breathing exercises combined with bodily relaxation. Kellner (1975) reviewed the extensive data and concluded that these studies showed several differences in outcome between patients treated with hypnosis and those treated by other methods. In the second study, good results were achieved in spite of one-half of the physicians having been inexperienced in hypnosis; moreover, patients in the control groups in both studies were given treatments that are believed to be effective. In the first study, a new effective bronchodilator was prescribed with the suggestion that the new treatment would be helpful, and, in the second study, the patients in the control group were treated with breathing exercises, relaxation, and, probably inadvertently, suggestion was also employed.

Hypnotic suggestions combined with pharmacotherapy apparently had beneficial effects on the course of bronchial asthma. This effect appeared to be more noticeable in patients who were good hypnotic subjects; the results were somewhat better with female patients and when the treatment was carried out by experienced hypnotists. Much work on the use of hypnosis in asthma done by Kroger (1964), Bohnert (1965), Brown (1967), Rose (1967), and Moore (1967) yielded evidence that hypnosis and systematic desensitization were of considerable value in the treatment of asthma. Moorefield (1971) demonstrated improvement in all but 1 of 9 asthma patients, using a combination of hypnosis and systematic desensitization. During hypnosis, the interrelationship between the emotions and the autonomic nervous system was stressed; that is, how, under tension, the autonomic nervous system causes constriction of the bronchi with increased secretions. Also stressed was the observation that, as the ability to breathe increases, tension and anxiety lessens and confidence grows as a function of the depth of the hypnosis.

Earlier, Maher-Loughman et al. (1962) carried out a controlled study of hypnosis in adult asthmatics over 6 months. The 55 patients who completed hypnotherapy had a significant reduction in wheezing and need for bronchodilators. Those who were easy to hypnotize achieved the best results, whereas those who were difficult achieved the least. Patients who only went into a light stage of hypnosis showed poor results, whereas those who were able to attain medium or deep hypnosis showed distinct improvement. Significantly, patients who readily mastered autohypnosis did still better.

Numerous therapists have treated asthma with hypnoanalysis (Ambrose and Newbold 1958, Magonet 1960, Marchesi 1949, Raginsky 1960, Rosen 1953, Van Pelt 1949). Abreaction under hypnosis may reduce attacks of status asthmaticus. For chronic cases of asthma, autohypnosis together with steroids and evocation of conflicts is often helpful. Asthmatics who became "adrenalin-fast'' have been relieved by hypnotherapy directed toward understanding the responsible psychogenic factors (Raginsky 1960).

In children afflicted with asthma, it has been reported that in a control series, reassurance by psychotherapy was slower and less certain in its effects than hypnotherapy (Magonet 1960). In both series, parents had to be treated concurrently. Parents can be taught to give suggestions to neutralize the anxiety-provoking situations. Reinforcement suggestions under hypnosis are usually necessary long after recovery has occurred. Perloff and Spiegelman (1973) used hypnosis in a child's allergy to dogs. Smith and Burns (1960) carried out a controlled study of hypnosis on asthmatic children and they did not find it effective. However, the children in this study had long-standing illnesses and received only a few hypnotic sessions. For adults, a superficial uncovering type of hypnotherapy often is successful. Prolonged sleep can alleviate severe asthmatic attacks. The authors use relaxation to regulate breathing and train all patients in sensory-imagery conditioning. About 60 per cent of carefully selected cases can be helped by these methods.

MacLaren and Eisenberg (1960) studied a group of 50 carefully selected asthmatics who showed no response to medical therapy and who had overt signs of emotional instability. Hostile, skeptical individuals or those who had advanced lung disease were rejected. They noted that if suggestions directed toward the patient's breathing in unison with the operator's counting was followed, the breathing soon became slower and quieter. Strong suggestions for relaxing the chest usually eliminated breathing difficulties. Sensory-imagery conditioning that involved relaxing experiences were employed. Posthypnotic suggestions that the bronchial tubes were opening helped relax the breathing. Scene-visualization technics oriented around the patient's seeing himself in a protected and comfortable position were most effective.

Their results, however, showed a high number of relapses brought about by exposure to a strong antigen or respiratory infection. In the emotionally disturbed asthmatics, stress precipitated severe attacks. They concluded that for more lasting results, threats to the individual's emotional stability had to be uncovered, or the person's fears of such threats had to be corrected by psychotherapy.

When fear of choking, which is commonly noted in these patients, was neutralized by reassurance and relaxed breathing exercises, 75 per cent of the relapsed patients improved. Others were asked to ventilate their emotions prior to the attacks. Using an abreactive technic, the therapists had their patients relive anxiety-provoking situations, but without affect. One in eight could not be hypnotized readily, and one in three could be hypnotized but received little if any benefit. Two out of three obtained relief, varying from temporary to sustained effects.

Many deaths occur with steroids (Clarkson 1937), and this alone makes the assessment of the potentialities of hypnosis more rather than less urgent. Edwards (1960) reports that hypnosis worked either by decreasing airway resistance or by a psychological effect (decreased awareness of airway resistance). The expiratory phase in human beings is particularly "overloaded" because it underlies the entire complex of speech; hence, breathing is the first manifestation of suffering. The involvement expresses itself as an alteration in the tonus of the smooth muscles of the bronchi.

Another report extolled the dramatic saving of an elderly man's life by hypnosis (for a severe case of status asthmaticus, [Sinclair-Gieben 1960]). Other observations deserve mention: typical attacks of bronchial asthma were produced hypnotically, and the attacks thus provoked were immediately terminated by appropriate hypnotic suggestions. This indicates that bronchial asthma results from a conditioned reflex to harmful external and internal stimulation.

The reader should not infer that our results are always as dramatic as the following cases.

> A 42-year-old male who had failed to respond to cortisone and psychoanalysis was cured in several sessions. The patient was induced into somnambulism on the first visit. It was suggested that any time that he felt an attack coming on, he would induce autohypnosis. While in this state, he was to re-experience an actual relaxing episode from the past. Much to the patient's surprise (as well as the authors'), he was promptly relieved of all symptoms such as wheezing, coughing, and choking sensations. It is possible that his bronchial manifestations may have been a conversion-hysteria reaction and, as such, dramatically responded to a "magical gesture." This patient was seen over a period of 3 years, and no significant relapses occurred. It is conceivable that his exaggerated response to tension and anxiety (later a marital conflict was uncovered) was due to a conditioned autonomic excitability. The hypnosis interrupted the conditioned pattern, and the subsequent superficial psychotherapy under sensory-imagery conditioning served to reinforce the apparent cure.

> Even more dramatic was the case of a 78-year-old woman who was seen by us in consultation at a distant hospital. This patient was in an oxygen tent and was in extremis; coarse râles were audible in the hospital corridor. Hypnosis, autohypnosis, and sensory-imagery conditioning were taught to her at the first session, which lasted 4 hours. Immediately the labored breathing subsided and râles were no longer heard except by stethoscopic examination. She was removed from the oxygen tent and, much to the surprise of her four consultants, she left the hospital the next day. She was "cued" to respond to posthypnotic suggestions over the telephone because she lived in another city. This patient has been seen monthly during the past year and there has been no return of her symptoms. She also lost 35 pounds with a dietary and hypnotic approach. When last seen, she was quite active for a person of her years, very happy and looking forward to a useful life. No attempt was made to understand her personality difficulties, and not even superficial exploration was attempted.

There may be an asthma potential or a building up of emotional tension which may modify the allergic mechanisms responsible for some asthmatics. Or they may precipitate asthma by means of a central nervous system control of bronchiolar function. A physiologic mechanism is also posited, such as a deficiency or blockade in the beta-adrenergic system, which interacts with the parasympathetic and immune systems (Knapp 1975).

The slower, deeper, and more regular breathing that ensues from hypnorelaxation is beneficial in controlling asthma attacks. Hypnotic imagery, such as Image II (mountain cabin), involving deep breathing of "cool, clean, fresh, crisp, pure" air with resultant overwhelming relaxation of the rib cage is good for conditioning proper breathing. The hypnotic recall of undisturbed, allergy-free breathing will, in time, produce this type of breathing.

Our experience indicates that hypnosis, imagery conditioning, and behavior modification therapy reduces anxiety, decreases effects of destructive emotions, and raises the threshold for offending allergens and other factors that precipitate asthma. Hippocrates was probably right when he said that asthmatics must guard against strong anger.

ALLERGY

Psychogenic factors certainly play an important role in precipitating allergic as well as asthmatic manifestations. The "rose asthma" case is a typical example. In 1881, an asthmatic woman was exposed to a paper rose under glass. Her eyes watered, her nose ran, and she began to wheeze. This experiment recently was repeated with careful pulmonary measurements. When it was suggested, "You are breathing in something that gives you asthma," over 50 per cent of subjects showed a definite increase in airway resistance. Some cases developed wheezing attacks.

Allergic reactions are frequently associated with stress. Urticaria can be precipitated by traumatic life situations. There are significant differences between acute and chronic urticaria; specific allergens are not present in the latter. Hypnosis has been employed to prevent asthmatic attacks in individuals susceptible to certain allergens even though skin tests remained positive. Attacks were produced when these patients were shown an artificial flower or a picture of one. Wheals resulting from a cutaneous reaction to eggs have been suppressed by hypnosis. Though not confirmed, it has been concluded that hypnotic suggestions, to some degree, influence cutaneous allergic reactions.

The above data indicate that injections (widely used) may help because of a placebo effect. Lowell (1960) believes that the rationale for injection therapy has not been validated to exclude coincidental factors, chance, or bias. He states:

> We cannot rule out the possibility of a happy coincidence—the initiation of treatment in a year of less intense exposure to pollen, instruction in allergic cleanliness and in the intelligent use of drugs, the allaying of anxiety, the spontaneous lessening of the patient's level of clinical sensitivity and, last but by no means least, the suggestion that accompanies the ritual of injection therapy. These, individually or in combination, might explain many a success without invoking any

specific therapeutic or prophylactic merit for the solution that we put into the syringe.

REFERENCES

Ambrose, G., and Newbold, G.: A Handbook of Medical Hypnosis. London, Baillière, Tindall and Cox, 1958.

Bohnert, P.: A review of the concepts of hypnosis. Paper given at the Eighth Annual Scientific Meeting of the Amer. Soc. Clin. Hypn., Chicago, 1965.

Brown, E. A.: Hypnosis in the treatment of bronchial asthma. Paper given at the Tenth Annual Meeting of the Amer. Soc. Clin. Hypn., New York City, 1967.

Cautela, J. R.: Use of behavior therapy. Paper given at the A.P.A. Meeting in San Francisco, 1968.

Clarkson, A. K.: The nervous factor in juvenile asthma. Brit. Med. J., *2:*845, 1937.

Cooper, A. J.: A case of bronchial asthma treated by behavior therapy. Behav. Res. Ther., *1:*351, 1964.

Dekker, E. and Groen, J.: Reproducible psychogenic attacks of asthma: a laboratory study. J. Psychosom. Res., *1:*58, 1956.

Dekker, E., Pelser, H. E., and Groen, J.: Conditioning as a cause of asthmatic attacks. J. Psychosom. Res., *2:*97, 1957.

Dunbar, H. F.: Emotions and Bodily Changes. New York, Columbia Univ. Press, 1938.

Edwards, G.: Hypnotic treatment of asthma. Brit. Med. J., *2:*492, 1960.

————: The hypnotic treatment of asthma. *In* Eysenck, H. J. (ed.): Experiments in Behavior Therapy. pp. 407–431. London, Pergamon, 1964.

Freeman, E. H., Feingold, B. F., Schlesinger, K., and Gorman, E. J.: Psychological variables in allergic disorders: a review. Psychosom. Med., *26:*543, 1964.

French, T., and Alexander, F.: Psychogenic factors in bronchial asthma. Psychosom. Med. Monog., *2:*34, 1941.

Herxheimer, H. and Prior, F. N.: Further observations on induced asthma and bronchial hyposensitization. Internat. Arch. Allergy and Appl. Immunol., *3:*189, 1952.

Kellner, R.: Psychotherapy in psychosomatic disorders. Arch. Gen. Psychiat., *32:*1021, 1975.

Kroger, W. S.: Current status of hypnosis in allergy. Annals of Allergy, *22:*123, 1964.

Lowell, F. C.: American Academy of Allergy: Presidential Address. J. Allergy, *31:*185, 1960.

Lyons, H. A., McFadden, C. R., Lupanello, T., and Bleecher, E. R.: Emotions in asthma. Reported at Am. Coll. of Physicians, Boston, 1968.

MacLaren, W. R. and Eisenberg, B. C.: Hypnosis in the treatment of asthma. Paper read at the Pan American Med. Assoc., May 5, 1960.

Magonet, A. P.: Hypnosis and asthma. Internat. J. Clin. Exp. Hypn., *8:*121, 1960.

Maher-Loughnan, G. P. et al.: Controlled trial of hypnosis in the symptomatic treatment of asthma. Brit. Med. J., *2:*371, 1962.

Marchesi, C.: The hypnotic treatment of bronchial asthma. Brit. J. Med. Hypn., *1:*14, 1949.

Moore, N.: Behavior therapy in bronchial asthma: a controlled study. J. Psychosom. Res., *9:*257, 1965.

————: Behavior therapy in bronchial asthma. J. Psychosom. Res., *9:*257, 1967.

Moorefield, C. W.: The use of hypnosis and behavior therapy in asthma. Amer. J. Clin. Hypn., *13:* 162, 1971.

Perloff, M. M. and Spiegelman, J.: Hypnosis in the treatment of a child's allergy to dogs. Amer. J. Clin. Hypn., *15:*269, 1973.

Raginsky, B. B.: The use of hypnosis in internal medicine. Presented at Pan Amer. Med. Ass., May, 1960.

Rose, S.: A general practitioner approach to the asthmatic patient. Amer. J. Clin. Hypn., *10:* 30, 1967.

Rosen, H.: Hypnotherapy in Clinical Psychiatry. New York, Julian Press, 1953.

Sinclair-Gieben, A. H.: Treatment of status asthmaticus by hypnosis. Brit. Med. J., *2:*1651, 1960.

Smith, J. M. and Burns, C. L.: The treatment of asthmatic children by hypnotic suggestion. Brit. J. Dis. Chest., *54:* 78, 1960.

Turnbull, J. W.: Asthma conceived as a learned response. J. Psychosom. Res., *6:*59, 1962.

Van Pelt, S. J.: Hypnotherapy in medical practice. Brit. J. Med. Hypn., *1:*8, 1949.

Vaughan, W. T.: Practice of Allergy, St. Louis, C. V. Mosby, 1939.

Walton, D.: The application of learning theory to the treatment of a case of bronchial asthma. *In* Eysenck, H. J. (ed.): Behavior Therapy and the Neuroses. pp. 188–189. Oxford, Pergamon, 1960.

SUGGESTED READINGS

Bartlett, K. A.: Hypnotic treatment of a novocaine allergy. Amer. J. Clin. Hypn., *12:*222, 1970.

British Tuberculosis Association: Hypnosis for asthma. A controlled trial. Report of the research committee of the British Tuberculosis Association. *4:*71–76, 1968.

Brown, E. A.: The treatment of bronchial asthma as viewed by the allergist. J. Asthma. Res., *3:*101–119, 1965.

Collisom, D. R.: Hypnotherapy in the management of asthma. Am. J. Clin. Hypn., *11:*6–11, 1968.

Hanley, F. W.: Individualized hypnotherapy of asthma. Am. J. Clin. Hypn., *16:*280–285, 1974.

Sutton, P. H.: A trial of group hypnosis and autohypnosis in asthmatic children. Brit. J. Clin. Hypn., *1:*11–14, 1969.

31

Dermatological Disorders

The role of emotional factors in cutaneous disorders has been described by numerous authors (Rothman 1945, Sulzberger and Zaidens 1948, Wittkower and Russell 1953). The nervous system apparently is capable of directing repressed emotional forces to appropriate target organs. The site selected is determined by a local tissue vulnerability plus a correlation between the nature of the emotional stimulus and the type of physiological response. Why the skin lesions vary with the type of conflict, and from person to person, appearing and disappearing during the life span of the same person is, at present, poorly understood.

The skin mirrors the inner self. It is richly endowed with emotional symbolism. Such expressions as "thick-skinned" and "thin-skinned" may mean "insensitive" and "sensitive," respectively. "To get under my skin" and "itching to do something" are common expressions; if the latter is not carried out, it may lead to actual itching and scratching. The epidermis and the nervous system originate from the ectoderm and, since both are nurtured by a mesenchymal derivative composed of vascular connective tissue, it is only logical to assume that there is interaction between the skin and the autonomic nervous system.

NEURODERMATITIS

One of the most common disorders is neurodermatitis. That there is such a disorder at all, which can be correlated with emotional upsets, strongly implicates emotional factors. Numerous remedies have been suggested. However, no specific therapy is available (Van Scott and Farber 1971). An operant approach was described by Walton (1960). Scratching was extinguished in a chronic case. Those close to the patient were told to ignore her condition. When she no longer received reinforcement in the form of attention, the problem subsided.

HYPNOTHERAPY

Zhukov (1961) illustrated the effects of hypnosis in a large series of cases versus a control group. Long-term follow-up showed substantial improvement over the controls. Horan (1950) and Twerski and Naar (1974) noted that hypnosis significantly improved chronic neurodermatitis.

> Mrs. R. L., aged 44, was referred to us with an acute neurodermatitis of the neck, involving the upper portion of the chest and the back. The patient was refractory to all medicaments. Glove anesthesia was employed for relief of the intractable itching. Posthypnotic directions were given for the patient to feel sensations of warmth and coldness over the involved areas. Direct suggestion for improvement in her skin was not given at any time. The neurodermatitis had developed immediately after her daughter had announced her engagement to a young man of another faith; this upset Mrs. R. L. terribly. The daughter was referred to a psychiatrist in an attempt to delay the marriage; she was able to work through her feelings toward the young man and finally decided it would not be feasible to marry him. The mother's neurodermatitis promptly improved. However, during the period that her daughter was receiving psychotherapy, hypnosis afforded Mrs. R. L. considerable relief from her itching, nervous tension, and anxiety. Hypnotherapy was employed only as an adjunctive procedure.

PSORIASIS

Reference has been made to the importance of psychological factors in the precipitation of skin disorders, including aggravation of psoriasis (Dunbar 1943, Wittkower (1946), Weiss and English 1949, Obermeyer 1955, Farber, Poissant 1963, Bright and Nall 1968). We could not find references to use of behavior therapy for psoriasis.

HYPNOTHERAPY

However, there are several reports on the effectiveness of hypnosis (Kline 1954, 1958, Zhukov 1961, Bethune and Kidd 1961, Luthe and Schultz 1969, Frankel and Misch 1973). In most cases success was obtained by sensory imagery to produce such altered changes in the skin as hot or cold and/or constriction or expansion of the psoriatic lesions. The purpose of these suggestions was to experience different or comforting sensations. Frankel and Misch (1973) describe a case in which the sensory imagery under hypnosis was selected to replicate a real-life experience that had been beneficial to the patient's condition in the past.

Under hypnosis, a 37-year-old man suffering from widespread psoriasis was given suggestions to revivify feelings experienced in his skin when sunbathing—an activity which had always cleared up the lesions in the past. The patient practiced self-hypnosis 5 or 6 times a day for a few minutes each time and the psoriatic lesions markedly improved.

A permissive hypnotic technic was described by Kline (1954). Kline's sensory-imagery technic for psoriasis is as follows: During light hypnosis the patient was told that she would be able to feel warm and cold sensations throughout the body. After this was accomplished, she was instructed to feel sensations of heaviness, lightness, constriction, and expansion in all the areas of her body where she had the psoriasis. Then she was told to feel warm and cold sensations only in the lesions. This was followed by localized sensations of lightness, heaviness, constriction, and expansion. Thus a regular treatment sequence of sensations were developed: warmth, cold, lightness, heaviness, constriction, and expansion, followed finally by normal sensation and relaxation.

Posthypnotic directions were given for experiencing this pattern of sensations daily. In addition she was instructed that whenever convenient she would visualize those areas of her body which had lesions and she would revivify each response suggested in the hypnotic and the posthypnotic treatment pattern. Training in scene visualization had been undertaken at hypnotic and nonhypnotic levels. She was able to achieve both the posthypnotic sensations and the imagery activity with relative ease. The length of time for both the pattern of sensations and the imagery would vary somewhat but averaged about 3 minutes for the sensations (entire pattern), and about 1 minute for the imagery. Through such patient-centered hypnosis and sensory imagery, similar to the technics described in Chapter 34 on pain, the patient learns to control his feedback systems.

STANDARDIZED IMAGES

The authors have found that the hypnotic reliving of feelings in the afflicted skin experienced under conditions of strong heat is often therapeutic in psoriasis. Images involving heat on the skin from the sun are I (beach), V (desert), VII (farm), X (pool), XIII (lake), and XVI (scuba). Images involving heat from a fire are II (mountain cabin), XIV (thunder shower), and XXII (hayloft). Both sets of images work well to produce this sensation. We have found Image VIII (jungle scene) to be most effective for shrinking various types of lesions. This particular image includes the fantasy of shriveling to less than pinpoint dimensions. Alterations in the body image are then directed toward condensation of the lesions.

ECZEMA AND OTHER DISORDERS

Brown and Bettley (1971) compared effects of psychiatric and dermatologic treatment with dermatological treatment alone. Patients who had relevant psychological events preceeding the onset of the eczema had a significantly better outcome with psychiatric therapy. Zhukov (1961) reported dramatic results with rest and hypnosis.

HYPNOTHERAPY

The effectiveness of hypnotherapy for alopecia areata, dermatitis, eczema, hyperhidrosis, pruritus, lichen planus, herpes simplex, pemphigus, verrucae, and other dermatologic disorders has been reviewed (McDowell 1959). A psychosomatic etiology for many of these disorders is posited. The well-known phenomena of goose pimples, sweating, blanching, and temperature changes in the skin following psychological stimuli constitute further corroborative evidence.

Direct hypnotic suggestion has been able to produce erythema, blisters, wheals, urticaria, tumefaction, congestion, hemorrhage, and various sensory effects ranging from anesthesia to hyperesthesia, cold to hot, and itching to pain. However, organic skin manifestations do not respond as well to mere suggestion per se as to hypnotic sensory-imagery conditioning, as demonstrated by Kline (1958) and by Frankel and Misch (1973). This enables the individual to react to a hallucinated stimulus as if it were a reality perception. The ability to relieve organic changes varies from one individual to another, depending upon the degree of autonomic control established by hypnotic conditioning (Block 1927).

Hypnosis has relieved itching in refractory cases of intractable eczema (Zhukov 1961), nevus, lichen planus, and hyperhidrosis (Fernandez 1955, 1956). There are several favorable reports on its use in chronic ichthyosis (Mason 1952, Schneck 1954). Others (Kepecs and Robin 1955) have investigated the relationship of masochism to itching. A typical personality profile has been postulated (Cleveland and Fisher 1956). Acne has been cured by hypnosis merely by suggesting that thinking of the word "scar" would symbolize an ugly facial appearance; thus, picking and spreading of the lesions were thereby prevented (Hollander 1959). Kenward (1963) maintains that emotional problems are associated with acne vulgaris; the mechanisms are not known.

PRURITUS ANI AND VULVAE

There is extensive literature (Alexander 1959, Rosenbaum 1945, Witkower and Russell 1953) on the psychosomatic aspects of pruritus ani and pruritus vulvae. We have had gratifying success with hypnotherapy used for direct symptom-removal in pruritus vulvae. Kroger and Freed (1951), in discussing the treatment of pruritus vulvae, have reviewed the older literature dealing with hypnosis, hypnonarcosis, and hypnoanalysis.

The primitive erotic pathways developed during infancy and childhood, when masturbation is commonly employed, are utilized during adulthood to express unrelieved sexual tensions by means of the genitals. Pruritus occurs as often in virginal girls as in married women; frigidity plays an important role in the latter; "necking" and "heavy petting" results in genital tensions in the former. Some women rub their legs together to obtain relief, "onanistic prurique," from the itching. Tickling and itching, as pleasurable sensations, only emphasize the intimate connection between sexual feelings and the modification of skin sensibility. Hence, it is not surprising that masturbation equivalents are engrafted on an actual itching dermatosis. By such measures, the scratching obviates guilt.

Some people utilize their pruritus masochistically to express inward rage over their inability to obtain love and affection. By such measures, the dependency and the subsequent hostility are denied and masked by a facade of cooperation and submissiveness. The unrelieved frustration and hostility are then activated in overt symptoms such as irascibility, insomnia, fatigue, anorexia, bodily pains, and an attitude of "If I don't get some relief soon, I might just as well be dead." These typical depressive reactions only cover the real, underlying emotional difficulties.

WARTS

Numerous investigators (Block 1927, Bonjour 1927, Dunbar 1946, Clark 1965, Tenzel and Taylor 1969, McDowell 1949, Surman, Gottlieb, and Hackett 1972) have found that 60 to 70 per cent of warts respond to suggestive therapy. Sulzberger and Wolf (1934) state: "The fact that suggestion, without recourse to any other therapy, cures an appreciable percentage of warts stands established." There have been many types of lay-healing, from "charming" away warts by bizarre and mysterious procedures to using prayers and incantations. Ullman (1959) and Ullman and Dudek (1960) in an excellent monograph on the subject, assayed the use of hypnosis—since it emulated lay-healing—for the treatment of warts. In 8 out of 15 deeply hypnotized patients, a complete remission of the warts occurred in contrast with 2 cures in 47 patients who could not be deeply hypnotized. This is clinically corroborated in a series in which half of the body of each individual was treated and the other half was used as a control (Sinclair-Gieben 1959). Cures were obtained in 10 out of a total of 15 patients on the treated side in from 5 weeks to 3 months. Directive hypnotherapy played a significant role in catalyzing the curative process in certain patients with warts. Keller (1975) found conflicting results and attributed this to studies that differed in design. When the design was different, results could not be replicated. Asher (1956) observed that response depended largely on the degree of hypnotizability. On the whole, both agree that hypnosis and, perhaps to a lesser extent, waking suggestion accelerate remission of warts. We recently had a case of condylomata accuminata that was resistant to all other forms of therapy, but readily responded to sensory imagery conditioning, namely, that the vulvar area would "seem" to be normal. Additionally, "heat transfer" and "glove anesthesia" were employed.

SPECIALIZED HYPNOTIC TECHNICS

The intensified hypnotherapeutic relationship, combined with the therapist's ability to release a sufficiently strong affect, often results in dramatic recovery. In dermatologic disorders, it appears that the greater the patient's conviction of cure, the less the physician's suggestive power is required, probably because of the ability of the skin to respond to emotions. However, lack of conviction on the part of the therapist leads to poor results and frequently makes the anxious patient worse. Hypnotherapy also often can potentiate x-ray therapy, ointments, and drugs.

Direct hypnotic suggestions relieve itching and scratching if given in a convincing manner as follows:

Immediately upon coming out of hypnosis, your itching (or pain, pimples, rash) will disappear. More effective is the method of telling the hypnotized subject, You are enveloped in a layer of cotton which acts as a protective coating. This wonderful feeling will remain for several hours (or all day); your skin will feel fine until your next visit.

When this approach is used, it is advisable to enhance the psychological suggestions (ideosensory) by the physiologic effect (ideomotor) of touching the area with the hand. Reinforcement is usually necessary at weekly or monthly intervals.

Hypnonarcosis has been employed to relieve chronic itching dermatoses. Various types of dermatitis have been cured by prolonged hypnosis—6 or more days of continuous "hypnotic sleep." Follow-up studies, however are meager. With reference to other methods for treatment of itching, one can, by hypnotic suggestions, exaggerate the condition. If the itching can be increased, it can be decreased! A systematic attempt then is made to "wean" the patient from the need to itch and scratch, by symptom-substitution or by symptom-transformation. Through conditioning under autohypnosis, the itch can be displaced or transferred to another portion of the body. The new symptom naturally is easier to remove than the long-standing one.

An interesting technic to relieve itching is to suggest a negative sensory hallucination. This can be accomplished as follows:

The patient is to imagine, while under hypnosis, that as he looks at his lesions he "sees" that the skin looks and feels as normal as any other area of the body devoid of lesions. Success with this approach requires the somnambulistic state or one closely allied to it. One can remark, "Look at your right wrist; you can begin to speculate on whether or not that area will look like your left wrist, which does not have any involvement. Now, keep looking at the left wrist; notice the texture of the skin—it also feels perfectly normal, does it not?" (The patient nods his head in agreement.) "Every time you look at this wrist you will observe that this area on your right wrist is becoming as normal-looking as your left wrist. You may also close your eyes, and in your 'mind's eye' see or imagine that the lesions have disappeared—the skin is normal in appearance. However, you may keep just as much of the itching on the involved area of the wrist as you wish to retain. You do not have to get rid of this itching all at once but, rather, allow it to disappear slowly." The patient is given another posthypnotic suggestion such as: "You might raise the question whether you wish this lesion (on the wrist) or that lesion (one near the elbow) to disappear first. Also, you might begin to consider the possibility of just when this will occur. Will it be tomorrow, a week from tomorrow, or several weeks from now? At any rate, the more you keep thinking about this under autohypnosis, the more likely the rash will go away."

Motivation, belief, and confidence are readily established when these permissive hypnotic technics are employed. Dependency on the therapist is minimal when autohypnotic conditioning is used. Specialized hypnotic technics can be employed. Revivification, automatic writing, dream interpretation, and other projective technics are often effective in the dissolution of refractory skin disorders. The patient is asked to revivify the disturbing experiences that preceded the onset of his symptom. Discussion of feelings associated with these experiences can help resolve emotional conflicts associated with the skin disorder. Abreaction, with education and reassurance, generally obviates the need for depth psychotherapy.

Of particular value is the engrafting of an artificial conflict calculated to produce a given specific emotional attitude which might elicit a specific skin reaction. When applicable and wisely used, hypnotherapeutic technics can alter the prognosis of many refractory cases of dermatologic disorders. The following case histories are illustrative.

Mrs. M. A., aged 37, was referred for dermatitis factitia of 7 years' duration. Various types of dermatologic therapy were ineffective. The patient also had had several years of intensive psychotherapy, also without appreciable success. Her entire body was scarred, particularly the face and the neck. Since extensive exploration of her personality had been fruitless, symptom substitution was employed in the following manner. After she had been taught autohypnosis, it was suggested that she should get herself a large doll made of rubber that resembled skin. Since most of the picking of her skin occurred while she was trying to fall asleep at night, she was to keep the doll at her side and pick it "to her heart's content." After posthypnotic suggestions to this effect were given to her over a 3-week period, she gradually shifted the digging and the clawing from herself to the doll. The number of fresh excoriations diminished. However, the self-mutilation of the skin was still being produced during most of her daytime activities. Through further posthypnotic suggestions, she was advised that she could twitch one or all of the fingers on either hand as often as she wished; this kept her fingers busy and reduced the intensity of the picking. Within 2 weeks all picking of her skin had stopped. The frequency of the finger-twitching was then gradually reduced by posthypnotic suggestions. At the end of approximately a month she was twitching her finger only about 2 or 3 times a day. She revealed that she had always masturbated, was completely frigid with her husband, and felt extreme guilt over deceiving him about this for many years. Through re-education and reassurance, she was informed that her guilt over masturbation and simulation of orgasmic responses was completely unwarranted. She stated, "I like the sex act and I am very much in love with my husband, but I am not getting the satisfaction I think I am supposed to have in my vaginal area." It was emphasized that sexual response could not be reduced to a mechanical act and also that the fact that she loved her husband was of more importance than localization of the climax. Through further resolution of her unhealthy sexual attitudes, she stopped masturbating. Within 3 months, she realized that she no longer had a need to stimulate her genitals artificially or to pick at her skin to compensate for unrelieved sexual tensions. Although she never achieved any other type of sexual response than a clitoric one, both the finger-twitching and the face-picking subsided. At the end of a 1-year follow-up there was no recurrence. Her sexual response was still unchanged.

DISCUSSION

In this chapter we have reviewed the older and more recent literature on the use of hypnosis for dermatological disorders. As yet there are few reports, mostly anecdotal, on the use of learning principles and behavior modification in this area.

Choice of psychotherapeutic technic and the results obtained are mediated by the personality pattern and the type of psychopathological skin disorder present. Those with strong emotional fears exacerbating their condition should respond well to systematic desensitization under hypnosis (reconditioning). It appears that patients with certain personality characteristics benefit from psychotherapy, although it is not certain how the psychotherapy contributes to the improvement. However, it seems advantageous to try our hypnobehavioral model with those patients whose dermatological disorders have not responded to routine medical care. More follow-up data and controlled studies are needed on a larger population sample.

REFERENCES

Asher, R.: Respectable hypnosis, Brit. Med. J., *1:*309, 315, 1956.

Alexander, R. P.: Contribution to the psychological understanding of pruritus ani: report of a case. Psychosom. Med., *21:*182, 1959.

Bethune, H. C. and Kidd, C. B.: Psychophysiological mechanisms in skin diseases. Lancet, *II:*1419, 1961.

Block, B.: Ueber die heilung der warzen durch suggestion. Klin. Wchnschr., *6:*2271, 1927.

Bonjour, J.: Cure of condylomata by suggestion. Schweiz. Med. Wchnschr., *6:*2272, 1927.

Brown, D. G. and Bettley, F. R.: Psychosomatic treatment of eczema: a controlled study. Brit. Med. J., *2:*729, 1971.

Clark, G. H.: The charming of warts. J. Invest. Derm., *45:*15, 1965.

Cleveland, S. E. and Fisher, S.: Psychological factors in the neurodermatoses. Psychosom. Med., *18:*209, 1956.

Dunbar, H. F.: Psychosomatic Diagnosis. New York, Paul B. Hoeber, 1943.
————: Emotions and Bodily Changes. p. 343. New York, Columbia Univ. Press, 1946.
Farber, E. M., Bright, R. D., and Nall, M. L.: Psoriasis: a questionnaire survey of 2,144 patients. Arch. Derm., *98:*248, 1968.
Fernandez, G. R.: Hypnotism in the treatment of the stress factor in dermatological conditions. Brit. J. Med. Hyp., *7:*21, 1955–56.
Frankel, F. H. and Misch, R. C.: Hypnosis in a case of long-standing psoriasis in a person with character problems. Internat. J. Clin. Exp. Hypn., *21:*121, 1973.
Hollander, M. D.: Excoriated acne controlled by posthypnotic suggestion. Amer. J. Clin. Hypn., *1:*122, 1959.
Horan, J. S.: Management of neurodermatitis by hypnotic suggestion. Brit. J. Med. Hypn., *2:*43, 1950.
Keller, R.: Psychotherapy in psychosomatic disorders. Arch. Gen. Psych., *32:*1021, 1975.
Kenward, J. F.: Psychiatric considerations in acne vulgaris. Ill. Med. J., *124:*427, 1963.
Kepecs, J. G. and Robin, M.: Studies on itching: I. Contributions toward an understanding of the physiology of masochism. Psychosom. Med., *17:*87, 1955.
Kline, M. V.: Psoriasis and hypnotherapy: a case report. J. Clin. Exp. Hypn., *2:*318, 1954.
————: Freud and Hypnosis: The Interaction of Psychodynamics and Hypnosis. New York, Julian Press, 1958.
Kroger, W. S. and Freed, S. C.: Psychosomatic Gynecology. Philadelphia, W. B. Saunders, 1951.
Luthe, W. and Schultz, J. H.: Autogenic Therapy. Vol. II. Medical Applications. New York, Grune and Stratton, 1969.
Mason, A. A.: A case of congenital ichthyosiform erythrodermia of brocq treated by hypnosis. Brit. Med. J., *2:*422, 1952.
McDowell, M.: Juvenile warts removed by the use of hypnosis. Bull. Menninger Clin., *13:*124, 1949.
————: Hypnosis in dermatology *In* Schneck, J. M. (ed.): Hypnosis in Modern Medicine. pp. 101–115. Springfield, Charles C Thomas, 1959.
Obermeyer, M. E.: Psychocutaneous Medicine. Springfield, Ill., Charles C Thomas, 1955.
Poissaint, A. F.: Emotional factors in psoriasis. Psychosomatics, *4:*199, 1963.
Rosenbaum, M.: Psychosomatic factors in pruritus. Psychosom. Med., *7:*52, 1945.
Rothman, S.: The role of the autonomic nervous system in cutaneous disorders. Psychosom. Med., *7:*90, 1945.
Schneck, J. J.: Ichthyosis treated with hypnosis. Dis. Nerv. System, *15:*211, 1954.
Sinclair-Gieben, A. H. and Chalmers, D.: Evaluation of treatment of warts by hypnosis. Lancet, *2:*480, 1959.
Sulzberger, M. B. and Wolf, J.: The treatment of warts by suggestion. Med. Record, *140:*552, 1934.
Sulzberger, M. B. and Zaidens, S. H.: Psychogenic factors in dermatologic disorders. M. Clin. N. Amer., *32:*669, 1948.
Surman, O. S., Gottlieb, S. K., and Hackett, T. P.: Hypnotic treatment of a child with warts. Amer. J. Clin. Hypn., *15:*12, 1972.
Tenzel, J. H. and Taylor, R. L.: An evaluation of hypnosis and suggestion as a treatment for warts. Psychosomatics, *10:*252, 1969.
Twerski, A. and Naar, R.: Hypnotherapy in a case of refractory dermatitis. Amer. J. Clin. Hypn., *16:*202, 1974.

Ullman, M.: On the psyche and warts: I. Suggestion and warts: a review and comment. Psychosom. Med., *21:*473, 1959.

Ullman, M. and Dudek, S.: On the psyche and warts: II. Hypnotic suggestion and warts. Psychosom. Med., *22:*68, 1960.

Van Scott, E. J. and Farber, E. M.: Disorders with epidermal proliferation. *In* Fitzpatrick, T. B., et al. (eds.): Dermatology in General Medicine, pp. 219–231. New York, McGraw-Hill, 1971.

Walton, D.: The application of learning theory to the treatment of a case of neurodermatitis. *In* Eysenck, H. J. (ed.): Behavior Therapy and the Neuroses. pp. 272–274. Oxford, Pergamon, 1960.

Weiss, E. and English, O. S.: Psychosomatic Medicine: The Clinical Application of Psychopathology to General Medical Problems. ed. 2. Philadelphia, W. B. Saunders, 1949.

Wittkower, E.: Psychological aspects of psoriasis. Lancet, *1:*566, 1946.

Wittkower, E. and Russell, B.: Emotional Factors in Skin Disease. New York, Hoeber, 1953.

Zukov, I. A.: Hypnotherapy of Dermatoses in Resort Treatment. *In* Winn, R. B. (ed.): Psychotherapy in the Soviet Union. New York, Philosophical Library, 1961.

SUGGESTED READINGS

Clark, G. H.: The charming of warts. J. Invest. Derm., *45:*15, 1965.

Mason, A. A.: Hypnotism for Medical and Dental Practitioners. London, Secker and Warburg, 1961.

Scott, M. J.: Hypnosis in Skin and Allergic Diseases. Springfield, Charles C Thomas, 1960.

Stankler, L.: A critical assessment of the cure of warts by suggestion. Practitioner, April–June, *198:*690, 1967.

32

Psychosomatic Cardiovascular Disorders

High blood pressure, or hypertension, affects over 23 million Americans a year and is the leading cause of strokes fatal to 200,000 Americans anually. Research indicates a delicate balance between emotional stability and cardiovascular disorders (Keegan 1973, Raab 1966, Wolf 1966). The older literature on hypnosis, particularly the Russian, describes numerous experiments accelerating or decelerating the heart, establishing reflex changes and also vasomotor responses. The heart rate could be altered without changing the respiratory rhythm. This data was later corroborated by Deutsch and Kauf (1923). They suggested an exciting experience upon which a simultaneously suggested amnesia was engrafted for it. A marked increase in the pulse rate, similar to the experience suggested during hypnosis, occurred when the exciting experience was repeated at nonhypnotic levels.

ROLE OF CONDITIONING

Platonov (1959) describes how other investigators produced conditioned cardiac reflexes combining a pain stimulus to the skin (UCS) with the sound of a buzzer (CS). He also discusses how conditioned heart reflexes were established in reaction to various pharmacological agents such as morphine, nitroglycerin, adrenalin, and strophantin. Also, arterial pressure in response to a bell was subsequently obtained when the conditioned subject himself, rather than the experimenter, uttered the word "bell." The reader is referred also to the later work on conditioning of the cardiovascular system by hypnosis (Heyer 1925, Schultz 1932). Dunbar (1946) discusses in detail an extensive literature on

351

arrhythmias, bradycardia and tachycardia, angina pectoris, and sudden death due to psychogenic factors.

Studies of heart rate conditioning substantiate neurophysiologic linkage between cerebral activity and cardiovascular functioning (Lacey 1959). These are a clear demonstration of treating a physiological function (heart beat) as an operant behavior determined by its consequences. Lang, Stroufe, and Hastings (1967) showed that when subjects received visual feedback about their own heart rate, they were able to maintain their heart rate response within prescribed limits in contrast to a control group that did not receive feedback. Shearn (1962) reported similar results in a study where delay of shock was made contingent on accelerated heart rate. Ascough and Sipprelle (1968) also demonstrated that spontaneous increase and decrease in heart rate can be brought under control of operant verbal conditioning. Commercial television programs and money were used in one study to reinforce the acceleration and deceleration of heart rate (Scott et al. 1973).

Using psychological procedures to lower blood pressure is of recent origin in the behavior literature. However, hypnotherapists have long been aware that blood pressure, in part, largely is determined by the autonomic nervous system and that its control could be altered by voluntary or conscious influences. It is interesting to note, however, that the disciplines of Yoga and Zen have been able to produce such alterations for hundreds of years (Anand et al. 1969, Solier and Axolt 1969). Yet, only recently have attempts been made at influencing blood pressure through use of operant conditioning procedures (Miller 1969, Miller et al. 1970, Benson et al. 1971).

ESSENTIAL HYPERTENSION

Hypnotherapy

Essential hypertension can be reduced through muscular relaxation and completely eliminated during hypnosis (Jana 1967; Deabler, Fidel, and Dillenkoffer 1973). Deabler et al. achieved decrease in both systolic and diastolic pressures through hypnosis. Suggestions were made for deeper breathing and exhaling synchronized with the imagery of descending a flight of stairs. Concomitantly counting downward from 10 to 0 interspersed with further suggestions of bodily relaxation, drowsiness, and heaviness of legs, arms, and body were associated with deeper and deeper states. Their patients also responded well to the learning of self-relaxation and self-hypnosis, which were used to continue beneficial effects after hospitalization.

Many of our own hypertensive patients have reported a drop in blood pressure once they began practicing self-hypnosis. Patients seldom come with the presenting problem of high blood pressure, but find their pressure decreases as a result of the hypno-relaxation they are practicing for other problems. Few realize that hypnosis can be used to reduce essential hypertension. Schultz (1930a) showed that the systolic and diastolic blood pressure would drop on an average of 40 and 30 mm respectively in a single session of autogenic training. With consistent training the average blood pressure level was lowered considerably. He points out the prophylactic possibilities of the method.

Brady, Luborsky, and Kron (1974) significantly reduced blood pressure in 3 out of 4 patients with essential hypertension through metronome-conditioned relaxation (MCR), a disguised hypnotic induction technic. This consisted in lying down for half an hour with eyes closed for several sessions while listening to a tape recording. The tape consists of instructions and suggestions to relax the muscles of the body. In addition, directions to "relax" and "let go" of the muscles are paced with the rhythmic beats of an auditory metronome set at 60 beats per minute. Other cardiological applications of hypnosis have been described (Collison 1970).

Posthypnotic suggestions, together with sensory-imagery conditioning under autohypnosis, also potentiate drug therapy to reduce blood pressure. This cannot be lightly dismissed as "nothing but suggestion" as in this state conditioned phenomena such as disturbed feedback mechanisms, faulty associative learning patterns, and harmful stimuli can be significantly altered. This type of patient-centered hypnotherapy is more effective than directive hypnosis, and also is superior to the old bromides such as, "You must take it easy and learn to relax." Or, "Why don't you just quit worrying?" Dunbar (1943) was among the first to call attention to a coronary-prone personality profile. More recently it has been postulated that the hard-driving, ambitious, choleric "type A" personality is far more prone to cardiovascular disorders than his imperturbable and patient "type B" brother (Friedman and Rosenman 1974).

BEHAVIOR THERAPY AFTER MYOCARDIAL INFARCTION

Recently, Suinn (1974) successfully conducted a pilot program to directly alter type A behaviors and reactions to these behaviors in 10 postinfarction patients. He assumed that the type A patient continuously exposes himself to stress-arousing situations by behaviors such as forcing himself to meet deadlines, competitiveness and drive, and rapid pacing of activities. He also proposed that the type A person finds it difficult to alter his behavioral patterns because of anxiety aroused when such behaviors are reduced, a proposition with which we are much in agreement. Inactivity is anxiety-producing for this type of patient.

The pilot program called Cardiac Stress Management Training combined a modified Anxiety Management Training (Suinn and Richardson 1971) with visual-motor behavior rehearsal technics (Suinn 1972). Anxiety management training involved teaching patients to recognize physical/physiological cues of tension and the use of relaxation to alter the anxiety state. Visual-motor behavior rehearsal technics relied upon imagery as a means of helping patients to practice adaptive behaviors under the controlled conditions possible with imagery rehearsal.

HYPNOBEHAVIORAL THERAPY

A similar treatment in conjunction with hypnosis was used by the authors with a cardiac patient described below. The use of hypnosis deepens relaxation and intensifies appropriate imagery for behavior rehearsal.

Mr. M. came to therapy complaining of high blood pressure, which had been increasing in the past few years. He had suffered one mild heart attack and his doctor had warned him that if he did not slow down and take it easy he would drive himself to an early grave. Mr. M. was an accountant and always working under the pressure of a time schedule. He was good at his job and was in no danger of losing it, but he constantly worried about his ability to compete with younger men in the firm. He was actually afraid to relax for fear his productivity would decline. Relaxation to him meant inefficiency.

Hypnorelaxation and autohypnosis were taught the first session. Sessions using the beach, mountain cabin, and garden images were given to deepen his relaxation and develop his sensory recall. This was done so that the imagery rehearsal to be described would be very vivid. In conjunction with the standard images just mentioned, he was to practice while in hypnosis seeing himself totally composed and working at a steady but relaxed pace at his office desk. He was therefore imagogically rehearsing an adaptive behavior as well as desensitizing himself to the idea of working while relaxed. After three weeks' practice of hypnotic imagery rehearsal in which he pictured himself doing all aspects of his job in a relaxed state, it was time for reality testing. He was instructed to induce hypnorelaxation at work to actually test whether relaxation aided or impeded his performance. Much to his amazement, his efficiency greatly increased when he felt most comfortable. Once this fact was realized emotionally through actual testing, therapy proceeded rapidly. Increased productivity reinforced more relaxation on the job.

Rapid pacing of activities was further diminished by the teaching of time expansion via the space and farm images. This created the feeling that the patient had all the time in the world to accomplish his tasks and therefore had no need to rush. Mr. M. was instructed that whenever he found himself pushing he should quietly say to himself, "I have forever—I have all the time in the world." Also, whenever Mr. M. caught himself worrying about work he had yet to finish, he was to employ thought stopping merely by saying to himself "stop" as many times as was necessary to stop this line of thinking. Just as his negative thoughts, such as "I will never get this done in time," had been making him tense and harried, now his positive thoughts made him *feel* relaxed and at ease. After nine weekly sessions, Mr. M. had gained sufficient control over his thoughts and physical cues of tension to lower his blood pressure to a normal level.

ANGINA PECTORIS

Behavior Modification

Symptoms of angina pectoris disappeared in a 52-year-old obese male after three desensitization sessions. Angiography indicated that bypass surgery was not indicated. His anginal pain generally occurred while he was driving his car. His anxiety completely disappeared after he was desensitized by a specially constructed hierarchy of stimuli related to driving to work. He continued to drive and work without angina until his death 2 years later (Rapp and Thomas 1974). We are now trying this approach on Prinzmetal's (variant angina). We saw a physician whose angina improved after he used desensitization combined with heat transfer. The hand was made warm by imagining the fireplace in the cabin scene. The warm hand was placed on the precordium and paired with the relaxation response. It is well recognized that fright and anxiety can produce constriction with cardiac ischemia and resulting pain. Therefore, warmth paired with relaxation scenes possibly can improve the compromised coronary circulation and, at least partially, increase blood flow and prevent some degree of myocardial ischemia. This is a fertile field for research.

Hypnorelaxation Therapy

Others have reported a large series of postinfarction angina treated with hypnorelaxation. Adjuvant measures as vasodilating drugs, exercise, and salt restriction were employed. However, in two matched groups, Evans and Chapman noted distinct improvement in the hypnotically conditioned group.* Schultz (1930b), using autogenic training, reports on 37 cases of angina pectoris that became entirely symptom-free. These were followed over a period of 3 years.

PSYCHOGENIC CARDIAC DISORDERS

Paroxysmal tachycardia, extrasystoles, and arrythmias can be produced by spontaneous recall of traumatic memories. Fright, anxiety, and sudden shock are commonly associated with precordial pain. Deconditioning, consisting of pairing pleasant associations with fearful thoughts under hypnosis, often can relieve functional chest pain and other associated symptoms in tense and anxious patients.

Hypnotic Technics

Hypnotic age-regression, prior to onset of the symptom, has been successfully utilized to ameliorate and relieve arrhythmias due to rheumatic fever in childhood. When the symptoms are functional in origin, hypnotic symptom-removal is particularly effective. If the arrhythmias can be related to specific situations, the results are excellent if the patient is conditioned or stress-adapted so that he does not overreact to strong emotional stimuli. This is not surprising, as cortical regulatory mechanisms acting through specific nuclei of the

---

* Evans, A. and Chapman, J. D.: Personal Communication, 1972.

hypothalamus affect the rate and rhythm of the heart and often are responsible for premature beats and paroxysmal tachycardia.

Suggesting conflictual situations to hypnotized patients has resulted in either the production or the elimination of extrasystoles. Creation of serene feelings such as those produced by our images have eliminated the extrasystoles in good hypnotic subjects. Revivification of a combat scene, which resulted in abreaction of an affect-charged experience, produced complete recovery in a case of psychogenic heart disease. These cases, as well as others discussed in this volume, apparently confirm Pavlov's observations that *traces of past experiences are indelibly "etched" in the brain, and can be activated by the proper associational reflexes.* It also appears that when some degree of abreaction of highly charged emotional material is relived under hypnosis, the resultant deconditioning significantly aids recovery.

Hypnobehavioral Therapy of Cardiac Neuroses

Those suffering from cardiac neurosis can be helped by systematic desensitization. While the patient is under hypnosis, a hierarchy should be given at a pace appropriate for each patient. The hierarchy involves reading about cardiac illness, seeing episodes about cardiac illness in movies or on television, hearing about heart troubles from friends or relatives. Thus they relieve their own anxieties about heart attacks and original traumatic episodes. For those who do not respond, assertive training and thought stoppage are effective. Subassertive patients can be exposed to assertive principles through publications and special tape recordings. They can be taught to make assertive responses by use of modeling, role playing, and video feedback. Family therapy can be of benefit for those patients whose symptoms have a consequential response in one or more of the family members. Family members can be taught what their reactions to the patient's symptoms mean, and an attempt can be made to alter their reactions.

HYPNOTHERAPY IN ARRHYTHMIAS AND CAROTID SINUS SYNDROME

Direct suggestions under hypnosis have relieved cases of chronic palpitation. Raginsky (1960) reinduced a stoppage of the heart in a patient who had been operated on for a carotid sinus syndrome several years before. The cardiac arrest had not occurred since the surgery. It was reproduced by posthypnotic suggestions to revivify the "attack." It was re-experienced with all its original manifestations and intensity. In spite of the absence of the carotid bodies, the objective findings of cardiac arrest were demonstrable in the serial electrocardiograms!

CORONARY DISEASE

Coronary disease has reached epidemic proportions in America. There are few reports on the use of hypnotherapy for the adjunctive treatment of coronary heart disease. Sometimes there is no correlation between the degree of atherosclerosis and the degree of severity of the symptoms or even fatal outcome. Acute or chronic stress is a crucial factor in the production of coronary disease, especially if obesity, diabetes, hypertension, smoking, and hypercholesteremia—all righ-risk factors—are present. Emotional tension per se can elevate serum cholesterol up to 35 mg. in an hour. In some cases of coronary insufficiency, it is difficult to understand how a patient can do a large amount of physical work at times and yet be unable to walk up a flight of stairs. Some sufferers have attacks while performing light physical duties and yet have no difficulties during more strenuous tasks. One must consider that a conditioned reflex is involved. The number of foot-pounds of work does not always tell the whole story. The input overload upon a diseased heart accounts for the severity of the symptoms and even death. The cardiac output can be improved by appropriate hypnotic conditioning and behavior therapy, consisting of desensitization and imagery conditioning using our images.

Particularly pertinent are studies that show that hypnotic conditioning and sensory-imagery technics indicate that depression, anger, and fear are associated with an increase in the free fatty acids in the bloodstream. The responses equalled those experienced in real situations in the past. This is proof-positive that the ability to experience sensory recall is correlated with the ability to respond physiologically to hypnotically suggested emotions.

Many heart sufferers can live out their life spans if they recognize their limitations, learn how to relax, and develop new interests. To minimize acute anxiety produced by aggravating situations, positive hypnosuggestions can augment tranquilizers and sedatives. Hypnosis also mobilizes faith and the "will to live." Unfortunately, not every heart victim is susceptible to deep hypnosis. However, even light hypnosis potentiates narcotics and sedatives, and can help those who react poorly to these drugs. Unquestionably, thoughts of death and impending doom take their toll. Extreme mental anguish produces hyperventilation and thus interferes with blood oxygen tensions, increases norepinephrine output, and sets the stage for such acute exacerbations as heart failure.

POST-MYOCARDIAL-INFARCTION SYNDROME

The authors have had gratifying results in a selected number of patients with post-infarction syndrome. Strong reassurance and reeducation under hypnosis directed toward achieving better adjustment to their conditions together with development of glove anesthesia, relieved or reduced their fears and anxieties and thereby raised their pain thresholds. Those whose symptoms were ameliorated were advised to live within their limitations. They were carefully informed that the onset of shortness of breath and anginal pains was a warning signal to be heeded. All were checked and kept on routine medication by their physicians. Dietary control as well as salt reduction can be maintained by posthypnotic suggestions in those who have obesity, diabetes, or hypertension. It would be interesting to compare a group of acute coronary and postcoronary cases treated as above with those treated by standard medical procedures. Kavanaugh et al. (1970, 1973, 1974) combined hypnosis with exercise for post-myocardial-infarction patients with success.

Though hypnosis was not employed, Dunbar (1943) demonstrated that post-infarction patients who had received some type of psychotherapy outlived those who had not been similarly treated. This area, too, merits further investigation.

CONGESTIVE HEART FAILURE

In congestive heart failure, the attacks of dyspnea are more frequent during the night when the sensory threshold is lowered. Everyone advocates complete mental and physical rest, but no one teaches patients specifically how the former can be attained. During periods of increased emotional tension, patients with congestive failure have increased sodium and water retention. The sodium output may be 20 per cent less than normal, thereby leading to decreased cardiac reserve. In these patients, hypnorelaxation decreases stress, hyperventilation, and electrolyte retention, and often can stimulate the recovery forces to their maximum potential.

STANDARDIZED IMAGES

The 25 images described in Chapter 10 all serve to produce deep muscular relaxation. Images XVI (scuba), XVII (picnic), XIX (chalk cliffs), and XXII (hayloft) deal directly with gaining control over the circulatory system.

SEX AND THE POST-MYOCARDIAL-INFARCTION SYNDROME

A paucity of information exists in regard to the relation between sexual activity and heart disease. A review of 33 cardiology books discloses less than a thousand words on this subject. This is despite the fact that many victims of heart attacks have diminished libido and fear of death during intercourse. Anxiety remains with the heart sufferer for years. In spite of reassurance that sex is permissible, a high percentage of such patients have diminished sexual interests and coital frequency, complete or partial impotence, and a fear response that is conditioned into a phobia.

It is unfortunate that most physicians offer little or no advice regarding sexual activity or that those who do give only vague and nonspecific advice. The bulk of physicians speak in generalities and shift the ultimate decision to their patients. In addition to making these decisions, the patients usually have to spend a great deal of time with concern over weight loss, smoking control, regular exercise, less stressful work, and other prescribed limitations.

The cardiac patient reacts to sexual excitement in the same way as the nonafflicted patient. Cardiac output for both is increased during the orgasmic phase. The additional workload on an already overburdened heart generally results in an elevation of blood pressure and an increase in respiratory rate. During orgasm the average heart rate for the 50- to 60-year-old individual rises to about 125/min. and the blood pressure is increased by 20 mm, systolic. Anxiety triggers an additional rise, particularly during the initial sexual relationship. The rise is greatest at the beginning of the sex act. If the mental stress can be inhibited, the heart rate and blood pressure can be reduced. One strongly inhibiting factor shared by both the husband and wife is that the cardiac victim might die during the sex act. Though this may occur, it is infrequent.

For those patients suffering from angina, we prescribe $1/150$ grain of nitroglycerine before intercourse. Hellerstein (1968), who has monitored the parameters involved in angina and coronary disease, believes that the average sex act is equivalent in exertion to briskly walking up two flights of stairs. For a thorough review on this subject, the reader is referred to Hellerstein (1968), Hellerstein and Ford (1957), and Hellerstein et al. (1965).

The return of sexual desires is a good prognostic sign. It can expedite the post-infarction patient's return to normal activity. However, this kind of patient should not engage in sex without the advice of his physician. Stress testing can be used to predict 85 per cent of the normal maximum for a given individual. The clinical assessment by the physician can be a valuable adjunct to determine the fitness of the individual. In most cases, the period of abstinence should be 8 to 14 weeks. We advise that just as physical exercise is initiated slowly, sexual activity should be reactivated in similar fashion. At first the couple can just talk about it. Then they can engage in sensate focusing. If the pain occurs, the patient should stop and take a nitroglycerin tablet before continuing with coitus. Fear and anxiety over failure should be allayed. Patience is required. The nondemand situation with the female in the superior position should be resorted to initially. Female post-infarction patients experience the same fears and apprehensions. Regular exercise increases the heart's performance in response to excitement, pulse, and blood pressure.

We counsel our patients not to worry about failure after a period of abstinence. We even suggest that they should not expect too much initially and that they pinpoint the key areas of anxiety. Our aim is to establish a readjustment. Green (1975) states, ''Physiologically, emotional stress inhibits adaptation to exercise, alters renal salt and water excretion (possibly contributing to increased blood pressure), and may alter renal blood flow to increase blood viscosity—all causing increased cardiac work.'' He points out how the powerful pressor effect of emotion can be a causative factor in unexpected death. He cites data indicating that changes of ST-T alterations on an ECG during a Master's two-step test can be produced by subjecting patients to an emotional psychological interview.

We would like to include that discussion of sex should be initiated as soon as the patient's condition has stabilized; that his sexual activity should be guided by his tolerance exhibited during stress testing. Today there is sufficient information to arrive at safe conclusions as to just how much tolerance a patient has for sexual activity. Regular exercise and psychological rehabilitation can afford the coronary patient a healthy sex life. There is inadequate data on the possibility of sudden coital death. The physician would do well to understand the psychological factors involved in the marital relationship, which are often of equal importance to the cardiovascular status of the patient. The reader is referred to Green's excellent review article on the subject.

DISCUSSION

In all types of cardiac malfunction, whether essential hypertension, psychogenic cardiac disorders, coronary disease, post-infarction syndrome, or congestive heart failure, the primary objective of treatment is to reduce anxiety. This is done effectively through production of hypnorelaxation using the images described in Chapter 10. For the post-infarction patient, or the one having had by-pass surgery, who has a sexual problem or fear of death, desensitization with construction of a specific hierarchy often is helpful. Sensory recall of sexual experiences prior to the attack or to recovery from surgery can by revivification reduce anxiety and fear.

REFERENCES

Anand, B. K., Chhina, G. S., and Singh, B.: Some aspects of EEG studies in yogis. *In* Charles Tart (ed.): Altered States of Consciousness. pp. 503–506. New York, John Wiley & Sons, 1969.

Ascough, J. C. and Sipprelle, C. N.: Operant verbal conditioning of autonomic response. Behav. Res. Ther. *6:*363, 1968.

Benson, H., Shapiro, D., Tursky, B., and Schwartz, G.: Decreased systolic blood pressure through operant conditioning techniques in patients with essential hypertension. Science, *173:*740, 1971.

Brady, J. P., Luborsky, L., and Kron, R. E.: Blood pressure reduction in patients with essential hypertension through metronome-conditioned relaxation: a preliminary report. Behav. Ther., *5:*203, 1974.

Collison, D. R.: Cardiological applications of the control of the autonomic nervous system by hypnosis. Amer. J. Clin. Hypn., *12:*150, 1970.

Deabler, H. L., Fidel, E., and Dillenkoffer, R. L.: The use of relaxation and hypnosis in lowering high blood pressure. Am. J. Clin. Hypn. *16:*75, 1973.

Deutsch, F. and Kauf, E.: Psycho-physische Kreislaufstudien. I. Mitteilung. Ueber die Ursachen der Kreisläufanderugen bei Muskelarbeit. Ztschr. f. d. ges. exper. Med., *32:*197, 1923.

Dunbar, F.: Psychosomatic Diagnosis. New York, Paul B. Hoeber, 1943.

————: Emotions and Bodily Changes. New York, Columbia Univ. Press, 1946.

Engel, B. T.: Comment on self-control of cardiac functioning: a promise as yet unfulfilled. Psychol. Bull., *81:*43, 1974.

Friedman, M. and Rosenman, R. Type A Behavior and Your Heart. New York, Knopf, 1974.

Green, A. W.: Sexual activity and the postmyocardial infarction patient. Amer. Heart J. *89:*246, 1975a.

Hellerstein, H. K.: Exercise therapy in coronary disease. Bull. N.Y. Acad. Med., *44:*1028, 1968.

Hellerstein, H. K., and Ford, A. B.: Rehabilitation of the cardiac patient. J.A.M.A., *164:*225, 1957.

Hellerstein, H. K. et al.: Active physical reconditioning of coronary patients. Circulation, *32:*110, 1965.

Heyer, G. R.: Quoted in Dunbar, F.: Emotions and Bodily Changes. New York, Columbia University Press, 1946.

Jana, H.: Effect of hypnosis on circulation and respiration. Indian J. Med. Res., *55:*591, 1967.

Kavanagh, T. and Shephard, R. J.: Intensive exercise in coronary rehabilitation. Med. in Sci. and Sports, *5:*34, 1973.

Kavanagh, T., Shephard, R. J., and Doney, H. Hypnosis and exercise—a possible combined therapy following myocardial infarction. Amer. J. Clin. Hypn., *16:*160, 1974.

Kavanagh, T., Shephard, R. J., Pandit, V., and Doney, H.: Exercise versus hypnotherapy in the rehabilitation of the coronary patient. A preliminary report. Arch. Physiol. Med. Rehab., *51:*578, 1970.

Keegan, D. L.: Psychosomatics: toward an understanding of cardiovascular disorders. Psychosomatics, *14:*321, 1973.

Lacey, J. I.: Psychophysiological approaches to the evaluation of psychotherapeutic process and outcome. *In* Rubinstein, E. A. and Parloff, M. B. (eds.): Research in Psychotherapy. Washington, American Psychological Assoc., 1959.

Lang, P. J., Stroufe, L. A., and Hastings, J. E.: Effects of feedback and instructional set on the control of cardiac-rate variability. J. Exp. Psychol., *75:*425, 1967.

Miller, N. E.: Learning of visceral and glandular responses. Science, *163:*434, 1969.

Miller, N. E. et al.: Psychological aspects of hypertension: learned modifications of autonomic functions. Supplement I to Circulation Res., *26 & 27:*1, 1970.

Platonov, K.: The Word as a Physiological and Therapeutic Factor. Moscow, Foreign Languages Publishing House, 1959.

Raab, W.: Emotional and sensory stress in myocardial pathology. Am. Heart J., *72:*538, 1966.

Raginsky, B. B.: The use of hypnosis in internal medicine, paper presented at Pan American Med. Assoc., May 1960.

Rapp, M. S. and Thomas, M. R.: 3 'Desensitization' sessions dispel angina. Medical Tribune, Dec. 12, 1974.

Schultz, J. H.: Psychologische Bemerkungen zur Therapie der Angina pectoris. Deutsche Med. Wchnschr., *56:*311, 1930.

————: Psychologie und Psychotherapie bei Herzschwache. Med. Welt, *4:*1321, 1930.

————: Das Autogene Training. Leipzig, Thieme, 1932.

Scott, R. W. et al.: The use of shaping and reinforcement in the operant acceleration and deceleration of heart rate. Behav. Res. Ther., *11:*179, 1973.

Shearn, D.: Operant conditioning of heart rate. Science, *137:*530, 1962.

Sollier, A. and Axolt, G.: Japanese Archery: Zen in Action. New York, Walker-Weatherhill, 1969.

Suinn, R.: Behavior rehearsal training for ski racers. Brief report. Behav. Ther., *3:*519, 1972.

————: Behavior therapy for cardiac patients. Behav. Ther., *5:*569, 1974.

Suinn, R. and Richardson, F.: Anxiety Management Training: A non-specific behavior therapy program for anxiety control. Behav. Ther., *4:*498, 1971.

Wolf, S.: Emotional stress and the heart. J. Rehab., *32:*42, 1966.

SUGGESTED READINGS

Blanchard, E. B., and Scott, R. W.: Behavioral tactics for clinical cardiac control. *In* Calhoun, K., Adams, H., and Mitchell K. (eds.): Innovative Treatment Methods in Psychopathology. New York, John Wiley & Sons, 1973.

Engel, B. T. and Melmon, L.: Operant conditioning of heart rate in patients with cardiac arrhythmias. Conditional Reflex, *3:*130, 1968.

Luthe, W.: Autogenic therapy: excerpts on application to cardiovascular disorders. *In* Barber, T. X. (ed.): Biofeedback and Self-Control: Aldine Annual 1971. pp. 437–457. Chicago, Aldine-Atherton, 1971.

Miller, N. E.: A Psychologist's perspective on neural and psychological mechanisms in cardiovascular disease. *In* Zanchetti, A. (ed.): Neural and Psychological Mechanisms in Cardiovascular Disease. Milan, Italy, Casa Editrice, 1972.

Nuland, W.: The use of hypnotherapy in the treatment of the postmyocardial infarction invalid. Int. J. Clin. Exper. Hypn., *16:*139–150, 1968.

Raginsky, B. B.: Temporary cardiac arrest induced under hypnosis. Int. J. Clin. Exper. Hypn., *8:*181–194, 1960.

Shapiro, D., et al.: Effects of feedback and reinforcement on the control of human systolic blood pressure. Science, *163:*588, 1969.

Weiss, T. and Engel, B.: Operant conditioning of heart rate in patients with premature ventricular contractions. Psychosom. Med., *33:*4, 1971.

Yanovsky, A. G.: The feasibility of alteration of cardiovascular manifestations in hypnosis. Am. J. Clin. Hypn., *5:*8–16, 1962.

33

Migraine Headache

ETIOLOGIC FACTORS

Migraine headaches have been a subject of study and discussion for thousands of years. Hippocrates used the expression "hemicrania," and Galen mentioned this entity in his writings. Gradually "hemicrania" evolved into our present word "migraine" (Friedman 1968). The migraine syndrome has been defined by many clinicians and investigators (Friedman and Merritt 1959, Goodell 1967). The outstanding feature of the migraine syndrome is periodic headache, usually unilateral in onset, which may become generalized. The headaches are associated with irritability and nausea and often with photophobia, vomiting, constipation, or diarrhea. Tension headaches generally result from chronic muscle contraction and have a close relationship to emotional conflicts. Onel et al. (1961) have shown that blood flow in the affected muscle is increased. Thus, both migraine and tension headaches could possibly be ameliorated by regulation of blood flow via the automatic nervous system.

Many causes have been suggested, such as vasoconstriction (Wolff 1948), vasodilatation leading to a combination of distention and altered sensitivity that results in pain (Ostfeld, Chapman, Goodell, and Wolff 1956), heredity (Grant, Bruce-Pearson, and Comeau 1936), and allergy (Vaughan 1939). Miscellaneous factors that have been suggested are electrolyte imbalance, histamine sensitivity, elevated serotonin levels (Ostfeld 1960), anoxia, vitamin and hormonal deficiencies, ocular malfunctions, and chronic intestinal disorders (Friedman 1959). Other biochemical correlates associated with migraine have been reviewed by Kroger (1963).

Although the precise mechanisms responsible for the migraine syndrome have not yet been elucidated, emotional tensions are precipitating factors in most instances. Likewise, the existence of a "migraine personality" cannot be satisfactorily substantiated even though many headache sufferers are compulsive, rigid, hostile, and perfectionistic.

These authors wish to advance a speculative hypothesis for the currently accepted vascular basis for migraine headache. We postulate that when we once walked on all fours, the head or cephalic portion of the body was functionally significant, especially for feeling states involving fright and rage reactions (head lowered to charge at an opponent). During our evolutionary development, the somatic manifestations of emotions involving rage continued to be displaced cephalad. Thus, this deeply repressed response may occur as an atavism in those unable to express rage. In such predisposed individuals, the blood rushes to the head, with chronic vasodilatation and subsequent vasoconstriction. The blood vessels become hard, tender, and rigid, and this produces a steady ache accompanied by spasm and pain of the neck muscles (Kroger, 1963). Hannington-Kiff (1974) remarks that "in no other region of the body is there a greater emotional attribute of pain than in the head." He posits that the head receives all the senses and also projects speech and facial expression; therefore, the migraine is largely a plea for help, and the head is chosen as the site for expression of pain.

OPERANT CONDITIONING; BIOFEEDBACK AND AUTOGENIC TRAINING

Miller (1969) presented research with animals showing that heart rate, gastrointestinal contractions, blood pressure, and the rate of saliva and urine formation can be directly controlled through operant conditioning technics by way of the autonomic nervous system. In human beings there is evidence for voluntary control of the autonomic nervous system through the training technics of Yoga (Green, Ferguson, Green, and Walters 1970), biofeedback training (Engel and Melmon 1968; Green, Green, and Walters 1971; Weiss and Engel 1971; Schwartz, Shapiro, and Tursky 1971), and the work of Schultz and Luthe (1969) on autogenic training, in treating migraine. Schultz and Luthe (1969) reported that the majority of their patients responded with lessened frequency and intensity of headaches with autogenic training excercises. A number of patients reported a cure after several months of practice and learned to interrupt the onset of an attack by starting autogenic exercises as soon as prodromal symptoms appeared.

Biofeedback training, a recently developed technic, holds promise of accelerating psychosomatic self-regulation of autonomic functioning. This technic, when combined with autogenic training, is called autogenic-feedback training. The method uses visual and auditory devices to show the subject what is happening to normally autonomic bodily functions as he attempts to influence them by his use of mental, emotional, and somatic visualization (Green, Green, and Walters 1971). One physiological function experimented with was increasing the hand temperature as an index to the voluntary control of the autonomic nervous system.

The technic of autogenic-feedback training for therapy of migraine was developed by Sargent, Green, and Walters (1973). In their study, 28 patients suffering from migraine and tension headaches used hand warming exercises to ameliorate or abort their headaches. This treatment was based on the authors' prior observation that a research subject found that her sudden recovery from a migraine attack coincided with an increase in hand temperature of 10 degrees F in 2 minutes. They conclude, "regulation of blood flow to the hands seems a useful treatment for migraine attacks." Graham (1975) found that hand-warming coupled with hypnosis was as effective as biofeedback training. It is the suggested relaxation that undoubtedly affords relief.

Another technic called contingent electromyographic (EMG) auditory feedback training has been found to be a promising method of reducing the frequency and intensity of tension headache (Wickramasekera 1972). Sustained contraction of the scalp and neck muscles appears to be associated with tension headache (Ostfeld 1969, Wolff 1948). Electromyographic feedback is useful in the induction of muscular relaxation (Budzynski and Stoyva 1969; Green, Walters, Green, and Murphy 1969). Budzynski, Stoyva, and Adler (1970) described an EMG instrument and feedback training procedure that reduced intensity of tension headache. Wickramasekera (1972) replicated this procedure under more control. He trained five female subjects suffering from chronic headache to relax their frontalis area with EMG feedback. The purpose of the EMG feedback system is to enable the subject to monitor his muscle tension by means of an analog information feedback system. The subject hears a tone with a frequency proportional to the EMG activity in the relevant muscle group. The subject is instructed to keep the tone low by relaxing this muscle group. Subjects receiving contingent EMG feedback reduced the frequency and intensity of headache activity, but subjects who received noncontingent but nonfrustrative EMG feedback did not reduce headache activity. Andreychuk and Skriver (1975) studied three groups treated by biofeedback training for hand-warming, biofeedback training for alpha enhancement, and training for self-hypnosis. There were no significant reductions in headache rates, and there were no significant differences between the first two groups. The high scorers on the hypnotizability scale showed significant reduction in the headache rates. They believe that although relaxation was the crucial variable involved, the greater improvement in highly suggestible patients supports a placebo explanation. This study on 33 patients indicates the need for exercising care about the outcome of biofeedback research, especially when dealing with psychosomatic illnesses. A more important finding is the need for ascertaining the role of suggestibility in any studies where mediating variables such as subject-expectations come into play.

HYPNOTHERAPY

The possibility of such physical factors as brain tumor, sinusitis, and other organic conditions must be ruled out before instituting any type of therapy. The psychogenic factors involved in tension headache or migraine respond readily to hypnotherapy, particularly cluster headaches (atypical facial neuralgia). There are numerous reports on this approach (Ambrose and Newbold 1958; Eisenbud 1937; Harding 1959; Horan 1953; Raginsky 1959; Van Pelt 1949; Wolberg 1948; Anderson, Basker, and Dalton 1975). The authors also have used directive hypnotherapy for menstrual migraine and for headaches associated with premenstrual tension.

The purpose of all treatment is to relieve tension and raise the pain threshold. Should analgesics or local methods of therapy fail, hypnosis is the method of choice, especially if it is combined with autohypnosis, time distortion, and glove anesthesia. Kroger (1963) has discussed the use of these as well as the technics of brief hypnotherapy for the treatment of headache, including glove anesthesia. Symptom-substitution, symptom-transformation, symptom-amelioration, and symptom-utilization are described in detail. Limitations and contraindications are also discussed. Rarely is formalized depth psychotherapy indicated in resistant cases of migraine, as the results are about the same as with directive hypnotherapy, which is less time-consuming and less expensive. Hypnotic relaxation, imagery conditioning combined with behavioral technics enable the patient to understand how he is reacting to his life situations and what he can do about facing his problems with more equanimity.

Many drugs recommended for migraine headache have little more than a placebo effect. Friedman (1959) states:

> In treatment of headache it is well to remember that the efficiency of any drug depends upon many factors. The emotional factors influencing results of treatment depend upon the personality of the patient, the method in which the medicine is applied, and the doctor-patient relationship. The personal influence of the physician is most important.

The following is an interesting case of intractable migraine which responded favorably to hypnotic intervention:

> The patient was a 33-year-old married woman who had recently lost an 8-year-old daughter from cancer. Headaches developed soon after this unfortunate occurrence. Hypnosis and glove anesthesia were only partially effective, but within 2 months the following data were elicited: she had conceived the daughter before marriage and always felt that she "had to marry her present husband." She became guiltladen and frigid following her tragedy and believed that "God took my

child from me because I sinned.'' Her deep-seated resentment of her mate as well as her faulty sexual responses were worked through, the latter facilitated by hypnosis.

Often formalized psychotherapy and in-depth probing is not necessary in the treatment of migraine. These authors have seen many cases in which the mere reduction of the patient's anxiety level through hypnosis is sufficient to eliminate the headaches. The following is such a case:

> M.B. was an attractive, very intelligent 44-year-old woman who complained of severe headaches accompanied by blurred vision and nausea lasting 3 to 4 days per episode. Headaches were frequent and averaged three per month. She had first become afflicted 9 years prior when she was slapped on the back by a friend while choking on some food from laughing at a dinner joke. The condition was diagnosed as occipital neuralgia and she had been treated by many therapists for the disorder and had years of physiotherapy, over 20 nerve blocks, and heavy medication including codeine and Demoral. Several other somatic difficulties had also ensued at this time, and the patient had had over 11 surgical operations.
>
> Discussion with the patient showed her to be well adjusted socially. She had 5 children, aged 4, 11, 14, 17, and 18, and her home life was happy. The emotional and sexual relationship with her husband was excellent. She was still active in spite of her headaches and had a zest for life. Hypnosis was begun the second session and the patient proved to be an exceptionally good subject. She responded well to Image IV for glove anesthesia, getting numbness on her first attempt. After the fourth session, she reported having cut her medication in half. The patient terminated after the fifth session, reporting that her headaches were gone. Whenever she would feel the onset of tension she would induce hypnotic relaxation and prevent the production of a headache. She had developed the ability to discriminate the anxiety state preceding her headaches so that this sensation of initial anxiety became a cue for her to induce relaxation. A 1-year follow-up showed her to be in good health and no longer plagued by headaches. In this case it had not been necessary to locate sources of stress in the patient's life and eliminate them. Her living conditions remained virtually unchanged, but her ability to cope and handle everyday stressors was greatly enhanced through application of relaxation technics.

STANDARDIZED IMAGES

Muscle relaxation necessary for the elimination of migraine can be gained through practice of the 25 images listed in Chapter 10. The throbbing, pulsating pain due to vasocongestion in the head and neck region can be eliminated by directing the blood from that area to other areas of the body. Glove anesthesia described in Image IV can be used to divert the blood from this region directly by producing numbness and anesthesia. The suggestion for warmth in another part of the body will also divert blood from the afflicted area with a resultant loss of vasocongestion there. Images IX (pool), X (Arctic), XVI (scuba), XVII (picnic), XIX (chalk cliffs), and XXII (hayloft) all involve training in gaining control over the circulatory system.

Although there is a considerable body of literature on the use of hypnosis in the treatment of migraine headache, there is a paucity of such references in the behavioral literature. The articles in the latter area are largely limited to the use of instrumental feedback control in the alleviation of headache. There is no doubt that physiological responses can be controlled by biofeedback. This does not mean, however, that such methods are clinically significant for the treatment of headache. It has been our experience that use of images to produce warmth, numbness, and relaxation can be therapeutic, especially when combined with many of the sophisticated hypnotic technics described in this volume.

REFERENCES

Ambrose, G. and Newbold, G.: A Handbook of Medical Hypnosis. London, Baillière, Tindall and Cox, 1958.

Anderson, J. A. D., Basker, M. A., Dalton, R.: Migraine and hypnotherapy. Int. J. Clin. Exp. Hypn., *23:*48, 1975.

Andreychuk, T. and Skriver, C.: Hypnosis and biofeedback in the treatment of migraine headache. Int. J. Clin. Exp. Hypn., *23:*172, 1975.

Budzynski, T. H. and Stoyva, J. M.: An instrument for producing deep muscle relaxation by means of analog information feedback. J. Applied Behav. Anal., *2:*231, 1969.

Budzynski, T. H., Stoyva, J. M. and Adler, C.: Feedback induced muscle application to tension headache. J. Behav. Ther. Exp. Psychiat., *1:*205, 1970.

Eisenbud, J.: The psychology of headache: a case studied experimentally. Psychiat. Quart., *11:*592, 1937.

Engel, B. T. and Melmon, K. L.: Operant conditioning of heart rate in patients with cardiac arrhythmias. Cond. Reflex., *3:*130, 1968.

Friedman, A. P. and Merritt, H. H.: Headache; Diagnosis and Treatment. Philadelphia, F. A. Davis, 1959.

———: The migraine syndrome. Bull. NY Acad. Med., *44:*45, 1968.

Goodell, H.: Thirty years of headache research in the laboratory of the late Dr. Harold G. Wolff. Headache, *6:*158, 1967.

Graham, G. N.: Hypnotic treatment for migraine. Int. J. Clin. Exper. Hypn., *23:*165, 1975.

Grant, R. T., Bruce-Pearson, R. S., and Comeau, W. J.: Observations on urticaria provoked by emotions, by exercise and by warming the body. Clin. Sc., *2:*252, 1936.

Green, E. E., Ferguson, D. W., Green, A. M., and Walters, E. D.: Preliminary report on the voluntary controls project: Swami Rama. The Menninger Foundation, June, *15:*13, 1970.

Green, E. E., Green, A. M., and Walters, E. D.: Voluntary control of internal states: psychological and physiological biofeedback and self-control. In Barber, T. X. et al. (eds.): Aldine Annual. Chicago, Aldine-Atherton, 1971.

Green, E. E., Walters, E. D., Green, A. M. and Murphy, G.: Feedback technique for deep relaxation. Psychophysiology, *6:*372, 1969.

Hannington-Kiff, J. B.: Pain Relief. Philadelphia, J. B. Lippincott, 1974.

Harding, H. C.: Hypnosis and migraine or vice versa. Paper read at the 11th Annual Scientific Meeting of the Soc. Clin. Exp. Hyp., San Francisco, August, 1959.

Horan, J. S.: Hypnosis and recorded suggestions in the treatment of migraine. J. Clin. Exp. Hypn., *1:*7, 1953.

Kroger, W. S. Hypnotherapeutic management of headache. Headache, *2:*50, 1963.

Miller, N. E.: Learning of visceral and glandular responses. Science, *163:*434, 1969.

Onel, Y., Friedman, A., and Grossman, J.: Muscle blood flow studies in muscle contraction headaches. Neurology, *11:*935, 1961.

Ostfeld, A. M.: Migraine headache. J. Amer. Med. Assoc., *174:*110, 1960.

————: The Common Headache Syndrome: Biochemistry, Pathophysiology, Therapy. Springfield, Illinois, Thomas, 1969.

Ostfeld, A. M., Chapman, L. E., Goodell, H., and Wolff, H. G.: Studies in headache: a summary of evidence implicating a locally active chemical agent in migraine, p. 356. Tr. Am. Neurol. A., 81st Meeting, 1956.

Raginsky, B. B.: Chapter on Hypnosis in Medicine, pp. 28–54. *In* Schneck, J. M. (ed.). Hypnosis in Modern Medicine. Springfield, Charles C Thomas, 1959.

Sargent, J. D., Green, E. E., and Walters, E. D.: Preliminary report on the use of autogenic feedback training in the treatment of migraine and tension headaches. Psychosom. Med., *35:*129, 1973.

Schultz, J. H. and Luthe, W.: Autogenic Therapy. Vol. I. New York, Grune & Stratton, 1969.

Schwartz, G. E., Shapiro, D., and Tursky, B.: Learned control of cardiovasuclar integration in man through operant conditioning. Psychosom. Med., *33:*57, 1971.

Van Pelt, S. J.: Hypnotherapy in medical practice. Brit. J. Med. Hyp., *1:*8, 1949.

Vaughan, W. T.: Practice of Allergy. St. Louis, Mosby, 1939.

Weiss, T. and Engel, B. T.: Operant conditioning of heart rate in patients with premature ventricular contractions. Psychosom. Med., *33:*301, 1971.

Wickramasekera, I.: Electromyographic feedback training and tension headache: preliminary observations. Amer. J. Clin. Hypn., *15:*83, 1972.

Wolberg, L. R.: Medical Hypnosis, vol. I. New York, Grune and Stratton, 1948.

Wolff, H. G.: Headache and Other Head Pain. New York, Oxford Univ. Press, 1948.

SUGGESTED READINGS

Blumenthal, L. S.: Hypnotherapy of headaches. Headache, *2:*197–202, 1963.

Dengrove, E.: Behavior therapy of headache. J. Am. Soc. Psychosomatic Dent. & Med., *15:*41–48, 1968.

Hanley, F. W.: Hypnotherapy of migraine. J. Can. Psychiat. Assn., *9:*254–257, 1964.

Lutker, E. R.: Treatment of migraine headache by conditioned relaxation: A case study. Behav. Ther. *2:*592, 1971.

Mitchell, K. R. and Mitchell, D. M.: Migraine: An exploratory treatment application of programmed behavior therapy techniques. J. Psychosom. Res., *15:*137, 1971.

Roberts, A. H., Kewman, D. G., and MacDonald, H. Voluntary control of skin temperature: Unilateral changes using hypnosis and feedback. J. Abnorm. Psychol. *82:*163, 1973.

34

Pain

CLASSIFICATION

Pain in one form or another accounts for the bulk of patients seeking medical assistance. Pain can be acute or chronic, organic or psychologic, and, of course, mild or severe. There are two broad classifications. The first and smallest group has pain that is definitely connected with cancer and other organic diseases. The second, and by far the largest, consists of pain associated with chronic benign conditions or "algias." The latter are of psychogenic origin, but are masked by a bewildering array of presenting complaints.

The first group often responds to appropriate neurosurgical intervention directed toward altering the affective quality of pain. The second group challenges the diagnostic acumen of the therapist and generally requires a multidisciplinary team approach for diagnosis and therapy. The latter group is particularly amenable to hypnobehavioral therapy. This is not to imply that organic pain syndromes cannot be helped to some degree by a psychological approach, difficult as it may seem. We shall direct our attention in this chapter to those with "pain illusion," a term coined by Crue (1973).

THEORETICAL ASPECTS

Crue (1975) points out that pain is not a primary sensory modality like hearing or sight, and that it is readily altered by perceptual and cognitive factors. Also the various mechanisms underlying the modulation of pain are extremely complex, and at present, inadequately understood. He states there is no such thing as a pain fiber per se or even a pain neurone in the peripheral nervous system, nor is it understood how pain is transduced from the end organs in the skin and received centrally. Furthermore, he contends that the theoretical mechanisms to explain pain such as the *specificity* and *pattern* theories are inadequate. The former proposes that a mosaic of specific pain receptors project to a pain center in the brain. The latter postulates that the intensity of the stimulus and central summation or intensity of the bombardment of impulses are the critical determinants of pain.

Melzack and Wall (1965) failed to unify these theories. They developed the concept of a "gate" in the region of the dorsal horn inputs. It is here that the small-diameter nerve fibers related to perception of pain conduct excitatory pain signals. Also it is here that large-diameter afferent nerve fibers generally associated with touch and proprioception modulate transmission of pain messages from the spinal cord to the brain, mostly via the dorsal columns.

The "gate theory" only explains pain from the periphery and also contains serious omissions. For instance, Crue (1973) stresses that the neuropathies such as trigeminal neuralgia associated with spontaneous pain are characterized by either a predominant small-fiber loss or depletion of all sizes. Melzack and Wall (1970), however, recognize the effects of the emotions on pain. They state:

> If the patient is allowed to think about something else or if other stratagems to keep the pain under control are employed, slowly rising temporal [pain] patterns are susceptible to central control. [More relevantly, they noted that relaxants, tranquilizers, sedatives, suggestion, placebos and hypnosis exert a profound influence on pain, but unfortunately the relative neglect of the motivational and cognitive contributions to pain has made these forms of therapy suspect, seemingly fraudulent.] . . . These methods deserve more attention than they have received.

Hannington-Kiff (1974) points out that Kroger and DeLee (1957) "made the prophetic remark that the mechanism of hypnoanalgesia is probably the result of keeping synapses open in the spinal cord so that noxious stimuli do not reach the higher centers. The language is different but the suggestion that the block is in the spinal cord is a remarkable anticipation of the gate control theory of Melzack and Wall" (p. 88–89).

Much research has been performed by laboratory means to produce artificial pain. Such experiments cannot be equated with real pain inasmuch as significance of the latter differs from person to person depending on numerous variables. The mode of action of all non-pharmacological methods of pain relief is the result of the central nervous system's being directed to the region affected through increment of regional nervous inputs. Also, distraction of the C.N.S. renders it incapable of evaluating noxious stimuli. Since the C.N.S. can only deal with a comparatively limited amount of information at any one particular moment, local application of electrical stimuli and acupuncture alleviate pain by distraction even though "gating" mechanisms may be implicated. Melzack (1971) concedes that the general effect of distraction plays an important role.

However he contends that one pain can suppress another by a "central biasing mechanism" in the brain stem's reticular formation. This part of the corebrain reduces pain by inhibition and cuts short C.N.S. activity after any sensory stimulus. It has recently been formulated that analgesia may be due to release of enkephalin in the brain. It is a morphine-like substance.

However, these theoretical formulations do not explain how meditation, hypnosis, and altered states of consciousness mitigate pain. "Pathways" for hysterical anesthesia exist, and mobilization of these can obtund pain. This exciting area will be dealt with below in detail. Omitted from this discussion, but pertinent, are the memory traces of pain (Ansell and Bradley 1973), reactivation of pain memory traces due to increased synaptic connectivity (Illis 1973), role of early perceptual experiences in the degree of response to pain (Melzack and Scott 1957), and the manner in which neurophysiologic pathways (Lewin 1972), cultural and religious factors influence pain (Lambert et al. 1960).

Additionally, allowing for variations in responses in human beings, the *pain threshold* is more dependent on physiological factors (Gelfand 1964) whereas the *pain tolerance* is influenced largely by psychological ones (Sternbach 1968, 1974). Lending further credence for adjunctive use of hypnobehavioral therapy are observations that dorsal column stimulation, chordotomy, and transcutaneous electrical stimulation often do not relieve pain (Shealy 1974). To improve management of refractory patients, he resorted to such other suggestive procedures as antogenics, gymnastics, percutaneous stimulation, and vigorous massage. Crue and Felsoory (1974) also noted that one of the mechanisms for the effectiveness of transcutaneous high cervical "electrical chordotomy" for chronic pain syndromes might be due to suggestion. One of their patients undergoing electrical chordotomy had significant reduction in pain, which lasted for several days even though no current whatsoever was delivered!

PAIN AND THE PLACEBO EFFECT

Beecher (1949, 1959) has studied the placebo effect associated with pain. He has noted that the presence or absence of anxiety, fear, and apprehension, and the meaning of the pain sensation are the crucial factors that determine pain. Benson and Epstein (1975) stress that the placebo effect is a neglected asset in amelioration of pain. Evans (1973) demonstrated that reduction of chronic anxiety, either as a personality trait or as acute situational anxiety, potentiated analgesic placebo effects. This corroborates our thesis that anxiety-mediating relaxation will raise pain tolerance. A dedicated physician, merely by empathy, reassurance, and inculcation of faith, can relieve over 60 per cent of pain by suggestive procedures. Patients suffering from organic pain of terminal cancer are more likely to respond to a placebo or any other type of suggestive therapy because of high motivation to be relieved of pain. They also do better than those with chronic benign pain syndromes.

OPERANT CONDITIONING

Skinner's (1953) operant conditioning explains how pain behaviors are mediated. Fordyce (1973) utilizes these concepts. Accordingly, all ways by which pain is signaled are termed operants. These operants are controlled by the consequences immediately following the expressions of pain. When an operant is systematically followed by a favorable consequence or positive reinforcer, that operant is likely to reoccur in response to a similar stimulus. If not reinforced, the operant will diminish. If followed by an aversive consequence such as punishment, the operant usually will likely extinguish. For instance, a husband using pain for obtaining sympathy from his wife will stop his learned maladaptive behavior if his spouse is instructed *not* to sympathize with him.

Therefore, instead of asking a patient to exercise to tolerance and then rewarding expressions of the resulting pain with rest and attention, Fordyce (1973) prescribes an exercise schedule below his proven tolerance. This insures that the rest and attention are positive reinforcers of exercise and not pain. The patient nearly always works up past his original tolerance limit and moves steadily on to whatever upper limit is prescribed. Fordyce sees other expressions of pain as patterns of learned behaviors either being positively reinforced or being used to avoid the pain itself. Such behaviors may be drug-dependence or refusal to leave the sickbed. Fordyce's approach here is to withdraw the positive reinforcers of such conduct in the face of pain and to reward activity or avoidance of "well" behavior on the patient's part.

For drug-dependent individuals, he switches from a regimen in which medication is the reward for complaints of pain to one in which the drugs are administered at a set time no matter how the patient feels. With this shift, according to Fordyce, it becomes a relatively simple matter to gradually reduce the active ingredients in the medication. Pain behavior also may be inadvertently reinforced by physicians who prescribe medication for use when needed (p.r.n.). Since the positive consequences of medication are contingent upon the occurrence of pain behavior, the patient may complain of pain in order to get the medication. The base rate for the giving of medication first must be determined according to the patient's needs. Then the medicaments are prescribed on a schedule so that the medication will be given whether or not the patient exhibits pain behavior at that time. The final step is a gradual decrease in dosage.

As we see it, a primary point of operant conditioning is to take the patient's attention from his pain. We do this and also instruct relatives and significant others to refrain from using the word *pain*. However, we are restricted by the amount of environmental manipulations possible, as we do not have an inpatient population sample. We therefore lay more emphasis on dealing with the pain itself. Since hypnosis facilitates manipulating the symptom (see cases below) more than the environment, it has great utility in the alleviation of pain.

Then, too, the protective inhibition produced by hypnosis revives cortical cells disturbed by such noxious processes as pain (Platonov 1959). These are potent factors in mitigating chronic pain. Hilgard and Hilgard (1975) present a considered assessment of the role of hypnosis in relation to pain as based both on studies in the experimental laboratory and in clinical practice.

HYPNOTIC CONDITIONING

Also, the structured nuances of our induction procedure builds in, by successive approximations, increasing control over the primary signaling system activities. These feedback systems as described in Chapter 4 consist of the nonlearned involuntary states of heaviness, tightness, lightness, stiffness, limpness, and relaxation; these are "digital" notions: on or off, present or not present. This induction procedure thus lays the foundation for putting under higher CNS control other desired feeling states or notions such as numbness, coldness, or warmness. Such notions are enhanced by our images as described below. These images function by analogy; they are "analog" notions, as they are learned, voluntary and secondary signaling system activities. By appropriate thoughts, ideas, or words, they are capable of calling forth the desired "instinctual" feeling states—all so essential for obtaining pain relief.

Furthermore, our induction procedure is characterized by extraverbal suggestions or double-bind maneuvers which practically force the patient to go into a hypnorelaxed state. Each feeling suggested is always paired with the phrase,

if you wish to get rid of your discomfort (we never use the word *pain* because it is a loaded word) you will allow your eyes to get *heavy*, lids to stick *tight*, you will feel *relaxed*, your arm will be *light*, *limp* or *stiff* (depending on steps in the induction), hand will be *numb* and woodenlike.

Additionally, suggestions of *warmth, cold, dryness,* and *wetness* are continually interspersed with assurances that the patient will attain the desired effects if he first can induce the simple feeling states. We know of no other technic that pairs the various steps of the induction procedure with the therapeutic goals. Motivation is thus readily obtained. In essence, behavioral response is formed and shaped by the responses to bring about compliant behavior. Patients also accept the suggestions as the result of their criticalness being bypassed.

Hypnotic phenomena such as time distortion (see case below) can be employed to condense time for duration of the painful attacks. Time expansion can be used for lengthening the intervals between painful episodes. Another very useful hypnotic phenomenon for obtunding pain is glove anesthesia. Age regression, age progression, hypnotic amnesia and depersonalization are valuable adjuvants.

BACK PAIN

This discussion will be limited to back pain of psychosomatic origin. The most common method of relieving this kind of backache by the combination of a psychodynamic and hypnobehavioral approach is illustrated in the following case:

Mrs. D.C., aged 20, had a severe backache for more than 3 months resistant to medicaments and physical therapy. No organic factors accounted for the symptom. Her backache began shortly after she was defeated for president of her club. She partially relieved her discomfort by "glove anesthesia." Subsequent hypnotic sessions were devoted to teaching her time distortion and systematic desensitization. An anxiety hierarchy was constructed, primarily oriented around her inability to express herself in her interpersonal relationships. She was also taught how to neutralize the anxieties when she communicated with others. Assertive training involved the construction of the following four-step hierarchy: (1) under hypnosis the patient "saw" herself in a social situation complimenting and being able to accept compliments from others. When she was able to do this successfully without experiencing anxiety, the second step or image was given. (2) The patient visualized herself in a small group beginning and maintaining conversations first with one individual and then other individuals. She was instructed to change and vary the social situations during practice sessions at home. (3) The patient was to see herself at her club meeting expressing to the chairwoman how she was really feeling about an injustice done to her. This was to be done in a manner that would not result in retaliation, punishment, or feelings of guilt. (4) The patient was to imagine herself in an intimate gathering at a friend's house where she is asked to do a favor she does not wish to do. She politely refuses and thus avoids being taken advantage of by others, a fault in her character which had been causing her much anxiety. After a month's work on the images of this hierarchy, she was able to achieve a closer and more rewarding relationship with other individuals. She no longer felt "used" and much of her tension had subsided. Hypnosis facilitated the desensitization process. She was able to see the images more clearly and achieve greater relaxation, which she effectively paired with anxiety-eliciting situations. Her husband was advised not to reinforce her pain by inordinate sympathy. During the next eight sessions she discussed her anxieties in stepwise fashion under hypnosis. This allowed her to ventilate her feelings with greater equanimity; the backache disappeared.

Such assertive training and conditioning should be given all individuals who feel inferior and uncomfortable in social situations. The lack of good social skills is one of the most common sources of anxiety among patients, regardless of their presenting problem.

Rhoads and Feather (1974) described a similar case in which desensitization and assertive training were used to successfully treat a woman who had severe pain, anxieties, and fainting spells. She also had a long history of abdominal pain which necessitated several exploratory operations—all showed no organic reasons for her pain. The course of therapy was continued irregularly over a

2-year span with ultimate recovery. However, back pain of emotional origin can be treated hypnotically by switching the symptom to another less incapacitating one. Through the induction of an artificial conflict, another target organ can be suggested for a symptom-equivalent to replace the original conversion reaction. For example, it can be suggested that the back pain be transferred to the stomach. This is not done by direct suggestion but by suggesting a new conflict associated with anxiety and fear. The symptom of backache is thus temporarily maintained until the emotional needs for it are worked through. If the patient develops the new symptom, it is indicative that he is willing to yield the old one. The fact that the symptom can be manipulated indicates a favorable prognosis. Also, the newly acquired symptom can be removed more readily than the long-standing conditioned one. These technics have been described more fully by Erickson (1954). The reader also is referred to the chapter on backache (Kroger 1951), which discusses the psychodynamic, differential diagnoses, and comprehensive treatment of this common affliction.

ABDOMINAL PAIN

Abdominal pain is treated in a manner similar to that described for backache. The case described below is typical. Many individuals with chronic benign pain have had previous operations for diminution of their pain. Some of these patients are "polysurgical addicts." Many are not aware of their deep-seated need for an operative assault. Such persons usually have masochistic guilt feelings for which the surgery serves as punishment, atonement, and, finally, the license to commit new offenses. As a rule, there is improvement for several months following such obtuse "therapy," after which the patient again produces new symptoms and demands further surgery. These people are referred to as "injustice collectors"; they engineer their own defeat so they can suffer. This "pleasure-in-displeasure syndrome" is more commonly referred to as psychic masochism (Bergler and Kroger 1954). The psychic masochist, on an unconscious level, enjoys the pain. He uses it to control his environment in a neurotic fashion to make up for his inability to cope with his problems on a mature and realistic level. He also repetitively uses the pain for expiation for real or fancied sins, thus developing a repetition-compulsion pattern.

Mr. C.C., aged 50, had a persistent pain in the right lower quadrant. He had had an appendectomy, gastric resection, removal of the gallbladder, and two chordotomies, without relief. After he was trained in autohypnosis and glove anesthesia, he was instructed to shift the pain to the left side of the abdomen by symptom-transformation. Within four sessions, at weekly intervals, he had a well-developed pain area in the left lower quadrant. Further posthypnotic suggestions were directed toward reducing the intensity of the pain in this region

At this point the technic of "thought stopping" was employed. Whenever he felt pain in this area he was to subvocally shout "STOP" and redirect his attention to one of the standard relaxing images described earlier in this book. In time the onset of pain automatically triggered a relaxing image and redirection of attention. Concomitantly, the masochistic need for the pain was worked through during subsequent sessions. He revealed that he felt he had to punish himself to atone for guilty fears and aggressive reactions toward his wife who constantly rejected him sexually. He felt he was growing old and unattractive and feared the loss of potency. The emotional needs for the symptom were made clear to him. This patient was seen over a period of 9 months. Much attention was directed toward the marital and sexual relationship. He made a complete recovery after his marriage became more harmonious.

PSYCHOPHYSIOLOGIC ASPECTS OF PAIN

Bonica (1974) has described the pathophysiological aspects of pain in detail. Hannington-Kiff (1974) has concisely presented the basic scientific aspects of pain as well as an overview of the clinical management of various pain syndromes. Pain often can be established as a conditioned pattern. The mere mention of a word repetitively associated with certain physiologic and psychologic reactions elicits these reactions even though the original stimulus has been forgotten. Thus, a word does not become meaningful until an associational bond between it and some conditioned or unconditioned stimulus takes place in the cortex. In the adolescent girl, for instance, the word *curse* acquires a definite meaning after it has been associated with the pain of menstruation. After that, the appropriate conditioned reaction to the word *curse,* in susceptible females, automatically produces the pain reaction. Discomfort can be increased by posthypnotic suggestion, and pain can be decreased by the same method (Platonov 1959). More important, autohypnotic suggestions can elicit the same reactions as posthypnotic suggestions via sensory-imagery conditioning. This is an important factor in successful management of pain by hypnobehavioral therapy.

DIAGNOSIS

The design of hypnobehavioral therapy depends upon the differential diagnosis of the pain. The patient often uses exaggerated metaphors to describe the character and onset of the discomfort. If there is a dull, dragging pain in the lower abdomen, difficult to diagnose, and always intensified when the patient is tired, one can be reasonably sure that the pain is of emotional origin and, therefore, that the patient has a good chance of responding to therapy. This is especially true if other and secondary symptoms, involving numerous organ systems, are present.

If the pain is constant, not relieved by rest, or is associated with throbbing and burning sensations in the abdomen, an organic etiology can be suspected, especially if the pain appears to serve no psychic purpose. Hypnoanalgesia can even be used as a palliative measure for organic pain refractory to conventional therapy. If the pain is of psychosomatic origin, hypnotherapy should be employed, either for behavioral change or understanding the emotional needs for the symptom (Conn 1949). There can be no question, however, of "functional" versus "organic" pain. To the apprehensive patient, all pain is real, irrespective of the cause. It should never be pooh-poohed or minimized.

Abdominal pain of obscure origin also may be the first sign of an incipient psychosis or deep-seated neurosis. Many prepsychotics are medical "shoppers." Gynecologists are apt to see many such patients; women who are not having so much "female trouble" as they are having trouble "being females."

HANDLING THE PATIENT

The authors' preliminary remarks to the patient proceed somewhat as follows:

We know you have the discomfort. It is not imaginary. We look at it as being real. Also we are well aware of the problems it has caused you and your family. We are anxious to help alter your reactions to your discomfort. However, remember that you are the one who developed your discomfort, therefore, you are the only one who can remove it. Hypnosis, which we shall teach you, by itself does not cure but merely facilitates therapy. It's your mind, your body, and your problem. Your problem resulted from learning negative, destructive, and harmful conditioned response patterns. Now, we realize you are willing to cooperate to your utmost. Therefore, you can reverse these faulty responses by substituting positive, constructive, and healthy conditioned response patterns through autosuggestions. We also will teach you other technics for decreasing your discomfort. We know you will put forth the necessary efforts for working with us. This will make your life more meaningful and, we hope, lessen your reaction to your discomfort.

Although such statements are an oversimplification, they help establish motivation and good rapport. The questions that follow are worded so as to elicit a desired response:

"How much of your discomfort do you really wish to keep?" the therapist asks. The patient of course answers, "None of it," and the therapist is thus able to remark, "Well, then, you are highly motivated to obtain relief, are you not?" Such a double-bind remark forces the patient to take a stand in the affirmative. She is then asked, "What are you trying to prove by the discomfort?" Invariably the patient will remark, "I don't know, Doctor." This makes the patient realize that she will have to talk about her innermost secrets if she wishes to get well. She is then asked, "How rapidly do you wish to get rid of your discomfort?" The reply is foreordained, and the patient's cooperation is assured. Finally, she is asked, "How would you feel without the discomfort?" This mobilizes faith and hope that recovery is pos-

sible. As stated in an earlier chapter, before beginning an induction procedure, the therapist should remove the popular misconceptions associated
with being hypnotized. He should stress that the patient is always in control.

BRIEF HYPNOTHERAPY BY SYMPTOM-REMOVAL

When pelvic pain is relieved by the glove anesthesia method or posthypnotic
suggestions, the improvement can be reinforced through sensory-imagery conditioning. If relief is obtained only for the duration of the hypnosis, this beneficial effect can be re-experienced long after dehypnotization by posthypnotic
suggestions. This helps break up the vicious reflex and is an important incentive toward further recovery.

A 32-year-old patient who complained bitterly of severe left lower quadrant
pain following a left salpingo-öophorectomy, was relieved of her symptoms by
posthypnotic suggestions directing her to actually relive or re-experience how
her pelvis felt before the onset of the symptom. Under autohypnosis she also
increased the duration of the glove anesthesia by approximately 15 minutes per
day until a comfortable feeling in the pelvis was established as a relatively permanent effect.

Another patient's intractable pain due to inoperable carcinoma of the cervix was
mitigated by the above technics, together with the use of time-distortion. She was
trained to "condense" time (making 10 minutes of clock time seem like 2 minutes of subjective or experiential time), and was thus able to telescope an attack
into 2 minutes. As a result, the need for opiates was drastically decreased, and
she remained fairly comfortable until she expired.

Another sufferer with pelvic pain due to psychogenic dysmenorrhea was given
a posthypnotic suggestion to remember what it felt like to be without discomfort,
to the end that she would be able to alter the character of the cramps in 2 or 3
months. The extraverbal suggestion implied is, "You might consider the possibility of being without your cramps for 2 or 3 menstrual periods." If relapses are anticipated, the condition of their occurrence can be suggested. Thus, the symptom
becomes a part of a cooperative endeavor rather than a manifestation of non-
compliance.

If a patient mentions that she is getting worse, this idea can be accepted and
negated by remarking, "Since you are worse, don't you think it's time for a
change?" This maneuver accepts but redefines the patient's statement and also
obviates active or passive resistances. In addition, guidance, reassurance, reeducation, and engrafting of new patterns of healthy thinking (reconditioning)
under hypnosis helps raise the pain threshold to anxiety-provoking stimuli. In
this approach, the patient is not ordered to yield the symptom. Rather, its
dissolution is in accordance with her wishes and needs. Here, a permissive hypnotic approach is mandatory. This approach as well as the technics of
symptom-manipulation, as mentioned, were pioneered by Erickson (1954).

BRIEF HYPNOTHERAPY BY SYMPTOM-SUBSTITUTION

Where direct hypnotic symptom-removal of the pain is unsuccessful, one can, through appropriate posthypnotic suggestions and amnesia in good hypnotic subjects, substitute another neurotic disability similar in type to the existing one, but yet nonincapacitating in character. This shifts the patient's behavior into more cooperative activity, and motivates her to follow other posthypnotic suggestions. Also, diverting attention from a severe anxiety-provoking symptom to a less noxious one produces less preoccupation with present difficulties. Symptom-substitution also temporarily satisfies the personality's needs for some type of neurotic disability.

A 38-year-old hypochondriacal widow, referred after a negative physical examination, complained of a myriad of vaguely defined pains that radiated from the pelvis down the thighs. She was taught hypnosis, autohypnosis, and glove anesthesia. All afforded some respite from her pelvic distress. Following the engrafting of a protective posthypnotic amnesia, it was suggested that she would have a dull, aching pain in both arms. On the next session, she complained of her inability to work (she was a legal stenographer) stating, "I couldn't type ever since you hypnotized me. What did you do to me?" Again hypnotized, it was suggested, "The pain in your arms will disappear within 2 or 4 days. It will be gone when I see you next· month, or next year, and even when I see you in 5 years." These extraverbal suggestions involving "age progression" implied that she was going to be all right in the future. This is more effective than saying, "Don't worry, your pain will disappear soon." Some of the patient's conflicts were then worked through. Then, after being shown that she was using the pain to call attention to her loneliness, sexual frustration, and sacrifice necessary to be breadwinner for her 3 children, she was able to deal with her life situations more realistically. The pelvic pain, as well as her other symptoms, were reduced in intensity as soon as she realized the secondary gain value of her symptoms that satisfied her neurotic needs. But she also was glad to give up the more incapacitating symptom, which had been artificially induced.

Poorly motivated patients respond well to symptom-substitution because loss of their symptom does not interfere with their defenses. Often, too, the defenses and ego strength of the patient can be strengthened by supportive hypnotherapy.

BRIEF HYPNOTHERAPY BY SYMPTOM-TRANSFORMATION

With symptom-transformation, some degree of anxiety is continually utilized and ultimately transformed into feelings that permit healthy adjustment. The character of the symptom is not changed, but merely transformed to a less disabling one. The suggestions for the new symptom are given in a complex manner in order to divert the patient from thinking of the old symptom.

A 21-year-old female complained of a heavy, dull pain that began in the vaginal area several weeks after marrying a male who had premature ejaculation.

The vague discomfort radiated to the back and lower pelvic region. Culdoscopic examination was negative. Her pelvic distress seemed to be associated with her lack of sexual satisfaction. Each fiasco increased the heavy feeling in her pelvis. After her husband's potency problem was remedied, she derived some satisfaction from intercourse. However, she still had considerable pelvic pain. She readily entered into deep hypnosis, and was given the posthypnotic suggestion that she would have *less* sexual satisfaction now that her mother-in-law, whom she greatly resented, was living under the same roof. Posthypnotic amnesia for this suggestion was instituted. Her pelvic pain was relieved by transforming her anxiety into a stronger anxiety reaction—the resentment and dissatisfaction toward her mother-in-law. She now transferred her aggression from her husband to the mother-in-law. She thus gave up the pelvic pain, which had been symbolically used as "organ language" to voice her protests over her pseudofrigidity. She also began to understand more about the *needs* for her undue hostility toward her mother-in-law. And after reviewing and talking about these feelings and attitudes, she realized that she was displacing her deep-seated resentments from her husband to his mother. Such desensitizing hypnotic technics accomplish more than exhortations to effect a change of attitude.

Illustrative of the value of symptom-transformation is the case of a 45-year-old patient who, because of intense hostility for her sexually inadequate and alcoholic mate, developed pelvic pain. The intensity of the distress seemed to be correlated with his crude sexual advances made during his drinking bouts. Through posthypnotic suggestions and amnesia, she was instructed that her pain would localize into her vagina. This suggestion was readily accepted, because she now had an alibi for avoiding sex with her husband. During subsequent visits her hostility toward her husband was discussed. She was given the following posthypnotic suggestions: "You will gradually lose the pain in your pelvis. Perhaps you might consider just how much pain you would like to transfer to your vagina?" This was like asking her, "How much pain do you really wish to keep?" She could still use the vaginal pain to retaliate against her husband. However, there was no doubt that she would be relieved of her symptom, that it was just a matter of degree, and that she would have to accomplish the task at her own pace. When some portion of the symptom can be kept, the patient is more apt to give up the rest of it eventually. A specific time limit is not set. In this case, psychotherapy was recommended for the husband, but was refused. Though the patient never recovered fully, she was able to adjust to her life situations and not react to them with neurotic symptoms. Symptom-transformation should not be attempted until the patient can develop autohypnosis and posthypnotic amnesia. Attainment of these are proof positive that she will comply to other suggested sensory alterations.

BRIEF HYPNOTHERAPY BY SYMPTOM-INTENSIFICATION

The hypnotherapist can add a much larger repertoire of technics to potentiate any type of conditioning for control of pain. *Dissociation* for the part of the body involved can be induced to relieve pain in good hypnotic subjects. Distraction or *misdirection of attention,* that is, getting the patient to concentrate on body areas not involved, often can reduce the fear and dread associated with the original and reoccurring painful experience. We also have used emotional flooding or *hypnotic intensification* of the affective component of the pain with moderate success. If the pain can be increased volitionally, it can be decreased in intensity in the same manner.

We have had little or no lasting success with instrumental biofeedback training on a small sample of patients suffering from intractable pain. Likewise our results with electrosleep have been disappointing for a wide variety of pain problems.

BRIEF HYPNOTHERAPY BY SYMPTOM-AMELIORATION

In hypnobehavioral therapy for pain relief, the degree of success is generally proportionate to the amount of practice. Furthermore, all suggestions should be directed toward the target behaviors that need to be decreased. The sophisticated hypnobehavioral therapist tries to have his patient accept a suggestion, regardless of whether or not decrement of pain has occurred. For instance, if a patient reports that she had 10 or 25 minutes *less* pain, the groundwork is then laid for further recovery if she concedes that this has occurred. This is referred to as *symptom-amelioration.*

During symptom-removal by any one of the brief therapeutic methods described above, reinforcement is often necessary to maintain pain reduction. Powerful reinforcement also is provided by the therapist's conviction in the efficacy of his methods. The hypnobehavioral approach for pain relief can be combined with neurosurgical procedures, pharmacological approaches, physical therapy, exercises, and occupational therapy. It also can be used with such sophisticated methods as percutaneous radiofrequency denervation of the spinal facets, dorsal column stimulation, high cervical electrical chordotomy, transcutaneous electrical stimulation, and acupuncture. Although we feel that acupuncture has a high content of suggestion, this approach can be combined with the hypnobehavioral model. We shall discuss the rationale for its effectiveness in Chapter 35.

OTHER TYPES OF THERAPY

There are other technics such as the very deep Yoga or Y-state of hypnosis (Meares 1960) for relieving pain. There is a definite correlation between the depth of hypnosis and degree of pain relief. There are such other methods as transcendental meditation, autogenic training, and progressive relaxation. However, these differ from the authors' hypnorelaxation technics. Our approach is directed to having the patient recall past experiences identical to the desired feeling states that can provide pain relief. For instance, recalling numbness for glove anesthesia, is the other side of the coin of hysterical anesthesia—a well described clinical entity.

There are numerous other pain syndromes that often can respond to hypnobehavioral therapy. These are degenerative arthritis, particularly those with chronic cervical syndromes, phantom limb and stump pain, atypical facial pain, peripheral neuropathies, partial or complete injury of the spinal cord, and the discomfort noted in Reynaud's or Berger's disease and other circulatory disorders. Our best results were attained in degenerative osteoarthritis and other arthritic conditions. Arthritis is very susceptible to suggestive procedures. Thousands of sufferers are helped by such procedures as the wearing of copper amulets, faith healing, visiting uranium mines, and spa therapy.

On the basis of our empirical observations, a high percentage of pain sufferers can achieve symptomatic control by hypnobehavioral therapy. The technics include the hypnotic phenomena mentioned in pages 18–24 as well as the various types of symptom-manipulation, desensitization, and operant conditioning. These are flexible and should be adapted to the needs of the patient. In refractory patients, hypnosis offers greater therapeutic leverage than slower and more cumbersome psychotherapeutic methods—many of which are "hypnosis in slow motion."

CONTRAINDICATIONS AND LIMITATIONS

Hypnobehavioral therapy is the safest of all healing methods, especially when employed for relief of pain. The dangers are virtually nonexistent. One contraindication that is now unwarranted is the belief that hypnosis is dangerous (Kroger 1961, 1963) because it only produces temporary symptomatic relief of pain. This does not occur with the sophisticated and permissive technics described above. It is the patient who removes the symptoms, and only the neophyte and the physician who plays God think otherwise. This is a far different situation from the concept that hypnobehavioral therapy consists of pulling the rug from under the patient's feet by dramatically removing the symptom.

Another unwarranted criticism leveled against hypnobehavioral therapy is that the underlying psychodynamics of the pain are not elicited by the procedure. It is obvious that we rely on psychodynamic and conditioning concepts and this combination in no small measure accounts for the success of hypnobehavioral therapy. However, the majority of pain problems are simply conditioned processes (Heron 1962) that have been developed and learned. In many cases, learning the removal of an unadaptive response pattern—the pain—will result in a generalization or "ripple effect" and the elimination of other associated symptoms. The physician, however, should not promise more from therapy in pain problems than can be reasonably accomplished.

STANDARDIZED IMAGES

Image V (mountain cabin) is used with pain problems to develop glove anesthesia. This enables the patient to transfer numbness to the afflicted area. Images VI (space), VII (farm), XI (clock), and XII (bluebird) are also used to produce time distortion. The patient is told to expand the periods when he is free of pain and condense those episodes when pain is present. Image I (beach) and VIII (jungle) are used to develop dissociation. Here the patient is able to dissociate or detach himself from the area of discomfort. For example, at the end of Image VIII he is instructed to shrink until he sees the areas of discomfort contracting to almost pinpoint areas. If a patient is suffering from breast pain following mastectomy, the removed breast, for example, can be dissociated from the body image, and along with this, the pain as well. Image XXV (autumn) may be used to regress the patient back to a time when he was not experiencing pain. Finally it should be remembered that all the images listed in Chapter 10 serve to produce relaxation, which heightens the patient's pain threshold.

REFERENCES

Ansell, G. B. and Bradley, P. B.: Macromolecules and Behavior. London, Macmillan, 1973.

Beecher, H. K.: Resusitation and Anesthesia for Wounded Men. Springfield, Charles C Thomas, 1949.

Beecher, H. K.: Measurement of Subjective Responses. London, Oxford Univ. Press, 1959.

Benson, H. and Epstein, M. D.: The Placebo Effect. J.A.M.A., *232*:1225, 1975.

Bergler, E. and Kroger, W. S.: Kinsey's Myth of Female Sexuality. New York, Grune and Stratton, 1954.

Bonica, J. J.: Recent Advances On Pain: Pathophysiology and Clinical Aspects. Springfield, Charles C. Thomas, 1974.

Conn, J. H.: Hypnosynthesis: Hypnosis as a unifying interpersonal experience. J. Nerv. Ment. Dis., *109*:9, 1949.

Crue, B. L.: Pain. Los Angeles County Medical Society Bulletin. *102*:10–15, 1973.

————: Pain: Research and Treatment. New York, Academic Press, 1975.

Crue, B. L. and Felsoory, A.: Transcutaneous high cervical "electrical cordotomy". Minnesota Medicine, *57*:204, 1974.

Erickson, M. H.: Special techniques of brief hypnotherapy. J. Clin. Exp. Hypn., *2*:109, 1954.

Evans, F. J.: Placebo response in pain reduction, *In* Bonica, J. J. (ed.): Pain. New York, Raven Press (Advances in Neurology, 4, 1973).

Fordyce, W. E.: An operant conditioning method for managing chronic pain. Postgraduate Medicine, *53*:123, 1973.

Fordyce, W. E. et al.: Operant conditioning in the treatment of chronic pain. Arch. Phys. Med. Rehab., *54*:399, 1973.

Fordyce, W. E., Fowler, R. S., and Delateur, B.: An application of behavior modification technique to a problem of chronic pain. Behav. Res. Ther., *6*:105, 1968.

Gelfand, S.: The relationship of experimental pain tolerance to pain threshold. Canad. J. Psychology, *18*:36, 1964.

Hannington-Kiff, J. G.: Pain Relief. Philadelphia, J. B. Lippincott, 1974.

Heron, W. T.: A confusion of verbs: To use and to need. Am. J. Clin. Hypn., *4*:211, 1962.

Hilgard, E. and Hilgard, J. R.: Hypnosis in the Relief of Pain. Los Altos, Wm. Kaufman, 1975.

Illis, L. S.: Regeneration in the Central Nervous System. Lancet, *1*:1035, 1973.

Kroger, W. S.: Hypnoanesthesia in Obstetrics, Gynecology and Obstetrics. Ed. by C. H. Davis, and B. Carter. Hagerstown, W. W. Prior, 1959.

————: Psychosomatic Gynecology: Including Problems of Obstetrical Care. Philadelphia, W. B. Saunders, 1951.

————: Techniques in Hypnosis, J.A.M.A., *172:*675, 1960.

————: It's A Wise Hypnotist Who Knows Who is Hypnotizing Whom. West. J. Surg, Obst. Gynec., *69:*132, 1961.

————: Clinical and Experimental Hypnosis. Philadelphia, J. B. Lippincott, 1963.

————: Hypnosis for relief of pelvic pain. Clinical Obst. and Gynec., *6:*763, 1962.

————: Sensory Processing and Control in Higher Nervous Systems Functioning. Bioengineering Symposium. Marquette Univ. Press, 1966.

Kroger, W. S. and DeLee, S. T.: Use of hypnoanesthesia for cesarian section and hysterectomy. J.A.M.A., *163:*442, 1957.

Lambert, W. E., Libman, E. and Poser, E. G.: The effect of increased salience of a membership group on pain tolerance. J. Personality, *28:*350, 1960.

Lewin, R.: Pain and Hypnosis. New Scientist, *7:*585–586, 1972.

Meares, A.: A System of Medical Hypnosis. Philadelphia, Saunders, 1960.

Melzack, R.: Phantom limb pain: Implications for treatment of pathologic pain. Anesthesiol., *35:*409, 1971.

Melzack, R. and Scott, T. H.: The effects of early experience on the response to pain. J. Comp, Physiol. Psychol., *50:*155, 1957.

Melzack, R. and Wall, P. D.: Pain mechanisms: a new theory. Science, *150:*971, 1965.

————: Psychophysiology of Pain. Int. Anesth. Clin., *8:*31, 1970.

Platonov, K. I.: The Word as a Physiological and Therapeutic Factor. Moscow, Foreign Languages Publishing House, 1959.

Rhoads, John M. and Feather, Ben W.: The applications of psychodynamics to behavior therapy. Am. J. Psych. *131:*17, 1974.

Schultz, J. H. and Luthe, W.: Autogenic Training. New York, Grune and Stratton, 1959.

Shealy, C. N.: Six years' experience with electrical stimulation for control of pain. Advances in Neurology. Bonica, J. J. (ed.): Vol. 4: International Symposium on Pain. New York, Ravens Press, 1974.

Skinner, B. F.: Science and Human Behavior. New York, Macmillan, 1953.

Sternbach, R. A.: Pain; A Psychophysiologic Analysis. New York, Academic Press, 1968.

————: Pain Patients—Traits and Treatment. New York, Academic Press, 1974.

SUGGESTED READINGS

Cheek, D. B.: Therapy of persistent pain states: Part 1, neck and shoulder pain of five years' duration. Amer. J. Clin. Hypn., *8:*281, 1966.

Crasilneck, H. B. and Hall, J. A.: Clinical hypnosis in problems of pain. Amer. J. Clin. Hypn., *15:*153, 1973.

Erickson, M. H.: The interspersal hypnotic technique for symptom correction and pain control. Amer. J. Clin. Hypn., *8:*198, 1966.

Field, P. B.: Effects of tape-recorded hypnotic preparation for surgery. Internat. J. Clin. Exp. Hypn., *22:*54, 1974.

————: Pain as a puzzle for psychology and physiology. Amer. Psychologist, *24:*103, 1969.

————: Pain: its reduction and production under hypnosis. Proc. Amer. Philosophical Soc., *115:*470, 1971.

Levit, H. I.: Depression, back pain and hypnosis. Amer. J. Clin. Hypn., *15:*266, 1973.

McGlashan, T. H., Evans, F. J., and Orne, M. T.: The nature of hypnotic analgesia and placebo response to experimental pain. Psychosom. Med., *31:*227, 1969.

Melzack, R.: The puzzle of pain. New York, Basic Books, 1973.

Sacerdote, P.: Psychophysiology of hypnosis as it relates to pain and pain problems. Am. J. Clin. Hypn., *10:*236–243, 1968.

Veldesy, F. A.: Pain and hypnosis. Am. J. Clin. Hypn., *5:*153–157, 1967.

Schwarcz, B. E.: Hypnoanalgesia and hypnoanesthesia in urology. Surg. Clin. N. Amer., *45:*1547, 1965.

Scott, D. L.: Hypnoanalgesia for major surgery. Amer. J. Clin. Hypn., *16:*84, 1973.

Werbel, E. W.: Use of posthypnotic suggestions to reduce pain following hemorrhoidectomies. Amer. J. Clin. Hypn., *6:*132, 1963.

35

Hypnoanalgesia in Obstetrics and Surgery

HYPNOSIS IN CHILDBIRTH

There is an extensive literature, reviewed by Kroger and DeLee (1943), Kroger (1951, 1959, 1960), Winkelstein (1958), Clark (1956), August (1960), Moya and James (1960), Tom (1960), Kroger and Steinberg (1961), Guéguen (1962), and Davenport-Slack (1975), showing that hypnosis can be an effective agent for obtunding pain in childbirth. Properly prepared women need have no more discomfort than they are willing to bear. One of the authors (WSK) has had extensive experience in training prepartal patients in groups. A desensitization technic was employed to psychologically immunize the patient against fear, anxiety, and surprise. Parturients, especially primiparae, were rehearsed during the prenatal training period for what to expect during labor and delivery. This training automatically raises the pain threshold in susceptible patients. The Lamaze (1958), Dick-Read's Natural Childbirth (1953), Psychoprophylactic Relaxation, Huttel et al. (1972), and the Velvoski (1960) methods are all forms of desensitization training using distraction or a great deal of misdirection of attention and waking hypnosis. Preparation for childbirth also teaches patients to relax during labor. As a result of relaxation and knowing what to expect, anxiety and fear are decreased. For a fuller explanation, the reader is referred to Kroger (1951, 1952, 1963), and Davenport-Slack (1975).

In general, hypnosis and prenatal training result in less medication and calmer behavior during labor and delivery. Davenport-Slack (1975), after carefully evaluating obstetrical hypnosis, concludes that the benefits cannot be attributed solely to the relaxation training, breathing exercises, and verbal suggestions; rather that the preparations raise the expectancy levels so that patients have to behave in a certain way, and that as a result, they will require less medication. These factors, as well as the degree of control a woman has over her own labor and delivery, seem to be a central factor in accounting for a less painful and more successful outcome.

However, the purpose of the prenatal training either by hypnosis or other conditioning technics is not to eliminate analgesia or anesthesia, but rather to reduce the need for excessive chemoanesthesia. The relaxation and decrease in pain also helps make childbirth a more rewarding and fulfilling experience. The perfect prescription for painless childbirth, therefore, is a combination of local (novocain infiltration) and vocal (positive reinforcing suggestions) support. Another potent factor is the rapport established with the obstetrician. His presence while the patient is in active labor is easily the equivalent of ¼ gr. of morphine. These tenets have been validated by numerous clinicians. There are disadvantages and limitations (Kroger 1963, Kroger and Steinberg 1961). Hypnoanalgesia is by no means intended to be a panacea. In carefully chosen patients, however, it can greatly reduce the fear of labor and the need for noxious drugs, thereby decreasing fetal and maternal morbidity and mortality.

HYPNOSIS IN SURGERY

There are many reports of various surgical procedures performed solely under hypnoanesthesia (Kroger 1960, Esdaile 1957, Bartlett 1971, Bernstein 1965, Marmer 1969, Van Dyke 1970). The technics and goals are similar to those described for labor and delivery. Postoperative complications are reduced and there are numerous advantages and disadvantages. These have been reviewed by Kroger (1963) in detail.

Gruen (1972) reported the successful application of systematic self-relaxation and autosuggestion to neutralize postoperative reactions in a coronary bypass surgical procedure performed on himself. He felt the recovery period was smoother than average and he required less medication for pain relief. He familiarized himself with all details of the operative experience and the preoperative and postoperative periods. He spent considerable time studying the reactions of patients in the intensive care unit. Autosuggestions focused on feeling happy and comfortable after the operation and on a quick return to normal physiological functions. He found that the preoperative preparation raised the pain threshold, and that autosuggestions were more effective than heterosuggestions. Marmer (1969), on a much larger series involving lobectomies and other major surgical procedures, noted siimilar results.

ACUPUNCTURAL ANALGESIA

With the recent advent of acupunctural analgesia (A.A.) for performing major surgical procedures, interest has been renewed in hypnoanesthesia. Acupuncture, as practiced in China, indicates the effectiveness of suggestive procedures in mitigating the pain of major surgery in selected patients. Western scientists are now alerted that preoperative medication and anesthesia can be markedly reduced by the Chinese approach.

Kroger (1972a,b; 1973a,b; 1974; 1975) in numerous publications has also explained how acupunctural analgesia works in terms of a paradigm that includes the basic principles of conditioning theory, autogenic training, and hypnosis. He contends that Chinese acupunctural analgesia (A.A.) and hypnoanesthesia have many common denominators. Both effectively reduce or eliminate conventional analgesia and anesthesia in selected patients. The success rate is higher in China because the antecedent cultural variables and inculcation by Maoistic doctrine in a regimented society bring about compliant behavior without overt motivational variables and cooperation being necessary. He believes that such compliance will be obtained in Western society only if strong and similar sociopolitical reward inducements are offered. Thus, he contends that some of the motivating factors responsible for A.A. are a kind of operant conditioning.

Acupunctural analgesia and hypnoanesthesia differ only in their method of induction; for the former, needles are used instead of words. Both are effective through their use of distraction or misdirection of attention, which helps bypass criticalness. Other similarities are establishment of good rapport, strong motivation, increased receptivity to suggestions, and the belief and confidence compounded into conviction—all account for the broad spectrum of psychobiologic experiences dealing with well-known placebo responses.

The advantages, disadvantages, indications, and contraindications for surgical anesthesia of each method are identical. If scientists of the East and West would realize that hypnosis is not a "trance-like" or "sleep" state and that it does not necessarily require a formal induction procedure, they would better understand some of the dynamics involved in A.A.—a remarkable breakthrough in anesthesiology. Neither method should be regarded with skepticism. As more serious scientists familiar with hypnotic technics exchange information on theoretical and clinical levels with traditional Chinese medical workers, it will be obvious that A.A. is chiefly "suggestion in slow motion," that is, hypnosis.

Case Histories

The following examples clearly illustrate the effectiveness of hypnoanesthesia and the similarity with A.A. for major surgical procedures. In all of the cases briefly described below, a large spinal needle was easily passed through the arm, breast or abdominal tissues to reinforce the patient's expectations and convictions that the "anesthesia" for the desired surgery would be effective.

Kroger and DeLee (1957) reported the first cesarian-hysterectomy ever performed in the world solely under hypnoanesthesia. The patient experienced no subjective discomfort and conversed with all in attendance. She watched the birth of her baby and saw her uterus removed. Her subjective experiences were identical to those of patients undergoing acupunctural analgesia. She stated, "You get a feeling of detachment. As it becomes complete, your arms and legs feel heavy, then numb, then as if they dropped off. Then you start floating. Your senses do not respond to pain stimuli."

A large tumor was removed from the breast of a 20-year-old patient under hypnoanesthesia alone. The surgeon, Dr. Silverstein, remarked, "I have never seen such remarkable relaxation of the tissues—they were like butter—and a radical mastectomy could undoubtedly have been performed without analgesia or anesthesis" (Kroger 1963).

One of us (WSK) hypnotized an unselected patient for an extensive breast operation which was painlessly performed without anesthesia at St. Vincent's Hospital, New York City, before a closed telecast of the 10th Postgraduate Assembly of the New York State Society of Anesthesiologists. The surgeon, Dr. Mitty, noted the marked relaxation of the tissues, decrease in bleeding, and absence of pain reflexes and discomfort. He stated "I easily could have performed more extensive surgery. I would not have believed it if I had not actually done and seen it" (Kroger 1953).

Kaplan and Kroger performed a subtotal thyroidectomy on a patient under hypnoanesthesia (Kroger 1953). No pre- or postoperative medication was required. The patient talked amiably to the surgical team throughout the surgery, had a glass of water immediately after the operation, jumped off the table, and wanted to walk to her own room. At no time during the 70 minutes did she have the slightest pain. She stated, "the scalpel felt like a feather being drawn across my neck."

The AMA film catalog lists a motion picture of this last case, entitled *Hypnosis in Thyroidectomy,* as well as one entitled *Hypnosis in Obstetrics.** An earlier book *Childbirth With Hypnosis* (Kroger and Steinberg, 1961) describes the hypnotic technics for pain relief and compares "natural childbirth" and psychoprophylactic relaxation to hypnosis.

IMPORTANCE OF AUTOGENIC TRAINING

In all of the above four cases, an adaptation of autogenic training for surgery was used. This method, consisting of a rehearsal technic, was first described by Schultz (1954), a German hypnotist-physician. Rehearsal of the entire surgical procedure preoperatively blocks the neurophysiological pathways involved in transmission of pain. Thus, receptors in the higher brain centers, when experientially conditioned under autogenic training or autohypnosis, protect the patient from surprise, apprehension, fear, and tension and raise the pain threshold (Kroger and DeLee 1957). Often a hypnotic induction was not required when rehearsal by autogenic training, was employed in highly motivated patients. During the latter method, every detail in the surgery was fully described while

---

* Films distributed by Wexler Film Co., 802 No. Seward, Hollywood, Calif.

the patient was under deep hypnosis. During a typical session the patient was told:

"Now your skin is being sterilized." [At this time the abdomen is swabbed with an alcohol sponge.] "I am now stretching the skin and the scalpel is going through the skin." [The line of incision is lightly stroked with a pencil.] "Now the tissues are being cut. Just relax. You feel nothing, absolutely nothing. Your breathing is getting slower, deeper and more regular. Each side of the incision is being pulled on by a retractor." [Skin and muscles are pulled laterally from midline.] "Now a blood vessel is being clamped." [A hemostat is clicked shut.] "You feel absolutely no discomfort. You are calm, quiet, and relaxed. Your breathing is getting slower, deeper, and more regular. Just relax! Now I am going deeper and I am going to enter the abdomen cavity." [For the peritoneum, suggestions of relaxation and assurances of complete pain relief are repeated several times.] "Just relax. Become deeper and deeper relaxed; your heartbeat is slower and more regular. You feel nothing. Absolutely nothing." [Since the viscera are relatively insensitive, the patient has to be prepared for the discomfort produced by pulling and torsion of the uterus. The steps for closure of the peritoneum, muscles, fascia, and skin are also described in a similar manner. There are really only three places where pain can be expected: the incision of the skin and peritoneum and the clamping of the peritoneal reflection of the viscera.]

At the Friendship Hospital in Peking, this form of autogenic training is used as a prelude to acupunctural anesthesia. Patients are rehearsed several days before surgery. The assigned surgeons describe the entire procedure to be performed. In the surgical suite, patients are shown how they will be operated upon, what the acupuncturist will do, and what effect the needles will have. Then the patients talk to other patients who have had acupuncture. Finally, at the patient's option, he is given acupuncture needles to experiment with at home.

An indication of the potent effect of the rehearsal during the autogenic training was illustrated when the only time one of the author's patients complained of pain was when the towel clips were being placed on the abdomen prior to the skin incision. This minor detail was inadvertently omitted from the rehearsal. That two other patients had similar experiences indicates how well perceptual and cognitive experiences can be organized (Kroger and DeLee 1957) into a variety of altered responses depending on the range of the learning process.

LIMITATIONS OF HYPNOANESTHESIA

Hypnoanesthesia per se, like A.A., is recommended only for selected patients. These constitute less than 10 per cent of all patients requiring major surgery. Hypnosis has a much wider field of application when used to potentiate or reduce chemoanesthesia or analgesia. In this capacity it can facilitate the induction of anesthesia. Due to marked reduction in anxiety, fear, and tension, anoxia is diminished. In good patients, hypnosis also can obviate the traditional use of preanesthetic medicaments and thus lessen respiratory depression.

MECHANISMS OF HYPNOANESTHESIA

Though the mechanism of hypnoanesthesia is as yet poorly understood, current research indicates that the pain, perceived in the tissues, does not reach the pain receptors in the higher brain centers during hypnosis. With the higher cortical centers unexcited during deep hypnosis, the vegetative nervous system is able to maintain homeostatsis and thus raise the adaptive response of the organism to stress. Further psychophysiologic investigations also are needed to elucidate the mechanisms by which hypnosis reduces neurogenic shock in surgery.

REFERENCES

August, R.: Hypnosis in Obstetrics. New York, McGraw-Hill, 1960.

Barlett, E. E.: Hypnoanesthesia for bilateral öophorectomy—a case report. Amer. J. Clin. Hypn., *14:*122, 1971.

Bernstein, M. R.: Significant values of hypnoanesthesia: three clinical examples. Amer. J. Clin. Hypn., *7:*259, 1965.

Bonica, J. J.: Therapeutic Acupuncture in Peoples Republic of China. J.A.M.A., *228:*1544, 1974.

Clark, R. N.: A training method for childbirth utilizing hypnosis. Amer. J. Obs. Gynec., *72:*1302, 1956.

Davenport-Slack, B. Obstetrical hypnosis and natural childbirth: A comparative evaluation. Internat. J. Clin. Exp. Hyp., *23:*266, 1975.

Dick-Read, G.: Childbirth Without Fear: The Principles and Practice of Natural Childbirth. Rev. ed. New York. Harper and Row, 1953.

Esdaile, J.: Introduction and supplemental surgical cases. W. S. Kroger (ed.): *In* Hypnosis in Medicine and Surgery. New York, Julian Press, 1957.

Gruen, W.: A successful application of systematic self-relaxation and self-suggestions about postoperative reactions in a case of cardiac surgery. Internat. J. Clin. Exp. Hypn., *20:*143, 1972.

Guéguen, J.: Childbirth under hypnosis (methods and results). Gynec. et Obstet., *61:*92, 1962.

Huttel, F. A., Mitchell, I., Fischer, W. M., and Meyer, A. E.: A quantitative evaluation of psychoprophylaxis in childbirth. J. Psychosom. Res., *16:*81, 1972.

Kroger, W. S.: Psychosomatic Gynecology; Including Problems of Obstetrical Care. Philadelphia, W. B. Saunders, 1951.

―――: "Natural Childbirth." Is the Read Method of "Natural Childbirth" Waking Hypnosis? Med. Times, *80:*152, 1952.

―――: Hypnosis in obstetrics. *In* B. Carter (ed.): Obstetrics and Gynecology. Hagerstown, Harper and Row, 1959.

―――: Hypnoanesthesia in Surgery. West J. Obst. Gynec. 1960. *68:*73, 1960.

―――: Clinical and Experimental Hypnosis. Philadelphia, J. B. Lippincott, 1963.

―――: More on Acupuncture and Hypnosis. Soc. Clin. Exp. Hyp. Newsletter, *13:*2, 1972a.

―――: Hypnotism and Acupuncture. J.A.M.A. *220:*1012, 1972b.

————: Acupunctural analgesia: its explanation by conditioning theory, autogenic training & hypnosis. Am. J. Psy. *130:*855, 1973a.

————: The scientific rationale for acupunctural analgesia. J. Psychosom. *14:*191, 1973b.

————: Current status of acupuncture in surgery, gynecology and obstetrics. *In* Greenhill, J. P. (ed.): Yearbook of Obstetrics & Gynecology. Chicago, Year Book Publications, 1974.

————: Pain, Acupuncture & Hypnosis. Read at symposium on acupuncture at Hahnemann Medical College, April 3, 1975.

Kroger, W. S. and DeLee, S. T.: The Hypnoidal State as a Safe Amnesic, Analgesic & Anesthetic Agent in Obstetrics. Am. J. Obst. Gynec., *46:*635, 1943.

————: Cesarian-hysterectomy under hypnosis. J.A.M.A., *163:*442, 1957.

Kroger, W. S. and Steinberg, J.: Childbirth With Hypnosis. New York, Doubleday, 1961.

Lamaze, F.: Painless Childbirth: Psychoprophylactic Method. L. R. Celestin (trans.). London, Burke, 1958.

Mandy, A. J., Mandy, T. E., Farkas, R., and Scher, E.: Is natural childbirth natural? Psychosom. Med., *14:*431, 1952.

Marmer, M. J.: Hypnosis and Anesthesia. Springfield, Ill., Charles C Thomas, 1969.

Moya, F. and James, L. S.: Medical hypnosis for obstetrics: Clinical and biochemical evidence indicates that cautious and competent administration is required. J.A.M.A., *174:*2026, 1960.

Schultz, J. H.: Some remarks about technics of hypnosis as anesthesia. Brit. J. Med. Hypnotism, *5:*23, 1954.

Tom, K. S.: Hypnosis in obstetrics and gynecology. Obstet. Gynec., *16:*222, 1960.

Van Dyke, P. B.: Some uses of hypnosis in the management of the surgical patient. Amer. J. Clin. Hyp., *12:*227, 1970.

Velvovski, I., Platonov, K., Plotitcher, V., and Chougom, E.: Painless Childbirth Through Psychoprophylaxis. Moscow, Foreign Lang. Publ. House, 1960.

Winkelstein, L. B.: Routine hypnosis for obstetrical delivery: An evaluation of hypnosuggestion in 200 consecutive cases. Amer. J. Obs. Gynec., *76:*152, 1958.

SUGGESTED READINGS

Anderson, M. N.: Hypnosis in anesthesia. J. Alabama Med. Assn., *27:*121–125, 1957.

Ball, T. L.: The psychoprophylactic preparation of pregnant women for childbirth in the Union of Soviet Socialist Republics. Trans. N.Y. Acad. Sci., *22:*578, 1960.

Betcher, A. M.: Hypnosis as an adjunct in anesthesiology. N.Y. State J. Med., *60:*812–822, 1960.

Chertok, L.: Psychosomatic Methods in Painless Childbirth. New York, Pergamon, 1959.

Crasilneck, H. B., McCranie, E. J., and Jenkins, M. T.: Special indications for hypnosis as a method of anesthesia. J.A.M.A., *162:*1606–1608, 1956.

Hirsch, H.: The Family. Section on Pregnancy and Preparation for Labor, New York, S. Karger, 1975.

Katz, R. et al.: Pain, acupuncture and hypnosis. *In* Bonica, J. J. (ed): Advances in Neurology, *4:*819–825. New York, Raven Press, 1974.

Li, C. L. et al.: Acupuncture and hypnosis: effects on induced pain. Experimental Neurology, *49:*272–280, 1975.

Van Dyke, P. B.: Hypnosis in surgery. J.Abd. Surg., *7:*1–5, 1965.

36

Gastrointestinal Disorders

ETIOLOGIC FACTORS

The imagination plays an important role in digestive upsets; for instance, merely hearing a description of a nauseating smell or even thinking about swallowing castor oil can induce vomiting in highly susceptible persons. Radiographically, it has been demonstrated that gastric contractility varies with emotional affects. Under fluoroscopy, we have observed Yogins who, at will, could contract their duodenal sphincter. Common gastrointestinal disorders with a large emotional overlay amenable to hypnobehavioral therapy are peptic ulcer, gastritis, colitis, pylorospasm, diarrhea, and constipation. Other conditions responding to this approach are glossitis, bizarre oral tastes, globus, dysphagia, cardiospasm, dyspepsia, aerophagia, anorexia, ptyalism, nausea and vomiting, pyrosis, bloating, and flatulence; all have a high content of severe anxiety.

ROLE OF CONDITIONING

Recent research indicates that physiological functioning of the gastrointestinal tract can be conditioned to environmental events. All human acts have observable motor aspects and physiological components that can be assayed. When a person enacts a social role consisting of aggressive, hostile, calm, or loving behavior, there are measurable concomitants in heart rate, blood pressure, psychogalvanic reflex, and respiration rate. In this chapter we will deal primarily with therapy based on learning theory rather than on the physical approach, which is outside the scope of this book.

It has been repeatedly demonstrated that most physiological functioning (e.g., cardiovascular, gastrointestinal) can be respondently or classically conditioned (Cannon 1929, Gantt 1964, Lacey 1956, Liddell 1956, Mahl 1949, Malmo 1950). More recently, it has been demonstrated that physiological functioning can be instrumentally as well as classically conditioned. Unelicited autonomic responses can be strengthened by the presentation of reinforcement *after* their emission, that is, as operants (Engel and Hansen 1966, Engel and Chism 1967, Kemmel and Hill 1960, Kimmel and Kimmel 1963, Mandler, Preven, and Kuhlman 1962, Razran 1961, Miller and DiCara 1967).

TREATMENT

Patients with functional gastrointestinal symptoms usually state, "I have always had a nervous stomach." Repeated physical examinations are consistently negative for pathology. Reassurance that an organic involvement does not exist improves gastrointestinal functioning in many chronic sufferers. Some others are "polysurgical addicts," having had some type of abdominal surgery or a long history of digestive upsets or food intolerance. Vacations, hospitalization, dietary measures, and reduction of family or business worries often ameliorates the symptoms. Our hypnobehavioral model stresses not only relaxation but desensitization, assertive training, role playing, and modeling—all help correct faulty behavior patterns. Alberti and Emmons (1974) emphasize that reduction in guilt and anxiety experienced by nonassertive persons who learn to be assertive often results in elimination of physical symptoms of gastrointestinal disorders.

PEPTIC ULCER

Etiologic Factors

Peptic ulcers often occur following severe burns, shock, and anoxemia. Thus, stress activates adrenergic responses, and the resultant corticotropin output interfers with normal functioning of the parietal cells in the stomach. Other factors, such as heredity, age, previous adverse conditioning to stress, and the nutritional state also can affect the mucosa. A careful history and physical examination is mandatory in all cases of ulcer.

Hypnobehavioral Therapy

Initially, hypnobehavioral therapy should assess the relationship between the character of the emotional upsets and the symptoms. If the patient is seen during an attack, questioning should be directed toward the type of mood, thoughts, or environmental stimuli that preceded the onset of the symptom. In good hypnotic subjects, one can revivify specific situations or thoughts that once triggered the symptoms. In this manner, the patient develops a clearer understanding of how stressful stimuli exacerbate and maintain the chronicity of the symptom.

The patient is asked to identify and enumerate those anxiety-provoking emotional situations connected with his symptoms in the order of their importance. Under hypnosis, reciprocal inhibition and desensitization technics are used to "immunize" him against these harmful influences. He is asked to imagine and discuss the least aggravating conditions first and the more serious ones later. He also is advised that during autohypnosis he can use these new learnings to facilitate removal of his maladaptive behaviors. Then a constructive plan for dealing with the causes of frustration, anxiety, and tension is discussed. Also, pleasant imagery paired with partaking of distasteful food often is helpful. This conditioning can readily be facilitated by posthypnotic suggestions. Some ulcer patients are dependent and have strong needs for recognition. For these, assertive training and sensory imagery conditioning directed to "seeing" themselves reacting favorably are valuable. Utilizing ongoing self-reinforcement, such as telling himself he is doing well and becoming more relaxed, especially benefit those whose personalities are either meek or passive-aggressive.

Moody (1953), using controls, noted improvement in 20 patients treated only by directive hypnosuggestive procedures. The rapid mobilization of faith and confidence by hypnosis, together with the establishment of corrective emotional attitudes and the fulfilling of dependency needs all played an important role in facilitating recovery. Zane (1966) also hypnotically controlled ulcer pain.

Hypnosis in the form of prolonged "sleep" may be of value for those ulcer patients refractory to our approach. Andreev (1960) described how prolonged hypnotic "sleep" for several weeks is more conducive to relaxation than continuous intravenous sodium amytal. One disadvantage is that a trained person has to be in constant attendance. The patient is dehypnotized only for evacuation and feeding. In this way, the organism is maintained at complete physiologic rest. Stress is eliminated and the ulcer has a good chance to heal. Follow-up psychotherapy, however, often is necessary to prevent relapses.

COLITIS

Etiologic Factors

Emotional maladjustments are closely related to colitis and can certainly aggravate the associated pain, bloating, and diarrhea. These symptoms often are associated with depression, headaches, irritability, and anorexia. Most sufferers have fears and unresolved anxieties. Those who usually are nonassertive in their interpersonal relationships are referred to as "having no guts." They can be helped by assertive training and learning how to cope with their anxieties and tensions.

Hypnobehavioral Therapy

Hypnorelaxation, with positive reinforcing suggestions involving reassurance, helps some colitis sufferers face their conflicts; these generally involve social and occupational maladaptive behaviors. However, some respond poorly to this type of conditioning as well as to behavior modification and other psychotherapeutic procedures. Others may improve on any regimen, but relapse rapidly. The approach we use is similar to the one described for the ulcer patient. Byrne (1973), Dias (1963) recommend hypnosis for bowel syndromes.

The following illustrates a combined hypnobehavioral and psychodynamic approach in a selected case of colitis:

Mrs. E.H., aged 34 and the mother of two children, complained of persistent bowel spasm, bloating, diarrhea, and lassitude present for 6 years. Medications were of little help. Her father was a top industrialist who never spent much time with her; her mother was an aggressive woman who dominated the patient. As a result, she resented her parents. After marriage, she displaced some of her tensions to her husband, but since he too was very dominating, she began to clam up and suppressed her ambivalent feelings toward him. It was at this time that her bowel symptoms became unbearable.

She was taught to relieve pain and spasm by glove anesthesia. It was suggested that her symptoms would decrease in intensity if she paired pleasant and relaxing images with her symptoms. This sensory imagery conditioning enlisted her active participation and, after she mastered this technic, some of her symptoms improved. It was further suggested that she remember the specific emotions associated with the onset of symptoms. After becoming aware of the patterns that seemed to initiate the symptoms, she utilized her capacities to learn, react, and respond to her feelings without suffering abdominal cramping. Using assertive training under hypnosis, she imagined speaking up to her hypercritical and demanding spouse. Within a month she was able to talk to her husband without anxiety, guilty fears, or self-recrimination. These needs were worked through on a superficial level, and it was pointed out that if she wished further improvement, she would have to "quit beating her head against the wall." After several months of therapy at hypnotic and nonhypnotic levels, she began to understand the masochistic nature of her behavior and what it meant in terms of her unhappy domestic situation. She discussed the possibility of divorce with her husband if he would not change his hypercritical attitudes. Her bowel upsets became less frequent but never completely disappeared. Therapy was suggested for her husband, but was refused. Although this patient was not cured, she at least made a partial adjustment to a difficult situation by learning how to assert herself.

ULCERATIVE COLITIS

Etiologic Factors

Nearly all investigators agree that psychogenic factors play an important role in the cause and maintenance of ulcerative colitis, especially with reference to the exacerbations of the symptoms. The physical aspects of the disease are serious and should not be neglected. Here, too, as for the colitis sufferer, one must find out how and why the patient reacts to his deep-seated emotional problems in this manner. A combined medical and psychological approach is always indicated.

Hypnobehavioral Therapy

Hypnobehavioral therapy requires a sympathetic understanding of the patient's plight, strong reassurance, even stronger persuasion and encouragement, and a thorough discussion of the patient's problems. Many of these patients feel that their prognosis is hopeless, so the major objective is to continually reinforce their confidence and outlook toward life. However, without controls, it is difficult to determine how much these patients are helped by any type of psychotherapy. Symptoms of a few have been arrested, probably temporarily. Most deteriorate rapidly and require successive resections of the bowel.

> Mr. L.S., a 40-year-old writer, developed all the signs and symptoms of ulcerative colitis when faced with a scenario assignment. He worried over his inability to write (he was considered excellent). In spite of medical therapy and his wife's encouragement, his attacks became more frequent.
>
> When first seen, he was resistant to hypnotic induction. It was suggested that the same emotional factors that prevented him from being hypnotized undoubtedly also were associated with his symptoms. He revealed that he feared being controlled by another person; he could not assert himself in such a dilemma. It was emphasized that he could better understand his situational anxiety and responses if he could be hypnotized. Following this "explanation," he readily entered a medium state of hypnosis. Since there seemed to be a clear-cut connection between his work and his symptom, it was decided to limit the therapy to overcoming the frustrations and guilt reactions brought about by his lack of assertiveness and concomitant aggressive feelings. Scene visualization was utilized to give him more confidence in his interpersonal relationships. Such conditioning allowed his imagination full rein to role-play what he could do to reduce his anxiety and guilt. He developed a better attitude toward his work, his superiors, and his family. His bowel symptoms decreased in intensity. Unfortunately, he was transferred to another city and had to terminate the therapy.

DIARRHEA

Emotionally-caused diarrhea often responds to hypnobehavioral therapy and dietary and medical measures. It generally occurs in sensitive and unstable persons. Episodes usually follow stress, tension, and anxiety. The urge to defecate immediately after eating or drinking suggests that a trigger-like gastrocolic reflex is responsible. One of the most refractory cases the authors have seen responded to intensive hypnobehavioral therapy directed toward the patient's facing his problems.

> A very successful business executive, aged 46, had diarrhea and painful abdominal spasms immediately after eating and drinking. The symptoms generally occurred when dining in restaurants or away from home. As a result, he was un-

able to eat out, to travel, or to perform many of his duties unless he was close to a lavatory. His symptoms began after he discovered that his wife, who had been frigid toward him, had been unfaithful. Following this episode, he became guilt-laden while he was having intimate relations with his secretary. Exacerbations of diarrhea were noted whenever he had to discuss problems with his superiors or when aggressive behavior was required when dealing with business associates. Through autohypnosis he utilized self-exploration and sensory-imagery conditioning (imagining he could perform dreaded tasks). He also received psychotherapy to overcome his passive-dependent tendencies, to deal objectively with his wife's problems, and also to work through his guilt over his extramarital relations. Less than a year after the start of therapy (approximately 30 sessions) his diarrhea subsided. He took assignments that he formerly was unable to fulfill. Glove anesthesia also materially assisted in controlling the abdominal cramps.

CONSTIPATION

Obstinate constipation that does not respond to laxatives can be helped by posthypnotic suggestions and sensory-imagery conditioning. One cannot merely suggest under hypnosis that the patient will have a bowel movement at a certain time but, rather, one can suggest that all the subjective sensations associated with a normal evacuation will be experienced; these are "rehearsed" during autohypnosis.

The rectal sphincter is under autonomic as well as volitional control, which provides this area with a "time sense." One usually develops the desire for defecation as the result of a well-established habit pattern. When this pattern is disturbed, constipation often results. Patients are first trained in hypnosis and autohypnosis. Then, during autohypnosis, the patient describes in minute detail what a normal evacuation feels like to him. All relevant details such as the time and the nature of the "call to stool" signal, and the type of spasms or tenesmus at the rectal spincter are elicited. Posthypnotic suggestions then are given that the exact sensations will be experienced during the next few days.

GALLBLADDER DYSFUNCTIONS

Dysfunction of the gallbladder may result from disturbances of the sphincter mechanism that is regulated in part by autonomic impulses, or from functional derangements in other portions of the biliary tract. Symptoms arising from a normally functioning gallbladder without stones frequently indicate a psychosomatic involvement.

Emotional factors can produce distension of the gallbladder, colic, and jaundice, and the resultant stasis also contributes to stone formation. This syndrome has responded to environmental manipulation, hypnobehavioral therapy, and sedative drugs. Glove anesthesia and opiates are the methods of choice for short-term relief of pain. In the presence of intermittent substernal pain, further search for such physical factors as reflex coronary spasm should be made.

DYSPHAGIA

Involuntary vomiting and fear of throwing up are fairly common presenting problems. Weitzenhoffer (1974) discusses the use of hypnosis in diaphragmatic clonus. Lait (1972) gives one of the more recent accounts of treatment in hypnotherapy for a case of recurrent vomiting. These people often have a long history of "nervous stomach" and are sensitized to food in general. They react to all sources of tension with an upset stomach. Often the fear of throwing up is not realistic and the patient seldom if ever vomits. He is however, traumatized by the idea that he may up-chuck in public and this limits his social activities. A slight feeling of nausea becomes the cue for the thought, "I might throw up in front of all these people," and this thought produces extreme anxiety and increased nausea. In cases such as this, the patient is instructed to practice hypnotic construction of images in which he sees himself throw up in given social situations. The pairing of hypnotic relaxation with such an image desensitizes him to the *thought* of throwing up in public, which is the source of most of the anxiety.

> The authors recall one case in which a 45-year-old female would not allow her husband to penetrate her vagina for fear she would throw up. Due to some very unpleasant sexual experiences in her adolescence the thought of penetration made her nauseous. In hypnosis, she imagined being penetrated by her husband and vomiting all over him. When sufficiently desensitized to this image, the patient permitted her husband to penetrate. She did not throw up and the fear dissipated.

In other cases, the fear of throwing up is well founded and the patient is unable to keep his food down. It is difficult to determine whether such a problem is operant or respondent, hysterical or psychophysiological. A person may develop a gagging, nauseated response through classical conditioning or as a response to situations that are followed by reinforcement. Wolf et al. (1965) report work with a 9-year-old retarded girl who was permitted to leave the classroom and return to the dormitory when she had vomited on her dress. The maximum number of instances of vomiting on a single day was 21. The treatment program involved shaping desirable classroom behavior with praise and candy, ceasing such reinforcement when she vomited (time out from reinforcement), and keeping the patient in the classroom until the end of the period (extinction). The rate of vomiting declined to zero in an orderly manner over a period of 30 class days.

The following case is illustrative of our hypnobehavioral model in the treatment of actual vomiting.

> R.P. was a 23-year-old male. Three years ago he forced himself to vomit after every meal to lose enough weight to successfully get out of the draft. He went from 136 pounds to 105. However, the gagging became reflexive after a year of practice and he could no longer control it. Presently he was throwing up after every meal. When the gagging became involuntary, he had become deeply involved in left-wing politics. He read all of Marx in one summer and felt he was a

genius to have absorbed so much in such a short time. As a result he had tremendous pressure to be productive. At this time, eating while reading improved his concentration. The more he threw up, the more he was able to eat and the greater his concentration became. He thought that blood was diverted from his brain during digestion and that throwing up of the food would rechannel the blood back to the brain. It was pointed out that the patient was afraid to start eating again for fear he would lose the energy and concentration he felt necessary for realizing his ambitions.

In addition to improving his concentration, the dysphagia was discovered to have other secondary gains. The problem kept him from having a normal sexual life. As he stated, "How else am I going to discipline myself?" All he could do was read and write. Also, R.P. reported he had not been sick a day since the onset of the dysphagia; he had no more headaches or hayfever, felt physically strong, and required much less sleep than before the onset of the malady. Also, he now felt a need to deviate, to be revolutionary, and to rebel. If he started eating again, his parents would see it as a victory to their side, a return to the middle-class, bourgeois way of doing things.

Much discussion and clarification of motives and feelings was necessary to bring the patient to the intellectual and emotional decision that he wanted to stop the gag reflex despite the consequent loss in secondary gain. At this point, hypnosis was initiated. The patient had stated on several occasions that eating allayed his anxiety. The more he could eat, the more relaxed he became. Unfortunately he resorted to dysphagia in order to enable him to eat even more and the price for relaxation was too high. Here is an excellent example of using the consummatory response to reduce anxiety. Therapy was directed at getting the patient to reduce anxiety by using the other responses incompatible with anxiety—sexual arousal and relaxation—rather than consumatory behavior.

When R.P. first began practicing self-hypnosis he experienced an initial stage of depression and lethargy. Although frequency of gagging was still constant, he was not throwing up as much each time. His present means of creating concentration and mental energy (gagging) was being destroyed and a period of adjustment was ensuing. The patient had reported that masturbation was infrequent as he was seldom "horny" and that he would masturbate only to "release anxiety." In this patient's case, the sexual climax would be a far better form of release than throwing up, so he was instructed to increase his masturbatory activities. He was also given specific hypnotic sexual imagery to increase his libido.

After 3 weeks, R.P.'s energy level began to increase. He still complained, however, that his compulsion to produce and prove his genius was exerting a great strain on him. Imagery for time expansion was then incorporated to enable the patient to feel less time pressure; he kept his desire to produce, but he did not feel the constant push and pressure of a time schedule that previously was creating so much tension. Soon he reported that he had more energy, less depression, and that he had resumed writing his book. After 6 more months of practice with relaxing and hypnotic sexual imagery, the patient's anxiety level was sufficiently reduced such that the gagging was back to voluntary control.

DISCUSSION OF HYPNOBEHAVIORAL THERAPY

Hypnobehavioral therapy, as described, has proved to be beneficial to many patients who were unable to respond to a wide variety of medical measures. This approach has afforded considerable relief of pain, spasms, and such other related disorders as heartburn, nausea, pylorospasm, eructations, and other symptoms. Sensory-imagery conditioning and glove anesthesia (Image IV) are valuable adjunctive procedures. Time expansion (Images VI and VII) enables the patient to "wind down." People with such disorders are usually on a treadmill: much concerned over meeting deadlines and schedules. The suggestion that one minute will seem like ten gives them the *feeling* that they have plenty of time to accomplish their tasks, and they therefore relax.

Hypnosis relaxes many anxious and disturbed patients, reduces their tension, helps relieve the irritability caused by a strict dietary program, and also increases the likelihood of cooperation with the medical regimen.

REFERENCES

Alberti, R. E. and Emmons, M. L.: Your Perfect Right: A Guide to Assertive Behavior. Impact, San Luis, Obispo, 1974.

Andreev, B. V.: Sleep Therapy in the Neuroses. New York, Consultants Bureau, 1960.

Byrne, S.: Hypnosis and the irritable bowel: case histories, methods and speculation. Amer. J. Clin. Hypn., *15:*263, 1973.

Cannon, W. B.: Bodily Changes in Pain, Hunger, Fear, and Rage. ed. 2. New York, Appleton, 1929.

Dias, M. M.: Hypnosis in irritable colon. Rev. Brasil Med., *20:*132–134, 1963.

Engel, B. T. and Chism, R. A.: Operant conditioning of heart rate speeding. Psychophysiology, *3:*418, 1967.

Engel, B. T. and Hansen, S. P.: Operant conditioning of heart rate slowing. Psychophysiology, *3:*176, 1966.

Gantt, W. H.: Autonomic conditioning. *In* Wolpe, J., Salter, A., and Reyna, L. J. (eds.): The Conditioning Therapies, pp. 115–124. New York, Holt, Rinehart, Winston, 1964.

Haggard, H. W.: Devils, Drugs, and Doctors. New York, Harper, 1929.

Kimmel, E., and Kimmel, H. D.: A replication of operant conditioning of the GSR. J. Exp. Psychol., *65:*212, 1963.

Kimmel, H. D. and Hill, F. A.: Operant conditioning of the GSR. Psychol, Rep., *7:*555, 1960.

Lacey, J. I.: The evaluation of autonomic responses: toward a general solution. Annals N.Y. Acad. Sci., *67:*123, 1956.

Lacey, J. I., Bateman, D. E., and VanLehn, R.: Autonomic response specificity. Psychosom. Med., *15:*8, 1953.

Lait, V. S.: A case of recurrent compulsive vomiting. Amer. J. Clin. Hypn. *14:*196, 1972.

Liddell, H. S.: Emotional Hazards in Animals and Man. Springfield, Charles C Thomas, 1956.

Mahl, G. F.: Chronic fear and gastric secretion of HCL in dogs. Psychosom. Med., *11:*30, 1949.

Malmo, R. B.: Experimental studies of mental patients under stress. *In* Reymert, M. L. (ed.): Feelings and Emotions. pp. 169–180. New York, McGraw-Hill, 1950.

Malmo, R. B. and Shagass, C.: Physiologic study of symptom mechanisms in psychiatric patients under stress. Psychosom. Med., *11:*25, 1949.

Mandler, G., Preven, D. W., and Kuhlman, C. K.: Effects of operant reinforcement on the GSR. J. Exper. Anal. Behav., *5:*317, 1962.

Miller, N. E. and DiCara, L.: Instrumental learning of heart-rate changes in curarized rats: shaping and specificity to discriminative stimulus. J. Comp. Physiol. Psychol., 63:12, 1967.

Moody, H.: An evaluation of hypnotically induced relaxation for the reduction of peptic ulcer symptoms. Brit. J. Med. Hypnotism, 5:23, 1953.

Pavlov, I. P.: Experimental Psychology. New York, Philosophical Library, 1957.

Razran, G.: The observable unconscious and the inferable conscious in current Soviet psychophysiology: interoceptive conditioning, semantic conditioning, and the orienting reflex. Psychol. Rev., 68:81, 1961.

Weitzenhoffer, A. M.: Limited hypnotherapy of a case of diaphragmatic clonus. Amer. J. Clin. Hypn. 16:147, 1974.

Wolf, M. M., Birnbrauer, J. S., Williams, T., and Lawler, J.: A note on apparent extinction of the vomiting behavior of a retarded child, pp. 364–366. *In* Ullmann, L. P. and Krasner, L. (eds.): Case Studies in Behavior Modification. New York, Holt, 1965.

Zane, M. D.: The hypnotic situation and changes in ulcer pain. Am. J. Clin. Hypn., 14:292–304, 1966.

SUGGESTED READINGS

Eichorn, R., and Tractir, J.: The effects of hypnotically induced emotions upon gastric secretions. Gastroenterology, 29:432–438, 1955.

Leonard, A. S., Papermaster, A. A., and Wangensteen, O. H.: Treatment of postgastrectomy syndrome by hypnotic suggestion J.A.M.A., 165:1957–1959, 1957.

PART SEVEN

Evaluation

37

Failures and Limitations

FAILURES

When discussing failures of the hypnobehavioral model, it is not intended to compare the success of this model with that of more traditional approaches or with control groups involving subjects who received no treatment. The validity of this model relates simply to whether changes in a single patient's behavior are lawfully related to the therapeutic operations that were intended to produce them. If the procedures changed a given feeling or behavior, the model was considered to be working. The results of the therapeutic operations must be meaningfully related to the operations themselves.

We favor a concentrated, controlled study of individual cases in determining the merit of a treatment technic. We are in accord with Chassan (1960, 1961) who states, "It is certainly not as generally recognized as it ought to be that *the intensive statistical study of a single case can provide more meaningful and statistically significant information than, say, only endpoint observations extended over a relatively large number of patients*" (Chassan 1960, p. 178; italics in original). Edgington (1966, 1967) offers a similar viewpoint.

If a therapeutic procedure fails to produce change in the patient, the fault lies in the experimental technic and not in the patient. This holds true unless, of course, the patient terminates prematurely before giving the treatment a chance. A large majority of our failures were patients who expected overnight miracles from the hypnobehavioral approach or who were not willing to exert the effort needed to practice the imagery. Merely attending the therapy sessions is often insufficient without practice at home. For the determined patients who did do their homework and still did not receive relief from their presenting problem, the fault lies in the method of application of the conditioning principles involved. The therapist is responsible here: the principles are sound, but they must be properly and ingeniously applied. A different therapist using the same model could possibly have produced better results in these cases. However, even in those cases where the presenting problem remained, the patients always reported deriving benefit from the therapy in terms of feeling generally more relaxed and better able to cope with everyday problems and irritations.

LIMITATIONS

The requisites for the successful employment of the hypnobehavioral model consist simply of a willing patient with some modicum of intelligence, and a confident and skillful therapist. The rapport established between supplicant and healer, the strength of the interpersonal relationship, the wisdom, judgment, and clinical experience of the therapist, the expectant attitudes or mental set of the patient—all catalyze the behavioral dynamics associated with successful treatment.

The hypnobehavioral model cannot be used on those individuals who still regard hypnosis according to a Svengali-Trilby-Rasputin model. Most of these individuals also are looking for a magical gesture. We see no limitations to the application of the hypnobehavioral approach to clinical problems. If animals with their limited cognitive and perceptual abilities are subject to change through appropriate application of learning principles, then it follows that humans as a result of their superior cortical development can have their response patterns even more readily modified.

However, even though learning principles alter response patterns and specific behavior, learning theory per se often is inadequate to deal with complex problems. Critics question the duration of behavior modification, recognizing that lasting personality changes often are not effected. Adding hypnotic technics to behavior modification enables some patients to apply self-reinforcement when necessary. Also, they can transfer or generalize the beneficial effects of behavior modification by the various types of symptom-manipulation we have described. Finally, they have greater capacity for self-control and self-management as the result of the hypnotic imagery conditioning.

Naturally, the limitations of this model depend upon the knowledge that the therapist has in the fields of behavior therapy and hypnosis. Other limitations are the lack of imagination and resourcefulness on the part of the therapist to construct an appropriate hierarchy for desensitizing or counterconditioning maladaptive behaviors. Psychological immunization requires appropriate timing as to when and how the patients are exposed to anxiety-provoking stimuli. If the patient is advanced too rapidly along a hierarchy, anxiety will supersede relaxation and nullify therapeutic gains.

We have mentioned that some may criticize behavior therapy as mechanistic and nonhumanistic. Others will still continue to criticize hypnosis as being too simplistic. It must be remembered, however, that the goal of this model is not to force or inflict the therapist's values on the patient but merely to aid the latter in actualizing his own values by better utilization of his own inner resources.

Initially, behavior therapy was thought to be only applicable for desensitization of phobic symptoms. With increasing research, behavior therapy is now being applied to a broad spectrum of problems. Likewise, hypnosis was originally thought to be inapplicable for thought disorders such as schizophrenia and for people of limited intelligence. Recent research, however, shows that schizophrenics (Chap. 28) and mental retardates (Chap. 29) can be hypnotized. The combination of behavior modification and hypnotherapeutic technics provides an armamentarium that can be used to combat an ever increasing range of presenting problems. Also, behavior therapy is not incompatible with psychodynamic therapy. Although we do not practice psychoanalysis, the reader will recognize that we have used many of its fundamental tenets in our discussion of hypnoanalytic technics. As wisely stated by Marmor (1973),

> Behavior therapists deserve much credit for having opened wide the armamentarium of therapeutic strategies . . . by doing so, they have forced dynamic psychotherapists into a reassessment of their therapeutic techniques and their effectiveness—a reassessment that in the long run can only be in the best interests of all psychiatrists and their patients.

We also have heard the criticisms of those who fear the development of "man the manipulator" with reference to behavior modification. Were not the same warnings made regarding hypnosis as a powerful control mechanism by scientists in high places as well as imaginative novelists? We fear that uncritical opposition to the hypnobehavioral approach will prevent many disturbed individuals from having their abnormal behavior beneficially modified. We also fear that uncritical opposition to behavior modification programs will deprive mental retardates and socially maladjusted individuals of opportunities to develop new behaviors that will benefit them. We strongly support the development of review committees to insure that behavior modification programs are sensible, reasonable, and likely to be effective. The American Medical Association did this in 1958 when hypnosis was met with the irrational prejudice that was educated ignorance. The reader will agree that banning behavior modification technics because they supposedly can subvert the population is irrational and unacceptable.

Throughout this book we have presented cases illustrating our successes with a wide variety of problems. Our model is not a panacea. We have had dramatic successes and we also have had many dramatic failures. We are cognizant that the initial wave of enthusiasm accorded any new procedure contributes to its success. Therefore, we hope that other researchers will build upon this model and validate the rationale for its efficacy. As our knowledge increases and new technics are developed, our failure rate will decrease.

REFERENCES

Chassan, J. B.: Statistical inference and the single case in clinical design. Psychiatry, *23:*173, 1960.

————: Stochastic models of the single case as the basis of clinical research design. Behav. Sci., *6:*42, 1961.

Edgington, E. S.: Statistical inference and nonrandom samples. Psychol. Bull., *66:*485, 1966.

————: Statistical inference from N-1 experiments. J. Psychol., *65:*195, 1967.

Marmor, J.: quoted in Is conditioning enough?, Medical World News, *14:*39, 1973.

Task Force Report No 5; Behavior Therapy in Psychiatry, American Psychiatric Assoc. Washington, D.C., July, 1973.

Wolpe, J. et al.: Current status of systematic desensitization. Amer. J. Psychiat., *130:*961, 1973.

SUGGESTED READINGS

Marks, I. M.: Current status of behavioral psychotherapy: theory and practice. Am. J. Psych., *133:*253–265, 1976.

Shapiro, A. K.: The behavior therapies: therapeutic breakthrough or latest fad? Am. J. Psych., *133:*154–159, 1976.

38

Hypnobehavioral Therapy: Present and Future Implications

At present there is a growing interest in the comparative study of Eastern and Western philosophies. The ancient wisdom of the Eastern beliefs is directed toward the internal processes of the organism. Self-realization is the goal. The Western world stresses external values, particularly materialistic goals. However, even though advocates have been making extravagant claims for their therapeutic efficacy, it will take considerable time to incorporate the fundamental principles of the Eastern philosophies into a Western frame of reference. Westerners have long been concerned with measurement and calibration—that which they can see and quantify. In contrast, the Eastern philosophies have directed their attention to subjective feelings—that which is intangible and unmeasurable.

BIOFEEDBACK AND LEARNING

In several chapters of this book we have mentioned how recently developed biofeedback technics control various physiologic processes. These include functions that were considered wholly involuntary, such as heart rate, blood pressure, and brain waves. Unfortunately, the studies have been poorly designed to rule out the influence of task-motivated suggestions and expectant attitudes. Nor have adequate follow-ups been carried out on a large enough population sample.

Segal (1975) optimistically believes that such instrumental devices will enormously accelerate the learning process and that self-regulation of the human organism is practically unlimited. Schwartz (1973) even more glowingly states:

By means of immediate, augmented feedback (with its associated increased bodily awareness), the patient may be able to learn new ways of coping behaviorally with his environment, or he may be able to alter his life style in such a way as to keep his physiological processes within safer limits.

Hopefully, with the future development of more sophisticated technology and instrumentation this may occur.

RATIONALE FOR BIOFEEDBACK

As intimated below, most of the results accounting for the success with biofeedback technics are closely related to the relaxation therapies. For instance, Brady (1975) warns that a placebo effect has not been ruled out. Orne (1975) comments that it is interesting that biofeedback researchers are now talking about the influence that suggestion, motivation, and emotions have on results. He comments, "This is another instance where a new technique is introduced and found to be wanting, by itself, so it is combined with older, proven therapies but is presented as a new package. . . ." Melzack (1975) showed that patients receiving alpha training alone for pain relief showed virtually no results. It was the distraction, strong suggestion, and hypnorelaxation training that reduced the anxiety and, therefore, the pain. In the future, people will turn to their *inner life* seeking desperately for new resources to help them cope with their problems. There will be greater stress on meditation processes in which *internal* feedback control and imagery will play an important role in attaining desired behavioral responses.

MEDITATIVE STATES

The reader should not be confused by the supposed differences between hypnosis, Zen, Yoga, and other Eastern healing methodologies. Although the ritual for each differs, they are fundamentally the same and are based on similar principles of conditioning (Kroger 1966). Gastaut (1969), after studying EEG patterns of Yoga and Zen disciples, regarded these alterations in awareness as autohypnotic states. Gellhorn and Kiely (1972) have also noted a common EEG and neurophysiologic basis for mystical states of consciousness. That hypnosis and such Eastern methodologies as Shintoism, Taoism, the Samadhic state of Yoga, and the Satori state of Zen have existed for several thousand years and now are being increasingly accepted indicates that they will play a meaningful role in modulating thought processes. They are here to stay, and they are modalities that American psychotherapy must eventually incorporate.

ALTERED STATES OF CONSCIOUSNESS

The behavioral technics of desensitization using scene visualization and hypnosis have also stimulated renewed interest in attaining altered states of consciousness for modifying behavior. We are certain that, through use of more precise technics, finer sensory discriminations will be made so that these states can facilitate therapy. There also will continue to be a burgeoning interest in guided affective imagery, fantasy encounter, and the use of standardized images similar to those described in Chapter 10. Meditation as a potent modality for changing behavior has certainly withstood the test of time. This is dramatically illustrated by the world-wide interest in Transcendental Meditation (T.M.), another method for achieving autohypnosis (Wallace 1970). Daniels (1975) has utilized hypnosis, behavior therapy, and T.M. for reducing severe anxieties.

The subjective experience of some practitioners of T.M., Zen, or Yoga resembles in many respects the heightened sensory awareness and uniqueness of perceptual and cognitive experiences of many LSD users. Patients undergoing hypnotic sensory-imagery conditioning report similar experiences. It has been noted that in states of meditation, habituation of the orienting reflex is delayed or abolished. This suggests that in some way the lack of habituation of alpha blocking by sensory input is a correlate of heightened perceptual sensitivity. Clearly, then, in unusual degrees of deep meditation and imagery conditioning, subjects can induce "ecstasy" or cortical excitation by adequate training.

These meditative states also show a remarkable parallel to REM sleep and dreaming. Both involve a state of cortical and visceral arousal associated with inhibition of skeletal muscle tone in trunk and limbs. A loss of distinctiveness in spatial orientations and vivid perceptual imagery with condensation of imagined persons and events are correlates of both dreams and the ecstasy state. The deepest, or plenary hypnotic state achieved through sensory-imagery conditioning shows the same parallel (Calloway 1975). Skeletal muscle tone in trunk and limbs are inhibited, and patients often stagger and waver from the couch to the desk on leaving the session. The time sense is distorted, expanded, or concentrated—in some cases, abolished. Perceptual or sensory imagery is incredibly vivid.

More study of the similarities between these states of altered consciousness is needed, as is study of their relationship to certain psychotic states. A group of anxiously depressed, impulse-driven, drug-dependent adolescents and young adults was observed to have replaced drug use with daily practice of Zen or of Transcendental Meditation (Gellhorn and Kiely 1972). While detailed physiological or objective psychological studies to support the fact of changes in their central nervous system balance are lacking, there is clinical evidence of significant emotional and behavioral change. These people report a heightened sense of *inner-directed self-control* as a result of meditation practice in opposition to the anxiety-provoking *loss of control* experienced under the influence of drugs. Most people suffering from emotional problems are concerned over fear of loss of control. The feeling of control gained over mastery of sensory functioning is very therapeutic. There was also evidence of much improved clarity in cognitive function and in emotional-behavioral integration. Therefore, we can see that, more and more, therapy will be directed toward helping the patient to help himself—toward teaching him how to gain control over his biological and emotional functioning so that he can maintain and reinforce appropriate responses and positive feeling states. The goal of self-reinforcement and self-hypnosis is self-control!

FUTURE IMPLICATIONS

Hypnosis, behavior therapy, and some of the tenets so well enunciated by Freud will merge as a practical psychology. A new concept, in part, has been expressed by the humanistic psychology movement lead by Maslow, Perls, May, and others. Even though this movement has differed from Skinnerian behaviorism and Freudian psychoanalysis, it has a high content of suggestion, hypnosis, or both. For instance, Maslow refers to "peak experiences " which are defined as vivid moments when one's vision is characterized by remarkable clarity and meaningful thoughts. Such experiences are associated with self-fulfillment, creativity, goal-directed achievements, or the reverie that one is in harmony with the universe. These goals are identical with the *transcendence of normal volitional capacities* characterizing hypnosis.

We believe that the "new-psychology" rising like a phoenix from the three above-mentioned disciplines will be directed to how man can best utilize his images, visions, or both, of what he is and what he can do to fulfill his potentials. The images described in our book should trigger a growing interest in the expansion of sensory awareness through sensory conditioning and thus enhance creativity, learning, and the ability to solve problems.

American psychology and psychiatry are splintered by many different movements—all of which seem to help patients to some degree or another. Among the more popular are Gestalt, the Human Potential Movement, Bioenergetics, Sensory Awareness, Transpersonal Psychology, Psychosynthesis, Autogenic Feedback Training, Rolfing, Zen, and Yoga. These are all part of the newer movement, which grew out of opposition to traditional psychotherapies. We are familiar with all of these various technics, and because of our knowledge of hypnosis, we unequivocally state that they all have a high content of suggestion, hypnosis, or both in effecting cures.

In time, therapists will become desensitized to the mystique surrounding hypnosis. Recognition of this core that underlies all forms of therapy will lead to the dissolution of the confusion and dissonance which has caused the fragmentation of American psychology and psychiatry. Masserman (1971), a noted American psychiatrist, in the welcoming address to the American Society for Clinical and Experimental Hypnosis emphasized this point when he spoke on "Hypnosis, the Misnamed Source of All Interpersonal Therapies."

The fundamental needs for the future as well as the present are quantitative indices and criteria for assessing efficacy of existing therapeutic modalities. Controlled comparative studies are needed to evaluate the combination of hypnosis and behavior therapy, in regard to clinical improvement. Many cases treated by our model, even though apparently successful, often may go into remission. Knowledge of neurochemical and electrophysiologic substrates of behavior is now available. Also, there are computer technics involving signal analysis, multivariate classification, and other technics for interpreting such peripheral signals from the central nervous system as the E.E.G., E.M.G., and other physiological patterns. This holds promise for developing noninvasive diagnostic tools for differentiating behavioral disorders, particularly those associated with C.N.S. abnormalities.

These technics should have far-reaching relevance for therapy of such mental disorders as depression and sociopathic and psychopathic behavior. It is also obvious that future scientists will require accurate physiologic measurements of normal and abnormal behavior. Until this is available, there is little hope of establishing psychotherapy as an exact science. We foresee that current research in anatomical mapping of the brain will make it possible to delineate various centers mediating specific behavioral responses. Stimulation of numerous centers is now being done. Sexual and satiety centers are being stimulated in animals. Focal abnormalities already are being dealt with with pinpoint precision. Examples are cryosurgery or chemopallidectomy for Parkinson's disease and electrode implantations for stimulating pleasure centers for pain relief in terminal cancer patients. However, we are not concerned that man might be conditioned by rewards and punishments through electronic brain stimulation to be controlled like robots by push buttons. Rather, we strongly feel that the hypnobehavioral model used as promulgated in this book should afford a safe and comprehensive method for controlling emotions and behavior in the alleviation of human suffering.

REFERENCES

Brady, J. P.: Claims for biofeedback as a therapy method disputed. Clinical Psychiatric News, *3:*8, 1975.

Calloway, E.: Psychiatry today. West. J. Medicine, *122:*349, 1975.

Daniels, L. K.: The treatment of psychophysiological disorders and severe anxiety by behavior therapy, hypnosis and Transcendental Meditation. Am. J. Clin. Hypn., *17:*26, 1975.

Gastaut, H.: Hypnosis and presleep patterns. *In* Chertok, L. (ed.): Psychophysiological Mechanisms of Hypnosis. pp. 40–44. New York, Springer-Verlag, 1969.

Gellhorn, E. and Kiely, W. F.: Mystical states of consciousness: neurophysiological and clinical aspects. J. Nerv. Ment. Dis., *154:*399, 1972.

Kroger, W. S.: Comparative evaluation of Zen, Yoga, Judaism with conditioning technics and psychotherapy. Excerpta Medica, *119:*175, 1966.

Masserman, J.: Hypnosis, the misnamed source of all interpersonal therapies. Address given to Am. Soc. Clin. Hypn., Oct. 13, 1971.

Melzack, R.: The promise of biofeedback: Don't hold the party yet. Psychology Today, *9:*18, 1975.

Orne, M.: Claims for biofeedback as a therapy method disputed. Clinical Psychiatric News, *3:*8, 1975.

Schwartz, G. E.: Biofeedback as therapy: some theoretical and practical issues. Amer. Psychol., *28:*666, 1973.

Segal, J.: Biofeedback as a medical treatment. J.A.M.A., *232:*179, 1975.

Wallace, R. K.: Physiological effects of transcendental meditation. Science, *167:*1751, 1970.

Index